8/06

WORLD ERAS

VOLUME 10

WEST AFRICAN KINGDOMS

500 – 1590

WORLD ERAS

VOLUME 10

WEST AFRICAN KINGDOMS
500 – 1590

PIERRE-DAMIEN MVUYEKURE

A MANLY, INC. BOOK

GALE®

THOMSON

★

GALE

Detroit • New York • San Diego • San Francisco • Cleveland • New Haven, Conn. • Waterville, Maine • London • Munich

World Eras
Volume 10: West African Kingdoms, 500–1590
Pierre-Damien Mvuyekure

Editorial Directors
Matthew J. Bruccoli and Richard Layman

Series Editor
Anthony J. Scotti Jr.

LIBRARY OF CONGRESS CATALOGING-IN-PUBLICATION DATA

West African kingdoms, 500–1590 / edited by Pierre-Damien Mvuyekure.
  p. cm.—(World eras; v.10)
"A Manly, Inc. book."
    Includes bibliographical references and indexes.
    ISBN 0-7876-6047-7 (alk. paper)
    1. Africa, West—History—To 1884.
    I. Mvuyekure, Pierre-Damien. II. Series.

DT476.W48 2003
966′.02—dc21   2003008079

Printed in the United States of America
10 9 8 7 6 5

ADVISORY BOARD

To Anathalie Mukagasana, Anita Bwiza, Michael Mugaba Jeni, and Malcolm-Aimé Musoni
To the victims of the Rwandan genocide, including my mother, uncle, and other relatives

CONTENTS

ABOUT THE SERIES

PROJECT DESCRIPTION

Patterned after the well-received *American Decades* and *American Eras* series, *World Eras* is a cross-disciplinary reference series. It comprises volumes examining major civilizations that have flourished from antiquity to modern times, with a global perspective and a strong emphasis on daily life and social history. Each volume provides in-depth coverage of one era, focusing on a specific cultural group and its interaction with other peoples of the world. The *World Eras* series is geared toward the needs of high-school students studying subjects in the humanities. Its purpose is to provide students—and general reference users as well—a reliable, engaging reference resource that stimulates their interest, encourages research, and prompts comparison of the lives people led in different parts of the world, in different cultures, and at different times.

The goal of *World Eras* volumes is to enrich the traditional historical study of "kings and battles" with a resource that promotes understanding of daily life and the cultural institutions that affect people's beliefs and behavior.

What kind of work did people in a certain culture perform?

What did they eat?

How did they fight their battles?

What laws did they have and how did they punish criminals?

What were their religious practices?

What did they know of science and medicine?

What kind of art, music, and literature did they enjoy?

These are the types of questions *World Eras* volumes seek to answer.

VOLUME DESIGN

World Eras is designed to facilitate comparative study. Thus, volumes employ a consistent ten-chapter structure so that teachers and students can readily access standard top-ics in various volumes. The chapters in each *World Eras* volume are:

1. World Events
2. Geography
3. The Arts
4. Communication, Transportation, and Exploration
5. Social Class System and the Economy
6. Politics, Law, and the Military
7. Leisure, Recreation, and Daily Life
8. The Family and Social Trends
9. Religion and Philosophy
10. Science, Technology, and Health

World Eras volumes begin with two chapters designed to provide a broad view of the world against which a specific culture can be measured. Chapter 1 provides students today with a means to understand where a certain people stood within our concept of world history. Chapter 2 describes the world from the perspective of the people being studied—what did they know of geography and how did geography and climate affect their lives? The following eight chapters address major aspects of people's lives to provide a sense of what defined their culture. The ten chapters in *World Eras* will remain constant in each volume. Teachers and students seeking to compare religious beliefs in Roman and Greek cultures, for example, can easily locate the information they require by consulting chapter 9 in the appropriate volumes, tapping a rich source for class assignments and research topics. Volume-specific glossaries and a checklist of general references provide students assistance in studying unfamiliar cultures.

CHAPTER CONTENTS

Each chapter in *World Eras* volumes also follows a uniform structure designed to provide users quick access to the information they need. Chapters are arranged into five types of material:

- **Chronology** provides an historical outline of significant events in the subject of the chapter in timeline form.
- **Overview** provides a narrative overview of the chapter topic during the period and discusses the material of the chapter in a global context.
- **Topical Entries** provide focused information in easy-to-read articles about people, places, events, institutions, and matters of general concern to the people of the time. A references rubric includes sources for further study.
- **Biographical Entries** profiles people of enduring significance regarding the subject of the chapter.
- **Documentary Sources** is an annotated checklist of documentary sources from the historical period that are the basis for the information presented in the chapter.

Chapters are supplemented throughout with primary-text sidebars that include interesting short documentary excerpts or anecdotes chosen to illuminate the subject of the chapter: recipes, letters, daily-life accounts, and excerpts from important documents. Each *World Eras* volume includes about 150 illustrations, maps, diagrams, and line drawings linked directly to material discussed in the text. Illustrations are chosen with particular emphasis on daily life.

INDEXING

A general two-level subject index for each volume includes significant terms, subjects, theories, practices, people, organizations, publications, and so forth mentioned in the text. Index citations with many page references are broken down by subtopic. Illustrations are indicated both in the general index, by use of italicized page numbers, and in a separate illustrations index, which provides a description of each item.

EDITORS AND CONTRIBUTORS

An advisory board of history teachers and librarians has provided valuable advice about the rationale for this series. They have reviewed both series plans and individual volume plans. Each *World Eras* volume is edited by a distinguished specialist in the subject of his or her volume. The editor is responsible for enlisting other scholar-specialists to write each of the chapters in the volume and for assuring the quality of their work. The editorial staff at Manly, Inc., rigorously checks factual information, line edits the manuscript, works with the editor to select illustrations, and produces the books in the series, in cooperation with Gale Group editors.

The *World Eras* series is for students of all ages who seek to enrich their study of world history by examining the many aspects of people's lives in different places during different eras. This series continues Gale's tradition of publishing comprehensive, accurate, and stimulating historical reference works that promote the study of history and culture.

The following timeline, included in every volume of *World Eras,* is provided as a convenience to users seeking a ready chronological context.

TIMELINE

This timeline, compiled by editors at Manly, Inc., is provided as a convenience for students seeking a broad global and historical context for the materials in this volume of World Eras. It is not intended as a self-contained resource. Students who require a comprehensive chronology of world history should consult a source such as Peter N. Stearns, ed., The Encyclopedia of World History, sixth revised edition (Boston & New York: Houghton Mifflin, 2001).

CIRCA 4 MILLION–1 MILLION B.C.E.
Era of *Australopithecus*, the first hominid

CIRCA 1.5 MILLION–200,000 B.C.E.
Era of *Homo erectus*, "upright-walking human"

CIRCA 1,000,000–10,000 B.C.E.
Paleolithic Age: hunters and gatherers make use of stone tools in Eurasia

CIRCA 250,000 B.C.E.
Early evolution of *Homo sapiens*, "consciously thinking humans"

CIRCA 40,000 B.C.E.
Migrations from Siberia to Alaska lead to the first human inhabitation of North and South America

CIRCA 8000 B.C.E.
Neolithic Age: settled agrarian culture begins to develop in Eurasia

5000 B.C.E.
The world population is between 5 million and 20 million

CIRCA 4000–3500 B.C.E.
Earliest Sumerian cities: artificial irrigation leads to increased food supplies and populations in Mesopotamia

CIRCA 3000 B.C.E.
Bronze Age begins in Mesopotamia and Egypt, where bronze is primarily used for making weapons; invention of writing

CIRCA 2900–1150 B.C.E.
Minoan society on Crete: lavish palaces and commercial activity

CIRCA 2700–2200 B.C.E.
Egypt: Old Kingdom and the building of the pyramids

CIRCA 2080–1640 B.C.E.
Egypt: Middle Kingdom plagued by internal strife and invasion by the Hyksos

CIRCA 2000–1200 B.C.E.
Hittites build a powerful empire based in Anatolia (present-day Turkey) by using horse-drawn war chariots

CIRCA 1792–1760 B.C.E.
Old Babylonian Kingdom; one of the oldest extant legal codes is compiled

CIRCA 1766–1122 B.C.E.
Shang Dynasty in China: military expansion, large cities, written language, and introduction of bronze metallurgy

CIRCA 1570–1075 B.C.E.
Egypt: New Kingdom and territorial expansion into Palestine, Lebanon, and Syria

CIRCA 1500 B.C.E.
The Aryans, an Indo-European people from the steppes of present-day Ukraine and southern Russia, expand into northern India

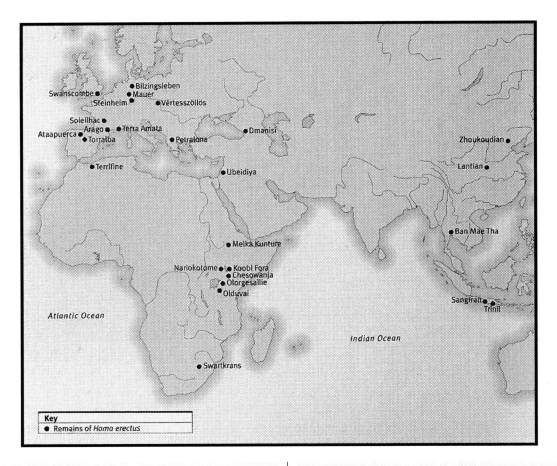

Key
● Remains of *Homo erectus*

CIRCA 1500 B.C.E.
Phoenicians create the first alphabet

CIRCA 1400-1200 B.C.E.
Hittites develop the technology of iron smelting, improving weaponry and agricultural implements as well as stimulating trade

CIRCA 1200-800 B.C.E.
Phoenicians establish colonies throughout the Mediterranean

CIRCA 1122-221 B.C.E.
Zhou Dynasty in China: military conquests, nomadic invasions, and introduction of iron metallurgy

CIRCA 1100-750 B.C.E.
Greek Dark Ages: foreign invasions, civil disturbances, decrease in agricultural production, and population decline

1020-587 B.C.E.
Israelite monarchies consolidate their power in Palestine

CIRCA 1000-612 B.C.E.
Assyrians create an empire encompassing Mesopotamia, Syria, Palestine, and most of Anatolia and Egypt; they deport populations to various regions of the realm

1000 B.C.E.
The world population is approximately 50 million

CIRCA 814-146 B.C.E.
The city-state of Carthage is a powerful commercial and military power in the western Mediterranean

753 B.C.E.
Traditional date of the founding of Rome

CIRCA 750-700 B.C.E.
Rise of the polis, or city-state, in Greece

558-330 B.C.E.
Achaemenid Dynasty establishes the Persian Empire (present-day Iran, Turkey, Afghanistan, and Iraq); satraps rule the various provinces

509 B.C.E.
Roman Republic is established

500 B.C.E.
The world population is approximately 100 million

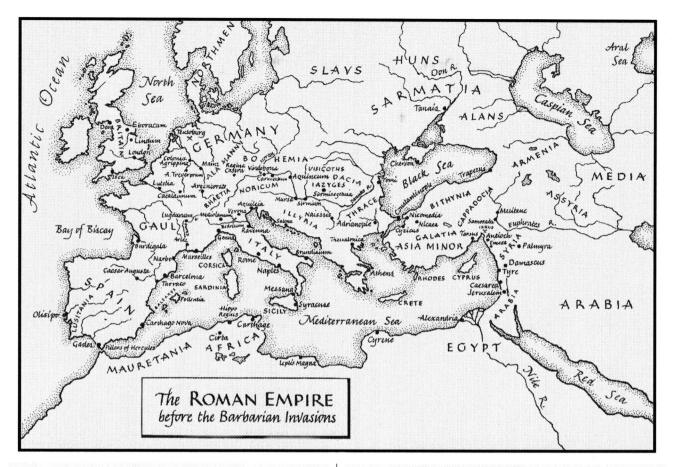

The ROMAN EMPIRE
before the Barbarian Invasions

CIRCA 400 B.C.E.
Spread of Buddhism in India

338-323 B.C.E.
Macedon, a kingdom in the central Balkan Peninsula, conquers the Persian Empire

323-301 B.C.E.
Ptolemaic Kingdom (Egypt), Seleucid Kingdom (Syria), and Antigonid Dynasty (Macedon) are founded

247 B.C.E.-224 C.E.
Parthian Empire (Parthia, Persia, and Babylonia): clan leaders build independent power bases in their satrapies, or provinces

215-168 B.C.E.
Rome establishes hegemony over the Hellenistic world

206 B.C.E.-220 C.E.
Han Dynasty in China: imperial expansion into central Asia, centralized government, economic prosperity, and population growth

CIRCA 100 B.C.E.
Tribesmen on the Asian steppes develop the stirrup, which eventually revolutionizes warfare

1 C.E.
The world population is approximately 200 million

CIRCA 100 C.E.
Invention of paper in China

224-651 C.E.
Sasanid Empire (Parthia, Persia, and Babylonia): improved government system, founding of new cities, increased trade, and the introduction of rice and cotton cultivation

CIRCA 320-550 C.E.
Gupta dynasty in India: Golden Age of Hindu civilization marked by stability and prosperity throughout the subcontinent

340 C.E.
Constantinople becomes the capital of the Eastern Roman, or Byzantine, Empire

395 C.E.
Christianity becomes the official religion of the Roman Empire

CIRCA 400 C.E.
The first unified Japanese state arises and is centered at Yamato on the island of Honshu; Buddhism arrives in Japan by way of Korea

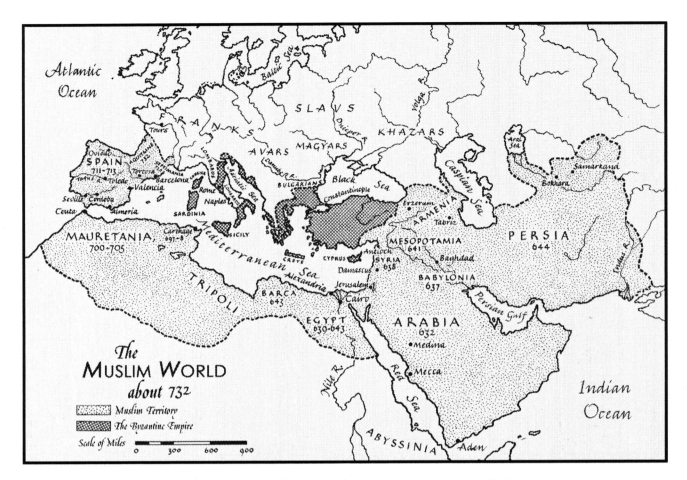

The MUSLIM WORLD about 732

Muslim Territory
The Byzantine Empire

Scale of Miles
0   300   600   900

CIRCA 400 C.E.
The nomadic Huns begin a westward migration from central Asia, causing disruption in the Roman Empire

CIRCA 400 C.E.
The Mayan Empire in Mesoamerica evolves into city-states

476 C.E.
Rome falls to barbarian hordes, and the Western Roman Empire collapses

CIRCA 500-1500 C.E.
Middle Ages, or medieval period, in Europe: gradual recovery from political disruption and increase in agricultural productivity and population

618-907 C.E.
Tang Dynasty in China: territorial expansion, government bureaucracy, agricultural improvements, and transportation and communication networks

632-733 C.E.
Muslim expansion and conquests in Arabia, Syria, Palestine, Mesopotamia, Egypt, North Africa, Persia, northwestern India, and Iberia

CIRCA 700 C.E.
Origins of feudalism, a political and social organization that dominates Europe until the fifteenth century; based on the relationship between lords and vassals

CIRCA 900 C.E.
Introduction of the horseshoe in Europe and gunpowder in China

960-1279 C.E.
Song Dynasty in China: civil administration, industry, education, and the arts

962-1806 C.E.
Holy Roman Empire of western and central Europe, created in an attempt to revive the old Roman Empire

1000 C.E.
The world population is approximately 300 million

1096-1291 C.E.
Western Christians undertake the Crusades, a series of religiously inspired military campaigns, to recapture the Holy Land from the Muslims

1200-1400 C.E.
The Mali Empire in Africa dominates the trans-Saharan trade network of camel caravans

1220-1335 C.E.
The Mongols, nomadic horsemen from the high steppes of eastern central Asia, build an empire that includes China, Persia, and Russia

CIRCA 1250 C.E.
Inca Empire develops in Peru: civil administration, road networks, and sun worshiping

1299-1919 C.E.
Ottoman Empire, created by nomadic Turks and Christian converts to Islam, encompasses Asia Minor, the Balkans, Greece, Egypt, North Africa, and the Middle East

1300 C.E.
The world population is approximately 396 million

1337-1453 C.E.
Hundred Years' War, a series of intermittent military campaigns between England and France over control of Continental lands claimed by both countries

1347-1350 C.E.
Black Death, or the bubonic plague, kills one-quarter of the European population

1368-1644 C.E.
Ming Dynasty in China: political, economic, and cultural revival; the Great Wall is built

1375-1527 C.E.
The Renaissance in western Europe, a revival in the arts and learning

1428-1519 C.E.
The Aztecs expand in central Mexico, developing trade routes and a system of tribute payments

1450 C.E.
Invention of the printing press

1453 C.E.
Constantinople falls to the Ottoman Turks, ending the Byzantine Empire

1464-1591 C.E.
Songhai Empire in Africa: military expansion, prosperous cities, and control of the trans-Saharan trade

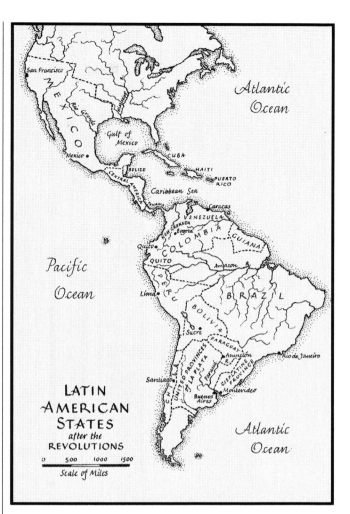

LATIN AMERICAN STATES after the REVOLUTIONS

Scale of Miles

1492 C.E.
Discovery of America; European exploration and colonization of the Western Hemisphere begins

CIRCA 1500-1867 C.E.
Transatlantic slave trade results in the forced migration of between 12 million and 16 million Africans to the Western Hemisphere

1500 C.E.
The world population is approximately 480 million

1517 C.E.
Beginning of the Protestant Reformation, a religious movement that ends the spiritual unity of Western Christendom

1523-1763 C.E.
Mughal Empire in India: military conquests, productive agricultural economy, and population growth

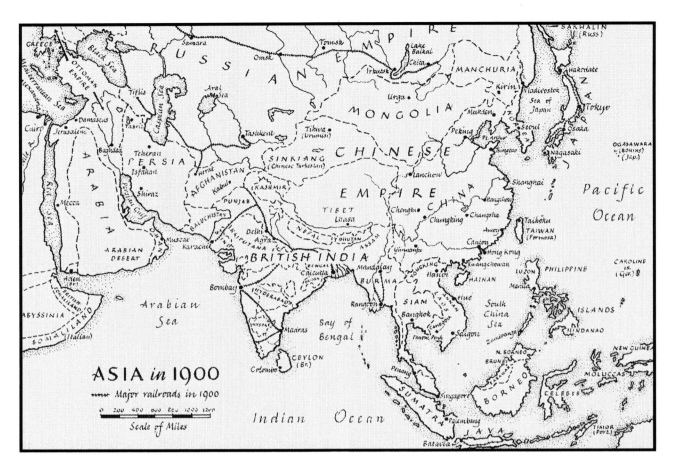

1600-1867 C.E.
Tokugawa Shogunate in Japan: shoguns (military governors) turn Edo, or Tokyo, into the political, economic, and cultural center of the nation

1618-1648 C.E.
Thirty Years' War in Europe between Catholic and Protestant states

1644-1911 C.E.
Qing Dynasty in China: military expansion and scholar-bureaucrats

1700 C.E.
The world population is approximately 640 million

CIRCA 1750 C.E.
Beginning of the Enlightenment, a philosophical movement marked by an emphasis on rationalism and scientific inquiry

1756-1763 C.E.
Seven Years' War: England and Prussia versus Austria, France, Russia, Saxony, Spain, and Sweden

CIRCA 1760-1850 C.E.
Industrial Revolution in Britain is marked by mass production through the division of labor, mechanization, a great increase in the supply of iron, and the use of the steam engine

1775-1783 C.E.
American War of Independence; the United States becomes an independent republic

1789 C.E.
French Revolution topples the monarchy and leads to a period of political unrest followed by a dictatorship

1793-1815 C.E.
Napoleonic Wars: Austria, England, Prussia, and Russia versus France and its satellite states

1794-1824 C.E.
Latin American states conduct wars of independence against Spain

1900 C.E.
The world population is approximately 1.65 billion

1914-1918 C.E.
World War I, or the Great War: the Allies
(England, France, Russia, and the United States)
versus the Central Powers (Austria-Hungary,
Germany, and the Ottoman Empire)

1917-1921 C.E.
Russian Revolution: a group of Communists
known as the Bolsheviks seize control of the
country following a civil war

1939-1945 C.E.
World War II: the Allies (China, England, France,
the Soviet Union, and the United States) versus the
Axis (Germany, Italy, and Japan)

1945 C.E.
Successful test of the first atomic weapon; beginning
of the Cold War, a period of rivalry, mistrust, and,
occasionally, open hostility between the capitalist
West and Communist East

1947-1975 C.E.
Decolonization occurs in Africa and Asia as European powers relinquish control of colonies in
those regions

1948
Israel becomes the first independent Jewish state in
nearly two thousand years

1949
Communists seize control of China

1950-1951
Korean War: the United States attempts to stop
Communist expansion in the Korean Peninsula

1957 C.E.
The Soviet Union launches *Sputnik* (fellow traveler of
earth), the first man-made satellite; the Space Age
begins

1965-1973
Vietnam War: the United States attempts to
thwart the spread of Communism in Vietnam

1989 C.E.
East European Communist regimes begin to falter,
and multiparty elections are held

1991 C.E.
Soviet Union is dissolved and replaced by the
Commonwealth of Independent States

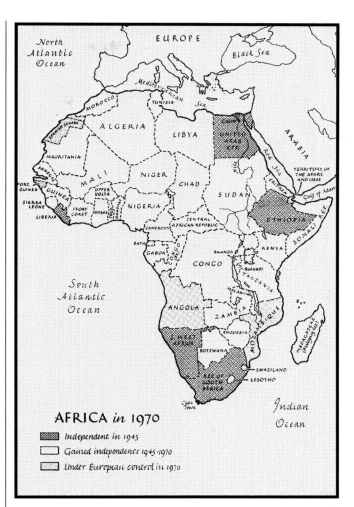

AFRICA *in* 1970
▓ Independent in 1945
□ Gained independence 1945-1970
▒ Under European control in 1970

2000 C.E.
The world population is approximately 6 billion

INTRODUCTION

Myths and Misinformation. From the beginning of recorded history, Africa has conjured up images of "darkness," barbarism, laziness, and ignorance, but also wonder and wealth (human and material resources to be exploited). Among the influential Europeans who fostered the image of Africans as "ignorant savages" were philosophers David Hume and Immanuel Kant. Writing during the European Enlightenment period of the mid eighteenth century, they argued that Africans had achieved little of any significance. In a long footnote to his 1754 essay "Of National Characters," Hume wrote: "I am apt to suspect the negroes and in general all other species of men (for there are four or five different kinds) to be naturally inferior to the whites. There never was a civilized nation of any other complexion than white, nor even any individual eminent either in action or speculation. No ingenious manufactures amongst them, no arts, no sciences." In 1764 Kant opened his essay "On National Characteristics" by declaring, "The Negroes of Africa have by nature no feeling that arises above the trifling." What is more, he reiterated Hume's challenge to find any accomplishment capable of demonstrating that "a Negro has shown talents." Even among those Africans who had been taken to other countries as slaves, he argued, "not a single one was ever found who presented anything great in art or science or any other praise-worthy quality," albeit poor white persons could pull themselves up from "the lowest rabble." Furthermore, Kant characterized Africans' religion as a widespread "religion of fetishes" wrought in trivial idolatry, in which a few words endow a "bird feather, a cow's horn, a conch shell, or any other common object" with power. Kant concluded that "blacks are very vain but in the Negro's way, and so talkative that they must be driven apart from each other with thrashings." There is no question that Hume's and Kant's ideas about Africa and Africans influenced the European colonial enterprise in Africa, including the so-called "civilizing mission" carried out by the European missionaries. It is equally true that

Hume and Kant based their observations on insufficient, secondhand evidence.

The Truth About Africa. This volume about West African kingdoms and empires between 500 and 1590 C.E. shows that Africans had complex religious systems, advanced artistic cultures, important centers of learning, and sophisticated systems of government. They knew science, mathematics, and technology. They traveled abroad in Africa, Asia, Europe, and the Americas. They communicated and traded not only with their neighbors but with countries around the world. Like all the volumes in the *World Eras* series, this one is a cross-disciplinary reference book, with a global perspective and a strong emphasis on daily life, social history, and cultural history. Providing in-depth coverage of how West Africans of the period 500–1590 lived and interacted with other peoples of the world, this volume is a reliable, engaging reference resource that encourages research and prompts comparisons to the lives of people on other times and places. Although there are several good books, reference works, and encyclopedias on Africa in general and West African kingdoms and empires in particular, there is no other single book that brings together in one volume discussions of West African geography, arts, communication, transportation, exploration, social class, economic and political systems, military developments, daily life and leisure activities, family structures, religion, philosophy, science, technology, and medicine.

Powerful Leaders and Great Empires. Described by the Arabs as *bilad al-Sudan* (land of the blacks), West Africa is often called the Sudan. During 500–1590 this region experienced tremendous progress in the arts, learning, trade, commerce, food production, science, and technology in kingdoms and empires ruled by a succession of mighty kings and emperors. Those who specialize in the history of ancient Africa know that Africans relied on oral traditions to chronicle events and pass on information to succeeding generations. The majority of the contemporary written documents about the region are accounts in Arabic, some by West Africans but many by visitors to the region from North Africa and Asia Minor. Both oral and written sources usually focus on the lives and deeds of great military and political leaders. Like the medieval European artisans who built the great cathedrals there, the great West African artists of the years 500–1590 were anonymous craftspeople. The same is true of everyday West Africans. Though historians and archaeologists have gleaned information about how they organized their families and conducted their daily lives, the names and deeds of these individuals went unrecorded.

Ghana: The First Great Empire. The wealthy kingdom of Wagadu arose in the third century, with its capital at Kumbi Saleh (in present-day southeastern Mauritania), which later became the capital of the Empire of Ghana. By 500, several major urban centers had sprung up in West Africa, and during the eighth century the city of Gao (in the modern nation of Mali) developed as a terminus for the trans-Saharan trade, which was largely based on the exchange of North African salt for West African gold. Though modern scholars call this expanding empire "Ghana," historians such as D. T. Niane and J. Suret-Canale, in their *Histoire de l'Afrique Occidentale* (1961), have concluded that the word *ghana* meant "war chief" and referred to the ruler, not the empire; they add that *ghana* may be derived from *kaya maghan* (king of the gold). By the middle of the eighth century Ghana had emerged as a powerful state, owing its prominence to the control it exerted over the burgeoning caravan trade. In 990, Ghana had 200,000 warriors and captured Audaghost, a strategically important Muslim oasis city (in present-day Mauritania), which served as a stopping place for trans-Saharan caravans. By 1068 the Empire of Ghana was the largest, wealthiest, and strongest state in West Africa. Around 1076, however, it fell to the Almoravids, Berber Muslims from North Africa under the leadership of Abu Bakr. Tunka (ruler) Menim of Ghana was allowed to maintain his throne while being compelled to pay tribute to the Almoravids. The Almoravids controlled Ghana until 1088, and the empire never regained its earlier power.

The Empire of Mali. The next state to exert a major influence over the region was a Susu kingdom that arose in the twelfth century. It reached the height of its power under Sumanguru, whose army captured Kumbi Saleh in 1203. Within a few decades, however, the Susu kingdom was eclipsed by Mali, which emerged as a major empire and exerted its control over the gold and salt traders. The founder of this empire, Sundiata (also known as Mari-Diata) and his grandnephew Mansa Musa are perhaps the best-known, most-mythologized rulers of ancient West Africa. Sundiata was crippled as a child, but one day he miraculously recovered movement in his legs and was able to walk. In 1230, he overthrew his uncle and ascended to the throne of Kangaba, and

five years later he defeated Sumanguru at the Battle of Kirina. In 1240, Sundiata captured and destroyed Kumbi Saleh and moved his capital from Djeriba to Niani (in present-day Guinea). In the Epic of Sundiata and other oral traditions of West Africa he is described as a great warrior who not only founded the Empire of Mali but also established its control over all the Western Sudan from Takrur in the west to the borders of Songhai in the east. Under Mansa Kankan Musa (ruled 1312–1337) the Empire of Mali experienced its golden age and reached its greatest territorial extent, expanding in all directions and absorbing the territories of the old Empire of Ghana. Mansa Musa is well known for his pilgrimage to Mecca in 1324. He traveled with a caravan of 60,000 people, including 12,000 servants, and 300 camels, each carrying 300 pounds of gold. Mansa Musa's pilgrimage to Mecca increased the reputation of the Mali Empire as a wealthy state and a major center for Islamic scholarship, especially in Timbuktu. But after Mansa Musa's death, his son and successor Mansa Magha (ruled 1337–1341) could not stop the Mossi (of Yatenga) from sacking Timbuktu twice. During the same period, Songhai recovered some of the autonomy it had lost to Mali under Mansa Musa. After 1360, the Empire of Mali was in decline and several of its territories were raided by the Mossi, the Tuaregs, and others. By 1450, Massina, Timbuktu, and Walata no longer paid tribute to the emperor of Mali.

The Empire of Songhai. In 1468, Sunni Ali (the Great) captured Timbuktu from the Tuaregs and founded the Empire of Songhai, which by 1475 had replaced Mali as the most important state in West Africa. Songhai grew to be as large as Western Europe, and its civilization rivaled that of any other in the world. Under its rule, between 1490 and 1590, West African gold traffic reached its pinnacle. A great warrior, Sunni Ali was celebrated for his economic reforms and military innovations, but he is also remembered for his destruction of Timbuktu and his cruelty to its inhabitants. In 1492 he was thrown from his horse and drowned while trying to cross a river during a battle. He was replaced by his general Askia Muhammad Toure, who ruled Songhai as Askia Muhammad I (Askia the Great) until 1528. Askia Muhammad is credited with tripling the size of the Empire of Songhai, promoting commerce and trade, and building the first professional army in West Africa. Under him, the University of Sankore became one of the greatest centers of learning in the world. Askia Muhammad I was overthrown by his son Askia Musa in 1528. Between then and 1539 Songhai was ruled in quick succession by three weak sons of Askia Muhammad, and the empire was in decline during this period. Askia Ishaq (ruled 1439–1549) halted this decline by eliminating all his rivals, but the end of the Songhai Empire was near by the time of his death. The Moroccan invasion of 1590–1591 ended the hegemony of the Empire of Songhai, but a weakened and fragmented empire continued to exist until 1690.

Other Kingdoms and Rulers. Other kingdoms and empires that played important roles in the history of West Africa during the period 500–1590 include Kanem and Bornu (sometimes ruled together and called Kanem-Bornu), the Hausa states, and the Yoruba states of Benin, Ile-Ife, and Oyo. Mai Idris Alooma, who ruled Bornu from about 1570 until sometime between 1600 and 1617, is known as a great leader, a military innovator, an astute administrator, and a devout Muslim. He also established diplomatic relations between his kingdom and the Ottoman Empire. Queen Amina (ruled 1566–1610) of Zazzau was reputed to be as capable and as fearless a warrior as a man.

West African Scholars. West Africa also had important scholars during the period 500–1590. Mahmoud al-Kati (1468 – circa 1593), a Soninke writer and historian who held a doctorate in Islamic Law from Sankore University in Timbuktu, is believed to be the first West African scholar to write a history of the Western Sudan. Ahmad Baba (1556–1627), another erudite scholar from Timbuktu, is known to have written fifty-six books on Islamic theology and law as well as on Arabic grammar. Another scholar from Timbuktu, 'Abd al-Rahman al-Sa'di (1569 – circa 1655), wrote the second history of the region by a West African, chronicling the fall of Timbuktu to Moroccan forces in 1591.

West Africans and Their Geography. West Africans have always faced geographical challenges, including hot temperatures and dust storms. During the years 300–1550, the world was in an extended period of drought. The Sahara expanded southward. Water levels reached record lows in the Senegal River, the Niger River, and Lake Chad, the major sources of water for the farmlands of the Sahel and savanna, where most West African food crops are grown. As a result people migrated southward in the region, searching for arable land and reliable water supplies. People also migrated to avoid subjugation to conquering empires. The more-or-less constant migration during the period affected the abilities of states to produce enough food to feed their populations, and the results included political instability and shifts of the balance of power. Yet, despite such hardships, West Africans managed to grow enough food to sustain great empires and advanced civilizations.

The Arts. During the period 500–1590, the crafts of smelting and working iron and other metals were widespread in West Africa, and sculptors fashioned realistic figures, including representations of humans, from brass, bronze, and gold—as well as terra-cotta and ceramics. As in other parts of Africa, art for art's sake was nonexistent. Art in West Africa was characterized by a sort of *dulce et utile*—it was beautiful and useful; it instructed and entertained. For example, the Akan, or Ashanti, gold weights of the fifteenth and sixteenth centuries were used on scales to weigh gold dust, and they were valued as beautiful artworks. Highly developed architectural styles also combined beauty and function. The West African arts of body adornment and cloth weaving communicated an individual's "story," including his or her social status and role in a particular society. While European history of this period was largely written, much of West African history and culture—as well the lineages of West African rulers—was passed on through the performance arts at the royal courts and in rural and urban areas. The griots—who functioned as storytellers, poets, and musicians—were oral historians, "living libraries" and depositories of history. West Africans possess a significant body of folklore and epic traditions that rival those of the Greeks. The best-known epic of the 500–1590 period is the Epic of Sundiata, narrated by a griot.

Communication, Transportation, and Exploration. West Africans were not "isolatoes." During the years 500–1590, they communicated among themselves, as well as with other regions of Africa and the world. It is believed that, before the arrival of Muslim and Arab scholars, West Africans already had some writing systems, such as Akan and Mande scripts. With the introduction of Islam to West Africa, beginning in the eighth century, came Arabic writing, which spurred the development of centers of religion and learning in cities such as Timbuktu and Djenné. Trans-Saharan trade routes connected West Africa to cities such as Tripoli and Cairo in North Africa and Mecca in Asia Minor, and West African cities such as Timbuktu, Djenné, and Gao along the Niger River developed into flourishing centers of commerce, trade, and cultural exchange. North African travelers such as Ibn Battuta, who visited Mali in 1352–1353, and Leo Africanus, who visited Songhai in 1512–1515, helped to educate the world about West Africa. In addition to crossing the Sahara, West Africans are believed to have explored the Atlantic Ocean and may have reached South America as early as 500 C.E. Arabic historians recorded accounts of Abubakari II of Mali and his 1311 westward voyage across the Atlantic. Increased communication also had nefarious effects on West African states during this period, two of which are slavery and European colonization along the Atlantic coast of West Africa. The first African slaves were taken to Europe in approximately the eleventh century, and in 1518 Spanish slave traders transported the first African slaves to the West Indies.

Social Class and the Economy. It would be a mistake to contend that the rise and decline of such great empires as Ghana, Mali, Songhai, and Kanem-Bornu depended solely on the trans-Saharan gold trade or on the introduction and expansion of Islam in the region. State formation was based around and dependent on centers of food production and metallurgy, as well as control of gold sources and trade routes. Social distinctions were often based on occupations, and many trades were the exclusive preserves of specific families or clans. Slavery existed in West Africa during the period 500–1590, but it was not practiced on as large a scale as the Atlantic Slave Trade of the sixteenth century. Mostly war captives, slaves were used largely as agricultural labor. A slave could rise from slavery and become a ruler, as did two emperors of Mali, Sakura (ruled circa 1285 – circa 1300) and Sandiki (ruled 1388–1390).

Politics, Law, and the Military. West Africans were astute political leaders, staunch supporters of the law, and brilliant military organizers and strategists. Much of the history of West Africa during the 500–1590 period is dominated by its rulers' military prowess, conquests, and assertion of their will over less-powerful states. Contrary to some beliefs, however, they were not tyrants. There is ample evidence that elaborate procedures existed to hold the king's power in check. It was understood that rulers exerted their power for the welfare of all citizens, not for individual gain. Furthermore, citizens had the right to representation in councils of elders or village assemblies, which kept power decentralized. During this period West African states were guided by the rule of laws that were undergirded by traditional legal systems and, later, by Islamic jurisprudence. Citizens enjoyed fundamental human rights, including the rights to live, work, and receive a fair trial.

Daily Life and the Family. Soil and climate conditions were major influences on the daily lives of West African families during the years 500–1590. For example, high temperatures lead to a rapid loss of water and salt, and much effort was expended in replenishing these basic needs. Areas where crops could grow well and people could fish and hunt experienced a tremendous, sustained population growth. Regarding entertainment, West Africans enjoyed music, dance, and other performance arts as part of their daily life and leisure. Sporting entertainments included hunting, horseback riding, rowing, stick fighting, and wrestling. The typical West African family unit consisted not only of a husband, wife, and children but also of the extended family. In this family unit, children learned about respect for their elders and love of family, and they were taught rituals and celebrations that connected the past to the present and future, as well as skills to use later in life. While young boys were trained by older men and young girls by mothers and aunts, not all tasks were gender specific.

Religion and Philosophy. When European colonizers and missionaries arrived in Africa, they created and perpetuated the stereotypical notions that Africans had no knowledge of God and could not formally process reflections about their human experiences. Africans lacked logical reasoning, the Europeans maintained, and could boast of no Plato or Aristotle. Therefore, colonizers and missionaries not only tried to downgrade and suppress African oral traditions and religious beliefs but also called practitioners of traditional religions "pagans" and characterized their rituals as sorcery or witchcraft. Before the Europeans arrived, Muslims had also tried to replace traditional religions with their own, but African traditional religions survived; for West Africans practiced these new faiths alongside their traditional religions.

Traditional Beliefs. Ancient West Africans usually believed in a supreme God who was omnipotent and omniscient—such as Onyame for the Akan, Chukwu for the Igbo, Da for the Fon, and Olorun/Olodumare for the Yoruba. Some lesser gods and goddesses were believed to act as messengers between the supreme God and the humans. For example, Esu (Esu-Elegba for the Yoruba) or Legba (for the Fon) was known to deliver rituals and sacrifices from the humans to the gods. Several West African deities—including Esu, Olorun, Ogun (the god of iron and war), Shango (the god of thunder and lightning), and Obatala (a human deified for his heroic deeds)—have crossed the Middle Passage to the Americas (Brazil, Cuba, Haiti, Jamaica, and Trinidad, as well as New Orleans, Chicago, and New York), where worship of them exists in a syncretic relationship with Christianity.

Philosophy. West African metaphysics and ethics are closely linked to the traditional religions of the region. West Africans believed that the past still exists in the present and future and that death was only a transitional phase. As a matter of fact, the domain of the living was never far from that of the dead. In Chinua Achebe's well-known novel *Things Fall Apart* (1958), the reader learns that during festivals, masquerades, and other religious ceremonies the dead cross back and forth between their world and that of the living. Explications of philosophical concepts are found in the tales of trickster-gods, riddles, proverbs, fables, myths, and oral traditions, as well as in the writings of scholars from great centers of learning such as Timbuktu, Sankore, and Gao.

Science and Technology. Even before the introduction of Arabic learning, West Africans were not ignorant of mathematics, science, and technology. For example, they had developed forms of non-Euclidean geometry such as fractals (based on pattern repetitions). The well-known Ifa divination was based on a form of fractal geometry. West Africans had also mastered the technology of metallurgy. Medicine men and women, diviners, and priests passed on healing arts, and the Dogon people had a caste of priest astronomers. With the arrival of Muslims, West Africans profited from the extensive knowledge of the Arabs in the fields of science, mathematics, and medicine. In the 1200s the University of Djenné became a famous center of scholarship and learning for medicine and surgery. In 1400 the University of Timbuktu was a flourishing center for Islamic studies, science, medicine, and mathematics; around 1500, some 25,000 scholars are believed to have resided in Timbuktu.

Acknowledgments. Editing this volume has been a challenging and enriching experience. I would like to thank the authors of the chapters: Pita Ogaba Agbese, Edwin Kweku Andoh, Diedre L. Badejo, Pade Badru, Donna J. Davis, Emmanuel Chukwudi Eze, David L. Horne, and Carole Shelley Yates. In addition to writing the chapter on "The Family and Social Trends," Pade Badru contributed "Sports" to "Leisure, Recreation, and Daily Life." I would not have taken on this assignment if it had not been for John Kirby, who made me aware of the project and believed in my ability to edit this volume. I thank my department at the University of Northern Iowa for encouraging me and assigning a graduate assistant to help me with the chapter on selected events outside West Africa. All those colleagues who sympathized with me during the hard work of bringing this book to fruition also deserve my thanks. Finally, I thank my wife, Anathalie Mukagasana, and my children, Anita, Michael, and Malcolm-Aimé, for their love, patience, and understanding.

Pierre-Damien Mvuyekure,
University of Northern Iowa
Cedar Falls, Iowa

PERMISSIONS

TEXT

"Ashanti Proverbs and Sayings Cast in Brass" (pp. 138–139), "Some Dahomean Riddles" and "Some Dahomean Proverbs" (p. 144),"How Twins Came Among the Yoruba" (p. 265), "Anansi Proves He Is the Oldest" (p. 283), "Shango and the Medicine of Eshu" (p. 297), and "Oranmiyan, the Hero of Ife" (pp. 300–301). Permission to reprint granted by the Emma Courlander Trust.

"How the Spider Obtained the Sky God's Stories" (pp. 290–291) and "How Diseases Came to the Ashanti" (p. 328), from Radin, Paul, ed.; *African Folktales & Sculpture*. Copyright © 1952 by Bolingen Foundation. Reprinted by permission of Princeton University Press.

ILLUSTRATIONS

Pp. 85, 130, and 343: Reproduced by permission of UNESCO.

Pp. 102 and 206: Stephenie Hollyman ©2003.

P. 106: © Margaret Courtney-Clarke/CORBIS.

P. 208: The Metropolitan Museum of Art, Gift of Mr. and Mrs. Klaus G. Perls, 1990. (1990.332) Photograph, all rights reserved, The Metropolitan Museum of Art.

P. 214: The Metropolitan Museum of Art, Gift of Mr. and Mrs. Klaus G. Perls, 1991. (1991.17.10) Photograph, all rights reserved, The Metropolitan Museum of Art.

P. 217 (left): The Metropolitan Museum of Art, Gift of Mr. and Mrs. Klaus G. Perls, 1991. (1991.17.25) Photograph, all rights reserved, The Metropolitan Museum of Art.

P. 217 (right): The Metropolitan Museum of Art, Gift of Mr. and Mrs. Klaus G. Perls, 1991. (1991.17.20) Photo-graph, all rights reserved, The Metropolitan Museum of Art.

P. 226 (left): The Metropolitan Museum of Art, Gift of Mr. and Mrs. Klaus G. Perls, 1991. (1991.17.22) Photograph, all rights reserved, The Metropolitan Museum of Art.

P. 226 (right): The Metropolitan Museum of Art, Gift of Mr. and Mrs. Klaus G. Perls, 1991. (1991.17.26) Photograph, all rights reserved, The Metropolitan Museum of Art.

P. 237: Photograph by Lester Wunderman. The Metropolitan Museum of Art, Gift of Lester Wunderman. Photograph, all rights reserved, The Metropolitan Museum of Art.

P. 240 (top left): The Metropolitan Museum of Art, Gift of Lester Wunderman, 1977. (1977.394.64) Photograph, all rights reserved, The Metropolitan Museum of Art.

P. 240 (top right): The Metropolitan Museum of Art, Gift of Lester Wunderman, 1977. (1977.394.66) Photograph, all rights reserved, The Metropolitan Museum of Art.

P. 269 (left): The Metropolitan Museum of Art, The Michael C. Rockefeller Memorial Collection, Bequest of Nelson A. Rockefeller, 1979. (1979.206.121) Photograph, all rights reserved, The Metropolitan Museum of Art.

P. 269 (right): The Metropolitan Museum of Art, Gift of the Kronos Collections in honor of Martin Lerner, 1983. (1983.600a,b) Photograph, all rights reserved, The Metropolitan Museum of Art.

P. 304: The Metropolitan Museum of Art, Gift of Mr. and Mrs. Klaus G. Perls, 1991. (1991.17.32) Photograph, all rights reserved, The Metropolitan Museum of Art.

ACKNOWLEDGMENTS

This book was produced by Manly, Inc. Karen L. Rood, senior editor, was the in-house editor. She was assisted by Anthony J. Scotti Jr., series editor.

Production manager is Philip B. Dematteis.

Administrative support was provided by Ann M. Cheschi and Carol A. Cheschi.

Accountant is Ann-Marie Holland.

Copyediting supervisor is Sally R. Evans. The copyediting staff includes Phyllis A. Avant, Caryl Brown, Melissa D. Hinton, Philip I. Jones, Rebecca Mayo, and Nancy E. Smith. Freelance copyeditor is Brenda Cabra.

Editorial associates are Amelia B. Lacey, Michael S. Martin, Catherine M. Polit, William Mathes Straney, and James F. Tidd Jr.

Permissions editor and database manager is Amber L. Coker.

Layout and graphics supervisor is Janet E. Hill. The graphics staff includes Zoe R. Cook and Sydney E. Hammock.

Office manager is Kathy Lawler Merlette.

Photography supervisor is Paul Talbot. Photography editor is Scott Nemzek.

Digital photographic copy work was performed by Joseph M. Bruccoli.

SGML work was done by Linda Dalton Mullinax.

Systems manager is Donald Kevin Starling.

Typesetting supervisor is Kathleen M. Flanagan. The typesetting staff includes Patricia Marie Flanagan, Mark J. McEwan, and Pamela D. Norton.

Walter W. Ross supervised library research. He was assisted by Jo Cottingham and the following librarians at the Thomas Cooper Library of the University of South Carolina: circulation department head Tucker Taylor; reference department head Virginia W. Weathers; reference department staff Brette Barron, Marilee Birchfield, Paul Cammarata, Gary Geer, Michael Macan, Tom Marcil, Rose Marshall, and Sharon Verba; interlibrary loan department head John Brunswick; and interlibrary loan staff Robert Arndt, Hayden Battle, Alex Byrne, Jo Cottingham, Bill Fetty, Marna Hostetler, and Nelson Rivera.

WORLD ERAS

VOLUME 10

WEST AFRICAN KINGDOMS

500 – 1590

WORLD EVENTS:
SELECTED OCCURRENCES OUTSIDE WEST AFRICA

by PIERRE-DAMIEN MVUYEKURE

500*	• The civilization of the kingdom of Teotihuacán in Mexico is at its height.
500*-600*	• In the Gupta empire of northeastern India, mathematicians develop the decimal system, and great Sanskrit epics and Hindu art works are created. • Indians in Peru make music with flutes, horns, tubas, and drums.
502-549	• Emperor Wudi, founder of the Southern Liang dynasty, rules southern China.
507	• Clovis I, king of the Franks (rules 481–511), kills Visigoth king Alaric II (rules 484–507) in battle and seizes his kingdom of Toulouse. • By this date the Germanic people known as the Alemanni are burying their dead in wooden coffins.
510	• Under Theodoric the Great, the Italian Ostrogoths occupy Provence, which they hold until 563.
511	• On the death of Clovis I, king of the Franks, his realm is divided among his sons, Theuderic I, Chlodomir, Childebert I, and Chlothar I (also known as Lothair).
516	• Sigismund, son-in-law of Theodoric the Great, becomes king of Burgundy.

*DENOTES CIRCA DATE

WORLD EVENTS 500-1590

517
- After converting to Buddhism, Emperor Wudi helps to establish it in China.
- In India, Aryabhata I compiles a manual of astronomy.

518
- Justin I becomes Roman emperor, ruling the remaining, eastern (Byzantine) empire.

519
- Through the efforts of Emperor Justin I and Pope Hormisdas, the first schism between the Western and Eastern Christian Churches ends.

520
- Latin grammarian Priscian writes *Institutiones Grammaticae* (Grammatical Foundations), which has a major influence on the teaching of Latin and grammar in general throughout the European Middle Ages.

523
- Hilderic succeeds Thrasamund as ruler of the Vandal kingdom (in modern-day Tunisia).
- Pope John I joins with Emperor Justin in an attempt to force Arian Christians (who deny the divinity of Jesus Christ) to convert to orthodox Christianity.

524
- Frankish kings Chlodomir, Childebert I, and Chlothar I invade Burgundy; Sigismund and Chlodomir are killed.

525
- Caleb of Abyssinia conquers the Yemen.

526
- On the death of Theodoric the Great, his son Athalaric becomes king of the Ostrogoths. Like his father, Athalaric is nominally subject to the emperor in Byzantium but is the de facto secular ruler of Italy.
- Pope John I dies while imprisoned by Theodoric the Great, an Arian who was angered by John's opposition to his religious beliefs.

527
- Emperor Justin I dies and is succeeded by his nephew Justinian I, who rules until 565.

529
- Attempting to rid the Byzantine Empire of paganism, Justinian I closes the one-thousand-year-old School of Philosophy in Athens.
- Known as the father of Western monasticism, Benedict of Nursia founds the Benedictine Order at Monte Cassino, where he builds a monastery.

*DENOTES CIRCA DATE

WORLD EVENTS 500-1590

530
- Gelimer deposes Hilderic and becomes king of the Vandals.

531-579
- During the reign of Persian king Khosrow I, the Sasanian Empire undergoes a cultural and artistic renaissance.

532
- Emperor Justinian commissions the principal church of Constantinople, the Hagia Sophia.

533
- Byzantine general Belisarius defeats the Vandal king Gelimer, conquering the North African provinces that the Vandals took from the western Roman Empire in about 429.
- Belisarius captures Sicily, using it as a base from which to conquer large portions of Italy, including Rome, for the Byzantine Empire by 540.

539-562
- The Byzantine and Sasanian Empires are at war.
- Empress Theodora of Byzantium introduces long white dresses, purple cloaks, gold embroidery, tiaras, and pointed shoes.

542
- Transported by rats from Egypt and Syria, a plague hits Constantinople and spreads all over Europe.

543
- Disastrous earthquakes shake the whole world.

546
- Ostrogoth king Totila captures Rome, which is retaken by Byzantine general Belisarius.

550
- Totila conquers Rome for the second time and goes on to take most of the rest of Italy and Sicily. As Byzantine power gradually declines in the West, the influence of the papacy begins to grow.

552
- Led by General Narses, the Byzantines defeat the Ostrogoths in the Battle of Taginae, killing King Totila and embarking on a march through Italy.
- Emperor Justinian sends missionaries to China and Ceylon with instructions to smuggle silkworms home to the West, marking the start of the European silk industry.

* DENOTES CIRCA DATE

WORLD EVENTS 500-1590

553
- Narses retakes Rome and Naples for the Byzantines, ending Ostrogoth rule there.

558
- Chlothar I, the last surviving son of Clovis I, reunifies the kingdom of the Franks under his rule.

561
- On the death of Chlothar, the Frankish kingdom is divided among his four sons, leading to war among the brothers.

565
- On the death of Justinan I, his nephew becomes Emperor Justin II.

567
- Leovigild, king of the Visigoths, drives the Byzantines from Spain.
- As a result of the feud among Chlothar's sons, the Frankish kingdom is partitioned into Austrasia (Lorraine, Belgium, and the right bank of the Rhine; capital Metz), Neustria (in France; capital Soissons), and Burgundy (a separate kingdom ruled by the king of Neustria).

568
- The Lombards conquer large portions of Italy, permanently ending Byzantine rule in those regions.

570*
- Muhammad, the founder of Islam, is born in Mecca.
- The Persian troops of the Sasanian Empire overthrow the Abyssinian rulers of the Yemen.

572-574
- Byzantine troops invade the Sasanian Empire, whose troops counterattack and capture several important Byzantine cities.

574
- Driven to insanity by the Sasanian conquests, Emperor Justin II is convinced to adopt General Tiberius as his son and co-emperor, Tiberius II Constantinus.

578
- On the death of Justin II, Tiberius II Constantinus becomes sole emperor of Byzantium.

581-604
- Founder of the Sui dynasty (581–618), Emperor Wendi rules China. By the end of the 580s he has unified northern and southern China.

*DENOTES CIRCA DATE

WORLD EVENTS 500-1590

582
- Just before his death Byzantine emperor Tiberius II Constantinus names Maurice, the commander of his Persian victories, as his successor.

587
- The first Buddhist monastery is founded in Japan.

590*
- General Bahram usurps the Sasanian throne and forces the young king Khosrow II to seek asylum with the Byzantines, who send an army to restore him to his throne.

597
- Kent becomes the first Anglo-Saxon kingdom to convert to Christianity.

600*
- Tibet begins to coalesce into one state.
- Smallpox spreads to China and then to Asia Minor and southern Europe.

602
- Phocas kills Byzantine emperor Maurice and succeeds him.

604
- The first church bell is installed in Rome.

610*
- The Prophet Muhammad has the first of many visions in which the message of the Quran is revealed to him.

613
- The Frankish kingdoms are re-united under Chlothar II, son of Chilperic I of Neustria.

614
- Persian troops of the Sasanid empire conquer the Byzantine cities of Damascus and Jerusalem and take the Holy Cross.

616
- Egypt is overrun by the Sasanids.

618
- Yangdi, the last emperor of the Chinese Sui dynasty, is overthrown by Li Yuan, who becomes the first emperor of the Tang dynasty.

*DENOTES CIRCA DATE

WORLD EVENTS 500–1590

622
- After they are driven out of his native city of Mecca, the Prophet Muhammad and his followers settle in Medina, where he founds a house of worship, or mosque, in the courtyard of his home. This year becomes year one in the Muslim calendar.

- Prince Shotoku of Japan dies, having served as regent for his aunt Empress Suiko (rules 592–628) since the beginning of her reign.

623
- The first Muslim military expeditions are launched from Medina.

626
- Chinese emperor Li Yuan's second son, Li Shimin, kills his brothers and forces his father to abdicate in his favor. He becomes Emperor Taizong.

- Bishop Paulinus of Kent goes on a mission to Northumbria, where he converts King Edwin and many of his subjects.

626–628
- The Celtic Christian Church of southern Ireland adopts the Roman Christian form of worship. Northern Irish churches make the change in 692.

628
- Having achieved a decisive victory against the Sasanids at the Battle of Ninevah in December 627, Byzantine emperor Heraclius I is able to end a war that has continued off and on for decades. Khosrow II is deposed and executed. The Byzantines recover all the territory conquered by the Sasanids, which includes Jerusalem and Alexandria, as well as the Holy Cross.

- After the surrender of Mecca to a Muslim force, the Prophet appoints his first resident governor away from Medina, thus making the Muslim polity a territorial state and establishing the practice of making an annual pilgrimage *(hajj)* to Mecca from Medina.

630*
- The Anglo-Saxon kingdoms of East Anglia and Wessex are converted to Christianity.

- Mahendravarman I dies. Under his reign, which began circa 600, the Pallava dynasty of southern India reached the height of its power.

630
- The first Japanese embassy is established in the Chinese capital of Chang'an.

632
- The Prophet Muhammad dies. His successor is Caliph Abu Bakr (rules 632–634). During his reign he begins a series of campaigns in Byzantine and Sasanid (Persian) territory.

*DENOTES CIRCA DATE

WORLD EVENTS 500-1590

633
- Because of a revival of paganism in Northumbria after the death of King Edwin in 632, his successor, Oswald, invites the monk Aidan of Iona to spread Christianity throughout northern England. The mission begins the temporary ascendancy in England of Celtic Christianity over that of the Roman Church.

634
- Damascus falls to Muslim forces.
- On the death of Abu Bakr, 'Umar ibn al-Khattab (rules 634–644) becomes caliph.

634-642
- In successful battles against the Byzantines and Sasanids, the Muslims conquer Syria, Palestine (including Jerusalem in 638), Egypt, Iraq, and Iran.

635
- A Nestorian missionary arrives in the Chinese capital of Chang'an, where he is received by Emperor Taizong, allowed to preach, and given a church (638). The Nestorians are a Christian sect centered in Persia who believe the divine and human natures of Jesus Christ are independent—two persons only loosely united.

639
- On the death of Chlothar II's son Dagobert I, the Frankish kingdoms are divided. Chlothar gave Austrasia to his son Sigibert in 632 and now leaves Neustria and Burgundy to his son Clovis II. Though members of the Merovingian dynasty continue to rule in name until 751, power passes to nobles known as mayors of the palaces: Ebroïn in Neustria and, in Austrasia, Pepin I of Landen, founder of what becomes known as the Carolingian dynasty.

640
- After Byzantine Egypt falls to the Muslims, thirty thousand papyrus scrolls are found in the library of Alexandria, whose book-copying industry is subsequently destroyed. As a result, Alexandria ceases to be the center for Western culture.

642
- Kubrat, king of the Bulgars, dies, and his five sons divide their people into five hordes, three of which are absorbed into other peoples over the next few decades. Bezmer, or Bat-Bayan, leads his horde north, where it eventually settles around the confluence of the Volga and Kama Rivers. Asparukh leads his horde westward, eventually crossing the Danube River.

643
- Muslims conquer Tripoli.
- King Rothari codifies the laws of the Lombards.
- The Soga family of Japan kills Prince Shotoku's son Yamashiro Oe and his family.

*DENOTES CIRCA DATE

WORLD EVENTS 500-1590

645
- Prince Nakano Oe and Nakatomi Kamatari stage a coup in Japan, killing the Soga family and re-establishing the power of the royal family.

646
- The Japanese royal family institutes the Taikwa reforms, re-establishing a central Japanese state and limiting the power of the nobility.
- A Byzantine fleet recaptures Alexandria.

647
- Harsha dies, and his empire in northern India, which he has ruled since 606, breaks up.

650*
- Two Slavic tribes, the Croats and the Serbs, settle in Bosnia.
- Turkic tribes known as the Khazars conquer the Bulgars of the Volga region in southern Russia.

651
- Yazdigard III, the last Sasanid ruler, dies as the Muslim conquest of his empire becomes complete.

653
- Muslims complete their successful attempt to seize Armenia from the Byzantines.

655
- A Muslim navy defeats a Byzantine fleet off the coast of Lycia (in present-day Turkey).
- The Chinese concubine Wu Zhao marries Emperor Gaozong (reigns 649–683) and becomes empress. By 660 she, not her husband, is the real ruler of China.

656-661
- During the first Muslim civil war Mu'awiyah becomes the first Muslim caliph of the Umayyad dynasty (660), establishing his capital in Damascus, which becomes the political and cultural center of the Muslim world.

657-659
- The western Turks disperse, some traveling across southern Russia and eventually reaching Hungary, others going to India.

660
- The Korean kingdom of Paekche is invaded by China.

664
- Though at first Roman and Celtic Christian missionaries worked together in Britain, differences have developed, especially over how to calculate the date of Easter. The Synod of Whitby firmly establishes Roman Christianity as the dominant religion of England.

*DENOTES CIRCA DATE

WORLD EVENTS 500-1590

668
- Constans II is killed during a mutiny of his troops in Syracuse and is succeeded by his son Constantine IV, who reigns until 685 during a period in which the Byzantine Empire is under constant attack, not only from the Muslim Empire but also from Bulgar and Slavic peoples of the Balkans.

- China forces Korea to become a vassal state.

672
- The death of Emperor Tenji, who has ruled Japan since 668, sparks warfare over the succession. Tenji's younger brother is victorious and rules as Emperor Temmu.

674-678
- Constantinople is besieged by Arab naval forces. The conflict ends with a truce that lasts thirty years.

675
- China completes its conquest of the Korean Peninsula.

680-711
- Visigoth authorities intensify their persecution of Spanish Jews and try to compel them to convert to Christianity.

681
- The Byzantine Empire recognizes by treaty that the land between the Balkans and the Danube is under the control of Asparukh's horde of Bulgars, delimiting the territory in which the modern state of Bulgaria was later created and weakening the hold of the Avars in the region.

681-687
- The Anglo-Saxon kingdom of Sussex is converted to Christianity.

681-692
- During the second Muslim civil war the Umayyads successfully defend their control of the caliphate.

681-737
- The Khazars are embroiled in a series of wars with the Muslim Empire and eventually withdraw north of the Caucasus Mountains, where they provide a buffer between the Muslims and eastern Europe.

683
- On the death of Emperor Gaozong of China, Empress Wu becomes the de facto ruler of China, finally usurping the throne outright in 690.

685
- Justinian II succeeds his father, Constantine IV, to the throne of the Byzantine Empire.

*Denotes Circa Date

WORLD EVENTS 500-1590

688
- Justinian II and Caliph Abd al-Malik sign a treaty declaring the Byzantine island of Cyprus neutral territory. The two empires hold the island jointly for almost three hundred years though both sides frequently violate the treaty.

693
- The Muslims win a major victory over Byzantine forces in the Battle of Sevastopol.

695
- Leontius seizes the Byzantine throne from Justinian II, initiating two decades of instability in the empire.

698
- Muslims capture and destroy the Byzantine port of Carthage in North Africa.
- The Byzantine army overthrows Emperor Leontius and places Tiberius II on the throne.

700*
- By this date the Lombards of Italy have converted from Arianism to orthodox Roman Christianity.

705
- In China, Empress Wu is forced to abdicate in favor of her son Emperor Zhongzong.
- With the help of the Bulgars, Justinian II reclaims the Byzantine throne.

711
- King Roderick of Spain is defeated by Berber general Tariq ibn Ziyad, who has been invited into Visigoth Spain by Roderick's rival for the throne. By 719 the invaders reach the Pyrenees, making nearly all of Spain a Muslim state and granting Jews the civil rights they did not possess in Christian Spain.

712
- Samarqand, in Turkestan, is occupied by the Arabs, who make the city a center of Muslim culture and one of the earliest sites of the Muslim papermaking industry, which spreads from China to the Muslim world during the first half of the eighth century.
- Muhammad ibn Kasim establishes a Muslim state in Sind (India).

712-744
- During his reign Lombard king Liutprand steadily reduces Byzantine territory in Italy.

716-719
- Charles (the Hammer) Martel, illegitimate son of Pepin II of Heristal and grandfather of Charlemagne, establishes himself as mayor of Austrasia and Neustria and sets out to reassert Frankish authority in southern Gaul.

*DENOTES CIRCA DATE

WORLD EVENTS 500-1590

717
- Leo III forces the abdication of Theodosius III and is proclaimed Byzantine emperor, ruling until his death in 741.

717-718
- For thirteen months Muslim naval forces besiege Constantinople in an unsuccessful attempt to take the city and crush the power of the Byzantines.

718-721
- Visigoth noble Pelayo establishes the Christian kingdom of Asturias.

720
- Muslim troops cross the Pyrenees into France, seizing Narbonne.

725
- The Chinese capital of Chang'an is the largest city in the world. Constantinople is the second largest.
- Southern France is ravaged by Muslim troops.

727
- China and Tibet begin a full-scale war. Though a settlement is reached in 730, fighting between China and Tibet flares up again within ten years and continues off and on for several decades.

729-749
- During his reign, the devout Emperor Shomu establishes Buddhist temples and monasteries in every province of Japan.

730
- With the help of the Lombards, Ravenna successfully rids itself of Byzantine rule, while Venice helps Byzantium to keep other parts of its Italian territory.

732
- Charles Martel leads Frankish soldiers to victory in the Battle of Tours, checking the Muslims' northward advance into Europe.

735-736
- Charles Martel drives the Muslims from Burgundy.

740
- The unity of the Muslim caliphate is destroyed when the Berbers of Morocco revolt and set up their own government.

741
- On the death of Charles Martel, his lands are divided between his sons: Carloman becomes mayor of Austrasia, and Pepin III (the Short) gets Neustria.

*DENOTES CIRCA DATE

WORLD EVENTS 500-1590

741
(CONT'D)

- On the death of Leo III, his son Constantine V becomes Byzantine emperor.

744

- On the northern border of China, the Uighur Turks establish an empire that remains a powerful force in the region until 840.

745

- Emperor Constantine V defeats Muslim troops at several important battles in northern Syria.

747

- With the support of Pope Zacharias, Pepin III (the Short) becomes king of all Carolingian holdings.

749

- Not long before his death the Buddhist monk Gyogi promotes the belief that Shinto, the native belief system of Japan, and Buddhism are two aspects of the same religion, leading to the gradual amalgamation of the two faiths.

- In the midst of a third Muslim civil war (746–752), a rival, Abbasid caliph, Abu al-'Abbas, is proclaimed in Iraq.

750

- On the death of Marwan II, the last caliph of the Umayyad dynasty, Abu al-'Abbas is proclaimed the first caliph of the Abbasid dynasty, which remains at least nominally in power until the Mongol siege of Baghdad in 1258.

751

- The Muslims conquer western Asia after defeating China in the Battle of Samarqand.

- Supported by Pope Zacharias, Pepin III (the Short) deposes Childeric III, the last Merovingian king.

- The Lombards take Ravenna from the Byzantines.

752

- Yang Guozhong—a relative of Emperor Xuanzong's favorite concubine, Yang Guifei—begins to dominate the Chinese court.

754-755

- Pepin III (the Short) provides military aid to the Pope in his disputes with the Lombards.

755-756

- An Lushan, the powerful military governor of three provinces on the northwest frontier of China, proclaims himself emperor. Emperor Xuanzong flees the capital city of Chang'an.

*DENOTES CIRCA DATE

756
- Pepin III (the Short) returns to Italy, defeating the Lombards and making the Donation of Pepin, which establishes the basis for a papal state (and the temporal power of the papacy) as well as setting up the Franks as the protectors of the papacy.

757
- An Lushan is assassinated by his son, but his followers continue their rebellion until 763. From this time until its fall in 907, the Tang dynasty is too weak to assert any authority.

759
- Frankish troops force the final withdrawal of Muslim troops from southern France, as Pepin III (the Short) conquers Septimania and reasserts Frankish authority in Aquitaine, extending his kingdom south to the Pyrenees.

762-763
- Uighur Turks attack Chinese rebel forces and sack the eastern capital at Loyang. After a Uighur leader is converted to Manichaeism, it becomes the state religion of the Uighur empire.

763
- Caliph al-Mansur moves his capital from Damascus to the new city of Baghdad.
- A Tibetan army invades China and briefly occupies Chang'an.

764
- Civil war erupts in Japan after the powerful Buddhist priest Dokyo, backed by former empress Koken, eliminates his main political rival, Oshikatsu. Emperor Junnin is deposed, and Koken takes the throne as Empress Shotoku. During her reign, which lasts until 770, Dokyo is prime minister and high priest of state.

768
- Pepin III (the Short) dies, and his kingdom is divided between his two sons, Charles (Charlemagne) and Carloman.

770
- On the death of Empress Shotoku of Japan, the powerful Fujiwara family places Emperor Konnin on the throne, considerably lessening the influence of the wealthy and powerful Buddhist establishment on Japanese politics. The Fujiwaras remain a major force in Japanese government until the mid twelfth century.

771
- On the death of Carloman, the kingdom of the Franks is reunited under Charlemagne, who establishes his capital at Aachen (Aix-la-Chapelle).

772-804
- Charlemagne's troops engage in a difficult but ultimately successful campaign to conquer Saxony.

*DENOTES CIRCA DATE

WORLD EVENTS 500-1590

773-774
- Invading Italy at the request of Pope Adrian I, Charlemagne defeats the Lombards, annexes their Italian kingdom, and fulfills his father's promise of creating a papal state in Italy.

775
- After the death of Constantine V, the Byzantine throne goes to his son Leo IV.

775*
- Monks on the Scottish island of Iona begin what is now known as the Book of Kells, an illuminated manuscript of the four Gospels in the ornate Celtic style. After Vikings (Norsemen) raid the island in 802, the book is taken to the Abbey of Kells in Ireland, where it is probably completed.

778
- The rear guard of Charlemagne's forces, led by Roland, is ambushed by Basques as they return from an unsuccessful mission against Muslims in Spain. The battle is later the basis for *La Chanson de Roland* (The Song of Roland), the oldest French epic poem, written in the early twelfth century.

778-824
- Borobudur Temple in Java is built as a microcosm of the universe according to the ideas of Mahayana Buddhism.

780
- On the death of Leo IV, ten-year-old Constantine VI inherits the Byzantine throne. His mother, Empress Irene, becomes his regent.

781
- Charlemagne gives the throne of Italy to his son Pepin and makes his son Louis I (the Pious) king of Aquitaine.
- Byzantine forces suffer a major loss to Muslim troops in Asia Minor.
- Emperor Kammu ascends the Japanese throne.

782
- Charlemagne has 4,500 Saxon hostages beheaded at Verdun; around 785 he issues the "Capitulatio de partibus Saxoniae" (Ordinance for the Saxon Regions), intended to force the Saxons to accept Frankish rule and convert to Christianity.

786-809
- During the rule of Caliph Harun al-Rashid, Muslim culture is in what some scholars have called its "Golden Age," while political unrest is rife throughout the caliphate.

787
- The first recorded incursion of Danes takes place in England, beginning a long series of European raids by Danes, Norsemen, and Swedes, known collectively as Vikings.

*Denotes Circa Date

WORLD EVENTS 500-1590

788
- Idris proclaims an independent Shiite Muslim kingdom in Morocco to rival the Sunni Muslim caliphate, founding the Idrisid dynasty that rules Morocco until 926.
- Charlemagne conquers Bavaria.

790
- The Byzantine army forces Empress Irene into retirement, but Constantine VI recalls his mother two years later and makes her coruler.

792
- The Bulgars win a major victory against the Byzantines.

797
- Empress Irene orders her son, Constantine VI, overthrown and blinded; she becomes sole ruler of the Byzantine Empire.

800
- In Rome on Christmas Day, Pope Leo III crowns Charlemagne "Emperor of the Romans," an attempt to signal the birth of a Christian Empire (the precursor of the Holy Roman Empire) to rival the Muslim and Byzantine Empires and to equal ancient Rome in its power and glory.

802
- High-ranking Byzantine officials depose Empress Irene and place Nicephorus I on the throne.

804-806
- Muslim forces conduct a series of raids on Anatolia, Cyprus, and Rhodes.

809
- King Krum of the Bulgars begins a war with the Byzantines and conquers the city of Sophia.
- The first public hospital is established in Baghdad and is soon followed by similar institutions of healing and teaching in other Muslim cities.

810
- Danish king Godfred is killed during a military campaign in Frisia. During his reign, he prevented Charlemagne from expanding his realm northward into Denmark.

811
- Emperor Nicephorus I is defeated and killed in a costly battle with the Bulgars. Emperor Michael I Rhangabe is also unsuccessful in stopping their advance on Constantinople.

811-827
- A fourth Muslim civil war greatly weakens the power of the Abbasid caliphs.

*DENOTES CIRCA DATE

WORLD EVENTS 500-1590

812
- The Byzantines sign a treaty with Charlemagne that allows them to keep their territory in southern Italy, Venice, and Dalmatia.

813
- The Byzantine army deposes Emperor Michael I Rhangabe and places Leo V (the Armenian) on the throne.

814
- Charlemagne dies and is succeeded by his last surviving son, Louis I (the Pious).

817
- Byzantine Emperor Leo V (the Armenian) wins a major victory over the Bulgars at the Battle of Mesembria and forces them to sign a thirty-year peace treaty.

819-999
- Though nominally subordinate to the increasingly weak Abbasid caliphs in Baghdad, the Samanid dynasty rules Iran.

820
- Emperor Leo V (the Armenian) is assassinated, and Michael II, the first emperor of the Phrygian dynasty, is placed on the Byzantine throne.

826
- Muslims from North Africa conquer and plunder Crete, using it as a pirate base until 961, when it is recaptured by the Byzantines.
- Benedictine monk Ansgar begins his mission to convert Scandinavia to Christianity.

832
- Abbasid Caliph al-Ma'mun sends troops to put down a peasants' revolt in Egypt.

833
- On the death of al-Ma'mun, his brother al-Mu'tasim becomes caliph. During his eleven-year reign, he becomes the first caliph to hire Turkish mercenaries, a move that eventually weakens the power of the caliphs.

838
- Muslims sack Marseilles.
- Louis I (the Pious) gives Neustria (modern northwestern France) and Aquitaine to his son Charles II (the Bald).
- King Egbert of Mercia achieves a major victory over invading Vikings (Danes) and their Cornish Briton allies at the Battle of Hingston Down.

*DENOTES CIRCA DATE

WORLD EVENTS 500-1590

840* • Vikings (Norsemen) found the towns of Dublin and Limerick on the Irish coast as bases for trade with their homeland.

840 • Louis I (the Pious) dies. His son Lothar I begins efforts to gain control of all Carolingian lands.

840-841 • Though Venice is still nominally a part of the Byzantine Empire, the great trading city is essentially self-ruling by this time.

841 • Lothar I is defeated by his brothers, Louis II (the German) and Charles II (the Bald), at the Battle of Fontenoy.

• France is invaded by Vikings (Norsemen), who settle in the region that becomes known as Normandy. By 843 these "Normans" have reached to the shores of the Mediterranean Sea.

842 • Louis II (the German) and Charles II (the Bald) renew their alliance against Lothar I in the Strasbourg Oaths. Charles makes his declaration in *lingua romana* (Old French), and Louis makes his in *lingua teudisca* (Old German), creating a manuscript that documents an early stage in the evolution of the modern German and French languages.

• Michael III ascends the Byzantine throne with his mother, Theodora, as regent.

843 • The Treaty of Verdun gives Lothar I control of northern Italy and Lorraine; Louis II (the German) receives the lands east of the Rhine River; Charles II (the Bald) becomes the king of the West Franks (modern-day France).

843-845 • Tang emperor Wu-tsung, a Taoist, persecutes Buddhists, Manichaeans, Nestorians, and Maddens (members of a Persian sect), ending a long period of general religious tolerance in China. Only Buddhism survives.

• Vikings (Norsemen) sack Paris.

843-858 • Kenneth I McAlpin is the first king to rule both the Scots and the Picts.

846 • Muslims sack Rome, damaging the Vatican.

850*
*DENOTES CIRCA DATE • Groups of Jews settle in Germany. The Yiddish language begins to develop from Hebrew, Aramaic, and German roots.

WORLD EVENTS 500-1590

850*
(CONT'D)

- Under Vijayawada, who reigns until 870, the prosperous Hindu Cola (or Cholla) dynasty of Tamil kings begins its territorial expansion in southern India.

- The Chinese have discovered how to make gunpowder; the formula is first published in 1040.

851

- Egbert's successor, Aethelwulf, defeats a Viking (Danish) army that has attacked Canterbury and London but is having difficulty defending the long, unfortified English coastline from repeated raids.

855

- Lothar I dies. His lands are divided among his three sons: Louis II is given Italy; Charles gets Provence; and Lothar II obtains Lotharingia (modern-day Lorraine).

856

- Bardas becomes de facto ruler of the Byzantine Empire.

858

- Fujiwara Yoshifusa, father-in-law of the emperor of Japan, becomes the first commoner to serve as regent when his nine-year-old grandson, Seiwa, takes the throne.

- The Muslims expel the Vikings from the Spanish port of Algeciras.

859

- Supported by the caliphate, Ashot I establishes the Bagratid dynasty in Armenia and rules essentially free of outside influence.

860*

- Viking (Norse) explorers discover Iceland.

860

- Sailing down the Dnieper from Kiev to the Black Sea, the Russians launch an unsuccessful naval attack on Constantinople.

862-885

- Byzantine missionaries Cyril and Methodius preach Christianity among the Slavs of Moravia and Bohemia. Cyril adapts the Greek alphabet to the Slavic tongue, and it becomes known as the Cyrillic alphabet.

865

- Boris I of Bulgaria is converted to Christianity, eventually affiliating with the Eastern Church.

- Louis II (the German) divides his kingdom among his three sons: Carloman (Bavaria and Carinthia), Charles the Fat (Swabia), and Louis the Younger (Franconia, Thuringia, and Saxony).

***DENOTES CIRCA DATE**

WORLD EVENTS 500-1590

866
- Emperor Seiwa of Japan achieves his majority, but his grandfather continues to serve as regent, inaugurating nearly two centuries of clan dominance known as the Fujiwara period (866–1160).

- A Viking (Danish) army of nearly three thousand men attacks England and captures Northumbria.

- Bardas is murdered by Basil, a favorite of Byzantine emperor Michael III.

866-910
- During his reign, Alfonso III (the Great) of the kingdom of Asturias expands his realm to include León and Castile and other territory as far south as the Duero River, thus setting in motion the "Reconquista," the Christian recapture of Spain from the Muslims.

867
- Basil orders Emperor Michael III deposed and murdered, replacing him on the throne as Emperor Basil I, the founder of the Macedonian dynasty.

868
- The Buddhist *Diamond Sutra*, the first known full-length printed book, is produced in China.

868-872
- As the Abbasid caliphate grows weaker, the Tulunid dynasty comes to power in Egypt.

869
- Lothar II dies, and his lands are divided between his uncles Louis II (the German) and Charles II (the Bald).

871
- Having already captured York and East Anglia, Vikings (Danes) raid London and meet fierce resistance in Wessex. Late in the year Alfred (the Great) becomes king of Wessex and negotiates a temporary peace.

871-879
- Taking advantage of internal dissent within the Muslim Empire, the Byzantines engage in sporadic border warfare with the Muslims and make some inroads.

874-883
- A series of popular uprisings challenges the government of Tang emperor Hsi-tsung (rules 873–888).

875
- Louis II dies; Charles II (the Bald) invades Italy and is crowned Emperor of the Romans.

- Byzantine forces capture Bari in southern Italy. They later take Tarentum (880) and Calabria (885), re-establishing a large foothold on the peninsula.

*DENOTES CIRCA DATE

WORLD EVENTS 500-1590

876
- Charles II (the Bald) attempts, but fails, to take the territory of Louis II (the German), who dies in August. His son Louis III (the Younger) defeats his uncle at the Battle of Andernach on 8 October. Louis's son Charles III (the Fat) becomes king of Swabia.

877
- The death of Charles II (the Bald) leaves the Empire in a state of anarchy. His son Louis II (the Stammerer) agrees to rule the West Franks but refuses to become emperor.
- Extending its domain into Syria, the Tulunid dynasty of Egypt seizes Damascus.
- A band of Danish marauders kills King Constantine I, who has ruled Scotland since 862; he is succeeded by Eocha, who rules until 889.

878
- Vikings led by the Danish king Guthrum are defeated by King Alfred the Great at the Battle of Edington in Wiltshire. Alfred establishes the Peace of Wedmore, in which Guthrum accepts Christianity and agrees to withdraw to the "Danelaw," England north of Watling Street from Chester to London and the Thames from London to the sea.

879
- After the death of Louis II (the Stammerer) his sons divide the kingdom of the West Franks. Louis III becomes king of the North, and Carloman rules the South.

882
- Charles III (the Fat) becomes king of all the East Franks.
- On the death of Louis III, Carloman becomes sole ruler of the West Franks.

884
- Following the death of Carloman, Charles III (the Fat) becomes ruler of all Charlemagne's empire except Provence.

885-886
- Vikings (Norsemen) lay siege to Paris, which is defended by Count Eudes (Odo). Charles III (the Fat) fails in his attempt to aid Eudes.

886
- After repelling a Danish invasion of Kent in 885, Alfred the Great captures London and is acknowledged as king of all England south of the Danelaw.
- Basil I dies and is succeeded as Byzantine emperor by his son Leo IV (the Wise), who has been co-emperor since 870.

887
- The final separation of Germany and France occurs after Charles III (the Fat) is deposed. His nephew Arnulf becomes king of the East Franks (Germany).

*DENOTES CIRCA DATE

WORLD EVENTS 500-1590

888
- Eudes, Count of Paris, is elected king of the West Franks. Another faction backs Charles III (the Simple), younger brother of West Frankish kings Louis III and Carloman, and a five-year civil war ensues in France.

889
- The Pechenegs, a Turkic people, enter the area between the Don and lower Danube Rivers, driving the Magyars to the eastern edges of their territory.
- Boris I retires to a monastery and is succeeded as ruler of the Bulgars by his son Vladimir.

889-900
- During the reign of Donald II in Scotland, the Danes increase their efforts to conquer and settle Scottish territory.

891
- Fujiwara Mototsune dies, and Emperor Uda, whose mother is not a Fujiwara, refuses to appoint a new kampaku. Having ascended the Japanese throne in 887, Uda rules independently of the Fujiwaras until his death in 897. He is supported in his efforts by the powerful scholar-poet-politician Sugawara Michizane (later deified as Tenjin).
- Arnulf of Germany defeats the Vikings (Norsemen) at the Battle of the Dyle (in present-day Belgium).
- With the help of the Magyars, Arnulf attacks the Moravians, who are making incursions into Germany.

893
- Charles III (the Simple) becomes king of France and rules from Laon. He is the last Carolingian king to exert any true authority in France.
- Boris I comes out of retirement, puts down a revolt against his son Vladimir, deposes and blinds him, and makes his son Simeon I (the Great) king of the Bulgars.

894
- In Japan, Sugawara Michizane convinces Emperor Uda that diplomatic relations with China are undesirable because of growing Near Eastern influence there. Although unofficial contact between the two countries continues, this breaking of official ties marks the end of some three centuries of Chinese influence on Japanese culture.

894-924
- Simeon I (the Great) of Bulgaria engages in a series of wars with the Byzantine Empire, but he is never able to take Constantinople.

895*-896*
- Driven from southern Russia by the Pechenegs (a Turkic people), the Magyars, led by Arpad, settle in Hungary, where they subjugate the resident Slavs and Huns.

*DENOTES CIRCA DATE

WORLD EVENTS 500-1590

899-924
- During his reign Edward the Elder, son of Alfred the Great, extends his kingdom to include nearly all of England, including most of the territory controlled by the Danes.

899-955
- The Magyars conduct raids throughout central Europe.

900*
- The Mayas abandon their settlements in the lowlands of Mexico, but their cities in the Yucatán Peninsula continue to flourish for several more centuries.
- By this time the last inhabitants of Teotihuacán, near present-day Mexico City, have abandoned what is left of their once-great city, devastated by fire some 150 years earlier. They have been driven away by the arrival of war-like peoples such as the Toltecs.
- The Chimú kingdom arises in the Moche Valley of Peru.

902
- The Byzantine island of Sicily falls to the Muslims after a long series of raids that began in 827.

905
- The Tulunid dynasty of Egypt is overthrown by the army of Abbasid caliph al-Muk.

907
- After another Russian raid on Constantinople, a delegation led by Prince Oleg arrives there to discuss a trade agreement, which is signed in 911.
- The Magyars begin raids in Germany and Italy.
- Khitan Mongol leader A-pao-chi proclaims himself ruler of the Khitans, and by 916 he has created a Chinese-style dynasty to rule a nation that includes Mongolia and much of Manchuria.

907-960
- After the fall of the Tang dynasty, the Five Dynasties rule in a fragmented China.

909
- The Fatimid dynasty comes to power in North Africa.

911
- Charles III (the Simple) cedes to the Norseman Rollo the Duchy of Northmen (Normans), which becomes known as Normandy. Rollo converts to Christianity, is baptized Robert, and becomes Charles's vassal. Charles gains control of Lorraine.
- On the death of Louis III (the Child), the last Carolingian king of the East Franks, Germany splinters into many smaller principalities.

***DENOTES CIRCA DATE**

WORLD EVENTS 500-1590

913
- Leo VI's seven-year-old son, Constantine VII (Porphyrogenitus), becomes Byzantine emperor and reigns until 959.

914
- Bulgar ruler Simeon I (the Great) extends his power in the Balkans through raids in Macedonia, Albania, and Serbia.

915
- Supported by a Byzantine navy and led by Pope John X, a united Italian army defeats a Muslim force in southern Italy.

915*
- The Berbers of North Africa found Algiers on the site of an ancient Phoenician city and make it an important center of Mediterranean commerce.

919*
- Chinese flamethrowers are ignited by gunpowder, marking its first documented use in battle.

919
- Henry I (the Fowler), Duke of Saxony and the strongest opponent of Conrad I, is elected king of Germany. He subsequently forms an alliance with Charles III (the Simple) of France.

920
- Romanus I (Lecapenus) is made co-emperor of the Byzantine Empire with his son-in-law Constantine VII (Porphyrogenitus) and becomes de facto ruler of the empire.

922*
- The Volga Bulgars convert to Islam.
- Robert, Duke of Paris, seizes the crown of France from Charles III (the Simple).

923
- Charles III (the Simple) kills Robert in a battle at Soissons, only to be captured by Hebert, Count of Vermandois, in whose custody he dies in 929. Robert's son-in-law Rudolf, Duke of Burgundy, becomes king.

924
- Edward the Elder dies and is succeeded by his son, Aethelstan, who creates political unity in England during his fifteen-year reign.

925
- Simeon I (the Great) proclaims himself tsar of all the Bulgars, presiding over the first Bulgarian Empire. Having proclaimed the independence of the Bulgarian Church from Constantinople, he is recognized by the Pope but not by the Byzantines.

*DENOTES CIRCA DATE

WORLD EVENTS 500-1590

926
- In return for helping the Juchens of Manchuria to conquer northern China, Khitan ruler A-pao-chi is given the northeast corner of China, which includes the city of Beijing.

928
- The Umayyad ruler of Muslim Spain takes the title of caliph in opposition to the Fatimids and the Abbasids.

936
- On the death of Henry I (the Fowler), his son, Otto I (the Great), becomes king of Germany.
- King Rudolf of France dies and is succeeded by the son of Charles III (the Simple), Louis IV, who is king in name only while King Robert's son, Hugh the Great, actually rules the kingdom.

939
- Vietnam gains its independence from China.

943-954
- During his reign, Malcolm I of Scotland drives the Danes from the English city of York, extending his kingdom south into the northern counties of England.

944
- Romanus I (Lecapenus) is deposed by his sons Stephen and Constantine, who force him to become a monk. After exiling Romanus's sons in 945, Constantine VII (Porphyrogenitus) becomes sole ruler again, but the Byzantine Empire is largely governed by the powerful general Bardas Phocas, who is under the influence of Constantine's wife, Empress Helena, and her favorite, Basil.

945
- Svyatoslav I succeeds his father, Igor, as grand prince of Kiev.
- The Buyids, an Iranian dynasty, capture Baghdad and place the Abbasid caliphs under virtual house arrest. The Buyids rule as amirs while allowing the Abbasids to remain as figurehead caliphs.

947
- The Khitans of northeastern China proclaim the Liao dynasty, which rules that portion of their empire until 1125.
- Quetzalcóatl, revered by the Toltecs as a god, is born in Mexico.

950*
- Toltecs invade the Mayan city of Chichén Itzá in the Yucatán Peninsula of Mexico. They build their capital, Tollan, near the modern Mexican city of Tula.

*DENOTES CIRCA DATE

WORLD EVENTS 500-1590

951
- Otto I (the Great) of Germany invades Italy.

954
- On the death of Louis IV of France his eldest son, Lothaire, becomes king. The kingdom is controlled by Hugh the Great until 956 and then by Hugh's uncle, Archbishop Bruno of Cologne, brother of King Otto I (the Great) of Germany.
- King Eadred wrests the northern counties of England from Scottish rule.

955
- The Magyars attempt another invasion of Germany, but they are defeated at the Battle of the Lechfeld and driven back into Hungary.
- A treaty between Ordoño III and 'Abd al-Rahman-al-Nasir secures the independence of the Spanish kingdoms of Leon and Navarre.

957
- Olga, regent for her son, Grand Prince Svyatoslav, is baptized in Constantinople and begins efforts to convert Russians to Christianity. She is later canonized as the first saint of the Russian Orthodox Church.

959
- Byzantine emperor Constantine VII (Porphyrogenitus) dies and is succeeded by his son Romanus II, who allows the eunuch Joseph Bringas to run affairs of state and leaves military affairs to Nicephorus Phocas, son of Bardas Phocas.

960
- Zhao Kuanyin stages a coup in China, defeating an army of Chinese and Khitans to become Emperor Taizu, the first emperor of the Song dynasty. During his reign, which lasts until 976, Taizu begins the reunification of the Chinese empire.

960*
- King Harald Bluetooth of Denmark converts to Christianity.

961
- The Muslims lose Crete to the Byzantines.

962
- Otto I (the Great) of Germany becomes Emperor of the Romans.

963*
- Duke Mieszko I becomes the first ruler of Poland, founding the dynasty later called the Piasts.

963

***DENOTES CIRCA DATE**
- After the death of Byzantine emperor Romanus II, the imperial army places Nicephorus II Phocas on the throne.

WORLD EVENTS 500-1590

965	• The Byzantines take control of Cyprus.
966-969	• With the aid of Prince Svyatoslav of Kiev, the Byzantines defeat the Bulgars. Svyatoslav refuses to cede his conquest to the Byzantines and announces plans to establish a Russo-Bulgarian empire.
969	• The Byzantines retake Antioch, in northern Syria, from the Muslims, who have held it since 638.
	• Nicephorus II Phocas is murdered in a plot devised by his wife, Empress Theophano, and his trusted lieutenant John Tzimisces, who becomes Emperor John I Tzimisces.
	• The Fatimids complete their invasion of Egypt and send troops into Palestine and southern Syria.
971	• Prince Svyatoslav of Kiev invades the Byzantine Empire, where he is defeated by John I Tzimisces and forced to evacuate Bulgaria. John annexes eastern Bulgaria to the Byzantine Empire.
975*-1025*	• *Beowulf*, an Old English epic that has evolved over several centuries, is written down for the first time.
976	• On the death of John I Tzimisces, Basil II and Constantine VIII, sons of Romanos II and Theophano, become the rulers of the Byzantine Empire.
976-997	• During his reign, Song emperor Taizong completes the reunification of the Chinese empire.
977	• Sabuktigin becomes governor of the town of Ghazna (modern Ghazni in eastern Afghanistan), founding a Turkish dynasty that rules until 1186 over an empire that eventually includes much of Iran and Afghanistan, as well as northwestern India.
978	• Otto II of Germany puts down a revolt by Henry II of Bavaria.
	• King Edward (the Martyr) of England is assassinated at Corfe Castle while visiting his brother, who becomes King Aethelred II.

*DENOTES CIRCA DATE

WORLD EVENTS 500-1590

980
- Samuel becomes tsar of Bulgaria, establishing his capital in Macedonia and gradually extending his empire into Byzantine territory in the northern parts of present-day Albania and Greece.

980-1013
- Aethelred II fails to halt a series of Danish invasions of England, earning the byname "the Unready."

982
- Muslim forces defeat the troops of Otto II near Stilo in southern Italy.
- Norseman Erik the Red discovers Greenland, establishing Norse colonies there in 986.

983
- On the death of Otto II, his three-year-old son Otto III becomes king of Germany. His mother and grandmother rule as regents until he comes of age in 994.
- On the death of King Lothaire, his weak son Louis V becomes king of France.

986
- Sabuktigin invades India, introducing Islam in that region.
- Blown off course during a storm, Icelander Bjarni Herjulfsson and his crew make the first recorded European sighting of the North American continent.

987
- The last Carolingian king of the West Franks, Louis V, dies and is succeeded by Hugh Capet, the founder of the Capetian dynasty of France.

989
- With the help of Prince Vladimir of Kiev, Byzantine emperor Basil II puts down a revolt led by his generals Bardas Phocas and Bardas Skleros. Basil rewards Vladimir with the hand of his sister Anna, on the condition that he and his subjects convert to Christianity. A mass conversion of Russians to Eastern Christianity follows.

989-992
- The Poles conquer Silesia. On succeeding his father, Duke Mieszko I, in 992 Boleslaw the Brave continues to expand Polish territory.

994
- Danes led by Sweyn I (Forkbeard) invade England and impose tribute.

995
- Fujiwara Michinaga becomes head of his clan and de facto ruler of Japan, struggling to suppress rebellions by warrior families who resent the Fujiwaras' centralized control of the nation.
- Military victories at Aleppo and Homs strengthen the Byzantines' position in Syria.

*DENOTES CIRCA DATE

WORLD EVENTS 500-1590

996
- Emperor Basil II recovers Byzantine holdings in Greece by defeating Tsar Samuel of Bulgaria at the Battle of Spercheios River.

- Hugh Capet of France dies and is succeeded by his son Robert II (the Pious).

- Hoping to rule an empire that rivals ancient Rome, Otto III of Germany answers an appeal from Pope John IV for help in putting down a rebellion of Roman noble Crescentius II by invading Italy and having himself declared king of Lombardy. Reaching Rome after Pope John's death, Otto engineers the election of his cousin Bruno of Carinthia as Pope Gregory V, the first German pope. In return, Gregory crowns Otto III Emperor of the Romans. After Otto returns to Germany, Crescentius returns to Rome and installs his own candidate as Pope.

997-998
- Otto III re-invades Italy, returns Gregory V to the papacy, and makes Rome his capital.

998-1030
- During the reign of Mahmud of Ghazna, the Ghaznavid Empire reaches its greatest extent.

999
- The Althing, or Icelandic assembly, declares that all Icelanders must abandon the old Norse religion in favor of Christianity.

1000*
- The Incan civilization begins to develop in South America.

- Struggles between rival religious groups begin to weaken the Toltec state of central Mexico.

- Among the Eastern Woodlands peoples in the northwestern part of present-day New York State, the introduction of corn sparks the development of the Owasco culture, the foundation of the groups that later become the Five Iroquois Nations: the Mohawks, Senecas, Onondagas, Oneidas, and Cayugas.

- The Navajo and Apache peoples from the far north in Canada arrive in the American Southwest, where they encounter Pueblo Indians, including the Zuni and Hopi, who have been in the region for thousands of years. The Navajo learn agriculture, weaving, and artistic styles from the Pueblo tribes, but the Apache remain mostly hunter-gatherers.

- At Cahokia, near present-day East St. Louis, Illinois, members of the group archaeologists call Mississippians begin building the largest earthen structures in pre-Columbian North America. Cahokia becomes a prosperous and influential city, with a population that eventually reaches about twelve thousand people.

- Maori people settle New Zealand following long voyages across the Pacific Ocean.

1000
- Leif Eriksson, son of Erik the Red, converts to Christianity during a visit to Norway.

- The Danes, led by Sweyn I, kill King Olaf I Tryggvason of Norway at the Battle of Svolder, making Norway part of Denmark.

*DENOTES CIRCA DATE

WORLD EVENTS 500-1590

1000 (CONT'D)	• Otto III of Germany recognizes Duke Boleslaw the Brave as the sovereign ruler of Poland. He is formally crowned King Boleslaw I in 1024.
1001	• Leif Eriksson and his crew sail to places they call Vinland, Helluland, and Markland, possibly Nova Scotia, Labrador, and Newfoundland.
1001-1002	• Romans rise up against Otto III, who calls on his cousin Henry of Bavaria for help. Otto dies before Henry's troops arrive, and his cousin becomes King Henry II of Germany.
1002	• Duke Boleslaw the Brave seizes Bohemia, beginning a series of wars with Germany that lasts until 1018.
1004	• Muslim raiders sack Pisa.
	• Thorfinn Karlsefni and his wife, Gudrid, lead an expedition of about 130 people from Greenland to the North American continent, landing possibly at Baffin Island, traveling south, and settling along what was probably the Gulf of St. Lawrence. After three years they abandon the settlement they call Vinland and return to Greenland. Thorfinn and Gudrid's son, Snorri (born circa 1005), may be the first European born in mainland North America.
1009	• The Fatimids destroy the Church of the Holy Sepulchre in Jerusalem.
1013	• Aethelred II (the Unready) flees to Normandy, leaving the rule of England to Danish king Sweyn I. After Sweyn dies in early 1014, Aethelred returns to the throne and rules until his death in 1016.
1014	• Rajendra becomes king of a Cola empire that includes southern India, the Laccadive and Maldive Islands, and northern Ceylon (Sri Lanka). During his thirty-year reign he extends the northern boundaries of his kingdom, completes the invasion of Ceylon, and conquers portions of the Malay Peninsula and Archipelago.
	• The victory of King Brian Boru's forces over the Norsemen at the Battle of Clontarf marks the end of Viking domination in Ireland.
1016*	• The victory of Malcolm II Mackenneth (rules 1005–1034) over a Northumbrian army at the Battle of Carham makes him the first Scottish king to rule over a country with roughly the same boundaries as modern Scotland.

*DENOTES CIRCA DATE

WORLD EVENTS 500-1590

1016
- On the death of Aethelred II (the Unready) in April, his son Edmund II (Ironside) becomes king in the midst of a massive Danish invasion. On his death in November, Canute I (the Great) of Denmark become king of all England, which he rules until 1035.

- The Pisans and Genovese drive the Muslims from Sardinia.

1018
- On the death of his father, Sweyn I, Canute I (the Great) of England becomes Canute II of Denmark.

- In the Treaty of Bautzen, Boleslaw of Poland retains Lusatia and Misnia and returns Bohemia to Henry II of Germany. Boleslaw then expands eastward by defeating Grand Prince Yaroslav I the Wise of Kiev.

1022
- Henry II defeats the Byzantines in southern Italy.

- The Byzantines, who have been annexing portions of Armenia since 968, gain possession of the Armenian kingdom of Vaspurakan, and the ruler of the Armenian kingdom of Ani is compelled to make Emperor Basil II heir to his estates.

1024
- On the death of Henry II, his cousin Conrad II becomes king of Germany; in 1027 he is crowned Emperor of the Romans.

1025-1028
- After the death of Basil II, his brother, Constantine VIII, rules the Byzantine Empire until his death three years later.

1026
- The Danes repel an invasion by Sweden and Norway.

1028
- The death of Fujiwara Michinaga begins the decline of Fujiwara control in Japan.

- Canute the Great of England and Denmark becomes king of Norway.

- After the death of Constantine VIII, his daughter Zoë becomes de facto empress of the Byzantine Empire, ruling until 1050 with a succession of three husbands, the first of which is her father's handpicked successor, Romanus III (Argyropolus).

1031
- Conrad II defeats the army of Mieszko II of Poland, making it a fief of the Holy Roman Empire.

- Robert II (the Pious) of France dies and is succeeded by his son Henry I.

*DENOTES CIRCA DATE

WORLD EVENTS 500-1590

1034
- The chosen successor of his maternal grandfather, Malcolm II (rules 1005–1034), Duncan I becomes king of Scotland, though, according to Scottish rules of succession, his cousin Macbeth has a stronger claim to the throne.

- Byzantine emperor Romanus III (Argyropolus) dies, reputedly poisoned by his wife, Empress Zoë, who marries Romanus's young chamberlain and makes him Emperor Michael IV (the Paphlagonian).

1035
- Harold I (Harefoot), the illegitimate son of Canute I (the Great), becomes regent in England and seizes the throne outright in 1037.

1039
- Conrad II dies and is succeeded as king of Germany by his son Henry III (the Black), who is crowned Emperor of the Romans in 1046. During his reign, which lasts until 1056, Henry controls Poland, Bohemia, and Saxony.

1040
- Macbeth kills Duncan I in battle and becomes king of Scotland.

- Danish king Hardecanute, the legitimate son of Canute I (the Great), invades England and takes the throne from his half brother Harold.

- Byzantine troops crush a Bulgar uprising. Bulgaria is incorporated into the Byzantine Empire.

1041-1042
- On the death of Michael IV (the Paphlagonian), Empress Zoë elevates her favorite, Michael V (Kalaphates), who attempts to make himself sole emperor by exiling Zoë to a convent. Members of the nobility depose Michael, blind him, and imprison him.

1042
- Edward the Confessor, son of Aethelred the Unready, takes the throne of England on the death of his half brother Hardecanute; Edward rules England until 1066.

- Byzantine empress Zoë marries Constantine IX (Monomachus), elevating him to emperor.

- General Georgios Maniakes fends off a Norman invasion of Byzantine holdings in southern Italy.

1054
- Malcolm, son of Duncan I of Scotland, and Siward, Earl of Northumbria, defeat Macbeth in battle, forcing him to yield part of southern Scotland to Malcolm.

- Angry at Pope Leo IX's support for Norman incursions in Byzantine southern Italy, Patriarch Michael Kerularios of Constantinople anathematizes the Roman Church, an act widely regarded as the beginning of the final schism between the Western and Eastern Christian Churches.

*DENOTES CIRCA DATE

WORLD EVENTS 500-1590

1054-1092
- The Muslim Almoravid dynasty of North Africa establishes its domain in Morocco and western Algeria.

1055
- On the death of Constantine IX (Monomachus), Empress Theodora reasserts her claim to rule the Byzantine Empire.
- Saljuk Turks capture northern Syria, Palestine, and central Iraq, where their capture of Baghdad gives them control over the Abbasid caliphs, who continue in their role as figureheads and religious leaders while the Saljuks wield political power as sultans.

1056
- Henry III dies and is succeeded as king of Germany and Emperor of the Romans by six-year-old Henry IV, who reigns until 1106.
- On the death of Empress Theodora in August, Michael VI (Stratioticus) becomes the Byzantine emperor. He is deposed the following August by members of the military aristocracy, who put Isaac I Comnenus on the throne.

1057
- With the assistance of the English, Malcolm kills Macbeth in battle and later this year becomes Malcolm III Canmore of Scotland.

1059
- Pope Nicholas II (reigns 1059–1061) decrees that seven cardinal (pre-eminent) bishops should be solely responsible for electing a new pope, thus eliminating any secular ruler from the selection process. The Church, however, is unable to enforce this ruling until the papal election of 1085.
- Byzantine emperor Isaac I Comnenus abdicates in favor of Constantine X (Ducas).

1060
- Henry I of France dies and is succeeded by his son Philip I.

1061
- Norman brothers Robert and Roger Guiscard begin a long campaign to capture Sicily from the Muslims. The invasion is not entirely complete until the fall of Muslim forces at Messina in 1091. In 1072 Roger becomes Roger II, Count of Sicily.

1064
- The Saljuks gain control over a large portion of Armenia, completing their invasion by 1071.

1066
- On the death of Edward the Confessor, Harold Godwinsson becomes king of England and defeats an invading army led by King Harald Hardrada of Norway at the Battle of Stamford Bridge (25 September) in Yorkshire.

*DENOTES CIRCA DATE

WORLD EVENTS 500-1590

1066
(CONT'D)
- Norman troops under William the Conqueror land on the southern coast of England and defeat Harold Godwinsson's weary army at the Battle of Hastings (14 October). Harold Godwinsson is killed, ending Saxon rule of England. William the Conqueror is crowned William I of England on Christmas Day and rules until 1087.

1067-1085
- During his reign Emperor Shenzong of China nationalizes the production and distribution of agricultural products.

1071
- The Saljuks defeat and capture Byzantine emperor Romanus IV Diogenes at Malazgirt (Manzikert), gaining control over much of Anatolia (the Asian part of Turkey). This victory begins a major expansion of the area influenced by Islam.
- Michael VII (Ducas) becomes sole ruler of the Byzantine Empire.

1072
- William I (the Conqueror) invades Scotland and forces the Scots to pay homage to him.
- The Normans take Palermo.

1074
- Michael VII (Ducas) calls on the Saljuks for help against Roussel de Bailleul, a Norman mercenary who is trying to establish his own kingdom in Asia Minor, thus paving the way for the Saljuks' conquest of the rest of Anatolia.

1075
- Saljuk ruler Malik Shah subdues Syria and Palestine.

1076-1122
- Pope Gregory VII and Emperor Henry IV and their successors engage in the long dispute known as the Investiture Controversy, a power struggle over whether secular rulers have the right to select and install bishops.

1078
- Rival generals, Nicephorus Bryennius in Albania and Nicephorus Botaneiates in Anatolia, march on Constantinople to claim the throne. Michael VII (Ducas) abdicates, and Botaneiates becomes Emperor Nicephorus III.

1080*
- An Armenian state is established in Cilicia.

1080-1086
- During his reign Canute IV (later Saint Canute) of Denmark is known for his patronage of several churches.

*DENOTES CIRCA DATE

WORLD EVENTS 500–1590

1081
- General Alexius Comnenus seizes the Byzantine throne, ruling as Alexius I Comnenus until 1118.

1081–1085
- Led by Robert Guiscard and his sons, Bohemond and Roger Borsa, Normans from southern Italy invade Byzantine territories in western Greece (1081), Macedonia (1083), and Corfu (1083). Alexius I Comnenus wins the support of Venice by granting it extensive trading privileges (1082). The Normans abandon their invasion in 1085, after the Byzantine and Venetian fleets defeat them near Corfu.

1083
- Christian king Alfonso VI of León and Castile takes Madrid from the Muslims.

1085
- Alfonso VI captures Toledo from the Muslims.

1085–1086
- The Almoravid dynasty of North Africa sends its forces into Spain, where they halt Alfonso's advance into Muslim territory but fail to retake Toledo.

1087
- William I (the Conqueror) is fatally wounded in a fall from a horse during warfare with Philip I of France. His son William II (Rufus) succeeds to the throne of England.

1093
- During a raid into England, Malcolm III Canmore is killed; his brother Donald Bane seizes the Scottish throne.

1094
- Spanish mercenary soldier Rodrigo Díaz de Vivar (El Cid) captures Valencia from the Muslims in Spain.
- Donald Bane of Scotland is deposed by Malcolm III Canmore's son Duncan II, but soon thereafter Donald Bane has his nephew killed and retakes the throne, ruling until 1097, when he is deposed in favor of Duncan's brother Edgar, who rules Scotland for the next twenty years.

1095
- Responding to a call from Alexius I Comnenus for help against the Saljuks, Pope Urban II calls for a Crusade to claim the Holy Land for Christianity.

1096–1099
- Crusader victories during the First Crusade enable Alexius I Comnenus to recover the western coast of Anatolia for the Byzantines, but rather than turning over all conquered territories the Crusaders establish the Latin Christian kingdoms of Jerusalem, Edessa, Antioch, and Tripoli—which only grudgingly acknowledge the Byzantine emperor as their overlord. The Crusaders take Jerusalem in 1099 and massacre its Muslim inhabitants.

*DENOTES CIRCA DATE

WORLD EVENTS 500-1590

1100*	• Inuits, a people of North America, settle in northern Greenland.
1100	• William II (Rufus) of England is killed while hunting. His brother Henry I (Beauclerc) becomes king and rules until 1135.
1100*-1300*	• Tahitian chiefs make a series of voyages to the Hawaiian Islands. • Germans expand eastward into the Slavic territory between the Elbe and Oder Rivers.
1100-1125	• During his reign, Chinese emperor Huizong is known as a patron of the arts.
1104	• Alfonso I (the Battler) becomes king of Aragon and Navarre, ruling until 1134. • Crusaders take Acre.
1104-1113	• England and France are at war over English lands on the Continent.
1105	• Henry IV of Germany abdicates and dies a year later. His son succeeds him as Henry V of Germany and, in 1111, as Emperor of the Romans.
1108	• Philip I of France dies and is succeeded by his son Louis VI (the Fat).
1113*-1150*	• During his reign Khmer king Suryavarman II builds Angkor Wat, a huge temple complex in his capital city.
1116-1120	• England and France are again at war.
1118	• Alfonso the Battler captures the province of Saragossa in northeast Spain, which Muslims have held for nearly four hundred years.
1120	• Construction begins on Chartres Cathedral in France, one of the greatest examples of Gothic architecture. It is essentially completed by 1220.

*DENOTES CIRCA DATE

WORLD EVENTS 500-1590

1120s
- Arabic works on mathematics, optics, and astronomy are introduced into Europe.

1120-1121
- John II Comnenus continues his father's campaign against the Saljuks and recovers still more of Anatolia for the Byzantines.

1122
- John II Comnenus defeats the Pechenegs, finally alleviating their threat to the Byzantine Empire.

1123
- John II Comnenus defeats the Serbs.

1124
- John II Comnenus defeats the Hungarians.
- David I, the last son of Malcolm III Canmore to ascend to the Scottish throne, succeeds his brother Alexander I, who has ruled Scotland since 1107.

1125*
- The Berber Almohad dynasty comes to power in Morocco; by 1147 they gain control of all Almoravid territory in North Africa.

1125
- Henry V dies without an heir. After a battle over the succession, Lothar, Duke of Saxony, emerges as King Lothar II of Germany and is crowned Emperor of the Romans in 1133.

1126
- The Juchens of Manchuria conquer the northern portion of the Song Empire in China.

1127
- Chinese prince Gaozong escapes from Juchen invaders and rules the portion of the Chinese empire that lies south of the Yangtze River, establishing the Southern Song dynasty, which rules the South until 1279. During this period the Song government prints paper money, a practice continued by the Yuan dynasty (1279–1368).
- Henry I of England compels his barons to accept his only living child, Matilda, the widow of Emperor Henry V, as the heir to his throne.

1130
- Roger II becomes ruler of the newly formed kingdom of Sicily. He patronizes many scientific projects, including the creation of sophisticated maps.

*DENOTES CIRCA DATE

WORLD EVENTS 500-1590

1135
- On the death of Henry I of England, his nephew Stephen, a grandson of William the Conqueror, seizes the English throne, though he has earlier recognized the claim of Henry's daughter, Empress Matilda, now the wife of Geoffrey Plantagenet, Count of Anjou. A civil war breaks out between forces loyal to Stephen or Matilda.

1137
- Byzantine troops complete a three-year campaign to conquer Cilician (Little) Armenia, which has been under the control of the Latin Christian state of Antioch. Raymond of Antioch is forced to do homage to the Byzantine Empire.
- Louis VI (the Fat) of France dies and is succeeded by his son Louis VII (the Young).
- Following the death of Lothar II in 1137, Conrad III is elected king of Germany.

1138
- David I of Scotland invades England on Matilda's behalf and is defeated at the Battle of the Standards.

1139
- Matilda arrives in England at the head of an army.
- Alfonso I of Portugal secures the independence of his kingdom from León. During his reign, which lasts until 1185, he has several important victories over the Muslims.

1141
- Stephen of England is captured by Matilda's forces in February, and in June she travels to London to claim the throne. Before she can be crowned at Westminster, however, the people of London become enraged by her arrogance and drive her from the city. In September her troops suffer a major defeat at Winchester, and two months later Stephen is released. He gradually defeats Matilda, who finally flees to Anjou in 1148.

1143
- On the death of John II Comnenus, his son Manuel I Comnenus becomes Byzantine emperor.

1145
- Pope Eugenius III calls for the Second Crusade.

1146-1158
- Normans from Sicily occupy Tripoli in North Africa.

1147
- European troops led by Louis VI of France and Conrad III of Germany arrive in the East for the Second Crusade, which ends in 1149, after their poorly coordinated offensive accomplishes little of importance. Relations between the Crusaders and the Byzantines worsen.

* DENOTES CIRCA DATE

WORLD EVENTS 500-1590

1147
(CONT'D)
- Yury Vladimirovich Dolgoruky, prince of Suzdal, founds the city of Moscow.

1150*
- Imported Muslim musical instruments begin to influence western European music.
- The Spanish epic *Cantar del mio Cid* (Poem of the Cid) recounts the deeds of a hero based on Castilian warrior Rodrigo Díaz de Vivar during warfare to recapture Valencia from the Muslims in 1094.
- After Aztecs destroy the Toltec capital of Tollan, the Toltec Empire goes into decline.

1150-1151
- The Ghurids sack the capital of the Ghaznavid empire.

1152
- On the death of his uncle Conrad III, Frederick I (Barbarossa) is elected king of Germany. During his thirty-eight-year reign, he leads six expeditions into Italy.

1152-1154
- The Byzantines defeat the Hungarians, who have attempted to take Serbia and Bosnia.

1153
- Matilda's son, Henry of Anjou, invades England; Stephen recognizes him as heir to the throne.

1154
- On the death of Stephen, Henry of Anjou becomes Henry II of England. Reigning until 1159, he is the founder of the House of Plantagenet, which rules England until 1485.

1155
- Pope Adrian IV crowns Frederick I (Barbarossa) Emperor of the Romans.

1156
- Pope Adrian IV (an Englishman) issues the Donation of Ireland, which is interpreted as granting to Henry II of England the right to invade and establish sovereignty over the island.
- Civil war breaks out in Japan as retired emperor Sutoku attempts unsuccessfully to regain power from his brother, reigning emperor Go-Shirakawa. The emperor is backed by samurai warriors led by Taira Kiyomori and by the Fujiwaras, who—despite their support of the winning side—continue to lose influence as the Taira family begins its ascent.

1157*
- King Erik of Sweden begins invading Finland, which becomes a battleground for nearly a century as Sweden and Russia vie for influence and control over the region.

***DENOTES CIRCA DATE**

WORLD EVENTS 500-1590

1157
- In Moscow, Prince Yury Vladimirovich Dolgoruky begins building the fortifications that become the Kremlin.

1158
- Emperor Frederick I (Barbarossa) crowns Vladislav II king of Bohemia.

1158-1159
- The Byzantines send a military expedition against the Latin Christian kingdom of Antioch and force its ruler, Raymond, to renew his homage to the Byzantine Empire.

1160
- Minamoto Yoshitomo and Fujiwara Nobuyori are defeated in their coup attempt against the Taira family, ending the Fujiwara period in Japan and leaving Taira Kiyomori in control of the entire country.

1162
- During his second campaign in Italy, Frederick I (Barbarossa) destroys Milan after a nine-month siege.

1167
- Cities in northern Italy form the Lombard League in opposition to Frederick I (Barbarossa)'s fourth invasion of Italy.

1167-1168
- The Lombard League rebuilds Milan.

1170
- Chrétien de Troyes writes Arthurian legends such as *Lancelot*.
- Archbishop Thomas Becket is murdered at Canterbury Cathedral in England because of his resistance to King Henry II's demands for greater royal control over the clergy.

1170-1171
- Acting on the Donation of Ireland (1156), English troops invade Ireland.

1171
- Known to Western Europeans as Saladin, Salah al-Din al-Ayyubi (reigns 1171–1193) overthrows the Fatimid rulers of Egypt and proclaims himself sultan, founding the Ayyubid dynasty that rules Egypt, Syria, and parts of Arabia until 1260.

1172
- The Almohads force the Almoravids to surrender Seville and soon control all Muslim Spain.

*DENOTES CIRCA DATE

WORLD EVENTS 500-1590

1173
- Construction begins on the bell tower for the cathedral of Pisa, which is completed in 1174 and becomes known as the Leaning Tower of Pisa.

1174
- The Toltec Empire of central Mexico falls after internal chaos and invasions by less-civilized nomads.

1174-1186
- Salah al-Din embarks on a successful campaign to unite Egypt, Syria, Palestine, and northern Mesopotamia under his rule.

1175-1176
- The Venetians and Normans form an alliance against the Byzantines, forcing them to pay a heavy indemnity.

1176
- Supporting Pope Alexander III, the Lombard League defeats Frederick I (Barbarossa) at Legnano.

- Byzantine emperor Manuel I Comnenus attacks the Saljuks and suffers a severe defeat at the Battle of Myriocephalon. Though the Byzantines achieve some military success in 1176, the Battle of Myriocephalon is often identified as a harbinger of the fall of the Byzantine Empire.

1177
- In the Peace of Venice, Frederick I (Barbarossa) acknowledges Alexander III as Pope.

1178
- Frederick I (Barbarossa) becomes king of Burgundy.

1179
- The Mayan city of Chichén Itzá is burned and destroyed.

1180
- Louis VII (the Young) dies and is succeeded on the French throne by his son, Philip II Augustus.

- Taira Kiyomori places his two-year-old grandson on the throne of Japan as Emperor Antoku, provoking a rebellion led by Minamoto Yoritomo, whose father Kiyomori had executed after his coup attempt in 1160.

- Manuel I Comnenus dies and is succeeded as Byzantine emperor by his eleven-year-old son, Alexius II Comnenus, whose mother, Mary, daughter of Raymond of Antioch, serves as regent. She entrusts the government to Manuel's unpopular nephew Alexius.

- Philip II Augustus of France expels the Jews from all the territory he controls.

*DENOTES CIRCA DATE

WORLD EVENTS 500-1590

1182-1202
- During his reign as king of Denmark, Canute VI expands Danish influence to Pomerania, Holstein, and Mecklenburg.

1183
- Andronicus I Comnenus, a cousin of Manuel I Comnenus, seizes the Byzantine throne from Alexius II Comnenus, has him strangled, and marries his thirteen-year-old widow.

1185
- The Minamoto clan of Japan defeats the Tairas and establishes the Kamakura shogunate. During this period of feudalism, which lasts until 1333, powerful military governors known as shoguns (generals-in-chief) are the real rulers of Japan.

- Isaac Comnenus, Byzantine governor of Cyprus, declares himself the independent ruler of the island.

- King William II (the Good) leads his Norman Sicilian troops across Greece and occupies Thessalonica, the second most important city of the Byzantine Empire. News of the defeat sparks a revolt in Constantinople. Andronicus I Comnenus is killed by a street mob. Isaac II Angelus seizes the throne.

1185-1191
- The Byzantines drive the Normans from Greece and the Balkans.

1186
- Henry VI, son of Frederick I (Barbarossa), marries Constance, daughter of the late Sicilian king Roger II, and assumes the throne of Sicily.

1186-1188
- The Byzantines are unable to put down a revolt in Bulgaria that leads to the establishment of a new Bulgarian state north of the Balkans.

1187
- After defeating Christian Crusaders at Hittin in Palestine, Salah al-Din retakes Jerusalem for the Muslims.

1189
- On the death of Henry II of England, his eldest son, Richard I (the Lion-Hearted), becomes king.

- Richard I (the Lion-Hearted), Frederick I (Barbarossa), and Philip II Augustus of France lead the Third Crusade, which lasts until 1192.

1190
- On the way to the Holy Land, Frederick I (Barbarossa) drowns in the River Saleph in Cilicia; Henry VI, his son, succeeds him and is crowned Emperor of the Romans in 1191.

*DENOTES CIRCA DATE

WORLD EVENTS 500-1590

1191
- Richard I (the Lion-Hearted) conquers Cyprus. He arranges to sell it to the Knights Templars, but after they cannot meet his price, Richard's ally Guy of Lusignan, the dispossessed king of the Crusader kingdom of Jerusalem, eventually becomes ruler of Cyprus.

- Crusaders led by Richard I (the Lion-Hearted) and Philip II Augustus take Acre, in the kingdom of Jerusalem, and slaughter the inhabitants.

1192
- After Latin Christian forces fail to retake Jerusalem, the Third Crusade ends. Richard and Salah al-Din negotiate a three-year truce that allows the Crusaders to keep Acre and a strip of land along the coast and to have free access to Jerusalem. While returning from the Crusade, Richard I is captured by Leopold, Duke of Austria, and is held for ransom until February 1194.

- Muslim Ghurid leader Mu'izz al-Din returns to win a great victory that opens the way for his subordinates to establish Ghurid control over northern India.

- On the death of Japanese emperor Shirakawa II, Minamoto Yoritomo seizes power and names himself shogun; Japan is ruled by a shogunate for the next seven hundred years.

1194
- Richard I (the Lion-Hearted) returns to England and begins a war against Philip II Augustus, who has been preparing to attack Richard's French lands.

1195
- Isaac II Angelus is deposed and blinded by his brother Alexius III, who seizes the Byzantine throne. During his reign, which lasts until 1203, the already decaying government and military bureaucracy of the empire collapses completely.

1197
- After the death of Emperor Henry VI, civil war breaks out between rivals for the German crown: Henry's brother Philip of Swabia, who is supported by France, and the ultimately successful Otto of Brunswick, who is backed by England.

1199
- Richard I (the Lion-Hearted) of England is mortally wounded while making war against Philip II Augustus in France. His successor is his brother John I (Lackland), who continues the war.

1200*
- Kabbalism, a Jewish mystic philosophy, develops in southern Europe.

- The Chimú kingdom builds an impressive capital at Chan Chan in the Moche Valley of Peru. The Chimú kingdom begins a period of expansion around 1370, becoming the most powerful civilization in Peru before the rise of the Incas.

- Khmer king Jayavarman VII builds the temple complex Angkor Thom in his capital city.

*DENOTES CIRCA DATE

WORLD EVENTS 500-1590

1200
- John I of England and Philip II Augustus of France sign the Peace of Le Goulet, in which Philip recognizes John's claim to all Richard's lands in return for financial and territorial concessions.

1200*-1250*
- French poet Guillaume de Loris writes the first part of *Roman de la Rose* (Romance of the Rose).

1201
- Pope Innocent III recognizes Otto of Brunswick as Otto IV, king of Germany.

1202
- Hostilities resume between England and France. By 1206 John I of England has lost Normandy, Anjou, Maine, and parts of Poitou.

1202-1204
- Boniface of Montferrat and Venetian doge Enrico Dandolo lead the Fourth Crusade.

1202-1241
- During the reign of Valdemar II, much of the Baltic region comes under the control of the Danes.

1203
- Motivated by the wish of Pope Innocent III to reunite the Byzantine and Roman Churches and by the long-standing trade disputes between the Venetians and the Byzantines, Latin Christian knights attack and pillage Constantinople. They depose Alexius III, and Alexius IV governs as a puppet of the Crusaders.

1204
- After the deposition and murder of Alexius IV, Alexius V (Ducas) seizes the throne. The Crusaders respond by sacking the city with such brutality that the Pope and the Crusade movement are discredited.

- The Crusaders place Baldwin I of Flanders on the throne of the Latin kingdom that controls Constantinople until 1261. Boniface of Montferrat is made king of Thessalonica, and the Venetians gain control of important harbors and islands on their trade routes.

- Members of Byzantine royal families establish enclaves at Trebizond on the Black Sea, Epirus in northwest Greece, Nicaea in Anatolia, and elsewhere, but the Byzantine Empire never recovers from the sack of its capital.

1206
- Temujin, great-grandson of Mongol leader Kabul Khan, is proclaimed Genghis Khan (Emperor within the Seas). Uniting the Mongol tribes into a single nation and forging them into a powerful fighting force, he rules until 1227.

- Muslim conquerors establish the Sultanate of Delhi in northwestern India, establishing a dynasty that rules until 1266.

*DENOTES CIRCA DATE

WORLD EVENTS 500-1590

1208-1209

- After the assassination in 1208 of Philip of Swabia, one of the claimants to the German throne, Pope Innocent crowns Otto IV Emperor of the Romans in 1209. In return, Otto recognizes Church territorial claims in central Italy.

- Pope Innocent III places England under interdict and excommunicates King John during a dispute over filling the vacant archbishopric of Canterbury. John finally accedes to the Pope's wishes in 1213.

- Theodore Lascaris establishes the empire of Nicaea, which becomes a Byzantine government in exile.

1209

- The Latin Christian Church launches an internal European Crusade in southern France against the Cathars, a Christian dualist sect.

1210

- Pope Innocent III excommunicates Otto IV for disputing some of the papacy's land claims.

1211

- Iltutmish (rules 1211–1236) founds the Sultanate of Delhi in northern India, the first Indian Muslim state.

- Led by Genghis Khan, the Mongols begin their invasion of the Chin state in northern China.

1212

- Frederick II, who has gained the support of Pope Innocent III, becomes king of Germany.

- At the Battle of Las Navas de Tolosa, the Christian kingdoms of León, Castile, Aragon, Navarre, and Portugal severely defeat the Almohad army, opening the way for the Christian conquest of southern Iberia.

- An army of thousands of adolescents is raised in France and Germany for the Children's Crusade to the Holy Land. Few, if any, of the children reach their destination, and a large number of them are sold into slavery in the East.

1213

- The Council of St. Albans, a meeting of prelates, earls, and barons, is held in an English abbey. Historians call it the precursor of the British Parliament.

1214

- Philip II Augustus of France and Frederick II of Germany defeat John of England and Emperor Otto IV at the Battle of Bouvines. Frederick becomes Emperor of the Romans (crowned 1220).

*DENOTES CIRCA DATE

WORLD EVENTS 500-1590

1215
- Genghis Khan captures Beijing.

- English barons meet with King John at Runnymede and force him to sign the Magna Carta, a feudal charter that limits the powers of the king and protects individual liberties.

1216
- At the request of rebellious barons, troops led by Prince Louis of France (later King Louis VIII) land in England. On the death of King John in October, his nine-year-old son becomes Henry III of England. A council of regency led by William Marshal, Earl of Pembroke, defeats the rebels and drives the French from England in 1217.

- The Cola empire of southern India begins to break up.

1218
- The Fifth Crusade begins, with efforts concentrated on Egypt. It ends in 1221 after Crusaders fail to take Cairo.

1218-1221
- The first Mongol invasions devastate Muslim Central Asia, Afghanistan, and northern Iran.

1219
- Control of the Kamakura shogunate in Japan passes from the Minamoto family to the Hojo family.

1220
- Genghis Khan completes his conquest of Persia.

1221
- The Chinese use gunpowder in shrapnel bombs.

1223
- On the death of Philip II Augustus of France, his son Louis VIII succeeds him.

- The Mongols defeat the Russian and Cuman forces at the Battle of the Kalka River in southern Russia but then return to Asia rather than continuing the invasion.

1226
- On the death of his father, Louis VIII, Louis IX (the Pious) becomes king of France and rules for forty-four years.

1227
- On the death of Genghis Khan, his three sons divide the empire among themselves with Ogodei, the eldest, as Great Khan, or overlord.

*DENOTES CIRCA DATE

WORLD EVENTS 500-1590

1228-1229	• Emperor Frederick II leads the Sixth Crusade. Capturing Jerusalem, Bethlehem, and Nazareth, he is proclaimed king of Jerusalem and signs a treaty with the Egyptians.
1233	• Pope Gregory IX establishes the Inquisition to rid the Church of heresy.
	• Emperor Frederick II captures Sicily.
1234	• The Mongols annex the Chin empire of northern China.
1237	• Mongol armies under Batu, grandson of Genghis Khan, renew their invasion of Russia, conquering the Volga Bulgars.
	• Frederick II defeats the Lombard League at Cortenuova in northern Italy.
1240*	• The Mongols capture Moscow and force its princes to accept them as overlords.
	• The Great Council of England begins to be called "Parliament."
1240	• Mongol troops take Kiev, ending their conquest of southern and central Russia. The western part of the Mongol Empire becomes known as the Golden Horde.
1241	• Mongol armies menace eastern Europe, successfully invading Poland and Hungary and reaching the Adriatic Sea.
1242	• Mongol troops withdraw from eastern Europe to their conquered Russian territory.
1244	• Jerusalem is recaptured by the Muslims.
1248	• Louis IX (the Pious) of France leads the Seventh Crusade, which ends in 1250. During this conflict Muslims use gunpowder against the Crusaders.
1250	• Frederick II dies while campaigning in Italy. In 1251 his son becomes Conrad IV of Germany.

*DENOTES CIRCA DATE

WORLD EVENTS 500-1590

1250*-1300*
- French poet Jean de Meun completes *Roman de la Rose* (Romance of the Rose).

1253
- The Venetians and the Genoese engage in ongoing naval warfare over trade rights in the eastern Mediterranean.

1254-1273
- The death of Conrad IV is followed by a long interregnum, during which many German princes struggle for power.

1258
- Mongol armies led by Hulegu take Baghdad, ending the Abbasid caliphate. Hulegu founds the Ilkhanid dynasty to rule Persia as part of the vast Mongol empire.
- An English committee draws up the Provisions of Oxford, establishing a baronial veto over decisions made by the king. In 1261 Henry III reneges on his oath to support the provisions, leading to the outbreak of a civil war known as the Barons' War.

1259
- Great Khan Mongke dies while leading his army in China and is succeeded by his brother Kublai.

1260
- Mongols sack Aleppo and Damascus but fail in their attempts to advance into Egypt.

1261
- Michael VIII Palaeologus of Nicaea conquers the Latin kingdom of Constantinople.

1264
- Henry III is captured by his brother-in-law, Simon de Montfort, Earl of Leicester, at the Battle of Lewes (14 May). Simon forces Henry to renew his pledge to the reforms of 1258.

1265
- With the help of troops from the Welsh borderlands, Prince Edward (later Edward I) comes to the aid of his father, Henry III, defeating and killing Montfort at the Battle of Evesham.

1266
- Turkish general Balban becomes sultan of Delhi, which he rules until 1287.
- Charles of Anjou, brother of Louis IX of France, defeats Manfred of Sicily at the Battle of Benevento and establishes himself as Charles I of Sicily.

*DENOTES CIRCA DATE

WORLD EVENTS 500-1590

1266-1273	• Thomas Aquinas writes his *Summae theologae* (Comprehensive Theology), a cornerstone of all subsequent Roman Catholic theology.
1268	• Charles I of Sicily captures Conradin, his rival claimant to Sicily, and has him beheaded in Naples.
1270	• Louis IX of France and Edward I of England launch the Eighth—and final—Crusade, which ends in 1271, having accomplished nothing. Louis dies in Tunis and is succeeded by his son Philip III (the Bold).
1271	• Kublai Khan proclaims the Yuan dynasty in China, establishing his capital at present-day Beijing. He rules until 1294. • Marco Polo leaves Venice to travel to China.
1272	• Henry III of England dies; called back from Crusade, Edward I assumes the throne in 1274 and rules until 1307.
1273	• Rudolf of Habsburg becomes Rudolf I, king of Germany and Holy Roman Emperor, establishing the Habsburg dynasty.
1274	• Kublai Khan's fleet is virtually destroyed while attempting to invade Japan.
1275	• Marco Polo arrives at the court of Kublai Khan and lives in his domains for the next seventeen years.
1279	• Kublai Khan completes his conquest of the Song kingdom in southern China, reunifying all of China under Mongol rule. • The last king of the Indian Cola dynasty dies.
1281	• Mongol hopes of conquering Japan are again dashed when a typhoon ("kamikaze") destroys Kublai Khan's great invasion fleet.

*DENOTES CIRCA DATE

WORLD EVENTS 500-1590

1281-1282
- Charles I of Sicily makes two attempts to wrest Albania from the Byzantines. His second invasion fails after a rebellion at home removes him from power. Defending his empire in the West prevents Emperor Michael VIII from protecting his eastern provinces from the Turks, and by Michael's death in 1282 they have advanced well into western Anatolia.

1282
- Edward I of England leads an army into Wales to put down a second revolt led by Welsh prince Llywelyn ap Gruffudd. Llywelyn is killed; his brother David is hanged, drawn, and quartered in 1283.
- Erik V (Glipping), the king of Denmark from 1259 to 1286, is forced to grant the nobles a constitution, which recognizes a national assembly and puts the king under its authority.

1285
- Philip IV (the Fair) succeeds his late father, Philip III (the Bold), as king of France.

1286
- On the death of Alexander III of Scotland, his granddaughter, Margaret "The Maid of Norway," daughter of King Eric of Norway, succeeds him.

1290
- Edward I expels the Jews from England.
- The death of young Margaret of Scotland sparks a two-year dispute over the throne.

1291
- Muslims capture Acre, the last Crusader outpost in Syria, ending the presence of Western Crusaders in the Middle East, except on Cyprus, which is ruled by the Knights of St. John of Jerusalem.

1292
- Supported by Edward I of England, John de Balliol, a descendant of David I's youngest son, becomes the successor to Alexander III (died 1286) after a long dispute over the Scottish throne.

1293
- The Pueblo peoples of the American Southwest abandon their cliff dwellings, moving southward and eastward and establishing new, large villages.
- Turkish leader Othman (for whom the Ottoman Empire is named) emerges as the prince of a border principality in northeastern Anatolia and begins to seize Byzantine territory.

1295
- Edward I of England calls the Model Parliament with the broadest representation to date, including clergy, knights, burgesses, and aristocrats as well as commoners representing shires, towns, and parishes.
- France and Scotland form an alliance to invade England.

*DENOTES CIRCA DATE

WORLD EVENTS 500-1590

1296
- Learning of the alliance between Scotland and France, Edward I of England invades Scotland and forces John de Balliol to abdicate the throne, which remains empty until 1306.

1297
- An army led by Scottish nobleman William Wallace defeats the English at Stirling Bridge.

1298
- Edward I sends another army against the Scots, who are defeated at the Battle of Falkirk.

1299*
- The Ottoman sultanate—later the largest, longest-lasting, and most institutional of pre-modern Muslim states—is established as a small principality in northwest Anatolia.

1302
- Flemish burghers defeat an army of French knights at the Battle of Courtrai (Battle of the Golden Spurs).
- Philip IV (the Fair) of France calls the first Estates-General, which has members from the clergy, nobility, and common people.

1303
- Pope Boniface VIII enters into a dispute with Philip IV (the Fair) of France, who has his agents kidnap the Pope. Boniface dies later this year.

1303-1307
- To fight the Turks, Byzantine emperor Andronicus I hires an army of Catalan mercenaries, who then attack Constantinople.

1306
- Another descendant of David I's youngest son, Robert I (the Bruce) murders his rival John Comyn, a nephew of John de Balliol, and is crowned king of Scotland.

1307
- Edward I of England dies and is succeeded by his son, Edward II.

1309
- Amid political factionalism in Italy, Pope Clement V moves the seat of the papacy from Rome to Avignon, France, where it remains until 1377.

1310
- Edward II is forced to accept the Lords' Ordinances, which require parliamentary consent to royal appointments, declarations of war, and the king's departure from the realm.

*DENOTES CIRCA DATE

WORLD EVENTS 500-1590

1311	• After failing to take Constantinople, the Catalans advance through Greece, conquer Athens, and create the Catalan Duchy of Athens and Thebes.
1314	• Robert I (the Bruce) defeats an English army at the Battle of Bannockburn, re-establishing Scottish independence. • Philip IV (the Fair) of France dies and is succeeded by his son Louis X (the Stubborn).
1315-1318	• Edward Bruce, brother of Robert I (the Bruce) of Scotland, invades Ireland and is crowned king; his attempt to wrest control of Ireland from the English ends when he is killed in battle in 1318.
1317	• Mongol rule in Persia begins to collapse.
1320	• Ghiyas-ud-Din Tughluq becomes sultan of Delhi, founding the Tughlaq dynasty.
1320-1328	• Byzantine emperor Andronicus II disinherits his grandson Andronicus, who responds by starting a civil war that devastates much of the empire. Andronicus II is finally forced to yield the throne to Andronicus III, who rules until 1341.
1321	• Dante completes his *Commedia* (Divine Comedy).
1322	• Forces loyal to Edward II defeat Thomas of Lancaster at Boroughbridge, Yorkshire. Edward has Lancaster beheaded and revokes the Lords' Ordinances. • Philip V (the Tall) of France dies and is succeeded by his brother Charles IV (the Fair).
1323	• Sweden and Russia sign the Treaty of Nöteborg, dividing Finland between them.
1325*	• The Mexica (Aztecs) build their great capital city of Tenochtitlán on the site of present-day Mexico City.
1326	• Queen Isabella of England, wife of Edward II and daughter of Philip IV of France, and her lover, exiled English baron Roger Mortimer, invade England.

*DENOTES CIRCA DATE

WORLD EVENTS 500-1590

1327
- King Edward II of England dies while imprisoned at Berkeley Castle, probably murdered. His fifteen-year-old son is crowned King Edward III. His fifty-year reign is marked by constant conflict with France.

- Othman I, ruler of Turkey, dies.

- Exiled from Florence, Petrarch (Francesco Petrarca) goes to Avignon, France, where he meets the woman he addresses as "Laura" in his sonnets.

1328*
- After an unsuccessful military campaign in 1327, Edward III of England signs the Treaty of Northampton, recognizing Scottish independence. Edward's seven-year-old sister, Joanna, is married to Robert I the Bruce's four-year-old son, David.

1328
- Charles IV (the Fair) of France dies without issue and is succeeded by Philip VI, son of Charles of Valois and a nephew of Philip IV.

1329
- On the death of Robert I (the Bruce), his son becomes David II of Scotland.

1330*
- The bubonic plague, or Black Death, begins to kill huge numbers of people in northeastern China. The epidemic is carried westward by traders, travelers, and nomadic peoples.

1330
- After a three-year regency during which England has been ruled by Roger Mortimer and Queen Isabella, Edward III overthrows their rule and has Mortimer executed.

1332
- With English support Edward de Balliol, son of John de Balliol, invades Scotland and seizes the throne. Young David II goes into exile in France.

1333
- Emperor Go-Daigo of Japan successfully overthrows the Kamakura shogunate, but his subsequent actions provoke civil war.

- Toghon Temur becomes the last Yuan (Mongol) emperor of China.

- The Mongol empire in Persia breaks into separate kingdoms, which are ruled by Ilkhanid princes until 1353.

1336
- Ashikaga Takauji, who has proclaimed himself shogun, drives Emperor Go-Daigo of Japan from the capital and places Kogon on the throne, establishing the Ashikaga shogunate, under which Japanese feudalism enters its golden age.

*DENOTES CIRCA DATE

WORLD EVENTS 500-1590

1337
- After losing all northwestern Anatolia to the Ottoman Turks, the Byzantines come to terms with the Ottomans and other Turkish emirs. The Byzantines then hire Turkish soldiers to help them against European enemies such as the Italians, Serbs, and Bulgars.

- Edward III of England, grandson of Philip IV of France, claims the French crown, which has gone to Philip IV's nephew Philip VI in 1328. Edward lands an army in Flanders, thus beginning the intermittent struggle known as the "Hundred Years' War" (1337–1453).

1340
- The Christian forces of Alfonso XI of Castile and Alfonso IV of Portugal defeat Granadan Muslim forces at the Battle of Rio Salado, retaining Castilian control over the Strait of Gibraltar and thwarting Muslim efforts to reclaim lost territory bordering the kingdom of Granada.

1341
- In the wake of widespread resentment of English control over King Edward de Balliol, David II returns from France and regains the Scottish throne.

- On the death of Andronicus III Palaeologus, his minor son John V Palaeologus becomes Byzantine emperor, and civil war breaks out in the empire.

1345
- The Ottoman Turks extend their conquest of Byzantine territory into Europe.

1346
- Bubonic plague reaches the Golden Horde, beginning the disintegration of Mongol rule in Russia.

- Stefan Dusan, king of Serbia since 1331, has himself crowned emperor of the Serbs and Greeks. He has already conquered much of coastal Albania and part of Greece, and by 1348 his empire includes all of northern Greece.

- In a major victory at the Battle of Crécy (26 August), English longbowmen and foot soldiers prove their superiority to French troops.

- The English defeat David II of Scotland at Neville's Cross (17 October) and take him as a prisoner to England, where he is held until 1357.

1347
- Bubonic plague reaches Constantinople and other parts of the Byzantine Empire.

- John Cantacuzenus, who has opposed the forces of John V Palaeologus in the Byzantine civil war, takes Constantinople and seizes the throne, reigning as John VI until 1354.

1348-1351
- Bubonic plague spreads throughout North Africa and Europe.

*DENOTES CIRCA DATE

WORLD EVENTS 500-1590

1349-1351
- Italian poet Giovanni Boccaccio writes *The Decameron,* set during the plague that ravaged Florence in 1348.

1350
- Philip VI of France dies and is succeeded by his son John II (the Good).
- Sixteen-year-old Javan ruler Hayam Wuruk seizes the throne of the Hindu state of Majapahit, bringing all Indonesia under Javan control.

1353
- Firuz Shah, sultan of Delhi, wages war against Bengal.

1353-1371
- The Laotian people live in unity under the leadership of Fa Ngum.

1354
- John V Palaeologus retakes Constantinople and forces the abdication of John VI Cantacuzenus as the Turks advance steadily on Byzantine territory.

1355
- Stefan Dusan is advancing on Constantinople when his sudden death puts an end to his efforts to expand the Serbian empire.

1356
- At the Battle of Poitiers, Edward the Black Prince, son of Edward III of England, defeats and captures King John II (the Good) of France.

1360
- The Treaties of Bretigny and Calais give Edward III full sovereignty over French lands he previously held as vassal to the king of France. In return, Edward renounces his claim to the French throne. John II of France is ransomed but remains in England, where he dies in 1364.

1364
- Charles V (the Wise) of France inherits the throne from his father, John II. Refusing to accept the provisions of peace agreements with England, he re-opens hostilities.

1367
- After a Brahman victory in the Battle of Vijayanagar, about four hundred thousand Hindus are slaughtered.

1368
- As the army of Zhu Yuanzhang advances on his capital, Yuan emperor Toghon Temur of China flees to Manchuria. Zhu Yuanzhang becomes Emperor Hongwu, establishing the Ming dynasty, which rules China until 1644.

*DENOTES CIRCA DATE

WORLD EVENTS 500-1590

1369
- Timur (Tamerlane), a Muslim Turkic leader, rises to power in Transoxania.

1370*
- The Chimú kingdom begins a period of expansion, becoming the most powerful civilization in Peru before the rise of the Incas.

1371
- David II dies and is succeeded by his cousin Robert II, the first Stuart king of Scotland.

1374
- John of Gaunt, Duke of Lancaster, becomes virtual ruler of England. He and his supporters are opposed by a faction led by Edward the Black Prince, heir to the throne of the aging Edward III.

1375
- The Mamluks complete their conquest of Armenia.

1375*-1400*
- Englishman Geoffrey Chaucer writes his *Canterbury Tales.*

1376
- Deposed Byzantine emperor John V Palaeologus is succeeded by his son Andronicus IV.
- At the Good Parliament of 1376, supporters of Edward the Black Prince impeach some of John of Gaunt's supporters, the first parliamentary impeachment of government officials in English history. The death of Prince Edward on 8 June, however, robs Parliament of the ability to deal with John of Gaunt.

1377
- Edward III of England dies and is succeeded by his grandson, ten-year-old Richard II, son of Edward the Black Prince. Until 1389, England is ruled by a council headed by John of Gaunt.

1378-1388
- England and Scotland engage in a series of border wars.

1378-1417
- After Pope Gregory XI moves the papacy back to Rome in 1377, there begins a period known as the Great Western Schism (1378–1417), during which cardinals in Rome and Avignon each elect their own pope.

1380
- The death of Charles V of France halts the gradual reduction of English territory in France. He is succeeded by his eleven-year-old son, Charles VI, who reigns until 1422, largely a figurehead for prominent members of the nobility.

***DENOTES CIRCA DATE**
- Prince Dmitry of Moscow defeats the Mongols at the Battle of Kulikovo.

WORLD EVENTS 500-1590

1382
- Mongol troops recapture and plunder Moscow.
- Leopold III of Austria obtains Trieste.
- The Turks capture Sofia.

1383-1385
- Timur conquers eastern Persia.
- Murad I occupies Salonika. The Turks now control most of the Byzantine Empire.

1391
- Manuel II, second son of John V Palaeologus, ascends the throne of a Byzantine Empire that for much of his reign is reduced to the cities of Thessalonica and Constantinople and the province of Morea.

1392
- Japanese shogun Ashikaga Yoshimitsu reopens trade with China and ends the imperial division of Japan by settling the succession dispute between rival branches of the imperial family.
- The Yi dynasty is established in Korea, where it rules until 1910.

1398
- Timur conquers Delhi.

1399
- Henry Bolingbroke—son of the late John of Gaunt, Duke of Lancaster, and, like Richard, a grandson of Edward III—deposes Richard II and rules England until 1413 as Henry IV, first king of the House of Lancaster.

1400*
- The Incan civilization begins a period of expansion that leads to its domination of the Andean region.
- The Five Iroquois Nations—the Mohawks, Senecas, Onondagas, Oneidas, and Cayugas—are formed in North America.

1401
- Timur conquers Damascus and Baghdad.

1402
- Several Ethiopian ambassadors arrive in Europe.

1402-1424
- During his reign, Ming emperor Yongle exacts tribute from Japan, moves his capital to Beijing, crushes the Mongols, and sends Chinese sailing vessels on expeditions to foreign lands, including Africa.

*Denotes Circa Date

WORLD EVENTS 500-1590

1404-1434
- Narameikhla rules Arakan, on the Bay of Bengal in southern Myanmar, as the first sovereign of the Mrohaung dynasty, which rules until the eighteenth century. Driven from his kingdom early in his reign, he regains it in 1430 and builds the new capital of Mrohaung.

1405
- Timur dies while trying to conquer China. His son Shah Rokh establishes the Timurid dynasty that rules Persia and Central Asia until the early sixteenth century.

1405-1433
- Chinese admiral Zheng He makes voyages of exploration to Southeast Asia, India, East Africa, Egypt, Ceylon, Indonesia, and the Persian Gulf.

1406-1407
- The Chinese invade and occupy Vietnam.

1413
- On the death of Henry IV, his son Henry V becomes king of England.

1415
- Henry V renews English claims to the crown of France and wins a major victory at the Battle of Agincourt.

1417
- The Council of Constance ends the schism in the papacy of the Roman Christian Church.

1417-1420
- After his success at Agincourt, Henry V of England forms an alliance with the Burgundian faction and conquers all of northern France. The Treaty of Troyes (1420) recognizes Henry as the regent and heir apparent to the mad king Charles VI (deposing the dauphin, later Charles VII) and arranges Henry's marriage to Charles VI's daughter Catherine.

1422
- Sultan Murad II of the Ottoman Empire lays siege to Constantinople and invades Greece.
- Henry V of England dies suddenly and is soon followed by Charles VI of France. The English proclaim Henry's nine-month-old son, Henry VI, king of England and France, while Charles's son Charles VII asserts his claim to the French throne, and fighting in France continues.

1423
- After proclaiming himself khan of the Mongols, Aruqtai assails northern China.

1425
- The Portuguese begin a series of voyages to explore the west coast of Africa.

*DENOTES CIRCA DATE

WORLD EVENTS 500-1590

1427-1428
- Under the leadership of Le Loi, the Vietnamese drive the Chinese from their nation. Le Loi is crowned emperor of Vietnam and rules it until he dies in 1443.

1428
- Scotland renews its alliance with France and sends troops to support Charles VII against the English.

1428-1440
- During his reign Itzcoatl makes the Aztecs the dominant nation in the valley of Mexico.

1429
- Joan of Arc leads French troops to end the English siege of Orléans and make possible the coronation of Charles VII at Reims.

1430
- Ottoman sultan Murad II captures Thessalonica.
- Joan of Arc is captured by Burgundians, who are allied with the English, at Compiègne on 23 May.

1431
- Joan of Arc is convicted of heresy and burned at the stake in Rouen. Henry VI of England is crowned king of France in Paris.

1434
- The Medici family rises to power in Italy, ruling Florence for most of the period from 1434 to 1737 (except for intervals in 1494–1512 and 1527–1530).

1436
- The forces of French king Charles VII retake Paris from the English.

1438-1471
- Led by Emperor Pachacuti Inca Yupanqui, the Incas greatly expand their territory.

1439
- Esen Taiji becomes chief of the Oyrat Mongols and begins expanding their territory into China and Korea.

1440-1469
- During the reign of Emperor Montezuma I, the Aztecs extend their territory to include much of present-day Mexico.

1444
- At the Battle of Varna, the Turks decisively defeat a Western army sent to aid the Byzantines, killing Vladislaw III of Poland and Hungary.

*DENOTES CIRCA DATE

WORLD EVENTS 500-1590

1445-1456	• Johannes Gutenberg invents a method of printing with movable type. Books from his press include the *Constance Mass Book* (1450) and the first printed Bible (1456).
1447-1449	• During the brief reign of Ulugh Beg, the Timurid empire reaches its cultural peak. After his death, the empire disintegrates.
1448	• Constantine XI Palaeologus inherits the throne. He is the last Byzantine emperor.
	• Ottoman sultan Murad II defeats the Hungarians at the Battle of Kosovo.
1449	• After the death of Borommaracha II, his son Trailok is crowned king of Thailand. During his forty-year reign, he extends his influence into the Malay Peninsula.
	• Led by Esen Taiji, the Oyrat Mongols capture Chinese emperor Zhengtong, holding him prisoner for a year. His brother becomes Emperor Jingtai and rules until 1457.
1450*	• The Incas build the city of Machu Picchu in Peru. It is inhabited for about a century and then abandoned.
1453	• Led by Sultan Muhammad II (the Conqueror), the Ottoman Turks take Constantinople, bringing about the fall of the Byzantine Empire.
	• The Hundred Years' War ends with England ceding to France all its French possessions except Calais.
1455	• The thirty-year Wars of the Roses begin in England between supporters of two rival claimants to the throne. The Lancastrians, who wear red roses, support King Henry VI. The Yorkists, who wear white roses, back Richard, Duke of York, who—as a descendant of Edward III's third son, Lionel, Duke of Clarence—has a better claim, according to the rules of primogeniture, than Henry, who is descended from John of Gaunt, Duke of Lancaster, Edward's fourth son.
1457	• As Emperor Jingtai is dying, former emperor Zhengtong re-ascends the throne and disposes of Jingtai.
1458	• After a two-year siege, Athens falls to the Ottoman Turks.
1460 ***DENOTES CIRCA DATE**	• Le Thanh Tong becomes king of Vietnam and introduces a Chinese-style government.

WORLD EVENTS 500-1590

1460
(CONT'D)

- Yorkist forces led by Richard Neville, Duke of Warwick, defeat the Lancastrians at the Battle of Northampton (10 July) and capture Henry VI, who comes to a compromise with Richard, Duke of York, by which Richard will succeed to the English throne on Henry's death. Angry that her son, Prince Edward, is thus disinherited, Henry's queen, Margaret of Anjou, gathers her own forces, who kill York at Wakefield in December.

1461

- York's son and heir, Edward, Duke of York, takes London and is proclaimed King Edward IV of England. Henry, Margaret, and their son flee to Scotland.

- Charles VII of France dies and is succeeded by his son Louis XI.

1462

- Ivan III (the Great) of Moscow becomes the first sovereign to rule a unified Russian nation. He reigns until 1505.

1463

- The Ottoman Turks complete their invasion of Bosnia.

1465-1470

- The Incas conquer the Chimú Indians of northern Peru.

1467

- The ten-year Onin War begins in Japan over who will succeed Shogun Ashikaga Yoshimasa.

1469-1471

- The Wars of the Roses resume in England. Edward IV's brother George, Duke of Clarence, and Edward's former ally Richard Neville, Duke of Warwick, depose Edward IV and return Henry VI briefly to the throne in 1470, but in 1471 Edward IV returns to England, defeats the Lancastrians, and resumes the throne. Henry VI's son Edward is killed in the fighting, and Henry is murdered in the Tower of London.

1471-1493

- During the reign of Topa Inca Yupanqui, Pachacuti's son, the Incan empire extends as far south as central Chile.

1474

- Queen Isabella, wife of King Ferdinand of Aragon, inherits the throne of Castile, leading to the union in 1479 of the two Spanish kingdoms under their joint monarchy.

1476

- Under the patronage of Edward IV, William Caxton sets up the first English printing press at Westminster. Among the roughly one hundred books he prints over the next fifteen years are Geoffrey Chaucer's *Canterbury Tales* (1477) and Sir Thomas Malory's *Morte Darthur* (1485).

*DENOTES CIRCA DATE

WORLD EVENTS 500-1590

1478
- Pope Sixtus IV authorizes the Spanish Inquisition to discover, and reform or punish, Christians who hold heretical or unorthodox beliefs, including converts to Christianity from Judaism or Islam who are suspected of retaining their prior beliefs and practicing those religions in secret.

1480
- Ivan III (the Great) repels the last Mongol advance on Moscow, ending Mongol power in Russia.

1482
- Portuguese navigator Diogo Cão locates the Congo River, initiating trade between Congo and Portugal and the Christianization of the Congolese.
- The Ottoman Turks complete their invasion of Herzegovina.

1483
- Tomás de Torquemada becomes Grand Inquisitor for the Spanish kingdoms of Castile, León, Aragon, Catalonia, Valencia, and Majorca. By 1498 he has had some two thousand "heretics" burned at the stake.
- On the death of Edward IV of England on 9 April, his twelve-year-old son, Edward V, becomes king, with his father's brother Richard, Duke of Gloucester, serving as lord protector. In June, Richard usurps the throne and is proclaimed Richard III.
- Louis XI of France dies and is succeeded by his son, Charles VIII.

1485
- In England, the Wars of the Roses begin anew as Yorkists angry with Richard III turn to the Lancastrian claimant, Henry Tudor, Earl of Richmond, whose forces defeat and kill Richard III at the Battle of Bosworth Field on 22 August. The victor ascends the throne as Henry VII, founder of the Tudor dynasty.

1486
- Henry VII of England unites the Houses of York and Lancaster by marrying Edward IV's daughter Elizabeth of York.

1487
- Spanish Christian troops seize Malaga from the Muslims.

1488
- James III of Scotland is deposed and killed. The rebels place his teenage son, James IV, on the throne.
- Portuguese navigator Bartolomeu Dias rounds the Cape of Good Hope at the southern tip of Africa, establishing the eastern sea route to Asia.

1489
- Cyprus comes under Venetian rule.

*DENOTES CIRCA DATE

WORLD EVENTS 500-1590

1491-1492	• Michelangelo sculpts two of his earliest works, *Madonna of the Stairs* and *Battle of the Centaurs*.
1492	• The Muslim kingdom of Granada falls to Spanish Christian forces, ending Muslim political rule in the Iberian Peninsula.
	• Seeking a westward route to Asia for the Spanish rulers Ferdinand and Isabella, Christopher Columbus discovers the Americas, reaching the Bahamas and Cuba.
	• Jews who refuse to convert to Christianity are expelled from Spain.
1493	• Following the death of Topa Inca Yupanqui, Huayna Capac emerges from a power struggle for the throne and rules the Incas until 1525.
1494	• Charles VIII of France conquers Naples, claiming he has inherited it through his father, but the Holy League (Holy Roman Emperor Maximilian I, Pope Alexander VI, Spain, Venice, Milan, and England) forces him to withdraw.
1495-1497	• Leonardo da Vinci paints *The Last Supper*.
1497	• Portugal expels Jews who refuse to convert to Christianity.
1497-1499	• Portuguese explorer Vasco da Gama commands an expedition around the Cape of Good Hope into the Indian Ocean. He reaches the southwestern coast of India in May 1498 before starting back to Portugal.
1498	• Charles VIII of France dies and is succeeded by his cousin Louis XII, son of Charles, Duke of Orléans.
1499	• French troops capture Milan. Ludovico, Duke of Milan, briefly controls the city in 1500, but the French recover it and continue to rule it until 1513.
	• After a renewal of warfare between the Turks and Venetians, the Ottomans destroy a Venetian fleet at Sapienza.
1500	• Portuguese mariner Gaspar de Corte Real explores the east coast of Greenland and the Labrador Peninsula.

*DENOTES CIRCA DATE

WORLD EVENTS 500-1590

1500
(CONT'D)
- Louis XII of France and Ferdinand II of Aragon agree to partition Naples, which they conquer in 1501. Late that year, after conflict between the two former allies, Naples comes under sole French rule until it falls to Spanish forces in 1503.

1501
- French troops enter Rome.
- Ismail I (1487–1524), Sheikh of Ardabil, seizes Persia and establishes the Safavid dynasty.
- Mengli Girai of Russia invades Lithuania.
- The first African slaves arrive in the West Indies, where they gradually replace Native Americans as laborers. Some Spanish-born blacks are imported as slaves by Nicolás de Ovando of Hispaniola.

1502
- Montezuma II succeeds his uncle Ahuitzotl as Aztec emperor of Mexico. Later this year he loses his empire to Spanish troops led by Hernán Cortés. Cortés imprisons Montezuma, who is then killed.
- Led by Khan Mengli Girai, the Crimean Tartars defeat the Mongol Great Horde of southwestern Asia and annex their lands.

1503
- Venice abandons the strategic port of Lepanto in Greece to the Turks and signs a peace treaty with them.
- Poland relinquishes the left bank of the Dnieper River to Russia.
- Zanzibar becomes a Portuguese colony.

1504
- In the Treaty of Lyons, Louis XII of France cedes Naples to Ferdinand II of Aragon; Naples remains under Spanish control until 1707.

1505
- On the death of Ivan III (the Great) his son, Vasily III, becomes ruler of Russia.
- Emperor Zhengde ascends to the throne of China and rules until 1521.

1506
- The sixth manikongo (ruler) of Kongo, Afonso I, converts to Roman Catholicism and promotes Portuguese colonization.

1506-1548
- During his reign Sigismund I, king of Poland and grand prince of Lithuania, establishes Polish suzerainty over East Prussia and annexes Mazovia (which includes the city of Warsaw) to Poland.

*DENOTES CIRCA DATE

WORLD EVENTS 500-1590

1508
- Pope Julius II, Holy Roman Emperor Maximilian I, Louis XII of France, and Ferdinand II of Aragon form the League of Cambrai to oppose the Venetian Republic, which the Pope excommunicates.

1509
- France crushes the Venetians at the Battle of Agnadello.
- Henry VII of England dies and is succeeded by his son Henry VIII.
- Commanded by Francisco de Almeida, a Portuguese navy destroys an Arab-Egyptian fleet off Diu, in northwestern Bombay, India.

1510
- Pope Julius II leaves the League of Cambrai, absolves Venice from excommunication, and allies himself with the Venetians in the hope of driving the French out of Italy.
- The Portuguese attack Goa, on the west coast of India, and establish a colony there.

1511
- Pope Julius II joins with Venice and Spain to form a Holy League against the French.

1512
- The French are forced out of Milan.

1512-1522
- Russia and Poland are at war over possession of Belarus, most of which remains under Polish-Lithuanian control.

1513
- Leading an unsuccessful Scottish-French invasion of England, James IV of Scotland is killed at the Battle of Flodden Field.

1515
- On the death of Louis XII of France, his nephew succeeds him as Francis I.
- Francis I takes Milan.
- Ottoman ruler Selim I seizes eastern Anatolia and Kurdistan.

1516
- On the death of Ferdinand II, his grandson becomes Charles I of Spain.
- In the Concordat of Bologna between Pope Leo X and Francis I, France is granted internal independence in ecclesiastical appointments.
- Ottoman emperor Selim I crushes Egyptian forces near Aleppo and annexes Syria.

*DENOTES CIRCA DATE

WORLD EVENTS 500-1590

1517
- Martin Luther nails his Ninety-five Theses, questioning the practices of granting indulgences, to the door of the Castle Church in Wittenberg, marking the beginning of the Protestant Reformation.

- Egypt and Arabia come under Ottoman suzerainty.

- Charles I of Spain approves slave trade in the Spanish South American colonies.

1518
- Thomas, Cardinal Wolsey, negotiates a Europe-wide peace treaty.

- The Barbary States of Algiers and Tunis are founded.

1519
- On the death of Emperor Maximilian I, his grandson Charles I of Spain becomes Holy Roman Emperor Charles V.

- Sailing for Spain, Portuguese navigator Ferdinand Magellan embarks on a voyage in search of a westward route to the spice islands of the East Indies.

1520
- Christian II of Denmark and Norway (rules 1513–1523) conquers Sweden and is crowned its king.

- On the death of Sultan Selim I, his son Suleyman I (the Magnificent) becomes ruler of the Ottoman Empire.

- Cuauhtémoc is crowned the last emperor of the Aztec Empire.

- Magellan rounds the tip of South America on 28 November, passing into the Pacific Ocean through the Strait of Magellan.

1521
- Ottoman troops seize Belgrade and advance into Hungary.

- After destroying the Aztec state, Cortés takes control of Mexico.

- Magellan is killed on Mactan Island in the Philippines.

1521-1566
- During the reign of Emperor Jiajing, the power of the Ming dynasty is in decline, and China is fraught with lawlessness, disorder, and nepotism.

1522
- Charles V grants Austria, Habsburg possessions in Germany, and Württemberg to his younger brother Ferdinand.

- Gustav Vasa becomes regent of Sweden.

- Sultan Suleyman I seizes Rhodes from the Knights of St. John.

*DENOTES CIRCA DATE

- Spanish Christian forces take Guatemala.

WORLD EVENTS 500-1590

1522
(CONT'D)

- Cortés hangs Cuauhtémoc.

- The remnants of Magellan's fleet reach Spain on 8 September, bearing the first Europeans to circumnavigate the globe.

1523

- The Chinese expel the Portuguese.

- Gustav Vasa establishes the independence of Sweden from Denmark and is elected King Gustav I Vasa.

1524

- In the Treaty of Malmo, Denmark validates the independence of Sweden.

1525

- German and Spanish troops defeat the French and Swiss at Pavia; Francis I of France is taken prisoner; Charles V becomes ruler of Italy.

- Mongol leader Babur, a descendant of Timur and Genghis Khan, marches into Punjab. By 1530 he is emperor of all northern India, founding the Muslim Mughal dynasty.

- On the death of Emperor Huayna, the Incan empire is divided between Huáscar and Atahuallpa.

1526

- In the Battle of Mohacs, the Ottoman Turks defeat the Hungarians, killing Louis II of Hungary; János (John) Zápolya and Ferdinand of Austria both claim the Hungarian throne.

1527

- Ferdinand becomes king of Bohemia and sole king of Hungary.

- Troops of the Holy Roman Empire pillage Rome, killing four thousand inhabitants and looting art treasures; Pope Clement VII is imprisoned for seven months.

- The Somali Muslim chieftain Ahmad Gran attacks Ethiopia.

- Mac Dang Dung defeats the Le dynasty and becomes ruler of Vietnam.

1529

- The viceroy of New Spain establishes his capital at Mexico City on the site of the Aztec capital of Tenochtitlán.

- Khayr ad-Din seizes Algiers, making it a base for Barbary pirates.

1530

- The Augsburg Confession establishes the basic doctrines of an independent Lutheran Church.

- Pope Clement VII crowns Charles V Holy Roman Emperor and king of Italy; this coronation is the last time a pope crowns a Holy Roman Emperor.

*DENOTES CIRCA DATE

WORLD EVENTS 500-1590

1530 (CONT'D)	• Having failed to convince Pope Clement VII to annul the marriage of Henry VIII and Catherine of Aragon, Cardinal Wolsey is arrested for treason and dies before his trial.
1531	• War erupts in Switzerland between Protestant Zurich and Catholic cantons; Protestant leader Huldrych Zwingli is killed at the Battle of Kappel.
1532	• Ottoman Sultan Suleyman I launches an unsuccessful invasion of Hungary. • Early this year Atahuallpa overthrows Huáscar and becomes ruler of the entire Incan empire. In November, Francisco Pizarro captures Atahuallpa, holds him for ransom, and once the demands are met, has him executed.
1533	• Parliament passes an act that clears the way for the annulment of Henry's marriage to Catherine of Aragon without the the approval of Pope Clement. Henry and the pregnant Anne Boleyn have already secretly married. The Pope excommunicates Henry. • Vasily III dies; his three-year-old son becomes Ivan IV (the Terrible) of Russia. • The Portuguese found a colony in Brazil.
1534	• The Act of Supremacy names Henry VIII "Supreme Head" of the separate Church of England. • Khayr ad-Din seizes Tunisia.
1535	• After refusing to swear an oath recognizing the annulment of Henry VIII's marriage to Catherine of Aragon and the validity of his marriage to Anne Boleyn, Sir Thomas More, Lord Chancellor of England, is tried for treason and executed. • Holy Roman Emperor Charles V seizes Tunis. • Antonio de Mendoza, viceroy of New Spain, introduces a printing press in Mexico, the first of its kind in the Western Hemisphere. • An army led by Incan ruler Manco Inca Yupanqui is defeated by the Spaniards in Peru. • Francisco Pizarro founds the city of Lima, Peru.
1536	• Queen Anne Boleyn is sent to the Tower of London, tried for treason, and executed. Henry VIII marries Jane Seymour.
1537	• Queen Jane Seymour dies after giving birth to the future Edward VI of England.

*DENOTES CIRCA DATE

WORLD EVENTS 500-1590

1538	• John Calvin is expelled from Geneva for promulgating his Protestant beliefs.
1539	• Afghan leader Sher Shah takes Bengal and defeats Mughal emperor Humayun at the Battle of Chausa, going on to become emperor of northern India. • Tabinshweti, of the Burman Toungoo dynasty, seizes Pegu in southern Myanmar.
1540	• Henry VIII marries his fourth wife, Anne of Cleves, in January. He has the marriage annulled in July and marries Catherine Howard.
1541	• Parliament proclaims Henry VIII king of Ireland and head of the Irish Church. • Ottoman sultan Suleyman I conquers the city of Buda and occupies part of Hungary. • With the help of the Portuguese arms, Ethiopia drives out Ahmad Gran's Somali army. Portuguese missionaries are sent to Ethiopia, where they convert its next two rulers.
1542	• Queen Catherine Howard is executed at the Tower of London. • On the death of James V of Scotland, the throne goes to his week-old daughter, Mary.
1543	• Polish astronomer Nicolaus Copernicus publishes his theory of a sun-centered universi. • Henry VIII marries his sixth wife, Catherine Parr. • Jesuit missionary Francis Xavier arrives in Japan.
1545	• Charles V, Ferdinand of Austria, and Suleyman I sign the Truce of Adriano. • The Spaniards discover silver at Potosí, Bolivia, and use Indian labor to mine it. • The Le dynasty of Vietnam retakes the Red River region.
1546-1548	• Angered by new laws that limit the privileges of the conquistadors, Ganzalo Pizarro, half brother of Francisco Pizarro, takes up arms against the colonial government of Peru. In 1548 he is defeated and executed.
1547	• Ivan IV becomes the first Russian ruler to assume the title *tsar* (caesar or emperor). • On the death of Henry VIII of England, his son succeeds him as Edward VI.

*DENOTES CIRCA DATE

WORLD EVENTS 500-1590

1548
- On the death of Sigismund I of Poland, his son Sigismund II Augustus, who has been coruler of Poland since 1530 and grand prince of Lithuania since 1544, becomes king of Poland. Reigning until 1572, he is the last king of the Jagiellon dynasty.

1550
- Led by Altan Khan, the Oyrat Mongols raid as far south as the outskirts of Beijing.

1550-1600
- Spain is at the peak of its political and economic power.

1551
- The Ottoman Turks capture Tripoli.

1552
- Ivan IV of Russia captures the khanate of Kazan on the Volga River; in 1556 he annexes the khanate of Astrakhan at the mouth of the Volga.

1553
- Edward VI of England dies, having been persuaded by the Protestant opposition to his Roman Catholic half sister, Mary Tudor (daughter of Henry VIII and his first wife, Catherine of Aragon), to name his first cousin Lady Jane Grey as his successor. She reigns for nine days before Mary's supporters claim the crown for Mary. During Mary I's reign, which lasts until 1558, she re-establishes Roman Catholicism in England, and some three hundred Protestants are burned at the stake for heresy.

1554
- Alarmed by the impending marriage of Mary I of England to the future Philip II of Roman Catholic Spain, Sir Thomas Wyat raises a revolt against her. After defeating and executing Wyat, Mary marries Philip, who rules jointly with her until her death in 1558.

1554-1555
- Sultan Suleyman I completes his invasion of Persia.

1556-1605
- During his reign, Emperor Akbar the Great, another descendant of Timur and Genghis Khan, spreads Mughal rule over most of the Indian subcontinent.

1558
- The English relinquish Calais, their last possession in continental Europe, to the French.

- On the death of Charles V (21 September), his brother becomes Holy Roman Emperor Ferdinand I, and his son becomes King Philip II of Spain.

- Mary I of England dies without issue and is succeeded by her Protestant half sister, Elizabeth I, daughter of Henry VIII and Anne Boleyn. Elizabeth, who rules until 1603, re-establishes the Anglican Church.

*DENOTES CIRCA DATE

WORLD EVENTS 500-1590

1558
(CONT'D)

- Fifteen-year-old Mary Queen of Scots marries Francis Dauphin of France, who succeeds Henry II as Francis II in 1559 and claims the thrones of Scotland and England.

1558-1583

- Seeking an outlet to the Baltic Sea for landlocked Russia, Ivan IV becomes involved in a protracted and largely unsuccessful attempt to conquer Livonia (in present-day Latvia and Estonia). Lithuania, Poland, and Sweden become involved in the war against Russia.

1559

- Christian III, king of Denmark and Norway, dies and is succeeded by his son Frederick II.

1560

- A group of Huguenots (French Calvinists) attempt to kidnap King Francis II, who dies later this year. His brother succeeds him as Charles IX.

1561

- Mary Queen of Scots, widow of Francis II, returns to Scotland from France.

- To obtain protection against the Russians, the Teutonic Knights who govern greater Livonia dissolve their order, placing Livonia proper under the protection of Lithuania and giving Courland to Poland, Estonia to Sweden, and Oesel to Denmark.

1562

- The massacre of a Protestant congregation in Vassy sparks a civil war in France, which ends in 1563. Further Wars of Religion take place sporadically between 1567 and 1598.

1563-1570

- Sweden, Denmark, Poland, and the Imperial city of Lübeck fight a war over the control of trade in the Baltic Sea.

1564

- On the death of Ferdinand I his son Maximilian II succeeds him as Holy Roman Emperor and rules until 1576.

1565

- Spain establishes its first permanent colonial settlement in the Philippines.

- Spanish troops aid the Knights of St. John in ending the Turks' siege of Malta.

1566

- On the death of Suleyman I (the Magnificent), his son Selim II becomes sultan of the Ottoman Empire and rules until 1574.

- Emperor Jiajing dies. By this time the Ming emperors of China have become figureheads.

*DENOTES CIRCA DATE

WORLD EVENTS 500-1590

1567
- Mary Queen of Scots is forced to abdicate in favor of her infant son, James VI.

- In Japan, Oda Nobunaga, a member of the Fugiwara family, overthrows the Ashikaga shogunate. Ruling until 1582, he unifies much of central Japan.

1568
- The Eighty Years' War begins as the Netherlands seek independence from Spain.

1569
- As the Livonia War continues, Lithuania forms a political union with Poland. The two states share a king and parliament but maintain separate legal codes and armed forces.

- Reacting to King Philip II of Spain's 1566 edict forbidding them their distinctive language, dress, and customs, the Moriscos (Spanish-Muslim converts to Christianity) rise up in Granada. After two years of conflict, Philip's half brother, Juan of Austria, crushes the rebellion, and the Moriscos are forceably dispersed throughout northern Spain. After 1609 some three hundred thousand Moriscos are deported to North Africa.

1570*
- The Japanese port of Nagasaki is opened to Western trade.

1570
- The Ottoman Turks capture Nicosia, Cyprus, from the Venetians, beginning a war with Venice that results in Turkish possession of Cyprus until 1878.

1570*-1600*
- Chiefs Hiawatha and Dekanawidah unite the Mohawk, Oneida, Onondaga, Cayuga, and Seneca tribes into the Iroquois League.

1571
- After repeated defeats during the 1560s, Altan Khan signs a treaty with the Chinese.

- Spanish colonialists in the Philippines found the city of Manila.

- The Ottoman Turks capture Famagusta, Cyprus; Spanish commander Juan of Austria destroys most of the Ottoman fleet off Lepanto in Greece.

1572
- Sigismund II Augustus of Poland and Lithuania dies childless. Henry of Valois, brother of Charles IX of France, is elected to succeed him.

- Some two thousand Huguenots die during the St. Bartholomew's Day massacre in Paris.

1573
- The Peace of Constantinople ends the war between the Ottoman Empire and Venice.

*DENOTES CIRCA DATE

WORLD EVENTS 500-1590

1573-1620	• Emperor Wanli's inattention to government contributes to the decline of the Ming dynasty in China.
1574	• After the death of Charles IX, his brother Henry of Valois abandons the throne of Poland to become Henry III of France.
1575	• The Poles elect Stephen Báthory, prince of Transylvania and son-in-law of Sigismund I, to be their new king. He reigns until 1586, successfully ending the Livonia War with Russia.
1578	• During an attempt to invade Morocco, King Sebastian of Portugal is slain at Alcazar. He is succeeded by his granduncle Cardinal Henry, who rules until 1580.
1579	• The Union of Utrecht establishes the Dutch Republic, which allies itself with England against Spain.
1580	• On the death of King Henry of Portugal, the Spanish invade the country. King Philip II of Spain, a nephew of Henry, becomes King Philip I of Portugal. Spain and Portugal remain united until 1640.
1581	• In a fit of rage, Ivan IV of Russia murders his son and heir, Ivan.
1581-1598	• The Russians conquer Siberia.
1582	• The Papal States, Spain and Portugal, France, the Netherlands, and Scandinavia adopt the Gregorian calendar, which corrects an error in the Julian calendar that has caused the beginning date for each season to regress almost one day per century. (That is, by 1582 the vernal equinox was occurring on 11 March instead of 21 March.)
1584	• Tsar Ivan IV (the Terrible) dies. He is succeeded by his infirm son Fyodor, who gives up most of his powers to his brother-in-law and successor Boris Godunov. Reigning until 1598, Fyodor is the last ruler of the Rurik dynasty, founded circa 862.
1586	• King Stephen Báthory of Poland dies. He is succeeded by Sigismund III Vasa, son of John III Vasa of Sweden and grandson of Sigismund I of Poland. After he becomes king of Sweden in 1592, Sigismund III unsuccessfully attempts to create a permanent union between the two countries, setting off a series of wars that lasts until 1660.

*DENOTES CIRCA DATE

WORLD EVENTS 500-1590

1587
- Mary Queen of Scots is tried for treason and beheaded in England.

- Toyotomi Hideyoshi issues a decree expelling Portuguese missionaries from Japan.

- Naresuan leads Thai troops in defeating invaders from Burma and Cambodia; he becomes king of Siam in 1590.

1588
- The English defeat a Spanish Armada sent to place Philip II on the British throne.

1588-1629
- During his reign, Abbas I (the Great) drives the Uzbeks and Ottoman Turks from Persia.

1589
- Henry III of France is assassinated by a Jacobin friar who questions his commitment to defending the Roman Catholic faith. Huguenot leader Henry of Navarre becomes the king of the Bourbon dynasty. Reigning until 1610, he converts to Catholicism to re-unify the country (1593) and grants religious freedoms to Protestants while recognizing Catholicism as the state church, thus ending the wars of religion in 1598.

1590
- Toyotomi Hideyoshi completes the unification of Japan begun by Oda Nobunaga.

*Denotes Circa Date

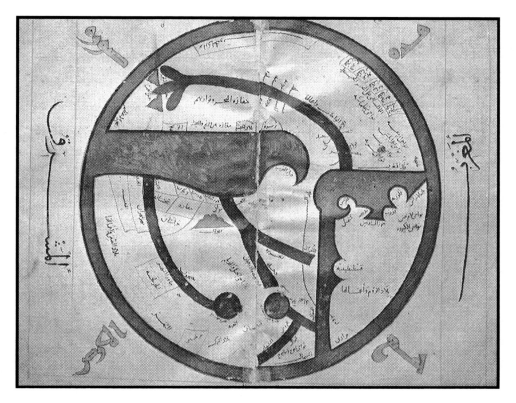

Ibn Hawqal's tenth-century world map (Suleymaniye Library, Istanbul)

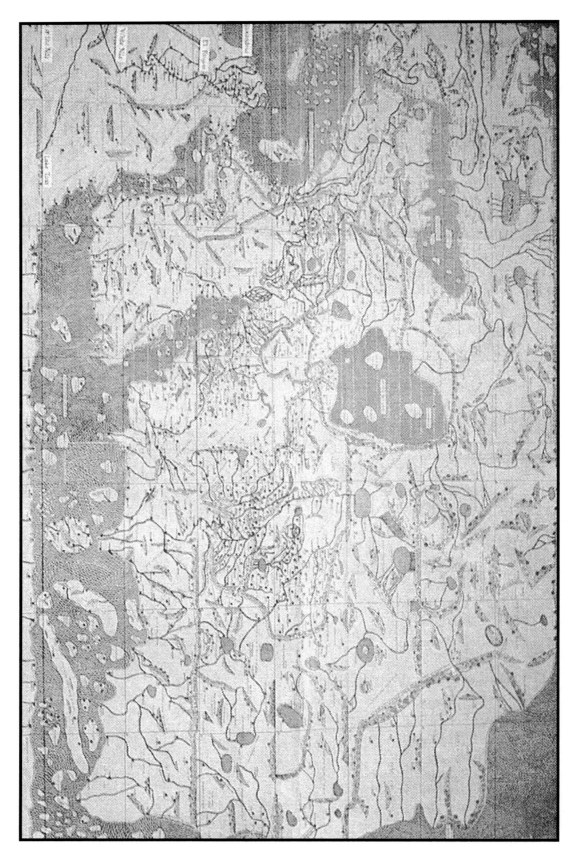

Al-Idrisi's twelfth-century map of the Mediterranean, Africa, and Asia (Bodleian Library, Oxford)

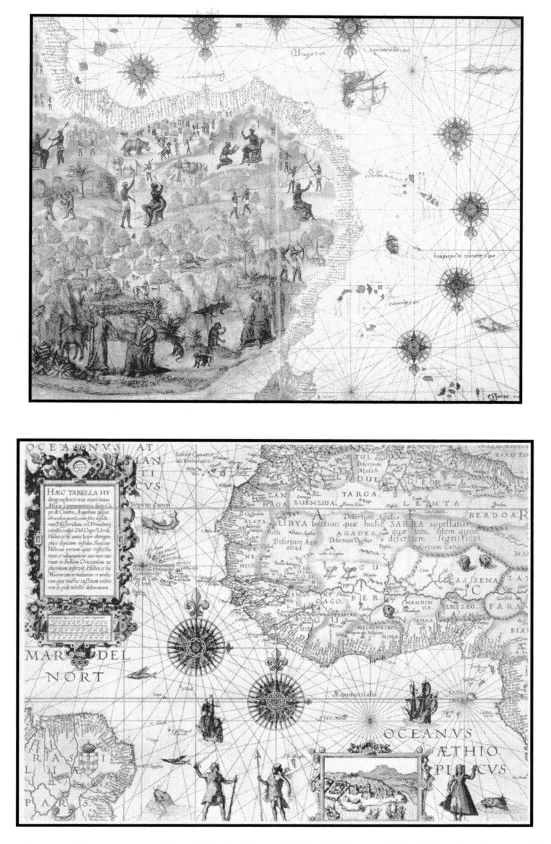

Two sixteenth-century European maps of West Africa: (top) from the Vollard Atlas, circa 1547, with South at the top; and (bottom) by Jan van Doetecum, circa 1595 (top: from Rosemarie Robotham, *Spirits of the Passage*, 1997; bottom: British Library, London)

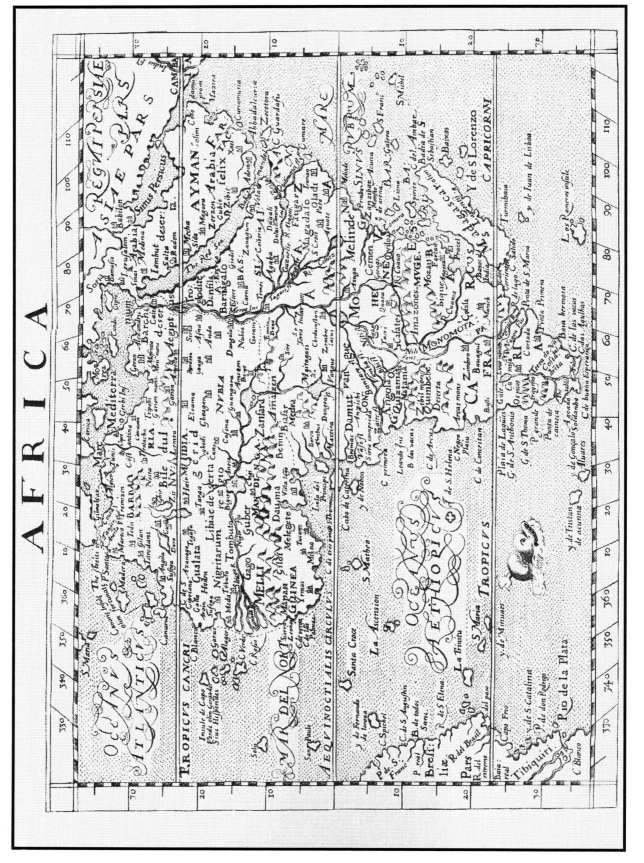

Map of Africa from *A Geographical Historie of Africa* (1600), the first English edition of the work for which Leo Africanus drew on his early-sixteenth-century visit to West Africa (from the 1969 Da Capo Press facsimile edition)

CHAPTER TWO

GEOGRAPHY

by DAVID L. HORNE

CONTENTS

Sidebars and tables are listed in italics.

IMPORTANT EVENTS OF 500-1590

500*
- For some two hundred years West Africa has been consolidated into states, urban confederations of villages and towns based on extensive use of iron technology; this manufacturing process has been employed at least since the fifth century B.C.E. and has required an extensive deforestation of woodlands near settled areas.

- Established in 400 by Mande speakers, the city of Djenné-Jeno is an important trading center. It is the first walled city-state in the Western Sudan along the Niger River, and the area may have been populated as early as the third or second century B.C.E.

- Mande speakers continue to migrate into the savanna areas of West Africa, spreading iron weapons, tools, and trade.

502
- The earliest documented trade in foodstuffs, salt, and gold along established routes in the Western Sudan dates from this year.

550*
- By this time trans-Saharan trade is conducted by camel caravans from northwestern Africa.

711
- By this date Muslim invaders and settlers have brought Islam to northwestern Africa and Spain.

770
- Al-Fazari of Baghdad completes the first written record of the existence of the Empire of Ghana, describing it as a state with gold resources and an economically diverse population.

800*
- By this date the trans-Saharan caravan trade from North Africa into and through the Western Sudan has discernibly expanded, and horses have been introduced into West African military campaigns; because they are expensive, horses are used only by elite military men and ruling social groups.

830
- Al-Khawarizmi produces the first known map of the world, including a small portion of West Africa.

833
- The first relatively accurate descriptions of Ghana, Gao, and Kanem depict them as states that trade extensively and indicate the evolution of political organization and territorial consolidation of the Western Sudan.

* DENOTES CIRCA DATE

IMPORTANT EVENTS OF 500-1590

872	• Al-Yaqubi's geographical history of the political state and populations of Ghana and Takrur includes descriptions of the man-made environment of these West African states.
903	• Ibn al-Faqih publishes a book that includes an accurate geographical description of a route from Ghana to Egypt and Mecca.
977	• Ibn Hawqal visits Ghana and records a description of how the population and geographical landscape have been influenced by the trans-Saharan trade as well as warfare and environmental pressures.
990	• Attempting to control the trans-Saharan trade, Berbers of North Africa seize the oasis city of Audaghost from the Empire of Ghana for the first time, causing rapid population movements away from the area and an abandonment of land resources.
1054	• Almoravid Berbers seize Audaghost for the second time and virtually destroy it, substantially redirecting the geopolitics of the area, causing the re-abandonment of an established and secure trading area and a new migration of resident long-distance-trade merchants and the financial infrastructure.
1067	• Al-Bakri writes the most detailed description of the Empire of Ghana in any extant Arabic manuscript.
1076	• Almoravids attack and sack Kumbi Saleh, the main capital of the Empire of Ghana, substantially weakening the state but not destroying it. Much of the resident merchant class leaves the city, causing a fundamental change in the geopolitics of the area.
1154	• Al-Idrisi publishes his description of Ghana, including the statement that the "king of Ghana was so rich that each of his horses was tethered with a gold nugget."
1337	• Al-Umari publishes his geographical history of the Empire of Mali.
1352-1353	• Ibn Battuta visits Mali and writes that the state has been decimated by succession disputes. Trade has been interrupted, and resident merchants have emigrated.

* DENOTES CIRCA DATE

IMPORTANT EVENTS OF 500-1590

1356
- Ibn Battuta publishes his account of his journey to Mali, which becomes the best-known geographical history of the Western Sudan during the fourteenth century.

1393
- Ibn Khaldun publishes his three-volume history, which includes firsthand accounts of Mali and the states of the Western Sudan.

1441
- The Portuguese initiate the European trade in slaves from West Africa.

1464-1492
- During his reign, Sunni Ali establishes the Songhai Empire, which lasts until 1591.

1481
- The Portuguese establish a trading post at Elmina on the West African coast as one of a series of commercial stations for the housing and transportation of slaves and other goods.

1492
- On the death of Sunni Ali, Muslim convert Askia Muhammad I (Askia the Great) seizes the throne of Songhai, establishing the dynasty of askias in Songhai. The expansion of the Songhai Empire causes mass migrations of indigenous populations, abandoning the land.

1500*
- By this time pastoral Fulani Muslims have begun to spread from the Senegal region eastward. These migrations fundamentally change the demographics of the Western Sudan.

1550
- Leo Africanus publishes an important firsthand account considered one of the most accurate and credible descriptions of the Western Sudan from this period.

1562
- In economic, maritime, and political competition with the Portuguese, Spanish, and Dutch, the British begin their trade in West African slaves.

1571-1603
- During his reign of the Kanem-Bornu empire, Mai Idris Alooma introduces firearms bought from the Moroccans and the Ottoman Turks. The economy of Kanem-Bornu relies on slave raiding in neighboring states.

1590
- Songhai troops armed with traditional weapons are no match for invading Moroccans carrying firearms. The Moroccans conquer Timbuktu in 1591.

* DENOTES CIRCA DATE

OVERVIEW

Geographical Challenges. To maintain itself and benefit its constituency, a successful state system has to overcome challenges from its natural geography over a sustained period of time. An understanding of the character and strength of a state system is always enhanced by paying attention to how it has handled its environmental issues. The early states of West Africa were created and maintained in the face of varied and adverse conditions. West Africa has some of the hottest temperatures in the world, as well as relentless dust storms and abrupt climate changes, which its people have faced with sustained environmental heroism. To create village collectives and Sudanic empires, the population had to be creative and vigilant. Large areas of virtually free, relatively arable land were often available, and population overcrowding was rarely an issue, as it often was in Europe during the same period. Yet, other challenging environmental circumstances created situations in which West Africans had to fight for basic survival.

Reliable Food Sources. The development of a lasting village collective or the formation of an expanding state requires reliable food production and sources of fresh water. Against considerable odds the people of the Sudan solved both problems by using river water and captured rainwater for growing food. At the same time they maintained a valued social place for formerly dominant hunter clans and made good use of natural resources.

Iron Technology and State Building. Each state had at least one organized clan collective whose members had mastered the production and use of iron farming tools and weapons. This expertise was the basis of uniting several villages under the suzerainty of that clan; then it expanded its reach over more populations and more territory. As a collective absorbed new populations, the problems of governmental administration, public safety, and public health became increasingly complex. Using slash-and-burn techniques that kept soils fertile, large tracts of land had to be cleared and plowed for growing food, and trees were used as building materials and for making the charcoal required in iron production. The need for land resulted in still more state expansion, which in turn brought even more people under its administration. At some point major empires such as Ghana, Mali, Songhai, and Kanem outran their administrative capacity and resources. Generally exacerbated by succession disputes, this weakness regularly spawned rebellions, attracted outside invasions, and eventually resulted in collapse. The earliest of the empires, Ghana, which lasted for many centuries, controlled its rate of expansion better than Mali, Songhai, or Kanem. These later major states were forced to rely increasingly on professional soldiers and cavalry to maintain state authority.

Migration. Societies threatened by expanding empires could either acquiesce, migrate, or fight. Frequently, state expansion resulted in the migration of an indigenous population, either because the invaders sought to avoid future insurrections by forcing inhabitants to leave their homes or because a conquered people voluntarily moved elsewhere to avoid subjugation. This constant movement contributed to instability and the underpopulation of strategic locations within the region. Thus, as early states attempted to balance challenging geographical circumstances with administrative, spiritual, military, and commercial interests, they succeeded grandly at first but ultimately collapsed.

TOPICS IN GEOGRAPHY

LAND AND WATER RESOURCES

Ancient Origins. West Africa was once part of the ancient continent of Gondwana, a single landmass that included Africa, North and South America, southern Asia, and Australia. That continent gradually moved and broke into its separate modern divisions. Africa sits on an extremely old land platform of fold-and-basin structures eroded and leveled by large variations in temperature and humid to arid climates. This environmental dynamic created unevenly distributed sedimentary formations of rough, sandy soil, vast low-lying plains, deserts, huge rift valleys and scattered but spectacular mountains created by volcanic activity. In West Africa, Mount Cameroon is 4,100 meters tall and is the only sizeable mountain in the region. In the western part of the region the primarily sandstone soils and river basins were produced as sedimentary formations.

The Sahara. At the northern edge of the region, the Sahara Desert has consistently challenged the inhabitants of West Africa. This relentlessly expanding region now covers more than fifteen degrees of geographical latitude on the continent. The Sahara has tremendously influenced the history of West Africa—not only as an obstacle to be overcome but also as a filter to limit overwhelming numbers of immigrants—but it has never been an impenetrable barrier to travel, trade, or communications.

The Sahel. One of the two principle vegetation zones in West Africa, the Sahel, or "Desert Shore," is on the southern edge of the Sahara Desert. It is a belt of semi-arid land that extends for more than 2,500 kilometers (approximately 1,750 miles) from near the Atlantic coast eastward beyond Lake Chad. In modern Africa, the Sahel extends from Senegal in the west, through the countries of Mauritania, Burkina Faso, Niger, and Chad. The largest flat surface on Earth, it has no distinctive mountains. Annual floodwaters and winds redeposit sand, silt, and dust in a dynamic, volatile, and relatively unpredictable pattern. Since at least the beginning of the first millennium, migrating groups of West Africans, especially the Mande speakers, have tried to cope with the environmental rhythms and nuances of the Sahel. This area of persistent hot temperatures, short and drought-resistant grasses (usually less than five feet tall), thorny shrubs, a few scattered acacia trees (the source of gum arabic), and oases is subject to periodic droughts, sandstorms, and quick bursts of heavy downpours. The annual rains, which have allowed agricultural subsistence and even surpluses for more than two thousand years, generally fall during only three to four months of the year (June through September) and deposit from ten to thirty inches of moisture onto the soil.

Sahel Water Sources. Farmers in this region have been almost totally dependent on this annual rainfall, except in the three parts of the Sahel that include the Senegal River basin in the extreme west, the Niger River bend basin in the middle of the Sahel, and the Lake Chad basin in the east. There, water for irrigation, drinking, fishing, waste removal, and other uses is a combination of rainwater and river or lake water, although evaporation regularly claims around 80 percent of river and lake water, especially during the long dry season, October to May. Except for the drought years, populations in the Sahel have been able to farm on land watered almost solely from the heavy rains that fall during the wet season, sometimes supplemented with well or swamp water. Throughout the 500–1590 period, settlers in the Sahel were able to live on agricultural grain production, livestock herding, and regional and long-distance trade, though the environment challenged them on an almost daily basis.

The Sudanic Grasslands. The second major vegetation zone is a savanna, or grassland, that stretches in a band below the Sahel near the Atlantic coast just south of the Gambia River and extends eastward through the Biu Plateau and the Jos Plateau just south of Lake Chad in the east. The Arabs called West Africa Bilad al-Sudan (Land of the Blacks), which was shortened to "Sudan." Today, that name is applied generally to the whole region, and the savanna is usually called the Sudanic grasslands. This savanna has gotten smaller in some areas because of desert and steppe desiccation resulting from man-made landscapes and natural processes, but it has spread in other areas because of frequent rain-forest burning. Thus, its exact location has changed since the 500–1590 period. Today it traverses Senegal, the Gambia, the middle of Burkino Faso, and Nigeria, through Chad. The Sudanic grasslands are broad humid plains that cover 75 percent of all of West Africa. They have been central to the evolution of food production, metallurgy, and civilization in the region. The Biu Plateau and the Jos Plateau, both between two thousand and four thousand feet, are the only highland elevations, and they were home to little, if any, early development in the area. Rainfall in the Sudanic grasslands averages approximately twenty to forty inches during a wet season of four to five months, and the grasses there regularly grow from five to ten feet high. These grasses are interspersed with both single, tall, woodland trees and clumps of fire-resistant trees, some growing as high as twenty to thirty feet. Thriving in an area where forest woodlands cannot, the grasses grow on savanna alluvial sediments with high erosion, poor drainage, and little moisture. On the Sahel and the Sudanic grasslands, pearl millet, sorghum, cowpeas, bambara groundnuts, calabash, and cotton were all developed indigenously, while on the savanna the ready availability of timber for firewood and metal smithing, wild fruits, and grassland and tree fowl provided other advantages.

Climate. Africa is considered the most consistently and uniformly hot of all the continents, particularly in the Maghrib region of northwestern Africa and the part of West Africa situated above the Equator. Here, the living conditions are influenced not by temperature alone but also by the amount of rainfall. The Sahara and West Africa are also affected annually by strong anticyclonic winds, which blow northeasterly, and harmattan winds, which blow hot, dry, sand-laden gusts over the entirety of the Sahel and most of the savannas westward from Lake Chad to Senegal.

Global Warming. Modern archaeologists have discovered that during the years 300–1550, particularly between 1100 and 1550, the world went through the Medieval Warm Period, during which global warming created increased precipitation and humidity in Europe and severe dry spells in the Amazon River basin of South America and the American Southwest. They have also connected this weather phenomenon to the major pandemic of bubonic and pneumonic plague (the Black Death) that began in China in the 1330s and swept westward across Asia, Europe, and North Africa until about 1350, recurring in 1361–1363, 1369–1371, 1374–1375, 1390, and 1400. In the Western Sudan during this period, abrupt, shifting patterns of hot winds and increased humidity brought much more rain in some areas while imposing severe, sustained drought conditions on other, once fertile regions. Lake Chad and the Niger fluctuated at record low levels, and the Sahara expanded, overwhelming hundreds of Sahelian

---

TRADE WINDS

The climate of West Africa is largely determined by two large air masses: a warm, dry, dusty air mass formed over the Sahara and a moist tropical air mass formed over the South Atlantic. The alternation of these air masses causes dry seasons and wet seasons in much of the region. Another aspect of these weather systems is the trade winds. As Akin Mabogunje explains, they were a major factor in delaying European exploration of the West African coastal region:

These winds in the north tend to blow from the north-east. In the south their initial direction is from the south-east, but on crossing the Equator they are forced to veer to the right and so become south-west in direction. Highly regular in their flow, they . . . have played very little part in the history of West Africa compared with their role in East Africa. There, the winds were of crucial importance for sailing boats coming from the shores of India and the Middle East to trade on the East African coastline. West Africa, on the other hand, lies on the offshore side of the north-east trades. While sailing boats from Europe from the time of Christopher Columbus came as far south as the Canary Islands in the hope of being speeded on their voyage to North America by the north-east trades, there was no wind to blow them in the opposite direction within the latitudes of West Africa. Besides, the coast of West Africa is not far from the doldrums of the equatorial low pressure belt. This belt moves north and south each year with the apparent motion of the sun. When the doldrums lie close to the West African coast from about April to September little wind blows, and sailing boats, like that of Coleridge's *Ancient Mariner*, were held up for days waiting for a gust of wind to blow their vessels out of the area.

Source: Akin L. Mabogunje, "The Land and Peoples of West Africa," in *History of West Africa*, edited by J. F. A. Ajayi and Michael Crowder, second edition, volume 1 (London: Longman, 1976), pp. 1–2.

---

communities and forcing their inhabitants to migrate in search of arable land and reliable water supplies.

Soil Conditions. Throughout the Western Sudan, the action of differing amounts of water and heat on sediment rocks has formed relatively shallow, tropical soils rich in iron oxide. Generally sandy or hardened clay, the soil is vulnerable to wind and water erosion. In part of the region the hardened, caked surface soil—sometimes called *bowe* soil—is of little agricultural value. In the savanna and part of the Sahel the structured, brown, and moist soils, protected from erosion by various grass and plant covers, produced the bulk of the food for virtually all the states of the Western Sudan during the 500–1590 period.

Lake Chad. In the eastern Sudan, the major water resource for Kanem-Bornu was Lake Chad, the seventh-

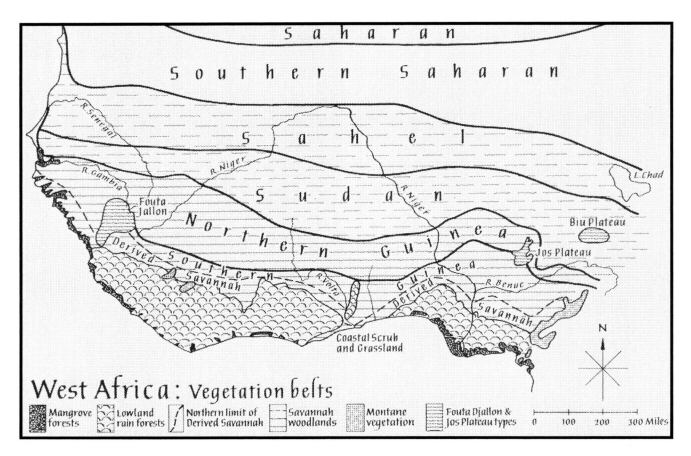

(Map by Leo Vernon; from J. F. A. Ajayi and Michael Crowder, eds., *History of West Africa*, 1971)

largest lake in the world and the fourth-largest lake and basin in Africa. Lake Chad annually goes through rather extreme increases and decreases in size, as determined principally by the length and intensity of Sahelian dry-season heat and by the amount of southern highlands rainfall. Typically, the lake may go from a shallow low of ten thousand kilometers to a high of more than thirty thousand kilometers. It is fed from the southeast by the Chari and Logone Rivers, both of which originate in the Central African Republic and the Cameroonian highlands. The Chari River contributes the most water by volume to Lake Chad, an estimated 95 percent of its annual water supply. The Chari is approximately 1,200 kilometers in length and is fed by its tributaries: the Bahr Salamat, the Bahr Aouk, and the Bahr Sara Rivers. The Longone River, which meets the Chari in Chad, near the city of N'Djamena (which is around 1,200 kilometers, or 720 miles, northeast of the Atlantic Ocean), flows approximately 960 kilometers (570 miles).

Major Rivers. The western part of the region has the Senegal, Benue, Volta, Gambia, Faleme, and Niger Rivers. The Niger, at 4,184 kilometers (2,600 miles) in length, is the third-longest river on the continent and flows through virtually every environmental zone in the Western Sudan. The Senegal and Faleme were important in the origin and development of the early Takrur Empire, which rivaled the Empire of Ghana by the tenth and eleventh centuries. These rivers were both adjacent to Bambuk (in the western part of present-day Mali), the first major source of Sudanic gold. The Benue feeds the Niger River, and the Volta was instrumental in the rise of the Niani people of Mali. The Gambia was the western boundary of the Sudanic savanna zone. Though the Senegal, Benue, and Faleme lacked the overabundance of rapids and waterfalls that hindered navigation on most of the significant African rivers, these rivers were never recognized as major transportation assets to the population of the Western Sudan, principally because of delta swamps, large extremes in their annual flows, and river-blocking sandbars at their mouths.

The Niger River Basin. The Niger River and Lake Chad valleys are two of the six largest basins in the continent. In terms of hydrology, one of the biggest geographical influences on the history of the Western Sudan has been the Niger River and its delta system. The Niger basin extends from five to sixteen degrees north latitude. The river rises in the coastal mountains of Guinea, just 150 miles inland from the Atlantic Ocean; it flows northeast toward the Sahara Desert, entering Mali; after it reaches Timbuktu, it turns eastward for about 250 miles; then it loops in a southeasterly direction, flowing through the city of Gao into Niger and forming part of its border with Benin. The river ends in Nigeria, finally reaching the Gulf of Guinea, where it forms a huge delta system of spider-like outlets flowing through mangrove and sand. Bolstered by annual rainy-season flooding, the middle Niger flows through part of the Sahel and the semidesert region around Timbuktu. It is fed by the Benue River downstream. The middle Niger, which is also called the Niger Bend area, has attracted large residential populations throughout its history and figured prominently in every one of the ancient African kingdoms.

Sources:
S. Diarra, "Historical Geography: Physical Aspects," in *Methodology and African Prehistory*, edited by J. Ki-Zerbo, volume 1 of *General History of Africa* (London: Heinemann / Berkeley: University of California Press / Paris: UNESCO, 1981), pp. 316–332.

A. T. Grove, *The Changing Geography of Africa* (Oxford: Oxford University Press, 1989).

Akin L. Mabogunje, "The Land and Peoples of West Africa," in *History of West Africa*, edited by J. F. A. Ajayi and Michael Crowder, second edition, volume 1 (London: Longman, 1976), pp. 1–32.

Marijke van der Veen, ed., *The Exploitation of Plant Resources in Ancient Africa* (New York & London: Kluwer Academic / Plenum, 1999).

MIGRATION

Population Distribution. In the Western Sudan—with grasslands, savanna, and relatively limited agricultural areas unevenly distributed throughout the region—human migration and shifting populations were a constant part of the geopolitics and history. People migrated to take advantage of more-favorable land resources, to gain access to reliable fresh water, and to escape encroachments by the Sahara. They also migrated for religious purposes and to avoid warfare. Migrations affected the ability of land resources to support populations, shifted military advantages, changed the locations of staging posts for trade routes, and cre-

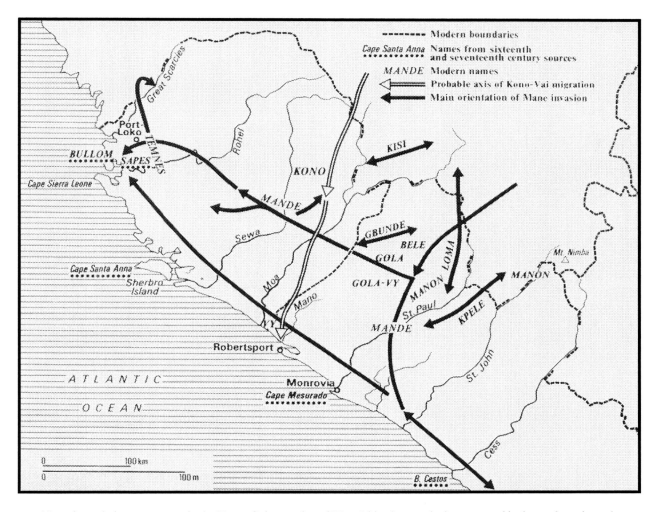

Map of population movements in the Upper Guinea region of West Africa from early times to roughly the tenth or eleventh century (from M. El Fasi and I. Hrbek, eds., *Africa from the Seventh Century to the Eleventh Century*, volume 3 of *General History of Africa*, 1988)

ated reliable and unreliable patterns of settlements for state formation. Four migratory peoples who strongly influenced development in the region are the Berbers, the Fulani, the Mande, and the Zhagawa and Kanuri.

The Berbers. The Berbers had learned to survive in the Sahara even before the introduction of the camel around the first century B.C.E. By the eighth century C.E., intrepid Berber camel caravans traveled all across the Sahara from the northern and western desert south across the Niger to the fringes of the West African forest. Known by several other names—including the Hawwara, the Massufa, the Lamtuna, the Djuddala, the Sanhadja, and eventually the Tuareg—the Berbers were a confederation of brown-skinned peoples who through constant migrations and demographic shifts became a human bridge connecting the Arabs, Europe, and the Black African kingdoms of West Africa. The great oasis trading town of Audaghost, which was eventually absorbed into the Empire of Ghana (and periodically reconquered by Berbers) was founded by migratory Berber traders, who also became effective intermediaries for spreading cultural practices and artifacts across the Sahara. This population also included the so-called Black Berbers—the Haratin—who moved from oasis to oasis throughout southern Morocco and Mauritania.

The Fulani. Also known as the Peul, the Fulbe, the Fula, the Fellata, and the Toucouleur, the Fulani expanded from southern Mauritania and into the Senegal River valley. The Fulani strongly influenced the state formations of Takrur and later Futa Toro and Futa Jallon. In association with their related neighbors, the Wolof and the Serer, they sent successive waves of migration east and south, integrating with and settling among other Sudanic peoples.

The Mande. The Mande (or Manding) peoples—including the Soninke, the Malinke (or Mandingo), the Wangara, the Sarakolle, the Marka, and the Dioula—have moved all over the Western Sudan from the Atlantic coast to the forests to the northern region. The Mande mixed with Niger Bend populations, founded the Ghana and Mali Empires, and formed a large proportion of the Songhai rulership. As a consequence of more than a millennium of migration, there are approximately two hundred Mande-related groups.

The Zhagawa and the Kanuri. On the Eastern Sudan the Zhagawa and the Kanuri, two related agricultural groups, developed as a result of the migrations of peoples fleeing climatic changes in the Sahara Desert and resettling in the challenging environment of the Lake Chad Basin. Some Saharan peoples, such as the Hausa, settled to the west of the lake, and the Zhagawa, the Kanembu, and the Kanuri settled to its east, where they developed the Kanem-Bornu polity. In the fifteenth and sixteenth centuries this state was involved in relent-less slave raiding, forcing large groups in the area to become refugees and abandon tracts of densely populated land in order to hide in scattered locations.

Sources:

F. De Medeiros, "The Peoples of the Sudan: Population Movements," in *Africa from the Seventh to the Eleventh Century*, edited by M. El Fasi and I. Hrbek, volume 3 of *General History of Africa* (London: Heinemann / Berkeley: University of California Press / Paris: UNESCO, 1988), pp. 119–139.

J. Devisse, "Trade and Trade Routes in West Africa," in *Africa from the Seventh to the Eleventh Century*, pp. 367–435.

S. Diarra, "Historical Geography: Physical Aspects," in *Methodology and African Prehistory*, edited by J. Ki-Zerbo, volume 1 of *General History of Africa* (London: Heinemann / Berkeley: University of California Press / Paris: UNESCO, 1981), pp. 316–332.

Akin L. Mabogunje, "Historical Geography: Economic Aspects," in *Methodology and African Prehistory*, pp. 333–347.

D. T. Niane, "Mali and the Second Mandingo Expansion," in *Africa from the Twelfth to the Sixteenth Century*, edited by Niane, volume 4 of *General History of Africa* (London: Heinemann / Berkeley: University of California Press / Paris: UNESCO, 1984), pp. 117–171.

WEST AFRICA AS A CULTURAL HEARTH

Centers of Innovation. During the Neolithic and post-Neolithic periods, places that scholars now call "cultural hearths" developed in various parts of the world. They were centers of innovation in areas such as food production, irrigation, the man-made environment, government, and religion. In effect, a cultural hearth was a regional "cradle of civilization," where distinct cultural traits, elements, and values were developed and shared. Cultural hearths greatly influenced surrounding regions; the closer an area was to the hearth the stronger the influence. All cultural hearths were urban, relative to the population density in the rest of their specific environments. They were situated close to rivers or lakes that flooded annually, and they used systematic agriculture and irrigation to produce surplus food supplies for a predominantly sedentary population. In turn, each had to adopt residential patterns and organized behavior to protect crops from animal and insect predators.

The Rise of Agriculture. All developed distinctive social stratifications based on a division of labor tailored to the material circumstances of their environments, and all developed rituals, rites, and sometimes multilayered religious processes associated with the different cycles of food production. All transformed their natural environments to build permanent dwellings—generally in mud, stone, or brick and mortar—and public structures. All developed managerial procedures to exploit their natural resources, and all eventually learned to use tools and weapons, either by making them—usually from bronze or iron or a combination of the two—or through developing strong trade relations with peoples who worked metals. All these cultures

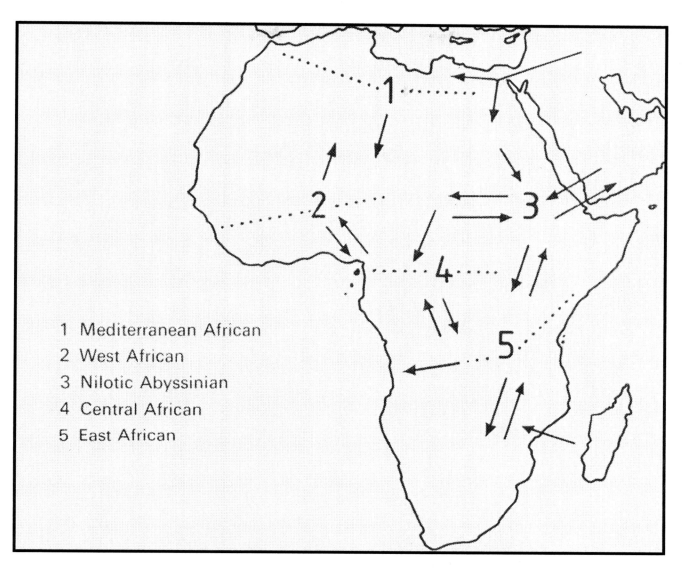

1 Mediterranean African
2 West African
3 Nilotic Abyssinian
4 Central African
5 East African

Map of African "cultural hearths" (from J. Ki-Zerbo, ed., *Methodology and African Prehistory*,
volume 1 of *General History of Africa*, 1981)

represented the triumph of agriculturalists over nomadic hunter-gatherers.

West Africa. In West Africa the basins of the Niger and Senegal Rivers and Lake Chad—along with smaller waterways such as the Faleme, Benue, and Volta Rivers—allowed the development of cultural hearths. The migration of various peoples into these regions, before and during the period 500–1590, led to the urban development of West African kingdoms and empires and the extensive utilization and spread of metallurgy. In turn, the clan-based skills of smelting and smithing iron and gold required persistent deforestation and repeated population adjustments.

Other Cultural Hearths. The valley of the Tigris and Euphrates Rivers in the Near East, the Nile in northeastern Africa, the Indus River in South Asia, the Huang He (Yellow River) and Yangtze in China, and the major rivers of Europe were also cultural hearths, which developed in parallel fashion, beginning with innovations in agriculture and continuing into state building, technical innovations, man-made alterations of the environment, warfare among competing states, and migrations sparked by political and religious conflicts as well as depletion of resources.

Sources:

Nehemia Levtzion, "The Early States of the Western Sudan to 1500," in *History of West Africa*, edited by J. F. A. Ajayi and Michael Crowder, second edition, volume 1 (London: Longman, 1976), pp. 114–151.

Akin L. Mabogunje, "Historical Geography: Economic Aspects," in *Methodology and African Prehistory*, edited by J. Ki-Zerbo, volume 1 of *General History of Africa* (London: Heinemann / Berkeley: University of California Press / Paris: UNESCO, 1981), pp. 333–347.

Detail from Abraham Crepques's 1375 map of West Africa showing Mansa Musa negotiating with an Arab merchant (Bibliothèque Nationale, Paris)

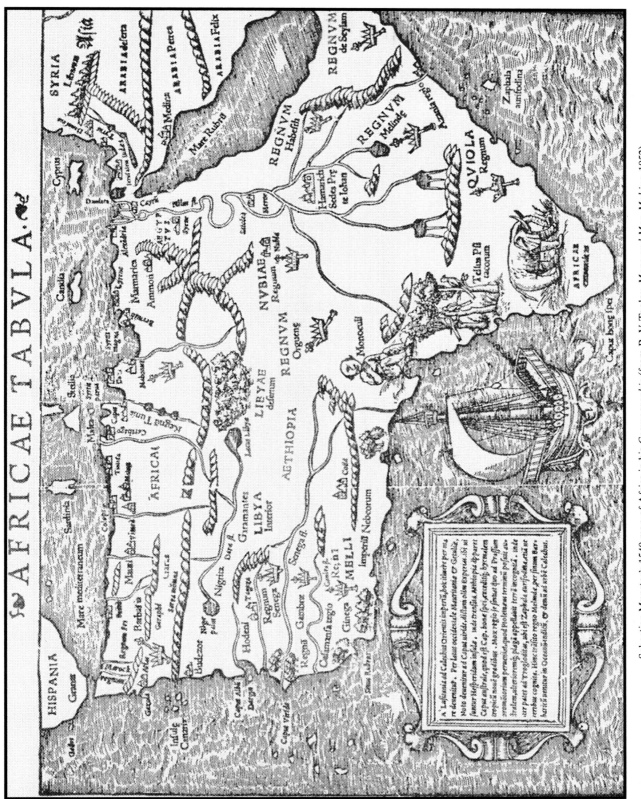

Sebastian Munster's 1540 map of Africa in his *Cosmographia* (from R. V. Tooley, *Maps and Map-Making*, 1952)

WEST AFRICA ON EUROPEAN MAPS

Early Maps and Geographical Descriptions. One way to trace the development of trade and cultural exchange between West Africa and the rest of the world is to look at the evolution of representations of the region in world maps. The fifth century B.C.E. voyages of the Carthaginian Hanno along the Atlantic west coast of Africa to establish a series of Phoenician trading posts resulted in the first recognized "European" on-site reports of the area. Hanno drew brief sketches, rather than actual maps, in his written accounts of the journeys. Exactly how far along the coast he sailed and the location of the area he called "Cerne" are still in dispute. However, it is known that Carthage already knew about the gold mines of the Western Sudan and had already established a trade network to acquire it. Hanno's voyages were attempts to solidify earlier contacts, but his efforts were not successful for any substantial period of time. A few years later, in 430 B.C.E., Herodotus described the Carthaginian coastal trade coordinated at Cerne. The Greek writer now known as Pseudo-Skylax built on Herodotus's version in 340 B.C.E. Neither Herodotus nor Pseudo-Skylax included maps in their narrative accounts. The first known attempt to map the Western Sudan was included in Claudius Ptolemy's second-century manuscript (published in 1477 and 1513). His "Tabula Quarta Africae," which included his vision of the Western Sudan, set the standard followed by virtually all subsequent European geographers until the Portuguese voyages to West, South, and East Africa in the fifteenth century. Although several Arab authors—including al-Khawarizmi in 830, Ibn Hawqal in 980, and al-Idrisi in 1192—used knowledge based on trade links across the Sahara to draw maps of West Africa that were fairly accurate spatially and conceptually, virtually all medieval European maps of West Africa were based only on ideas of the region, not on real data.

European Maps. The first relatively accurate European map of the Western Sudan, based on Mansa Musa's golden trip to Mecca in the fourteenth century, was the Catalan Map of the Sahara region, commissioned by Charles V of France and drawn by Abraham Crepques of Mallorca in 1375. The original is at the Bibliothèque Nationale of France. This map shows the Atlas Mountains of the Maghrib and a picture of Mansa Musa, the ruler of Mali in 1312–1337, with a golden crown and scepter and a large gold nugget in his hand as he engages in a trade negotiation with a merchant on a camel. There are three captions beside the drawing. The one to the right says, "This Negro King is called Musa Mali, Lord of Guinea. There is so much gold found in his country that he is the richest and most noble king in all the land." The caption just above the drawing says, "Through this place must pass all merchants who travel to the land of the Negroes of Guinea, which place is called the Valley of the Dra'a." The last caption says, "All of this land is occupied by people who veil their mouths; one can only see their eyes and they live in tents and ride in camel caravans. They also have control of beasts called Lemp from which they make fine war shields."

Increased Accuracy. Following the Catalan Map, European mapmakers got better at locations and distances in their maps of the Western Sudan. In 1570 Abraham Ortelius used firsthand maps of the West African coast drawn by Portuguese traders at the end of the fifteenth and the beginning of the sixteenth centuries for an accurate depiction of the West African coastline in his "Africae Tabula Nova" map. Ortelius was the leading mapmaker in the Netherlands at the time and began a "golden age" of cartography in Antwerp and Amsterdam, as the Netherlands became the primary production center for European mapmaking until well into the eighteenth century. A few years later, in 1595, one of his countrymen published the highly popular Gerardus Mercator Atlas Map of Northwest Africa, the first projection map, which added the details of the Western Sudan away from the coast. Continuing this tradition, Jodocus Hondius's 1602, 1628, 1633, and 1634 maps depicted Guinea and the Western Sudan better than previous maps and included Gao, Timbuktu, and the Empire of Songhai. Willem Blaeu's "Fezzae et Marocchi regna Africae celeberrima describebat Abrah" (1635) is an excellent rendition of Northwest Africa and the Sudan. European cartographers of the next century fairly routinely included accurate depictions of the Western Sudan in their maps.

PTOLEMY'S VIEW OF AFRICA

Well known for his theories that the Earth was flat and the center of the universe, Ptolemy influenced Western geography for more than a thousand years:

For many Europeans in the fifteenth century, the world looked much the same as it had to Ptolemy in the second century. His work on geography was the basis for most scholarship throughout the Middle Ages and into the Renaissance, before exploration and improved technology began to provide better information. . . .

In the Ptolemaic world view, Africa, Antarctica, and part of Asia were all joined, forming a large southern land mass marked simply "Terra Incognito." The exact shape of Africa was not known, and the northern part was depicted as much broader and squarer than it actually is.

Source: "The Eye of the Beholder: Western Maps of Africa," Yale Map Collection <www.library.Yale.edu/MapColl/afexbib.html>.

Sources:

Nehemia Levtzion, "The Early States of the Western Sudan to 1500," in *History of West Africa*, edited by J. F. A. Ajayi and Michael Crowder, second edition, volume 1 (London: Longman, 1976), pp. 114–151.

A. L. Mabogunje, "Historical Geography: Economic Aspects," in *Methodology and African Prehistory*, edited by J. Ki-Zerbo, volume 1 of *General History of Africa* (London: Heinemann / Berkeley: University of California Press / Paris: UNESCO, 1981), pp. 333–347.

WEST AFRICAN GEOGRAPHY AND REGIONAL INFLUENCES

Geographical Motivations for Change. From the sixth through the sixteenth centuries, five major factors motivated change in the Western Sudan: expansion of reliable food production, the establishment and stabilization of governments, the creation of control over intra- and interregional trade routes and shifts in who exerted such power, war and resulting migrations, and natural and man-made catastrophes. (Though they were manifested in different regional circumstances, these same five impetuses drove the evolution of Asian, European, Mesoamerican, and Near Eastern societies.) During the 500–1590 period, there developed a series of Sudanic-Sahel regional civilizations that were able to produce surpluses of foods such as millet, sorghum, rice, and other crops in the desert fringes, the savanna grasslands, the edges of the forest areas, and the basins of the Senegal and Niger Rivers and Lake Chad. These civilizations successfully adapted to regional soil conditions and seasonal variations of rainfall, as well as to the long series of environmentally motivated migrations of various peoples throughout the area. They organized villages and isolated settlements into larger units under unified clans with access to iron tools, weapons, and military resources, and innovated warfare and military preparedness. As intra- and interregional trade evolved, they provided effective protection of the trade routes and maintained control of the gold resources being exported to the north. They also managed to resolve the persistent problem of underpopulation in strategic areas. Because of their basis in agriculture and metalworking, these states required extensive destruction of forest areas for charcoal fuel and agriculture, as well as building. They fashioned large-scale public buildings from mud bricks, stone, and wood, substantially altering the West African landscape. The Empires of Ghana, Mali, Songhai, and Kanem-Bornu, the Mossi and Hausa-Fulani states, and other political units grew indigenously from consistently successful community adaptations to physical and material circumstances. As in other parts of the world at the time, they survived droughts, flooding, military incursions, plagues, and other catastrophes to create new social and technical achievements and move forward.

The Interplay of Geography and Food Production. The early states of West Africa inherited the best assets of the intertropical climatic zone (the area between the Tropics of Cancer and Capricorn) and its particular agri-

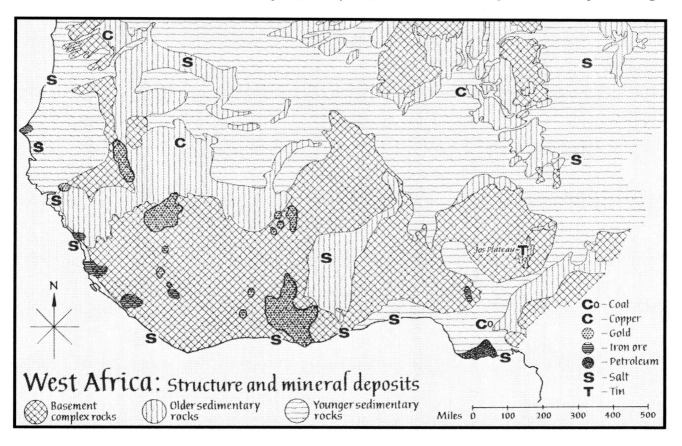

(Map by Leo Vernon; from J. F. A. Ajayi and Michael Crowder, eds., *History of West Africa*, 1971)

cultural features. The Sudan, for example, has one wet and one dry season each year, with heavy equatorial rains and flooding of river valleys during one part of the year and the aridity of frequent dust storms during the other. Throughout their histories the Empires of Ghana, Mali, and Songhai produced large food surpluses for their expanding populations. The southern savanna areas closest to the forest got at least six months of 1,500 to 2,000 millimeters of rainfall a year with consistently high temperatures. The central savanna got only 600 to 1,500 millimeters of rain during three to six months of the year, and those areas were consequently much drier than the southern savanna. The Sahel got only 600 millimeters of rain during less than three months of the year, but it and the central and northern savanna, particularly in the river valleys, formed one of the three primary centers in Africa for the early evolution and development of food production. Brown, sandy, structured soils called duricrusts, with strong concentrations of iron oxide and alumina mineral, were the agricultural foundation for the creation, expansion, and maintenance of the Sudanic states.

Agriculture and Economics. Growing millet, rice, sorghum, and vegetables, smoking and drying fish, along with cattle herding and horse keeping were regular components of the economies of Ghana, Mali, and Songhai. In the tenth and eleventh centuries Takrur, located in the middle Senegal River valley several miles away from the Atlantic coast, was the center of a rival production and trading system to that of Ghana. It dominated the Barisa-Silla towns and their hinterlands that lay on the fringes of the Galam-Bambuk goldfields, and its presence radically changed the production and movement of gold from the south to the north. In spite of extreme variations in soil type and mountainous obtrusions, Takrur had fertile farmland, as well as reliable river fishing and iron production and a relatively dense concentration of population. It was also the first Black-ruled Muslim state in the region. Kanem-Bornu, located in the relatively harsh climate of the eastern Lake Chad basin, has a diverse geography that makes it distinctive within the Sudanic pattern. Maximizing food production in this area required consistent labor-intensive farming on the clay soils of its alluvial plains, as well as fishing. The agricultural demands in this region were an important factor in Kanem-Bornu's massive commitment to slavery and slave raiding.

Sources:

Adu Boahen, with J. F. Ade Ajayi and Michae Tidy, *Topics in West African History*, second edition (Harlow, U.K.: Longman, 1986).

S. M. Cissoko, "The Songhay From the 12th to the 16th Century," in *Africa from the Twelfth to the Sixteenth Century*, edited by D. T. Niane, volume 4 of *General History of Africa* (London: Heinemann / Berkeley: University of California Press / Paris: UNESCO, 1984), pp. 187–210.

Philip de Barros, "Iron Metallurgy: Sociocultural Context," in *Ancient African Metallurgy: The Sociocultural Context*, by Michael S. Bisson, S. Terry Childs, de Barros, and Augustin F. C. Holl, edited by Joseph O. Vogel (Walnut Creek, Cal.: AltaMira Press, 2000), pp. 147–198.

F. De Medeiros, "The Peoples of the Sudan: Population Movements," in *Africa from the Seventh to the Eleventh Century*, edited by M. El Fasi and I. Hrbek, volume 3 of *General History of Africa* (London: Heinemann / Berkeley: University of California Press / Paris: UNESCO, 1988), pp. 119–139.

J. Devisse, "Trade and Trade Routes in West Africa," in *Africa from the Seventh to the Eleventh Century*, pp. 367–435.

S. Diarra, "Historical Geography: Physical Aspects," in *Methodology and African Prehistory*, edited by J. Ki-Zerbo, volume 1 of *General History of Africa* (London: Heinemann / Berkeley: University of California Press / Paris: UNESCO, 1981), pp. 316–332.

R. Haaland, "Man's Role in the Changing Habitat of Mema during the Old Kingdom of Ghana," *Norwegian Archaeological Review*, 13 (1980): 31–46.

Augustin F. C. Holl, "Metals and Precolonial African Society," in *Ancient African Metallurgy: The Sociocultural Context*, pp. 1–82.

I. Hrbek, "The Emergence of the Fatimids," in *Africa from the Seventh to the Eleventh Century*, edited by M. El Fasi and Hrbek, volume 3 of *General History of Africa* (London: Heinemann / Berkeley: University of California Press / Paris: UNESCO, 1988), pp. 314–335.

John Iliffe, *Africans: The History of a Continent* (Cambridge & New York: Cambridge University Press, 1995).

D. Lange and B. W. Barkindo, "The Chad Region as a Crossroads," in *Africa from the Seventh to the Eleventh Century*, pp. 436–460.

Nehemia Levtzion, *Ancient Ghana and Mali* (London: Methuen, 1973).

Levtzion, "The Early States of the Western Sudan to 1500," in *History of West Africa*, edited by J. F. A. Ajayi and Michael Crowder, second edition, volume 1 (London: Longman, 1976), pp. 114–151.

A. L. Mabogunje, "Historical Geography: Economic Aspects," in *Methodology and African Prehistory*, edited by J. Ki-Zerbo, volume 1 of *General History of Africa* (London: Heinemann / Berkeley: University of California Press / Paris: UNESCO, 1981), pp. 333–347.

Raymond Mauny, *Tableau géographique de l'Ouest africain au Moyen Age, d'après les sources écrites, la tradition et l'archéologie* (Dakar: IFAN, 1961).

D. T. Niane, "Mali and the Second Mandingo Expansion," in *Africa from the Twelfth to the Sixteenth Century*, edited by Niane, volume 4 of *General History of Africa* (London: Heinemann / Berkeley: University of California Press / Paris: UNESCO, 1984), pp. 117–171.

SIGNIFICANT PEOPLE

ABU UBAYD AL-AZIZ AL-BAKRI

1010-CIRCA 1075
GEOGRAPHER

Spanish Muslim. The son of a Muslim governor of the province of Huelva and Saltes in southwest Spain, al-Bakri spent most of his life in Cordoba, Spain, becoming an accomplished scholar and diplomat.

Geographer. Although he never visited West Africa, he wrote accurate descriptions of its land and peoples. His well-known descriptions of the ancient state of Ghana came from research in earlier written sources, including contemporary travel accounts of ship captains and navigators, and interviewing merchants who had visited the Western Sudan. He is known for his meticulous and thorough methodology. His best-known work is *Kitab al-masalik wa-'l-mamalik* (Book of Routes and Realms, 1068), which includes descriptions of the Empire of Ghana and the trans-Saharan trade routes that linked it to the Arab world.

Sources:
Nafis Ahmad, *Muslim Contribution to Geography* (Lahore: Sh. Muhammad Ashraf, 1972).

S. M. Ali, *Arab Geography* (Aligarh: Muslim University, 1960).

ABU ABD ALLAH MUHAMMAD IBN BATTUTA

1304-CIRCA 1378
TRAVELER

North African Muslim. Born in Tangier, Ibn Battuta spent more than thirty years of his life traveling throughout the Muslim world and recording his observations. His journeys covered more than seventy-five thousand miles and included visits to the capitals of every known Muslim ruler. Traveling by foot, on the backs of donkeys, camels, and horses, in boats and carts, and by any other means available, he reached as far away as Sri Lanka and parts of China in the east and north through Byzantium to Russia.

West African Travels. In 1352–1353 he visited Timbuktu and other parts of the Empire of Mali at a time when it was beginning to go into decline and the Songhai polity was coalescing to challenge it.

Later Life. Ibn Battuta spent the last two decades of his life as a *qadi* (judge) in Fez, Morocco. During that time he wrote memoirs of his travels. His *Rihlah* (Travels) is the best-known and most respected Arabic sources for descriptions and history of the Western Sudan in the fourteenth century.

Sources:
Ross E. Dunn, *Adventures of Ibn Battuta, A Muslim Traveler of the Fourteenth Century* (Berkeley: University of California Press, 1986).

Ibn Battuta, *Travels in Asia and Africa, 1325–1354*, 3 volumes, translated by H. A. R. Gibb (London: Routledge, 1929).

ABU ABD ALLAH AL-IDRISI

1099-1165 OR 1166
GEOGRAPHER

Early Years. Born to a Muslim in the Spanish enclave of Ceuta, on the North African side of the Strait of Gibraltar, al-Idrisi was educated in Cordoba. At age sixteen he began traveling through Muslim lands around the Mediterranean.

Court Geographer. Around 1145 Roger II (ruled 1105–1154), the Norman king of Sicily, invited al-Idrisi to Palermo to become his court geographer. There he was commissioned to write an encyclopedic compendium of geographic knowledge of the world, eventually producing *Nuzhat al-mushtaq fi ikhtiraq al-afaq* (Amusement for One Who Desires to Travel around the World, 1154), also known as *Kitab al-Rujari* (The Book of Roger). This work was a compendium of virtually all geographical data on the known world, including the Western Sudan. He also created the most scientifically accurate maps ever made to that time. Al-Idrisi's work supplanted that of Ptolemy, which had been the primary geographical authority in Europe for centuries. During his later years al-Idrisi made several revised versions of his geography. An abridgment of the Arabic original and an extremely influential Latin translation were published in 1592.

Sources:

J. H. Kramers, "Geography and Commerce," in *The Legacy of Islam*, edited by Thomas Arnold and Alfred Guillaume (Oxford: Clarendon Press, 1931).

G. Oman, "al-Idrisi," in *Encyclopedia of Islam*, CD-ROM version (Leiden: Brill, 1999).

ABU ABD ALLAH MUHAMMAD IBN MUSA AL-KHAWARIZMI

780-850
ASTRONOMER-MATHEMATICIAN

The House of Wisdom. Al-Khawarizmi was born in Kath Town, Khiva, on the Aral Sea and was appointed official astronomer to Caliph al Ma'mun, who in 830 established the Bayt al-Hikmah (House of Wisdom) in Baghdad for the study and translation of scientific and philosophical treatises. He invented the terms *algebra* and *algorithm,* and his works are responsible for introducing those concepts, as well as Arabic numerals (which the Arabs got from the Hindus), to European mathematicians.

Geography. Al-Khawarizmi revised and improved Ptolemy's geographic works and produced a map of the world that included a precise location for the Western Sudan. His *Kitab surat al-ard* (Book of the Image of the World) includes latitudes and longitudes for localities in the known world and is credited with laying the foundation for all subsequent Arabic geography.

Sources:

Nafis Ahmad, *Muslim Contribution to Geography* (Lahore: Sh. Muhammad Ashraf, 1972).

Seyyed Hossein Nasr, *Islamic Science: An Illustrated Study* (London: World of Islam Festival Publishing, 1976).

Nasr, *Science and Civilization in Islam* (London: Islamic Texts Society, 1987).

Ahmad Nazmi, "Some Aspects of the Image of the World in Muslim Tradition, Legends, and Geographical Literature," *Studia Arabistyczne i Islamistyczne,* 6 (1998): 87–102.

LEO AFRICANUS

1485-1554
TRAVELER

Spanish Muslim. Born al-Hassan ibn Muhammad al-Wizzaa al-Fasi, Leo Africanus was a native of Granada, Spain, and was educated in Morocco. As a young man he traveled all over North Africa and West Africa on trade and diplomatic missions with his father, visiting the Songhai Empire in 1513–1515.

Italy. On the way home from a 1516–1517 trip to Egypt, he was captured by Christian pirates, who gave him to Pope Leo X as a slave. Impressed with his slave's intellectual abilities, the Pope set him free and in 1520 convinced him to convert to Christianity, baptizing him Johannis Leo (John Leo). The Pope also persuaded Leo to write an Italian account of his travels, which he completed in 1526. Published in 1550 as *Descrittione dell'Africa* (Description of Africa), the book became the most famous and most widely quoted European work about Africa. It remained the most important source of European knowledge about West and North Africa for the next four centuries. The name by which Leo is known today, Leo Africanus (Leo the African), stems from his reputation for writing the "definitive" European book on Africa. Through his descriptions, Europeans formed an image of Timbuktu as an exotic, mysterious, ancient, and inaccessible locale, making it the subject of fantasy and legend for years to come.

Sources:

Leo Africanus, *The History and Description of Africa,* 3 volumes, translated by John Pory, edited by Robert Brown (London: Printed for the Hakluyt Society, 1896).

Amin Maalouf, *Leo Africanus,* translated by Peter Sluglett (New York: Norton, 1989).

DOCUMENTARY SOURCES

Al-Bakri, *Kitab al-masalik wa-'l-mamalik* (Book of Routes and Realms, 1068)—The most detailed description of the Empire of Ghana available in Arabic manuscripts.

Ibn Battuta, *Rihlah* (Travels, 1356)—The best-known Arabic account of the Western Sudan in the fourteenth century.

Ibn Hawqal, *Surat al-Ard* (Picture of the Earth, 988)—The best tenth-century description of the trans-Saharan caravan trade from Sijilmasa to Ghana and a valuable depiction of relations between Ghana and the Berbers; this work was an important methodological model for early Arab geographers.

Ibn Khaldun, *Kitab al-'ibar* (The Book of Historical Lessons, written 1374–1378, revised 1378–1404)—A valuable geographical and historical work that includes a geographical analysis of Mali and its relations with North Africa; the book collects information from other Arabic sources and draws on Ibn Khaldun's own travels and experiences in the Maghrib and the Western Sudan.

Al-Idrisi, *Nuzhat al-mushtaq fi ikhtiraq al-afaq* (Amusement for One Who Desires to Travel around the World, 1154)—The book that provided Europeans with information on the Western Sudan and its gold resources.

Mahmoud al-Kati, *Tarikh al-Fattash* (The Chronicle of the Seeker after Knowledge, started 1519)—The first of the two great geographical histories by West Africans, considered the beginning of authentic, written African voices regarding the early dynamics of the Western Sudan; this history, which was continued by two later generations of the Kati family, Muslim residents of Djenné, chronicles the geographical politics, history, and economics of the Western Sudan, particularly focusing on the later phases of the development of Mali and Songhai, making major use of oral histories.

Leo Africanus, *Descrittione dell'Africa* (Description of Africa, 1550)—The most important, accurate, and credible source for the history of the Western Sudan between Ibn Battuta's fourteenth-century account and those of nineteenth-century European explorers.

Al-Mas'udi, *Muruj al-Dhahab wa Ma'adin* (Meadows of Gold and Mines of Precious Stones, 947–956)—An early manuscript that connects the arrival of Islam in the Western Sudan with the prior existence of Sudanic state formation.

'Abd al-Rahman al-Sa'di, *Tarikh al-Sudan* (Chronicle of the Western Sudan, circa 1650)—The second West African history, based on oral traditions dealing with the struggle between the Songhai and the Mossi to control the middle Niger River region; written by a Timbuktu scholar, this text includes geographical descriptions and historical accounts of the Songhai Empire and nearby regions through 1655 and is considered a more comprehensive treatment than al-Kati's history.

Al-Umari, *Masalik al-absar fi mamalik al-amsar* (Pathways of Vision in the Realms of the Metropolises, 1338)—One of the primary Arabic sources (with the histories of Ibn Khaldun and Ibn Battuta) on Mali in the fourteenth century.

Ahmad ibn Abi Yaqubi, *Tarikh* (History, 872–873)—The earliest known Arabic work that provides a geographical depiction of the location, population, and political life of the states in the Western Sudan, especially Ghana, Gao (KawKaw), and Kanem.

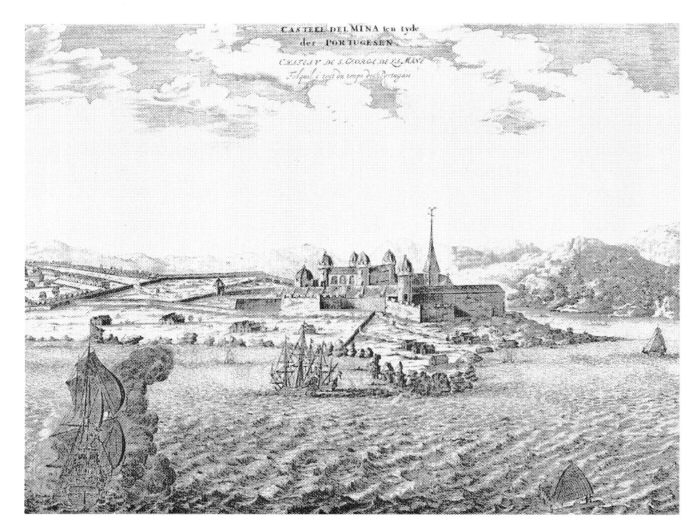

Elmina Castle (originally called São Jorge da Mina), a coastal trading fort built by the Portuguese during the late
fifteenth century in the present-day nation of Ghana (engraving from Olfert Dapper,
Naukreurige Beschrijvinge van Africa Gewesten, 1668; Musée Dapper, Paris)

THE ARTS

by DIEDRE L. BADEJO

CONTENTS

Sidebars and tables are listed in italics.

IMPORTANT EVENTS OF 500-1590

500*
- At Nok and neighboring villages (in modern-day northern Nigeria), a massive iron-smelting culture has already evolved; this culture has also created some of the earliest West African sculpture.
- The ancient Empire of Ghana (in present-day southeastern Mauritania and southwestern Mali), also known as Wagadu, with its capital at Kumbi Saleh, controls the trans-Saharan trade in gold, which is mined in the Wangara and Bambuk provinces of Ghana.
- The people of Ghana build stone and acacia-wood houses.

600*-699*
- The city-state of Kanem is founded near Lake Chad, probably by the Zaghawa people.

800*-899*
- The loosely united Soninke people form what later becomes the Songhai Empire. Artisans are associated with the ruling elite.

900*
- Bronze ceremonial objects are made by the Igbo-Ukwu people of Nigeria.

1000*
- Hausa people inhabit towns and villages in the iron-rich hills north of the confluence of the Niger and Benue Rivers, between Lake Chad to the east and the Niger bend to the west.
- Benin begins to expand, merging smaller fiefdoms into a powerful kingdom.
- New goldfields are found and mined at Bure on the upper Niger, attracting Almoravid raiders and invaders from the rising Empire of Mali, both of which threaten the stability of Ghana. Gold as art, adornment, and currency influences class formation.

1076
- Kumbi Saleh, the capital of Ghana, falls to Almoravid troops.

1100-1600
- Yoruba sculpture is in its Classic period.

1200*
- Artisans in Ile-Ife begin creating realistic bronze and terra-cotta sculptures of human heads.

1200*-1499*
- Despite some stylistic differences, the ceramics of Ile-Ife and Benin suggest a close historical link between the two cultures, which sets them apart from the ceramics of surrounding Yoruba and Edo territories.

* DENOTES CIRCA DATE

IMPORTANT EVENTS OF 500-1590

1240
- Sundiata, ruler of Mali, conquers Ghana and incorporates it into his empire.

1327*
- During the reign of Mansa Musa, the Jungereber mosque is built in Timbuktu, the capital of the Empire of Mali and an important trading city.

1400*
- Artisans in the Kingdom of Benin begin making high-quality bronze and brass sculptures.

1464-1492
- During the reign of Sunni Ali, Songhai reaches its ascendancy, occupying Timbuktu to secure the flow of trade and exchange of ideas and cultural artifacts through the region.

1571-1603
- During his reign Idris Alooma establishes himself as the greatest leader of the Kanem-Bornu Empire, greatly expanding its territory through a succession of military conquests.

* DENOTES CIRCA DATE

The Friday Mosque in the Malian trading city of Djenné, built circa 1300
(from Susan Denyer, *African Traditional Architecture*, 1978)

OVERVIEW

Nature and the Arts. An area of great human, natural, and climatic variety, West Africa is inhabited by indigenous and migrant populations that have lived for at least ten thousand years in an area larger than the United States. The geography and biodiversity of West Africa have inspired and challenged its people and contributed to their distinct and rich cultural heritage. In the north, the basins, oases, mountains, dunes, and blowing sands of the Sahara Desert influenced the attire of its nomadic peoples, as well as their architecture, folklore, and oral traditions. In the south, rivers and other waterways feature prominently in regional myths of origin and legends of conquest and resettlement. The rich colors, textures, and sounds of diverse flora and fauna in the forest region influenced its rituals and performances, its instrumental and human music, and the iconography and design of its visual arts and attire. The Saharan sands; the barks, fibers, and roots of the Sahel (the semidesert area on the southern fringe of the Sahara from Mauritania and Senegal to Chad); and the woods and metal ores of the forest are found in jewelry, musical instruments, sculpture, clothing, and decorative arts. While the different regions contributed to the artistic diversity of West Africa, they have also unified geographically scattered cultural groups. In fact, it is possible to argue that trade and migration across the Sahara unified east and west in the northern region of the continent. Similarly, waterways such as the vast Niger-Benue River system facilitated dialogue among cultures and peoples of many parts of West Africa. For instance, the forceful winds that carry Saharan sands across much of the region are associated with such deities as Oya, one of the many female deities of the Yoruba, an ethnic group of southwestern Nigeria and Benin.

Gender and the Arts. Captured in folklore and religion, the delicate balance of nature also contributed to perceptions of gender roles in the region. For example, the Yoruba goddess Oya, who is especially associated with tornadoes, lightning, and strong winds, is also connected with the power of female leadership. West African women as well as men passed on the culture and history of the region. As performers, visual artists, and historians, women chanted in shrines, played important roles at ritual and ceremonial occasions, and presided over births and deaths. West African men carved rock and wood and forged metals into statues, swords, gold weights, and jewelry. Both men and women maintained an elaborate oral literary tradition, including a body of folklore that has fascinated travelers and scholars for many centuries.

Domestic and Cultural Art. Art in West Africa is both functional and aesthetic. Most West African cultures have well-defined aesthetics with deep roots in their histories. Art and artistic expression permeated West African life in urban and rural settings. Local courts placed high value on fine arts and performance arts, and their creators were honored as courtiers who documented the spiritual dimensions of their culture as well as the lineages of royalty and local rulers. In a system where skills were passed down through guilds or designated families, some artists and their productions were protected by spiritual conventions as well as court alliances. Using a wide range of woods, metals, stones, and clay soils, West African sculptors and carvers played a prominent role in their communities and within the region. Most of their works had utilitarian purposes and were owned by commoners and ruling classes alike. Valued for aesthetic as well as practical reasons, Akan gold weights—cast from bronze or copper during the fifteenth and sixteenth centuries—were used with scales for weighing gold dust so it could serve as a means of exchange. Hence, the development of gold weights had a significant impact on commerce all across West Africa and the trans-Saharan trade routes.

Poets, Singers, and Musicians. Poets, singers, and musicians were local and regional historians and often performed as living "archives" as well as artists. They usually served the ruling class and their larger communities. There was a distinction, however, between professional and communal artists. Communal artists entertained and taught lessons of daily life through songs and poems drawn loosely from a wellspring of cultural motifs and images. Unlike communal artists, professional artists were strictly trained and were expected to adhere to specific conventions.

Depending on the culture, apprentices studied with master teachers, often with others of their age group, until they mastered a set of required basic skills; then they traveled to study with specialists in other guilds. This practice was evident among Mande and Yoruba oral historians and praise singers, who acknowledged their predecessors and teachers in the prologue to their performances.

Theater and Dance. Performance arts such as dance, mime, puppetry, and theater found expression in formal and informal, secular and sacred, settings. West African dancers combined strength and agility with narrative to create a distinctive art form. Throughout the region, dance, music, and theater merged into what is frequently called dance-drama. Spirit possession, religious belief, courtship, bravery, physical prowess, fertility, and sensuality were all subjects of dance-drama. Social commentary and humor were also expressed through dance-dramas, which often included mime and sometimes puppetry. Most often these performances were accompanied by spoken and visual forms of artistic expression as well. Animals such as horses were even used in re-enactments of historical events.

TOPICS IN THE ARTS

ARCHITECTURE

Architecture. A West African village, town, or city included a complex system of buildings, agricultural-pastoral spaces, storage and food-preparation centers, clusters of specialist industries, market centers, community common areas, and roadways intersecting according to definable patterns. In other words, architecture was more than structures. The functions and spatial relationships of buildings revealed much about the worldviews, lifestyles, and aesthetic values of the residents. Access to water and wood resources was an important factor in determining the location of a community. In several ethnic regions of West Africa, there are distinct networks of urban and rural settlements located for ease of access to water, wood, and resources for specialized crafts such as iron smelting as well as for the facilitation of trade in craftspeople's goods and other products.

The Compound. The plans of most cities, towns, and villages were based on the common idea of a compound, a group of related spaces that housed core and extended families. The many sociocultural organizational patterns and belief systems of different ethnic groups influenced building styles and the internal and external arrangement of dwelling spaces. As Roderick J. McIntosh has written,

> urban clusters reflect a different social contract. The settlements are occupied by ethnic or specialist corporate groups. As opposed to centralized power used to prevent class conflict and to maintain the privileges of the elite, the urban clusters present an opportunity for multiple agencies of authority, maintaining peace by a sense of belonging to the community within the larger horizontally-integrated urban system.

Settlements included architectural spaces for public rituals and performances, while family compounds had places for functions such as births and naming, betrothal, and marriage ceremonies, as well as wakes, funerals, second burials, parties, play, and other social gatherings. Within family living spaces, women's rooms often included storage spaces for daily culinary, domestic, and personal needs. Small gardens and family cooking facilities were frequently on the periphery or in adjacent outer spaces. The design and location of granaries and silos for food storage also followed distinct culturally and regionally defined patterns. In some cases, areas adjacent to compounds were reserved for small marketing activities or workshops for craftspeople. In other cases, family farmlands were located within walking distance of the main family dwelling. Areas for livestock were often located outside compounds. Particularly in villages and towns, some food-preparation areas—for tasks such as brewing beer or drying meats, fish, skins, and peppers—also lay beyond the compound in well-defined areas. Archaeological evidence and oral traditions indicate that West African family compounds, villages, towns, and urban centers were generally circular, rectangular, diamond, or oval in shape. Most were surrounded by fences, trees, bush, or open areas. Individual houses were often rectangular or round. In many instances, the walls and verandas of certain dwellings were decorated with specific designs and colors.

Two styles of traditional architecture: (top) an Impluvial-style compound in an Igbo village of southeastern Nigeria and (bottom) Hill-style dwellings in a Dogon village on the Bandiagara Escarpment, Ireli, Mali (top: from Susan Denyer, *African Traditional Architecture,* 1978; bottom: photograph © 2001 by Stephenie Hollyman)

Architectural Styles. West African architecture has always been influenced by climate and availability of materials, as well as by the worldview, lifestyle, and cosmological belief system of a given population. Susan Denyer has described three different styles of West African architecture—the Sudanese, Impluvial, and Hill styles—each of which was influenced by climatic and environmental factors. Although it is difficult to date their origins precisely, some archaeological evidence suggests that all three styles predate the Muslim influences of the tenth century and later and evolved before any contact with the eastern region of the Nile Valley or the European strangers along the Atlantic coastline.

Sudanese Style. Found predominately in areas between the Niger and Chad basins, the Sudanese style is characterized by four rectangular-shaped buildings around an open courtyard. Denyer cites archaeological evidence from northern Ghana to date the design of such structures before the arrival of Islam. The Sudanese style is more associated with urban environments than the Impluvial and Hill styles, in part because Sudanese buildings were constructed of various combinations of mud, brick, and stone—important building materials in dry areas where fire posed a constant threat. The courtyard is a common feature of the Sudanese style throughout the region, but building materials vary. Rectangular sun-dried mud bricks were common, but burned bricks (mud bricks hardened by heat from an open fire) were used throughout the Chad basin. The Hausa used pear-shaped mud bricks in their construction, while dwellings built of stone and mud mortar and then plastered with mud were common in Oualata. Roofs were usually flat and made of mud or dome-shaped vaulted designs made of mud or thatch. When mud roofs were used, they were supported by palm-frond joists and forms. In fourteenth-century Mali, roofs were shaped like camel backs, perhaps to mimic that dominant mode of transportation used by trans-Saharan travelers.

Impluvial Style. The Impluvial style developed in the forest zones. Iron Age houses excavated south of Lake Chad include many elements of this style. Like the Sudanese style, Impluvial-style construction is characterized by four rectangular buildings around a courtyard. The term *impluvial* refers to the use of the courtyard to collect water for the household, an important feature in an area where drinking and cooking water are scarce, particularly during the dry season. Draining rainwater from roofs into tanks or pots also helped to prevent erosion. Impluvial structures were built of mud and always had thatched roofs. Depending on location, the four buildings around a courtyard were either thatched separately and linked by a screen wall, or they were covered by one continuous roof that extended around the courtyard. A variation on this style includes abutting roof corners of the four buildings to form groins. Impluvial structures often included verandas, or the side of a room facing the courtyard was left open to allow for good ventilation while maintaining privacy. Potsherds were often used to make decorative pavements. Notable examples were created by the Ashanti, Yoruba, and Benin peoples. The Impluvial style was used in both rural and urban environments.

Hill Style. With some examples dating back to the ninth century, Hill-style architecture required intensive labor and technical skill. Remarkably similar Hill-style settlements may be found on highlands throughout Africa. West African Hill-style settlements were built by the Dogon of Mali, the Gwari on the Jos plateau of Nigeria, the Dagomba of Ghana, and residents of other mountainous areas. Though hill communities have sometimes been called inhospitable, they were often quite pleasant in terms of climate, aesthetics, and access to food and water. Stone appears to be the dominant material used in the construction of these dwellings, and it was especially common in the foundations, walls, terraces, and the walls of livestock enclosures. Houses were usually round with conical, thatched roofs. These communities typically housed dense populations.

Courtyard or Large-Compound Structures. Courtyard or large-compound structures are common throughout most of West Africa. The organization of compounds was based on social and philosophical beliefs as well as individual family needs. In polygamous and multigenerational households, the inner compound served, as it does today, as a center of socialization for children and as the location for family activities. Such compounds also exemplify the holistic view of West African lifestyles that incorporated family, food, child development, aesthetics, and art. Familial, cultural, and social organization influenced the outer living spaces of West Africans, suggesting their view of living as a creative act.

Communal Gatherings. Open space within the compound and external to it reflects the dominant belief in holding communal gatherings for festivals, celebrations, rites of passage, and other events. Where internal spaces are reserved for family and friends, the external spaces are the purview of the community at large and a constant reminder of the integral relationship among members of the village, town, or urban area. In some instances, special communal spaces may be reserved for rituals and royal ceremonies or for general public gatherings and local events. In some rural communities, ritual activities may be held within an adjacent designated forest space.

Palaces and Places of Worship. Palaces and palace compounds are distinguished from the homes of the general populace more by their size and location than by their style. While the style may be consistent with other buildings in an environment, features such as the size of the structure, the inclusion of additional functional structures, or the large size of the common area indicate the leadership role of the occupant. Cultural worldview and historical experi-

Examples of traditional Sudanese-style architecture in the old sections of (top) Djenné, Mali, and (bottom) Kano, northern Nigeria (top: from Anthony Atmore and Gillian Stacey, *Black Kingdoms, Black Peoples,* 1979; bottom: from Susan Denyer, *African Traditional Architecture,* 1978)

The Djingereyber Mosque in Timbuktu, Mali, designed by al-Sahili, circa 1528
(from Susan Denyer, *African Traditional Architecture*, 1978)

ence influenced the location of palaces and palace compounds. The marketplace or center of trade was frequently close to the seat of power in many rural and urban communities. In other instances, the location of central indigenous shrines or mosques determined the location of a ruling court and its entourage.

Sources:

Margaret Courtney-Clark, *African Canvas: The Art of West African Women* (New York: Rizzoli, 1990).

Susan Denyer, *African Traditional Architecture: An Historical and Geographical Perspective* (New York: Africana Publishing, 1978).

David Hughes, *Afrocentric Architecture: A Design Primer* (Columbus, Ohio: Greyden Press, 1994).

Elizabeth Isichei, *A History of African Societies to 1870* (Cambridge: Cambridge University Press, 1997).

Roderick J. McIntosh, "Early Urban Clusters in China and Africa," *Journal of Field Archaeology*, 18 (1991): 199–212.

Susan Keech McIntosh and Roderick J. McIntosh, *Jenne-jeno, An Ancient African City* <http://www.ruf.rice.edu/~anth/arch/niger/broch-eng.html>.

West Africa Architecture Album <http://www.dogon-lobi.ch/architecture album.htm>.

THE ART OF ADORNMENT

Body Designs. Perhaps one of the greatest African art forms is the adornment of the human body. Among many West African groups intricately designed jewelry, elaborate hairstyles, body decoration, and elegant attire combine to make human beings, especially women, living works of art. Representing individual, familial, and cultural concepts of beauty, many of these adornments have roots in the 500–1590 period of West African history.

Body Decoration. For centuries West Africans have turned the human body into living art through tattoos, decorative pigments, and scarification (a process whereby incisions are made in the skin to create patterns). While it is difficult to pinpoint the origins of these forms of body designing, the survival of masks and

scriptures that depict such decorations has helped scholars to determine that they date back to antiquity. Permanent body designing such as tattoos and scarification occurs at different intervals in an individual's life and contributes to his or her identification with a particular society, status, or role. In some cultures, tattooing is as much narrative as symbolism. Stories of courtship and marriage may be told through tattoos on women's bodies. Among Yoruba, Bambara, and Akan women, tattooing also communicates and enhances their place and value in their societies. Intricate designs painted with henna, indigo, and other dyes beautify and tell the stories of their wearers. Igbo women used a variety of natural dyes called *uli* to paint abstract and representational designs (also called *uli*) on each other's bodies as well as on the walls of houses. Yoruba women often used henna and other plant-derived dyes to tell personal and familial stories through designs on their hands, legs, and arms.

Scarification. Scarification also did more than enhance physical appearance. According to George Landow, it was believed to provide spiritual protection and to place an individual physically within a region or belief system. For example, the style of scarification on a thirteenth- or fourteenth-century Yoruba head conveys the balance, demeanor, and poise that characterize *iwapele* (good character) in Yoruba aesthetics and personal behavior. In fact, as Landow has explained, body designing is a sign of civilization: "Scarification, tattooing, and body piercing therefore parallel the characteristic African aesthetic emphasis upon composure, balance, and calm in an important way, for both represent ways of separating the human from the less-than-human—the animal, the natural." Catherine Cartwright Jones points out that "interlocking knotwork patterns are often used as metaphors for the Yoruba concept of the world as two distinct yet inseparable realms, *Aye* and *Orun*. *Aye* is the

A Nigerian woman being painted in a traditional *uli* line pattern, signifying that she is considered a good woman (photograph by Margaret Courtney-Clarke/CORBIS)

world of the living, *Orun* is the world of spirits and the afterlife." Thus, this style may be interpreted as a representation of the Yoruba saying that may be translated as "this world is a marketplace we visit, the other world is our home."

Hairstyles. Since antiquity, intricately patterned hairstyles have played an important role in the artistic, cultural, and social lives of African women and men. From the exaggerated emphasis placed on the head in ancient African sculpted, brass, and terra-cotta figures, scholars have deduced that the head and the hair carried deeply philosophical and spiritual meanings as well as indications of social status or role, identity, or age. So significant is the notion of hair and hairstyling in Yoruba cosmology that hair combs represent the relationship

between personal destiny and personal presentation. Even today, African hairstyling carries more than aesthetic meaning, particularly for those who exercise leadership and authority in spiritual matters.

Sources:
Rowland Abiodun, Henry J. Drewal, and John Pemberton III, eds., *The Yoruba Artist: New Theoretical Perspectives on African Arts* (Washington & London: Smithsonian Institution Press, 1994).

Margaret Courtney-Clarke, *African Canvas: The Art of West African Women* (New York: Rizzoli, 1990).

David Hughes, *Afrocentric Architecture: A Design Primer* (Columbus, Ohio: Greyden Press, 1994).

Catherine Cartwright Jones, *Traditional Yoruba Patterns* <http://reverndbunny.sphosting.com/yoruba.htm>.

George Landow, "Civilizing Scars" <http://www.scholars.nus.edu.sg/post/africa/scar.html>.

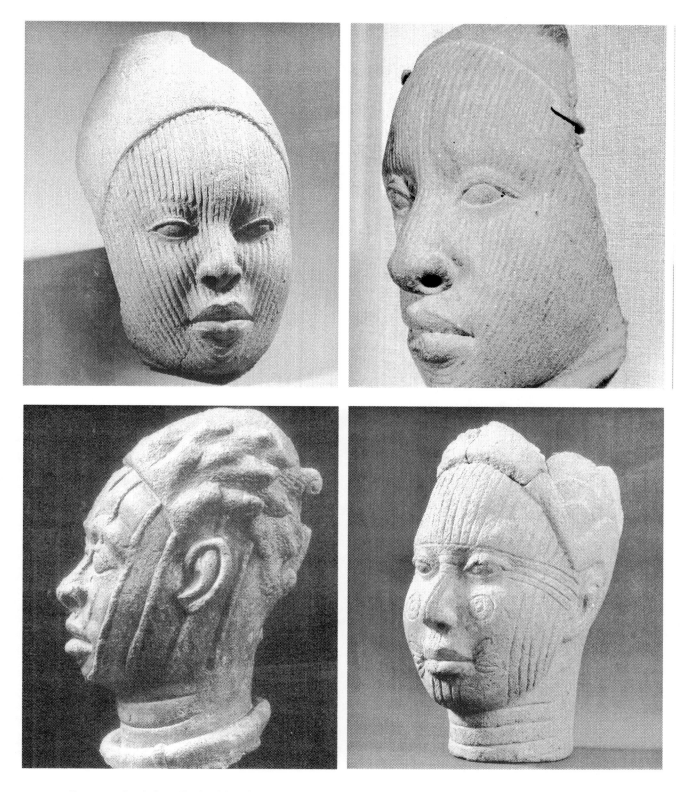

Terra-cotta heads from Ile-Ife with various patterns of scarification: top (left) circa 1000–1200, (right) circa 1100–1300; bottom (left) circa 1200–1400, (right) circa 1300–1500 (top left and bottom right: Obafemi Awolowo University, Ile-Ife, Nigeria; top right: Guennol Collection, Brooklyn Museum of Art; bottom left: Ethnological Museum, Berlin)

THE ART OF ATTIRE

Cloth Weaving. Archaeological and historical evidence suggests that the domestic cultivation of cotton and cloth weaving evolved around the third or second millennium B.C.E. in the middle Nile region. By the beginning of the Common Era both cotton and ceramic technologies had also developed in the Western Sudanic and Atlantic areas of West Africa. These technologies were passed on through guild systems. Young apprentices learned not only the skills necessary to practice the craft but also the taboos associated with protecting them. As weaving became an art, various ethnic cultures developed distinctive styles. Historical and archaeological records suggest that cloth weaving began with the use of raffia, specially treated fibers made from the bark of a tree called the raffia palm. Raffia cloth was followed by woven strips of cotton and other fibers. Archaeological evidence dates the use of these textiles in West Africa at least back to the eleventh century, when woven cloths were used in funerary rites in the area around the Bandiagara cliffs in present-day Mali. From Senegambia to the Niger long strips of cloth in diverse widths and patterns are still made. During the early years of African-European trade in the fifteenth century, these woven fabrics were so admired that Portuguese traders used them as currency along the western Atlantic coast of Africa.

Looms. With many variations, most West African woven cloth is still made by one of two dominant weaving technologies: either an upright single-heddle loom or a narrow-strip, double-heddle loom. (A heddle is a set of parallel strings that guides the warp, or lengthwise, threads on a loom.) The strips woven on these looms vary in width, length, and pattern. The strips are cut and sewn together edge to edge to make six-yard garments that are wrapped or sewn in a variety of styles according to cultural preferences. Although the basic interior design of the looms is similar, the outer construction varies from ground looms to upright looms and elaborate treadle looms. A few fragments of a single-heddle loom were found in the Igbo-Ukwu area among brass works that were carbon dated to the ninth century.

Cloth for the Elite. Akan and Ewe kente cloth, Yoruba aso oke, and Bambara bogolanfini, or mud cloth, are well known and popular West African textiles. The exquisite artistry of such traditional woven cloth was associated with ruling elites and the wealthy. According to Adu Boahen, the "enlightened and capable" Nana Obunumankoma, who ruled the flourishing Akan state of Bono for more than sixty years during the fifteenth century, imported weavers and embroiderers from the north, most likely from among the Fula. The weavers were commissioned to fashion attire for his court that reflected the growing wealth of the state, its rulers, and elders. Images representing Akan philosophical and spiritual beliefs, as well as state symbols, were embroidered onto the cloth. This tradition exists today in adinkra cloth. The court-sponsored Fula weavers influenced the local textile industry of Bono. According to Doran H. Ross, who cites the research of linguists and historiographers, Fula weaving and textiles had been spreading throughout West Africa since the eleventh century.

Attire as Literature. Art historian Robert Farris Thompson has suggested that designs created by some

A Yoruba ruler wearing coronation garb, bronze figure from Ile-Ife, circa 1200–1500 (Museum of Antiquities, Ile-Ife)

West African textile artists can be "read as ideographs related to a system of writing." In her unpublished photography exhibition "A Language of Their Own: Yoruba Women's Attire," Andrea Benton Rushing illustrated how clothing in Yoruba culture tells the story of a woman's social, marital, and economic status through the patterns and colors of the fabric and the style of the garment into which it is fashioned. Since the wearing of a certain cloth and style occurs within an extended family or cultural context, it also carries messages of familial or cultural connections. Nor is the language of attire unique to the Yoruba. In fact, dress in most West African societies communicates much about the wearer and her or his entourage. Indeed, the Dogon word for "woven material" is the same as that for "spoken word." Each ethnic group in West Africa created symbols to represent their cultural philosophies, epistemologies, and environmental realities. Specific colors also had different meanings for various ethnic groups. This combination of image and color often had historical as well as cultural significance, frequently locating a people in a time and place. In other words, those versed in a particular culture could "read" the cloth.

Kente Cloth. Although it is impossible to document the origins of Akan and Ewe kente weaving, it dates at least to the fourteenth century. Kente-cloth patterns are created using either weft (crosswise) or warp (lengthwise) weaving techniques, and Ross has estimated that there are more than five hundred designs in each technique. Bonwire, a town north of Kumasi in the modern nation of Ghana, was known for kente weaving and remains so today.

Bogolanfini. Because of drastic shifts in temperature in the environs of the Sahara Desert, heavier garments, including blankets, were needed there, and clothing was made from animal wool and skins, as well as from various treated woven cottons, including bogolanfini, made by the Bambara of Mali. The production of this cloth has always involved both men and women. In some societies the men wove the strips of cloth, and the women dyed it. In others both women and men wove the cloth. Made during the dry season, mud cloth is still handwoven and hand dyed. For centuries women have learned dyeing techniques from their mothers and passed them on to their daughters. They first soak the fabric in a solution made from a combination of various leaves, creating rich shades of mustard yellow, and then they apply black mud in various designs. The tannic acid in the leaf solution combines with the iron oxide in the mud to create a colorfast dye called iron tannate. For designs that include white, they apply caustic soda to some areas. Frequently, the designs and colors on the cloth indicate either a rite of passage or some significant event in the wearer's life—including women's experiences such as marriage, births of children, and competition among co-wives. The designs include fish bones, little stars, squares, and a series of concentric circles.

Aso Oke. Aso oke is a heavy woven cloth. Its date of origin is unknown. Historians do know, however, that it was worn in the courts of Oyo during the sixteenth century.

Other Patterns and Dyes. West African flora and fauna are the sources of raw materials for a variety of colorful natural dyes. One popular coloring agent is the deep blue dye obtained from the indigo plant, which is used throughout much of West Africa to create designs that are characteristic of each different ethnic tradition. For most West African peoples dyeing has always been a female enterprise. For example, as Marietta Joseph points out, among the Yoruba dyeing is under the aegis of Iya Mapo, the "protector of female trades and the custodian of indigo dyeing." The Yoruba hold in sacred respect those who transform raw materials into art, attire, and other material objects. Throughout West Africa, practitioners of this craft draw on a vast store of traditional knowledge about the natural resources of the local environment and chemical interactions among them, and they are recognized as bearers of cultural and ritual authority.

Sources:

Adire African Textiles <www.adire.clara.net/core.htm>.

Adu Boahen, *Topics in West African History* (London: Longmans, 1966).

Christopher Ehret, *The Civilizations of Africa: A History to 1800* (Charlottesville: University Press of Virginia, 2002).

Marietta Joseph, "West African Cloth," *African Arts*, 11, no. 2 (1978): 34–36.

Doran H. Ross, *Wrapped in Pride: Ghanaian Kente and African American Identity* (Los Angeles: UCLA Fowler Museum of Cultural History, 1998).

Robert Farris Thompson, *Flash of Spirit: African and Afro-American Art and Philosophy* (New York: Random House, 1983).

CARVING AND SCULPTURE

The Nok Culture. Flourishing between about 500 B.C.E. and 200 C.E. on the Benue plateau of present-day Nigeria, the ancient Nok culture produced some of the earliest examples of West African sculpture, terra-cotta figurines characterized by simple facial features and bulging eyes with pierced pupils. The art of these Iron Age people influenced evolving cultures north and south of the Niger-Benue confluence as well as east and west of the Niger and its delta area. Nok civilization is thus part of an extensive continuum that includes the Igbo-Ukwu, Ile-Ife (also called Ife), Owo, and Benin cultures, which developed after the year 500.

Metallurgy. According to Christopher Ehret, iron ore was in abundance at scattered sites throughout West Africa, and iron smelting had emerged independently within the region by the first millennium B.C.E. Ironworkers eventually became a protected class, or guild, who carefully guarded the knowledge of transforming iron ore into useful tools, ornaments, jewelry, and art. Ironwork also

Male and female figures with facial scarification on front and back of a bronze altar stand from Igbo-Ukwu,
Nigeria, circa 900–1000 (Nigerian Museum, Lagos)

contributed to improvements in agriculture and animal husbandry. In fact, the creative use of iron contributed greatly to the social, political, and economic well-being of West Africa. Ogun, the Yoruba deity of war and iron, is associated with hunters, warriors, carvers, and metalworkers. The earliest known examples of the related art of bronze casting date from around 900 C.E. They were made by the Igbo-Ukwu culture, located north of the Niger-Benue confluence. Bronze ceremonial objects dating from this era are known for their beauty and artistic sophistication. Like cloth weavers, bronze casters developed an iconography that communicated secular and sacred meanings. Like iron casters, bronze casters occupied an exalted sociocultural position.

"Lost Wax." Bronze casters among the Igbo-Ukwu and other West African peoples used the *cire-perdue*, or lost-wax, process, which is still employed today. The artist first carves a figure in wax and encases it in a heat-proof substance such as clay, leaving holes at the top and bottom of the mold. The wax is "lost" when molten brass or bronze is poured into the mold, melting the wax, which flows out of the mold. When the molten metal cools and solidifies, the mold is broken, revealing the sculpture inside.

The Igbo-Ukwu Culture. In addition to the tenth-century bronze objects, archaeological excavations at Igbo-Ukwu sites have uncovered other artifacts dating as far back as the ninth and tenth centuries. This culture made terra-cotta sculptures and copper items, as well as the intricately patterned bronze objects for which it is best known. The bronze and copper items may also indicate the significant wealth of Igbo-Ukwu and its rulers.

Ile-Ife. Art historian William Bascom notes that the bronze-casting techniques of Igbo-Ukwu are similar to those of a culture at Ile-Ife in southwestern Nigeria, which radiocarbon evidence places in about the same time period; yet, the two cultures have distinct artistic traditions. The bronze heads of classical Ile-Ife have a higher degree of naturalism than similar Igbo-Ukwu objects. Bronze and terra-cotta heads were made in Ile-Ife from the 1200s onward.

Benin. Beginning in the 1400s in the Kingdom of Benin in present-day western Nigeria, great artists produced high-quality bronze figures and heads. Only the obas (rulers) of Benin were allowed to own sculptures made of brass, and metalworkers were their servants. (Chiefs were permitted to own only ancestral figures

Zinc-brass head from the Kingdom of Benin, circa 1400–1600 (Ethnological Museum, Berlin)

made from terra-cotta.) There can be little doubt that the art of metal casting in Benin was an indigenous development fueled by the need for life-like images of royalty to be used in funerary rituals and the cult of ancestors from whom the kings derived their power and authority. Benin art was thus predominantly royal, and it was so closely tied to the rituals used in the service of divine kingship that it underwent few modifications over the generations.

Bambara Woodcarving. The Bambara, who have lived along the Niger River since before the year 1000,

are known for producing sculptures from wood as well as forged iron. Beautifully carved Chi Wara statues are among the best-known Bambara symbols. With intricately carved, elongated features they usually stand between twenty and twenty-six inches in height. The Chi Wara is a mythical antelope that taught people how to farm by using sticks to till the land. During ceremonies at planting and harvest times, dancers wear headpieces representing male and female Chi Wara, with the female carrying its offspring on its back. Symbolizing harmony and balance in human and natural life, Chi

Wara are believed to bring fertility to the land. Stylistically mimicking the movements of both antelopes and farmers, Chi Wara dancers perform sacred (ritual) and secular (historical) rites that re-enforce their cultural bonds and spiritual perspectives. The creation of Chi Wara still rests within a guild of carvers who enjoy high status and are invested with ritual and social authority.

Akan Gold Weights. Nana Obunumankoma, who ruled the Akan state of Bono for more than sixty years during the fifteenth century, is credited with exploiting the state's gold reserve and establishing gold dust as the local currency. He developed a system of weighing gold using standardized weights, which goldsmiths cast usually from bronze or copper by the *cire-perdue* method employed throughout West Africa. Gold weights served both economic and aesthetic purposes. As artistic expressions, gold weights were decorated with icons from Akan culture that conveyed cultural philosophy and values. Many of these images represented proverbs and maxims that reminded the users of the centrality of their culture in daily life. Like other metalworkers, goldsmiths were a privileged guild of master craftsmen. They were protected by the political leadership, and their works contributed to the creation of wealth in the state treasury. Goldsmiths and other metalworkers created staffs of authority and elaborate jewelry—including rings, necklaces, earrings, bracelets, and anklets—for the ruling elite. They also made household utensils.

Sources:

Rowland Abiodun, Henry J. Drewal, and John Pemberton III, eds., *The Yoruba Artist: New Theoretical Perspectives on African Arts* (Washington & London: Smithsonian Institution Press, 1994).

Akan Cultural Symbols Project <http://www.marshall.edu/akanart/>.

E. V. Asihene, *Apoo Festival* (Tema, Ghana: Ghana Publishing, 1980).

William Bascom, *African Art in Cultural Perspective: An Introduction* (New York: Norton, 1973).

Benin Bronze Mask <http://www.vilasart.co.uk/beninbronze.html>.

Christopher Ehret, *The Civilizations of Africa: A History to 1800* (Charlottesville: University Press of Virginia, 2002).

Angela Fagg, "Thoughts on Nok," *African Arts*, no. 3 (July 1994): 79–84.

William Fagg, *The Art of Western Africa: Sculpture and Tribal Masks* (New York: New American Library, 1967).

François Neyt, with the assistance of Andrée Désirant, *The Arts of the Benue: To the Roots of Tradition* (N.p.: Editions Hawaiian Agronomics, 1985).

Ernest E. Obeng, *Ancient Ashanti Chieftaincy* (Tema, Ghana: Ghana Publishing, 1988).

Paul Radin and Elinore Marvel, eds., *African Folktales & Sculpture*, revised and enlarged edition (New York: Pantheon, 1964).

G. T. Stride and Caroline Ifeka, eds., *Peoples and Empires of West Africa: West Africa in History 1000–1800* (London: Nelson, 1971).

CERAMICS AND POTTERY

Cultural-Historical Periods. Like weaving, pottery making evolved around the third or second millennium B.C.E. in the middle Nile region and existed in West Africa by the beginning of the Common Era. It is notable that Ile-Ife, Owo, and Benin shared the same "ceramic sphere" during the thirteenth, fourteenth, and fifteenth

Terra-cotta pots from Ile-Ife, circa 1200–1400 and circa 1300–1500 (Obafemi Awolowo University, Ile-Ife, Nigeria)

centuries. That is, as Akinwumi O. Ogundiran has explained, despite some stylistic differences between Ile-Ife and Benin, similarities in their ceramics from this period suggest a close cultural historical link between the two areas that distinguishes them from the ceramics of surrounding Yoruba and Edo territories. Ogundiran identifies "three major cultural-historical periods" of Ile-Ife and Benin society: the "pre-Classic," prior to the twelfth century; the "Classic," from the twelfth to the sixteenth century; and the "post-Classic," from the sixteenth through the nineteenth century.

The Pre-Classic Period. In the pre-Classic periods closely linked, yet independent, villages coordinated their interactions without dynastic rule. It may be that matrilinearity was prevalent in this period as evinced by the deified female rulers, whose stories have been passed down in such local oral traditions as the Osun and Yemoja narrative. With respect to the ceramic finds, archaeological evidence suggests occupation of the area from the sixth century. In some areas, consistency of ceramic style indicates cultural longevity and the presence of an indigenous population prior to the Oduduwa migratory era around the year 1000, when the Yoruba arrived in the area and largely displaced the indigenous population.

The Classic Period. The Classic period is characterized by the evolution of formal kingship traditions set in urban centers. An extensive cache of terra-cotta figures and potsherd pavements from this period has been uncovered. The Ile-Ife and Benin cultural sites of the Classic era are associated with specific decorative motifs that appear to indicate cultural preferences as well as changes within the cultural and/or external influences. Ogundiran points to similarities in jar rims and bowls as evidence of interaction between Ile-Ife and Benin from the thirteenth through the sixteenth centuries.

Designs. Like designs in textiles, those found on pottery communicate information to individuals versed in a specific culture. For example, corroborating oral narratives about religio-spiritual traditions of the period, the herringbone motif found on several ceramic vessels represents leaves, which are symbolic of ritual and religious ceremonies and ideologies. The production of ceramic vessels required a sophisticated manipulation of and experimentation with local soils, minerals, animal materials, and plants, and it resulted in the creation of beautiful art and artifacts of material culture.

Sources:

Adu Boahen, *Topics in West African History* (London: Longman, 1966).

Christopher Ehret, *The Civilizations of Africa: A History to 1800* (Charlottesville: University Press of Virginia, 2002).

François Neyt, with the assistance of Andrée Déirant, *The Arts of the Benue: To the Roots of Tradition* (N.p.: Editions Hawaiian Agronomics, 1985).

Akinwumi O. Ogundiran, "Filling a Gap in the Ife-Benin Interaction Field (Thirteenth–Sixteenth Centuries A.D.): Excavations in Iloyi Settlement, Ijesaland," *African Archaeological Review*, 19 (March 2002): 27–60.

Doran H. Ross, *Wrapped in Pride: Ghanaian Kente and African American Identity* (Los Angeles: UCLA Fowler Museum of Cultural History, 1998).

Barbara Thompson, *The Earth Transformed: Ceramic Arts of Africa*, The Virtual Research Center for African Ceramics Project, 2000 <http://bailiwick.lib.uiowa.edu/african-ceramic-arts/>.

CROSS-CULTURAL INFLUENCES

Artistic Influences. While most West African cultures of the period 500–1590 had distinct artistic expressions, interregional and trans-Saharan artistic influences were already apparent. Long-distance trade and military expeditions by the North African Almoravids spread not only Islam but Muslim art and culture, which came together with sub-Saharan intellectual and cultural influences at major commercial centers such as Djenné-Jeno and Timbuktu. Some musical forms and instruments of the Sahel and the eastern Sahara bear striking resemblances to those of Islamized cultures in the Western Sudan, part of the band of savanna or grassland stretching across the continent south of the Sahara. Trade, migration, the expansion of kingdoms, and the conquest of neighboring or peripheral peoples within West Africa also brought the commingling of cultural and artistic media, styles, and forms. For example, the complex mythology of the Yoruba-speaking peoples of Nigeria—who had migrated to Ile-Ife in southern Nigeria over several centuries and subsequently dispersed within the western region—is an amalgamation of both indigenous and imported cultural ideas and iconographies. Other cultural interactions account for the broad distribution of iron-smelting furnaces, the *cire-perdue* (lost-wax) method of brass sculpting, and heddle looms in West Africa.

Muslim Artistic Culture. Muslim influences may be found in the verbal and vocal styles, language, and iconography of many West African peoples. The Sahara and Sahel often acted as a bridge between the Nile Valley and Arabic cultures of eastern Africa and the Atlantic coastal and Sudanic cultures of western Africa. At its zenith, around 800–1100, Djenné-Jeno in Mali drew artists and intellectuals from as far away as the eastern Nile Valley and the Arabian Peninsula. The dynamic interactions of such diverse cultures greatly influenced court and common art in the region, and the resulting artworks drew attention to its greatness from the outside world.

Arabic Language. Arabic language and literature had a profound impact on West African artistic development. As trade and Islam spread, so did the Arabic language in both its oral and written forms. Arab traders and Islamized Africans brought the Quran (Koran), written in Arabic script. Djenné-Jeno became the site of intellectual exchange, religious study, and cultural evolution. Within the walls of its beautiful mosques, artists

Hausa minaret at the Gobirau Mosque in Katsina, northern Nigeria, constructed in the fifteenth century and rebuilt in 1702 (from Susan Denyer, *African Traditional Architecture*, 1978)

and scholars gathered to exchange ideas and to learn from the great minds of their era. Like other contemporary international cities of artistic and intellectual engagement, Djenné-Jeno attracted visitors from around the world.

Sources:
J. O. Hunwick, *Timbuktu & the Songhay Empire: Al-Sa'di's Ta'rikh al-sudan Down to 1613 and Other Contemporary Documents* (Leiden: Brill, 1999).

Timothy A. Insoll, "The Road to Timbuktu: Trade & Empire," *Archaeology*, 53, no. 6 (2000): 48–52.

LITERARY ARTISTS

Ancient Roots. Although it is impossible to date the origin of literary production in West Africa, it is possible to deduce from themes, settings, and the plethora of narrative styles that West African oral literary traditions have roots as ancient as those of the people who occupy the land. Literary production in West Africa involved a trained professional class of verbal artists as well as a nonprofessional class of gifted entertainers. A professional or nonprofessional was expected to possess a good voice, to be agile and rhythmic, and to demonstrate a mastery of one's cultural aesthetic. Both drew on an extensive cultural and historical repertoire of themes, images, metaphors, and styles. From present-day Mauritania to Cameroon, the literature of West Africa is a vast store of complex mythical and historical narratives. Most of these works are part of oral traditions, but others have been communicated through performance-art forms. For example, the epics of Sundiata and Ozidi are told through mime, vocal and instrumental music, dance, and poetry—all performed over a period of several days. Instruments such as the Yoruba dundun drums or the Akan horns, both of which mimic human speech, also have a literary function.

Professional Artists. Professional artists served the ruling and ritual classes and were often responsible for maintaining regional cultural and legal histories as well as the cosmologies that legitimized the authority of their patrons. The idea that narratives were simply passed from father to son and mother to daughter obscures the fact that literary novices underwent an extensive educational process during their training to become masters of the verbal and instrumental arts. In most areas of West Africa, classes of age-related youth were (and still are) trained by teams of master teachers who were responsible for insuring that their students were proficient enough to perform publicly. Talent, natural gifts, and affinity for a given undertaking were considered in the selection of students. Training lasted from ten to thirty years depending on the ability of the student and the area of specialization. In a social system dominated by guilds, a mediocre or weak performance embarrassed the guild of master teachers as much as it did the student.

Nonprofessional Artists. The repertoires of nonprofessional literary artists came from folkloric traditions and included animal tales, fables, songs, and narratives on themes such as drought, conquest, migration, resettlement, and a spectrum of social issues. In most parts of West Africa, talented narrators rose from among local villagers and were appreciated for their vocal, mime, or instrumental abilities. Voice and mime were especially important assets. These local artists drew from a storehouse of indigenous motifs and styles for their creative presentations to members of their communities, which included a wide range of forms from lullabies to morality tales to songs of social satire. Their efforts not only entertained but often reiterated important lessons. This pedantic aspect is particularly evident in West African animal tales, where the personifications of the tortoise, hare, spider, and duiker are lightly shrouded human characteristics. Similar folkloric characters and themes can be found in all world cultures. What makes West African tales distinctly African is the teller's narrative style, which usually involves a call-and-response engagement between performer and audience. Although there are differences throughout the region, there are many common features in all West African narrative styles.

Sources:

Uchegbulam N. Abalogu, *Oral Poetry in Nigeria* (Lagos, Nigeria: Nigeria Magazine, 1981).

S. A. Babalola, *The Content and Form of Yoruba Ijala* (Oxford: Clarendon Press, 1966).

Diedre L. Badejo, "The Orisa Principle: Divining African Literary Aesthetics," in *Orality, Literacy and the Fictive Imagination: African and Diasporan Literatures*, edited by Tom Spencer-Walters (Troy, Mich.: Bedford, 1999), pp. 45–70.

Badejo, "The Yoruba and Afro-American Trickster: A Contextual Comparison," *Presence Africaine* (3rd Quarter 1988): 3–17.

Marion Kilson, ed., *Royal Antelope and Spider: West African Mende Tales* (Cambridge, Mass.: Press of the Langdon Associates, 1976).

Isidore Okpewho, ed., *The Oral Performance in Africa* (Ibadan, Nigeria: Spectrum Books, 1990).

LITERATURE: ORAL TRADITIONS

Folklore. West Africa has a large body of folklore. Animal tales are probably the most common, with folktales about the tortoise, rabbit, or spider leading the way. Primarily viewed as entertainment, these stories often served the important purposes of educating children, reinforcing social mores and cultural values, and transmitting the general knowledge and cumulative observations of a given locality. Songs, proverbs, personification, and improvisation played significant roles in these narratives, and listeners quickly identified certain animals with specific characteristics and themes.

A CLEVER MAN

With its question-and-response format, this Mande folktale from what is now Sierra Leone is a good example of the sort of fables told by nonprofessional storytellers. The story not only illustrated the virtue of patience but also educated young people about the value of using intellect to solve problems and demonstrated the importance of understanding the relationships among animals, plants, and human beings.

At one time a man went walking with three things: a goat, a leopard, and hamper of cassava. They journeyed to three days. During this journey neither the man nor the animals ate anything; they all became extremely hungry. They continued to travel until they reached a large river. There was a law about crossing this river: a person could take only one load at a time across the river.

The man reached the river crossing with the goat, the leopard, and hamper of cassava. If the man crossed the river with the hamper of cassava, he would leave the goat and the leopard together, and the leopard would eat the goat. If he crossed the river with the leopard, the cassava and the goat would remain together, and the goat would eat the cassava.

What did he do?

When the man reached the river crossing and the law was explained to him, he first crossed the river with the goat and tied it up on the far side of the river before returning for the leopard. When the man crossed the river with the leopard, he untied the goat, recrossed the river with it, and tied it up again. Then he took the hamper of cassava, crossed the river with it, and placed it near the leopard, which would not eat the cassava. The man recrossed the river, untied the goat, and brought it across the river. Then the man continued his journey with his three possessions. This man showed cleverness by preventing the creatures from eating one another. He safely reached his destination with all three possessions. This is why cleverness is desirable.

Source: Marion Kilson, ed., *Royal Antelope and Spider: West African Mende Tales* (Cambridge, Mass.: Press of the Langdon Associates, 1976), p. 47.

THE GRIOT'S JOB

In the epic of Sundiata, a griot explains the importance of his role as historian and how his profession has been passed down in his family.

I am a griot. It is I, Djeli Mamoudou Kouyate, son of Bintou Kouyate and Djeli Kedian Kouyate, master in the art of eloquence. Since time immemorial the Kouyates have been in the service of the Keita princes of Mali; we are vessels of speech, we are the repositories which harbour secrets many centuries old. The art of eloquence has no secrets for us; without us the names of kings would vanish into oblivion, we are the memory of mankind; by the spoken word we bring to life the deeds and exploits of kings for younger generations.

I derive my knowledge from my father Djeli Kedian, who also got it from his father; history holds no mystery for us; we teach to the vulgar just as much as we want to teach them; for it is we who keep the keys to the twelve doors of Mali.

I know the list of all the sovereigns who succeeded to the throne of Mali. I know how the black people divided into tribes, for my father bequeathed to me all his learning; I know why such and such is called Kamara, another Keita, and yet another Sibibe or Traore; every name has a meaning, a secret import.

I teach kings the history of their ancestors so that the lives of the ancients might serve them as an example, for the world is old but the future springs from the past.

My word is pure and free of all untruth; it is the word of my father, it is the word of my father's father. I will give you my father's words just as I received them; royal griots do not know what lying is. When a quarrel breaks out between tribes it is we who settle the difference, for we are the depositories of oaths which the ancestors swore.

Source: D. T. Niane, *Sundiata: An Epic of Old Mali*, translated by G. D. Pickett (London: Longmans, 1965), p. 1.

For example, the tortoise, rabbit, and spider are usually perceived as physically weak members of the animal kingdom, but have strengths as well. As folkloric characters, these animals are broadly distributed throughout the region. All three are witty and humorous and often get the better of more powerful opponents. It is not difficult to understand their appeal to children, and the tales offer subtle encouragement for children to face their own challenges.

Other Secular Literature. Similar to folklore but differentiated by form and purpose, secular tales of origin, fables, songs, and stories with communal themes were usually narrated by nonprofessional storytellers. These literary texts often suggest indirectly migratory or relational connections among different towns, peoples, or villages. Tales of origin deal with natural features such as rivers, hills, or celestial bodies. They may entertain children, but they sometimes subtly teach limitations and restrictions to movement or warnings as well. At one time, these tales may have communicated common village or regional concerns and subtle messages about intraregional conflicts, or they may have augmented familial warnings about local animals and environmental dangers. The body of West African secular tales is dominated by stories with communal themes interspersed with proverbs and songs. These stories of life-cycle events such as births, naming ceremonies, puberty rites, marriages, and burials are woven into the fiber of folklore. Concepts of beauty, social satire, gender conflict, human foibles, and love of family, friends, and culture all resonate in West African folkloric traditions.

Epic Traditions. Epics are usually narrated by professional literary artists. Two historical narratives, the thirteenth-century epic of Sundiata, who ruled the Empire of Mali circa 1230–1255, and the Ozidi Saga of the Ijo of Nigeria, exemplify the complex oral literary traditions in West Africa.

Sundiata. The historic narrative of Sundiata was the preserve of a select class of professional literary artists, known as jeli (in Mande), or griots (in French), sworn to guarantee the veracity of their narrative. Nevertheless, they were expected to present the truth in an aesthetically pleasing and linguistically eloquent manner. In their narrative, history and art converged to stimulate the imagination, inspire the soul, and inform the mind. The narrative of Sundiata meets those cultural demands.

The Ozidi Saga. The Ozidi Saga of the Ijo people of southeast Nigeria is set in the ancient city-state of Orua, an Ijo town in the delta region of Nigeria. The story line focuses on competition for kingship and the treachery that follows. Filled with courtly intrigue, attempts to preserve family honor, and individual tragedy, this narrative is recounted over seven days. During this time the storyteller portrays eighty scenes or situations for an average of four hours per day, using spoken words, song, dance, mime, and various theatrical conventions. A distinctive cultural aspect of this epic is the mandate that the narrator must finish telling it in Orua, its place of origin, every time it is told. In his introduction to the epic, J. P. Clark-Bekederemo calls the Ozidi Saga "as much drama as narrative."

Proverbs. West African speakers of languages such as Wolof, Bambara, Yoruba, Igbo, and Akan consider conversations filled with proverbs to be linguistically rich and eloquent. The importance of proverbs in daily and ritual communications is expressed in a Yoruba proverb that says, "Owe l'esin oro, bi oro ba sonu owe li a fi nwa a" (Proverbs are the horses of communication, when the conversation goes astray, we steer it back with proverbs).

POWERFUL WOMEN IN THE OZIDI SAGA

This excerpt from the Ozidi Saga extols the power of women, as Ozidi's mother, Oreame, seeks to protect her young son from Azeza and his allies, who have killed Ozidi's father. Ozidi's grandmother also protects him by various methods, and God (Tamara in Ijo language) is also female.

Azeza arose once more.
"I am Azeza! Day has broken again!
Whatever day has broken is the day.
All night I exercised myself and now it is dawn.
This is the day I shall do battle.
Yes, Ozidi after all is but a boy.
His father himself fought with us until he tired, and did us no harm.
And when at that place we killed his father, I myself with my stick was first to hit him over the head, before the others fell on him.
Others were all scared of him and running away.
Yes, as I have this one eye, a twenty-eyed man is not my match.
The way my one leg is, a ten-legged man is no match for me.
The way my one hand is, this one hand of mine really is a miracle."
He stomped round and round.
So terrible was his show of force that Oreame flew off straight to God—scaled the skies until she arrived and asked God:
"O God!"
"Yes!"
"This battle my son is fighting with the people of Orua, what do you yourself think of it? Do you think that my son too should die on top of his father's head, do you think so?"
"Oh, Oreame, don't you see the fight is a just one in your hand? Go back and seek your battle.
Who knows nothing and comes to you, that person is your animal."
So she assured her.
After being assured, she said:
"Truly, O Mother! It is you molded us all.
I kneel to you."
Next, at one drop, she descended to earth—like wind she flew circling over rooftops and alighting [calling aloud]:
"Oh Ozidi, my son, my son!

Hand-all-man, foot-all-man, my son, my son, my son! O fit-to-fight, my son, my son, my son!
O fit-to-be-Captain, my son, my son, my son! O Ozidi, rise, rise, rise!"

Source: J. P. Clark-Bekederemo, ed. and trans., *The Ozidi Saga: Collected and Translated from the Ijo of Okabou Ojobolo* (Washington, D.C.: Howard University Press, 1991), pp. 82–83.

From the traditions of the Bambara griot to conversations at the social gatherings of families and friends, most West Africans revere the power of the word and hold in awe the culturally sophisticated speaker. In many instances speech is tailored to the status of the listener or the significance of the topic. More than just pithy sayings, proverbs transmit cultural ideals and enrich discourse. Hyperbole, personification, alliteration, and mythopoetic phraseology provide linguistic agility and humor. In their original languages West African proverbs are poetic and musical. For example, the Yoruba proverb "Amoron mo owe ni ilaja oron" (A wise person who knows proverbs can settle disputes) is both alliterative and lyrical in its expression of cultural philosophy. Proverbs are expressed not only verbally but also with Yoruba dundun drums and Akan horns, both of which are known for their ability to mimic the sound of human speech. The literary quality and style is aurally pleasing and rhythmically balanced through voice and instrument. For these reasons, the most culturally salient proverbs reverberate in drum and horn language as well as in artistic forms.

Sources:
J. O. Ajibola, *Owe Yoruba* (Ibadan, Nigeria: Oxford University Press, 1968).

J. P. Clark-Bekederemo, ed. and trans., *The Ozidi Saga: Collected and Translated from the Ijo of Okabou Ojobolo* (Washington, D.C.: Howard University Press, 1991).

Marion Kilson, ed., *Royal Antelope and Spider: West African Mende Tales* (Cambridge, Mass.: Press of the Langdon Associates, 1976).

D. T. Niane, *Sundiata: An Epic of Old Mali*, translated by G. D. Pickett (London: Longmans, 1965).

Kwesi Yankah, "Proverb Speaking As a Creative Process: The Akan of Ghana," *DeProverbio.com*, 6, no. 2 (2000) <www.deproverbio.com/DPjournal/DP,6,2,00/YANKAH/AKAN.html>.

MUSIC AS SPEECH

Dundun Drums. In his book on Yoruba drumming, Akin Euba explains that dundun drums mimic human speech, specifically Oyo or standard Yoruba dialect, thereby making the speech of the drums comprehensible to all Yoruba. Thus, the drums communicate proverbs, poetry, satire, and social commentary through actual words, not as code. Presenting a compelling argument for dating the beginning of the Yoruba dundun tradition to around the fourteenth century, Euba explains that memorized drum texts form a cumulative body of knowledge that serves as source materials for other literary forms and performance arts. Dundun drummers are particularly adept at speaking in proverbs that are relevant to particular contexts. In fact, as Euba points out, drum proverbs are used to elicit audience participation.

Akan Horns. Also known for their "talking drums," the Akan use ceremonial horns, Mmintia, to communicate in a language understood by Akan speakers. As Peter Kwasi Sarpong has pointed out, their language is "idiomatic, symbolic, and proverbial." Unlike the dundun drums, which are used for ceremonial and nonceremonial occasions, the Akan

AKAN DRUM POETRY

J. H. Kwabena Nketia has described the poetry of Akan talking drums:

The development of the poetic tradition has not been confined to the spoken voice. A great deal of Akan heroic poetry is conveyed through the medium of horns, pipes, and drums. Although drums are used in Akan society for making a limited number of announcements, they are also vehicles of literature. On state occasions poems of special interest are drummed to the chief and the community as a whole. These poems run into many scores of verses and fall into four groups.

First there are the poems of the drum prelude called the Awakening, *Anyaneanyane.* When a drummer is playing these poems he begins by announcing himself, closing the opening with the formula: "I am learning, let me succeed" or "I am addressing you, and you will understand."

He then addresses in turn the components of the drum—the wood of the drum, the drum pegs, strings, the animal that provides the hide of the drum: the elephant or the duiker.

Next he addresses the earth, God, the witch, the cock and the clockbird, ancestor drummers, and finally the god Tano. The cock and the clockbird are frequently referred to in drum texts because of the alert they give. They are like drummers who have to keep vigil while others are asleep.

When I was going to bed, I was not sleepy.
When I felt like sleeping, my eyes never closed.
All night he stood in his coop,
While children lay in bed asleep.
Early in the morning he was hailed:
"Good morning to you, Mr. Cock."
The Cock crows in the morning.
The Cock rises to crow before the crack of dawn.
I am learning, let me succeed.
Kokokyinaka Asamoa, the Clockbird,
How do we greet you?
We greet you with "Anyaado,"
We hail you as the Drummer's child.
The Drummer's child sleeps and awakes with the dawn.
I am learning, let me succeed.

The second group of texts are in the nature of panegyrics or eulogies. Abridged forms incorporating the names, praise appellations of individuals and greetings or messages are used in social situations—for example, in a dance arena. The chief use of these eulogies, however, is for honoring kings and ancestor kings on ceremonial occasions when their origin, parentage and noble deeds are recalled against a background of tribal history.

The third group of poems are those used for heralding the movements of a chief, for greeting people, for announcing emergencies and so on. When a chief is drinking at a state ceremony, the drummer drums a running commentary. If it is gin, he drums as follows:

Chief they are bringing it.
They are bringing it.
They are bringing it to you.
Chief you are about to drink imported liquor.
Chief pour some on the ground.
He is sipping it slowly and gradually.
He is sipping it in little draughts.

The last group of poems are the proverbs. These may be used separately or they may be incorporated into other poems or into drum pieces intended for dancing. Here are some proverbs of the Akantam dance:

Rustling noise by the wayside
Means what creature?
The wood pigeon, the wood pigeon.
Wood pigeon Seniampon,
He goes along the path eating grains of millet.
Condolences, wood pigeon.
    Duiker Adawurampon Kwamena
    Who told the Duiker to get hold of his sword?
    The tail of the Duiker is short,
    But he is able to brush himself with it.
"I am bearing fruit," says Pot Herb.
"I am bearing fruit," says Garden Egg.
Logs of firewood are lying on the farm,
But it is the faggot that makes the fire flare.
    Duiker Adawurampon Kwamena
    Who told the Duiker to get hold of his sword?
    The tail of the Duiker is short,
    But he is able to brush himself with it.
"Pluck the feathers off this tortoise."
Tortoise: "Fowl, do you hear that?"
    Duiker Adawurampon Kwamena
    Who told the Duiker to get hold of his sword?
    The tail of the Duiker is short,
    But he is able to brush himself with it.

The origin and storehouse of Akan poetry is the individual member of Akan society brought up on the traditions of his people, the individual who from childhood has been taught or has learned through social experience to use certain words and expressions, to regard some as beautiful, deep, proper, improper, correct, bad and so on; the individual who has been taught to understand and use the proverbs in his language, who has been taught to sing cradlesongs, dance songs, war songs and love songs, to drum and dance or to appreciate drumming and dancing; the individual who under emotional stress would quote a proverb, a familiar saying, a line or two of traditional oral poetry. But the function of the individual was not merely to act as a carrier of a tradition. He was also to maintain it by using it, by re-creating it, for each time he performed his set pieces he was in a sense giving the poetry of his people a new life.

Source: J. H. Kwabena Nketia, "Drum Poetry of The Akan People," in *A Treasury of African Folklore,* edited by Harold Courlander (New York: Crown, 1975), pp. 95–97.

Bronze figure of a royal musician, Kingdom of Benin, circa 1400 (British Museum, London)

Mmintia are reserved specifically for ceremonies for a king or chief. These horns chronicle the history and daily events of Akan leadership, including information about the queen mothers and their lineage responsibilities. Because their language is dominated by idiomatic and historical references, Akan horn messages are understood by a relatively small number of listeners.

Sources:

Akin Euba, *Yoruba Drumming: The Dundun Tradition* (Bayreuth, West Germany: Eckhard Breitinger, Bayreuth University, 1990).

Peter Kwasi Sarpong, *The Ceremonial Horns of the Ashanti* (Accra, Ghana: Sedco, 1990).

Kwesi Yankah, "Voicing and Drumming the Poetry of Praise: The Case for Aural Literature," in *Interdisciplinary Dimensions of African Literature,* edited by Kofi Anyidoho, Abioseh M. Porter, Daniel Racine, and Janice Spleth (Washington, D.C.: Three Continents Press, 1985), pp. 139–158.

THEATER AND DANCE

Festivals. African festivals integrate instrumental music, song, dance, mime, costuming, fine arts, and narrative performances. Preparations for a festival employ the talents of skilled artists and craftspeople. Carvers, smiths, weavers, cultural historians, poets, musicians, and dancers carefully plan annual celebrations and ritual performances. Most festivals occur over several days and offer an array of sacred and secular events at several venues. Festivals often attract people who have married outside their community, providing an occasion for families to reunite and for the ruler and his extensive organization to reconnect with his constituency. In a ritual context, festivals are a time of communal and individual healing, spiritual renewal, thanksgiving, and societal cleansing. Archaeological evidence, as well as the

Female and male Chi Wara headdresses, worn in a traditional Bambara dance-drama performed before each planting and harvest season (Art Institute of Chicago)

chronicles of the earliest Arab and European travelers, document that West African societies have engaged in these forms of spectacle for hundreds of years. Although scholars cannot locate the origins of West African ethnic festivals in specific periods, it is often possible to date the historic events they celebrate. Because the ritual and secular performances described by anthropologists and missionaries between the eighteenth and twentieth centuries allude to narratives that recount origins, migrations, conquests, defeats, and social reconstructions that occurred before 1590, it is considered likely that modern festival performances follow traditions established in ancient times.

The Osun Festival. The Osun Festival, which occurs annually in July and August in Osogbo, Nigeria, celebrates the founder of Osogbo, who was one of the wives of Shango, the fourth king of Old Oyo, who reigned around the fifteenth century. Both these historical personages became part of the Yoruba pantheon, Osun as a fertility goddess and Shango as the god of thunder and lightning. Osogbo grew into a bustling city that has served for many years as a link among the major Yoruba centers of spiritual and commercial activities, such as Ile-Ife, Ibadan, Ijebu, and Ilorin. The festival celebrates Osun as a woman of keen business acumen, a dyer, and an owner of brass, parrot feathers, and beads. As a sacred icon, Osun represents the quintessential portal of human existence through which life is given. She possesses a cool female principle whose nature balances the fiery male principle of Shango. A major purpose of the annual festival is to galvanize the community around its historic and cultural achievements, to inform the young about their heritage and the meaning of life, and to celebrate their rich traditions. Festivals such as these include re-enactments of important historic events, recitations of traditional poetry and epics, and the chanting of the oral praise poems known in Yoruba as *orile oriki*, which remind the ruling families and their subjects of their individual and collective responsibilities.

Dance-Drama. Described by early Arab and European travelers and traders, dance-drama has been an important and highly respected performance art form throughout Western Africa for many centuries. Dance-drama celebrates the ability of the dancer's body to "speak" to the audience and to engage in "dialogue" with musicians. Dancers, master drummers and other musicians, and singers communicated cultural histories and other social narratives through the integration of body movement, costume, instrumentation, song, and mime. In some instances dance-drama presentations also include the artistic efforts of community carvers, weavers, and drum makers. The carved-wood Chi Wara headpieces made by the Bambara, the jembe drums of the Wolof, or the egungun masks of the Yoruba dramatically enhance the aesthetics of performance in a manner that emphasizes the movement and kinetic energy of the human form.

Ancient Roots. By studying ancient artifacts, archaeologists and historians have discerned that dance-drama dates to the earliest years of settlement and cultural diffusion in the West African region. Images and icons of dancers and musicians are found in ancient wall paintings and carvings. Depictions of masquerading dancers are particularly prevalent. Rock paintings found in the middle Sahara and areas toward the Sahel and savanna regions illustrate that wearing masks and dancing are truly ancient performance arts. In these paintings, dancers portraying hunters are predominant, leading to the conclusion that subjects of these early dance-dramas were the exploits of hunter-heroes.

The Chi Wara. Performed at planting and harvest seasons, the Chi Wara dance-drama of the Bambara is an important example of a performance art associated with agriculture. According to Herbert Cole, the dancers perform "in the fields during hoeing contests and in the village square." Carved male and female Chi Wara (antelope) figures are worn atop the heads of the male dancers, who are completely covered with raffia. They dance in pairs representing male and female, the ultimate balance of the reproductive power of the universe, and reinforcing the Bambara worldview that bespeaks the mutuality of male-female fertility and survival in both earthly and spiritual realms. Bent forward throughout their performance, the dancers must exhibit agility and fitness as well as mastery of choreography to meet aesthetic and spiritual expectations of their audience. In fact, the spiritual and secular dimensions of Chi Wara dance-drama are equally significant. According to Cole, "Chi Wara headpieces link humans with the earth, sun, and water; reflect the union and cooperation of male and female; stimulate the growth of grain; and exemplify the virtues of primordial farming success and its repetition today."

Sources:

E. V. Asihene, *Apoo Festival* (Tema, Ghana: Ghana Publishing, 1980).

Diedre L. Badejo, *Osun Seegesi: The Elegant Deity of Wealth, Power, and Femininity* (Lawrenceville, N.J.: Africa World Press, 1996).

Peter Badejo, "The Bori Spirit Possession Dance," thesis, UCLA, 1980.

Eckhard Breitinger, ed., *Theater and Performance in Africa: Intercultural Perspectives* (Bayreuth: Bayreuth University, 1994).

Herbert M. Cole, *I Am Not Myself: the Art of African Masquerade*, Monograph Series, no. 26 (Los Angeles: Museum of Cultural History, University of California, Los Angeles, 1985).

Nehemia Levtzion, "The Early State of the Western Sudan to 1500," in *History of West Africa*, 2 volumes, edited by J. F. A. Ajayi and Michael Crowder (London: Longman, 1971, 1974), I: 120–157.

Isidore Okpewho, ed., *The Oral Performance in Africa* (Ibadan, Nigeria: Spectrum Books, 1990).

John Pemberton III and Funso S. Afolayan, *Yoruba Sacred Kingship: "A Power like that of the Gods"* (Washington & London: Smithsonian Institution Press, 1996).

SIGNIFICANT PERSON

ABU ISHAQ IBRAHIM AL-SAHILI

CIRCA 1290-1346
ARCHITECT

Early Life. Born in Granada, Andalusia (Muslim Spain), Abu Ishaq Ibrahim al-Sahili studied the arts and law in his native land. Known as a gifted poet, al-Sahili belonged to a well-established merchant family. His father was also known for his mastery of jurisprudence, especially inheritance law. Al-Sahili gained a reputation as a man of letters and an eloquent poet in Andalusia, which by the fourteenth century was known for its rich cultural and religious diversity. Jewish, Christian, and Islamic influences spread throughout the Iberian Peninsula and into North Africa and the Western Sahel. Al-Sahili left Granada around 1321 and began to travel in Egypt, Syria, Iraq, and Yemen.

Architect. In 1324 al-Sahili met the ruler of Mali, Mansa Musa, during his pilgrimage to Mecca. According to the chronicler al-Sa'di, Mansa Musa was so delighted by the poetry and narrative talents of al-Sahili that he invited him to return to Mali with him. Al-Sahili settled in the growing intellectual and commercial center of Timbuktu, where he built an audience chamber for Mansa Musa, demonstrating his talent as a skilled craftsman. Citing Ibn Battuta, J. O. Hunwick notes that the architectural style of the audience chamber resembled that of the Alhambra in Granada more than the local architecture. So impressed was Musa that he engaged the Andalusian to construct his new residence and the Great, or Djingereyber, Mosque in Timbuktu. While the residence has been lost to time, the Great Mosque still stands in Timbuktu. Hunwick posits that the "rounded arch, so reminiscent of the architecture of Muslim Andalusia, may, therefore have been an innovation of al-Sahili." Abu Ishaq Al-Sahili died in 1346 and is buried in Timbuktu. Although it is believed that he never married, he is said to have fathered several children who later resettled in Walata.

Sources:

J. O. Hunwick, "An Andalusian in Mali: A Contribution to the Biography of Abu Ishaq al-Sahili," *Paideuma*, 36 (1990): 59–66.

Hunwick, "The Islamic Manuscript Heritage of Timbuktu," unpublished paper, Inaugural Symposium of the Sudanic/Maghaaribi Studies Unit on Africa's Intellectual Caravan/Vilad as-Sudan Wa'L Maghaarbi, Poughkeepsie, N.Y.: Vassar College, 7–9 November 2002.

Hunwick, *Timbuktu and the Songhay Empire: al-Sa'di's Ta'rikh al-Sudan down to 1613 and other Contemporary Documents* (Leiden: Brill, 1999).

DOCUMENTARY SOURCES

Al-Bakri, *Kitab al-masalik wa-'l-mamalik* (Book of Routes and Realms, 1068)—An Arabic account of the culture, politics, and geography of the Empire of Ghana.

Ibn Battuta (1304 – circa 1378), *Rihlah* (Travels) — A travel account by a wide-ranging North African Muslim traveler, who visited the Empire of Mali in 1353, recording his observations of cultural and religious practices, customs, everyday life, politics, economic relations, and topography.

Mahmoud al-Kati, *Tarikh al-Fattash* (The Chronicle of the Seeker After Knowledge, started 1519)—The first history of the region by a West African, an important

contribution to the written literature of the region and a valuable source of information on its culture, especially in the Empires of Mali and Songhai.

Leo Africanus, *Descrittione dell'Africa* (Description of Africa, 1550)—An account of a Granadan's early-sixteenth-century travels in the Western Sudan, with information on the culture of Songhai.

'Abd al-Rahman al-Sa'di, *Tarikh al-Sudan* (Chronicle of the Western Sudan, circa 1650)—The second West African history by a native of the region with accounts of the Songhai Empire and nearby regions from their origins through 1655.

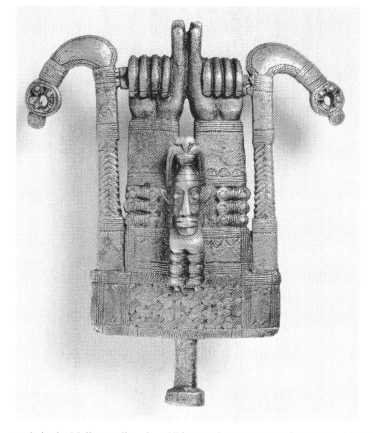

A royal ornament made in the Malian trading city of Djenné, circa 1000–1500 (Musée Barbier-Mueller, Geneva)

Seventeenth-century Akan brass gold weights, scale, and gold-dust box used in a measurement system devised by
Nana Obunumankoma, ruler of Bono, during the fifteenth century (Fowler Museum of Cultural History,
University of California, Los Angeles)

CHAPTER FOUR

COMMUNICATION, TRANSPORTATION, AND EXPLORATION

by CAROLE SHELLEY YATES

CONTENTS

Sidebars and tables are listed in italics.

IMPORTANT EVENTS OF 500-1590

500*
- Griots (storytellers, clan historians, and poets) preserve histories of clans and royal dynasties.
- West Africans begin exploring the Atlantic Ocean, and some reach South America.

700–800*
- The city of Gao, in the ancient kingdom of Mali, reaches its peak as a center of trade and cultural exchange.

700–1000
- The city of Djenné on the Niger River is at its peak as a trading center.

850*
- The powerful Empire of Ghana (in present-day southeastern Mauritania and southwestern Mali) engages in international trade in gold and salt.
- Islam and Arabic writing arrive in West Africa, brought by Muslim Berber traders and Islamic scholars from North Africa.

900*
- Trade routes are established to link the Lake Chad region to Tripoli, Cairo, and Mecca.

1000*
- Hausa and Yoruba states are founded.

1000*–1099*
- African slaves begin to appear in European countries.

1054
- Almoravid Berbers capture Audaghost, an important market town northwest of Timbuktu, and invade the Empire of Ghana.

1068
- Relying on reports of travelers and merchants, Spanish Muslim scholar al-Bakri writes a history of the Empire of Ghana.

1076
- Kumbi, the capital of Ghana, falls to the Almoravids.

1200
- The state of Benin is founded.

* DENOTES CIRCA DATE

IMPORTANT EVENTS OF 500-1590

1230
- Sundiata, a Malinke prince, defeats the Susu tribe, creating the foundation for the Empire of Mali.

1240
- Sundiata conquers the Empire of Ghana.
- Dunama II Dibbalemi, king of Kanem, sets up a Quranic (Koranic) school in Cairo for Kanuri students living there.

1255
- The Empire of Mali controls the gold and salt trade, with the city of Gao becoming a major commercial power.

1300
- The Yoruba cities of Ile-Ife and Benin thrive through trade with camel caravans.

1311
- Abubakari II of Mali sets off with two thousand ships, sailing west on the Atlantic Ocean and possibly reaching the Americas.

1312-1337
- During the reign of Mansa Musa, Mali expands across the western and central regions of West Africa.

1324
- Mansa Musa makes a pilgrimage to Mecca, attracting the notice of many Africans and Europeans with his great wealth.

1330
- The University of Sankore is established at the Sankore mosque in Timbuktu.

1353
- North African Muslim writer Ibn Battuta visits Mali and records his observations.

1375*
- Mali goes into decline.

1400*-1499*
- Royal delegations are regularly exchanged between West and North Africa and between Kanem-Bornu and Mediterranean and North African courts.
- Akan written script is used on gold weights.

* DENOTES CIRCA DATE

IMPORTANT EVENTS OF 500-1590

1415
- Timbuktu and Djenné have become great centers of Muslim scholarship.
- Quranic scholars from North Africa are hired to read, write, and teach Arabic in West African royal courts.

1430
- Portuguese mariners explore the Atlantic coast of West Africa. They are soon followed by other European explorers.

1441
- A Portuguese ship loaded with slaves returns to Europe, beginning the Atlantic slave trade.

1447
- Genoan traveler Antonio Malfante stays at Tuat (in present-day Algeria), a commercial center where traders from Tunis and Egypt exchange goods for West African gold.

1455
- Portuguese explorers set up sugarcane production on the islands of Madeira, off the Atlantic coast of West Africa.

1456
- Exploring the Atlantic coast of West Africa for Portugal, Venetian trader Alvise Cà da Mosto (Cadamosto) discovers the Cape Verde Islands, which become a holding place where many Africans are imprisoned before they are shipped as slaves to the Americas.

1464-1492
- The Songhai Empire is ruled by Sunni Ali, who asserts control over the main trade routes.

1468
- Sunni Ali conquers Timbuktu.

1471
- Portuguese explorers reach the Bight of Benin and establish a settlement at Elmina.

1493-1528
- During the reign of Songhai emperor Askia Muhammad, the city of Timbuktu reaches its height as a center of learning.

* DENOTES CIRCA DATE

IMPORTANT EVENTS OF 500-1590

1495
- Askia Muhammad makes a pilgrimage to Mecca and Medina with an army of one hundred foot soldiers and five hundred men riding horses or camels, displaying his great wealth and religious devotion.

1498
- On his third voyage Christopher Columbus finds evidence that suggests an African presence in the New World.

1500
- Trade expands between Europeans and Africans living along the Gulf of Guinea.

1507
- Trade expands between Sudan and Guinea.

1513
- Vasco Núñez de Balboa sees black people in Panama and believes they have come from Africa.

1513-1515
- Leo Africanus visits the Songhai Empire and later writes of sub-Saharan Africa, in a work that is translated into languages other than Arabic. Leo describes the uses of camel caravans and dugout canoes.

1518
- Spanish slave traders ship the first African slaves to the West Indies.

1519
- Mahmoud al-Kati of Timbuktu begins writing *Tarikh al-Fattash* (The Chronicle of the Seeker After Knowledge), the first history of West Africa by a black man.
- African slaves are imported to Spain.

1534
- Mali sends an ambassador to Portugal.

1544
- The Songhai Empire successfully defeats a Moroccan invasion force but continues to be plagued by northern forces and is finally conquered by Morocco in 1591.

1550
- European sea merchants and African coast states establish trading partnerships.

* DENOTES CIRCA DATE

IMPORTANT EVENTS OF 500-1590

1553
• English traders visit Benin for the first time. They bring metal pots and pans and buy a load of peppercorns.

1569
• 'Abd al-Rahman al-Sa'di is born. In the 1600s he writes *Tarikh al-Sudan* (Chronicle of the Western Sudan), one of the earliest and most important histories of West Africa.

1571-1603
• During his reign Idris Alooma greatly expands the Kanem-Bornu Empire, establishing diplomatic relations with Tripoli and Cairo and exchanging gifts with the Ottoman emperor in Constantinople (Istanbul).

1575
• Hausa states revolt against the Songhai Empire.

* DENOTES CIRCA DATE

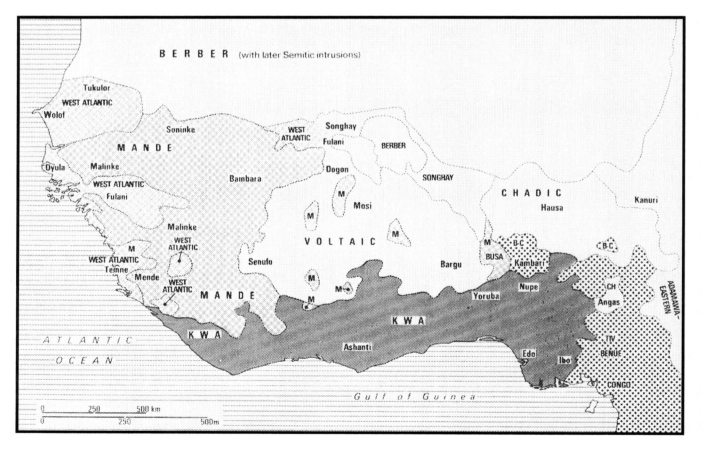

Map locating West African language groups (from M. El Fasi and I. Hrbek, eds., *Africa from the Seventh Century to the Eleventh Century*, volume 3 of *General History of Africa*, 1988)

OVERVIEW

The "Bright Age." While Europe was going through the Dark Ages and Middle Ages and then entering its Renaissance, West Africa was in its "Bright Age." The thriving kingdom of Ghana, founded near the Senegal and Niger Rivers, reached its peak in the tenth and eleventh centuries. Like the later West African empires of Mali and Songhai, Ghana had all the elements of a strong civilization, including a formal government, industry, urbanism, religion, arts, and commerce. These advanced civilizations south of the Sahara Desert were founded by indigenous peoples, not by Muslims from the north or by people from the Mediterranean region.

Historical Sources. The history of the West African kingdoms was passed on by oral traditions and some written sources that included what was called "the knowledge" of the people. Much of this information was subsequently lost. Many of the historical sources available to modern scholars are accounts by writers of Arabic, some of whom never visited West Africa. Often they based their information on stories from caravan traders or travelers, or on previous Arabic texts. The earliest firsthand Arabic account was Ibn Battuta's work about his 1353 visit to the kingdom of Mali. Later, in the early 1500s, the author known to Europeans as Leo Africanus wrote a firsthand account of communication, transportation, and exploration in the ancient kingdoms of West Africa based on his visit to the region in 1513–1515.

A River Lifeline. West Africa stretches from the Atlantic Ocean on the west to Lake Chad on the east and from the Sahel (the semidesert area on the southern fringe of the Sahara Desert) on the north to the Gulf of Guinea on the south. The major rivers of this region—the Niger, Senegal, Benue, and Volta—were the chief means of communication, transportation, and exploration during the period 500–1590. On these rivers natives carried their merchandise (primarily gold) north to trade with the Muslim nomad caravans that traveled south across the Sahara. The rivers also facilitated communication and served as a water source for agricultural and animal husbandry. Harvested grains, fruits, nuts, and cotton—as well as livestock and other products and raw materials—were also transported and traded along the rivers.

World Connections. Before the seventh century the dromedary camel's adaptability to desert travel had made possible extensive trans-Saharan trade. Trade routes crisscrossing North and West Africa were well established by the tenth and eleventh centuries, providing a direct commercial link that allowed the people of West Africa to trade their gold, kola nuts, cloth, and other goods for salt and commercial European products. North African Berber nomads with their flocks of camels were the first connection through which West Africans traded their gold for copper from north of the Sahara. The trade routes also brought West Africans news from North Africa and its Muslim cultures, which also included elements of Roman and Greek civilizations.

Muslim Influence. As reliable means of transportation increased the traffic on the trans-Saharan trade routes in West Africa, new religious and cultural ideas made their way along with trade goods from North to West Africa. By the end of the eleventh century many West African states situated along caravan routes had adopted Islam. The trade routes also brought Islamic scholars to cities such as Timbuktu and Djenné. In these places, Africans in high positions learned to read and write Arabic. Their literacy put the large West African empires on a more equal footing with North Africa, allowing better communication and influencing the intellectual life along the Niger River valley and in its primary cities. The urban elite was introduced to Arabic ideas and the study of astrology, astronomy, geography, and other sciences, as well as mathematics and grammar. Still, Arabic studies affected only a small fraction of West Africans and did not incorporate any of their native languages or culture. Most people of West Africa retained their own religions. Islam did not spread to the countryside until the latter part of the sixteenth century. Contrary to the beliefs of some Muslim writers of the period, West African empires did not become Muslim states.

European Exploration. Beginning in the fifteenth century, European exploration along the Atlantic coast of West Africa, which they called the "Atlantic Mediterranean," strongly influenced the destiny of West Africa. Europeans were attracted to West Africa by stories of its gold, and they wanted large expanses of land for growing crops such as sugarcane and wheat. In 1434, after the Portuguese, French, and Italians built ships capable of navigating in the strong currents and shallow waters around Cape Bojador (in the modern nation of Western Sahara), explorers were able to get closer to the source of gold along the Gulf of Guinea, the so-called Gold Coast near the Akan Forest. Some sugarcane production facilities were established in the 1450s on islands off the coast of North Africa. By this time Europeans had also established a base for the Atlantic slave trade.

Exploration by West Africans. Before Europeans began exploring West Africa, West African mariners were sailing westward on the Atlantic Ocean. Modern scholars, including Ivan Van Sertima, J. A. Rogers, and Leo Wiener, have uncovered evidence that seamen from Mali set off on voyages of exploration that took them to the Americas long before Christopher Columbus. When Columbus landed on the South American coast during his third voyage (1498), he and his men found evidence that suggested an African presence there. Other early explorers of the Americas also recorded stories about black mariners who had preceded them.

The Atlantic Slave Trade. The European practice of trading goods for African slaves developed not long after Portuguese explorers arrived in West Africa. For hundreds of years the Atlantic slave trade took millions of Africans away from their homes. From about 1530 to 1600, between two thousand and four thousand Africans were exported each year. In the 1600s Dutch, Danish, Swedish, and German companies joined the Portuguese, French, and English slave traders who were already operating in West Africa. By the second half of the seventeenth century, more than twenty thousand slaves were taken each year. The numbers increased in the eighteenth century to nearly sixty thousand slaves a year from all over Africa.

From Stability to Chaos. The 1054 invasion of Ghana by the fanatical Almoravid Muslims from North Africa set in motion centuries of change, during which stable social and political systems disintegrated into chaos. Some tribes fled to the south to avoid destruction. Other groups split off from Ghana and became part of the kingdom of Mali, which flourished in the thirteenth and fourteenth centuries, and the Songhai kingdom that followed it. Peoples who resisted involvement in these successor empires were continually pushed southward throughout this period. For example, the Akan group—which includes the Ashanti, the Fanti, and the Akim—moved south from the savanna region of West Africa to the coastal region of what is now the modern nation of Ghana to avoid being taken over by other tribes and to trade directly with the Portuguese. Other tribes also moved south to the Gulf of Guinea. Some scholars have connected this breakdown of social stability and constant uprooting of peoples to the success of the slave trade, which depended on the success of dominant tribes in capturing people who were not part of their clan or ethnic group.

TOPICS IN COMMUNICATION, TRANSPORTATION, AND EXPLORATION

COMMUNICATION: ORAL AND NONVERBAL TRADITIONS

The First Historians and Teachers. Long before the eighth century, when Muslim scholars began writing histories of West Africa in Arabic, the ancient kingdoms of West Africa relied on the oral tradition to pass on their histories. These accounts of villages and clans and genealogies of ruling families were kept by people now known as *griots,* a French word meaning "traditional minstrel," which probably replaced African words such as *dieli* in the Bambara language. Griots served as oral historians, storytellers, poets, dancers, musicians, and actors, teaching the clan its history and keeping the memories of their people. Each clan or village had its own griot. Royal families often hired griots to preserve their personal stories and events of their dynasty. According to an ancient Soninke epic, the first griot known by name was Gassire, who composed a praise song, or *pui,* that is said to recount the origins of the kingdom of Ghana. According to the North African Muslim traveler Ibn Battuta, who visited the Empire of Mali in 1353, the griot was one of the most important people in a West African royal court. He wrote that the position of king's griot was passed down in a family within the same clan. A griot acted as his ruler's main aide. When messengers arrived at a court, they gave their messages to the griot. The griot also taught the princes, led court musicians, and conducted ceremonies. Even after there were scribes in Mali, many messages were still communicated orally through griots.

Drum Talk. Drums are the most common instrument in Africa, and historically they played a significant communication role. The main kind of drum in West Africa is a tension drum with an hourglass shape. It is sometimes called a "talking drum" because its rhythm and sound mimic the human voice. Using it as a medium for communication, people in West Africa could communicate rapidly over long distances, reaching places a day's journey away with "drum talk." Especially in the thirteenth through the fifteenth centuries, administrators of the huge West African empires used drum talk to communicate with each other. Griots often used talking drums to describe the kings of an empire. A story passed down about an ill-favored Yoruba king says he first heard the public's demand for his departure through drum talk. Drummers also used drum talk as a musical form. At festivals and ceremonies, a drummer would find a particular rhythm for the dancers and use his rhythmic beating to communicate a message to the audience, who understood the drum vocabulary.

The Meaning of Clothing. Since ancient times the fabrics and patterns of West Africans' clothing have communicated much about the person wearing it. Sometimes the use of a certain kind of cloth conveyed a message. For example, the Asantehene, king of the Ashanti people in the southern forest area of West Africa, historically wore expensive silk cloth, conveying the message that he was "the most wealthy and powerful person in the kingdom." If others had worn the same cloth, they would have been challenging the king's power. This particular kind of cloth could have been kente made by weavers at the Ashanti court from silk fibers traded by Europeans on the trans-Saharan routes. The fabric was handwoven in many colors, patterns, and textures. Al-Bakri, an eleventh-century Spanish-Muslim geographer who based his history of West Africa on information from earlier writers, said that in Ghana only the king and his heir (his sister's son) could wear sewn clothes. Everyone else wrapped their bodies in large pieces of fabric. The designs woven into or printed on fabrics were also a means of communicating information about a person. The Akan peoples of the forested regions on the Gulf of Guinea developed a complex system of symbols that they used on their clothing.

GASSIRE'S LUTE

An ancient Soninke epic, the *Dausi*, explains how Gassire, a prince who is longing to succeed his father as king, became a griot instead. His lute will sing only after it is soaked in the blood of his sons, a metaphorical expression of the idea that great art is born of the artist's pain. The story mentions the four names of Wagadu, the original home of Mande-speaking peoples: Dierra, Agada, Ganna, and Silla.

Gassire's heart was full of longing for the shield of his father, the shield which he could carry only when his father was dead, and also for the sword which he might draw only when he was king. Day by day Gassire's rage and longing grew. Sleep passed him by. Gassire lay, and a jackal gnawed at his heart. Gassire felt the misery climbing into his throat. One night Gassire sprang out of bed, left the house, and went to an old wise man, a man who knew more than other people. He entered the wise man's house and asked: "Kiekorro! When will my father, Nganamba, die and leave me his sword and shield?" The old man said: "Ah, Gassire, Nganamba will die; but he will not leave you his sword and shield! You will carry a lute. Shield and sword shall others inherit. But your lute shall cause the loss of Wagadu! Ah, Gassire!" Gassire said: "Kiekorro, you lie! I see that you are not wise. How can Wagadu be lost when her heroes triumph daily? Kiekorro, you are a fool!" The old wise man said: "Ah, Gassire, you cannot believe me. But your path will lead you to the partridges in the fields, and you will understand what they say, and that will be your way and the way of Wagadu."

Hoooh! Dierra, Agada, Ganna, Silla! Hoooh! Fasa!

The next morning Gassire went with the heroes again to do battle against the Burdama. Gassire was angry. Gassire called to the heroes: "Stay here behind. To-day I will battle with the Burdama alone." The heroes stayed behind and Gassire went on alone to do battle with the Burdama. Gassire hurled his spear. Gassire charged the Burdama. Gassire swung his sword. He struck home to the right, he struck home to the left. Gassire's sword was as a sickle in the wheat. The Burdama were afraid. Shocked, they cried: "That is no Fasa, that is no hero, that is a Damo" (a being unknown to the singer himself). The Burdama turned their horses. The Burdama threw away their spears, each man his two spears, and fled. Gassire called the knights. Gassire said: "Gather the spears." The knights gathered the spears. The knights sang: "The Fasa are heroes. Gassire has always been the Fasa's greatest hero. Gassire has always done great

deeds. But to-day Gassire was greater than Gassire!" Gassire rode into the city and the heroes rode behind him. The heroes sang: "Never before has Wagadu won so many spears as to-day."

Gassire let the women bathe him. The men gathered. But Gassire did not seat himself in their circle. Gassire went into the fields. Gassire heard the partridges. Gassire went close to them. A partridge sat under a bush and sang: "Hear the *Dausi!* Hear my deeds!" The partridge sang of its battle with the snake. The partridge sang: "All creatures must die, be buried and rot. Kings and heroes die, are buried and rot. I, too, shall die, shall be buried and rot. But the *Dausi,* the song of my battles, shall not die. It shall be sung again and again and shall outlive all kings and heroes. Hoooh, that I might do such deeds! Hooh, that I may sing the *Dausi!* Wagadu will be lost. But the *Dausi* shall endure and shall live!"

Hoooh! Dierra, Agada, Ganna, Silla! Hoooh! Fasa!

Gassire went to the old wise man. Gassire said: "Kiekorro! I was in the fields. I understood the partridges. The partridge boasted that the song of its deeds would live longer than Wagadu. The partridge sang the *Dausi.* Tell me whether men also know the *Dausi* and whether the *Dausi* can outlive life and death?" The old wise man said: "Gassire, you are hastening to your end. No one can stop you. And since you cannot be a king you shall be a bard. Ah! Gassire. When the kings of the Fasa lived by the sea they were also great heroes and they fought with men who had lutes and sang the *Dausi.* Oft struck the enemy *Dausi* fear into the hearts of the Fasa, who were themselves heroes. But they never sang the *Dausi* because they were of the first rank, of the Horro, and because the *Dausi* was only sung by those of the second rank, of the Diare. The Diare fought not so much as heroes, for the sport of the day, but as drinkers for the fame of the evening. But you, Gassire, now that you can no longer be the second of the first [i.e. King], shall be the first of the second, and Wagadu will be lost because of it." Gassire said: "Wagadu can go to blazes!"

Hoooh! Dierra, Agada, Ganna, Silla! Hoooh! Fasa!

Gassire went to a smith. Gassire said: "Make me a lute." The smith said: "I will, but the lute will not sing." Gassire said: "Smith, do your work. The rest is my affair." The smith made the lute. The smith brought the lute to Gassire. Gassire struck on the lute. The lute did not sing. Gassire said: "Look here, the lute does not sing." The smith said: "That's what I told you in the first place." Gassire

GASSIRE'S LUTE (CONTINUED)

said: "Well, make it sing." The smith said: "I cannot do anything more about it. The rest is your affair." Gassire said: "What can I do, then?" The smith said: "This is a piece of wood. It cannot sing if it has no heart. You must give it a heart. Carry this piece of wood on your back when you go into battle. The wood must ring with the stroke of your sword. The wood must absorb down-dripping blood, blood of your blood, breath of your breath. Your pain must be its pain, your fame its fame. The wood may no longer be like the wood of a tree, but must be penetrated by and be a part of your people. Therefore it must live not only with you but with your sons. Then will the tone that comes from your heart echo in the ear of your son and live on in the people, and your son's life's blood, oozing out of his heart, will run down your body and live on in this piece of wood. But Wagadu will be lost because of it." Gassire said: "Wagadu can go to blazes!"

Hoooh! Dierra, Agada, Ganna, Silla! Hoooh! Fasa!

Gassire called his eight sons. Gassire said: "My sons, to-day we go to battle. But the strokes of our swords shall echo no longer in the Sahel alone, but shall retain their ring for the ages. You and I, my sons, will that we live on and endure before all other heroes in the *Dausi*. My oldest son, to-day we two, thou and I, will be the first in battle!"

Gassire and his eldest son went into the battle ahead of the heroes. Gassire had thrown the lute over his shoulder. The Burdama came closer. Gassire and his eldest son charged. Gassire and his eldest son fought as the first. Gassire and his eldest son left the other heroes far behind them. Gassire fought not like a human being, but rather like a Damo. His eldest son fought not like a human being, but like a Damo. Gassire came into a tussle with eight Burdama. The eight Burdama pressed him hard. His son came to help him and struck four of them down. But one of the Burdama thrust a spear through his heart. Gassire's eldest son fell dead from his horse. Gassire was angry, and shouted. The Burdama fled. Gassire dismounted and took the body of his eldest son upon his back. Then he mounted and rode slowly back to the other heroes. The eldest son's heart blood dropped on the lute, which was also hanging on Gassire's back. And so Gassire, at the head of his heroes, rode into Dierra.

Hoooh! Dierra, Agada, Ganna, Silla! Hoooh! Fasa!

Gassire's eldest son was buried. Dierra mourned. The urn in which the body crouched was red with blood. That night Gassire took his lute and struck against the wood. The lute did not sing. Gassire was angry. He called his sons. Gassire said to his sons: "To-morrow we ride against the Burdama."

For seven days Gassire rode with the heroes to battle. Every day one of his sons accompanied him to be the first in the fighting. And on every one of these days Gassire carried the body of one of his sons, over his shoulder and over the lute, back into the city. And thus, on every evening, the blood of one of his sons dripped onto the lute. After the seven days of fighting there was a great mourning in Dierra. All the heroes and all the women wore red and white clothes. The blood of the Boroma (apparently in sacrifice) flowed everywhere. All the women wailed. All the men were angry. Before the eighth day of the fighting all the heroes and the men of Dierra gathered and spoke to Gassire: "Gassire, this shall have an end. We are willing to fight when it is necessary. But you, in your rage, go on fighting without sense or limit. Now go forth from Dierra! A few will join you and accompany you. Take your Boroma and your cattle. The rest of us incline more to life than fame. And while we do not wish to die fameless we have no wish to die for fame alone."

The old wise man said: "Ah, Gassire! Thus will Wagadu be lost to-day for the first time."

Hoooh! Dierra, Agada, Ganna, Silla! Hoooh! Fasa!

Gassire and his last, his youngest, son, his wives, his friends, and his Boroma rode out into the desert. They rode through the Sahel. Many heroes rode with Gassire through the gates of the city. Many turned. A few accompanied Gassire and his youngest son into the Sahara.

They rode far: day and night. They came into the wilderness and in the loneliness they rested. All the heroes and all the women and all the Boroma slept. Gassire's youngest son slept. Gassire was restive. He sat by the fire. He sat there long. Presently he slept. Suddenly he jumped up. Gassire listened. Close beside him Gassire heard a voice. It rang as though it came from himself. Gassire began to tremble. He heard the lute singing. The lute sang the *Dausi*.

When the lute had sung the *Dausi* for the first time, King Nganamba died in the city of Dierra; when the lute had sung the *Dausi* for the first time, Gassire's rage melted; Gassire wept. When the lute had sung the *Dausi* for the first time, Wagadu disappeared—for the first time. . . .

Source: Leo Frobenius and Douglas C. Fox, *African Genesis* (Berkeley, Cal.: Turtle Island Foundation, 1983), pp. 112–119.

Ceremonial wooden drum, southeastern Nigeria, circa 1400–1600 (Ethnological Museum, Berlin)

The Honor of the Trousers. One of the highest awards the king of Mali could give for a job well done was the "Honor of the Trousers." The king presented civil servants and military persons with a pair of wide trousers. The size of the trousers correlated to the number and greatness of the subject's deeds. These pants were baggy in the hips and narrow in the leg, resembling those seen in illustrations for the *Arabian Nights.*

Languages. Most West Africans speak languages in the Niger-Congo language family. The first offshoot of the parent Niger-Congo language, breaking off around 3000 B.C.E., was probably the Mande branch, spoken in many parts of West Africa. The largest branch of this family is the Benue-Congo group, which includes the Bantu languages, spread by immigration to East and South Africa, as well as Yoruba, Igbo, and Edo, spoken mainly in Nigeria. Other Niger-Congo language groups are the Kwa branch, spoken in coastal regions from Liberia to Nigeria; the Gur branch, spoken in northern Nigeria and much of Côte d'Ivoire and Burkina Faso; the Ubangi and Adamawa branches, spoken across the northern part of Central Africa; the Atlantic branch, spoken from Liberia north to the desert above Dakar in Senegal; the Kru branch, spoken in southwestern Côte d'Ivoire and southern Liberia; the Ijoid branch, spoken in the Niger delta; and the Dogon branch, spoken in northeastern Mali. Smaller numbers of West Africans, primarily from northern Nigeria east toward Lake Chad, speak languages in the Chadic branch of the Afro-Asian family, which includes most of the languages of North Africa. The chief Chadic language of West Africa is Hausa, spoken in Niger and northern Nige-

ria. Other West Africans speak one of the Nilo-Saharan languages that are found from the great bend in the Niger River east to Ethiopia and parts of the upper Nile Valley, Uganda, and Kenya.

Languages around Lake Chad. The peoples living around Lake Chad, on the eastern edge of West Africa, speak two distinct languages, demonstrating what happens when a barrier to communication arises. The east and the west sides of the lake were both habitable, but swamps around the south side of the lake helped to keep the two different ethnic groups on either side of the lake from mingling. As a result, they developed two distinct language systems. The Hausa on the west side spoke the Chadic language Hausa, and the Kanuri people on the east spoke the Nilo-Saharan language that bears their name. The Hausa people apparently lived on the plains of Bornu west of Lake Chad for hundreds of years, and some scholars have speculated that their language may have been influenced by immigrants from the north. They were an agricultural people who grew food crops and cotton. They had contact with the outside world because these products were desired on the trans-Saharan trade route. Yet, they remained somewhat isolated, building fortified walled cities for protection from outside attacks and encircling these urban areas with farmland and homes. The Kanuri culture and language on the east side of Lake Chad was entirely different. In the twelfth century and later, they owned a large number of horses, and many were fighting men. As trans-Saharan trade routes became increasingly important, the Kanuri expanded their state, adding ethnic groups who spoke other languages.

THE NIGER-CONGO LANGUAGE FAMILY

About three-quarters of all Africans, including most West Africans, speak one of the languages in the sub-Saharan Niger-Congo family. With similar words for many common objects and actions, this family includes the following branches and languages:

Mande branch
Mandinka (Senegal, Mali, Guinea, Côte d'Ivoire)
Bambara (Senegal, Mali, Guinea, Côte d'Ivoire)
Dyula (Senegal, Mali, Guinea, Côte d'Ivoire)
Mende (Sierra Leone)
Kpelle (Liberia)

Benue-Congo branch
Bantu languages
Zulu (South Africa)
Xhosa (South Africa)
Fang (Cameroon)
Bulu (Cameroon)
Yoruba (Nigeria, Benin, Togo)
Igbo (Nigeria)
Edo (Nigeria)

Kwa branch
Ewe (Togo, Ghana)
Anyi (Côte d'Ivoire)
Baule (Côte d'Ivoire)
Akan languages
Ashanti (Ghana)
Fante (Ghana)

Gur branch
Mossi (Nigeria, Côte d'Ivoire, Burkina Faso)
Bariba (Nigeria, Côte d'Ivoire, Burkina Faso)
Gurma (Nigeria, Côte d'Ivoire, Burkina Faso)

Kru branch (Côte d'Ivoire and southern Liberia)

Atlantic branch
Temne (Sierra Leone)
Wolof (Senegal)
Fulani (Guinea, Nigeria, Cameroon)

Dogon branch (northeast Mali)

Ijoid branch
Ibibio (Niger Delta)

Source: Kwame Anthony Appiah and Henry Louis Gates Jr., eds., *Africana: The Encyclopedia of the African and African American Experience* (New York: Basic Civitas Books, 1999).

Sources:
J. F. A. Ajayi and Michael Crowder, eds., *The History of West Africa*, second edition, 2 volumes (New York: Columbia University Press, 1976, 1987).

Akan Cultural Symbols Project <http://www.marshall.edu/akanart/>.

Kwame Anthony Appiah and Henry Louis Gates Jr., eds., *Africana: The Encyclopedia of the African and African American Experience* (New York: Basic Civitas Books, 1999).

Carrie Beauchamp, *Social Fabric: Exploring the Kate Peck Kent Collection of West African Textiles*, University of Denver Museum of Anthropology, 2002 <http://www.du.edu/duma/africloth/>.

Patricia and Fredrick McKissack, *The Royal Kingdoms of Ghana, Mali, and Songhay: Life in Medieval Africa* (New York: Holt, 1994).

D. T. Niane, ed., *Africa from the Twelfth to the Sixteenth Century*, volume 4 of *General History of Africa* (Paris: United Nations Educational, Scientific and Cultural Organization, 1984).

Ivan Van Sertima, ed., *Blacks in Science, Ancient and Modern* (New Brunswick & London: Transaction Books, 1983).

COMMUNICATION: WRITTEN TRADITIONS

Ancient Writing Systems. Some nineteenth- and early-twentieth-century scholars believed that the ancient kingdoms of West Africa came into being because of invaders from the north and that West African culture developed because of Arab and Muslim influences. Later scholars, however, have demonstrated that West African kingdoms were developed by Africans and that some of their writing systems predate the arrival of the Muslims while others developed independently from Arabic influence. One indigenous writing system was the script invented by the Akan peoples, who lived in what is now south-central Ghana. During the fourteenth century, the Akan group controlled the gold trade and introduced standard gold weights made of brass for use in measuring gold dust. (These gold weights are sometimes called Ashanti gold weights after one of the best known of the Akan peoples.) The Akan kingdom grew during the 1500s, and by the latter part of that century, the Akan people had moved south to the Gulf of Guinea coast to trade directly with Europeans.

Gold-Weight Markings. Becoming well known for their beauty as well as their function, Akan gold weights were miniature records of the culture's knowledge. Akan script appears to be one of the earliest African writing systems. The Akan people may not have invented all of its marks, nor was it a complete alphabetic system. Some scholars believe the Akans contributed significantly to the ancient Saharan writing symbols of the Libyans. Made by people from several ancient West African states, the weights were marked with symbols that represent proverbs, sayings, riddles, and historic events. The symbols represented things that were important to the Akan people—things created by God and by man. The marks of Akan gold weights constitute a writing system because identical symbols were used and recognized by people with a common language over a large geographic area and because the symbols were combined in ways that created meanings that

AKAN GOLD-WEIGHT PROVERBS

Some gold-weight markings depict an action or scene in a proverb. Others are mnemonic, reminding people of proverbs but not illustrating them. The following list links some gold-weight markings with the proverbs they represent.

GOLD WEIGHT	PROVERB
A leopard attacking a hunter	It's better not to shoot at the leopard at all than to shoot and miss.
Two fighting birds	Two birds fighting with their beaks. (A disturbance, but no one gets injured.)
A man with a load of wood on his head	As long as a person has a head he cannot avoid carrying loads on it.
A shield (with or without a covering)	Even when the shield covering wears out the frame survives. (Men do not live forever, but their accomplishments remain behind.)
Birds on a tree	Only birds of the same kind gather together. (Comments on a person's background, his family or his reputation.)
A man scraping bark from a tree	The bark falls to the ground if the one who scrapes has no one to gather it up for him. (One should accept help if he needs it.)
A leopard	When rain falls on the leopard it wets him but does not wash out his markings. (A person's character does not change.)
A man playing a drum	When a drum has a drumhead, one does not beat the wooden sides. (Avoid far-fetched actions.)
A chief sitting on a chair or stool	When the head of the household dies, that is the end of the household. (No group can survive without good leadership.)
A scorpion	When a scorpion stings without mercy, you kill it without mercy. (A man responds according to the seriousness of his situation.)
A man with a gun	It is only when a gun has someone to cock it that it can be warlike.
Crossed crocodiles with a common stomach	Two crocodiles having a common stomach nevertheless fight over the food. (Persons with a common interest who compete. Also refers to the well-being of the family or the village.)
A crocodile with a fish in its mouth	If the fish in the water grows fat, it is in the interest of the crocodile.
A porcupine	A man does not rub backs with a porcupine. (Don't get involved with someone who can hurt you.)
An elephant-tail whisk	Short though the elephant's tail may be, he can flick away flies with it. (Handicaps or disadvantages are no excuse for lack of effort.)
A fowl's head protruding from a cooking pot	The head of a bird is recognizable in the soup even if the other parts are not. (Some things can't be covered up.)
A man throwing a stone at a bird in a tree	When a bird sits too long in the tree it may have a stone thrown at it.
A man with a hump on his back	If one has a hump on his chest or his back, there's nothing he can do about it. (Don't rail against what can't be changed.)
A hunter eating a mushroom	When the hunter returns from the forest carrying mushrooms, one need not ask him how he fared.
An elephant	If you follow the elephant you don't have to knock the dew from the grass.
A rooster	Rooster, do not be so proud. Your mother was only an eggshell.
A man holding a head in his hands (an executioner)	After a man has had his head cut off he no longer fears anything.
A man hanging by his neck	All the different forms of death are death.
A rooster and a hen	The hen knows when it is daybreak, but allows the rooster to make the announcement.
A child with his hand on a lion	There are still those who do not know a lion when they see one. (Innocence.)

AKAN GOLD-WEIGHT PROVERBS (CONTINUED)

GOLD WEIGHT	PROVERB
A man holding his stomach	Intestines do not help the belly. (That is, the belly is filled with intestines, but one can still be hungry.)
A bird caught in a snare	The bird caught in the snare is the one that sings sweetly.
A man smoking a pipe	Even a farmer has time to relax.
A man with a pipe in his mouth and a keg of gunpowder on his head	Because you carry gunpowder is no reason you should not smoke.
An okra fruit	An okra does not show its seeds through its skin. (A man's face does not reveal all he knows.)
A snail	To get at the meat of a water snail you must cut off the top and the bottom of the shell. (Nothing worthwhile is achieved without effort.)
Kola pods	The ant on the kola pod will not pick the kola to eat or sell. (A person who has something he doesn't need but won't let someone else have it.)
A guinea fowl	If a guinea fowl goes after a dead frog its hunger will only increase. (Dead frogs are tabooed. The meaning is that it is foolish to do something that does not have any prospect of success.)
A cartridge belt	The cartridge belt of Akowua was never known to be empty. (Akowua was a famous warrior. The meaning is that even if an enterprising person is in difficulty he will find a way to prevail.)
A clockbird	In his own forest the clockbird is supreme (even if nowhere else).
A canoe	The canoe must be paddled on both sides. (Cooperation makes for success.)
Fowls eating a cockroach	A cockroach has fallen among the fowls. Or: Fowls will not spare a cockroach that has fallen among them. (One who is at the mercy of his enemy should not expect consideration.)
A sankofa bird with turned head, looking backward	Regrets are useless.
A man digging up a stump	A stump that could hurt you is dug out by the roots (not merely cut off at the top).
Doves sitting around the bowl of an oil lamp	After a man has eaten he will drink.
A man with an axe, carrying wood on his head	A poor man must go out and cut firewood.
An antelope with horns sloping far to the back	"Had I known that." (It is futile to regret what has passed.)
A man with gun in hand standing before a trap, a dead monkey slung over his shoulder	If one person had not helped me, another would have helped me. (One way or another one achieves something. If the hunter had not shot the monkey he would have caught game in his trap.)
A man lying on his stomach and a man lying on his back	If I who am lying on my back cannot see the Sky God, how can you, lying on your stomach, do so?
Two old men shaking hands	Represents two friends, Adu and Amoako, once men of wealth, who have met again after years of separation, only to find out that they both are now poor.
A man helping another man climb a tree	A man with no friends has no one to help him up.
A snake with a bird in his mouth	Although the snake has to crawl on his belly, God has given him wings.
A leopard with a porcupine in his mouth	An animal that the leopard has not been able to eat, its carcass will not be eaten by the cat.
Two men, their heads together	One head does not exchange ideas.
A tortoise holding a baby tortoise in its mouth	The tortoise does not have milk to give but it knows how to take care of its child.
A tortoise	If hair is so easy to grow why doesn't the tortoise have any?

Source: "Ashanti Proverbs and Sayings Cast in Brass," in *A Treasury of African Folklore*, edited by Harold Courlander (New York: Crown, 1975), pp. 130–133.

Page from a manuscript for *Tarikh al-Sudan* (Chronicle of the Western Sudan, circa 1650) by 'Abd al-Rahman al-Sa'di, who lived in Timbuktu during the final decades of the Songhai Empire (from Basil Davison, *The Growth of African Civilization*, 1967) could be interpreted. Some 135 symbols have been identified, and researchers have found instances in which symbols were put together in patterns to function as a word or a phrase. Some gold weights were marked with individual symbols while other weights had extensive text on them.

Mande Script. Another example of written communication in ancient West Africa is the script of the Mande, or Mandinka-speaking, people, who have lived at the headwaters of the Niger and Senegal Rivers since 5000 B.C.E. It may have developed from a proto-Mande script used by ancestors who lived in the Sahara when it was fertile land, before the Christian era. It was a kind of syllabary; that is, each written symbol represents a syllable. The script was apparently used to help merchants record their transactions along the trans-Saharan trade routes. The ancient Mande people wrote this script on stone, wood, or dried palm leaves, using ink made from soot and liana, a climbing plant or vine.

Arabic Writing. Islam was introduced into West Africa from the north after the eighth century. The *ulama'*, educated religious teachers and professors of Islam, traveled with the trade caravans and brought Islam first to the Soninke people in the kingdom of Ghana. By the eleventh century, Islam had spread to many states near trade routes. Islamic scholars also brought the written language of Arabic. The empires of Ghana, Mali, and Songhai welcomed and tolerated the Muslims and their religion, allowing them to teach people about their religion and culture and to create religious and educational institutions. In 1068 the Spanish-Muslim geographer al-Bakri wrote in his *Kitab al-masalik wa-'l-mamalik* (The Book of Routes and Realms) that Ghana had two towns on opposite sides of the river, one for the king, Tunka Manin, and the other for the Muslims. Muslims served West African rulers as jurists, scholars, and interpreters. Kings of the West African empires hired Muslim scholars and writers, who brought to their courts knowledge of North Africa and other parts of the world.

Written Histories. One service these Muslim scholars from the north provided was to record the history of a royal household, information previously handed down by oral tradition. For example, during the first half of the thirteenth century, court chroniclers began writing the history of the Kanem-Bornu royal line, beginning in the late tenth century. This history was continually updated until the end of the Sefuwa dynasty in the nineteenth century. Although the kings at first relied on Muslim scholars from the north to do their reading and writing, West Africans subsequently learned Arabic and used it for written communications. The first black men to write histories of West Africa in Arabic were Mahmoud al-Kati, who wrote *Tarikh al-Fattash* (The Chronicle of the Seeker After Knowledge) and 'Abd al-Rahman al-Sa'di (1569–1655), who wrote

Tarikh al-Sudan (Chronicle of the Western Sudan) in the 1600s.

Centers of Learning. By the beginning of the tenth century, Muslim teachers were residing in the trading city of Gao. In the following century there were many Muslim missionaries working in the Sudanic region and probably teaching some West Africans to read and write Arabic. After Mansa Musa (reigned 1312–1337), of the Empire of Mali, hired scholars of the Quran (Koran), Islamic schools began to appear in Mali, reaching their highest number at the peak of the successor Empire of Songhai in the fifteenth century. At this time, the Songhai Empire was the size of western Europe and equal to any civilization of its day. Timbuktu and Djenné were important centers of learning, with mosques and schools run by religious men. In the sixteenth century Muslims in West Africa wrote on a wide range of subjects, including religion, history, and moral issues. Firsthand descriptions of these centers of learning may be found in Leo Africanus's description of his visit to the Songhai Empire around 1513–1515. He wrote that the capital city of Niani had "many mosques, priests, and professors who teach in the mosques." Concerning Timbuktu, he noted:

> there are numerous judges, professors, and holy men, all being handsomely maintained by the king, who holds scholars in much honour. Here, too, they sell many handwritten books from North Africa. More profit is made from selling books in Timbuktu than from any other brand of trade.

The Sankore Mosque. The wealth and fame of West African rulers such as Mansa Musa attracted North African scholars to their capital cities, including Timbuktu. The Sankore mosque, which Mansa Musa had built in Timbuktu during the 1330s, became renowned as a center for higher education. Its library, which burned in the nineteenth century, is said to have included copies of all the important works of Muslim learning. Studies there included the humanities (theology, exegesis, tradition, and jurisprudence), grammar, rhetoric, logic, astrology, astronomy, history, and geography.

The Learned Class. Through learning to read and write Arabic and gaining access to the extensive Arabic literature of science (including world geography), an elite group of West Africans became well connected with the outside world. The general prosperity created by trade made it possible to bring scholars from the north to towns of the Sudan (savanna) and the Sahel. This Arabic learning, however, was reserved for those in royal courts and commercial centers and did not include native languages, history, and cultures. It was therefore a marginal part of the whole culture. Although Arabic writers of the time portrayed Mali, Songhai, and Bornu as Muslim states, their Islamic faith was largely superficial. When meeting with Muslims from North Africa, West African kings acted like pious Mus-

Akan brass weights used for weighing gold dust, circa 1400–1800 (Private Collection, London)

lims, but in their interactions with their subjects they professed belief in their traditional religions.

Sources:

Ayele Bekerie, *African Writing Systems*, John Henrik Clarke Africana Library, Cornell University, 1998 <http://www.library.cornell.edu/africana>.

Pekka Masonen, "Trans-Saharan Trade and the West African Discovery of the Mediterranean," in *Ethnic Encounter and Culture Change: Papers for the Third Nordic Conference on Middle Eastern Studies*, edited by M'hammed Sabour and Knut S. Vikor (Bergen: Nordic Society for Middle Eastern Studies, 1997), pp. 116–142.

D. T. Niane, ed., *Africa from the Twelfth to the Sixteenth Century*, volume 4 of *General History of Africa* (Paris: United Nations Educational, Scientific and Cultural Organization, 1984).

Odyssey/Africa Online, Michael C. Carlos Museum of Emory University, Memorial Art Gallery of the University of Rochester, Dallas Museum of Art 2002 <http://www.carlos.emory.edu/ODYSSEY/AFRICA/>.

Ivan Van Sertima, ed., *Blacks in Science, Ancient and Modern* (New Brunswick & London: Transaction Books, 1983).

COURTESY AND HOSPITALITY

Clan and Village Communication. After the year 500, the populations of Soninke towns in the kingdom of Ghana averaged about 500 to 1,500 people. Larger cities, such as Kumbi Saleh, developed as centers of trade on the Niger and Senegal Rivers while about 80 percent of the people lived in small farming compounds and worked the land cooperatively. Several farming compounds where families worked together formed a clan and from it a village. A village leader appointed by the local king assigned land to each family as needed. One family might be assigned to grow food on a piece of land, while another received the right to harvest fruit from trees growing on the same property. If a disagreement arose about who could do what, families could go to the local king for a decision or to the king in the capital city. Writing in 1068, the Spanish Muslim geographer al-Bakri noted that in one West African town, when the king sat to eat a meal, a drum was beaten and women came to dance for the king. No one else in the town could do anything until the king was done eating. After the scraps from his meal were thrown into the river, the king's aides shouted loudly so that people knew they could proceed with their daily activity.

Respect for Kings. The writers of Arabic works about West Africa, either from firsthand observations or from travelers' reports, often mentioned the courtesy and hospitality of the people of Ghana, Mali, Songhai, Kanem-Bornu, and Hausa. For example, during his journey across the western Sudan (1352–1353) Ibn Battuta observed the protocol for greeting a ruler at court. He wrote that when Mansa Sulaiman (ruled 1341–1360) of Mali asked to see one of his subjects, that person took off his clothes and put on rags, took off his clean turban and put on a dirty one. He then approached the king holding up his true garments with his trousers halfway up his leg as a gesture of submission. The subject then beat the ground with his elbows and prepared to listen to the ruler in the position of someone

performing a *rak'a* (a unit of Islamic prayer involving recitation and bowing). If the king talked to the subject, he uncovered his back and sprinkled a handful of dust on his head and back, as if washing with water. This behavior was considered good manners among the people of Mali. Whenever the ruler spoke to a subject, everyone present took off their turbans to listen. When someone provided a report of his accomplishments to the king, others expressed their agreement by pulling back the strings of their bows and released them with a "twang." If the king replied, "You have spoken the truth," the subject again bared his back and sprinkled himself with dust.

King-to-King Greetings. The great leaders of the ancient world did not always greet one another as equals. Al-Umari (1301–1349) of Damascus, the author of a history of the Mamluk administration of Egypt and Syria, wrote about the meeting between the Sultan al-Malik an-Nasir (ruled 1293–1341) of Egypt and Mansa Musa (ruled 1312–1337) of Mali, basing his account on a story from Emir Abu l-Abbas Ahmad ibn al-Had, who escorted distinguished guests, perhaps the court griot. Al-Umari wrote that in 1324, during his pilgrimage to Mecca, Mansa Musa visited the sultan's court at the Citadel in Cairo. When he arrived in the sultan's royal presence, Mansa Musa was instructed to kiss the ground in greeting and honor. He "refused outright saying: 'How may this be?' Then an intelligent man who was with him whispered to him something we could not understand and he said: 'I make obeisance to God who created me!' Then he prostrated himself and went forward to the sultan. The sultan half rose to greet him and sat him by his side." In recognition of Mansa Musa's greatness, the sultan treated him with honor, but he did not always let Mansa Musa sit in his presence. He did give Mansa Musa a gray horse with a covering of yellow satin and many camels and equipment. In return Mansa Musa sent many gifts to the sultan.

Hospitality to Travelers. Ibn Battuta, author of one of the most reliable works about West Africa during his time, wrote that during his journey through the kingdom of Mali, travelers did not need to carry food or money. Instead they carried pieces of salt, glass trinkets, and some spices, especially cloves. When travelers came to a village, the women of the village allowed them to exchange these commodities for as much milk, chicken, flour, rice, and cowpea meal as they wanted. He also wrote about the generosity and hospitality of the people. On arriving in one town he met a man of "noble virtues," who gave him a cow as a welcome gift. In that same town, an interpreter sent Ibn Battuta a bullock; another man gave him two sacks of *funi* (plants) and a gourd filled with *gharti* (a fruit similar to a pear); and someone else in the town gave him rice. After such generosity, Ibn Battuta was surprised when Mansa Sulaiman sent him only "three loaves of bread and a piece of beef fried in *gharti* and a gourd containing yogurt." Hav-

FON RIDDLES AND PROVERBS

The Fon people who lived in Togo before they migrated to present-day Benin, where they founded the kingdom of Dahomey in the seventeenth century, are known for their riddles and proverbs.

RIDDLES

Hole within hole, hair all round, pleasure comes from inside.
(Answer: A flute being played by a bearded man.)

A thing leaves the house bent over and returns home straight.
(Answer: A water jar.)

A thing is naked going out, but returning, the body is covered with clothes.
(Answer: Corn.)

My father eats with his anus and defecates through his mouth.
(Answer: A gun.)

One throws a thing across the hedge, and it falls in one heap.
(Answer: A frog.)

A large hat in the midst of weeds.
(Answer: A latrine.)

One thing falls in the water with a loud voice, another falls in the water with a soft voice.
(Answer: A bottle of oil, a carrying basket.)

PROVERBS

The big do not eat out of the hand of the small.

He who makes the gunpowder wins the battles.

War lies in wait on a narrow path.

A snake bit me; I see a worm and I am afraid.

If one wants to catch a large fish he must give something to the stream.

Mawu [the creator] sent sickness into the world but he also sent medicine to cure.

When one is at sea he does not quarrel with the boatman.

The fish trap that catches no fish is brought back to the house.

Source: "Some Dahomean Riddles," "Some Dahomean Proverbs," in *A Treasury of African Folklore*, edited by Harold Courlander (New York: Crown, 1975), p. 183.

ance for the remainder of his stay and—at the end of Ramadan—more money.

Sources:

Kwame Anthony Appiah and Henry Louis Gates Jr., eds., *Africana: The Encyclopedia of the African and African American Experience* (New York: Basic Civitas Books, 1999).

Pekka Masonen, "Trans-Saharan Trade and the West African Discovery of the Mediterranean," in *Ethnic Encounter and Culture Change: Papers for the Third Nordic Conference on Middle Eastern Studies*, edited by M'hammed Sabour and Knut S. Vikor (Bergen: Nordic Society for Middle Eastern Studies, 1997), pp. 116–142.

Patricia and Fredrick McKissack, *The Royal Kingdoms of Ghana, Malik, and Songhay: Life in Medieval Africa* (New York: Holt, 1994).

Mary Penick Motley, *Africa, Its Empires, Nations, and People* (Detroit: Wayne State University Press, 1969).

D. T. Niane, ed., *Africa from the Twelfth to the Sixteenth Century*, volume 4 of *General History of Africa* (Paris: United Nations Educational, Scientific and Cultural Organization, 1984).

Ivan Van Sertima, ed., *Blacks in Science, Ancient and Modern* (New Brunswick & London: Transaction Books, 1983).

DESERT TRAVEL

Connections to the World. Despite the apparent barrier created by the Sahara Desert, West Africa has been connected to the Mediterranean and lands to the east for more than a thousand years. Although no surviving written documents state exactly when trade exchanges began across the Sahara Desert, historians and archaeologists have found evidence that the kingdom of Ghana was becoming an important commercial center by the year 300. North African coins dating from that period have been found in West Africa, and historians have found proof that some camel-caravan routes from North Africa to the Sahel were established around the same time. By the year 400 more extensive travel had resumed between West Africa and Egypt. This connection had existed much earlier, when the Sahara was more of a wetland than a desert before 2500 B.C.E., but the southern movement of the desert had cut off West Africa from Egypt until the advent of camel travel, which became common in North Africa during the third century C.E. and spread into the savanna region of West Africa by the end of that century.

Travel before the Camel. The camel made it possible for the Berber nomads of North Africa to trade farther south of the Sahara and into the Sahel. Before the camel, there was some trade using horses and bullocks. Some historians deduced the existence of this earlier trade across the Sahara after rock paintings of small two-wheeled, horse-drawn chariots, like those used circa 1000 B.C.E. – 500 C.E. along the Mediterranean coast of North Africa, were found at Fezzan, in southwest Libya, during the early 1930s. Yet, in the early 1970s, some critics disputed this theory, arguing that these small carts had barely enough room for a driver, let alone enough space to carry anything heavy over a long distance. In addition, no horse skeletons dating to that period have been found in the vicinity of Fezzan. Others explain the rock paintings not as historic documentation

ing thought the king would give him cloth and money, Ibn Battuta later confronted Mansa Sulaiman, saying he had been in Mali for two months and had not received a welcome gift. The king then gave him a house and an allow-

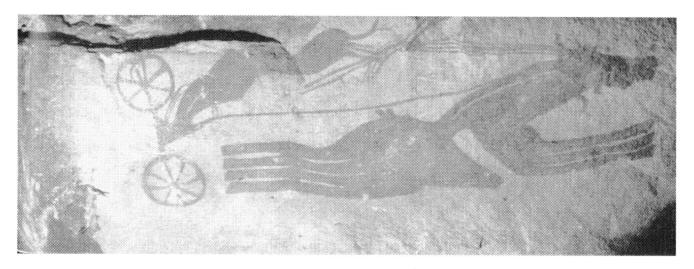

Ancient rock painting of a horse-drawn chariot in southwestern Libya, which some scholars interpret as evidence that trans-Saharan trade may have developed before 500 C.E. (Werner Forman Archive, London)

but as an artistic expression similar to art found over a wide region from the Mediterranean to south of the Sahara. While the debate continues, it is certain that beasts of burden such as horses, bullocks, and donkeys are less suited than camels to carrying heavy loads for long distances under desert conditions.

Camel Caravans. Although donkey caravans were used to carry merchandise to and from all points across West Africa, for the most part camels made trans-Saharan travel possible. Berber nomads from the north were skilled at crossing the Sahara Desert. The camel provided everything they needed: transportation, milk, wool and hides for clothing and shelter, and meat. From the south, merchants of the West African empires also began to use camel caravans, often with one hundred or more camels, to carry cloth and gold to North Africa, from whence those commodities reached Europe and Asia.

Dromedaries. The Granadan writer Leo Africanus, who traveled through much of West Africa in 1513–1515, explained that dromedaries, or one-hump camels, were better suited than two-hump Bactrian camels to carry heavy loads and be ridden. The dromedary was introduced into the Greco-Roman Empire from Asia and spread throughout the Arabian Peninsula and North Africa. Well adapted to desert travel, these camels have double rows of eyelashes, hairy ear openings, and nostrils that can be closed—all providing protection from sun and sand. They can endure heat, and they can drink up to twenty-five gallons of water at a time, which enables them to travel several days without food or water. Camels can sometimes, however, be short-tempered. They are known to bite, spit, kick, run away, or refuse to move. As early as the year 500, caravan leaders often hired crews specifically trained to work with camels.

Distances Traveled. Merchants traveling by camel caravan were away from home for long periods of time. A caravan traveled at about three miles an hour, moving from one oasis to the next. During the hottest part of the day, when temperatures soared to about 130 degrees, travelers remained at these rest areas. They continued their travels after the sun set. Writing in 903, the Iranian Ibn al-Faqih said it took forty nights to cross Egypt and seven years to travel across West Africa. Ibn Hawqal, writing in 967, said that to travel from Sijilmasa in southeastern Morocco to

USES FOR CAMELS

Yaqut al-Hamawi (1179–1229) was born in Byzantium, sold as a slave to a Syrian merchant, and later educated in Arabic and freed, traveling in Iran, Iraq, Syria, and Egypt. In his *Mujam al-Buldan* (Dictionary of Countries, 1212) he described merchant caravans traveling from Sijilmasa (in southeastern Morocco) to the kingdom of Ghana and explained how the camels often saved travelers' lives:

On their way they cross desert plains, where the *samum* (noxious) winds dry up the water inside the water skins. They employ an artful means to carry water in the desert in order to survive. Thus they take with them unloaded camels, which they cause to thirst for one day and one night before they reach the water place, and then they let them drink a first time, and a second until their bellies are quite full. Then the camel drivers urge them on and when the water in the skins has evaporated, and they are in need of water, they slaughter a camel and save their lives with what is in its stomach. Then they hasten on their way until they reach another watering place and they fill their water skins there.

Source: Nehemia Levtzion and J. F. P. Hopkins, eds., *Corpus of Early Arabic Sources of West African History*, translated by Hopkins (Cambridge: Cambridge University Press, 1981).

Audaghost, an oasis and market town northwest of Timbuktu, took two months.

Desert Travel. Writing in 1068, the Spanish Muslim geographer al-Bakri carefully described the route across the desert from Tamdult in northwestern Africa to Audaghost as a four-stage journey, traveling from one well to another. He wrote that the first watering place was four fathoms deep and travelers passed through a narrow ravine with the camels walking single file. Next they made a three-day journey through the hills of Azwar, a stony region where camels could easily become lame but where the travelers had the advantage of shade from trees that grew there but not in the rest of the desert. At the next watering place, al-Bakri wrote, travelers had to dig a well, which quickly filled in again with sand. Three more days of travel took them to the next large well, called Win Haylun, and in three more days they found rainwater under a rock in the sand. At each stop, travelers had to be sure the water was drinkable, not brackish. Writing in 1154, the Moroccan Muslim al-Idrisi told a story he had heard from a reliable traveler about nomadic Berbers who drank water from underground springs they located in the desert. The Berbers were well known for their desert knowledge. It was said that they could dig in the sand with their hands to find the underground springs and that they could smell a handful of earth and determine if there was water below.

Sources:

Leo Africanus, *The History and Description of Africa*, 3 volumes, translated by John Pory, edited by Robert Brown (London: Printed for the Hakluyt Society, 1896).

N. Levtzion and J. F. P. Hopkins, eds., *Corpus of Early Arabic Sources of West African History*, translated by Hopkins (Cambridge: Cambridge University Press, 1981).

Pekka Masonen, "Trans-Saharan Trade and the West African Discovery of the Mediterranean," in *Ethnic Encounter and Culture Change: Papers for the Third Nordic Conference on Middle Eastern Studies*, edited by M'hammed Sabour and Knut S. Vikor (Bergen: Nordic Society for Middle Eastern Studies, 1997), pp. 116–142.

Patricia and Fredrick McKissack, *The Royal Kingdoms of Ghana, Malik, and Songhay: Life in Medieval Africa* (New York: Holt, 1994).

EXPANDING TRADE ROUTES

Early Trade Routes. By the year 500, the kingdom of Ghana relied on trading iron and gold to buy salt mined in the Sahara Desert and merchandise from north of the desert. Camel caravans traveled the trade routes with their cargo. The nomadic Berbers of North Africa called the part of the continent south of the Sahara *Bilad al-Sudan* (Land of the Black Peoples), and the entire region of West Africa became known as the Sudan. One of the earliest trade routes followed by the northern traders linked the salt mines of Taghaza (an oasis in the Sahara), to Walata on the southern edge of the Sahara, and to other points in West Africa, including the important trading center of Djenné and the goldfields further south. During the latter part of the ninth century a route developed further west, linking

A TRANSPORTATION ENTERPRISE

During the thirteenth century, the five Maqqari brothers developed a successful business in communication and transportation along a trans-Saharan trade route. The brothers from Tlemcen (in northwest Algeria, near the Moroccan border) created ways to ease the strenuous, dangerous journey across the Sahara Desert from Sijilmasa in southeast Morocco through the oasis of Taghaza to the West African market town of Walata on the southern edge of the desert. The Maqqari brothers dug and maintained wells along the route and also provided caravan guides. Two brothers stayed in Tlemcen and received goods from European traders. Another brother lived in Sijilmasa, where he gathered information about markets and prices in North Africa and the Sudan. With this information, he could maximize profits by shipping particular goods when they were most in demand. The other two brothers lived in Walata, where they distributed merchandise from the north to the local traders and sent local goods by caravan to their brothers in the north. Their enterprise apparently found favor with Mali officials, who encouraged the brothers to trade throughout the country.

Source: J. F. A. Ajayi and Michael Crowder, eds., *The History of West Africa*, second edition, 2 volumes (New York: Columbia University Press, 1976, 1987), I: 143.

the Moroccan cities of Tangier, Fez, and Sijilmasa to the West African market towns of Audaghost and Walata. From those towns, merchants could take other routes along the Senegal and Niger Rivers to reach other parts of the region. The Arab writer al-Hussan recorded in 950 that in Fezzan, a region of southwestern Libya, gold was exchanged for copper, which was traded for more gold further south. Writing a century later, al-Bakri told of a caravan from Morocco carrying more than two thousand brass rods to be traded south of the Sahara. Other items traded across the desert included horses, textiles, glass beads, ivory, and kola nuts.

Trade Routes by 1500. In the eastern part of West Africa, by the year 900, the Kanuri people around Lake Chad in the kingdom of Kanem-Bornu had set up trade routes that circled north to Tripoli and east to Cairo and Mecca and back to Lake Chad. After 1000, merchants traded from Timbuktu north to Tunis and the Mediterranean Sea. From Timbuktu, trade spread all across the Sahel and savanna regions south of the Sahara and along the major rivers, the Senegal, Niger, and Benue. These river routes made it fairly easy to get merchandise to Djenné and Gao. By around 1300, the forest areas along the Gulf of

West African slaves washing gold ore in the Spanish West Indies; from a circa 1590 manuscript for Sir Francis Drake's
Natural History of the West Indies (Pierpont Morgan Library, New York)

Guinea coast in West Africa were connected with the major trading centers. The cities of Ile-Ife and Benin in present-day Nigeria were thriving trading centers in the 1300s and 1400s. Ile-Ife traded ivory, gold, pepper, kola nuts, and slaves north to other Niger River communities and further along the trans-Saharan routes. Some of the caravans on the trade routes were quite large. Visiting West Africa in the mid fourteenth century, Ibn Battuta wrote of seeing Egyptian-made cloth in Walata as proof that trade existed between West Africa and Egypt. He also heard that a huge caravan of more than twelve thousand camels passed near Tadmekka in the Sahel every year.

Control of Trade Routes. After 500, the West African kingdom that controlled the trade routes held the power in the region. In the ninth century, the ancient kingdom of Ghana controlled a region of goldfields called the Wangara, between the upper Niger and Senegal Rivers. From the Wangara, vast quantities of gold were traded north across the Sahara Desert in return primarily for salt and cloth from North Africa. Ancient Ghana went into decline following conquest of its capital city by Muslim Almoravids from North Africa in 1076. By the mid thirteenth century the great Empire of Mali had arisen to control the gold trade and trade routes. The shift in power from Ghana to Mali created a southward shift in trade from the Sahel toward the savanna, and Timbuktu replaced Walata as the main end point for desert caravans. By the mid fifteenth century, Mali had been absorbed by the even larger and more powerful Songhai Empire, which asserted its control over the trade routes. By this time the primary source of West African gold was farther south than Wangara, in the Akan forest in present-day Ghana, with Djenné as the starting point of the southward routes to this region.

Slave Labor. By the sixteenth century, slavery had been a fact of life in West Africa for thousands of years. Often slaves were captives taken during wars or other people from outside the tribe. Frequently, they rose in rank, became administrators, and sometimes gained their freedom. In certain situations merchants used slaves instead of pack animals. In the sixteenth century Leo Africanus wrote that when merchants from Wangara traveled to Bornu with gold, the roads were too rough for camels so their loads were transported by slaves, who were usually made to walk ten to twelve miles a day. Leo saw two such caravans in one day. The slaves carried not only merchandise but also food for their masters and the soldiers who guarded them. Salt bars were carried on camelback across the Sahara to towns in the Sahel and then transported further south by Muslim traders called Wangara after the goldfields. Their merchandise was sometimes carried by donkeys or bullocks, but they also used slave porters, who carried wares on their heads often as far as the Akan gold mines. In Yoruba, where the environment was not conducive to raising small draft animals, trade activities depended on footpaths and human caravans.

Changes in Transportation Needs. Losing control of the trans-Saharan trade routes contributed to the fall of the Ghana, Mali, and Songhai Empires. The end of Songhai domination was foreshadowed in 1544, when Sultan Muhammad al-Mahdi of Morocco demanded that Songhai ruler Askia Ishaq I hand over the gold mines. Ishaq refused, and the Songhai army successfully repelled a Moroccan invasion. Trans-Saharan trade continued profitably for the Songhai until Moroccan troops conquered their empire in 1591. This disruption of trans-Saharan trade routes, coupled with development of successful trade between Europeans and West Africans along the southern Gulf of Guinea coast, changed transportation patterns in the region. As trade to North Africa became much less profitable, the cities that had grown up along the trans-Saharan trade route were eventually abandoned.

Sources:

Leo Africanus, *The History and Description of Africa*, 3 volumes, translated by John Pory, edited by Robert Brown (London: Printed for the Hakluyt Society, 1896).

J. F. A. Ajayi and Michael Crowder, eds., *The History of West Africa*, second edition, 2 volumes (New York: Columbia University Press, 1976, 1987).

Kwame Anthony Appiah and Henry Louis Gates Jr., eds., *Africana: The Encyclopedia of the African and African American Experience* (New York: Basic Civitas Books, 1999).

Brian Catchpole, *A History of West Africa in Maps and Diagrams* (London: Collins Educational, 1983).

Pekka Masonen, "Trans-Saharan Trade and the West African Discovery of the Mediterranean," in *Ethnic Encounter and Culture Change: Papers for the Third Nordic Conference on Middle Eastern Studies*, edited by M'hammed Sabour and Knut S. Vikor (Bergen: Nordic Society for Middle Eastern Studies, 1997), pp. 116–142.

Mary Penick Motley, *Africa, Its Empires, Nations, and People* (Detroit: Wayne State University Press, 1969).

TRANSPORTATION BY WATERCRAFT AND HORSEBACK

Canoes. Dugout canoes are still the main means of water transportation in West Africa. Dugout canoes, each made from a single tree, were seen by European explorers in the fifteenth century and had apparently been in use for centuries. In the latter part of the fifteenth century Europeans who traveled on the Niger River reported seeing canoes made from the trunks of two large trees that had been hollowed out and joined together across the middle. A mid-seventeenth-century explorer of that river said that his three camels were carried in one such canoe. Used widely over hundreds of miles on the Niger, canoes changed little over the centuries. Leo Africanus also described canoe travel during his 1513–1515 journey through West Africa. He wrote that, after 15 June, the Niger River flooded for forty days, creating good conditions for merchant travel. At the high point of the river he saw many men in a "barke pass over the land of Negros." He later wrote that the Niger overflowed during July, August, and September, "at which time the merchants of Tombuto [Timbuktu] conueigh [convey] their merchandize hither in certaine Canoas or narrow boats made of one tree, which they rowe all the day long, but at night they binde them to the shore, and lodge themselves upon the lande." A *zopoli* dugout canoe with thirty or even forty-eight rowers was often used. It was apparently the kind of vessel that greeted and then attacked Alvise Cà da Mosto, when he was exploring the West African coastline for Portugal in 1455. In forty-eight-man vessels, twenty-four men rowed while the other twenty-four rested. In this way, the crew could travel night and day. Such a vessel also had a waterproof awning to protect provisions stored in the center of the craft.

River Navigation. The 2,600 miles of the Niger River—which flows in a great arc from Guinea northeast and east through Mali, and southeast through Niger and Nigeria into the Gulf of Guinea—and its tributaries were the major east-west trade routes of West Africa. These river routes—as well as the Senegal River, which flows northwest from Guinea into the Atlantic Ocean—were links to the north-south trans-Saharan trade routes that took gold from West Africa to North Africa and from there into Europe. In addition, gold was transported along the Black Volta River, which rises in Burkina Faso and flows into Lake Volta in the modern nation of Ghana. All these waterways were navigable mainly during the rainy season, which typically occurred in July, August, and September. For much of the rest of the year,

West African horsemen: terra-cotta statue from Djenné-Jeno, Mali, circa 1000–1400 (Private Collection); zinc-brass figure from the Kingdom of Benin, Nigeria, circa 1500–1600, possibly Oba Esigie, who ruled Benin from 1504 until about 1550 (Ethnological Museum, Berlin)

waterfalls, rapids, sandbars, and swamps deterred the passage of boats. Even in the wet season, the Niger between Djenné and Timbuktu was shallow and not navigable by boats with sails. Some boats were propelled by pushing poles against the bottom of the river to move the boats forward. All along the river systems dugout canoes were the most common watercraft. Traders carried yams, cloves, cows, and goats by boat as far as possible into the interior of West Africa. The Hausa people who lived near the fork of the Niger and Benue Rivers (in present-day Nigeria) traded leatherwork and textiles with central Sudan and North Africa, conveying merchandise between the savanna area south of the Sahara and the forest regions along the Guinea coast. They probably traded from early times with Niger delta cities such as Oyo, Ile-Ife, and Benin.

Coastal Trade. As coastal trade between Europeans and the ethnic groups of the forest regions along the Gulf of Guinea grew more important than the trans-Sahara trade after 1500, coastal peoples began to gain power and influence. For instance, in 1553–1554 English traders bought merchandise along the Gold Coast that included 400 pounds of top-quality gold, 36 barrels of peppercorns, and 250 elephant tusks. Coastal people no longer had to rely on traders from the West African interior to transport their goods to buyers. Now they could sell directly to Europeans and avoid middlemen.

Horses. From early times in West Africa, owning a horse was a sign of prestige. Leo Africanus wrote that the horses he saw near Timbuktu were not well-bred, noting that merchants had "nags" they used for travel. Leo felt the best horses were the Arabian horses that came from the nomadic Berbers in North Africa. If a West African king heard horses were arriving on the trade routes, he commanded that a certain number be set aside for him so he could choose the best horses for himself. Of course, Leo wrote, the king was willing to pay a liberal price. Often horses (and other merchandise) sold for a lot more in Gao than they were purchased for in North Africa. According to Leo, horses bought in Europe for 10 ducats were sold in Gao for 40 to 50 ducats.

Trading Horses for Slaves. Even though they were expensive, Leo indicated that it was fairly easy to buy good horses in West Africa. He wrote that the king of Bornu traded slaves to the Berbers in exchange for the best Arabian horses, sometimes paying fifteen to twenty slaves for one horse. Many horses arrived in West Africa through this kind of trading. Because kings typically got slaves after raiding another tribe or village, Leo noted that sometimes merchants had to stay in West Africa for three or more months, waiting for a king to return from a war in which he had captured enough slaves to pay for his horses.

Uses for Horses. Many rulers of the Ghana, Mali, Songhai, and Kanem-Bornu Empires had large cavalries. In the mid thirteenth century Kanem-Bornu is said to have raided other tribes with a military force that included one hundred thousand horses and a huge number of fighting men. Horses also provided some entertainment in the ancient kingdoms of West Africa. In the Numidian Desert, Leo Africanus observed races between ostriches and Arabian horses, known for their swiftness and agility. People placed bets on the animals and the horses usually won. According to Leo, some West African tribes used horses for war and travel, while the Arabians in the desert and people of Libya also used horses for hunting. When they were used for this purpose, people did not use them for riding.

Sources:

J. F. A. Ajayi and Michael Crowder, eds., *The History of West Africa*, second edition, 2 volumes (New York: Columbia University Press, 1976, 1987).

Basil Davidson, with F. K. Buah and the advice of Ajayi, *A History of West Africa to the Nineteenth Century*, revised edition (Garden City, N.Y.: Anchor/Doubleday, 1966).

Leo Africanus, *The History and Description of Africa*, 3 volumes, translated by John Pory, edited by Robert Brown (London: Printed for the Hakluyt Society, 1896).

Pekka Masonen, "Trans-Saharan Trade and the West African Discovery of the Mediterranean," in *Ethnic Encounter and Culture Change: Papers for the Third Nordic Conference on Middle Eastern Studies*, edited by M'hammed Sabour and Knut S. Vikor (Bergen: Nordic Society for Middle Eastern Studies, 1997), pp. 116–142.

D. T. Niane, ed., *Africa from the Twelfth to the Sixteenth Century*, volume 4 of *General History of Africa* (Paris: United Nations Educational, Scientific and Cultural Organization, 1984).

Ivan Van Sertima, ed., *Blacks in Science, Ancient and Modern* (New Brunswick & London: Transaction Books, 1983).

TRAVELERS FROM WEST AFRICA

Physical Conditions. Some modern scholars have pointed out that as early as the year 500 the watercraft of ancient West Africa were suited to transatlantic travel. Because West Africa is only 1,600 miles from South America with islands in between, this voyage would not have been as long or arduous as the one Polynesians made around the year 400 across the Pacific Ocean to Easter Island off the coast of Chile. Furthermore, currents running along the west coast of Africa loop westward toward the Americas. Some modern scholars have suggested that a ship could sail from Africa to the Americas almost without any navigation. In 1500, for example, the Portuguese fleet of Alvares Cabral was caught in a storm off the coast of West Africa and ended up in Brazil. Although anthropologists, archaeologists, and historians have uncovered evidence to suggest an early West African presence in the New World, not all scholars agree, with some arguing that transatlantic voyages by ancient West Africans were not technically possible.

An Explorer from Mali. Early Arabic histories of West Africa include accounts of westward voyages across the Atlantic. The best-known account was written by al-Umari (1301–1349), who recorded a story of Atlantic voyages by West African seamen during the reign of Mansa Abubakari II, king of Mali in 1300–1311. Al-Umari heard about Abubakari from Ibn Amir Hajib, governor of old Cairo, who got the information from Abubakari's half brother and successor, Mansa Musa (ruled 1312–1337). Abubakari sent two large fleets westward across the Atlantic, commanding the second one in 1311. They never returned to West Africa.

Africans in the New World. Though Abubakari's voyage is the best documented, he was probably not the first African to set out for the New World, and evidence of an early African presence there has been found in several sources. Preserved in the footnotes of Spanish and Portuguese documents from the New World, oral traditions of Native Americans and Guinea Africans told of Africans in South, Central, and North America when the Europeans arrived. On his third voyage (1498), which took him along the coast of South America, Christopher Columbus reported that natives brought his men cotton handkerchiefs woven in symmetrical patterns and colors like those he had seen in Guinea and along the rivers of Sierra Leone, when he had traveled there in 1483. These handkerchiefs were also worn in the African fashion as head wraps or loincloths. He had already heard stories from the Indians of the island of Hispaniola about communities of black people on

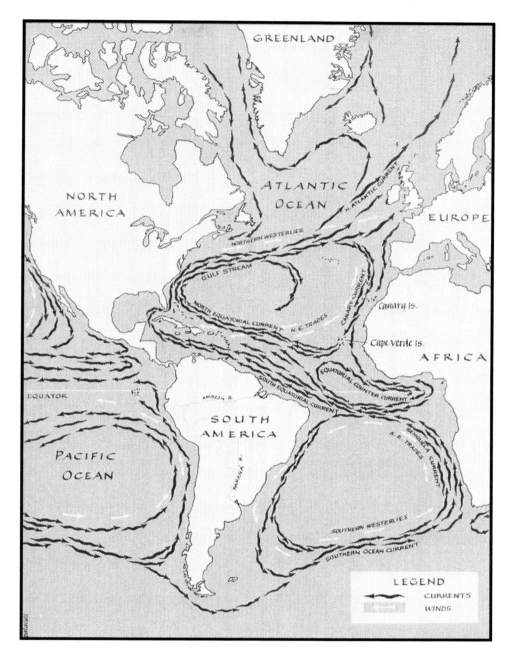

Map of Atlantic trade winds and currents, which facilitate ocean travel from Africa to the Americas (map by Rafael Palacios; from Ivan Van Sertima, *They Came Before Columbus,* 1976)

the South American coast. In the nineteenth century French anthropologist Armand de Quatrefages pointed out that these small isolated settlements were located along the South American seaboard in places that coincided with the ending points of transatlantic currents. Columbus also heard about African traders from Guinea (Ghana) who had brought spears with points made of "gua-nin," which when assayed proved to be an alloy of gold, silver, and copper that was common in West Africa. When Vasco Nuñez de Balboa discovered the Pacific Ocean in 1513, he reported seeing Africans in Panama. Archaeologists have found statues with African features, some dating as early as 700–800

B.C.E., in Mexico among the Olmecs, who lived eighteen miles inland from the Gulf of Mexico. Portraits of black Africans done in clay, gold, and stone have also been found in pre-Columbian strata of digs in Central and South America, and some South and Central American archaeologists now believe that Africans were in the Americas before Columbus. In February 1975 a Smithsonian Institution team reported finding two African male skeletons in the U.S. Virgin Islands in a soil layer that dated to 1250 C.E. A study of the teeth of these skeletons showed their characteristics to be consistent with those of people in early African cultures.

Royal Delegations. The rulers of the many kingdoms in North and West Africa routinely corresponded, exchanged delegations, and traded among each other. In the ninth century, the Rustamid imam of Tahert on the north end of a trans-Saharan trade route sent a delegation with special gifts to the "king of blacks," probably the ruler of Gao. These sorts of visits continued, and in the fourteenth century royal delegations were regularly exchanged between West and North African capitals. News of various events was communicated in a timely manner for those days of caravan travel and communication. A year after the conquest of Tlemcen by Marinid Sultan Abu l-Hasan in 1337, Mansa Musa of Mali sent a royal delegation to congratulate the sultan. Another delegation was sent from Mali to congratulate the sultan for the conquest of Constantine in 1349. Also in the fourteenth century, the ruler of Kanem sent delegates on an official mission to present many gifts to kings in North Africa. These ambassadors traveled along a trade route that led directly from Lake Chad to the Mediterranean. In 1391 Mai Abu Amr Uthman ibn Idris, the ruler of Bornu, corresponded with Sultan Barkuk of Egypt. By the fifteenth century Benin was an important power in West Africa. Oba Ewuare (ruled 1440–1473) of Benin wanted to know more about Europe than his Portuguese visitors could tell him, so he sent one of his chiefs to find out. Ewuare was an accomplished, literate ruler who was said to have traveled much in Guinea and even to have gone to the Congo.

Early Pilgrimages to Mecca. The kings of Kanem-Bornu and other kingdoms were converted to Islam by Muslims from North Africa who traveled south with merchant caravans. Many rulers made the hajj (pilgrimage) to Mecca. Dunama I of Kanem-Bornu made the pilgrimage twice and drowned in the Red Sea on his third journey to Mecca around 1150. Arabic writer Ibn Sa'id wrote in 1252–1253 that Dunama II Dibbalemi, king of Kanem during the first half of the thirteenth century, was an Islamic reformer known for his holy wars and Muslim good works. He is thought to have made a pilgrimage to Mecca, and he probably established the *madrasah* (Quranic school) of al-Rashiq in Cairo during the 1240s for Kanuri students in that city. Rulers of Mali also made pilgrimages. The first one was made by Mansa Uli (ruled 1255–1285) during the 1260s. Mansa Sakura went to Mecca and visited Cairo, dying on the way home, possibly around 1300. The best-known hajj of a Mali ruler was performed by Mansa Musa in 1324, when he carried so much gold to Mecca that he upset the economy for many years after. Askia Muhammad I (ruled 1493–1528) of Songhai was well known for his 1495 pilgrimage, on which he was accompanied by an army of one thousand infantrymen and five hundred men riding horses and camels. He carried with him 300,000 pieces of gold—one-third for his expenses, one-third as alms and support for an inn for Sudanese pilgrims in Mecca, and

one-third to purchase food and supplies. Common people from West Africa seldom made pilgrimages to Mecca until after the fifteenth century, the time at which Islam moved out of the courts and started to become established in the beliefs of the people.

Students in Morocco and Spain. West Africans also traveled for the purpose of religious study. After West Africans began to convert to Islam, some went abroad to well-known Islamic universities. In the twelfth century, some West African students studied in Spain and Morocco. In the thirteenth, West African students were studying at Al-Azhar University in Cairo. These students studied subjects such as geography, religion, literature, and economics and returned home with worldviews broadened by their experiences.

Sources:

J. F. A. Ajayi and Michael Crowder, eds., *The History of West Africa*, second edition, 2 volumes (New York: Columbia University Press, 1976, 1987).

Basil Davidson, with F. K. Buah and the advice of Ajayi, *A History of West Africa to the Nineteenth Century*, revised edition (Garden City, N.Y.: Anchor/Doubleday, 1966).

Pekka Masonen, "Trans-Saharan Trade and the West African Discovery of the Mediterranean," in *Ethnic Encounter and Culture Change: Papers for the Third Nordic Conference on Middle Eastern Studies*, edited by M'hammed Sabour and Knut S. Vikor (Bergen: Nordic Society for Middle Eastern Studies, 1997), pp. 116–142.

D. T. Niane, ed., *Africa from the Twelfth to the Sixteenth Century*, volume 4 of *General History of Africa* (Paris: United Nations Educational, Scientific and Cultural Organization, 1984).

J. A. Rogers, *Africa's Gift to America* (New York: Futuro Press, 1961).

J. Spencer Trimingham, *History of Islam in West Africa* (London, Glasgow & New York: Oxford University Press, 1962).

Ivan Van Sertima, *They Came Before Columbus* (New York: Random House, 1976).

Van Sertima, ed., *African Presence in Early America* (New Brunswick, N.J.: Journal of African Civilizations, 1987).

VOYAGES TO WEST AFRICA

Twelfth- and Thirteenth-Century Explorers. Though knowledge of West Africa had been carried along trans-Saharan trade routes to North Africa, and from there to Europe for hundreds of years, West Africa was not explored by sea until the twelfth century, when Arabic sources recorded several attempts to sail along its coastline. Writing in 1154, Moroccan geographer al-Idrisi told about some Muslim adventurers who set off from Lisbon, Portugal and may have reached the Canary Islands, which lie off the Atlantic coast from the southwestern corner of Morocco. The thirteenth-century historian Ibn Sa'id said that Muslims explored the West African coast during the twelfth century, probably in search of a good source for the "tunny fish" that were a main food for Moroccans. North Africans, however, did not put much capital or effort into such seafaring ventures because the trans-Saharan trade route was a well-established and efficient means of supplying their needs for most West African goods and materials.

Portuguese traders depicted on a brass plaque made in the Kingdom of Benin, Nigeria, circa 1500–1600
(Ethnological Museum, Berlin)

Therefore, much of the exploration along the west coast of Africa was financed by European countries, especially Portugal and Italy, which were particularly attracted by West African gold and by its suitability for growing crops such as sugarcane.

Early Portuguese Exploration. Portuguese explorers landed on the shores of West Africa during the 1430s, after they had begun to build ships that could navigate the shallow waters and strong currents around Cape Bojador, which lies just below the Canary Islands, in the modern nation of Western Sahara. These Portuguese caravels, which weighed far less and were more maneuverable than Venetian cargo ships, could sail with the Atlantic winds and travel up rivers. Gil Eannes was the first Portuguese mariner to round Cape Bojador, making his journey in 1434. After Alvise Cà da Mosto discovered the Cape Verde Islands off the coast of Senegal in 1456, the Portuguese established a town on São Tiago, the principal island. Writing in the next century, Leo Africanus reported that a large number of African slaves—many of whom had converted to Christianity—were on the Cape Verde Islands, where their jobs were to "till the earth, water the sugarcanes, and serve both in the cities and in the country." Cà da Mosto and Diogo Gomes explored the Gambia River on separate expeditions for Portugal in 1455 and 1456 and wrote accounts of their travels. After this time, Portugal, and other countries, continued to send small fleets on annual expeditions.

Italian Exploration. In 1447 the Genoan merchant Antonio Malfante stayed for a time at Tuat, a Saharan oasis that had become an important commercial center where traders from Tunis and Egypt exchanged goods for Sudanese gold. His letter to a friend reported what he heard there about sub-Saharan Africa. In 1469 a Florentine, Benedetto Dei, reportedly traveled up the Niger River by boat to Timbuktu.

Later Portuguese Exploration. In 1471 some Portuguese ships landed at Shama on the southern "Gold Coast" of West Africa, so-called because of its proximity to the Akan goldfields, and the Portuguese established their first settlement, at Elmina in the modern nation of Ghana. When they visited the wealthy and powerful kingdom of Benin in 1486, the Portuguese were impressed with the size of the empire and its ruler's skills. As the largest political system of Guinea at the time, Benin traded far and wide. It exported cotton, spices, kola nuts, shea butter, hides, civet musk for making perfumes, and ivory. It imported salt, horses, copper, silver, dried dates and figs, beads, glassware, and other manufactured goods. During the Portuguese explorations of the early fifteenth century, sailors acted like pirates, taking goods and prisoners from the West African mainland, but by the end of the century, Europeans and West Africans had developed a trading partnership. For the most part, the African empires along the coast were too strong to be pushed around or exploited.

Exploration and Changes in Trade. In 1488 Portuguese explorer Duarte Pacheco Pereira brought horses, cotton goods, and other merchandise to trade for gold and slaves along the southern coast of West Africa. Like Cà da Mosto before him, Pacheco Pereira observed weather problems, including heavy summer rains and winds that allowed ships to sail only at certain times of the year. These poor weather conditions kept Europeans from developing the gold trade to the extent they wanted. Exporting African slaves for sugarcane production, however, turned out to be the most profitable trade venture for Europeans.

Exploration and a Shift in Trade Routes. The arrival of Europeans on the southern coast of West Africa in the late 1400s corresponded with the rise in power of the city of Ile-Ife on the Niger River at the edge of the tropical forest. Its rulers controlled the trade with Europeans in ivory, gold, pepper, kola nuts, and slaves from the interior along the Niger River. By 1500, however, the center of power had shifted to Benin, where the Portuguese traded maize and pineapples that they brought from Central and South America. By 1600, the long-established trans-Saharan trade routes had become less important for the West African economy than the new trading places all along the western and southern coasts. Events in North Africa also contributed to this change. Between 1471 and 1514 the Portuguese took several Moroccan ports of the Atlantic, and during this period of civil unrest the city of Sijilmasa at the northern end of the western caravan routes fell into decline. After driving the Muslims from their last outpost in Spain in 1491, Spanish Christians were also fighting the Muslims of North Africa, who at the same time were beginning to come under attack from fellow Muslims, the Ottoman Turks, who completed their conquest of Tunisia in 1575. As a result, travel along the caravan routes became dangerous, and trade shifted to the southern coast of West Africa.

Sources:

J. F. A. Ajayi and Michael Crowder, eds., *The History of West Africa*, second edition, 2 volumes (New York: Columbia University Press, 1976, 1987).

Kwame Anthony Appiah and Henry Louis Gates Jr., eds., *Africana: The Encyclopedia of the African and African American Experience* (New York: Basic Civitas Books, 1999).

Brian Catchpole, *A History of West Africa in Maps and Diagrams* (London: Collins Educational, 1983).

Basil Davidson, *The Lost Cities of Africa* (Boston & Toronto: Little, Brown, 1959).

Mary Penick Motley, *Africa, Its Empires, Nation, and People* (Detroit: Wayne State University Press, 1969).

D. T. Niane, ed., *Africa from the Twelfth to the Sixteenth Century*, volume 4 of *General History of Africa* (Paris: United Nations Educational, Scientific and Cultural Organization, 1984).

SIGNIFICANT PEOPLE

MANSA ABUBAKARI II

1300-1312?
EMPEROR OF MALI

Expanding an Empire. A grandson of a daughter of the great ruler Sundiata (reigned 1230–1255), the founder of the Keita dynasty, Mansa (emperor) Abubakari became ruler of Mali in 1300. His younger half brother was Kankan Musa, who later became the famous Mansa Musa. As ruler of one of the largest empires in the world at that time, Abubakari sought to increase the power and influence of Mali even further. While his brother was interested in extending the borders of the empire to the east, toward Cairo, Abubakari apparently focused on westward expansion by exploring the waters to the west of his kingdom. Unlike most medieval Europeans, Muslim geographers such as Abu Zaid, al-Masudi, al-Idrisi, al-Istakhri, and Albufeda had concluded that the Atlantic Ocean was not the western edge of the world, and their ideas may have come to Abubakari through scholars at the great Muslim university in Timbuktu.

The First Fleet. According to oral tradition, Abubakari gathered shipbuilders and watermen from all over his empire. He is said to have had different boat designs built so that if one failed, another might succeed. Al-Umari recorded the story Mansa Musa told in Egypt in 1324:

> The monarch who preceded me would not believe that it was impossible to discover the limits of the neighboring sea. He wished to know. He persisted in his plan. He caused the equipping of two hundred ships and filled them with men, and of each such number that were filled with gold, water, and food for two years. He said to the commanders: Do not return until you have reached the end of the ocean, or when you have exhausted your food and water.

According to al-Umari, only one ship returned. Its captain reported to Abubakari that he had watched as the other ships sailed on, entered a broad current in the midst of the ocean, and disappeared. Instead of following them, he turned around and returned home.

The Second Fleet. Abubakari then decided to build a fleet of two thousand boats and to command it himself. He conferred power on Musa, specifying that if he did not return after a reasonable amount of time, Musa should inherit the throne. In 1311 Abubakari set out with his fleet down the Senegal River and headed west in the Atlantic. He never returned to Mali, and his brother became Mansa Musa in 1312.

Sources:

Basil Davidson, *Lost Cities of Africa* (Boston: Little, Brown, 1959).

J. Spencer Trimingham, *History of Islam in West Africa* (London, Glasgow & New York: Oxford University Press, 1962).

Ivan Van Sertima, *They Came Before Columbus* (New York: Random House, 1976).

Van Sertima, ed., *African Presence in Early America* (New Brunswick, N.J.: Journal of African Civilizations, 1987).

OBA ESIGIE

DIED 1550
KING OF BENIN

Communicator. A ruler with many skills, Oba (king) Esigie was known for his hospitality, literacy, and abilities as a communicator. Benin was one of two major, wealthy Yoruba states west of the lower Niger delta. During his reign, which began in 1504, Esigie established peaceful relations with Portuguese ambassadors as well as the Christian missionaries who had come from Lisbon at the request of his predecessor, Oba Ozolua, in 1486. In 1516 missionary Duarte Pires reported that Oba Esigie was a man of learning who could speak and read Portuguese and practiced astrology (which then included what is now known as the science of astronomy). Oba Esigie maintained a strong connection to Portugal throughout his reign, and in 1540 he sent an ambassador to the Portuguese capital.

European Trade. Oba Esigie encouraged extensive trade with the Europeans but kept Benin independent of European rule. During his reign, selling slaves to the Portuguese, the French, and later the English became a major business in Benin, whose armies captured people from other West African kingdoms for this purpose. At this time the Portuguese described Esigie's capital as a city with a nine-mile wall around it. As several historians have pointed out, this description reveals that Benin was a wealthy trading center, but its great wall suggests that it had many enemies and was plagued by unrest and instability.

Changing Royal Succession. By Esigie's time the rulers of Benin had strengthened the governing power of the oba. Oba Esigie continued this trend by waging a successful war against the group of noblemen who had the power to choose the king of Benin and changing the rules of royal succession so that the throne was inherited by the oba's eldest son.

Sources:

Kwame Anthony Appiah and Henry Louis Gates Jr., eds., *Africana: The Encyclopedia of the African and African American Experience* (New York: Basic Civitas Books, 1999).

William Farquhar Conton, *West Africa in History*, 2 volumes (London: Allen & Unwin, 1965, 1966).

Basil Davidson, with F. K. Buah and the advice of Ajayi, *A History of West Africa to the Nineteenth Century*, revised edition (Garden City, N.Y.: Anchor/Doubleday, 1966).

MAHMOUD AL-KATI

1468–CIRCA 1593

HISTORIAN

Soninke Writer. Mahmoud al-Kati was the first West African scholar to write an important history of the Western Sudan, *Tarikh al-Fattash* (The Chronicle of the Seeker After Knowledge). Al-Kati was a member of the Soninke tribe who learned to read and write Arabic, the language of West African scholars in his time.

Travel to Mecca. As a member of the Soninke tribe, al-Kati was a descendant of the rulers of the ancient Empire of Ghana and shared this lineage with Askia Muhammad the Great, ruler of Songhai in 1493–1528. When al-Kati was twenty-five, he became a member of Askia Muhammad's personal staff. In 1495 al-Kati went with the emperor on his hajj to Mecca. Askia Muhammad apparently stayed in Mecca and Cairo for two years, during which al-Kati observed and wrote about the events and people they encountered.

Scholar. After they returned from Mecca, al-Kati became a doctor of Islamic law at Sankore University in Timbuktu. He began writing *Tarikh al-Fattash* in 1519 when he was 51 years old. Though he is said to have lived

to the age of 125, he did not complete the work. His sons and grandsons who were also scholars continued the work of recording the history of the Songhai Empire and Timbuktu to about 1665. No original manuscript of al-Kati's history has survived, and in extant copies it is often difficult to distinguish his observations from commentary by other writers.

Tarikh al-Fattash. The word *tarikh* may be translated as "presenting oral traditions," which is what al-Kati did. He did use some texts by contemporary Arabic scholars, but he also wrote much original work based on unwritten historical sources. Living through most of the sixteenth century—when the Songhai Empire was at its peak—al-Kati recorded the histories of the rulers and the powerful Empires of Ghana, Mali, and Songhai, covering their geography, towns, and cultures over the centuries.

Sources:

J. F. A. Ajayi and Michael Crowder, eds., *The History of West Africa*, second edition, 2 volumes (New York: Columbia University Press, 1976, 1987).

Basil Davidson, with F. K. Buah and the advice of Ajayi, *A History of West Africa to the Nineteenth Century*, revised edition (Garden City, N.Y.: Anchor/Doubleday, 1966).

Nehemia Levtzion, *Ancient Ghana and Mali* (New York: Harper & Row, 1973).

Patricia and Frederick McKissack, *The Royal Kingdoms of Ghana, Mali, and Songhay: Life in Medieval Africa* (New York: Holt, 1994).

Mary Penick Motley, *Africa, Its Empires, Nations, and People* (Detroit: Wayne State University Press, 1969).

'ABD AL-RAHMAN AL-SA'DI

1569–CIRCA 1655

HISTORIAN

West African Writer. 'Abd al-Rahman al-Sa'di wrote *Tarikh al-Sudan* (Chronicle of the Western Sudan), the second important history of West Africa by a native of the region. Al-Sa'di was of Andalusian descent and a learned citizen of Timbuktu. He said he wrote the book because of the sad events he saw during his childhood, a period in which the Songhai Empire was often at war with Morocco. His history was published in about 1650 in Arabic, the literary language of his day.

A History of Triumph and Defeat. In the preface to his book al-Sa'di described "the ruin of learning and its utter collapse" under the Moroccan invaders, who completed their conquest of the empire in 1591:

> And because learning is rich in beauty and fertile in its teaching, since it instructs men about their fatherland, their ancestors, their history, the names of their heroes and what lives they lived, I asked God's help and decided to set down all that I myself could learn on the subject of the Songhai princes of the Sudan, their adventures, their story, their

achievements and their wars. Then I added the history of Timbuktu from the time of its foundation, of the princes who ruled there and the scholars and saints who lived there, and of other things as well.

Other information in *Tarikh al-Sudan* includes early traditions and legends of ancient Ghana and Mali.

Sources:

J. F. A. Ajayi and Michael Crowder, eds., *The History of West Africa,* second edition, 2 volumes (New York: Columbia University Press, 1976, 1987).

Basil Davidson, with F. K. Buah and the advice of Ajayi, *The Growth of African Civilization; A History of West Africa 1000–1800,* revised edition (London: Longmans, 1967).

Nehemia Levtzion, *Ancient Ghana and Mali* (New York: Harper & Row, 1973).

Patricia and Fredrick McKissack, *The Royal Kingdoms of Ghana, Mali, and Songhay: Life in Medieval Africa* (New York: Holt, 1994).

Mary Penick Motley, *Africa, Its Empires, Nations, and People* (Detroit: Wayne State University Press, 1969).

MANSA SAKURA

DIED 1300?

EMPEROR OF MALI

The Slave Who Became Emperor. Unlike most rulers of the ancient West African kingdoms, Sakura did not come from royal lineage. Starting life as a slave, he was freed, possibly after arriving at the royal court, and subsequently became a government official. After the weak-minded and sadistic Mansa Khalifa (ruled 1274–1275)—a degenerate member of the Keita dynasty founded by the great ruler Sundiata—was deposed and killed, the nobles made the easily controlled Abu Bakr their new ruler. On his death, possibly in 1285, Sakura seized the throne and managed to restore order to the deteriorating kingdom.

Conquest and Trade. Mansa Sakura was a powerful leader known for exploring lands and incorporating them into the kingdom of Mali. He extended the empire along the Gambia River to the sea and also encouraged trading activities. After a hiatus during the years of instability, merchants from North Africa began traveling to Mali again.

Pilgrimage. Sakura followed the example of other great rulers of Mali and made a hajj to Mecca. While on this journey, he visited Cairo. Sakura died on his way home from the pilgrimage, possibly around 1300. Some sources said he was killed at Tajura. The throne returned to the legitimate heirs of the Keita dynasty.

Maintaining the Empire. Because of this restoration, some historians have interpreted Sakura's takeover as an attempt to ensure the survival of the Keita dynasty rather than an attempt to establish his own dynasty. Slaves in royal courts often held positions of power. In fact, a king's power was based heavily on the loyalty of his slaves. Slaves of strong kings obeyed their ruler, but those of weak kings often seized control.

New Ideas. During Sakura's reign, North African diplomats visited Mali, and Islamic scholars came to teach in court schools. Among the ideas they brought from North Africa were the beliefs that the Atlantic Ocean was not on the edge of the world and that new lands beyond this sea were waiting to be explored. This impetus to exploration inspired Sakura's successor, Abubakari II, to set out on his westward journey across the Atlantic Ocean in 1311.

Sources:

Nehemia Levtzion, *Ancient Ghana and Mali* (New York: Harper & Row, 1973).

J. Spencer Trimingham, *History of Islam in West Africa* (London, Glasgow & New York: Oxford University Press, 1962).

Ivan Van Sertima, *They Came Before Columbus* (New York: Random House, 1976).

DOCUMENTARY SOURCES

Al-Bakri, *Kitab al-masalik wa-'l-mamalik* (The Book of Routes and Realms, 1068)—A geographical work by a Spanish Muslim who never visited West Africa and based his detailed descriptions of the region on oral and written accounts by travelers; al-Bakri included material on the kingdom of Ghana, the trans-Saharan trade network, how nomads found water in the desert, the communication role of clothing, and the importance of Arabic scholars in preserving West African history.

Alvise Cà da Mosto (1432–1488), *Una opera necessaria a tutti li nauiga[n]ti chi vano in diuerse parte del mondo* (A Guide for All Navigators Who Wish to Travel Safely; Venice: Printed by Bernardino Rizus, 1490)—A travel account by a Venetian who explored the Madeira and Canary Islands and the coast of West Africa for Portugal in 1455 and 1456; he traveled partway up the Gambia River.

Yaqut al-Hamawi, *Mu'jam al-duldan* (The Dictionary of Countries, 1229)—A list of place names with information from people in different time periods including Ibn Hawqal and Al-Bakri; Yaqut traveled and visited libraries in Iran, Iraq, Syria, and Egypt; his work includes a description of merchant caravans and their use of camels in the desert.

Ibn al-Faqih, *Mukhtasar Kitab al-Buldan* (Abridged Book of the Muslim World, 903)—An encyclopedia of the Muslim world that includes a description of a transportation route from Ghana to Egypt and estimates of the length of time it took to travel some desert trade routes.

Ibn Battuta (1304 – circa 1378), *Rihlah* (Travels)—A generally reliable account of twenty-four years of travel through much of the Muslim world, including West and East Africa, India, Ceylon, Sumatra, and perhaps China; his eyewitness reports of his trip to West Africa describe how trade caravans traveled across the desert and include stories of generosity and hospitality; he also wrote about court etiquette and the role of griots.

Ibn Hawqal, *Surat al-Ard* (The Picture of the Earth, 988)—A geographical work based on the author's travels in the Maghrib and Spain; the work describes Sijilmasa and its trade with the Sudan, a route from Sijilmasa to West Africa, and how the caravans traveled from oasis to oasis across the Sahara.

Ibn Khaldun, *Kitab al-'ibar* (The Book of Historical Lessons, written 1374–1378, revised 1378–1404)—A well-known "universal history" that describes the connections and communications between Mali and North Africa from the eleventh through the fourteenth centuries.

Al-Idrisi, *Kitab Nuzhat al-Mashtaq fi Ikhtiraq al-Afaq* (Amusement for One Who Desires to Travel Around the World, 1154)—A book written by a Muslim geographer for the Norman Christian king of Sicily, Roger II, and often called *Kitab al-Rujari* (The Book of Roger); this book includes maps of the geographic regions of the western Sudan, some material from Al-Bakri, and some new information on trade routes, how nomads found water in the desert, and the explorations of Portuguese sailors in the Atlantic; Al-Idrisi's work became part of the *Diwan*, the recorded history of Kanem-Bornu.

Mahmoud al-Kati, *Tarikh al-Fattash* (The Chronicle of the Seeker After Knowledge, started 1519)—a history of the ancient Empires of Ghana, Mali, and Songhai including geography, towns, and culture; important work on West Africa and the first written by a native.

Leo Africanus (1485–1554), *Descrittione dell'Africa* (Description of Africa, 1550)—A firsthand account of the travels of an author born in Granada as al-Hassan ibn Muhammad al-Wizzaa al-Fasi through the Sudan in 1513–1515; the work includes extensive, accurate information on various modes of transportation in West Africa, including dugout canoes, horses, and camels; it also discusses the role of Arabic scholars in teaching people in Timbuktu to read and write Arabic.

'Abd al-Rahman al-Sa'di, *Tarikh al-Sudan* (Chronicle of the Western Sudan, circa 1650)—the second history of West Africa, written by a native of Timbuktu, the work includes early traditions and legends of ancient Ghana and Mali, information on the Songhai princes, and a history of Timbuktu.

Al-Umari, *Masalik al-absar fi mamalik al-amsar* (Pathways of Vision in the Realms of the Metropolises, 1338)—A work of history and geography that includes a history of Mali in the fourteenth century, which is based on information provided by people who lived there and by Egyptian officials who met Mansa Musa during his 1324 pilgrimage to Mecca and visit to Cairo.

An Arab merchant traveling a trans-Saharan trade route; illumination from a 1237 Baghdad manuscript for the *Maqamat* (Assemblies) of al-Hariri (Bibliothèque Nationale, Paris)

Bankoni drummer, Mali, circa 1100–1500 (from Jean-Baptiste Bacquart, *The Tribal Arts of Africa,* 1998)

SOCIAL CLASS SYSTEM AND THE ECONOMY

by DAVID L. HORNE

CONTENTS

Sidebars and tables are listed in italics.

IMPORTANT EVENTS OF 500-1590

500
- Mande-speaking peoples are migrating into the savanna region of West Africa, bringing iron weapons and tools and establishing patterns of trade. Within their social groups there is a clear division of labor in agriculture and social differentiation based on possession of iron weapons and status within the trading process.

502
- West Africans have been trading foodstuffs, salt, and gold along intra- and interregional trade routes.

550
- By this date, camel caravans from the Maghrib (Northwest Africa) are engaged in trans-Saharan trade with West Africa.

711
- The Muslims complete their conquest and colonization of Northwest Africa and Spain.

770
- Al-Fazari of Baghdad writes about the economically diverse people and gold resources of the Empire of Ghana in the first surviving record of this wealthy West African state.

800*
- West African states begin to employ cavalry in their military campaigns.
- The trans-Saharan caravan trade between North and West Africa has greatly expanded.

872-873
- Yaqubi's geographical history of Ghana and Takrur includes a description of the differences in economic status between Muslim traders and the local people.

977
- Ibn Hawqal visits Ghana and writes about the extensive banking system that underwrites the trans-Saharan trade.

990
- Berbers invade the oasis trading city of Audaghost from the Empire of Ghana in an attempt to control the trans-Saharan trade.

1054
- Almoravid Berbers attack Audaghost for the second time and virtually destroy it.

1076
- Almoravids sack Kumbi Saleh, the main capital of the Empire of Ghana, weakening, but not destroying, the state. Many members of the merchant class leave the city.

* DENOTES CIRCA DATE

IMPORTANT EVENTS OF 500-1590

1154
- Al-Idrisi writes about the great wealth of Ghana.

1180
- Led by Sumanguru, the Susu clan seizes control of southern territories that have been part of the Empire of Ghana. Basing their power on their possession of horses and iron weapons, the Susu try to establish protection for trade and commerce.

1225*
- The Hausa city-states increase in power as the Empire of Ghana enters its final decline.

1230
- Sundiata seizes the throne of Kangaba (a small state in present-day Guinea on a tributary of the Niger River), founding the Keita dynasty.

1235
- Sundiata defeats Sumanguru at the Battle of Kirina, establishing the basis for the Empire of Mali, in which the resident merchant class expands and thrives.

1255
- The death of Sundiata is followed by lengthy succession disputes and temporary economic disruption in the major cities of Mali.

1285
- Sakura, a loyal slave of the royal household, seizes the throne of Mali, restoring stability to trading operations and reviving the confidence of Muslim and local merchants.

1307-1337
- During the reign of Mansa Musa, a member of the Keita dynasty, the Empire of Mali reaches its greatest size.

1324-1325
- Mansa Musa makes a pilgrimage to Mecca, depressing the economy of Egypt for more than a year because of the oversupply of gold he brings there on his journey.

1337
- After the death of Mansa Musa, Mali enters another period of economic instability.

1352-1353
- Ibn Battuta visits Mali, observing the economic and political consequences of succession disputes.

* DENOTES CIRCA DATE

IMPORTANT EVENTS OF 500-1590

1388	• The court slave Sandiki seizes control of the government in Mali.
1390-1391	• A member of the Keita clan reclaims control in Mali and restores viability to the economy.
1441	• The Portuguese begin the European trade in slaves from West Africa. African slaves become a profitable economic commodity.
1464-1492	• During his reign, Sunni Ali establishes the Songhai Empire, which lasts until 1591.
1481	• The Portuguese establish the Elmina trading post on the West African coast. It becomes one of a series of way stations for slaves and other goods.
1492	• After the death of Sunni Ali, the Muslim convert Askia Muhammad I (Askia the Great) seizes power in Songhai, establishing a dynasty of askias. During his reign the economic status of participants in the creation of commodities, including merchants and financiers, is substantially enhanced.
1500*	• Pastoral Fulani Muslims from the Senegal region are migrating eastward, increasing the economic complexity of the Western Sudan, particularly in terms of trading.
1528	• Askia Muhammad is deposed by several of his sons, who then engage in succession disputes that destabilize the Songhai state, bringing economic disorder and lack of protection for merchants. As a result, a large-scale emigration of the commercial class begins.
1562	• The British enter the West African slave trade in economic, maritime, and political competition with the Portuguese, Spanish, and Dutch.
1571-1603	• During his reign in the Kanem-Bornu empire, Mai Idris Alooma supplies his troops with firearms purchased from the Moroccans and the Ottoman Turks.
1590	• Armed with traditional weapons, Songhai troops are easily defeated by Moroccans carrying firearms. The Moroccans capture Timbuktu in 1591, causing the fall of the Songhai Empire.

* DENOTES CIRCA DATE

OVERVIEW

Contemporary Icons. Popularized by Africanists and African historians since the 1960s as a sequential triad of trade-based empires, ancient Ghana, Mali, and Songhai have become icons of African history and culture. Although much of what has been written about these rulerships is fairly credible, a significant portion remains within the realm of mythmaking rather than accurate history. For example, though the hypothesis about Greek, Roman, or Arab-Muslim origins of these empires has generally been dispelled, it has been replaced by the myth that these three kingdoms—and Kanem-Bornu—represent radical departures from the surrounding political realities of the Western Sudan. On the contrary, these three rulerships are expanded versions of the basic Sudanic *kafu*—the groupings of clans and lineages in villages under a single clan head—that were characteristic of Mande speakers and their neighbors, who dominated the residential and migratory populations of the Western Sudan. The Takrur, Susu, Dagomba, Kiri, Do, Hausa, and Kanem-Bornu states, among others, are similar examples of polities that resulted from consistent food surpluses and population expansion based on the *kafu*.

Metallurgy and State Building. Each state had its own dominant clans with territorial and financial ambitions, and each had access to extensive ironworking populations, who produced tools, trade goods, and weapons. In fact, the creation of large and small Sudanic states was based not only on military forces using weapons made by ironworkers but also on the ability to apply the spiritual beliefs associated with metalworking to creating social and political syntheses. Each state used military innovation, traditional beliefs regarding authority, and existing clans or lineages of skilled craftsmen for the purpose of expanding and maintaining control over local populations. Yet, none was a police state so the regular population participated in intra- or interregional commercial relationships over a sustained period of time.

Other Myths. A second myth is that the Sudanic rulerships can best be understood by analogies to European monarchy. Thus, scholars regularly discuss West African empires in terms of kings, princes, courts, nobles, and vassals, rather than *kaya maghan, mansa, dia, mai,* and askia—the titles of the rulers of these West African states, which came from dominant clan names and do not correspond neatly to European titles. A third myth is that the rulerships of Ghana, Mali, and Songhai were each ended abruptly by a single major catastrophic event—the Murabitun, or Almoravid, attack on Ghana in the eleventh century, the Songhai attack on Mali in the fifteenth, and the Moroccan invasion of Songhai in the sixteenth—and that the three rulerships replaced each other in succession, adding more territory over time. The rise and evolution of each state was far more complicated than such an outline suggests. Succession disputes fundamentally undermined the maintenance of any state in the Western Sudan. None effectively solved this basic weakness in the state-building pattern. Also, relentless warfare and the coastal slave trade substantially reduced populations of the savanna, forest, and Sahel from the fifteenth through the nineteenth centuries. Without expanding populations, state building in the region could not occur, and established states or empires could not be sustained.

Trade. A fourth myth is that the rise of the three western Sudanic rulerships was almost exclusively a function of the evolution and expansion of the trans-Saharan caravan trade, while a fifth is that gold was the only metal of importance in the economic history of those rulerships. According to this view, its importance in the Western Sudan was limited to its status as one of the two principal commodities of the trans-Saharan caravan trade and its symbolism of elite wealth. The history of the Western Sudan cannot be reduced to an account of the significance of the trans-Saharan caravan trade and the associated spread of Islam in the region. Those two factors were undeniably crucial to the development of the Western Sudan, but they were no more important than the ability to grow a regular surplus of food in the region and its enablement of sustained population expansion, the tradition of the *kafu* political unit, military innovations in weaponry and tactics, and the evolution of metallurgy in the region, working not only gold—which had a significance far beyond its status as one of the two staple commodities of the caravan trade—but especially iron and frequently copper.

Ghana. Like Mali and Songhai, Ghana was founded and governed by indigenous tribal groups. According to Arab authors, by the eleventh century its boundaries enclosed the huge area occupied by present-day southeast Mauritania and almost all of western Mali. A trading state that grew into an empire, its accepted origins go back to approximately 300 C.E. Based on the written records of Muslim travelers, who dubbed ancient Ghana the "land of gold," from 700 until the mid 1200s Ghana was prosperous, and its capital at Kumbi Saleh (located approximately 222 miles north of present-day Bamako, in the country of Mali) was a major, central market for trading in Ghanaian gold, ivory, iron and leather goods, and slaves for salt, copper, dried fruit, textiles, clothing, and mechanical tools and equipment. This capital was divided into two cities located approximately six miles apart, with dwelling huts in the space between them. In the larger city were located the ruler's residence and houses for thousands of his constituents, all surrounded by a high stone wall. The second city was a merchant city for foreigners, including Muslims. Archaeological digs at Kumbi Saleh have uncovered two-story cement houses of sixty-six by forty-two square feet in size, with more than seven rooms—as well as iron lances and knives, nails and arrow tips, farming tools, scissors, painted pottery, and glass weights for measuring gold.

Rise and Fall of an Empire. During the medieval period, when Ghana was in its ascendancy, its gold was a highly valued and relentlessly sought-after commodity in Spain and large portions of North Africa. Kumbi Saleh and Audaghost, the other main town of Ghana, a trading center situated in a desert oasis, were major urban areas with populations of more than ten thousand people. The dominant ethnic group during Ghana's rise to prominence and its sustained prestige was the Soninke. Ghana was significantly weakened after the successful sacking of Kumbi Saleh in 1076 by the North African Muslim soldiers of Abu Bakr and the Almoravids. A few years later, however, the Soninke revived Ghana by re-establishing Kumbi Saleh as a thriving entrepôt (intermediary trade center). Ghana survived being absorbed temporarily by the Susu around 1180–1203, but around 1240 Sundiata Keita sacked and razed Kumbi Saleh, essentially what remained of the Ghanaian state system as a dominant force in the region. As its population thinned beyond a critical point, it contracted back toward its basic *kafu,* but it did not "disappear." It still had iron technology and effective food-production pro-

cesses. It still had a collection of clans and lineages, a military presence, and autonomy. The later expansion of Mali did absorb the previous territories associated with ancient Ghana, and the basic constituency of the larger empire was still Mande speakers, but Mali did not "succeed" Ghana.

Mali. Sundiata established Mali, which evolved to control the Sahel region currently occupied by the African states of the Gambia, Senegal, Guinea, Mali, and portions of Burkino Faso, Mauritania, and Niger. Its capital city was Niani, and its major cities were Gao, Djenné, Walata, and Timbuktu. Its dominance extended from approximately 1240 until around 1500, as its territory expanded through trade, treaty, and conquest. The indigenous population anchoring medieval Mali was the Mandinke, and included the Kangaba and the Susu. The caravan trade was primarily responsible for the wealth and luxury of Mali, notwithstanding the fact that the majority of the population engaged in agriculture and herding. By 1500, competing tribal factions, including the Songhai people, who originated around the eastern bend of the Niger River, had conquered enough Malian territory to cause major constriction, but not the "disappearance," of the once great state.

Songhai. Throughout the last part of the fourteenth century, Songhai had been growing and competing with Mali, especially in terms of the caravan trade and gold collection. By the time its size and influence overwhelmed Mali, Songhai reached from the Atlantic Ocean on the west to the Niger River bend area of present-day central Nigeria on the east, and included the area now occupied by Guinea, the Gambia, Burkina Faso, Mali, Mauritania, Niger, Senegal, and part of Nigeria. With Gao as their capital, the rulers of Songhai also continued to enhance the prestige of Timbuktu and Djenné. The inglorious end of Songhai has regularly been dated to its military defeat at the hands of a Moroccan army at the battle of Tondibi in 1591, which forced the Songhai economy into a downward spiral of instability.

Kanem-Bornu. To the east of these three "empires" lay the Hausa-Sefuwa kingdoms of Kanem and Bornu. Established by the eighth century and reaching an expanded territorial range that included the Lake Chad region and territory halfway to the Nile by the thirteenth century, Kanem, and its successor state, Bornu, evolved as a kind of African feudal power in the Central Sudan area. Though they lacked the gold-producing areas that created the power base in the west, these two states gained control of the north-south caravan trade and the east-west trade to the Nile Valley.

TOPICS IN SOCIAL CLASS SYSTEM AND THE ECONOMY

THE ECONOMIC CONTEXT FOR STATE BUILDING

Organized Societies. During the first twelve hundred years of the Common Era, there appeared a procession of large, indigenously organized societies in the western, central, and eastern sections of West Africa, generally in the vicinity of the Senegal and Niger River basins or the region around Lake Chad. These societies included ancient Ghana, the Susu, Gao, Mali, Songhai, Kanem-Bornu, the Takrur, the Do or Dodugu, the Hausa, Kiri, the Mossi, and the Dagomba.

The Impetus for Empires. Though the rise and fall of Ghana, Mali, Songhai, Kanem-Bornu, the Hausa city-states, and the rest of the West African rulerships are frequently attributed to the trans-Saharan trade and the expansion of Islam, these factors alone do not explain the history of the region. It is true that trans-Saharan trade was of crucial importance in the origins and growth of those states, particularly regarding the regular acquisition and accumulation of wealth by the commercial and ruling elites, and the spread of Islam had both external and internal influences on Sudanic history. In fact, the caravan trade and Islam were no more significant than at least five other crucial factors: the regular production of food surpluses and an associated population growth, the *kafu* basic political unit in the West African savanna, widespread knowledge of iron metallurgy, the economics of military innovations, and the singular significance of gold.

Food Production and Climate. With their annual wet and dry seasons, the savanna and Sahel of West Africa are subject to two extremes in weather: heavy equatorial rains causing the flooding of river valleys and dry Harmattan dust storms. The southern savanna area closest to the forest gets 1,500 to 2,000 millimeters of rainfall a year for more than six months, along with high temperatures. The central savanna and the northern savanna or steppe known as the Sahel, particularly the river valleys, were one of the three primary centers in Africa for the early evolution and development of food production. From their brown, sandy, structured soils called duricrusts, with strong concentrations of iron oxide and alumina mineral content, came the sorghum, millet, and rice that were staples of the West African diet.

Food Production and Migration. During the first millennium before the Common Era, many clusters of peoples gravitated toward these fertile areas, resulting in concentrations of settlements and cultivation in several defensible locations. As their populations expanded, they reached the point of requiring adjustments to residential organization. One such large migrating population was the Soninke, a Mande-speaking people, who moved from their original desert/Sahel habitat called Wagadu, situated in an area of unstable climate and geography. According to oral traditions, Wagadu had a seven-year drought just before the beginning of the Common Era. Ostensibly because of that extended dry period, the Soninke migrated in stages over a large part of the Western Sudan, from the Gambia east through Songhai territory. A large group of them settled within the central-northern savanna belt and established the ancient state of Aoukar, later called Ghana. This kind of migration occurred in many other parts of West Africa. In areas where the soils supported successful agriculture, reliable food surpluses produced concentrated populations, which created highly evolved societies, such as Ghana and the other large Sudanic states.

Kafu Organization. Among Mande speakers, the basic state in the Western Sudan started with a clan or kinship lineage who acknowledged a common founding ancestor and inhabited an identifiable territory, with boundaries that were sometimes overt (such as sections of rivers or clusters of trees) but in other cases amorphous. As chief or clan head *(dugutigi),* the group might select either a patriarch who was recognized as a direct descendant of the first clan settler or a person who had demonstrated skills and clan integrity. They also elected a council of elder-advisers. The chief's functions included the distribution of group wealth and land usage and the adjudication of disputes. As the embodiment of the spiritual identity of his clan, the chief or clan head was not allowed discretionary power within this traditional arrangement; instead he was guided and circumscribed by lineage custom and accepted clan values. An extra-clan rulership was a collection of several clans or lineage groups under a dominant clan and chief that had grown wealthy or large enough to impose an artificial order on the larger collective, either by a well-equipped military or by secret societies within the dominant clan group. The chief of this collected group of clans, the *fama* or *farin*, was the master protector of the land and the political authority over the collective body. The combined body of clans, lineages, villages, and/or microstates was called the *kafu*. The name of the chief's home village generally became the name of the *kafu*.

Bases for State Building. John Iliffe has called the *kafu* "the enduring political community of the savanna, the building-block with which larger . . . polities were constructed." The clan and the *kafu* represented the essential localism of West African state-building processes. Empire builders who overextended their reach could easily lose their authority by moving too far from their power base in the *kafu*. Instead of being destroyed, however, the West African empire was most frequently reduced back to its root *kafu*, as was the case with Ghana, Mali, Songhai, the Susu, and most other states that achieved a zenith and then declined. The majority of the general histories of these rulerships have reported their abrupt devastation and end because of a single violent clash, but, in fact, the societies continued unabated, although much reduced.

Iron. Mande-speaking cultivators—including the Soninke, Wangara, Wakore, Sarakolle, Susu, Malinke, and Dyula—generally used iron tools and iron weapons. According to evidence found in excavations at Djenné-Jeno in the Niger bend area, they had been doing so since at least the third century B.C.E. At least thirteen iron-smelting furnaces dating from the fifth to the third centuries B.C.E., have been found in Taruga and the Baruchi Plateau of contemporary Nigeria. Taruga was part of the Nok-culture sites, which include examples of the oldest African sculptures of the human form. Additional evidence, dating from the sixth to the fourth centuries B.C.E., has been found at Nsukka in southern Nigeria, as well as in Cameroon, Gabon, and the Republic of the Congo. Iron hoes, axes, digging sticks, knives, and other implements helped these areas in the production of the food surpluses necessary for a sustained population increase, contributing to the spread of Mande speakers throughout the savanna and eventually into the forest areas of West Africa.

Metallurgists. Ironworkers—smiths and smelters, in particular—were an indispensable part of every centralized state. Ironworkers produced objects that had symbolic and practical values in the traditional societies of the Sudan-Sahel, including bridewealth, essential farming tools, and technologically advanced weapons of war. They had both economic and spiritual power within West African societies, and at times, political power. Among Mande speakers, the blacksmith was a mythical hero who "descended from the sky and brought fertilizing water to a parched land." Traditionally, blacksmiths and smelters were typically seen as the bringers of life and civilization through the forging stone (mother stone) and the anvil. Iron brought life-affirming agricultural tools and weapons of defense, but at the same time it was seen as a threat to those who did not embrace it and wanted to get rid of it. In general, ironworkers were highly respected, sometimes feared, craftsmen within their communities, but Muslim

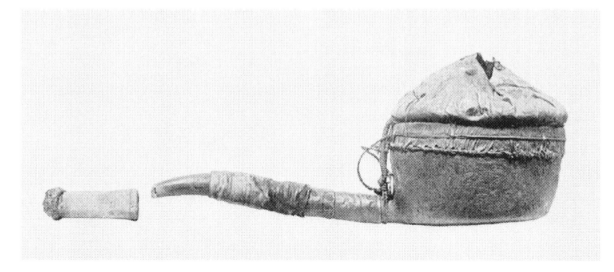

Traditional bellows used by ironworkers in West Africa (British Museum, London)

populations increasingly disparaged them, believing that they clung to traditional magic and superstition. In traditional societies ironworkers stimulated an increase in social differentiation and stratification because of the increasing specialization of skilled labor their work required.

Metallurgy and State Building. Some scholars, such as R. Haaland and Augustin F. C. Holl, believe that the "intensification of iron production is directly associated with the rise of Ghana (and the other successive rulerships) as a centralized state" and that the central authority had either to control the process and volume of iron production in its immediate region or to control access to that process, if it intended to maintain its superiority in that region and continue to expand its boundaries. A persistent tension existed because clan chiefs and rulers were both in competition and in alliance with iron craftsmen. Ironworkers were not only necessarily a pre-existing part of the population base from which a rulership was expanding, but they might be a crucial part of a population the rulership was trying to capture and as such had to be absorbed into whatever *kafu* had growth ambitions. Like the *fama*, or ruler, metallurgists were believed to have great spiritual and magical power within the clans. Through the investiture process, the *fama* was transmuted to semi-divine status with all of its attendant ceremony and trappings. Iron smelters and smiths transmuted "ordinary" sand and rock into precious metal in the shapes of farming tools, weapons, body decorations, trade goods, and other implements.

Metallurgy and Migration. The Mema region, situated on a large floodplain approximately one hundred kilometers northwest of the Niger Delta, was the central area for iron production in Ghana and, later, Mali. Excavations there from the 1950s through the 1990s have uncovered evidence of periods of increased intensity and concentration of ironworking for weapons, tools, and jewelry from 342 to 970, from 1025 to 1225, and from 1310 to 1550. More than one hundred mines and ironworking sites were found, including ninety-four village mounds and fifteen smelting/slag areas. Evidence at Mema also shows a sharp decrease in the number of settlements in the region during the thirteenth to the fifteenth centuries, as the trade routes and military expansion shifted northeastward within the Empire of Mali. As the population thinned, the Mema area still produced significant iron implements, but at a much reduced level.

Bonds between Metallurgists and Rulers. The rulers of Ghana, Mali, Songhai, and the other Sudanic states regularly attempted to bond the two realms of traditional spiritual power by claiming expertise as ironsmiths and smelters and simultaneously asserting the divine right to rule, as did the thirteenth-century Susu ruler Sumanguru. In war, he was reputed to be invulnerable to iron because he was a divine master of that metal. To cement the loyalty of ironworkers, rulers frequently married daughters of smiths or

smelters, ignoring the ironworker clans' restrictions of endogamy (marriage within one's own clan or group). Others—like Sumanguru's vanquisher, Sundiata—who were not ironworkers, publicly allied themselves with smiths and smelters to maintain their loyalty. According to the oral *Epic of Sundiata*, the young Sundiata took refuge in Mema, a significant ironworking area, where he had become a favorite of the *fama*. When he returned to Kiri (Mande) to establish the Keita dynasty and the beginnings of the Mali Empire, he was at the head of a Mema iron-equipped army, which then defeated one of the best militaries in the region at that time: Sumanguru's Susu army of excellently equipped soldiers, including many with chain-mail armor.

Ironworker Advisers. Sundiata had learned how to pay homage and give respect to the ironworker clans, keeping ironworker elders among his closest advisers. Such elders essentially controlled the production of iron tools and weapons in the region, and thus they could significantly influence the success of food production and the outcome of battles. Staying on good terms with ironworker elders was thus good policy, lest the elders curse the state administration by refusing to serve that rulership. In recounting the final battles of Sundiata and Sumanguru, *The Epic of Sundiata* comments on the fields of iron-smelting furnaces at the gathering places of opposing forces.

Metallurgy and War. Access to large quantities of quality ironwork was critical to the success of West African states and empires. The greater the state expansion, the more manpower and weaponry were needed to maintain, defend, and continue the spread of state influence. In the Western Sudan, hunter and secret-society protective clans often provided the military forces with chiefs and *fama* needed to defend their territory and sometimes to establish a sphere of influence over other villages and clans. When called on for work as mobile warriors, these groups used tactics and strategies borne of their forest and tracking experience. Before the eighth century they generally used iron-tipped weapons such as spears, arrows, and knives, which gave them a distinct advantage over those who did not have access to iron armaments. The advantage also went to the side that either had ironworker clans associated with it or had immediate access to such clans—as well as to the side that brought the greatest number of combatants to a show of force. Since a throwing spear or arrow, for example, was used only once, it took sustained effort to produce weapons in the great numbers required for a war. A regular part of military campaigns was seizing control of the opposition's ironworks or scuttling them by chasing away ironworkers and destroying their furnaces, forges, stones, and living quarters. Before the ninth century, most large armies in the Sudanic area, including that of Ghana, were essentially infantry and archers who engaged in close combat with weapons such as stabbing spears, axes, clubs, and

Terra-cotta statues of cavalrymen from the Bamako region of Mali, circa 1300–1500
(from Bernard de Grunne, *Terres cuites anciennes de L'Ouest Africain*, 1980)

hammers. Overwhelming numbers and superior tactics usually carried the day, sometimes along with psychological duplicity or trickery.

Cavalry. In the ninth and tenth centuries, the horse was introduced to Sudanic warfare, and rulerships that supplemented their infantry and archers with well-trained cavalry earned the advantage in combat. Ghana added cavalry to its military but was never able to use it to full advantage. It overextended itself by having to station garrisons of soldiers in trading cities to protect routes, merchants, and merchandise, while also having to fight incessant little wars and a few major wars against the Almoravids. As documented in accounts of the Battle of Kirina (1235), by the end of the twelfth century and the beginning of the thirteenth, the Susu and early Mali had chain-mail armor for chest protection, iron helmets for head protection, established societies of cavalry horsemen wearing clan emblems, and slave infantrymen in substantial numbers. By the fourteenth century, the Songhai had added a large river navy to their military forces, while maintaining the traditional aspects of the Sudanic fighting army. Mali at its peak and Songhai had permanent standing armies, which practiced and drilled and stood ready to defend or attack quickly. The last metallic innovation, which neither Mali nor Songhai accepted, was the gun. It was the weapon that gave the invading Moroccans their victory in 1590–1591. In all

other cases in the Western Sudan, the states with the best ironworks generally triumphed. Ultimately, all this military activity had a tremendous impact on the well-being, quality of life, and business stability of the merchant class. Continued warfare was usually bad for business, although all sides in a dispute usually allowed traders to move freely, even through ferocious fighting.

Metallurgical Property Rights. Ironworking and other skilled crafts were nearly always regarded as the property of a particular lineage or clan. In Ghana, Mali, Songhai, and most of the other states, ironworkers belonged to hereditary occupational castes that observed relatively strict rules of endogamy. They were widely recognized as separate and distinct "mystery" groups within Sudanic societies, and they most frequently lived in their own villages some distance from the main body of settlement, in special, restricted quarters within a particular settlement. Mastering smelting and smithing required years of apprenticeship, and because they were full-time professions in larger societies—such as Ghana, Mali, and Songhai—they took significant numbers of men away from farming, leaving much more of the agricultural work to be done by women, children, and war-captive slaves. Smelting and smithing were primarily dry-season work, as was most savanna-Sahelian agriculture. Men were the smelters and smiths while women and children helped by providing them with food and drink, mining for ore, gathering wood to make charcoal for the smelting process, and locating clay for the furnaces or tuyeres (pipes through which blasts of air were delivered to forges or furnaces). Ironworkers were generally paid extremely well. Payment was most frequently in food, livestock (including horses), metal coins, cowrie shells, gold pieces, and/or iron bars. Given their prestige in their communities, it was not unusual for enterprising ironworkers to achieve political authority over clans and villages, become involved in extensive trade networks, or enter into relatively large-scale slave holdings. The importance of the ironworkers to West African societies, large and small, cannot be overestimated.

Metallurgical Production. For everyday military, ceremonial, ritual, and traditional use, ironworkers made knives, machetes, sickles, digging sticks, walking canes, nails, hoes, axes, chain mail, arrow and spear tips, swords, daggers, lances, finger guards for bowmen, bits, stirrups, spurs, saddle parts, harpoons, fishhooks, picks, pokers, hammers, adzes, chisels, tongs, woodcarving tools, portions of boats and war canoes, leatherworking tools, needles for weaving, pottery tools, neck and leg chains for slaves, bracelets, anklets, necklaces, hairpins, rings, earrings, gongs, bells, noisemakers, thumb pianos, cymbals, flutes, royal staffs, ceremonial hammers, anvils, double gongs, crowns, metal for clothing and embroidery, circumcision knives, and many other objects.

Iron Smelting and Forging. The iron-smelting process included prospecting for ore, mining it, transporting it or arranging for it to be transported, preparing the sand or rock ore, acquiring and transporting wood charcoal and the proper clays for construction or repair of the tuyeres and furnaces, making and maintaining the pot or bag bellows and the foundry roofs and shelters, loading and lighting the furnace, operating the bellows, overseeing all elements of the smelt, and, finally, extracting the iron bloom (a malleable lump of metal) for the blacksmith to form into usable tools and weapons, usually heavy implements such as axes and hoes. For objects such as lighter tools, knives, and jewelry, the smelter broke the iron bloom, reworked and purified it, and put it into preforms. Rituals, prayers, and sometimes songs and dances were also part of the process. In addition to forging, the smith also had to acquire and prepare charcoal, get and transport a large stone anvil, produce a smith's stone and tools, construct a crucible furnace to rework the bloom, and select clays and use them to construct his bellows, tuyeres, and shelter.

Gold. Throughout its millennium of existence, the trans-Saharan caravan trade remained a dangerous undertaking. Besides natural perils such as violent dust storms, venomous snakes and scorpions, disappearing trail signs, poisoned waterholes, dromedary incapacity, human illnesses, "heat insanity," and deaths of indispensable guides, various bandits and disgruntled caravan workers were

threats to travelers' lives and livelihoods. A one-way north-south trip generally took a minimum of two months and could take up to six months. Caravan travel required planning, organization, financial backing, strategic provisioning, and faith in an established network. Because the risks were so great, a caravan journey was not undertaken without the expectation of substantial profit. Though caravan merchants traded for leather goods, harem slaves, cloth, iron bars, and southern foodstuffs, including the kola nut, the only item whose value made their dangerous journey worthwhile was gold. The desire for direct access to West African gold, or at least control of access to the forest-dwelling producers of gold, was one of the principal stimuli for outside intervention in West Africa. As early as the late eighth century, Arab writings and European maps called ancient Ghana "land of gold," and finding ways to acquire it became a major compulsion for outside forays into the region, whether hostile or hospitable. Ivan Hrbek has reported that "the control of the western gold route, not the colonization of the whole Maghrib, was the primary aim of the North African policy of the Fatimids," the first Arab dynasty to establish the political unity of all North Africa.

The Gold Standard. For most of the period 500–1590 West Africans seem to have been less interested in gold than in copper, which they more frequently sought after for rituals and adornment, but outside the region, in North Africa, gold had been viewed as a commodity of prestige and significant worth and had been a recognized standard of international trade since at least 1800 B.C.E. Egypt, the world's first major source of gold, was probably responsible for providing the Romans and Assyrians with their initial supplies of the malleable, noncorrosive, shiny metal. By the time of the Phoenician voyages along the West African coast in approximately 1200 B.C.E. the existence of its gold had become known worldwide and begun to attract the earliest of many generations of Arab empire builders, European explorers, and various other conquerors. Although by the seventh century C.E. gold had been discovered in ancient Gaul (France) and a few places in central Europe, Europe never became a consistent and reliable source of gold. Raymond Mauny has estimated that West Africa was one of the main sources of European gold throughout the medieval period up to the discovery of the Americas. In fact, finding and acquiring gold was one of the prime motivations for the Spanish, Portuguese, Dutch, English, and French voyages of exploration that began in the fifteenth century. Nehemia Levtzion adds that during the Middle Ages "two thirds of the world's production of gold came from the Sudan to replenish the raw material needed for the European mints."

Securing and Controlling Gold Sources. Starting in the eighth century C.E. and continuing through the seventeenth, a succession of Muslim Arabic and Berber clans and kinship associations—including the Abbasids, the Fatimids, the Aghlabids, the Umayyads, the Almoravids (Murabitun), and the Almohads—competed with each other in attempts to impose religious, political, and economic unification on all North Africa, Spain, and other parts of southern Europe, or on significant portions of the region. Each of these groups made strong efforts to consolidate clan-based dynasties and Muslim empires, using increasing degrees of Islamic fundamentalism as the publicly announced reasons for their expansion and absorption of people and territory. The recorded histories of these groups focus on their religious motives and say little about the role of gold as an inducement for their conquests. The trans-Saharan caravan trade is a central subject in the great majority of these histories, but they usually explain attempts to control West African trading cities such as Audaghost, Djenné, and Gao as exerting "a more correct" Muslim presence. Yet, Muslim "religious war" in West Africa clearly benefited the invaders financially. For example, the Almoravids' invasions of the Sudan decimated the Ghanaian trading city of Audaghost in 1054, destroying its ability to control the gold trade with North Africa. The *kafu* of Takrur, to the west of Ghana, greatly benefited by the absence of Audaghost. Throughout the eleventh century the rulership of Takrur was both a valued ally of the Almoravids and a competitor of Ghana in the gold trade. For the short term, eliminating the competition increased the regularity and volume of gold exports for the Almoravids. However, the gold regions of Ghana remained beyond their control, so in 1076 they destroyed Kumbi Saleh, the capital city of Ghana. Again, their chief aim was consolidation of direct access to and control of the gold-producing regions of ancient Ghana.

The Demand for Gold. The importance of West African gold should not be underestimated. Because of continued competition among dynasties, to remain in power for any length of time an Arab ruler had to maintain expensive land and sometimes naval forces. Their traditional sources of gold imports—initially Asia and Egypt—could not provide enough of the metal at the levels needed to pay these troops. Once the existence of gold in Ghana and a competing *kafu*, Takrur, became known to the Arabs, they began to see that region as the best source for the large quantities of gold they needed. By the eighth and ninth centuries, gold from the Sudanic areas became readily available through an expanded caravan trade. The primary source of the financing for the various Arab armies became Sudanic gold, which was used for minting high-grade imperial coins. The foundation of the banking system that sponsored and underwrote the trans-Saharan caravan trade became Sudanic gold, as did the basis of the entire monetary system of the Arab African world.

Gold Purification and Minting. In the Muslim world, as in the Roman traditions that the Muslims in small part

SUNDIATA AND THE IRONWORKERS

In his *Tarikh al-Fattash* (The Chronicle of the Seeker After Knowledge, begun in 1519), the first history of West Africa by a native of the region, Mahmoud al-Kati included a version of the oral *Epic of Sundiata* that explains the origins of Sundiata's close relationship to ironworkers:

Sogolon . . . gave birth to the crippled son Sundjata and she and her son were treated with contempt by the rival-wife who gave birth to Nare Maghan's eldest son and heir, Dankaran-Tuma, who succeeded his father when he died. With the help of a town blacksmith, who made iron supports for his legs, Sundjata was able to stand up on his feeble legs and walk like other young men. He studied the warrior and hunter traditions of his mother's clan and gathered many young men around him. The mother of Dankaran-Tuma is said to have grown in jealousy and envy over Sundjata and made attempts on his life. This caused Sundjata and his mother to go into exile away from the Malinke town of his birth. They were rejected by many Malinke chiefs because they feared the vengeance of Dankaran-Tuma, but were taken in by the king of Mema, an iron town. Soon thereafter the Malinke were conquered and oppressed by Sumanguru Kante of the Susu, who killed Dankaran-Tuma. Envoys sought out Sundjata to return and save his people. Sundjata left Mema with thousands of troops and mounted hunters granted to him by his benefactor, the king of Mema. He and Sumanguru Kante met at the great battle of Kirina, and because of magic and trickery, Sundjata eventually prevailed. Sumanguru's wife had revealed his secrets to Sundjata. Sumanguru was a master of iron and could not be killed or wounded with weapons or arrows from that great metal. Sundjata put poison from a white cock's tail into the wine drank by Sumanguru and so made the great warrior king weak and dispirited. Sundjata's less numerous forces carried the day. Following that great battle, all the chiefs of the Malinke met at Ka-ba and swore allegiance to Sundjata, who wore his hunter clothing. Each chief was appointed by Sundjata and the independent Malinke chiefdoms became the Mali empire under the Keita clan of Sunjata.

Source: Nehemia Levtzion, *Ancient Ghana and Mali* (London: Methuen, 1973).

imitated, the minting of coins was a symbol of regal authority and a consistent demonstration of ruling-class monopoly. For Muslim leaders, gold coinage became a sign of one's prestige within the expanded Muslim community, so individual rulers regularly and fervently competed with each other over acquiring unobstructed access to gold supplies for their mints, the purer the gold the better. By the mid tenth century, the Fatimids had started a boom in gold-coin minting and made West African gold famous. It was regarded as the highest grade of gold because it could normally go straight to coinage without "purification"— smelting to remove impurities and naturally occurring alloys. Sudanic gold was easy to smelt and mold into various shapes and was relatively rare. It came in specks, dust, nuggets, and lumped ore from alluvial goldfields in the Senegal, Niger, Volta, Casamance, and Faleme Rivers, and the forest areas fed by Lake Chad. It also came from labor-intensive seasonal shaft mining in the Sudanic region. Archaeological data reveals that there were thousands of gold-working shafts in the Sudanic region from the tenth century through the seventeenth. In order to regularize the importing of this gold, the Fatimids made the Sijilmasa-Ghana route the main avenue for the gold trade for at least two centuries, from the eighth through the tenth. This route included Audaghost, part of the Ghanaian Empire, as the primary intermediate stop because of its access to water and fresh supplies.

Gold Coins. The Fatimids worked this route with the intention of building a gold reserve in their treasury and acquiring the amounts of gold they needed to mint and distribute reliable gold coinage that would earn them international credibility. From Sijilmasa in southeastern Morocco, gold went to the Fez, Tangier, Spanish Cordoba, Sicily, Italy, Portugal, Sardinia, and Corsica. From the tenth century onward, various other Arab rulerships also used West African gold for minting coinage. Thus, the intensity of the trans-Saharan caravan trade was most often determined by the gold requirements of the gold-minting dynasties in North Africa, Spain, and Egypt, including not only the Fatimids but also the Aghlabid governors of Tunisia, eastern Algeria, and Sicily in the ninth century; the Umayyads of Spain in the tenth; the Zirids of Tunisia, eastern Algeria, and Granada in the tenth and eleventh centuries; and the Almoravids and Almohads of North Africa and Spain in the eleventh through thirteenth centuries.

Gold Transactions with the Arab World. According to archaeological evidence, written transaction records, and historical estimates, in 904–905 approximately 100,000 gold dinars were minted from an estimated 400 kilograms of gold in Egypt. In 1009–1010, 40,000 gold dinars were struck in Umayyad Spain, using approximately 160 kilograms of gold. J. Devisse has estimated that more than 250,000 ounces were exported to Arab North Africa and Egypt in 1400, 500,000 ounces in the fifteenth century, and 850,000 in the sixteenth. Gold exports to these Muslim regions declined to 500,000 ounces in the eighteenth century and 400,000 in the nineteenth, as coastal trade with Europeans siphoned off more and more West African products. Mauny has estimated that, during the 500–1590 period, the annual gold production and export from Ghana, Mali, and Songhai was 4 metric tons from the Bure fields, 500 kilograms from the Galam fields, 200 kilograms

from the Poura-Lobi fields, 4 metric tons from the Gold Coast and Ivory Coast, and 300 kilograms from Kpelle-Sierra Leone. Other historians have disputed some or all of those estimates. For example, J. B. Kiethega says Poura-Lobi, in present-day Burkina Faso, never exceeded an average production and distribution of 50 kilograms per year between the fifteenth and nineteenth centuries.

Gold for Europe. Arabic states required 2 to 3 tons of West African gold annually from the tenth through the seventeenth centuries. Approximately forty camels could carry this amount comfortably, but most trans-Saharan caravans were much larger than forty camels, and there were usually at least ten to fifteen caravans a year from the tenth through the seventeenth centuries. Clearly, then, more gold than what was required by Arab Africa was being transported, most likely to be sent into various parts of Europe via international trade. Once Europeans developed the ships and navigational technology to open up maritime trade with West Africa, they no longer needed North African middlemen. According to Portuguese records, during the fifteenth and sixteenth centuries that European country acquired approximately 42,185 kilograms of gold from Mande traders along the coast of West Africa. By this sea route, more than 550,000 ounces of gold had been exported to all of Europe by 1600, and 1,500,000 ounces had been sent to that continent by 1700.

Domestic Gold. Both iron and gold were strategically necessary in the state-building processes of the Western Sudan. As the *kafu* in Ghana, Mali, Songhai, and the other states got larger through increased access to iron and gold products, these rulerships needed still more gold and iron to sustain themselves. The greater the expansion, the greater the need for iron and gold. The Western Sudanic states did not mint gold coins, and they based their monetary systems on cowrie shells, cattle, and copper products, not on gold. Yet, they did use gold to pay for imported horses, chain-mail armor, exotic swords, and other armaments. Maintaining large armies, even nonstanding armies as in ancient Ghana, was expensive. States needed to station garrisons in provinces to collect taxes and tribute, as well as to provide protection for traders and the trade routes. Gold and eventually slaves became the accepted currency to pay for these services. Additionally, the Sudanic states established "spheres of influence" over the gold-producing areas; they did not have direct control of them. The Sudanic states were middlemen in the gold trade, further distancing the North African dynasties from direct access to the gold they continually sought.

Sources:
Philip de Barros, "Iron Metallurgy: Sociocultural Context," in *Ancient African Metallurgy: The Sociocultural Context,* by Michael S. Bisson, S. Terry Childs, de Barros, and Augustin F. C. Holl, edited by Joseph O. Vogel (Walnut Creek, Cal.: AltaMira Press, 2000), pp. 147–198.

F. De Medeiros, "The Peoples of the Sudan: Population Movements," in *Africa from the Seventh to the Eleventh Century,* edited by M. El Fasi and I. Hrbek, volume 3 of *General History of Africa* (London: Heine-

Akan gold traders (Dyula-Wangara) and their interpreter (top) and Akan canoes bringing merchandise to a
Dutch ship (bottom); illustrations from Pieter de Maree's 1602 account of his journey to West Africa
(from Timothy F. Garrard, *Akan Weights and the Gold Trade*, 1980)

mann / Berkeley: University of California Press / Paris: UNESCO, 1988), pp. 119–139.

J. Devisse, "Trade and Trade Routes in West Africa," in *Africa from the Seventh to the Eleventh Century*, edited by M. El Fasi and I. Hrbek, volume 3 of *General History of Africa* (London: Heinemann / Berkeley: University of California Press / Paris: UNESCO, 1988), pp. 367–435.

R. Haaland, "Man's Role in the Changing Habitat of Mema During the Old Kingdom of Ghana," *Norwegian Archaeological Review*, 13 (1980): 31–46.

Augustin F. C. Holl, "Metals and Precolonial African Society," in *Ancient African Metallurgy: The Sociocultural Context*, pp. 1–82.

John Iliffe, *Africans: The History of a Continent* (Cambridge & New York: Cambridge University Press, 1995).

Nehemia Levtzion, *Ancient Ghana and Mali* (London: Methuen, 1973).

Raymond Mauny, *Tableau géographique de l'Ouest africain au Moyen Age, d'après les sources écrites, la tradition et l'archéologie* (Dakar: IFAN, 1961).

THE ECONOMIC CONTEXT OF POPULATION AND SOCIAL CLASS

Population Growth in Ghana. Evidence from excavations, written texts, and oral histories indicates that the population of ancient Ghana increased from 300 through 1000. Growth rates differed from year to year—sometimes coming in major spurts, sometimes incrementally—based on territorial conquests, migration, and indigenous births. By the end of the tenth century, Ghana probably had more than two million residents living in a territory that covered more than 250,000 square miles. This empire was organized into a confederation of semi-autonomous chieftaincies and clan-based states that recognized the authority of the ruler (or *tunka*) and paid him tribute and/or taxes.

Feeding the Empire of Ghana. In order to feed this expanding populace and produce the surpluses needed for intraregional and interregional exchange, Ghana grew millet, sorghum, and rice for its starches, and used animal meat (mainly beef and guinea fowl), fish, stewed groundnuts, or palm oil for protein. It imported salt, an important component of diet in its hot climate. The division of farm labor generally involved the men clearing the land and tilling and hoeing it with iron tools, while women and children weeded and cropped with similar implements. Everyone took part in the harvest.

Social Stratification in Ghana. By the eighth and ninth centuries, social differentiation and stratification in Ghana was apparent in food, clothing, and occupation. Excavations in Audaghost have uncovered evidence that the merchant and administrative classes, including the northern expatriate communities, generally ate imported wheat, dates, raisins, dried and locally grown figs, grapes, other fruits, beef, and mutton. By contrast, the common people usually ate millet durra, often mixed into griddle cakes, and dried camel meat. In other parts of ancient Ghana, the regular diet of the indigenous population was millet durra, rice, fresh and smoked fish, and cattle meat. The well-to-do often wore cotton and woven clothes, some finely decorated, while the lower classes wore woolens and animal skins. The well-to-do owned imported glazed oil lamps, cups, vases, decorated and glazed perfume holders, glass beads, glass goblets, silver, and jewelry set with amazonite and garnet. Occupational categories in Ghana included the ruler and his officials (such as provincial heads and advisers), artisans and craftsmen, builders and architects, hunters and herdsmen, merchants, smiths (iron, copper, and gold), potters, and agricultural laborers, many of whom were war-captive slaves. Blacksmiths and metallurgists (and to a somewhat lesser extent hunters and archers) had high status in Ghanaian society.

Food Production in Mali. According to al-Umari and Ibn Battuta, both of whom visited Mali in the mid fourteenth century, Mali regularly produced food surpluses, so incoming travelers were not required to bring their own provisions. Estimated at more than five million people, the Malian population comprised mostly agriculturalists and animal herders. Millet was grown in the drier terrain—which got only two to three months of rain annually—again with men doing the ground clearance and hoeing and women and children the cropping and weeding. Rice was grown in the Niger Valley floodplains, in Sankarani, in the Senegal River valley, and in the Karabu region. Some vegetables and beans were also grown, along with sorghum. Each year, according to Mande tradition, the first crop of millet, sorghum, rice, vegetables, and (particularly from the forest areas) yams was dedicated to the ruler (or *mansa*) of Mali. Not to do so was commonly recognized as an act of disrespect and rebellion against the ruler. Fishing and raising cattle, sheep, and goats were specialties of individual

MALI IN THE FOURTEENTH CENTURY

In 1513–1515 a North African traveler who later became known as Leo Africanus visited Mali, which was then part of the Songhai Empire, and described the enterprises and religious activities he observed there:

In this kingdome there is a large and ample village containing to the number of six thousand or mo families, and called Melli, whereof the whole kingdome is so named. And here the king hath his place of residence. The region it selfe yeeldeth great abundance of corne, flesh, and cotton. Here are many artificers and merchants in all places and yet the king honourably entertaineth all strangers. The inhabitants are rich, and haue plenty of wares. Here are great store of temples, priests, and professours, which professours read their lectures onely in the temples, because they haue no colleges at all. The people of this region excel all other Negros in witte, ciuilitie, and industry, and were the first that embraced the law of Mahumet.

Source: Robert O. Collins, *Western African History* (Princeton: Wiener, 1990).

clans or peoples. For example, the Fulani raised cattle, while the Somono of the upper Niger and the Bozo and the Soninke near Gao were fishing experts who usually smoked and dried fish to preserve it. Mali also used slaves for work on farms controlled by career soldiers, administrative authorities, or the mansa himself. Virtually all these slaves were war captives. In the markets that existed in nearly all villages, towns, and trading cities, smoked and dried fish were regular commodities, as were raw cotton and woven cotton cloth.

Social Stratification in Mali. As with metallurgy, craft production such as indigo dyeing and leatherworking was limited to specific clans. Those not in particular occupational clans were restricted by law from engaging in such work. This practice created divisions that resemble social classes. There was a hierarchy of occupational clan status, with a clan specifically for the ruling mansa and clan associations specifically for elite soldiers (sometimes called the "nobility of the quiver"), horse breeders, cavalrymen, weavers, carpenters and mud-clay masons, urban and rural traders (the Dyula), priests, metalsmiths and smelters, and many others. Each clan had distinct privileges, rights, and leverage within the society. This hierarchy was essentially a more complex version of the social structure of Ghana and other Sudan-Sahel states. The clans were not class divisions but rather social-economic relationships approximating caste groups based on Mande custom and tradition. Because of their monopolies on specific commodities, the craft clans often became quite wealthy. A wealthy clan or lineage sometimes absorbed other clans into a larger *kafu*.

Expatriates and Slaves. In two particular instances, social classes were a distinct part of Malian society. The first was the class of expatriate traders residing in the northern trading towns of the Mali empire, especially Taghaza, Djenné, and Niani, the Malian administrative capital. As they had in ancient Ghana, these merchants lived as a discernible, interest-pursuing class of Muslim clerics, teachers, bankers, and businessmen. They had a strong influence on Malian government economic and religious policies, but little leverage or clout outside urban areas or within the ranks of indigenous Malians. The second was the slave class. In Mali, slaves made up a great proportion of the standing military, particularly the infantry. Slaves were porters, laborers accompanying the Dyula donkey caravans into the forest areas, and agricultural workers on large farms. One slave-soldier, Sakura, who had served as a military officer under Sundiata, seized the rulership of Mali in the late thirteenth century during a period of leadership instability and expanded the borders of Mali to their greatest historical limits. During his reign, he increased the ability of the government to protect caravan routes and resident merchants and completed the empire-building design of Sundiata.

Food Production in Songhai. In Songhai, the typical Sudanic pattern of population synthesis and differentiation of Ghana and Mali continued, with some significant additions and on a much larger scale. The consistent production of millet, rice, sorghum, lentils, fish, cattle, and goats was carried on generally through the same customs and clan occupations. Food surpluses were frequent, and

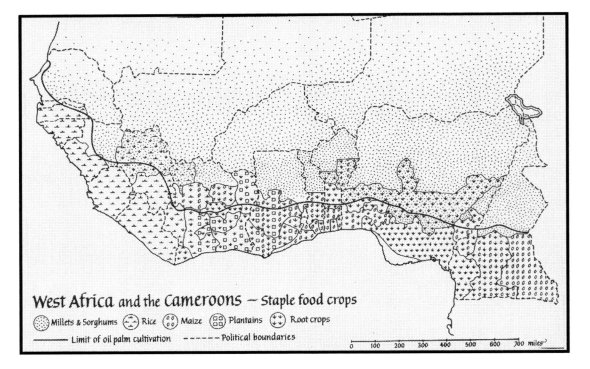

West Africa and the Cameroons — Staple food crops

Millets & Sorghums Rice Maize Plantains Root crops

——— Limit of oil palm cultivation   ------ Political boundaries

0 100 200 300 400 500 600 700 miles

(Map by Leo Vernon; from J. F. A. Ajayi and Michael Crowder, eds., *The History of West Africa*, 1971)

periods of famine were exceedingly rare during the two-hundred-year history of Songhai. With access to an extensive array of iron tools and implements from an expanded metallurgical population, local farmers, fishermen, and cattle raisers generally sold extra foodstuffs in village and urban markets and bought salt, cloth, iron tools, glassware, footwear, copper products, and sometimes jewelry.

Social Stratification in Songhai. The utilization of slaves increased; hierarchical distinctions among social groups became less amorphous; and a more organized standing army provided better protection of lives and property. Large groups of agricultural slaves grew millet, sorghum, and rice on estates owned or controlled by rulers, rich merchants, officials, and Muslim clerics. The military included thousands of slaves. The elite *suna* guards of the askia (ruler) were nearly always slaves. Slaves were also messengers, mosque builders, porters, movers, domestic help, and wet nurses. Songhai society was divided into rulers and administrators; military leaders and career soldiers; resident foreign traders; Muslim clerics, learned men, and judges; mobile traders; clan craft guilds and secret societies, especially metallurgists; clan chiefs and headmen; and indigenous farmers, fishermen, and animal husbandmen. Subject clans and peoples paid tribute. The government levied taxes on slave produce, imported and exported trade goods, agricultural harvests, fishing bounties, and herds of animals. In addition, clan heads had to provide warriors for yearly military campaigns.

Urban and Rural Society in Songhai. There was a discernible difference between urban society and rural society in Songhai. They were interdependent but virtually autonomous from one another. There were at least thirty-five cities in Songhai, the largest being Timbuktu (approximately eighty thousand people), Djenné (approximately forty thousand people), and Gao toward the east (approximately one hundred thousand people). Timbuktu was the economic and intellectual center of Songhai, while Djenné was the headquarters for commercial contact between the forest and savanna areas, and Gao was the political capital with links to the Hausa city-states and Egypt. Songhai's urban areas imported luxury goods, woven and tailored clothing, fine jewelry and glassware, exotic perfumes and spices, books, rare silver items, and many horses. They often paid for horses with slaves, generally eleven to fifteen slaves for one horse. The cities were highly diverse in population, with Berbers, Dyula-Wangara (Mande-speaking traders), Soninke, Fulani, Hausa, Mossi, and other groups regularly engaging in daily transactions and activities and speaking to each other primarily in Songhai, Mande, and Arabic languages. The rural areas, which included hundreds of villages and towns, maintained their Mande-based matrilineal traditions, most frequently administered their own tribunals of justice, elected and supported their own clan chiefs, grew their own foodstuffs, paid homage to

whatever askia happened to be in charge, and traded with the Dyula-Wangara. They generally rejected Islam and did not agree to give up any of their traditional sovereignty in spite of demands and dictates from the city dwellers.

Sources:

S. M. Cissoko, "The Songhay from the 12th to the 16th Century," in *Africa from the Twelfth to the Sixteenth Century*, edited by D. T. Niane, volume 4 of *General History of Africa* (London: Heinemann / Berkeley: University of California Press / Paris: UNESCO, 1984), pp. 187–210.

I. Hrbek, "The Emergence of the Fatimids," in *Africa from the Seventh to the Eleventh Century*, edited by M. El Fasi and Hrbek, volume 3 of *General History of Africa* (London: Heinemann / Berkeley: University of California Press / Paris: UNESCO, 1988), pp. 314–335.

John Iliffe, *Africans: The History of a Continent* (Cambridge & New York: Cambridge University Press, 1995).

Nehemia Levtzion, "The Early States of the Western Sudan to 1500," in *History of West Africa*, edited by J. F. A. Ajayi and Michael Crowder, second edition, volume 1 (London: Longman, 1976), pp. 114–151.

THE ECONOMICS OF STATE OPERATION

Horses. As early as the third-century Wagadu *kafu* in the Sahel, which led to the Ghanaian empire, horses were a regular part of building and maintaining a state. For most of the Sudanic states, the cavalry was acknowledged as the best striking force. It had a military advantage over all other forms of fighting in the region until the introduction of firearms in the late sixteenth century. Cavalrymen rode locally bred or imported horses, but imported horses were considered superior mounts. Leo Africanus, who visited the Songhai Empire in 1513–1515, reported on the breeding of small, short horses in Ghana and Timbuktu. These horses were generally used as transportation for resident merchants and for sundry purposes by the ruler. Larger, better-quality horses were imported from the Maghrib and were used for royal ceremonies and parades, as presents for the ruler's favorites, and as mounts for the state cavalry. Because of their relative rarity and military importance, imported horses often cost more than camels during the fifth through the eleventh centuries, and it was up to each ruler to pay for the animals. Despite their expense, documents from the period indicate that there were more than ten thousand horses in Mali, mostly for cavalrymen, including special mounts for cavalry captains. Songhai also had a large cavalry.

Portuguese Imports. In the fifteenth century, the Portuguese discovered that horses were in great demand by the Wolof, Malinke, and other groups in West Africa and supplied them by the hundreds. The Portuguese, in fact, provided horses and guns to many coastal chieftainships, exacerbating a slave-raiding pattern that was already established before the Portuguese arrived in the area. Especially in the fourteenth through eighteenth centuries, horses and guns were most frequently exchanged for slaves. In Kanem-Bornu, the more horses and guns one had, the more slave raids one could conduct; and captured slaves were then traded for still more horses and guns.

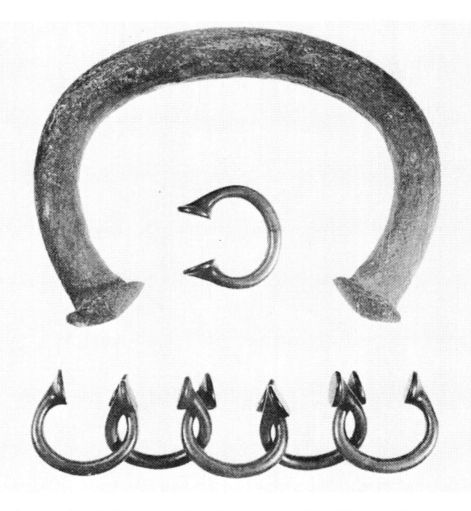

Copper manillas, which became a medium of exchange between West Africans and Europeans in the fifteenth century (British Museum, London)

State Income from Trade. For the states of the Western Sudan, intra- and interregional trade, including trans-Saharan trade, was protected, monitored, and taxed by the government but operated by local and foreign residents. Taxes and fees on trade goods provided consistent government income. Ghana did not integrate the network of villages (the *kafu* system) and lesser states of the Sahel/savanna into one unit of commercial interchange. Mali and Songhai, however, established and maintained a monetary system involving cowrie shells as currency for food and small items and gold—or frequently copper and iron bars—as the medium of exchange for long-distance intra- and interregional trade items. The use of cowries as currency in Mali and Gao was observed by al-Umari during the 1340s and Ibn Battuta during the 1350s. They were also widely used in urban centers such as Timbuktu. Other media of exchange were actual trade goods. Thus, salt was most frequently exchanged directly for gold; copper was an important currency in fourteenth-century Kanem-Bornu and Takedda; and pieces of cloth were treated as currency in Zawila, Takrur, and Kanem-Bornu. Also, since gold coins and gold dust were the standard medium of exchange throughout North Africa from the eighth century onward, gold was both the main currency for trade transactions and the primary item of trade in Audaghost, Tadmekka, Djenné, and Gao, as well as in other areas of West Africa.

Ethics and Economics. Government officials responsible for monitoring and protecting trade seem to have understood that a reputation for fair dealing was crucial for continuing to fill the state coffers with tax moneys. The Portuguese trader Fernandes described the regular process of trading with the Dyula-Wangara (Mande-speaking itinerant merchants) as a matter of great trust between the participants. No receipts or written agreements were necessary; credit was commonly extended for periods of up to a year, based on the Dyulas' standard practice of going to commercial centers such as Niani, Djenné, and Timbuktu once a year for business transactions. If a debtor died in the interim, his son or daughter would make sure that the debt was paid. It was also a standard practice among the rulers of Ghana, Mali, and Songhai to protect the property of resident traders who died. The accepted procedure was for the ruler to contact a responsible person from the deceased's clan to hold the property until a legitimate heir came to claim it, or, if the deceased were a

Muslim, to have an Islamic cleric or *qadi* dispense the property according to Muslim law.

Fair Treatment. Rulers promoted the idea that complaints of unfair treatment and price gouging would be quickly investigated and resolved. Officials responsible for commercial transactions were held to a high standard. If they made financial miscalculations, they were dismissed and made to pay anyone they had shortchanged. Theft and dishonesty were typically punishable by death or forced enslavement.

State Operation and Land. The sort of feudal land management and serfdom that developed in medieval Europe did not occur in the Western Sudan. According to Nehemia Levtzion, the factors that caused such a system to occur in Europe did not exist in West Africa. Throughout the period 500–1590, there was no overpopulation or land shortage in West Africa, as there was in Europe. In fact, there was a recurring shortage of population associated with frequent migration, and one of the central necessities of state building in the Western Sudan was the ability to marshal concentrations of population over a sustained period of time through military might. In the states of the Western Sudan, a government's ability to exact taxes, tribute, public service, and labor from constituents was never based on control and distribution of land but rather on access to loyal hunter and warrior clans armed with iron weapons and horses.

State Operation and the Slave Trade. The principal income producer for Kanem-Bornu in the Central Sudan was the slave trade. By the fifteenth century the city of Zawila, between Kanem and Tripoli, had become the best-known slave market in the Sahara-Sudanic region, and it maintained that reputation through the eighteenth century. For most of the 500–1590 period, the slave trade was far less important in the Western Sudan. There it was necessary to maintain relative peace and security for the long-distance and regional trade routes so that gold, the chief source of state income, could be transported freely through the region and beyond. Slave raids created instability and a more or less constant state of hostilities. Little peace meant little trade. Too far east of the main goldfields to derive any income from the gold trade, the Central Sudanic states turned to slave trading to produce income. Repeated, intensive slave raiding, however, encouraged massive flights of populations, terror, relentless warfare, and institutional instability. For this reason there were far fewer states in the Central Sudan than in the West.

The Trans-Saharan Slave Trade. At least by the seventh century, West African slaves were being sent to North Africa. By the eleventh and twelfth centuries, slaves from the Western Sudan were identified in Cordova and Algecira, Spain, and by the fourteenth century they were in Catalan, Valencia, Majorca, Marseille, Montpellier, Naples, Genoa, and Venice. Slaves from Kanem-Bornu, many of whom were captured in the neighboring Mossi-Dagomba region, were taken to Morocco. Slaves from Gao were

brought to Tripoli. From there they were often traded to Barca, Tunisia, Sicily, the North African coast, and Andalusia, as well as to Portuguese planters on Arguin Island (off the coast of Mauritania). Large numbers of slaves from the Western Sudan became loyal bodyguards for various rulers in North Africa as well as house servants and eunuchs. They also served as soldiers for the Almoravids in the conquest of the Maghrib, the Sahara, and Spain.

Slavery in the Western Sudan. Slaves in the Western Sudan were usually captives from wars waged for purposes other than taking slaves, but there were some relatively limited slave-raiding forays, and slaves were also acquired through direct purchase and bartering. In the fifteenth century, Dyula merchants (Mande-speaking West African traders) even went to the Portuguese slaveholding castle at Elmina and bought slaves who had been captured elsewhere along the coast. More frequently, however, the Dyula sold slaves to the Portuguese. In his *Tarikh al-Fattash* (The Chronicle of the Seeker After Knowledge, begun in 1519), Mahmoud al-Kati wrote that Mali and Songhai established slave villages specifically to grow rice, millet, sorghum, and other products for the rulers. This history mentions a Songhai farm where more than two hundred slaves—under four slave headmen and a slave village chief—were assigned to produce at least a thousand sacks of rice for the reigning askia. Any amount over that obligation could be kept and distributed at the discretion of the slave village chief, so the farm chief and the headmen became quite well-to-do. However, when such slaves died, any assets they had accumulated went to the askia. Household slaves deemed loyal were frequently trusted with the utmost responsibilities in the Western Sudanic states.

The Atlantic Slave Trade. By the late fifteenth century the Portuguese and other European slave merchants had begun bypassing North African middlemen and buying slaves directly along the West African coast. Slave trading became more profitable in that region at the same time the Almoravids were once again disrupting the trade routes to the north. The results were increased warfare and instability and ultimately the fall of the Songhai Empire.

Sources:

Nehemia Levtzion, *Ancient Ghana and Mali* (London: Methuen, 1973).

D. T. Niane, "Mali and the Second Mandingo Expansion," in *Africa from the Twelfth to the Sixteenth Century*, edited by Niane, volume 4 of *General History of Africa* (London: Heinemann / Berkeley: University of California Press / Paris: UNESCO, 1984), pp. 117–171.

THE TRANS-SAHARAN CARAVAN TRADE

Origins. As Adu Boahen has explained, the trans-Saharan caravan trade began to take place on a regular basis during the fourth century, as an expanded version of the pre-existing intra- and interregional trade among peoples of the forest, savanna, Sahel, and Sahara. While Ghana was an integral part of the early trans-Saharan trade, neither it nor any other Western Sudan state was built by, or specifically

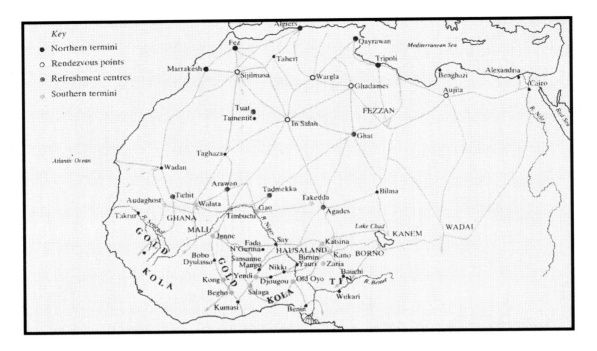

Trans-Saharan trade routes (map by Oxford Illustrations; from
Adu Boahen, *Topics in West African History*, 1986)

for, the trans-Saharan trade. Fundamentally important to the success of the Empire of Ghana between the eighth and twelfth centuries, this trading system reached its peak during the fourteenth through sixteenth centuries, during the heydays of the Mali and Songhai Empires.

Routes. There were seven primary north-south routes, six principal forest routes, and two west-east routes. During the 500–1590 period, routes rose and declined in importance depending on the empire in power and the amount of security it could maintain for traders and trade routes.

North-South Routes. To obtain gold from the Bambuk goldfields—particularly during the ascendency of Ghana and the competing state of Takrur—traders from Fez and Marrakesh in Morocco traveled what is sometimes called the Audaghost Trail through Sijilmasa and Wadan to Azukki or Audaghost and from there to Kumbi Saleh in Ghana, or to Takrur. For gold from the Bure fields, especially when the Empire of Mali was at its height, merchants traveled from Fez through Sijilmasa, Taghaza (or Tuat) and Tichitt-Walata, to Timbuktu and Djenné. Another route to gold from the Bure fields led from Algiers through Wargla, In Salah, and Arawan to Timbuktu. For gold from the Lobi-Pourra fields traders left Qayrawan in Tunisia and traveled through Wargla, In Salah, Tadmekka, and Timbuktu to Gao, a route particularly active during the Songhai Empire. From Tripoli, caravans traveled through Ghadames, Ghat, and Takedda or Agades to the Hausa cities of Katsina or Kano. Another route began in Tripoli and passed through Fezzan, Bilma, and Kanem to the Bornu city of Bauchi. Finally, from Cyrenaicain or

Aujila in eastern Libya a route led through Wadai to Bornu. Not counting Cairo, Egypt, there were five major starting or ending points for the trade in the north (from which some gold and other products were regularly transported into the Mediterranean and Europe): Marrakesh, Fez, Algiers, Qayrawan, and Tripoli. There were also five major rendezvous stations where merchants gathered money, camels, drivers, guides, water, provisions, and trade goods for the journey south: Sijilmasa, In Salah, Wargla, Ghadames, and Aujila.

West-East Routes. There were two routes from Timbuktu or Gao to Egypt. One went through Takedda, Agades, Bilma, and Tibesti to Cairo. The other ran through Takedda, Ghat, Fezzan, and Aujila to Cairo. Also called the Gao or Mecca Road, this second route was the preferred route and was also used by West African Muslims on pilgrimages to Mecca.

Southern Routes. From the end points of the camel-caravan routes, trade goods were carried farther south to the forest regions by donkeys, human porters, or canoes. One route from Kumbi Saleh went through Diara, down the Senegal and Faleme Rivers to the Bambuk goldfields. Another led from Kumbi Saleh to Kangaba, down the Niger to the Bure goldfields. From Djenné one could travel through Bobo, Dyulasso, Kong, and Begho to Kumasi (in the modern nation of Ghana). From Kano a road led through Zaria and Old Oyo to Benin. Another road went from Katsina through Kano and Bauci to Wukari.

Economic and Social Consequences. The establishment of regular trade routes stimulated the development of various monetary systems in the Western Sudan, which used cowrie shells (from the Maldive Islands), strips of cotton cloth, minted gold dinars from North Africa, standard weights of gold dust, kola nuts, glass beads, and salt as currency. Trade also created a need among the indigenous *kafu* to control the centers of strategic productivity. For example, the Empire of Ghana extended its territory as far north as Audaghost in an attempt to secure direct access to salt production, while it simultaneously maintained direct linkages to the Bambuk goldfields across the Senegal River. Mali went even further north, capturing Taghaza for its salt mines and incorporating Bure, in the Niani region, for direct access to its gold. Songhai seized Takedda in the desert, mainly for its salt and copper, so the Songhai rulership could maintain direct control of salt and gold production at opposite ends of its territories.

Trade and State Building. Trans-Saharan trade also provided strong motivation for the formation of large Sudanic states and empires to protect traders and trade routes, which in turn brought in the necessary wealth to conduct wars of population and territorial expansion, to acquire horses and superior iron weaponry, to send thousands of soldiers into battle, and to outfit and maintain garrisons of soldiers in conquered provinces. The need for places where business could be transacted promoted increased urbanization in the Sudanic and Sahelian areas, from villages to walled cities and commercial centers with populations in excess of one hundred thousand residents. The rise of trade strongly promoted the specialization of clans and the establishment of clan "monopolies" in particular crafts, crucially important in iron smelting and smithing. Finally, the trans-Saharan trade brought the Sudanic states and their access to gold to the attention of the world outside the insular West African region.

Trade Commodities. Salt, gold, and slaves were the essential commodities throughout the 500–1590 period. Cloth also became an important trade good. A viable cloth-production industry began around the eleventh century in Djenné, Takrur, Timbuktu, and Gao and lasted well into the eighteenth century. By the thirteenth century, Timbuktu was reported to have more than twenty-six tailor shops with approximately one hundred apprentices in training at each one. The first cloth was made for local and intraregional consumption only, but production gradually became large enough and skilled enough to create textiles for regular export. The Western Sudan also imported European and Moroccan cloth and clothing, especially from the eleventh century onward. These textiles were generally for the elite—including resident foreign merchants, rulers, and highly placed administrative staff—rather than the local population. Modern archaeological excavations in the region have uncovered remains of silk clothing, presumably from commercial contacts with China or the Mongol Empire through the Maghrib. By the fifteenth

century, the Portuguese were bringing in large quantities of cloth to pay for the slaves and gold. Copper from southern Morocco and the Byzantine Empire was also imported to the Sahel and the Western Sudan, as were silver, tin, lead, perfumes, bracelets, books, stone and coral beads, glass jewelry, and drinking implements. In addition to gold, slaves, and cloth, the Western Sudan exported animal hides, civet musk, spices, ambergris, kola nuts, and shea butter (used for cooking oil, lamp lighting, and soap manufacture). Kola nuts became one of the primary sources of income for Mali and Songhai. Dyula-Wangara traders carried them from their forest source to the savanna and Sahel in pouches of wet leaves to keep them fresh. They did not become an important product of international trade until the nineteenth century, but they were widely traded in the Western Sudan from the twelfth century onward. Known by several different names—"the nut," "bitter fruit," "carob of the Sudan," and *goro*—kola nuts became important enough to be given as special presents by one ruler to another and to his honored guests. Kola nuts were frequently used in rituals, ceremonies, and celebrations. They were chewed to relieve thirst in desert caravans, and they were such a popular stimulant that their use by West Africans sometimes approximated addiction.

Pattern of Trade. By the eleventh century a typical caravan included one thousand camels. It might, for example, set out from Sijilmasa loaded with salt from Taghaza, foodstuffs, cloth, perfumes, and other goods from the Maghrib. Its next stop was Wadan, an oasis in the present-day nation of Mauritania, where some of the goods were sold and new items purchased; then the caravan went to Walata or Tichitt on the southern edge of the Sahara, and finally it went on to Timbuktu. From there the salt and other products would likely be taken by canoe to Niani or Djenné, where the salt was broken into smaller pieces and carried into the forest areas via the slave porters and donkeys of the Dyula-Wangara. These itinerant merchants traded the salt and other items from the north for forest gold, kola nuts, animal hides, and other products and then returned to Djenné, Niani, and Timbuktu. The number of camels on a return journey to Sijilmasa was typically less than half the number that arrived in Timbuktu because gold and other forest products were less bulky and much lighter in weight than the blocks of salt.

The Dyula-Wangara Trading Network. Only a small group of people in each state participated in long-distance trade in the Western Sudan. The bulk of the population was fishermen, herdsmen, agriculturalists, and hunter-soldiers. One group that was essential to the trade process was the itinerant Mande-speaking traders known as the Dyula or the Wangara, who from at least the eighth century operated trade routes along the upper Niger River from Timbuktu and across the Senegal. During the thirteenth and fourteenth centuries, they traveled into the

JEWISH MERCHANTS

In 1447 a Genoan merchant named Antonio Malfante visited the Saharan oasis of Tuat and wrote a letter in which he described the life of the Jewish merchants there:

There are many Jews, who lead a good life here, for they are under the protection of the several rulers, each of whom defends his own clients. Thus they enjoy very secure social standing. Trade is in their hands, and many of them are to be trusted with the greatest confidence. This locality is a mart of the country of the Moors, to which merchants come to sell their goods: gold is carried hither, and bought by those who come up from the coast. This place is Tamentit, and there are many rich men here. The generality, however, are very poor, for they do not sow, nor do they harvest anything, save the dates upon which they subsist. They eat no meat but that of castrated camels, which are scarce and very dear.

Source: G. R. Crone, trans. and ed., *The Voyages of Cadamosto and other Documents on Western Africa in the Second Half of the Fifteenth Century* (London: Printed for the Hakluyt Society, 1937).

Akan forests, as gold trade shifted from the upper Gambia and Casamance area of Bambuk to Bure. After the arrival of Europeans along the coast of West Africa, their routes took them southward from Niani to Worodugu along the Côte d'Ivoire and the Gambia Valley to the western Atlantic coast, to the Portuguese fortress at Elmina and other European trading posts; they also traveled eastward into Hausaland. In fact, they attempted to dominate the role of commercial middleman throughout the region, linking Guinea, the northeast, and the northwest along the Djenné-Be'o-Bonduku route, establishing routes across the Gambia and Casamance Rivers, and connecting Bondu, Kedougou, Futa Djallon, Niokholo, and Dantilia. Leo Africanus, who visited the Songhai Empire in 1513–1515, described these itinerant merchants selling their wares throughout West Africa, and German explorer Heinrich Barth found them living and trading among the Hausa at Katsina in the nineteenth century. The Portuguese reported that Dyula-Wangara trading activities between the coast and the Sahel were so important that Europeans who hoped to have successful commercial ventures in the region should accommodate their plans to the habits of those indigenous traders or risk unnecessary disruptions in the flow of trade goods.

Insular Clan. The Dyula-Wangara have been described as a rather insular, endogamous clan of occupational merchants who characteristically married within their own group and traveled as whole families along established commercial routes. Their small to large donkey caravans carried books, slaves, cotton cloth, iron bars, kola nuts, gold, salt, perfumes, beads, cowries, and copper, among other items. They apparently enjoyed a special status in a broad area of West Africa and were allowed to travel even through war zones without fear of harm from either side of the combatants. The Dyula-Wangara were recognizable by several other names in West Africa, including Marka among the Bambara, Yarse among the Mossi-Dagomba between Djenné and the Ashanti region, and Malinke-Mori in Guinea and the Ivory Coast region. By the seventeenth century, they were also called Kong, Bobo-Dyulasso, Buna, Bonduku, Black Volta Gonja, Diakhanke, and "Mary Bucks" (marabouts) after towns and settlements they founded with those names.

African Jews. From the twelfth century onward, significant numbers of Jews residing in Morocco helped to finance and expand the trans-Saharan trade. They migrated from southern Morocco, especially Wadi Dara, into the Sahel. By the fifteenth century, Jews made up roughly half the population of Sijilmasa in southeastern Morocco, the central city for the trans-Saharan trade going to Ghana and the rest of the Western Sudan. Becoming well known as merchants, financiers, goldsmiths, and silversmiths, they invested in long-distance trade along the principal routes from Sijilmasa to Walata through Taghaza. In addition to organizing caravans, they operated sections of the continuous traders' market in Sijilmasa, and they exported goods to Europe, Egypt, and other areas. Jewish goldsmiths and silversmiths also resided in Walata and Audaghost, and the oral traditions of Mauritania credit them with introducing goldsmithing in the Sahel and savanna. Gold from the Sahel was regularly exported north in twisted threads and coils that were fashioned by Jewish goldsmiths or smiths they had taught.

Sources:

Adu Boahen, with J. F. Ade. Ajayi and Michae Tidy, *Topics in West African History,* second edition (Harlow, U.K.: Longman, 1986).

Robert O. Collins, *Western African History* (Princeton: Wiener, 1990).

J. Devisse, "Trade and Trade Routes in West Africa," in *Africa from the Seventh to the Eleventh Century,* edited by M. El Fasi and I. Hrbek, volume 3 of *General History of Africa* (London: Heinemann / Berkeley: University of California Press / Paris: UNESCO, 1988), pp. 367–435.

Raymond Mauny, *Tableau géographique de l'Ouest africain au Moyen Age, d'après les sources écrites, la tradition et l'archéologie* (Dakar: IFAN, 1961).

SIGNIFICANT PEOPLE

ABU BAKR IBN UMAR

CIRCA 1025-1087
ALMORAVID LEADER

Invader of Ghana. Abu Bakr was governor of Wadi Da'ra and the brother of Yahya ibn Umar, military commander of the Almoravids, who seized the oasis of Audaghost from the Empire of Ghana in 1054. After his brother's death in 1059, Abu Bakr became the primary commander of the army, invading and sacking Kumbi Saleh, which served as the center of Ghana's governmental and commercial operations, in 1076. Abu Bakr's military campaigns in Ghana seriously disrupted the economic stability of the empire, as well as its significance to the trans-Saharan caravan trade.

Source:
J. F. A. Ajayi and Michael Crowder, eds., *The History of West Africa,* second edition, 2 volumes (New York: Columbia University Press, 1976, 1987).

TUNKA MENIN

CIRCA 1010-CIRCA 1078
RULER OF GHANA

A Model Ruler. Having become *tunka* (ruler) of Ghana in 1063, Menin was on the throne when al-Bakri visited the empire in 1067 and wrote his description of that Western Sudan polity. Tunka Menin was also the ruler when Almoravids led by Abu Bakr attacked Ghana and tried to destroy it. Tunka Menin's rulership is now used by historians as the model against which they measure the success and effectiveness of other West African statesmen of the 500–1590 period. He was highly respectful of the community traditions through which he had achieved his exalted position. He rode through community streets daily to hear his constituents' pleas and complaints, and he dispensed justice regularly. He also administered an economic system that controlled trans-Saharan and intraregional caravan traffic, providing income and wealth for himself and the merchant elites in Ghana. He protected the trade routes, provided ethical business leadership, and used magic and mystery to wrap himself in an aura of "divine kingship," which gave his many subjects a sense of divinely guarded safety.

Source:
J. F. A. Ajayi and Michael Crowder, eds., *The History of West Africa,* second edition, 2 volumes (New York: Columbia University Press, 1976, 1987).

SANDIKI

CIRCA 1346-1390
WAZIR OF MALI

From Slave to Ruler. Born a slave in the Mali court, Sandiki—in an act of loyalty that was presumably expected of such slaves—took over the rulership of the Malian empire at a time of civil war and instability from succession disputes. When Mansa Musa II, an ineffective leader, died in 1387, he was succeeded by a brother, Mansa Magha II, who was killed within a year. To preserve the rulership for the Keita dynasty, Sandiki first married the widowed queen mother and then usurped the throne. Mobilizing the army, he expanded the reach of the Malian Empire beyond the territory of the Songhai people, attacked the town of Takedda, and restored the confidence of the merchant businessmen in the security of the caravan trade routes.

Source:
J. F. A. Ajayi and Michael Crowder, eds., *The History of West Africa,* second edition, 2 volumes (New York: Columbia University Press, 1976, 1987).

ZAYNAB OF QAYRAWAN

CIRCA 1036-CIRCA 1090

POLITICAL STRATEGIST

Rise to Power. A daughter of a wealthy merchant residing in Qayrawan, a trading city in the Sus region of Tunisia, Zaynab married a Masmuda ruler of Aghmat when she was around sixteen years old. She later left him for Laqqut ibn Yusuf al-Maghrawi, a chief of the desert Zanata, who took over Aghmat. After the Almoravids overran the Zanatas in Aghmat, they executed Laqqut. Zaynab became a significant political figure when she married Abu Bakr, who introduced her to the intrigues of creating a Muslim empire. Abu Bakr divorced her when he was required to return to the desert for a lengthy military campaign, and she married Abu Bakr's cousin and eventual successor, Ibn Tashfin. Zaynab encouraged her new husband to buy West African slaves to increase his military manpower and avoid dependence on the Sanhaja Berbers. She convinced him to introduce drums and flags to his troops as a source of esprit de corps among his troops and to recruit his top commanders from among Abu Bakr's forces. Most important, she gave him the political strategy that probably saved his life when Abu Bakr came back from the desert to depose his dangerous and disloyal kinsman. Successful in the encounter, Ibn Tashfin became the head of the entire northern division of the Almoravids and carved out his own empire in Morocco and Spain. All this state-building activity increased demand for West African gold, which was needed in North Africa for minting coins and buying luxury goods.

Source:
I. Hrbek and J. Devisse, "The Almoravids," in *Africa from the Seventh to the Eleventh Century*, edited by M. El Fasi and Hrbek, volume 3 of *General History of Africa* (London: Heinemann / Berkeley: University of California Press / Paris: UNESCO, 1988), pp. 348–350.

DOCUMENTARY SOURCES

Al-Bakri, *Kitab al-masalik wa-'l-mamalik* (Book of Routes and Realms, 1068)—The most significant source of historical and geographical information about West Africa of all Arabic texts written before the thirteenth century; the most detailed description of ancient Ghana in all available Arabic manuscripts.

Ibn al-Faqih, *Mukhtasar Kitab al-Buldan* (Book of the Mystic Lands, 903)—A work that includes an original account of an important west-east route from Ghana to Egypt, which was used by West African Muslims on their way to Mecca.

Ibn Battuta, *Rihlah* (Travels, 1356)—The best-known Arabic account of a Muslim traveler's visit to the Western Sudan.

Ibn Hawqal, *Surat al-Ard* (Picture of the Earth, 988)—A geographical work that includes a detailed description of the trans-Saharan caravan trade from Sijilmasa to Ghana, an analysis of the desert Sanhaja, and a discussion of relations between Ghana and the Berbers.

Ibn Khaldun, *Kitab al-'ibar* (The Book of Historical Lessons, written 1374–1378, revised 1378–1404)—A "universal history" that includes excellent descriptions of Mali and its relations with North Africa, based on the author's own travels and experiences in the Maghrib and the Western Sudan and his research in earlier sources.

Al-Idrisi, *Kitab Nuzhat al-Mashtaq fi Ikhtiraq al-Afaq* (Amusement for One Who Desires to Travel Around the World, 1154)—A work written by a Muslim geographer for the Norman Christian king of Sicily, Roger II; often called *Kitab al-Rujari* (The Book of Roger), it provides vivid pictures of the gold resources in the Western Sudan and the dynamics of the trans-Saharan caravan trade.

Mahmoud al-Kati, *Tarikh al-Fattash* (The Chronicle of the Seeker After Knowledge, started 1519)—The first history of West Africa by a West African; the work was continued by two subsequent generations of the Kati family, who were converted Muslims living in Djenné.

Leo Africanus, *Descrittione dell'Africa* (Description of Africa, 1550)—The most important and credible source for the history of the Western Sudan between Ibn Battuta's fourteenth-century account and those of the nineteenth-century European explorers.

Al-Mas'udi, *Muruj al-Dhahab wa Ma'adin* (Meadows of Gold and Mines of Precious Stones, 947–956)—One of the major sources on the early history of Islam in West Africa as well as information on the states of the Western Sudan.

'Abd al-Rahman al-Sa'di, *Tarikh al-Sudan* (Chronicle of the Western Sudan, circa 1650)—The second West African history by a native of the region of seventeenth century; written by a scholar in Timbuktu, this history of the Songhai Empire and its neighbors from its origins through 1655 is considered more comprehensive than al-Kati's *Tarikh al-Fettash*.

Al-Umari, *Masalik al-absar fi mamalik al-amsar* (Pathways of Vision in the Realms of the Metropolises, 1338)—An important Arabic primary source on fourteenth-century Mali.

Ahmad ibn Abi Yaqubi, *Tarikh* (History, 872–873)—The earliest extant Arabic source on West Africa, including relatively accurate information on the political and historical dynamics of the states of the Western Sudan, especially Ghana, Gao (KawKaw), and Kanem.

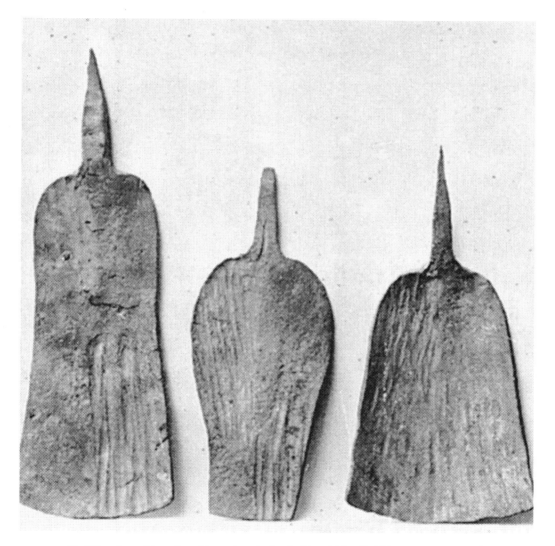

Traditional metal hoes found by archaeologists in West Africa (British Museum, London)

Cup engraved with the head of a Portuguese trader, Kingdom of Benin, Nigeria, circa 1500–1700
(from Jean-Baptiste Bacquart, *The Tribal Arts of Africa,* 1998)

POLITICS, LAW, AND THE MILITARY

by PITA OGABA AGBESE

CONTENTS

Sidebars and tables are listed in italics.

IMPORTANT EVENTS OF 500-1590

500*
- Major urban centers develop in several parts of West Africa.

750*
- Ghana emerges as a powerful state, one of several empires and kingdoms that flourish in West Africa during the Middle Ages. The rise of Ghana (in present-day southeastern Mauritania and southwestern Mali) coincides with the Islamization of several parts of West Africa.

850
- The Dya'ogo dynasty comes to power in the Takrur kingdom (in present-day Senegal); this dynasty is one of several that have long reigns over West African kingdoms.

980
- The Dya'ogo dynasty falls and is replaced by the Manna dynasty.

1020
- Berber troops from North Africa attack Ghana and are driven back. After this time the Berbers frequently attack their neighbors to the south, and West African states such as Songhai (in present-day Mali) and Bornu (west and south of Lake Chad) launch several military campaigns in retaliation.

1040
- War-jabi, king of Takrur, one of the earliest Muslim rulers of a West African kingdom, dies. Islam becomes increasingly important in the courts of some West African kingdoms. In several places it is imposed by force of arms by Muslim troops from North Africa.

1055
- Berbers destroy the oasis trading city of Audaghost as their forays against the Empire of Ghana become more frequent.

1056
- Abdullah ibn Yacin, an important religious figure of the Almoravid dynasty from North Africa, leads Takrur forces in an unsuccessful attack on their northern neighbor, Goddala.

1057
- On the death of Abdullah ibn Yacin, the powerful Almoravid empire splits into two rival parts.

1076
- Almoravids under military leader Abu Bakr conquer Ghana. Islam is imposed on the northern Soninke of Ghana, and many inhabitants of the empire migrate to other regions. Menim, the ruler of Ghana, is allowed to retain his throne, but he is forced to pay homage to the victorious Almoravids.

* DENOTES CIRCA DATE

IMPORTANT EVENTS OF 500-1590

1087
- Almoravid leader Abu Bakr dies.

1203
- A Susu army defeats Almoravid forces and drives them from Kumbi Saleh, the capital of Ghana.

1230
- Sundiata assumes power after staging a coup d'état against his uncle, ruler of the small state of Kangaba (in present-day Guinea on a tributary of the Niger River).

1235
- Sundiata defeats Sumanguru Kante, king of the Susu, at the Battle of Kirina—establishing the basis for the great Empire of Mali.

1240
- Sundiata captures Kumbi Saleh and destroys the city. Sundiata moves the capital of his new empire from Djeriba to Niani, in his home territory.

1255
- Sundiata dies, having ruled for twenty-five years. He is succeeded by his son, Mansa Uli (or Wali).

1285
- Sakura, a freed slave of the royal household, seizes power and proclaims himself emperor of Mali.

1300*
- Yoruba states such as Ile-Ife and Oyo (in present-day Nigeria) become important arts centers specializing in bronze casting.

1312-1337
- During the reign of Mansa Musa, the Empire of Mali reaches its largest size.

1324
- On a pilgrimage to Mecca, Mansa Musa and his entourage arrive at Cairo. Through this journey Musa solidifies the reputation of Mali as a wealthy West African state and enhances its status as a major center for Islamic scholarship.

1352-1353
- North African theologian and traveler Ibn Battuta journeys through West Africa, providing an eyewitness account of the splendor of the Mali Empire; his writings become an important source of information about economic and political developments in West Africa during the fourteenth century.

* DENOTES CIRCA DATE

IMPORTANT EVENTS OF 500-1590

1440
- Ewuare the Great ascends the throne of the Benin Kingdom. He rules for thirty-three years.

1444
- Portuguese sailors capture Africans for slave labor on the sugar plantations of Algarve, a province of southern Portugal. Trafficking in African men and women and shipping them to the Americas as slaves dominates African and European relations for several centuries.

1450*
- The kingdom of Bornu gains power and eventually becomes the most important political entity in the northeastern corner of West Africa, eclipsing the older Kanem empire in the same region.

1455-1456
- Alvise Cà da Mosto and Diogo Gomes explore the southern coast of West Africa for Portugal.

1468
- Sunni Ali captures Timbuktu and founds the Empire of Songhai.

1473
- Sunni Ali captures the city of Djenné after beseiging it for several years.

1481
- Burba Birain, ruler of the Wolof empire (in present-day Senegal), is deposed in a revolt organized by his half brothers. This sort of political intrigue and quarreling over succession is common in West African political entities that have not established formalized rules for succession.

1482
- The Portuguese build Elmina Castle (originally called São Jorge da Mina) in the gold-mining district along the West African coast (in the modern nation of Ghana). Elmina eventually becomes a major slaveholding fort during the transatlantic trafficking in African people.

1492
- Sunni Ali drowns during a military raid after having ruled the Songhai Empire for more than twenty years.

1497
- Askia Muhammad I (Askia the Great), ruler of Songhai, goes on pilgrimage to Mecca.

* DENOTES CIRCA DATE

IMPORTANT EVENTS OF 500-1590

1513
- Futa Toro, one of the largest cities of the Wolof empire, is captured by Dengella Koli's combined forces of Fulani and Mandinka (or Mandingo) soldiers.

- Al-Hassan ibn Muhammad al-Wizzaa al-Fasi, known to Europeans as Leo Africanus, visits West Africa with his uncle on a diplomatic mission for the sultan of Morocco. Leo's extensive writings about politics and society in West Africa are later published in Europe.

1535
- The Nupe (of present-day Nigeria) conquer and occupy the nearby state of Oyo. The ruling dynasty of Oyo flees to neighboring Borgu, where it remains in exile for about eighty years before returning to Oyo.

1562
- Englishman John Hawkins makes his first slaving expedition to West Africa and returns in 1564.

1570
- Idris Alooma ascends the throne of Bornu. Among the earliest West African kings to equip his soldiers with firearms, he brings Turkish military instructors to Bornu to teach his men how to use the weapons. These guns give Bornu a decisive advantage over its neighbors in warfare.

1590
- Moroccan forces armed with guns and cannons invade the Songhai Empire, crushing the Songhai army in 1591. This use of modern weapons changes the military balance between West Africans and invaders from North Africa, ending the hegemony of the three successive Empires of Ghana, Mali, and Songhai and dealing a severe blow to the trans-Saharan trade that has flourished for centuries.

* DENOTES CIRCA DATE

Bronze plaques from the Kingdom of Benin, Nigeria, sixteenth-seventeenth century: (top) guards outside
the oba's palace; (bottom) Oba Esigie (ruled 1504 – circa 1550) returning from war with the Igala
(top: Ethnological Museum, Berlin; bottom: British Museum, London)

OVERVIEW

Glorious Past. The grandeur of ancient Africa has been revealed in discoveries about its large and prosperous empires, efficient governing systems, major architectural projects, scientific and artistic advancements, and valuable mineral resources. Much attention has been focused on ancient Egypt, Kush, and Meroe, but all parts of Africa contributed to its cultural heritage. West Africa is known, among other things, for its state building. Between 400 and 1600 powerful empires such as Ghana, Mali, Songhai, Bornu, and Benin exerted widespread influence. Their rise to prominence was based on factors including astute political leadership, effective and efficient bureaucracies, well-organized armies, and strong economies.

Historians, Empires, and Kingdoms. Large empires and kingdoms tend to capture the imagination of historians because these political systems are more likely than small states to leave behind records of their accomplishments in sources such as oral traditions and epics, archaeological evidence, and written records of traders, travelers, and palace chroniclers. As they continue to collect evidence about the complex administrative and social systems of West Africa, historians are learning more about smaller political entities, whose past is no less interesting than the histories of empires. During the period 500–1590 millions of Africans were not part of the large political conglomerates that have so fascinated historians. Information about smaller political units and village democracies helps scholars to place the histories of empires within a larger context. After all, imperial systems were built through systematic incorporation of smaller political entities, which were important parts of the historical and political dynamics of West Africa.

Environment. In the course of African history, several ecological changes have had a profound impact on human settlement and migration as well as agricultural production. Among the most spectacular of these developments was the drying up of the Sahara region in the north-central part of the continent about 3000 B.C.E. As this region began to lose water and vegetation, it could no longer sustain its population, leading to mass migration from the region and surrounding areas. Many of the migrants settled in the West African savanna south of the desert, where ecological conditions were suitable for agriculture. In addition to crop production, the new settlers also raised livestock and used camels, horses, and donkeys to transport their goods from one place to another. This migration helped to shape the subsequent history of West Africa.

Gold, Salt, and the Trans-Saharan Trade. North of the savanna, the inhabitants mined salt and produced other commodities that were not readily available in the savanna. There and in the forests much further south in West Africa, large quantities of gold were mined. Beginning about 200 C.E., a complex network of trade developed between Africans north and south of the Sahara Desert. This trans-Saharan trade was structured around the exchange of gold, salt, grains, gum, hides and skins, books, silks, and an assortment of other commodities. While the direct participants in the trade were North Africans and West Africans, the tentacles of the trans-Saharan network extended much further, to include southern Europe, the Middle East, and Asia. For many kingdoms of West Africa—including the Empires of Ghana, Mali, and Songhai—the trans-Saharan trade was central to their politics, law, and military. For instance, standing armies were established for the purpose of conquering gold- and salt-producing regions as well as for providing protection and security along the trade routes.

The Trans-Saharan Trade and Empire Building. Inhabitants of West Africa were linked to far-flung places by several important east-west and north-south trade networks. Several empires rose and fell in connection with struggles to control them. Ghana, Mali, Songhai, and other large states of West Africa owed their fame and fortune to the influence that they exerted over trade along these caravan routes. States that lost their ability to control strategic locations along the route dramatically declined in power, wealth, and stature. Political entities that could impose their will on trade experienced a dramatic rise in power. Moreover, the benefits of the trade routes extended well beyond the African continent. Gold mined in West Africa was indispensable to the economy of Europe during this period. European states used gold not just as a means of exchange but as a stabilizer of currencies, and West African gold traded across the Sahara fueled European financial enterprises. Trans-Saharan trade was thus an important instrument for creating cultural linkages between West Africans and the rest of the world.

Timbuktu and Other Centers of Trade and Learning. Several emporia of politics, trade, and higher learning emerged along trade routes in West Africa, among them Timbuktu, Gao, Kano, Katsina, and Djenné. The best-known of these important West African cities was Timbuktu, which despite its strategic location was more than just a trading post. Above all, it was an intellectual center. At its mosques and places of higher learning, scholars provided instruction on subjects such as theology, rhetoric, grammar, literature, and Islamic law and jurisprudence. The fame of Timbuktu as a major center of Islamic higher learning attracted scholars from faraway places, including Cairo in Egypt, Fez in Morocco, and Mecca in Saudi Arabia. At Timbuktu and other major cities in West Africa, Islamic scholars taught courses to young people who sought knowledge and wisdom. The role of Timbuktu as a city of learning had important ramifications for the development of Islamic jurisprudence in West Africa.

Military Conquests. Much of the history of empires and kingdoms in West Africa deals with military conquests and practical demonstrations of military geniuses. Political leaders such as Sundiata, Mansa Musa, Idris Alooma, and Askia Muhammad I, ruling as emperors and kings, used superior military power and prowess to exert their will on other states or ethnic groups. Successful West African states imposed political, cultural, and sometimes religious hegemony over vast territories. Soninke, Kanuri, Edo, Hausa, and several other groups formed large, powerful, and complex kingdoms through military conquests. With superior military power and competent political leadership, such kingdoms were able to dominate less-powerful states, turning these vanquished entities into vassal states that had to pay tributes to their political overlords. Some of these empires lasted for several decades or even centuries while others rose and fell in quick succession. No political vacuum was left for long. As soon as one empire fell down, another rose in its place. Sometimes the decline was gradual rather than dramatic. For instance, Ghana was conquered by the Almoravids of North Africa in 1076, but remnants of the empire continued to survive for several more decades. Many West African kingdoms were built by the sword and met their demise through military campaigns mounted by their arch rivals. While some developed fine martial traditions with standing armies, others relied on citizen-soldiers who took up weapons only when necessary for the defense of their kingdom.

Military Heroes. Dramatic conquests by West African states have generated interesting folklore on the military commanders. According to Robert Edgerton, "in most of Africa south of the Sahara, warfare and the warrior-tradition were so inextricably tied to everything of importance—honor, wealth, religion, politics, even art and sexuality—that it is no exaggeration to say that most men's reputations, fortunes, and futures depended on their martial valor." Within this milieu of reverence for valor and military prowess, legends about martial exploits grew around certain political figures. Military victories of Sundiata, Idris Alooma, Sumanguru, Mansa Musa, Askia Muhammad I, and many others are celebrated, and these leaders have assumed larger-than-life stature. They are credited with the ability to confound their enemies and achieve success in the face of formidable obstacles. Appellations such as "outstanding magician," "invincible general," "fearless warrior," and "lion of the savanna" are attached to their names. Many of them were said to have used mystical powers to aid their military campaigns. Epics and songs composed in their honor extol their bravery, ruthlessness, and generalship.

Songs and Epics. There are many songs and epics on historic West African battles. Extolling the bravery and power of their protagonists, they provide graphic descriptions of military encounters between rival forces. Sometimes, battles are depicted as struggles between good and evil. A professional group of historians, storytellers, and musicians known as griots emerge to tell these stories and epics, and thus to transmit historical knowledge and legends from one generation to another.

TOPICS IN POLITICS, LAW, AND THE MILITARY

CONSTITUTIONAL MONARCHIES

Constitutional Safeguards. Because of the legends glorifying their heroic deeds and far-reaching influence, Mansa Musa, Sundiata, Idris Alooma, and other political leaders of ancient West Africa tend to be remembered as all-powerful tyrants. In fact, the power of West African kings was usually held in check by a large number of safeguards, and many African states of the period were constitutional monarchies. The nobility and other social classes worked to ensure that rulers did not overstep their bounds. A king could not make major political decisions without consulting a ruling council or some similar political institution. For instance, the oba (king) of Benin could not make important decisions, such as promulgation of new laws or declaration of war, without involving councils of state such as the *uzama* (the seven hereditary chiefs whose duties included installing the oba), *eghaevbo n'ogbe* (the town chiefs in the oba's cabinet), and the *eghaevbo n'ore* (the palace chiefs in the cabinet).

Checks on Power. Elaborate procedures were created as checks on the abuse of power. Taboos, such as preventing the king from owning private property or eating in public, were designed to hold the king under tight control. Part of the mystique of kingship in ancient Africa was the belief that the ruler was superhuman. He was not supposed to require human necessities such as eating and sleeping. Thus, the king should not have to amass public resources such as food for himself since he did not have to eat in the first place. In some places, traditions forbade rulers from leaving their kingdoms. Sanctions against an errant ruler included private and public admonitions, banishment, and outright removal from office. Among some West African communities, the ultimate sanction against a king who misruled his people was regicide. Among the Yorubas, the council of chiefs asked rulers who had abused their authority to "open the calabash" (that is, to commit suicide). In other places a bad ruler was subject to banishment. Some kingdoms held secret trials for rulers who had abused their

power, and in some cases secret societies were established to act as unseen checks on the kings' exercise of power. Among some other West African groups, mass migration from an oppressive ruler was a strategy against bad governance. This practice of abandoning an oppressive king is the source of the saying "No king can rule without the people." The right of the citizens to secede from an oppressive political environment was also enshrined in the political systems of West Africa. Where it was necessary to stage a revolt against an autocratic ruler, the revolt was aimed at removing him from office and rarely against the entire political system. In other words, the people removed an errant ruler but kept the royal institution. Despite such elaborate systems of checks against the abuse of power, there were, however, some cases in which rulers became tyrannical.

Promotion of the Citizens' Well-Being. An important feature of leadership in ancient Africa was the understanding that a ruler was not in office to serve his private ends but to advance the collective interests and general welfare of the people. The king's tenure was contingent on good governance. In some cases, if a king ruled well, he could rule for life. Poor leadership by the king delegitimized his rule and could subject him to forfeiting the kingship. It was clearly understood that obligations and responsibilities went with the ruler's exercise of power and authority. Both rulers and citizens accepted the notion that the ruler was not above the law. One of the duties of rulers was the allocation of land and other resources. Any resources that were unallocated were held in trust by the ruler for the entire community. He could not appropriate them for himself.

Principles of Power. Several important principles undergirded the use of power in the ancient states of West Africa. First, rulers and citizens alike understood that citizens surrendered their power to the king, but that he held it in trust only. Thus, the authority wielded by the king was not his personal authority but the collective power and

Two Igbo ruler-priests, circa 900–1000 (left: National Commission for Museums and Monuments, Nigeria; right: British Museum, London)

security of the people. Second, the purpose of giving power to the king was so that he could use it to advance the collective welfare and security of the community. The king's power was not meant for advancing his private or personal interests. Third, legitimate power could be exercised only on the basis of the people's consent, resulting in wide and extensive consultations among kings and citizens. Fourth, citizens reserved the right to take back their power from rulers who misused it. Thus, even though citizens made a conscious decision to surrender political power to the king, they had a right to participate in the making of public policies, and such right of popular participation could not be forfeited to the ruler. The principle of citizen participation in politics was widely enshrined. In some polities, the right to participate in public affairs was extended to all adults. In others, only adult males took part in public deliberations.

The Representative Principle. It was firmly established in West Africa that the people must have a voice on issues that touched their lives and material well-being. Ideally, each person would have been able to participate in public affairs and public choices that shaped his or her life. But geographical and other considerations did not always allow everyone to have direct participation in politics, and therefore the principle of representation was devised. Several types of representation were used. Sometimes representation was geographical; that is, a council of state was made up of members drawn from the political provinces of the state. Sometimes, age or gender was used as a basis of political representation, and often the principle of clan or family representation was used. Representation through a guild system was another method of political participation. The representative council usually arrived at decisions through a majority vote, but in many cases, strenuous efforts were made to reach a consensus decision. The principle of representation was also apparent in the manner through which a ruler was chosen. Typically, a body of kingmakers—whose membership was composed of regional, clan, or family representatives—selected their ruler from among several contestants. Members of the body of kingmakers were not themselves eligible for the kingship.

THE MAJESTY OF THE EMPEROR OF MALI

Foreign visitors to ancient West African kingdoms were often captivated by their rulers' wealth and majesty. The North African Muslim traveler Ibn Battuta, who visited Mali in 1353, described the majesty of its emperor, Mansa Sulaiman:

The Sultan's usual dress is a velvety red tunic. . . . he is preceded by his musicians, who carry gold and silver guitars, and behind him come three hundred armed slaves. He walks in a leisurely fashion, affecting a very slow movement, and even stops from time to time. On reaching the dais he stops and looks around the assembly, then ascends it in the sedate manner of a preacher ascending a mosque-pulpit. As he takes his seat the drums, trumpets, and bugles are sounded.

Source: Thomas Hodgkin, "Kingdoms of the Western Sudan," in *The Dawn of African History*, edited by Roland Oliver (London: Oxford University Press, 1968), p. 41.

Decentralization. In ancient Africa, power was generally decentralized and diffused. Power and authority were generally shared by three main institutions: the king and his cabinet or council, the council of elders, and the village assembly. The council of elders comprised heads of clans or lineages. The village assembly was often the highest decision-making group. Every adult had a right to participate in its deliberations. Some West African societies dispensed with the notion of hierarchical powers and recognized no rigid areas of authority. Others, particularly the major empires, had highly centralized political systems in which the king or emperor was extremely powerful. Power was sometimes decentralized on a territorial basis. It was common to divide an empire or kingdom into provinces, cantons, cities, and villages. For instance, ancient Ghana was divided into sixteen principalities. Kings or emperors appointed provincial governors and other high-ranking officials to administer these political subdivisions. Accountable to his ruler, an official sometimes lived in the political domain he administered, but in other cases he lived in the capital city and paid frequent visits to the area over which he had authority. While some officials were appointed to their posts by the ruling monarch, others ascended to their offices through hereditary rights. In places where the political system was decentralized on a territorial basis, local issues and administration were handled by district officials. In ancient West Africa, however, there were many autonomous communities that came under the jurisdiction of no centralized political structure. Some were loosely united by common languages or cultures, but the individual villages remained largely independent in political terms.

Sources:

George B. N. Ayittey, *Indigenous African Institutions* (Ardsley-on-Hudson, N.Y.: Transnational Publishers, 1991).

John A. A. Ayoade and Adigun A. B. Agbaje, eds., *African Traditional Thought and Institutions* (Lagos: Center for Black and African Arts and Civilization, 1989).

George E. Brooks, *Landlords and Strangers: Ecology, Society, and Trade in Western Africa, 1000–1630* (Boulder, Colo.: Westview Press, 1993).

Lester Brooks, *Great Civilizations of Ancient Africa* (New York: Four Winds Press, 1971).

Basil Davidson, *African Kingdoms* (New York: Time, Inc., 1966).

Cheik Anta Diop, *Precolonial Black Africa: A Comparative Study of the Political and Social Systems of Europe and Black Africa, from Antiquity to the Formation of Modern States*, translated by Harold J. Salemson (Westport, Conn.: Lawrence Hill, 1987).

Sylvia C. Finkley, *Africa in Early Days* (New York: Odyssey Press, 1969).

Thomas A. Hale, *Scribe, Griot, and Novelist: Narrative Interpreters of the Songhay Empire* (Gainesville: University of Florida Press, 1990).

Henri Labouret, *Africa before the White Man*, translated by Francis Huxley (New York: Walker, 1963).

Phyllis M. Martin and Patrick O'Meara, eds., *Africa*, third edition (Bloomington: Indiana University Press, 1995).

D. T. Niane, *Sundiata: An Epic of Old Mali*, translated by G. D. Pickett (London: Longmans, 1965).

Roland Oliver, ed., *The Dawn of African History* (London: Oxford University Press, 1968).

Oliver and Anthony Atmore, *The African Middle Ages: 1400–1800* (Cambridge: Cambridge University Press, 1981); revised as *Medieval Africa: 1250–1800* (Cambridge: Cambridge University Press, 2001).

Charlotte A. Quinn, *Mandingo Kingdoms of the Senegambia: Traditionalism, Islam, and European Expansion* (Evanston, Ill.: Northwestern University Press, 1972).

John Reader, *Africa: A Biography of the Continent* (New York: Knopf, 1998).

Walter Rodney, *A History of the Upper Guinea Coast, 1545–1800* (Oxford, Clarendon Press, 1970).

Ricky Rosenthal, *The Splendor That Was Africa* (Dobbs Ferry, N.Y.: Oceana Publications, 1967).

G. T. Stride and Caroline Ifeka, *Peoples and Empires of West Africa: West Africa in History, 1000–1800* (New York: Africana Publishing, 1971).

EMPIRES AND UNIFICATION

Multi-Ethnic and Multi-Cultural Kingdoms. The large empires of West Africa facilitated trade and political and cultural exchanges among a diverse population. These empires also encouraged millions of people to transcend territorial limits imposed by ethnicity and other primordial ties. Some kingdoms and empires were created through the initiative of a particular ethnic group, but ultimately most of these political entities were a mosaic of different ethnic and cultural backgrounds. In some cases, conquered peoples were assimilated by their conquerors. They adopted the cultures, languages, and religions of their rulers. In many cases, however, conquered peoples were allowed to maintain local authority while paying tributes to the new imperial rulers and acknowledging their overlordship. These peoples usually retained not only their political institutions but also their cultures, languages, and religions. The centralized administrative systems instituted by some

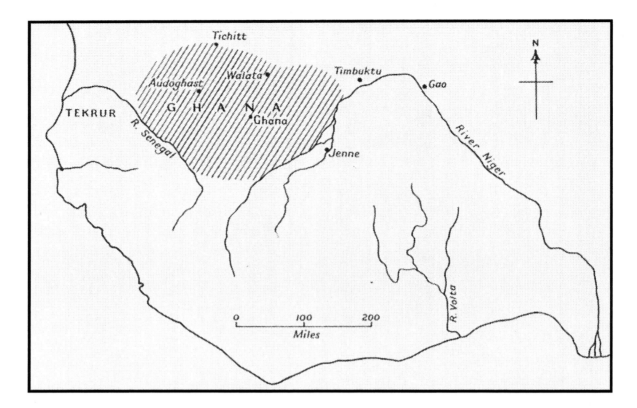

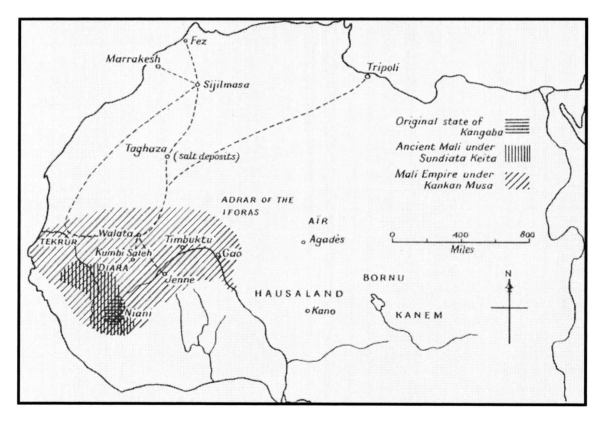

Territories of the Empires of Ghana and Mali (maps by K. C. Jordan, F.R.G.S.;
from Basil Davidson, *The Growth of African Civilization*, 1965)

West African states were a means of unifying such disparate peoples.

Socio-Economic Development. While West African states—Ghana, Mali, Songhai, Bornu, Benin, Kebbi, and many others—differed greatly in size and influence, they had several common features. Most were well organized. High officials were appointed to fulfill specific roles or to govern particular territories. Various strategies were devised to raise revenues for running the political systems, including import and export taxes, tributes, and land taxes. Many of the empires that emerged in West Africa from about 750 to 1590 placed a high premium on education. Naturally captivated by the wealth, majesty, and military prowess of the Songhai Empire when he visited in 1513, Leo Africanus also observed the intense demand for learning in Timbuktu and other major West African cities. In Timbuktu, he said, "more profit is made from the book trade than any other line of business." The empires actively promoted economic development. A variety of economic activities—such as iron smelting, cloth and basket weaving, gold works, agriculture, animal husbandry, fishing, and bronze production—were undertaken to spur growth and development. The general peace and stability engendered by the large West African states facilitated long-distance trade interactions, which in turn promoted economic development in most parts of the region. As a result of such interactions, the large political systems became the birthplaces of new ideas, new technologies, and novel production methods.

Diplomacy. West African states maintained extensive diplomatic contacts. For instance, Mansa Musa, who ruled the Empire of Mali in 1312–1337, opened diplomatic relations with Egypt and Morocco. His pilgrimage to Mecca in 1324, his active promotion of Islamic learning, and his close relationship with Muslim scholars helped to establish Mali as a bona fide Islamic state in the eyes of the Muslim leaders of North Africa and the Middle East, enhancing the diplomatic relationship of Mali with the outside world. Sometimes, diplomatic exchanges were facilitated through military victories. In other cases, princes and other royalty from defeated states were held hostage to prevent uprisings against conquerors. For example, Mansa Musa's soldiers captured two Songhai princes, Ali Kohlen and his brother, and held them hostage to ensure the good behavior of their conquered Songhai people.

The Enslavement of Africans. Between the middle of the fifteenth century and the end of the sixteenth century several factors came together to end the era of prosperity and stability. Berber incursions into West Africa disrupted the trans-Saharan caravan trade and ultimately led to the fall of the Songhai Empire in 1591, while the arrival of Europeans along the southern coastline of West Africa shifted the focus of trade, as well as the locus of power, from the great inland states to the coastal region, where Europeans soon found it more profitable to deal in human

---

THE WEALTH OF TIMBUKTU

Travelers in the West African empires described their grandeur. The North African traveler known as Leo Africanus, who visited West Africa in 1513, wrote a firsthand account of life in Timbuktu:

The inhabitants of Timbuktu are very rich, especially the foreigners who have settled in the country; so much so that the king gave two of his daughters in marriage to two merchants who were brothers, on account of their great wealth.

The rich king of Timbuktu has many plates and scepters of gold, some whereof weigh 1,300 pounds; and he keeps a magnificent and well-furnished court. When he travels anywhere, he rides upon a camel which is led by some of his noblemen: and so he does likewise when he goes to warfare, and all his soldiers ride upon horses. . . . They often have skirmishes with those that refuse to pay tribute, and, so many as they take, they sell unto the merchants of Timbuktu. . . .

Here are a great store of doctors, judges, priests and learned men, that are bountifully maintained at the king's cost and charges. And hither are brought divers manuscripts of written books out of Barbary, which are sold for more money than any other merchandise. The coin of Timbuktu is of gold without any stamp or superscription; but in matters of small value they use certain shells (cowrie shells) brought hither out of the kingdom of Persia.

Source: Margaret Shinnic, *Ancient African Kingdoms* (London: Arnold, 1965), pp. 60–61.

---

cargo than in commodities and natural resources. The transatlantic slave trade, through which Europeans, for hundreds of years, captured, enslaved, and transported millions of Africans to the Americas, had a profound impact on the African continent, creating devastation and economic stagnation for Africa and leaving the continent underdeveloped. The process began about 1441 when Antam Goncalvez of Portugal took Africans from the west coast of the continent and gave them to Prince Henry the Navigator of Portugal as gifts. Subsequently, other African captives were taken to Europe as household slaves for wealthy Europeans. The voyages of Christopher Columbus, and other European adventurers to the Americas, led to a great demand for labor with which to extract the huge wealth of the Americas. Europeans eventually settled on using Africans as slaves to cultivate sugarcane, tobacco, and cotton and to dig gold and silver. The Portuguese writer Gomes Eannes de Azurara described a group of African captives brought to work on sugar plantations in southern Portugal on 8 August 1444:

Some among them were tolerably light in color, handsome and well-proportioned; some slightly darker; others a

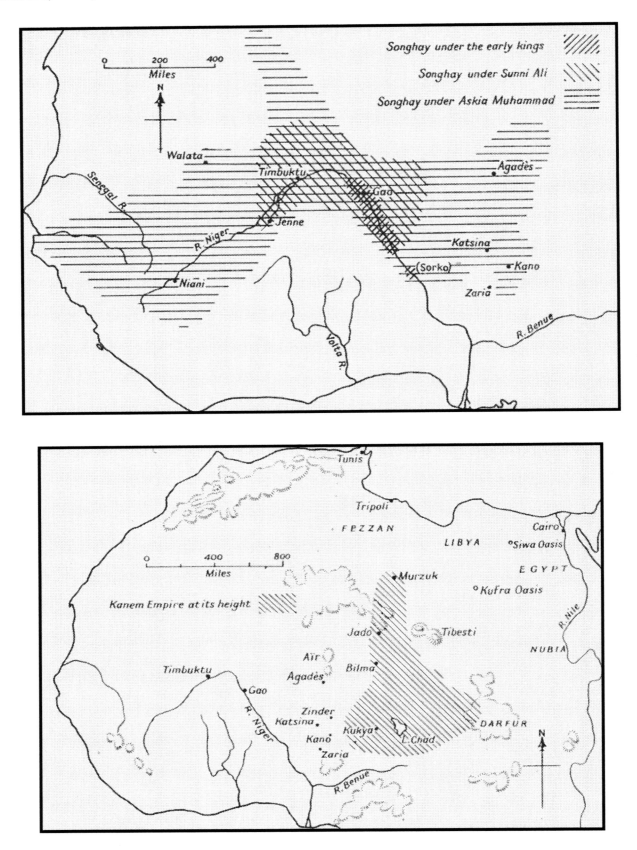

Territories of the Songhai and Kanem-Bornu Empires (maps by K. C. Jordan, F.R.G.S.;
from Basil Davidson, *The Growth of African Civilization*, 1965)

degree lighter than mulattoes, while several were as black as moles, and so hideous both of face and form as to suggest the idea that they were come from the lower regions. But what heart so hard as not to be touched with compassion at the sight of them! Some with downcast heads and faces bathed in tears as they looked at each other; others moaning sorrowfully, and fixing their eyes on heaven, uttered plaintive cries as if appealing for help to the Father of Nature. Others struck their faces with their hands and threw themselves flat upon the ground. Others uttered a wailing chant after the fashion of their country. . . . But their anguish was at its height when the moment of distribution came, when of necessity children were separated from their parents, wives from their husbands, and brothers from brothers. Each was compelled to go wherever fate might send him. It was impossible to effect this separation without extreme pain. . . .

Centuries of profitable exploitation of African labor enhanced European industrialization and economic development while greatly retarding the development of Africa.

Sources:

George B. N. Ayittey, *Indigenous African Institutions* (Ardsley-on-Hudson, N.Y.: Transnational Publishers, 1991).

John A. A. Ayoade and Adigun A. B. Agbaje, eds., *African Traditional Thought and Institutions* (Lagos: Center for Black and African Arts and Civilization, 1989).

George E. Brooks, *Landlords and Strangers: Ecology, Society, and Trade in Western Africa, 1000–1630* (Boulder, Colo.: Westview Press, 1993).

Lester Brooks, *Great Civilizations of Ancient Africa* (New York: Four Winds Press, 1971).

Basil Davidson, *African Kingdoms* (New York: Time, Inc., 1966).

Cheik Anta Diop, *Precolonial Black Africa: A Comparative Study of the Political and Social Systems of Europe and Black Africa, from Antiquity to the Formation of Modern States*, translated by Harold J. Salemson (Westport, Conn.: Lawrence Hill, 1987).

Sylvia C. Finkley, *Africa in Early Days* (New York: Odyssey Press, 1969).

Thomas A. Hale, *Scribe, Griot, and Novelist: Narrative Interpreters of the Songhay Empire* (Gainesville: University of Florida Press, 1990).

Henri Labouret, *Africa before the White Man*, translated by Francis Huxley (New York: Walker, 1963).

Phyllis M. Martin and Patrick O'Meara, eds., *Africa*, third edition (Bloomington: Indiana University Press, 1995).

D. T. Niane, *Sundiata: An Epic of Old Mali*, translated by G. D. Pickett (London: Longmans, 1965).

Roland Oliver, ed., *The Dawn of African History* (London: Oxford University Press, 1968).

Oliver and Anthony Atmore, *The African Middle Ages: 1400–1800* (Cambridge: Cambridge University Press, 1981); revised as *Medieval Africa: 1250–1800* (Cambridge: Cambridge University Press, 2001).

Charlotte A. Quinn, *Mandingo Kingdoms of the Senegambia: Traditionalism, Islam, and European Expansion* (Evanston, Ill.: Northwestern University Press, 1972).

John Reader, *Africa: A Biography of the Continent* (New York: Knopf, 1998).

Walter Rodney, *A History of the Upper Guinea Coast, 1545–1800* (Oxford: Clarendon Press, 1970).

Ricky Rosenthal, *The Splendor That Was Africa* (Dobbs Ferry, N.Y.: Oceana Publications, 1967).

G. T. Stride and Caroline Ifeka, *Peoples and Empires of West Africa: West Africa in History, 1000–1800* (New York: Africana Publishing, 1971).

GOVERNMENT AND RELIGION

The Fusion of Religious and Political Power. The practice of separating governmental power and religious authority was not a feature of politics in ancient West Africa. Political and religious leadership roles were frequently fused in one person. Ritual beliefs, myths, and dogmas were central to the exercise of power. The king was accountable both to the living and to the ancestors. As part of his responsibilities, he served as a mediator between his domain and the realm of the deceased, and the extent to which he maintained harmony between the temporal world of the living and the supernatural world of the ancestors was a measure of his success as a ruler. He was responsible for good order in society, which was partially created through harmony between its secular and nonsecular components. The king's powers were held in check by religious, as well as institutionalized, sanctions. He had a duty to serve the living and the dead. Both the king and the people believed that a ruler's transgressions could be punished by the ancestors. This notion that the ruler was answerable to the ancestors as well as the living was an important principle of governance, serving as a powerful check on the propensity to abuse power.

Islam. The introduction of Islam into West Africa during the eighth century had a profound impact on the political, economic, and religious life in some parts of the region. In some communities Islam modified the indigenous political system. For instance, the principles of Islamic jurisprudence increasingly became important elements in the administration of law and justice. With the introduction of Islam, political power in several parts of West Africa became organized on the basis of Islamic religious precepts. For example, matrilineal descent systems in societies converted to Islam were changed into patrilineal systems—a transformation that had a profound impact on the succession of rulers. Many West Africans in the Islamic empires were exposed to Arabic culture and Islamic scholarship. Islam was also a key component in the development of diplomatic and cultural ties between West Africa and the Middle East. In religious terms, however, the impact of Islam was not monumental. For a long time West African converts to Islam continued to practice their indigenous African religions as well. Rulers such as Sundiata skillfully combined Islamic faith with the worship of indigenous African gods. In Mali, Ghana, and several other West African kingdoms, Islam was practiced in the royal courts, but traditional African religions were dominant outside the palaces.

Muslim "Crusaders." Islam also changed the fundamental purpose and character of warfare in West Africa. In the early phase of its introduction to West Africa, Islam was propagated through peaceful means by Muslim

A Yoruba queen on a ceremonial vessel (top) and a Yoruba throne (bottom), fragment from a statue
of a ruler; terra-cotta objects from Ile-Ife, Nigeria, circa 1100–1500 (National Commission
for Museums and Monuments, Lagos [top] and Ile-Ife [bottom])

merchants. In its later phase it was imposed largely by force of arms. For the first time bloody wars of religious conversion were waged. Many North African invaders saw themselves as warriors for Allah in a region dominated by "nonbelievers." The Almoravids, Muslim militants from North Africa, believed in the doctrine of Islamic purity. They used military conquest to spread Islam in West Africa. In many places, people put up stiff resistance against the imposition of Islam, particularly in the gold-producing regions, where resistance to Islam was manifested through the refusal of the people to mine the desired quantities of gold for Muslim merchants and rulers.

Sources:

George B. N. Ayittey, *Indigenous African Institutions* (Ardsley-on-Hudson, N.Y.: Transnational Publishers, 1991).

John A. A. Ayoade and Adigun A. B. Agbaje, eds., *African Traditional Thought and Institutions* (Lagos: Center for Black and African Arts and Civilization, 1989).

George E. Brooks, *Landlords and Strangers: Ecology, Society, and Trade in Western Africa, 1000–1630* (Boulder, Colo.: Westview Press, 1993).

Lester Brooks, *Great Civilizations of Ancient Africa* (New York: Four Winds Press, 1971).

Basil Davidson, *African Kingdoms* (New York: Time, Inc., 1966).

Cheik Anta Diop, *Precolonial Black Africa: A Comparative Study of the Political and Social Systems of Europe and Black Africa, from Antiquity to the Formation of Modern States,* translated by Harold J. Salemson (Westport, Conn.: Lawrence Hill, 1987).

Sylvia C. Finkley, *Africa in Early Days* (New York: Odyssey Press, 1969).

Thomas A. Hale, *Scribe, Griot, and Novelist: Narrative Interpreters of the Songhay Empire* (Gainesville: University of Florida Press, 1990).

Henri Labouret, *Africa before the White Man,* translated by Francis Huxley (New York: Walker, 1963).

Phyllis M. Martin and Patrick O'Meara, eds., *Africa,* third edition (Bloomington: Indiana University Press, 1995).

D. T. Niane, *Sundiata: An Epic of Old Mali,* translated by G. D. Pickett (London: Longmans, 1965).

Roland Oliver, ed., *The Dawn of African History* (London: Oxford University Press, 1968).

Oliver and Anthony Atmore, *The African Middle Ages: 1400–1800* (Cambridge: Cambridge University Press, 1981); revised as *Medieval Africa: 1250–1800* (Cambridge: Cambridge University Press, 2001).

Charlotte A. Quinn, *Mandingo Kingdoms of the Senegambia: Traditionalism, Islam, and European Expansion* (Evanston, Ill.: Northwestern University Press, 1972).

John Reader, *Africa: A Biography of the Continent* (New York: Knopf, 1998).

Walter Rodney, *A History of the Upper Guinea Coast, 1545–1800* (Oxford: Clarendon Press, 1970).

Ricky Rosenthal, *The Splendor That Was Africa* (Dobbs Ferry, N.Y.: Oceana Publications, 1967).

G. T. Stride and Caroline Ifeka, *Peoples and Empires of West Africa: West Africa in History, 1000–1800* (New York: Africana Publishing, 1971).

HEREDITARY SUCCESSION AND POLITICAL INSTABILITY

Rules of Succession. Some West African kingdoms and empires had elaborate rules governing succession to the throne. Hereditary succession was quite common. In maternal societies, where descent was traced through the

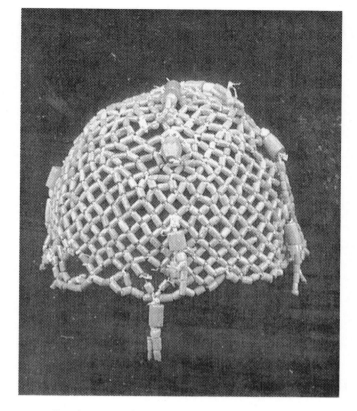

Royal crown made of coral, agate, and copper for Oba Ozolua, who ruled the Kingdom of Benin in the late fifteenth century (British Museum, London)

male line on the mother's side, the king was succeeded by a nephew, not his son. It was also common to choose the successor from among the direct descendants of the founder of the dynasty. In some places where hereditary succession was not recognized, the ruler was selected by a council of kingmakers. In other kingdoms, the next ruler was determined by a rotational system among two or several royal lineages. Some rulers were chosen on the basis of their physical vigor and leadership potential. In other cases, a proven record of achievement in war or other important activities was a criterion for selection. Strength of moral character was highly prized as a prerequisite for leadership.

Succession Disputes. Disputes over succession were particularly intense after the death of a founding emperor or king. In such cases, where the lines of succession were not yet clearly delineated or understood, arguments frequently arose among the founder's children or other relatives. Quite often, a breakdown in a line of succession led to usurpation or a coup d'état. If the battle for power among the ruler's descendants became particularly fierce, an outsider, such as a military commander, might dismiss all the contenders and make himself the ruler, in many cases creating a new ruling dynasty.

Abdication. A drastic sanction against the ruler was to force him to abdicate the throne. Even powerful leaders—

A terra-cotta head of a queen, Ile-Ife, circa 1100–1300, and a zinc-brass head of a queen mother, Kingdom of Benin, circa 1400–1600 (left: Museum of Antiquities, Ile-Ife; right: Ethnological Museum, Berlin)

such as Askia Muhammad I (Askia the Great), who ruled the Songhai Empire in 1493–1528—were not exempted from this sort of treatment. Despite Muhammad's genius in war and administration, he was forced, by his son Musa, to abdicate the throne. By 1528 Muhammad had become old and feeble and had lost his eyesight. He was exiled to a desolate island. Musa was assassinated three years after visiting such dishonor on his father.

Dynastic Struggles. When lines of succession were not clearly delineated or rulers were weak, divided loyalties and political intrigues were quite common, and intense power struggles were the result. Political rivalry at the center of an empire had major political consequences all the way to its fringes. In fact, dynasties were sometimes the first part of an empire to disintegrate when power at the center began to wane. Quarrels among contenders to the throne gave tributary states a chance to break away from their political overlords. Even when such breakaway attempts did not succeed, they could seriously weaken the power and authority of a ruling group. For example, in the Mali Empire, disputes over succession between the descendants

of Mansa Musa (ruled 1312–1337) and the descendants of Musa's brother Mansa Sulaiman (ruled 1341–1360) led to the breakaway of Songhai and Wolof. In other cases, trouble at the center encouraged tributary states to launch daring military raids on the declining empire. The Mossi made several such raids against Mali as quarrels over succession ravaged the empire. Political dissent at the center also gave powerful rival states an opportunity to initiate military aggression that challenged the hegemony of the troubled empire and sometimes created a new imperial power.

Breaking Up Empires. Even when succession disputes did not lead to the total collapse of an empire, they weakened it and inhibited its capacity to enforce its will on outlying territories. Tributary states were always seeking ways of regaining their freedom, and each time an opportunity presented itself, they did not hesitate to try to regain their lost sovereignty. When a major empire collapsed—like Ghana after 1076, Mali in 1468, and Songhai in 1591—tributary states sought to restore their independence. At the same time, however, a new potentate could attempt to

THE BURIAL OF A KING OF GHANA

In his *Kitab al-masalik wa-'l-mamalik* (Book of Routes and Realms, 1068) the Spanish Muslim geographer al-Bakri included a traveler's account of how the people of the Empire of Ghana buried a deceased ruler:

When the king dies, they build over the place where his tomb will be an enormous dome of wood. They bring him in on a bed. . . . At his side they place his ornaments, his weapons and the vessels from which he used to eat and drink. They also place there the man who had served his meals. They close the door of the dome and cover it with mats and materials and then they assemble the people, who heap earth upon it until it becomes like a large mound.

Source: Margaret Shinnie, *Ancient African Kingdoms* (London: Arnold, 1965), p. 49.

reconstitute the empire by forcing former tributary states to return to the fold. Some tributary states such as the Susu later rose to military prominence and formed their own empires by defeating their former imperial overlords. Such reversal of fortune was common in West Africa.

Political Instability. Overall, empires introduced political stability, which facilitated trade, diplomacy, and economic development. Large political systems could use their economic and military supremacy to maintain law and order. Nonetheless, the demise of a large empire created insecurity, poverty, disorder, disasters, violence, and general chaos and lawlessness. Vacuums created by the downfall of such political systems did not remain long unfilled.

Women and Politics. While women were not entirely excluded from politics, active participation in the public affairs of many West African states was largely the province of men. In several parts of the region, however, certain political institutions were reserved exclusively for women. For example, the queen mother was extremely powerful in Benin, Ashanti, and several other states. In Benin, she had the responsibility of grooming the successor to the oba (king). Nevertheless, to discourage her from meddling in palace politics, tradition required her to live several miles away from the capital city. In Bornu, women such as the king's mother, his wife, or a senior female relative such as his sister had important positions. Like their male counterparts in the nobility, they were given fiefs to administer. Among their responsibilities as fief holders were raising militia for the king, collecting taxes for the king and themselves, and hearing appeals from lower courts.

Sources:
George B. N. Ayittey, *Indigenous African Institutions* (Ardsley-on-Hudson, N.Y.: Transnational Publishers, 1991).

John A. A. Ayoade and Adigun A. B. Agbaje, eds., *African Traditional Thought and Institutions* (Lagos: Center for Black and African Arts and Civilization, 1989).

George E. Brooks, *Landlords and Strangers: Ecology, Society, and Trade in Western Africa, 1000–1630* (Boulder, Colo.: Westview Press, 1993).

Lester Brooks, *Great Civilizations of Ancient Africa* (New York: Four Winds Press, 1971).

Basil Davidson, *African Kingdoms* (New York: Time Inc., 1966).

Cheik Anta Diop, *Precolonial Black Africa: A Comparative Study of the Political and Social Systems of Europe and Black Africa, from Antiquity to the Formation of Modern States*, translated by Harold J. Salemson (Westport, Conn.: Lawrence Hill, 1987).

Sylvia C. Finkley, *Africa in Early Days* (New York: Odyssey Press, 1969).

Thomas A. Hale, *Scribe, Griot, and Novelist: Narrative Interpreters of the Songhay Empire* (Gainesville: University of Florida Press, 1990).

Henri Labouret, *Africa before the White Man*, translated by Francis Huxley (New York: Walker, 1963).

Phyllis M. Martin and Patrick O'Meara, eds., *Africa*, third edition (Bloomington: Indiana University Press, 1995).

D. T. Niane, *Sundiata: An Epic of Old Mali*, translated by G. D. Pickett (London: Longmans, 1965).

Roland Oliver, ed., *The Dawn of African History* (London: Oxford University Press, 1968).

Oliver and Anthony Atmore, *The African Middle Ages: 1400–1800* (Cambridge: Cambridge University Press, 1981); revised as *Medieval Africa: 1250–1800* (Cambridge: Cambridge University Press, 2001).

Charlotte A. Quinn, *Mandingo Kingdoms of the Senegambia: Traditionalism, Islam, and European Expansion* (Evanston, Ill.: Northwestern University Press, 1972).

John Reader, *Africa: A Biography of the Continent* (New York: Knopf, 1998).

Walter Rodney, *A History of the Upper Guinea Coast, 1545–1800* (Oxford: Clarendon Press, 1970).

Ricky Rosenthal, *The Splendor That Was Africa* (Dobbs Ferry, N.Y.: Oceana Publications, 1967).

G. T. Stride and Caroline Ifeka, *Peoples and Empires of West Africa: West Africa in History, 1000–1800* (New York: Africana Publishing, 1971).

INDIGENOUS LEGAL SYSTEMS

Human Rights. Respect for human beings was enshrined in the political and civil rights of West Africans, which included the rights of political participation, equal protection under the law, and freedom of speech and assembly. They also enjoyed the fundamental rights to earn a living and to receive a fair trial.

The Rule of Law. A major characteristic of ancient political systems in West Africa was the importance attached to the doctrine of the rule of law. Because people recognized that laws were made for the smooth running of the political system, there was widespread respect for the law and established judicial institutions. Rulers and the subjects were equally placed under the law. Laws were not arbitrarily made by an individual ruler or a handful of autocrats; they were enacted after a lengthy process of participation, including full public debates in which all adults participated. Every adult in a village belonged to the village assembly, the ultimate lawmaking body. In some African societies, laws could be made only on the basis of a general consensus. This lawmaking process not only created public

A traditional *toguna* (men's house), seat of local government in the Dogon village
of Tireli, Mali (photograph © 2001 Stephenie Hollyman)

awareness of the law but also conferred a sense of legitimacy on it. Laws were promulgated in the interest of the society as a whole and not as a mechanism for advancing or protecting the interests of a single person or of a particular segment of the population. Many checks and balances against the misuse of power ensured that most rulers had no authority to enact laws unilaterally. People who were found guilty of crimes were punished in several ways: public execution (in cases of homicide), incarceration, fine, and confiscation of property. Punishment was not arbitrarily meted out. It was exacted only after a trial and a finding of guilt. Sometimes, judicial decisions were enforced by members of an age-grade association, a group of people within a society who were born within a particular three- or four-year period.

Judicial Decisions. Several legal principles undergirded the judicial settlement of disputes in West Africa. Judicial decisions were based on established rules and precedents, not on arbitrary rulings of the adjudicators. Several states had elaborate legal codes that set standards for legal and ethical behavior. Judges carefully weighed the evidence following established procedures. An accused person was given ample opportunity to prove his innocence. He could hire an advocate to plead his case. Since oratory was important in the court proceedings, he was likely to seek out an advocate who was an eloquent speaker. For criminal offenses, the intent of the accused when the crime was committed was an important consideration in reaching a

verdict. For example, based on the legal principle of intent, a distinction was made between murder and manslaughter. The principle that an individual was responsible for his own actions was a fundamental element of justice in West Africa. While the principle of collective responsibility—under which all people related to the accused by blood were presumed to be responsible for his action—could be invoked, it was not universally applied in the region. Even where it was applied, it was not applicable to all offenses. In cases where a mentally ill person killed or injured another person, however, his family could be held responsible for the criminal behavior. In such cases the family had a duty to provide its sick member medical treatment or to restrain him. If it failed to carry out this duty, the family incurred liability for the person's crimes and must pay for the offense.

Punishment. The severity of a punishment was proportional to the enormity of the crime. Punishments for various offenses were also clearly specified. Mitigating circumstances led to reductions in fines or punishments, but intentional wrongs sometimes exacted double compensation. Unlawful homicide could result in the death penalty, and the relatives of the victim could demand material compensation from the perpetrator or his relatives. Incest was punishable by ostracism or even death. The penalties for burglary were flogging and the payment of restitution. In some cases, diligent care was exercised to ensure that only the perpetrator of a crime was punished for his or her

JUSTICE IN MALI

When the North African Muslim traveler Ibn Battuta visited Mali in 1353, he found much to praise in the justice system:

The Negroes possess some admirable qualities. They are seldom unjust, and have a greater abhorrence of injustice than any other people. Their sultan shows no mercy to anyone guilty of the least act of it. There is complete security in their country. Neither traveler nor inhabitant in it has anything to fear from robbers or men of violence. They do not confiscate the property of any white man who dies in their country, even if it be uncounted wealth.

Source: Thomas Hodgkin, "Kingdoms of the Western Sudan," in *The Dawn of African History*, edited by Roland Oliver (London: Oxford University Press, 1968), p. 41.

offences. For instance, a pregnant woman who was sentenced to death was not executed until after she had been delivered of the baby.

Channels for Judicial Settlement. Not all cases were submitted to established courts and tribunals. Some judicial disputes were settled through arbitration or informal moot courts composed of neighbors or friends. At such gatherings parties negotiated until a settlement was reached. Invariably, the settlement was a compromise between the two claims, and sometimes a ritual such as oath taking was used to bind the parties to the decision. Family disputes were arbitrated by family moots, composed of lineage leaders or family heads. Oracles were consulted in more-complex cases. For example, among the Igbos of what is now southeastern Nigeria, some cases were taken to the oracle Aro Chukwu. In certain instances, trial by ordeal was used.

Sources:
A. K. Ajisafe, *Laws and Customs of the Yoruba People* (London: Routledge, 1924).

Paul Bohannan, *Justice and Judgement among the Tiv of Nigeria* (London: Oxford University Press, 1957).

J. B. Danquah, *Gold Coast: Akan Laws and Customs and the Akim Abuakwa Constitution* (London: Routledge, 1928).

T. O. Elias, *Government and Politics in Africa*, revised and enlarged edition (Bombay & New York: Asia Publishing House, 1963).

Elias, *Groundwork of Nigerian Law* (London: Routledge & Kegan Paul, 1954).

Elias, *The Nature of African Customary Law* (Manchester: Manchester University Press, 1956).

Elias, *Nigerian Land Law and Custom* (London: Routledge & Kegan Paul, 1951).

M. Fortes and E. E. Evans-Pritchard, eds., *African Political Systems* (London: Published for the International Institute of African Languages and Cultures by the Oxford University Press, 1940).

William Burnett Harvey, *Law and Social Change in Ghana* (Princeton: Princeton University Press, 1966).

J. F. Holleman, *Shona Customary Law with Reference to Kinship, Marriage, the Family and the Estate* (Cape Town: Published in association with the Rhodes-Livingstone Institute and the Beit Trust by Oxford University Press, 1952).

P. P. Howell, *A Manual of Nuer Law Being an Account of Customary Law, Its Evolution and Development in the Court Established by the Sudan Government* (London: Oxford University Press, 1954).

Hilda Kuper and Leo Kuper, eds., *African Law: Adaptation and Development* (Berkeley: University of California Press, 1965).

Laura Nader, ed., *Law in Culture and Society* (Chicago: Aldine Press, 1969).

N. A. Ollennu, *Principles of Customary Land Law in Ghana* (London: Sweet & Maxwell, 1962).

ISLAMIC JURISPRUDENCE

Islam in West Africa. As Islam spread in West Africa, Islamic principles of jurisprudence influenced changes to indigenous systems of law and justice in some parts of the region. At the heart of Islamic law (the *shari'ah*) is the belief in its divine origin. Muslims hold that the fundamental sources of all laws are the Quran (Koran) and the Sunnan (singular: *Sunnah*), customs and legal pronouncements of the Prophet Muhammad and other members of the early Muslim community. In making a ruling an Islamic judge also consults consensus interpretations made in earlier cases and draws analogies from established laws. Nonetheless, the judge understands the supremacy of the Quran—the will of God as revealed through Muhammad—above all other sources. Each of the two branches of Islam, Sunni and Shi'a, has four major schools of law. The dominant school of Islamic law in West Africa is the Maliki, one of the Sunni schools.

Categories of Behavior. Islamic law divides behavior into five categories: (1) acts that Muslims are enjoined to perform, such as praying five times a day; (2) acts that are strictly forbidden *(haram)*, such as drinking alcohol; (3) acts that Muslims are advised, but not required, to perform, such as kindness and generosity to the poor; (4) acts from which believers are advised to refrain, including interpersonal issues, such as unethical business practices; (5) behavior that is morally neutral (most everyday activities). Under Islam, the second category, *haram*, is enforced by law.

Establishing Guilt. Under Islamic jurisprudence, the guilt of the accused can be established in several ways. The accused may confess to the charges, or guilt can be established through conclusive proof. Circumstantial evidence, if found to be strong enough, can also form the basis for conviction. Islamic law requires a minimum number of witnesses to a crime. For example, four adult male witnesses must testify to a charge of illicit sex, but two competent witnesses are sufficient for a charge of theft or brigandage. Analogical deduction may also be used to establish the guilt of the accused. For instance, pregnancy of an unmarried woman can be assumed to be proof of her engagement in illicit sex, unless she can demonstrate that her pregnancy resulted from rape or that she was deceived into having sexual intercourse. For the charge of consuming alcohol, the

Warrior chief, soldiers, and attendants; brass plaque from the Kingdom of Benin, circa 1500–1700.
The Metropolitan Museum of Art, Gift of Mr. and Mrs. Klaus G. Perls, 1990. (1990.332)
Photograph, all rights reserved, The Metropolitan Museum of Art.

court may not require a witness to the act of drinking. Under the Maliki school of jurisprudence, smelling alcohol on the accused or seeing the accused behave in an intoxicated manner is sufficient proof. Insanity may be used as a defense. If adequate testimony is provided that insanity prevented the accused from knowing he was committing a crime, then he cannot be convicted.

Punishment. The shari'ah prescribes a scale of fines and punishments for different offences. For example, an unmarried man who confesses to having illicit sex can be sentenced to one hundred lashes and a one-year jail term, but a married person who is convicted of the same crime may be stoned to death. A conviction for consuming alcohol results in eighty lashes from a cowhide whip. The willful wounding of another person may be visited with like retaliation. For instance, if the injured person loses an eye, the punishment may entail removing one of the offender's eyes. While the prescribed punishments for offences under Islam seem rather harsh, in reality the harshness of the punishment may be mitigated. For example, in flogging a person who has been convicted of drinking alcohol, the severe impact of the prescribed eighty lashes is lessened by the requirement that the flogger hold the whip between certain fingers and that he must also place an object under the armpit of the arm holding the whip.

Influence in West Africa. Islam has had a profound impact on law, the administration of justice, and jurisprudence in West Africa. In some parts of West Africa, Islamic law supplanted pre-Islamic law. Even where it did not completely nullify local laws, it defined new crimes and introduced new laws relating to matters such as inheritance, marriage, and contracts. Islam also had a major impact on jurisprudence through the introduction of new punishments, such as stoning for people convicted of adultery. Islamic law helped to create a degree of uniformity in the administration of justice throughout the ethnically and culturally diverse kingdoms and empires of West Africa. The presence of Islamic jurists in the palaces of some West African rulers also had a significant impact. While Islamic law brought some positive changes in West Africa, however, making apostasy from Islam an offense punishable by law constituted a diminution of religious freedom in the region.

Sources:
J. N. D. Anderson, *Islamic Law in Africa* (London: Cass, 1970).

Asaf A. A. Fyzee, *Outlines of Muhammadan Law*, fourth edition (Delhi & London: Oxford University Press, 1974 [i.e., 1975]).

MILITARY FORCES

Size of Military Forces. Many West African kingdoms built formidable military machines that were used for conquest of new territories and for the defense of an empire's territorial integrity. Large armies were kept for the purpose of political prestige. Empires and kingdoms were founded, extended, or defended by thousands of soldiers. Kaniaga had an army of 2,000 horsemen. Ghana had 200,000 soldiers, including 40,000 archers. Tilutane, the Lemtuna Berber leader, had an army of 100,000 camel-mounted men. Songhai had 12,500 cavalry and 30,000 infantry soldiers. Benin could mobilize as many as 100,000 soldiers in a day. In some instances, political alliances, family ties and personal ties, and astute diplomacy cemented relationships and obviated the need for large standing armies. Yet, overall, the military was an important institution in the states of West Africa.

Social Composition. West African armies were composed of soldiers from different social strata. The 4,000-man Moroccan army that invaded Songhai in 1590 was composed of an assortment of men, including Portuguese Christian soldiers captured by Morocco in a war against Portugal, European captives bought from North African pirates, and European mercenaries, as well as troops of Moroccan descent. In Benin the adult age-grade association constituted the warrior group. The core of the Bornu

BORNU EXPANSIONISM

During the fifteenth and sixteenth centuries, Bornu was a major expansionist power, and warfare was the main function of the state. According to historian Ronald Cohen,

as many as seven or eight military campaigns a year were not uncommon; this meant an expedition might leave Bornu every six or eight weeks during the dry season. With so much militarism the techniques of warfare elaborated accordingly. From at least the sixteenth century onward, Bornu imported muskets, swords, and chain-mail, which were vital and ancient parts of the Saharan trade, although such armaments were also manufactured by Bornu craftsmen as well.

The army itself was organized into regiments, representing a local area or an ethnic group under their own leaders, and they went into battle according to a well-laid-out military strategy. Campaigns were almost always conducted against walled towns. The shield bearers advanced first, then after it was felt that the poison arrows of the enemy were exhausted, the rest of the army would advance, either storming the walls or forcing the town dwellers to come out and fight—whereupon muskets and cavalry were used. Generally speaking, open encounters were quite unusual; the Bornu army was large, well disciplined, and well-equipped, while the town dwellers were weak in all these respects and would usually try to flee once the siege went against them. Fallen towns were then mercilessly looted and the inhabitants killed or enslaved.

After the campaign and the distribution of booty by the leaders, the army disbanded. Leaders of various territorial ethnic groups swore allegiance to the king and arranged for the next campaign to be held so many days hence. At that time, criers were sent around to local markets stating the date and place of rendezvous for the army. Able-bodied men were expected to go or send a representative bearing arms. A wife or female slave often accompanied each man to cook for him. But local townspeople were also expected to supply the army with food when it passed through their territory. However, it was preferred that the army be self-sufficient even to the point of digging their own wells. Discipline obviously posed some problems since the records indicate that at times, army morale was low, especially during long, arduous campaigns. However, it picked up very quickly when the prospect of booty was in evidence.

Source: Ronald Cohen, *The Kanuri of Bornu* (New York: Holt, Rinehart & Winston, 1967), pp. 23–24.

infantry was composed of slaves. In addition to these armed slaves, its forces included 3,000 armored knights and conscripted peasants armed with spears and bows and arrows. Tributary rulers were required to provide warriors to an imperial army. For instance, the ruler of Bornu did not maintain a large permanent force. Instead, he drew many

Benin warrior with a sword and bow, bronze figure, and an Ashanti archer, brass pendant or gold weight, both circa 1500–1700 (left: Ethnological Museum, Berlin; right: private collection)

fighters from conquered peoples or by imposing local levies. Several African states had professional soldiers. A few empires maintained full-time militaries and also had militias that could be called into active service as the situation warranted. In Mossi, a few security units were maintained on a permanent basis. Songhai maintained a standing army. Soldiers included knights, cavalry, foot soldiers and auxiliary soldiers of Tuaregs, infantry regiments, royal guards, and an armed flotilla. In many cases, West African armies were composed of citizen-soldiers who were drafted to fight and discharged from the military once a war was over. Even in states that had standing armies, if a particular military operation demanded more soldiers, the regular army was reinforced by the conscription of able-bodied young men. Military power was supplemented by military confederations and alliances. Military aid in the form of weapons or soldiers was extended to places outside the region.

Organizational Structure. Some West African armies, such as the Songhai army under Askia Muhammad I (ruled 1493–1528), were divided into territorial units. Some states divided the polity into four or more provinces. Each province had a governor who was responsible for law and order, defense, and the mobilization of citizens for warfare. In other cases, the military was organized on the basis of specialized functions, such as cavalry and infantry units, each with its own commander. Close coordination of the fighting forces was the responsibility of the supreme military leader.

Bravery and Gallantry. Military codes of honor emphasized valor, courage, and patriotism. Whether composed of conscripts, slaves, mercenaries, or volunteers, West African military forces usually fought gallantly. They learned bravery through discipline and epics of courageous ancestors. They took oaths of patriotism and were instilled with a spirit of fierce independence. Their sense of military honor demanded that they die rather than turn tail in the face of enemies. It is possible that stimulants such as kola nuts were distributed to soldiers to help them maintain a state of mental alertness. One famous example of bravery occurred during the reign of Askia Daud of Songhai (1549–1582), who sent forces to raid Hausaland. On one particular occasion, his twenty-four horsemen boldly attacked a force of four hundred Hausa soldiers at Katsina. Fifteen of Daud's men killed fifteen Hausa fighters and wounded nine others. Hausa forces captured several of Daud's men but sent the captives back to Songhai instead of killing them. The Hausa soldiers justified their magnanimity on the ground that such brave men did not deserve to be put to death. Another instance of bravery among Askia Daud's soldiers had a tragic outcome. Cheik Anta Diop has described the aftermath of a Moroccan defeat of elite Songhai foot soldiers: having been "taught not to run away in the face of overwhelming military odds," they sat on their shields and waited for the Moroccans, "who massacred them in this position without any resistance on their part."

Sources:

J. F. A. Ajayi and Michael Crowder, eds., *The History of West Africa*, second edition, 2 volumes (New York: Columbia University Press, 1976, 1987).

Bolanle Awe, ed., *Nigerian Women in Historical Perspectives* (Lagos: Sankore / Ibadan, Nigeria: Bookcraft, 1992).

E. W. Bovill, *The Golden Trade of the Moors* (London & New York: Oxford University Press, 1958).

Basil Davidson, *Old Africa Rediscovered* (London: Gollancz, 1959); republished as *The Lost Cities of Africa* (Boston & Toronto: Little, Brown, 1959; revised, 1970).

J. C. De Graft-Johnson, *African Glory* (London: Watts, 1954).

Cheik Anta Diop, *Precolonial Black Africa: A Comparative Study of the Political and Social Systems of Europe and Black Africa, from Antiquity to the Formation of Modern States*, translated by Harold J. Salemson (Westport, Conn.: Lawrence Hill, 1987).

Robert Edgerton, *The Fall of the Asante Empire: The Hundred Year War for Africa's Gold Coast* (New York: Free Press, 1995).

Jacob U. Egharevba, *A Short History of Benin*, second edition, revised and enlarged (Benin: Published by the author, 1953).

J. D. Fage, *An Introduction to the History of West Africa*, third edition (Cambridge: Cambridge University Press, 1962).

Sylvia C. Finkley, *Africa in Early Days* (New York: Odyssey Press, 1969).

Robin Law, *The Horse in West African History* (Oxford: Oxford University Press, 1980).

Wale Ogunyemi, *Queen Amina of Zazzau* (Ibadan, Nigeria: University Press, 1999).

Roland Oliver, ed., *The Cambridge History of Africa, Volume 3: from c. 1050 to c. 1600* (Cambridge, London, New York & Melbourne: Cambridge University Press, 1977).

Oliver and J. D. Fage, *A Short History of Africa* (Harmondsworth, U.K.: Penguin, 1962).

Elias N. Saad, *The Social History of Timbuktu: The Role of Muslim Scholars and Notables, 1400–1900* (Cambridge: Cambridge University Press, 1983).

Margaret Shinnie, *Ancient African Kingdoms* (London: Arnold, 1965).

John Spencer Trimingham, *A History of Islam in West Africa* (London: Published for the University of Glasgow by Oxford University Press, 1962).

Jan Vansina, *Kingdoms of the Savanna* (Madison: University of Wisconsin Press, 1966).

MILITARY LEADERS AND STRATEGIES

Military Leadership. Military leadership was drawn from various segments of West African social structure. Often, rulers had direct command of their forces and led their troops into battles. Emperor Nassere of the Mossi led an expedition against Ghana. Sumanguru and Sundiata in the

---

THE BATTLE OF KIRINA

The following description of Sundiata's famous 1235 defeat of Sumanguru illustrates how legends of warfare created larger-than-life heroes:

As Sundiata advanced with his army to meet Sumanguru, he learned that Sumanguru was coming against him with an army prepared for battle. They met in a place called Kirina. When Sundiata turned his eyes on the army of Sumanguru he asked, "What is this cloud on the eastern side?" They told him it was Sumanguru's army.

As for Sumanguru, when he looked in Sundiata's direction he exclaimed, "What is that mountain of stone?" And they told him "It is the army of Sundiata, which lies to the west of us."

Then the two columns came together and fought a murderous battle. In the thick of the fight, Sundiata uttered a great shout in the face of the warriors of Sumanguru. At once, these men ran to get behind Sumanguru. He, in turn, uttered a great shout in the face of Sundiata's warriors, all of whom fled to get behind Sundiata. Usually when Sumanguru shouted, eight heads would rise above his own.

When they had done this, Sundiata said to one of his captains, "Have you forgotten the taboo [that foretold Sumanguru's end]?" As soon as Sangaran Danguina [the captain] heard Sundiata's question he came to the front of the army, halted, grasped the [spear] armed with the spur of a white cock and threw it at Sumanguru. As soon as it had struck Sumanguru, Sangaran said, "This is the arrow of him who knows the ancient secrets. . . ." While he was saying this, Sumanguru vanished and was seen no more. Now he had had a gold bracelet on his wrist and this fell on that spot. A baobab tree grew out of it and carries the mark to this day. . . . As for Sundiata, he defeated the army of Sumanguru, ravaged the land of the Sosso and subjugated its people.

Source: Lester Brooks, *Great Civilizations of Ancient Africa* (New York: Four Winds Press, 1971), pp. 126–127.

---

thirteenth century and a host of other rulers at various other times and places led their armies into battles. In some kingdoms, such as Mossi, tradition forbade kings from leaving the capital city. The Mossi king Moro Naba had to appoint generals to lead his troops into battle. When Askia Muhammad II (ruled 1582–1586) of Songhai was unable to lead expeditionary forces to attack his neighbors because he was afflicted with a disease, he had to appoint generals to oversee the operations. High-ranking commanders might be rulers' relatives. Sumanguru's chief military general was his nephew, Fakoli Koroma. Even men from lowly backgrounds could ascend to the highest military ranks by proving their military skills in battle. The head of the Mossi cavalry, called

Early Igbo leader on horseback, circa 800–1000, and a Dogon cavalry chief, circa 900–1300
(left: National Museum, Lagos, Nigeria; right: Minneapolis Institute of Art)

Kidiranga naba, was usually from an ordinary family. In some cases, even slaves rose to top military leadership. The *Samande naba,* the general in charge of the Mossi infantry, was usually a slave. Many generals in the Songhai army were slaves. Slave generals played an important role in military and civil administration, often serving as members of the cabinet. The danger of a military composed of slaves was that slave warriors sometimes revolted and seized power. Such revolts created new ruling lineages and subordinated former power elites. Whether an army was led by a king, a freeman, or a slave, generalship was judged by intelligence, bravery, organizational ability, and astute leadership.

Figureheads. Africans created some symbolically useful offices whose holders had no power. Among the Ga, the Manste was said to have magical uses in war, but he was only "a small boy" in peacetime. Even in wartime, he never took part in battles. Instead, he sat on his stool apart from the fighting and was protected by a special bodyguard. The director of military operations, the Akwashontse, also headed a military court to which the Mantse was subject. It could order the beheading of an unsatisfactory Mantse.

Magic. Some military leaders enhanced their military skills with displays of magical powers. For instance, it was believed that Sundiata wielded magical powers to defeat his enemies, and his rival Sumanguru was "a smith and a renowned sorcerer" who used these gifts to enhance his military prowess. Oral traditions in Songhai painted Sunni Ali (ruled 1464–1492) as a foremost magician, who used his magical prowess to confuse his enemies in battle and win decisive victories in military campaigns. The fear that Ali struck in his enemies was best summed up by West African historian 'Abd al-Rahman al-Sa'di (1569–1655), who wrote that when Timbuktu faced an attack from Ali, "bearded men of ripe age [were] trembling with fright at the prospect of mounting a camel and tumbling to the ground as soon as the animal got to its feet."

Reconnaissance. Deceit and trickery were quite common in military reconnaissance. In 1582, Sultan al-Mansur of Morocco sent a messenger bearing gifts to the new ruler of Songhai, Askia Muhammad II. The Songhai learned later that the messenger was a spy, and soon after he returned home the Moroccan army attacked Timbuktu. Reconnaissance was frequently conducted at night, and soldiers on reconnaissance missions hid or disguised themselves as natives of territories under surveillance.

Tactics. Ambushes and massive two- or three-pronged attacks were used quite often. Attacks frequently came at night. Military lookouts climbed tall trees to see enemies from far away, and in some cases such lookouts directed the fighters below. Horses gave armies mobility and swiftness. Mande-speaking cavalrymen conquered an extensive territory in the Sahel, savanna, and savanna-woodland zones, founding many states and imposing their hegemony on subjugated peoples. Lat Dior of Cayor introduced a fighting tac-

tic in which his troops dug a hole in the ground for each soldier. The hole was then covered, except for a tiny space from which to aim a weapon. When a frontal assault was deemed futile, military commanders often resorted to guerrilla tactics. For instance, when Askia Nur of Songhai realized that he could not challenge head-on Moroccan forces who were equipped with guns and cannons, he used guerrilla tactics in an attempt to halt their southward advance. Long-distance attacks were sometimes used. In 1590 Sultan al-Mansur of Morocco sent his army of 4,000 men and 9,000 transport animals 1,500 miles to attack Songhai. Similarly, Askia Muhammad I (ruled 1493–1528) penetrated as far as Kano and Zaria, places far from Songhai. Around 1561 Bornu troops attacked Kebbi, which was more than 500 miles from their capital. Some military campaigns lasted a long time. In the eleventh century the Almoravids needed fourteen years to subdue Ghana. The difference between victory and defeat was not determined by superiority of weapons alone but by strategy and the numbers or skills of the people who could be deployed as fighters. Some military leaders had elite, or special, forces. Despite its relatively small size, Borgu was not defeated by the mighty Songhai army in 1505–1506.

Rules of Engagement. While some battles were quite brutal, they were fought on the basis of specified rules of engagement enacted to keep violence within controllable limits. Except in extreme circumstances, the fighters did not engage in wanton destruction of lives and property. In 1591, Mami ibn Barun, the Moroccan commander in Timbuktu, apologized to the inhabitants of the city for the excesses of his fighters.

Sources:

J. F. A. Ajayi and Michael Crowder, eds., *The History of West Africa,* second edition, 2 volumes (New York: Columbia University Press, 1976, 1987).

Bolanle Awe, ed., *Nigerian Women in Historical Perspectives* (Lagos: Sankore / Ibadan, Nigeria: Bookcraft, 1992).

E. W. Bovill, *The Golden Trade of the Moors* (London & New York: Oxford University Press, 1958).

Basil Davidson, *Old Africa Rediscovered* (London: Gollancz, 1959); republished as *The Lost Cities of Africa* (Boston & Toronto: Little, Brown, 1959; revised, 1970).

J. C. De Graft-Johnson, *African Glory* (London: Watts, 1954).

Jacob U. Egharevba, *A Short History of Benin,* second edition, revised and enlarged (Benin: Published by the author, 1953).

J. D. Fage, *An Introduction to the History of West Africa,* third edition (Cambridge: Cambridge University Press, 1962).

M. J. Field, *Social Organization of the Ga People* (Accra: Government of the Gold Coast Printing Press, 1940).

Sylvia C. Finkley, *Africa in Early Days* (New York: Odyssey Press, 1969).

Robin Law, *The Horse in West African History* (Oxford: Oxford University Press, 1980).

Wale Ogunyemi, *Queen Amina of Zazzau* (Ibadan, Nigeria: University Press, 1999).

Roland Oliver, ed., *The Cambridge History of Africa, Volume 3: from c. 1050 to c. 1600* (Cambridge, London, New York & Melbourne: Cambridge University Press, 1977).

Oliver and J. D. Fage, *A Short History of Africa* (Harmondsworth, U.K.: Penguin, 1962).

Elias N. Saad, *The Social History of Timbuktu: The Role of Muslim Scholars and Notables, 1400–1900* (Cambridge: Cambridge University Press, 1983).

Margaret Shinnie, *Ancient African Kingdoms* (London: Arnold, 1965).

John Spencer Trimingham, *A History of Islam in West Africa* (London: Published for the University of Glasgow by Oxford University Press, 1962).

Jan Vansina, *Kingdoms of the Savanna* (Madison: University of Wisconsin Press, 1966).

POLITICS AND THE MILITARY

Defense Expenditures. Given the large sizes of the armies maintained by West African states, a modern scholar might deduce that huge resources were expended on soldiers. In reality, however, the profits derived from invasions tended to offset the expense of the military action. Revenues from conquered territories supported defense expenditures and minimized the resources that the conquering state had to spend on its military. The victorious state typically imposed large tributes and heavy indemnities. Court fees and fines were important sources of revenues. Expenditures were also kept low by the practice of giving warriors shares in the booty.

Civil-Military Relations. In many cases, soldiers were not personal instruments of the rulers and thus could not be dispatched to do their personal bidding. The military was an organ of the state, which was not the private property of its ruler. The principle of civilian supremacy over the military was maintained through designated political institutions, and some safeguards were built into the political system with the intent of ensuring that a military commander did not usurp power. For instance, in some states, the military commander had to live far away from the capital city. In other cases, the military chief was an integral part of the king's cabinet.

Reasons for Military Deployment. Most West African leaders considered war a necessity for defense and territorial expansion, but many did not derive any particular pleasure from waging it. For example, it is said that Sundiata (ruled 1230–1255), the great ruler who used his military skills to extend vastly the borders of Mali, detested war.

Territory and the Spoils of War. Military campaigns were mounted to increase the territory of an empire and to acquire war booty, including gold, salt, cattle, and grain. Some states maintained home-guard units to provide security against such raids, as well as protection for women, children, and others left at home during major military campaigns. Defeated states were compelled to grant large political concessions to the victors. For example, after Moroccan forces defeated the soldiers of Askia Ishaq II of Songhai (ruled 1588–1591), he was forced to grant Morocco the right to import salt from Songhai. Other military missions were undertaken to capture women and

Bronze plaque of a court official holding a calabash, circa 1500–1700. The Metropolitan Museum of Art, Gift of Mr. and Mrs. Klaus G. Perls, 1991. (1991.17.10) Photograph, all rights reserved, The Metropolitan Museum of Art.

slaves or to punish conquered states that had refused to pay their obligatory tributes.

Demonstrations of Force. The military was also used as a demonstration of force against a potential foe. When Sultan al-Mansur asked Askia Ishaq II to cede the salt mines of Taghaza to Morocco, Ishaq responded by dispatching two thousand soldiers to raid the Moroccan city of Dra'a, instructing them not to kill anyone. This military action was intended to caution the sultan about the consequences of making an outrageous demand.

INTERNATIONAL DIPLOMACY

Abd al-Aziz al-Fishtali, an historian and diplomat at the court of Sultan al-Mansur of Morocco, wrote the following account of how an envoy from the great ruler Idris Alooma of Bornu made a blunder in 1612–1613 that nearly led to war:

Towards the end of the year 990 [according to the Muslim calendar] the envoy of the ruler of Borno—one of the kings of the Sudan—arrived at the court of the amir al-mu'minin (may God assist him) and brought, among the presents they were accustomed to bring on such occasions, over two-hundred young slaves, male and female. He found the sultan, amir al-mu'minin Mawlai Ahmad al-Mansur, at his military camp of Ra's al-ma' in the outskirts of Fez.

The purpose of the message with which his master had sent him was to request aid from the amir al-mu'minin in the form of troops, muskets and cannons in order to declare a holy war against the unbelievers who were near them in the remote parts of the Sudan. . . . But when the letter was put before the amir al-mu'minin it was discovered that there was a clear discrepancy and an obvious contradiction between its contents and what the envoy had said. That is to say, what the letter contained differed from what the envoy had uttered—a blunder caused by their deep-rooted ignorance and stupidity and the lack among them of specialists in the art of letter-writing owing to the general lack of knowledge of the basic sciences in their lands.

Before the arrival of this envoy, the amir al-mu'minin had resolved to direct his troops in that year to the subjugation of the lands of Taut and Tikurarin as a first step towards the conquest of the countries of the Sudan and the control of their kingdoms. He was determined to prosecute this object because he was confident of victory; for the troops at his disposal were numerous, his mission was widely acknowledged, and his word was effective throughout the countries of the West (Maghrib). It was for this reason that he took advantage of the discrepancy between the contents of the letter and the words of the envoy and offered this as an excuse to the ruler of Borno. The envoy returned to his master furnished with a present of well-bred horses and magnificent robes of honor.

And when the envoy reached his master and reported the excuse, the latter scorned the present and sent him back after making his object clear. The envoy found the amir al-mu'minin at his capital Marrakesh and the confusion was removed and the purpose (of the mission) expressed in clear terms. And now the amir al-mu'minin (may God assist him) came out openly with the truthful statement: namely that they should swear allegiance to him and offer their submission and obedience. He explained to them on the authority of the Sunna and the revealed Book, that the jihad which they professed and for which they showed an inclination and enthusiasm, is not incumbent upon them and they will not be rewarded for undertaking it, if they do not get the permission of the imam of the community–that is to say the amir al-mu'minin whom God has favored with descent from the Prophet. Verily, God has entrusted him with the defense of the Muslim realms and set him over and above the entire rulers and kings of the Earth through the Qurashite pedigree which constitutes one of the requisite qualifications for the Caliphate according to the consensus (ijma) of the scholars (ulama) of Islam who are the interpreters of the bright Sunna and the heirs of the prophets, blessing and peace be upon them.

Furthermore, he (may God assist him) ordered them to propagate his mission in their regions, and undertake the jihad against their enemies among the unbelievers in his name, and he made the supply of aid subject to the fulfilment of these conditions. The envoy accepted these conditions and declared that his master would accept them and would offer his submission. Then he said good-bye and departed.

Source: Bala Usman and Nur Alkali, eds., *Studies in the History of Pre-Colonial Borno* (Zaria: Northern Nigerian Publishing, 1983), pp. 171–172.

Holy Wars. In some cases, soldiers were used to wage religious or holy wars. Askia Muhammad I's (ruled 1493–1528) war against Emperor Nassere of Mossi in 1497–1498 was partly a holy war for the purpose of converting the Mossi to Islam. In general, however, even when a war was sparked by religious considerations, economic interests rather than religious fervor were the primary motivating factor.

Raids. Military raids, such as the Mossi incursions into Mali in the fourteenth century, weakened an empire even if the raiders did not seek territorial expansion. The campaigns of Sunni Ali (ruled 1464–1492) of Songhai against the Tuaregs, who had pillaged and massacred people in Timbuktu, were not meant for permanent occupations. Instead, they were quick raids in which soldiers looted what they could find and withdrew.

Bodyguards. Soldiers were also used to provide security for rulers and their royal households. Ibn Battuta observed during his 1353 visit to Mali that when the ruler, Mansa Sulaiman, moved about, three hundred armed slaves provided security. Similarly, on his 1497 pilgrimage to Mecca, Askia Muhammad I was accompanied by a bodyguard of five hundred cavalrymen and one thousand foot soldiers.

Civil Wars. Some wars in ancient West Africa were civil wars resulting from the disruption of the constitutional norms of succession. Like states in other parts of the world,

African empires and kingdoms were subjected to intrigues, rebellions, and resistance, general uprisings to gain political control or end tyrannical rule. Some succeeded while others were put down by force of arms.

A Tradition of Resistance. Frequent military incursions from outside the region helped to build a tradition of resistance among West African polities. For example, the Songhai and the Zarma fiercely resisted the series of invasions by Moroccan troops in the late 1500s. The same tradition helped to protect some West Africans against the transatlantic enslavement of Africans during the fifteenth to nineteenth centuries.

Sources:

J. F. A. Ajayi and Michael Crowder, eds., *The History of West Africa,* second edition, 2 volumes (New York: Columbia University Press, 1976, 1987).

Bolanle Awe, ed., *Nigerian Women in Historical Perspectives* (Lagos: Sankore / Ibadan, Nigeria: Bookcraft, 1992)

E. W. Bovill, *The Golden Trade of the Moors* (London & New York: Oxford University Press, 1958).

Basil Davidson, *Old Africa Rediscovered* (London: Gollancz, 1959); republished as *The Lost Cities of Africa* (Boston & Toronto: Little, Brown, 1959; revised, 1970).

J. C. De Graft-Johnson, *African Glory* (London: Watts, 1954).

Jacob U. Egharevba, *A Short History of Benin,* second edition, revised and enlarged (Benin: Published by the author, 1953).

J. D. Fage, *An Introduction to the History of West Africa,* third edition (Cambridge: Cambridge University Press, 1962).

Sylvia C. Finkley, *Africa in Early Days* (New York: Odyssey Press, 1969).

Robin Law, *The Horse in West African History* (Oxford: Oxford University Press, 1980).

Wale Ogunyemi, *Queen Amina of Zazzau* (Ibadan, Nigeria: University Press, 1999).

Roland Oliver, ed., *The Cambridge History of Africa, Volume 3: from c. 1050 to c. 1600* (Cambridge, London, New York & Melbourne: Cambridge University Press, 1977).

Oliver and J. D. Fage, *A Short History of Africa* (Harmondsworth, U.K.: Penguin, 1962).

Elias N. Saad, *The Social History of Timbuktu: The Role of Muslim Scholars and Notables, 1400–1900* (Cambridge: Cambridge University Press, 1983).

Margaret Shinnie, *Ancient African Kingdoms* (London: Arnold, 1965).

John Spencer Trimingham, *A History of Islam in West Africa* (London: Published for the University of Glasgow by Oxford University Press, 1962).

Jan Vansina, *Kingdoms of the Savanna* (Madison: University of Wisconsin Press, 1966).

WAR GODS AND RITUALS

War Gods. The notion that wars were sanctioned by the gods was a widely held belief in West Africa. Several communities had special deities responsible for war. For example, Adzobo is the divinity of war among the Fon-Ewe of the modern nation of Benin. For the Yorubas, Ogun, a lesser god associated with iron, is the patron god of warriors. Ogun's fearlessness is symbolized by the viper he carries, and Yoruba warriors were expected to emulate Ogun's bravery in battle. In the parts of West Africa where war gods were recognized, designated warriors frequently car-

ried emblems and symbols of these deities on the battlefield. Even where there were no specific gods of war, certain political leaders were thought to be imbued with magical powers that they used to their advantage in warfare.

Rituals. Before soldiers set out for battle, they propitiated war gods and the ancestors in general, hoping to obtain their blessings. Some states had special priests who mediated between rulers and the hidden forces of the universe with the intent of ensuring military success. Oblations were a popular means of seeking the intervention of supernatural forces on the battlefield. The Manes society built special villages exclusively for women who manufactured "medicine" for war. Rituals were also important for warfare and political control in West Africa. People consulted diviners and oracles for predictions about the outcome of battles. Sometimes spiritual consultations were used to determine the ideal day and time to launch an attack or to decide on military strategies. Many states in West Africa also performed rituals at the end of military operations, acknowledging the help of war gods and other mystical forces.

Martial Dancing and Music. War dance and music were fundamental to the military culture in West Africa, emphasizing the cultivation of esprit de corps among soldiers. Adzohu is a sacred war dance of the Fon-Ewe. The Djung Djung was a special war drum used by the Damel of Cayor. Battle hymns such as the Jonjon (glory to the warrior) were composed to cultivate camaraderie among the warriors. Bards frequently sang songs of praise for military heroes. Drumming and war songs extolled the skill, bravery, and military prowess of ancestors. These songs and rituals taught young soldiers to emulate the bravery and chivalry of past heroes. War songs and dances, along with military parades, also created opportunities for the community to express its gratitude to its brave fighters. Military culture involved preparations of warriors for battle and a period of debriefing after each conflict to ease the transition back to civilian life.

Sources:

J. F. A. Ajayi and Michael Crowder, eds., *The History of West Africa,* second edition, 2 volumes (New York: Columbia University Press, 1976, 1987).

Bolanle Awe, ed., *Nigerian Women in Historical Perspectives* (Lagos: Sankore / Ibadan, Nigeria: Bookcraft, 1992).

E. W. Bovill, *The Golden Trade of the Moors* (London & New York: Oxford University Press, 1958).

Basil Davidson, *Old Africa Rediscovered* (London: Gollancz, 1959); republished as *The Lost Cities of Africa* (Boston & Toronto: Little, Brown, 1959; revised, 1970).

J. C. De Graft-Johnson, *African Glory* (London: Watts, 1954).

Jacob U. Egharevba, *A Short History of Benin,* second edition, revised and enlarged (Benin: Published by the author, 1953).

J. D. Fage, *An Introduction to the History of West Africa,* third edition (Cambridge: Cambridge University Press, 1962).

Sylvia C. Finkley, *Africa in Early Days* (New York: Odyssey Press, 1969).

A palace priest and a court official with a protective charm, bronze plaques from the Kingdom of Benin, circa 1500–1700. Left: The Metropolitan Museum of Art, Gift of Mr. and Mrs. Klaus G. Perls, 1991. (1991.17.25) Photograph, all rights reserved, The Metropolitan Museum of Art. Right: The Metropolitan Museum of Art, Gift of Mr. and Mrs. Klaus G. Perls, 1991. (1991.17.20) Photograph, all rights reserved, The Metropolitan Museum of Art.

Robin Law, *The Horse in West African History* (Oxford: Oxford University Press, 1980).

Wale Ogunyemi, *Queen Amina of Zazzau* (Ibadan, Nigeria: University Press, 1999).

Roland Oliver, ed., *The Cambridge History of Africa, Volume 3: from c. 1050 to c. 1600* (Cambridge, London, New York & Melbourne: Cambridge University Press, 1977).

Oliver and J. D. Fage, *A Short History of Africa* (Harmondsworth, U.K.: Penguin, 1962).

Elias N. Saad, *The Social History of Timbuktu: The Role of Muslim Scholars and Notables, 1400–1900* (Cambridge: Cambridge University Press, 1983).

Margaret Shinnie, *Ancient African Kingdoms* (London: Arnold, 1965).

John Spencer Trimingham, *A History of Islam in West Africa* (London: Published for the University of Glasgow by Oxford University Press, 1962).

Jan Vansina, *Kingdoms of the Savanna* (Madison: University of Wisconsin Press, 1966).

WEAPONS AND FORTIFICATIONS

Defensive Fortifications. Fortresses, walls, ramparts, and guarded gates were built as defensive shields against invaders. The cities of Kebbi, Kano, and Djenné were fortified by walls. When invaders could not gain access to such protected cities, they often laid siege to them. The city of Djenné is said to have been held under siege by the Songhai forces of Sunni Ali (ruled 1464–1492) for more than seven years. During that long period Ali's soldiers cultivated crops outside the walled city. In the sixteenth century the seven layers of stone walls around Kebbi ensured the successful defense of the city against mighty Songhai forces.

Military Technology. Archeological findings have revealed that iron smelting and ironworking in West Africa

Chain-mail shirt worn by a Fulani or Kanuri cavalryman of northern Nigeria in the sixteenth century (Royal Ontario Museum, Toronto)

date back as early as 500 B.C.E. By that time the people of Nok had mastered ironwork technology. Early West African weaponry included spears, swords, cowhide shields, bows and arrows, clubs, and knives. Poisoned arrows were important weapons in the arsenal of West African armies. The kanta (king) of Kebbi was killed with a poisoned arrow in 1513. New technology over the years spurred military reforms. Similarly, changes in the economy and culture affected military preparedness and warfare. Sometimes, particular weapons proved militarily decisive. Ghanaian troops' use of swords against neighbors who fought with bars of ebony was a major factor in its successful territorial expansion in the eighth through tenth centuries. The Moroccans' use of cannons against the army of Songhai in 1590–1591 was the deciding factor in the fall of that great empire.

Mobility. The mobility of troops was enhanced by horses, camels, and canoes. On the Niger River, Lake Chad, and other major waterways of the region, naval flotillas were used in warfare. The Mande used horsemen during their territorial expansion. The military prowess of Sundiata (reigned 1230–1255), the great ruler of Mali, was enhanced through his acquisition of horses from the rulers of Mema and Mossi. In the epic 1235 battle at Kirina, Sundiata's cavalry gave him superiority over Sumanguru. The horses enhanced mobility, and the noise made by the galloping horses and clashing swords created terror and panic among Sumanguru's foot soldiers. The Songhai cavalry had a similar effect in 1609, when it terrified Moroccan troops so much that the whole army turned and fled. According to Cheik Anta Diop, "What frightened the Moroccans most in this encounter was the noise of the shields pounding against the legs of the horses when they were galloping." Once the Moroccans realized the source of the sound, however, they returned to the battlefield.

Firearms. When Portuguese sailors visited Benin in 1486, some Portuguese soldiers accompanied Oba Ozalua of Benin on military campaigns and demonstrated the efficacy of firearms. As a result, the oba became interested in acquiring such weapons, and in 1514 he sent an emissary to King Manuel of Portugal asking for Christian missionaries and cannons. Manuel sent a Christian cleric and a letter promising,

> When we see that you have embraced the teachings of Christianity like a good and faithful Christian, there will be nothing within our realms with which we shall not be glad to favor you, whether it be arms or cannon and all other weapons of war for use against your enemies; of such things we have a great store, as your ambassador Dom Jorje will inform you.

European and North African soldiers used firearms against West African fighters before West African kingdoms such as Benin and Bornu obtained European-made guns and used them to wage wars against other West African states.

In 1590–1591 Moroccan troops used 31,000 pounds of gunpowder in its defeat of the Songhai Empire. As Sultan al-Mansur of Morocco said to counselors who were trying to dissuade him from attacking Songhai, "today the Sudanese have only spears and swords, weapons which will be useless against modern arms. It will therefore be easy for us to wage a successful war against these people and to prevail over them." At the battle of Tondibi a Moroccan army of about 1,000 men easily defeated a Songhai army of 18,000 cavalry and 9,000 infantry. West African historian 'Abd al-Rahman al-Sa'di (1569–1655) provided a glimpse of the destruction which the Moroccan invasion of West Africa left in its wake: "security turned to fear, luxury was changed into affliction and distress, and prosperity became woe and harshness. People began to attack one another throughout the length and breadth of the kingdom, raiding and preying upon property, [free] persons and slaves. Such iniquity became general, spreading and becoming ever more serious and scandalous."

Sources:

J. F. A. Ajayi and Michael Crowder, eds., *The History of West Africa*, second edition, 2 volumes (New York: Columbia University Press, 1976, 1987).

Bolanle Awe, ed., *Nigerian Women in Historical Perspectives* (Lagos: Sankore / Ibadan, Nigeria: Bookcraft, 1992).

E. W. Bovill, *The Golden Trade of the Moors* (London & New York: Oxford University Press, 1958).

Basil Davidson, *Old Africa Rediscovered* (London: Gollancz, 1959); republished as *The Lost Cities of Africa* (Boston & Toronto: Little, Brown, 1959; revised, 1970).

J. C. De Graft-Johnson, *African Glory* (London: Watts, 1954).

Jacob U. Egharevba, *A Short History of Benin*, second edition, revised and enlarged (Benin: Published by the author, 1953).

J. D. Fage, *An Introduction to the History of West Africa*, third edition (Cambridge: Cambridge University Press, 1962).

Sylvia C. Finkley, *Africa in Early Days* (New York: Odyssey Press, 1969).

Robin Law, *The Horse in West African History* (Oxford: Oxford University Press, 1980).

Wale Ogunyemi, *Queen Amina of Zazzau* (Ibadan, Nigeria: University Press, 1999).

Roland Oliver, ed., *The Cambridge History of Africa, Volume 3: from c. 1050 to c. 1600* (Cambridge, London, New York & Melbourne: Cambridge University Press, 1977).

Oliver and Anthony Atmore, *The African Middle Ages: 1400–1800* (Cambridge: Cambridge University Press, 1981); revised as *Medieval Africa: 1250–1800* (Cambridge: Cambridge University Press, 2001).

Oliver and J. D. Fage, *A Short History of Africa* (Harmondsworth, U.K.: Penguin, 1962).

A. F. C. Ryder, *Benin and the Europeans, 1445–1897* (Harlow, U.K.: Longman, 1969).

Elias N. Saad, *The Social History of Timbuktu: The Role of Muslim Scholars and Notables, 1400–1900* (Cambridge: Cambridge University Press, 1983).

Margaret Shinnie, *Ancient African Kingdoms* (London: Arnold, 1965).

John Spencer Trimingham, *A History of Islam in West Africa* (London: Published for the University of Glasgow by Oxford University Press, 1962).

Jan Vansina, *Kingdoms of the Savanna* (Madison: University of Wisconsin Press, 1966).

SIGNIFICANT PEOPLE

QUEEN AMINA

1533?-1610
RULER OF ZAZZAU

A Fearless Warrior. Amina is the best known of the legendary Hausa queens who ruled kingdoms in the savanna region of West Africa. Probably born in 1533, she was the eldest daughter of a high-ranking government official of the king of Kufena, Bakwa Turunku, who in 1536 seized political power and made herself ruler of Zazzau (later known as Zaria) Much is known of Amina because of an anonymous book, *Amina, Sarauniya Zazzau* (Amina, Queen of Zazzau), written shortly after her death. Unlike other women of her time in Zazzau, Amina took a great interest in warfare and received extensive military training. Her reputation as a woman who was as capable as a man was derived largely from her prowess as a fearless warrior.

Political Skills. At an early age Amina developed an intense interest in politics and public affairs, acquiring political skills not only from her mother but from her grandfather, who was also a Hausa ruler. When Amina was sixteen years old, her mother named her *Magajiya* (heir apparent) of Zazzau, thus making her a member of the ruler's cabinet.

Military Prowess. After her mother's death around 1566, Amina's brother Karama, ascended the throne. Unlike Bakwa, Karama liked warfare and was interested in expanding the Zazzau empire. Within two years of becoming king, he had organized four major military campaigns. Amina fought in all four. It is said that she took delight in warfare and showed no interest in marrying any of her many suitors. Her bravery and skill as a fighter quickly established her as the leading warrior of Zazzau.

Queen Amina. When Karama died in 1576, the king-makers did not hesitate to appoint Amina as their next ruler. After only three months on the throne, Amina returned to the battlefield and fought in one military campaign after another until her death at Atagara in 1610. Amina expanded the territorial limits of Zazzau in both the south and the west. On the southwest, she invaded Nupeland and compelled its ruler to pay a tribute of eunuchs and kola nuts to Zazzau. Conquered territories were either incorporated into Zazzau or became its tributary states. Amina is remembered not only for her pioneering efforts as a woman warrior but also for her military innovations, including building fortified walls around Zazzau cities. She had a long reign as queen of Zazzau, ruling for thirty-four years.

Sources:

Bolanle Awe, ed., *Nigerian Women in Historical Perspectives* (Lagos: Sankore / Ibadan, Nigeria: Bookcraft, 1992).

Wale Ogunyemi, *Queen Amina of Zazzau* (Ibadan, Nigeria: University Press, 1999).

Hilary Rouse-Amadi, *Amina* (Zaria: Ahmadu Bello University Press, 1994).

OBA EWUARE OGIDIGAN

REIGNED 1440-1473
RULER OF BENIN

Ewuare the Great. Known as Oba (king) Ewuare the Great, Ewuare Ogidigan, who was originally named Ogun, ruled the kingdom of Benin from 1440 until his death in 1473. Ewuare had a reputation for being a brave and wise man. During his reign he expanded the territory of Benin to include 201 towns and villages. According to legend, Ewuare, who was the heir to the throne, and his brother, Uwaifiokun, were banished from Benin. After several years in exile, Ewuare sent his brother home to see if they would be recalled. Uwaifiokun was well received and ascended the throne. Ewuare then marched into Benin, killed the usurper, and set fire to Benin as punishment for his banishment. He subsequently took the name Ewuare (Owo ru are), which means "the trouble has ceased."

Ruler of Benin. Under Ewuare, the capital city of Benin was well organized and supported a large population. He built many roads and constructed nine gateways to Benin. Oral traditions extol Ewuare as a clever magician, doctor, and warrior who helped to make Benin one of the largest and best-known empires of ancient West Africa. Engaging in intense rivalry, Ewuare's two sons poisoned one another and died. After their death, the angry Ewuare banned sexual intercourse throughout the kingdom—an edict that resulted in mass migration.

Patron of the Arts. Ewuare encouraged artistic expression, particularly ivory and wood carving. He is credited as the inventor of the *Eziken*, a wind instrument, and is reputed to have established the Benin royal band, *Ema-Ode*. During his reign, the Portuguese made their earliest voyages to the West African coast and developed trade relationships with the people of Benin.

Source:
Ade Obayemi, "The Yoruba and Edo-speaking peoples and their neighbors before 1600," in *The History of West Africa*, edited by J. F. A. Ajayi and Michael Crowder, second edition, 2 volumes (New York: Columbia University Press, 1976, 1987), I: 196–263.

MAI IDRIS ALOOMA

REIGNED CIRCA 1570–CIRCA 1600–1617
RULER OF BORNU

Great Leader. Idris Ali, who was posthumously named Idris Alooma, was the greatest mai (ruler) of the kingdom of Bornu in the eastern-most part of West Africa. Much is known about Alooma's military exploits, because Ahmad ibn Fartuwa, the chief religious leader of Bornu, wrote elaborate accounts of his military campaigns.

Military Innovator. Like several other rulers of his time, Alooma was pre-occupied with military conquest and the territorial expansion of his domain, and he took several steps to enhance the professional competence of his military. He established a new military corps equipped with firearms and trained by Turkish instructors. He furnished his cavalrymen chain mail, quilted armor, and iron helmets and introduced a cavalry of camels as a transportation unit of the army. He also built larger boats for naval use. He repeatedly attacked a particular target to break down the defenders' resistance and morale while maintaining the morale of his own men with generous distribution of war booty.

Administration. Although his military prowess tends to overshadow his other accomplishments, Alooma was also a skilled administrator and a gifted diplomat. He carried out many reforms of the Bornu administrative system and separated the judiciary from the main bureaucracy. He created a court of appeals to review the judgments of lower courts.

Alooma's strategy for preventing the rebellion of conquered groups was a combination of mass expulsion and immigration. He changed the demographic profile of his empire by driving out recalcitrant groups and encouraging or forcing new groups from outside Bornu to settle in those areas. He also encouraged intermarriage between his subjects and women of conquered territories.

Diplomacy. Alooma established diplomatic relations with the Ottoman Empire, sending emissaries who extracted from the emperor a guarantee of security of life and property of Bornu travelers in Ottoman territory. He solicited the cooperation of the Ottoman ruler on a joint strategy to deal with the menace of Tuareg raids on trans-Saharan caravans.

Islamic Proselytizer. A devout Muslim, Alooma built many brick mosques in several parts of Bornu and enhanced the Islamic judicial system by appointing qualified judges to administer the law. He encouraged his subjects to fulfill their Muslim obligation to perform the pilgrimage to Mecca. The impact of Alooma's policies on pilgrimage can be deduced from the fact that his grandson, Mai Ali, made three pilgrimages to Mecca, taking thousands of Bornu pilgrims each time.

Source:
Ahmad ibn Fartuwa, *History of the First Twelve Years of the Reign of Mai Idris, Alooma of Bornu, 1571–1583*, translated by H. R. Palmer (London: Cass, 1970).

ASKIA MUHAMMAD I

REIGNED 1493–1528
RULER OF THE SONGHAI EMPIRE

Askia the Great. Widely known as Askia the Great, Askia Muhammad I was the most renowned ruler of the Songhai Empire. There is no doubt, however, that he had no constitutional right to ascend the throne. Muhammad was the chief minister to Sunni Ali (ruled 1464–1492), who on his death was succeeded by his son Abu Bakr Da'u (known as Sunni Baru). In 1493 Muhammad, who did not belong to the Songhai royal family, deposed Sunni Baru and made himself ruler. Muhammad violated the Songhai mode of succession because he did not possess the sacred symbols of national cults that constitutionally entitled the possessor to the throne. Furthermore, if—as was generally believed—Muhammad came from Soninke rather than Songhai lineage, he did not meet the ethnic eligibility requirement for succession.

Military Leader. Muhammad created a large standing army, as well as an imperial bodyguard consisting of 3,000 cavalrymen and archers. With the skillful use of horse cavalry, he used his formidable military might to enlarge the Songhai Empire, subduing the Mossi Empire in 1498 and justifying this conquest on the ground that their ruler had refused to accept Islam. After freeing the Songhai from the potential threat posed by the Mossi, Muhammad expanded the empire in several directions. He extended its northern reaches to the Sahara Desert.

Westward Expansion. In the west he incorporated much of the old Empire of Mali, beginning with the conquest of Bagana in 1499–1500. In 1502 he moved further west, capturing Diala. After failing in 1505 to breach the walled cities of Borgu—whose harsh terrain and tsetse flies made conditions difficult for Songhai horses—Muhammad conquered Galam in 1507.

Eastward Expansion. Muhammad was able to expand the imperial reach of Songhai as far east as Hausaland, easily capturing Hausa states such as Gobir, Katsina, and Zaria. Although Muhammad was not able to conquer another major Hausa state, Kano, he brought Kano under the ambit of Songhai imperial domination by making one of his daughters the wife of the ruler of Kano. Through this arrangement, his new son-in-law paid tribute equal to one-third of Kano's annual revenue to Songhai.

Alliance Building. Part of Muhammad's military genius consisted of skillful cultivation of military alliances with neighboring states. For instance, his alliance with the Kanta of Kebbi enabled him to fight against the Tuaregs at Air and Agades in 1516. He captured both cities and imposed his rule on their inhabitants.

Religious Leader. Muhammad was devoted to Islam. He is said to have been the first Songhai ruler to send his children to an Islamic school, and he insisted that his Muslim subjects observe Islamic injunctions. He introduced and enforced the wearing of the veil by Muslim women and the practice of keeping Muslim women in purdah. Despite his Islamic zealotry, however, Muhammad recognized the rights of his subjects to practice the religions of their choice and appointed a high priest to administer the religious affairs of his non-Muslim subjects.

Pilgrimage. In 1497–1498 Muhammad fulfilled one of the five pillars of Islam by going on hajj (pilgrimage) to Mecca. He took 300,000 pieces of gold, of which 100,000 were spent for charity in the holy cities. Such lavish gifts may have been designed to impress the people of Mecca with the power and wealth of Songhai; yet, they also seem to have been motivated by a genuine desire to show compassion to the poor. He also built a hostel in Mecca for Songhai pilgrims. During this journey, he persuaded the ruler of Mecca to appoint him the caliph of West Africa, a title that had both religious and political significance, lending legitimacy to his claim to the throne he had usurped from its true heirs.

A Lover of Learning. Muhammad encouraged Islamic learning through lavish patronage of Muslim clerics. He recruited Muslim scholars from Egypt and Morocco to teach at the famous Sankore Mosque in Timbuktu and set up cen-

ters of learning in various other cities, including Gao, Djenné, and Walata. Apart from the religious instruction, Islamic jurisprudence and basic bureaucratic skills were taught at these centers of learning. Islamic clerics also provided cultural and diplomatic linkages between Songhai and the Muslim world.

Astute Administrator. Muhammad was a talented administrator. Because he recognized that a ruler could not base his governance on military force alone, he tried to engender his subjects' consent to his governance by means such as allowing a measure of religious freedom in the empire. By permitting conquered non-Muslims to practice their religions, he avoided the possibility that his enemies could use religion to mobilize opposition to his rule. Muhammad centralized the administration of the empire and established an efficient bureaucracy, which was responsible for, among other things, tax collection and the administration of justice. He replaced some local rulers with members of his family or people personally loyal to him. He divided the kingdom into provinces with governors to oversee them. He set up a council of ministers and appointed high-level officials, including a commander of the fleet, a minister of forests and fisheries, and a master of the court.

Encouraging Agriculture and Trade. Muhammad built irrigation canals to enhance agricultural production. He showed his genius in administration by introducing common weights and measures throughout the empire, and he also appointed an inspector for each of its important trading centers. Given the dependence of the Songhai economy on trade, these innovations were important policy measures.

Loss of Power. Muhammad lived into his eighties, becoming blind and feeble. In 1528 several of his many sons staged a coup, deposing him and placing his son Musa on the throne. Musa was forced to abdicate in 1531, and the declining Songhai Empire was ruled by a succession of Muhammad's sons and grandsons until it fell to Moroccan troops in 1591.

Source:
J. O. Hunwick, "Songhay, Borno, and Hausaland in the sixteenth century," in *The History of West Africa*, edited by J. F. A. Ajayi and Michael Crowder, second edition, 2 volumes (New York: Columbia University Press, 1976, 1987), I: 264–301.

MANSA MUSA

REIGNED 1312-1337
RULER OF MALI

Man and Legend. Mansa (emperor) Kankan Musa is widely regarded as one of the wealthiest rulers in the medieval world, largely because of his lavish spending during his pilgrimage to Mecca in 1324. Among his own subjects, he was known as an able ruler who enlarged the territory of Mali to its greatest extent and restored order and prosperity to an empire that had gone into decline after the death of its founder, Sundiata, in 1255.

Restoration of a Dynasty. Musa was a member of the Keita dynasty, a direct descendant of Sundiata. During the period that followed Sundiata's rule, only Sakura, a slave of the royal household who had usurped the throne in 1285, had been an effective ruler. After Sakura was assassinated on his way from Mecca, around 1300, the throne was returned to the Keita dynasty.

Political and Economic Challenges. By the time Musa ascended to the throne in 1312, the general incompetence of most of his predecessors after Sakura had created major political and economic problems throughout Mali. The trans-Saharan trade, which constituted the basis for the economy of Mali, could not prosper in the face of chaos and lawlessness. Musa set out to restore law and order.

Governmental Reform. Musa revamped the judicial system and appointed competent judges. People dissatisfied with the decisions of the courts could bring their appeals directly to Musa. Dividing the empire into provinces and semi-autonomous kingdoms, Musa appointed generals and distinguished public servants as their governors. Rulers of conquered territories who pledged their loyalties to Musa were allowed to rule their territories as officials of Mali and its emperor and were required to send annual tributes to the emperor's court. Musa also maintained direct control over some parts of the empire. Each major town or city had its own administration presided over by a mayor, who was appointed by Musa and answerable to him.

Economic Measures. Recognizing the need for the sizable expenditures to maintain the large Malian military, Musa realized the need for a large revenue base. He introduced new forms of taxation and new methods for the efficient collection of existing taxes to ensure a bountiful treasury.

Religious Tolerance. Like other rulers of West African empires and kingdoms, Musa had to balance diverse political and religious interests. A devout Muslim, he had to show restraint in forcing Islam on his subjects. For example, the gold producers of Mali were not Muslims, and they resented any attempt to impose Islam on them. Often, they demonstrated their resentment by curtailing the production of gold. As al-Umari (1301–1349) of Damascus, who chronicled the 1324 meeting between Mansa Musa and the Sultan of Egypt, wrote:

> the sovereigns of this kingdom [Mali] have learned by experience that whenever one of them has conquered one of these gold towns, established Islam there and sounded the call to prayer, the production of gold dwindles and falls to nothing; meanwhile, it grows and expands in neighboring pagan countries. When experience had confirmed them in this observation, they left the gold country in the hands

of its pagan inhabitants and contented themselves with assuring their obedience and paying tributes.

Pilgrimage to Mecca. When Musa made his pilgrimage to Mecca in 1324, he displayed both his piety and his great wealth. He traveled with an entourage of 60,000 men, including 12,000 personal servants. Five hundred slaves each carried a six-pound gold staff, and eighty camels were each loaded with three hundred pounds of gold. When his entourage stopped in Egypt on the way to Mecca, Musa reportedly gave away so much gold that the price of gold plummeted in Cairo. He ran out of money on the way home and had to borrow some gold. His creditor accompanied him on the return journey and died along the way, but Musa paid the debt to the creditor's children.

Reverence for Learning. Musa loved learning and is reputed to have been the founder of the Sankore University in Timbuktu. Through the patronage of Muslim learned men and clerics, he helped to spread Islam in Mali. He attracted scholars from as far away as Egypt and the Near East.

Sources:

Lester Brooks, *Great Civilizations of Ancient Africa* (New York: Four Winds Press, 1971).

Nehemia Levtzion, "The early states of the Western Sudan to 1500," in *The History of West Africa*, edited by J. F. A. Ajayi and Michael Crowder, second edition, 2 volumes (New York: Columbia University Press, 1976, 1987), I: 114–151.

SUNDIATA

REIGNED 1230-1255

RULER OF MALI

Founder of an Empire. Also known as Mari-Diata, Sundiata is celebrated in West African oral tradition as the great warrior-king who established the territorial basis for the prosperous Empire of Mali. He is said to have been the twelfth and youngest son of the king of the small kingdom of Kangaba (in present-day Guinea on a tributary of the Niger River). According to legend, when the Susu king Sumanguru conquered Kangaba, he killed all the heirs to the throne except Sundiata, who was a crippled child and thought to have a doubtful future. Sundiata later made a miraculous recovery, regaining the use of his legs.

Empire Building. Sundiata became king in 1230, after staging a successful coup d'état against his uncle, and set about building an empire. He defeated Sumanguru at the Battle of Kirina in 1235, and by 1240 he had captured Kumbi Saleh, capital city of the old Empire of Ghana. He also gained control over the southern end of the trans-Saharan caravan routes and the Wangara goldfields between the upper Niger and the Senegal Rivers. Though he was a Muslim, Sundiata also practiced traditional ways and was reputed to have had enormous magical powers. Some of his military victories, including his defeat of Sumanguru, were attributed to his magic. Sundiata died in 1255, after ruling for twenty-five years.

Sources:

Nehemia Levtzion, "The early states of the Western Sudan to 1500," in *The History of West Africa*, edited by J. F. A. Ajayi and Michael Crowder, second edition, 2 volumes (New York: Columbia University Press, 1976, 1987), I: 114–151.

D. T. Niane, *Sundiata: An Epic of Old Mali*, translated by G. D. Pickett (London: Longmans, 1965).

SUNNI ALI

REIGNED 1464-1492

RULER OF SONGHAI

Restoration of a Dynasty. Sunni Ali was the descendant of Ali Kohlen, the elder of two Songhai princes who were held captive by Mansa Musa to ensure the good behavior of the conquered people of Songhai. Around 1335, Ali Kohlen and his brother managed to escape from Mali, and on returning home, Ali ascended his father's throne, founding the Sunni dynasty. Sunni Ali assumed the throne in 1464 and initiated the territorial expansion that was the basis for the Songhai Empire, which filled the power vacuum left by the disintegration of the older Empire of Mali.

Economic Reforms. Sunni Ali devoted considerable energy to warfare, but he also initiated political reforms that enhanced economic productivity. For instance, he increased from twelve to fifteen the number of captive states that were compelled to cultivate crops for the king. He also changed the quota of crop production. Instead of following the old practice of requiring each person to cultivate forty measures of land, he assigned two hundred measures of land to a group of one hundred cultivators.

Military Innovator. Ali was a military genius. He was the first leader in West Africa to use naval forces on the Niger River as part of a systematic strategy for conquest of new territories and defense of the empire. War boats regularly ferried his troops across the Niger.

Conquest of Timbuktu. Sunni Ali demonstrated his skill as a political strategist in 1467, when he made an alliance with Omar Muhammad Naddi, governor of Timbuktu, against Akil Ag Malwal of the Maghcharen Tuaregs. In 1468 Ali turned on Omar, who fled when he saw Ali and his forces, abandoning the city to Songhai. Ali's treatment of the people of Timbuktu contributed greatly to his reputation for excessive cruelty and vindictiveness. He organized a systematic destruction of Timbuktu over a two-year period. His forces pillaged the city and put to death a large number of inhabitants, including many of the scholars for which the city was famous. (Scholars who managed to escape the massacre were not lured back to the city until after Ali's death.)

The Siege of Djenné. In 1473 Ali used four hundred naval boats to end his siege of the city of Djenné, which—according to legend—lasted seven years, seven months, and seven days and inflicted great suffering in the people of the city. Ali did not destroy Djenné as he had Timbuktu. He spared the lives of the inhabitants of Djenné because he admired their bravery and fortitude in resisting his forces, if not for the more than seven years as legend has it, then certainly for a long time.

Great Warrior, Cruel Tyrant. Ali had immense energy and talent for warfare. In his march eastward to capture the kingdom of Borgu, he waged an incessant military campaign for ten years. The West African historian Mahmoud al-Kati (1468 – circa 1593) wrote:

> He was always victorious. He directed himself against no country without destroying it. No army led by him in person was put to rout. Always conqueror, never conquered, he left no region, town or village . . . without throwing his cavalry against it, warring against its inhabitants and ravaging them.

Ali governed Songhai for twenty-eight years, a period regarded by some as a time of unparalleled tyranny. Having successfully avoided death on the battlefield many times, Ali drowned while crossing a river during a military campaign in November 1492.

Source:

J. O. Hunwick, "Songhay, Borno, and Hausaland in the sixteenth century," in *The History of West Africa*, edited by J. F. A. Ajayi and Michael Crowder, second edition, 2 volumes (New York: Columbia University Press, 1976, 1987), I: 264–301.

DOCUMENTARY SOURCES

Al-Bakri, *Kitab al-masalik wa-'l-mamalik* (Book of Routes and Realms, 1068)—A geographical work by a Spanish Muslim who never visited West Africa and based his detailed descriptions of the region on oral and written accounts by travelers; al-Bakri included material on the kingdom of Ghana and the trans-Saharan trade network.

Pieter de Marees, *Beschryvinge ende historische verhael vant Gout koninckrijck van Guinea* (Description of Guinea; Amsterdam: Cornelis Claesz, 1602)—A Dutch mariner's description of his visit to West Africa.

Defensive walls built around the palace at Ngazargamu, Bornu, in 1548–1566
(from Basil Davidson, *The Growth of African Civilization*, 1965)

Bronze plaques of court officials in the Kingdom of Benin, circa 1500–1700. Left: The Metropolitan Museum of Art, Gift of Mr. and Mrs. Klaus G. Perls, 1991. (1991.17.22) Photograph, all rights reserved, The Metropolitan Museum of Art. Right: The Metropolitan Museum of Art, Gift of Mr. and Mrs. Klaus G. Perls, 1991. (1991.17.26) Photograph, all rights reserved, The Metropolitan Museum of Art.

LEISURE, RECREATION, AND DAILY LIFE

by EDWIN KWETU ANDOH

CONTENTS

Sidebars and tables are listed in italics.

IMPORTANT EVENTS OF 500-1590

600*-700*
- The Songhai people establish markets at Koukaya and nearby Gao (both in present-day Mali) on the Niger River, where they trade with foreigners as well as sell goods to local inhabitants.

900*-1000*
- Merchants travel busy trade routes across the Sahara between the Kingdom of Ghana (in present-day southeastern Mauritania and southwestern Mali) and Morocco.

1054
- The Almoravids, Berbers of North Africa and Spain, convert several West African dynasties to Islam, but the masses retain their original beliefs.

1076
- The Almoravids pillage Kumbi (in present-day Mali), the capital of the Kingdom of Ghana. The area goes into a decline that is hastened by the increasing barrenness of the land.

1095-1134
- During his reign King Gojemasu of Kano builds Kano City (in present-day Nigeria) as his capital.

1097
- Umme, Mai (sultan) of Kanem (north and east of Lake Chad), dies in Egypt during a pilgrimage to Mecca.

1150*
- King Yusa of Kano completes the walls surrounding Kano City.

1190*
- With the help of Tunis, Kanem ensures the safety of trans-Saharan trade routes.

1200*
- Nta, or Ntafo, ancestors of the Akan people, begin to disperse near Gonja (in the northern part of the modern nation of Ghana).
- During the reign of Eweka I, Oba (king) of Benin, a hereditary council is instituted to elect future obas.
- Fulani people begin to appear in the inland region of Borgu (in present-day Benin and Nigeria) and among the Hausa people (in present-day northwestern Nigeria and southern Niger).

1225*
- Christian and Jewish European merchants begin to travel the trans-Saharan route to trade with West Africa, chiefly for gold and ivory.

* Denotes Circa Date

IMPORTANT EVENTS OF 500-1590

1240
- Sundiata conquers the Kingdom of Ghana, incorporating it into Mali.

1250*
- Dunama ibn Umme (Dunama I), Mai of Kanem, drowns during a pilgrimage to Mecca.

1257
- Mai Dunama Dubalemi (Dunama II) of Kanem-Bornu (surrounding Lake Chad) sends a giraffe and other gifts to al-Mustansir, a ruler of the Berber Hafsid dynasty, in Tunis.

1260
- Ule, the first ruler of Mali to bear the title mansa (emperor), makes a pilgrimage to Mecca.

1280*
- Oguola, Oba of Benin, is at war with neighboring Igbo people in the southeastern part of present-day Nigeria.

1283*
- Rawa, son of Ouedraogo, founds the Mossi kingdom of Zandoma, later called Yatenga (in present-day Burkina Faso).
- The walls of Benin City (in present-day Nigeria) are built.

1293-1294
- Sakura, Mansa of Mali, goes on a pilgrimage to Mecca.

1300*
- The Ga people migrate from Benin to Accra (on the coast of the modern nation of Ghana).
- The Friday (main) mosque is built in the Malian city of Djenné, where Komboro Mana is chief.

1300*-1400*
- The Igbo people begin to migrate into the area that is now southeastern Nigeria.

1312-1337
- During the rule of Mansa Kankan Musa, Mali seizes the neighboring kingdom of Songhai.

1327*
- The Djingereyber mosque is built in Timbuktu, Mansa Musa's capital and an important trading city.

* DENOTES CIRCA DATE

IMPORTANT EVENTS OF 500-1590

1337-1341
- During the reign of Mansa Magha, son of Mansa Musa, Timbuktu is burned by the Mossi, who are beginning to form an empire to rival Mali, and he loses Gao to the Songhai.

1384-1388
- During the reign of Umar ibn Idris, the Bulala (a rival line of the ruling dynasty) conquer Kanem (north of Lake Chad), separating it from Bornu (west and south of Lake Chad).

1390-1410
- During his reign, Kanajeji, Hausa king of Kano, introduces the use of coats of mail and iron helmets in warfare.

1392
- Sultan Abu Bakr Liyatu of Bornu complains to Cairo about raiders from Egypt who sell his people as slaves.

1400*-1500*
- The Fulani begin to accept Islam and are later responsible for spreading it throughout much of West Africa.

1433
- Tuareg chief Akil, from the region north of the Empire of Mali (in the northern part of the modern nation of Mali), takes Timbuktu.
- The sending of West African ulama' (Muslim learned men) to study in Fez, a practice encouraged by Mansa Musa, is discontinued.

1450*
- Gold from Golam passes from Mali to Timbuktu, then to the Mediterranean via Touat (in present-day Algeria).
- Ozulua, crown prince of Benin, conquers Ijebu (in the western part of present-day Nigeria).

1463-1499
- During his reign, Muhammad Rimfa, King of Kano, extends the fortifications of the city of Kano and builds Dakin Rimfa (Rimfa's Palace).

1475*
- Prince Ginuwa of Benin founds the city of Warri (in present-day southern Nigeria).

1493-1528
- During his reign, Muhammad I of Songhai is the first ruler of that state to adapt the title askia.

* DENOTES CIRCA DATE

IMPORTANT EVENTS OF 500-1590

1493-1591	• While Timbuktu is controlled by the Songhai, Sankore mosque in that city develops into a center of learning.
1503	• The chief of the Efutu (a subgroup of the Guan people living in present day Ghana) and 1,300 of his subjects are baptized.
1504-1505	• Idris Katagarmabe succeeds his father as mai of Bornu and regains Kanem for the kingdom.
1504-1550	• Invited by Oba Esigie, the first Portuguese missionaries arrive in Benin.
1517	• The Songhai are defeated by the Hausa confederation, a major power east of the Niger River.
1557	• Manillas, brass or copper currency introduced by Europeans, have been circulating in West Africa since the end of the fifteenth century. The exchange rate is 80 manillas to 1 ounce of gold.
1562-1567	• British naval officer Sir John Hawkins makes regular voyages to West Africa, transporting slaves on cargo ships from Sierra Leone to the West Indies and Spanish colonies in South America.

* DENOTES CIRCA DATE

OVERVIEW

West African History. The recorded history of West Africa is largely devoted to powerful empires and the deeds of their rulers. Little of the information in these sources is directly related to the everyday lives and aspirations of the common men and women of the cities, forests, and savanna of the region. Furthermore, there are few written accounts of West Africa from before the year 1000, and the earliest documents for several regions were written even later. Archaeological research in West Africa has been conducted for a relatively short time, and the distribution of digs has been uneven. Information about the great empires of Ghana, Mali, and Songhai before 1500 comes mostly from Arabic documents of the period.

A Complex Culture. Despite incomplete records of West African everyday life, scholars have been able to piece together a picture of a diverse and complex culture that has often been misunderstood. During the years 500–1590, West Africans lived in ordered and democratic societies governed by powerful rulers. West African states and empires included the ancient Tekrur, Ghana, Mali, and Songhai Empires of the savanna; the Mossi, Nupe, Igala, and Jukun states of the middle zone; and the Ashanti, Dahomey, Yoruba, and Benin Kingdoms of the forest.

Climate and Daily Life. The lives of West Africans depended on existing soil and climate conditions, which determined what they ate and drank. Those in the southern part of the Sahara cultivated and gathered various plants while maintaining herds of cattle, sheep, or goats. People living close to bodies of water fished and gathered wild fruits, such as baobab and bananas. In the southern part of West Africa the soil was more fertile, and water was always available. All over the region, people went to markets to buy crops such as millet, yams, sorghum, maize, cassava, kola, palm, and rice. In the western and central parts of West Africa, cattle were the major source of dairy products and meat, but goats and sheep were also raised. Salt was an important part of West Africans' diet. In fact, it was crucial for survival, as body salt is rapidly lost in high temperatures. Water was of equal importance.

Clothes and Social Status. The people of some West African states were scantily clothed, while those in other states, especially in heavily Muslim areas, dressed in apparel that covered much of their bodies. Clothing and ornaments could communicate the theme of a festival, and they were also status symbols. Markedly different from those of common people, the clothes of people in a royal household conveyed the message that they should be treated with reverence. Elaborate hairstyles also enhanced their appearance. Among the people of the Empire of Mali, cosmetics and scarification (decorative marks made by scratching or cutting the skin) were often used to indicate status and wealth.

Entertainment. West Africans greatly valued music and dance, not just as forms of entertainment fraught with mystery and drama but also as intrinsic parts of their daily lives, expressing their religious sentiments and cultural pride. In various kingdoms traditional wind instruments, drums, brass bells, and gunfire (toward the end of the period) accompanied music, playacting, and magical tricks. Acrobatic dances attracted large audiences. West Africans played cerebral games such as Mancala, a game of counting and strategy that was popular among ordinary people as well as royalty. They enjoyed hunting as a sport as well as a means of food gathering. Developed as training for warfare, horseback riding, rowing, and stick fighting were also popular sports.

Construction. The nomads of West Africa usually lived in tents, and most of the ancient towns were built from mud fortified with sticks. In some places, however—such as ancient Ghana (in present-day southeastern Mauritania and southwestern Mali) and Zaghawa (in present-day eastern Chad and western Sudan)—stone buildings were constructed. In the capital of the Empire of Mali, Timbuktu (in modern Mali), and in Kanem-Bornu (around Lake Chad) some mosques was constructed of brick. For protection, West Africans built stockaded mud walls and filled ditches with spikes. After Europeans arrived to explore the region in the fifteenth century, they built castles for protection and the storage of trade goods.

Religion, Magic, and Taboo. God was an omnipresent, omniscient, and omnipotent presence in the daily lives of West Africans, who regularly acknowledged God as the sole provider of needed resources and their ultimate judge. Magic and witchcraft were also considered important tools for daily survival and were used mainly as protection from enemies. People regularly consulted spiritual specialists, who practiced sand divining and said prayers as well as providing charms and amulets. West Africans also placed emphasis on the observance of traditional taboos and moral values. As forms of social control, myths and legends helped to perpetuate societal beliefs and value systems by underscoring the consequences of flouting or showing disrespect for such traditions. Furthermore, myths and legends explained the origins of societies, giving legitimacy to a people's residence in the area of their origin. Instead of replacing earlier belief systems, Islam and Christianity were practiced alongside traditional religions and customs.

Warfare in Daily Life. During the years 500–1590 conflict touched every aspect of West African village life. Attacks and the fear of attacks created tension, subjection, and scarcity of food and other necessities. Some wars were motivated by economic reasons. For example, when Mansa Musa (ruled 1312–1337) of Mali seized the neighboring kingdom of Songhai in 1325, he was motivated by the desire to increase tax revenues in the form of produce, gold, slaves, and other trading items. Wars were also waged in the name of religion, as exemplified by the conquest of the Empire of Ghana in 1076 by the Almoravids of North Africa, who sought to spread the religion of Islam. In both sorts of wars, as well as in small-scale raids by neighboring villages, the well-being and material comforts of West Africans were negatively affected.

TOPICS IN LEISURE, RECREATION, AND DAILY LIFE

CLOTHING AND ORNAMENTS

Clothes. Because of the hot climate in West Africa, some of its peoples dressed scantily. In the Zaghawa kingdom (in present-day eastern Chad and western Sudan) around the year 1000, most ordinary people were almost naked, covering themselves partially with skins and painting their bodies. At about the same time, the forest peoples of the area stretching from the modern nation of Gambia to the western part of present-day Liberia wove fabrics mainly from the leaves of the screw pine and raffia palm, or they made bark cloth by soaking the inner bark of trees and then beating it so that the fibers became interlaced and thinner. While early societies often wore only woven-grass or bark-cloth waistbands, they gradually adopted elaborate garments that covered much more of the body. This change in the daily dress of West Africans was influenced by Islam, whose emphasis on modesty led Muslim converts to clothe themselves more fully than practioners of traditional African religions.

Textile Production. Weaving and other branches of the textile industry seem to have expanded in the western Sudanic region along with Islam. Muslim towns such as Timbuktu and Djenné had many workshops of weavers and tailors, who were often part of the Muslim elite. Around the year 1000, the people of Kano (in present-day Nigeria) began growing cotton and weaving it into fabric on narrow and broad looms. The Mandyaka of the Senegambia region wove fabric to create beautiful pagne cloth in many colors and patterns to wear wrapped around the lower part of the body. The Wolof people of the same region wove cotton cloth that was used as a medium of exchange, even for the payment of taxes. Beginning in the 1500s, there was a dramatic growth in textile design and manufacturing. Nearly every large village had spinners, weavers, cloth dyers, and tailors. As a result of trade, West Africans also wore European cotton textiles.

Clothes for Important Events. Costumes were sometimes worn to mark special occasions, especially in Mali, where the symbolism of dress—for both the nobility and ordinary people—was much more apparent than in other West African countries. For example, to commemorate his victory over the Susu of neighboring Kaniaga, circa 1235,

Yoruba shrine figure of a woman wearing an elaborate hairstyle and a lip plug (from Anthony Atmore and Gillian Stacey, *Black Kingdoms, Black Peoples: The West African Heritage,* 1979)

Traditional bogolanfini, or mud cloth, made by the Bambara, a Mande-speaking
people of Mali (Ethnology Museum, Berlin)

Sundiata, the great warrior who founded the Empire of Mali, rode in triumph among the Malinke chiefs of Mali wearing the costume of a hunter-king to stress his connections to the hunters' associations that unified the various Malinke clans and chiefdoms. Dress also denoted status, particularly to identify people of the royal household who should be treated with reverence. As in other kingdoms of the Sudanic region (the broad savanna, or grassland, that stretches across Africa between the Sahara Desert on the north and the forest zone to its south), the mansa, or ruler, of Mali and his court were richly dressed. The mansa was surrounded by a slave bodyguard, and seated before him were dignitaries who included the *farariya*, or commanders of the cavalry, to whom Mali owed much of its military superiority in the region. The mansa maintained their goodwill by giving them gold, imported Arabian horses, and luxurious clothing. They wore gold anklets and were given the privilege of wearing wider trousers than other dignitaries. Mansa Musa (ruled 1312–1337) dressed in even wider trousers, which were made from about twenty pieces of a kind of cloth that only he was allowed to wear. Emblematic of his power, his weapons—all made of gold—stood near his throne. A page stood on his left holding a silk umbrella surmounted by a dome and a gold falcon.

Protective Clothing. In Kano during the reign of Kanajeji (1390–1410), warriors began to wear iron helmets and coats of mail; quilted protection for horses was also introduced. Kano became the chief market and shipping center for "Morocco" leather manufactured from the hides of cattle from the western and central Sudanic region.

Travelers' Reports. When the North African Muslim traveler Ibn Battuta visited the Empire of Mali in 1353, he described how the people dressed for public prayers during the great Muslim festivals. They went to the prayer site, which was close to the ruler's palace, wearing well-made white clothes. Mansa Sulaiman (ruled 1341–1360), whom Ibn Battuta called a "sultan," wore a black turban and *tailasan* (mantle). Most people were allowed to wear the *tailasan* only during the two major Muslim festivals, but judges, preachers, and jurists could wear it daily. Ibn Battuta described a ceremony in which dress played an important symbolic role:

> The sultan emerges from a door in the corner of his palace with a bow in his hand and a quiver of arrows on his shoulders; on his head is a golden skull-cap, held in place by a golden turban which has edges as thin as knives, eight inches or more long. . . .
>
> When he calls one of his subjects at an audience, the man removes his clothes and puts on worn-out garments and replaces his turban by a dirty skull-cap. Then he enters raising his garments and pantaloons to halfway up his shins and comes forward in a submissive and humble way and strikes the ground hard with his elbows. . . . When one of them [the subjects] addresses the sultan and the sultan replies, the man removes the garments from his back and pours dust on his head and back like one washing with water.

Similar ceremonial recognitions of a ruler's power are thought to have been common in many parts of West Africa. The Dutch writer Willem Bosman, who arrived in West Africa during the late seventeenth century, reported in his 1705 account of his travels about an apparently long-standing practice at the court of the oba, or ruler, of Benin: "No man is allowed to wear any dress at all at court before he has been clothed by the king; nor let his hair grow before this has been done. There are men at the king's court, twenty and twenty-four years old, who without any semblance of shame go about naked, only wearing a chain of corals or jasper around their necks. But when the king gives them clothes, he usually presents them at the same time with a wife, thus making them from boys into men. After this time, they always wear clothes and let their hair grow without being obliged to shave it off with a knife any more."

Cosmetics and Scarification. Cosmetics and scarification were also used to communicate status and wealth. The oasis city of Audaghost was said to be so rich that the young women did not soil their hands with any kind of work but focused only on their looks and the condition of their skins by never exposing themselves to the harsh rays of the tropical sun.

Ornaments. West Africans wore ornaments with their everyday garments. Before the middle of the fourteenth century, cowrie shells were worn as accessories, and only later did some West Africans begin to use them as currency. In wealthy areas, such as Audaghost, even ordinary people wore gold ornaments, which were imported from the kingdom of Ghana. In some West African countries people wore rings, pendants, bracelets, and hairpins made from ebony, copper, and gold. The people of Nok, an ancient city in northern Nigeria, were particularly fond of accessorizing. The smooth stone and tin ornaments discovered in the region include jewelry worn on the neck, wrists, and the waist, as well as lip plugs and earlobe plugs. Royal families commissioned artisans to fashion rings, pendants, bracelets, and hairpins from gold, copper, ivory, and exotic woods. To glorify the monarchy of Kano, Muhammad Rimfa (ruled 1463–1499) initiated the royal use of *figinni* (ostrich-feather fans) and sandals. The Hausa, Nupe, and Yoruba peoples of present-day Nigeria wore caps (especially red ones) and copper armlets. In Ghana even domestic pets and beasts of burden wore ornaments. At the king's court, hounds often wore collars and bells made of gold and silver, and the bits and buckles of the horses' bridles, as well as the peaks of their saddles, were made of pure gold. The saddle cloths were sewn and edged with gold thread and held in place with gold bosses. Pages, counselors, and vassals wore gold, and the king adorned himself with as much as he could carry.

Hairstyles. From surviving sculpted heads scholars have concluded that some West Africans of the period 500–1590 wore elaborate hairstyles. The style on a recovered head in Nok resembles those worn by the present-day Kachicheri and Numana peoples living about thirty miles away. Some people of the Yoruba kingdom of Oyo shaved their heads or cut their hair short.

Sources:

J. F. Ade. Ajayi and Ian Espie, eds., *A Thousand Years of West African History: A Handbook for Teachers and Students* (Ibadan, Nigeria: University of Ibadan Press / London: Nelson, 1969).

Anthony Atmore and Gillian Stacey, *Black Kingdoms, Black Peoples: The West African Heritage* (London: Orbis, 1979).

Edward McNall Burns and others, *World Civilizations: Their History and Their Culture,* seventh edition, 2 volumes (New York: Norton, 1986).

Roland Oliver, ed., *The Cambridge History of Africa, Volume 3: from c. 1050 to c. 1600* (Cambridge, London, New York & Melbourne: Cambridge University Press, 1977).

FOOD AND DRINK

Diet. Rock paintings in the Sahara show that from early times domestic cattle and wild animals provided a stable source of food for West Africa. During the early part of the sixth century, people living along rivers and lakes caught fish and supplemented their diets by gathering wild vegetables and fruit. While some West Africans moved about in search of food, others domesticated animals—including cattle, goats, sheep, chickens, and dogs—and began to cultivate tropical crops such as millet, yams, and sorghum. Apart from hunting, fishing, and farming, people were also able to purchase food at local markets.

Fishing and Hunting. Some small fishing communities along the West African shoreline have existed since 1300. These fisherfolk exchanged ocean salt and dried fish with the farmers in the forests for yams, cattle, and goats. The people of Mali were great hunters and knew the secrets of the bush. Where crops grew plentifully and fishing or hunting was good, populations multiplied. The Songhai people were fishermen, farmers, and hunters—following complementary livelihoods. The dominant Songhai group,

Thatched-roof granaries in a traditional Dogon village of central Mali. Photograph by Lester Wunderman.
The Metropolitan Museum of Art, Gift of Lester Wunderman. Photograph, all rights reserved,
The Metropolitan Museum of Art.

fishermen called Sorko, navigated the great river in canoes that they also used as war craft. Their fishing and fighting expeditions took them to a part of the river where they hunted herds of hippopotamuses and nests of crocodiles.

Domestic Livestock. The inhabitants of Zaghawa (in present-day eastern Chad and western Sudan) raised cows, goats, camels, and horses. The forest peoples kept livestock such as cattle, pigs, and poultry, supplementing their meat supply through hunting and trapping. In the western and central Sudanic region, cattle were a major source of meat and dairy products and were used daily for transporting goods. Some of the people of Mali, especially those who moved south from the Sahara, remained nomadic, raising cattle, sheep, and goats. In some parts of Mali, however, the pasturage was unsuitable for four-footed animals, and all quadrupeds introduced there died. The nomadic Fulani people raised cattle but ate little meat, subsisting more on milk and butter in order not to deplete their stock. The people of the Hausa states, however, worried less about depletion of livestock and were known for holding feasts.

Food Crops. Even before plants such as maize, cassava, and sweet potatoes were introduced from the New World after 1500, the forest peoples especially were predominantly cultivators, depending on root crops such as yams, cocoyam, and legumes. They also cultivated kola trees and acquired palm products from their forest environment. In the area stretching from the Gambia to western Liberia, swamp and upland rice were grown. This indigenous African rice, known as *oryza glaberrima*, is believed to have been first cultivated around the middle Niger. The people of the Kingdom of Zaghawa grew mainly beans and wheat. Archaeologists digging at the ancient city of Djenné have discovered that rice, sorghum, millet, and various wild swamp grasses were cultivated there.

Fruits and Herbs. Various kinds of fruit were consumed daily. Travelers over the Sahara ate meagerly, usually dates and thin rounds of bread baked on cooking stones. The baobab, a large gourd-like fruit containing a pleasant, cool-tasting pulp around its seeds, was associated with Sundiata's victory over the Susu (1240) and thus popular in the Empire of Mali. To produce oil for cooking and other purposes, the Dogon, a people of the central plateau region of present-day Mali and Burkina Faso, pounded the fruit of the *hannea acida* tree. Groundnuts (peanuts) and their oil

THE SILENT SALT TRADE

Salt was dug from Sahara mines in large pieces of about 90 kilograms apiece, two of which could be carried by a camel. When the caravan reached Timbuktu, the salt was transferred to canoes and carried to Djenné. There it was divided into portions small enough for a man to carry one piece on his head. These porters traveled by foot in large groups, carrying their merchandise south for long distances. When they reached their destination they piled the salt in rows and then left the site to a spot a half-day's journey distant. While they were away another group of traders placed a quantity of gold by the piles and then left. Then the salt traders returned. If they were pleased with the amount of gold, they took it and left. If they wanted more gold they left the salt and the gold behind and waited for the second group of traders to add more gold. This trading went back and forth, with the addition of gold or the removal of some of the salt, until both parties were satisfied. Documented in many contemporary sources, this "silent trade," conducted without meetings and communication between the two parties, was a long-standing custom in many parts of Africa and was used in trading many different commodities.

Sources: J. F. Ade. Ajayi and Ian Espie, eds., *A Thousand Years of West African History: A Handbook for Teachers and Students* (Ibadan, Nigeria: University of Ibadan Press / London: Nelson, 1969).

Roland Oliver, ed., *The Cambridge History of Africa, Volume 3: from c. 1050 to c. 1600* (Cambridge, London, New York & Melbourne: Cambridge University Press, 1977).

were consumed by the peoples of the Senegambia region, who also used palm oil for culinary purposes, as did the Jukun, especially around Calabar, in southeastern Nigeria. Fruits such as bananas were also grown and consumed as part of the daily diet. Kola nuts were chewed daily and exchanged for other commodities. People also made daily use of herbs, ingesting medicinal leaves to heal wounds and cure diseases. The knowledge of herbs was a specialized skill that was believed to be handed down by the gods.

Salt. What many West Africans needed most on a daily basis was salt. Because of the heat and humidity in much of the region people lost body salt quickly through perspiration and had to replace it. In coastal regions some salt was extracted from seawater, but most of the salt in West Africans' diets was mined in the Sahara, at places such as Taghaza and Taodeni, and then transported in solid bars by Berber caravans to trading centers such as Timbuktu, where commodities such as salt and dates were traded for gold, grain, and kola nuts. The merchants of Mali took a

small piece of salt, mixed it with a little water, and drank some every day. The Hausa, Yoruba, and Nupe people used trona (hydrated sodium bicarbonate) as a salt substitute and for medicine.

Water. Certainly, water could not be replaced as a necessary aspect of the daily dietary intake of West Africans. To the south of Lake Chad, there are traditions of a race of "giants," the So (or Sao), who preceded the Kanuri inhabitants and made huge pots, which they used for storing water as well as for burials. Apart from acquiring water from naturally occurring rivers and lakes, West Africans also dug deep wells. The people of Audaghost had so much water that they could grow all kinds of fruits and vegetables.

Culinary Duties. Although women were responsible for the culinary duties in most, if not all West African states, the elderly—such as old men in the city of Audaghost—were also food preparation enthusiasts. Cooking meals required substantial effort, especially when pestles were used to pound foodstuffs. A Nok pestle has been scientifically dated to around 875.

Sources:

J. F. Ade. Ajayi and Ian Espie, eds., *A Thousand Years of West African History: A Handbook for Teachers and Students* (Ibadan, Nigeria: University of Ibadan Press / London: Nelson, 1969).

Anthony Atmore and Gillian Stacey, *Black Kingdoms, Black Peoples: The West African Heritage* (London: Orbis, 1979).

G. R. Crone, trans. and ed., *The Voyages of Cadamosto and Other Documents on Western Africa in the Second Half of the Fifteenth Century* (London: Printed for the Hakluyt Society, 1937).

Naomi Mitchison, *African Heroes* (London: Bodley Head, 1968).

HOUSING AND FURNISHINGS

Houses. Most West African towns and cities were built of mud, including the important Malian trading center of Djenné. Round mud huts with thatched or straw roofs were typical architecture, especially in the kingdoms of Ghana to the west and Songhai to the east. However, houses and the ruler's castle in the Sudanic kingdom of Zaghawa were made of gypsum, and in Ghana some houses, mosques, and schools were built from carved and joined stone. In the mid eleventh century, working from earlier sources, the Spanish Muslim geographer al-Bakri gave a detailed account of the Kingdom of Ghana, describing the houses in the capital, Kumbi Saleh (in present-day southern Mauritania). Built of stone, these houses had two stories, with the lower floor of each serving as a storeroom. They were built close together with narrow alleys between them. The city included a foreign quarter, inhabited by Muslim traders. There is also evidence of stone architecture in the middle Gambia valley, where archaeologists have found circles of dressed standing stones that are thought to belong to the period between 1300 and 1600. The nomadic Fulani lived in clusters of tents that could be collapsed and

Courtyard of a house at an archaeological dig in Ile-Ife, Nigeria, with a floor and altar paved with
pottery shards, and an artist's reconstruction of how the house may have looked circa 800–1400
(from Peter Garlake, *The Kingdoms of West Africa*, 1978; illustration by Yvonne McLean)

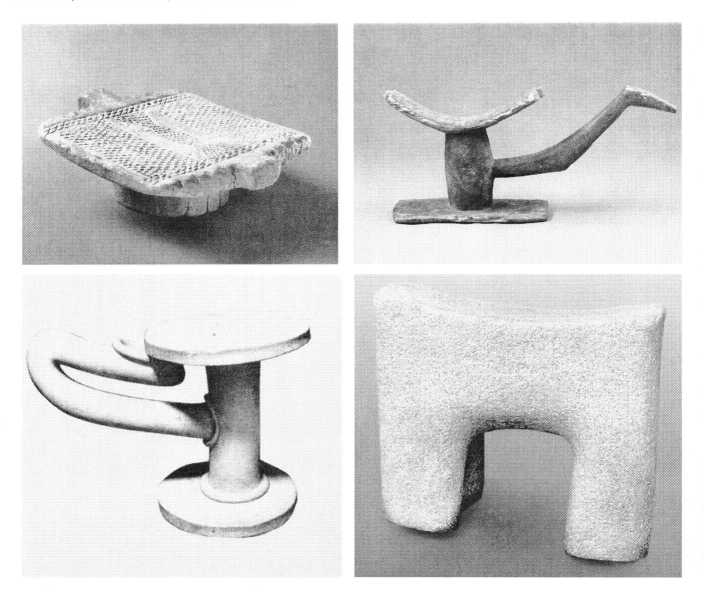

Dogon neck rests (top) from the Bandiagara Cliffs region of Mali, circa 1000–1200, and Yoruba stools (bottom) from Ile-Ife, Nigeria, circa 1100–1500. Top left: The Metropolitan Museum of Art, Gift of Lester Wunderman, 1977. (1977.394.64) Photograph, all rights reserved, The Metropolitan Museum of Art. Top right: The Metropolitan Museum of Art, Gift of Lester Wunderman, 1977. (1977.394.66) Photograph, all rights reserved, The Metropolitan Museum of Art. Bottom left: British Museum, London. Bottom right: National Commission for Museums and Monuments, Ile-Ife, Nigeria

moved. Shaped like beehives, these dwellings were usually pole frames covered with mats, leaves, or grass.

Djenné. Archaeological investigations by Roderick and Susan McIntosh at ancient Djenné on the Bani River (in the present-day nation of Mali) and neighboring sites in 1977, 1981, and 1994 have revealed a great deal about the economic and social complexity of that society, even before the beginning of relations with North African Muslims during the seventh and the eighth centuries. The city was located on relatively high ground. Most of its houses were circular huts made of straw and encrusted with clay quarried from the floodplain. Their cemeteries were organized, with corpses interred in huge burial urns and in simple pits. The city wall was 3.7 meters wide at the foundation and

stretched over a distance of 2 kilometers around the city. After the city became a major center for trade with North Africans, Muslim architectural influences resulted in the construction of rectilinear houses during the eleventh and the twelfth centuries. Constructed with sun-dried bricks and embellished with vaults and arches, buildings in Kano also show Muslim influences.

Religious Structures. Because religion played an important part in everyday life, places of worship, such as shrines and mosques, had prominent places in villages and cities. The North African traveler known in Europe as Leo Africanus visited Timbuktu in 1512 and later wrote of its great burned-brick mosque, which had been constructed by the order of Mansa Musa (ruled 1312–1337). It is believed to

DOGON VILLAGES

In West African cities and villages, buildings were arranged according to people's concepts of daily relations. The Dogon, for example, designed their villages according to kinship patterns and religious beliefs, revealing the way in which their spirituality permeated their everyday life. Anthony Atmore and Gillian Stacey have described how the Dogon situated and arranged their dwelling places:

Twins occupied a crucial position in their thinking, being used to explain dualities as male and female, and accordingly villages were often twinned, one being on the plateau above the escarpment, the other among the rocks at the foot of the almost vertical cliff.

. . . An ideal village would extend from north to south like the body of a man lying on his back. The head was the village council house, built on the chief square, which was the symbol of the primal field, cultivated by the earliest Dogon. On the north side of the chief square was the smithy—the smith being the bringer of civilization. To the east and the west there were houses where the women were secluded during menstruation; these were round like wombs and represented the hands of the village. The larger family houses were its chest and belly; the communal altars at the south of the village were its feet.

In the centre of the village were placed the stones for crushing the fruit of the *hannea acida* tree, from which the Dogon obtained most of their precious oil. These represented the female sexual parts of the village; beside them was the foundation altar, which was its male sex organ. Out of respect for the women this altar was frequently erected outside the confines of the villages.

Ideally, like the village as a whole, individual buildings were laid out in a way determined by the Dogon view of creation. The Dogon creation myths specify eight ancestors who after a time in human form were transformed into water spirits. The man's shelter and meeting house, which was generally built in the center of a village, had eight supports, representing these ancestors. The ground plan of these eight pillars resembled a serpent coiled along a broken line and surrounding the symbols of the seventh ancestor, the Master of Speech, and the eighth ancestor, who was the Word itself. . . .

Inside each house, the rooms represented the caves, or sections of the world inhabited by mankind. The vestibule, which belonged to the master of the house, represented the male partner of the couple, the outside door being his sexual organ. The big central room was the domain and symbol of the woman; the storerooms on each side were her arms, and the communicating door her sexual parts. The central room and the store-rooms together represented the woman lying on her back with outstretched arms, the door open and the woman ready for intercourse. The room at the back, which contained the hearth and looked out to the flat roof, showed the breathing of the woman, who lay in the central chamber. The ceiling above her symbolized the man, its beams representing his skeleton; their breath found its outlet through the opening above. The four upright posts were the couple's arms—those of the woman supporting the man, who rested his own on the ground. When a child was born, the woman in labor was seated on a stool in the middle of the room, her back to the north, and supported by other women. The infant was delivered on the ground and took possession of its soul in the place where it was conceived.

Source: Anthony Atmore and Gillian Stacey, *Black Kingdoms, Black Peoples: The West African Heritage* (London: Orbis, 1979), pp. 66, 69.

have been built by the Andalusian architect Abu Ishaq al-Sahili, who met Mansa Musa during his pilgrimage to Mecca (1324). According to historian Ahmad ibn Fartuwa, chief imam during the reign of the great ruler Idris Alooma (reigned 1571–1603) of Kanem-Bornu, Idris built brick mosques to replace mosques constructed of reeds in his capital of N'gazaragamu.

Walls and Other Barricades. Conflict and war were part of daily life in the West African kingdoms. Settlements were regularly attacked, not only by neighboring enemies but by North African Muslim forces and slave traders. The victors often exacted tribute as well as taking slaves and plundering property. For protection against such enemies and for territorial demarcation, stockaded mud walls and spiked ditches were sometimes constructed around villages or cities. Early Hausa social and political organization was always centered on the *birni*, a walled or stockaded town, rather than the *gari* (or *kauye*), a village or hamlet. Muhammad Rimfa, who ruled Kano between 1463 and 1499, found it expedient to extend the walls around his capital, which had been completely ringed by walls since about 1150. Chiefly in the southern part of West Africa, villages were built close to hills and mountains to which people could flee or in bushy areas with barricaded or camouflaged access routes. The pastoral Fulani, who lived in temporary tent camps, surrounded their settlements with thorn hedges to keep their cattle corralled at night. By 1490 the Europeans had also built castles for protection and the storage of the commodities acquired from trading with the Africans. One of the earliest examples is Elmina Castle of the Gold Coast, built in 1482.

Furnishings and Decor. West African craftspeople produced household objects for aesthetic, utilitarian, and religious purposes. While men dominated crafts such as sculpting, in most West African cultures women were in charge of making pots, and both sexes engaged in weaving. Sculptures were created from clay, bronze, brass, ivory, and wood. In houses at various sites archaeologists have also uncovered cooking utensils, stools, gongs, masks, and ornaments. Basic ideals of beauty were expressed through distinct symbols stamped into cloth, molded in high relief on the facades of buildings, or shaped into fine wood or metal sculpture. Complex notions of God and the universe were expressed in the intricate designs of royal thrones, scepters, swords, and craftsmen's tools. Glass, pottery, and stone plaques found in West African houses closely resemble those found in Muslim homes of the Maghrib (the region of North Africa bordering the Mediterranean). Small glass weights, suitable for use in weighing small quantities of valuable substances such as gold, have also been recovered. Some of the peoples of Senegambia used sweet-smelling gums as incense to perfume their living spaces as well as to cover up bad odors.

Royal Decor. In Mali, Mansa Musa's throne was a huge seat of ebony fit for a large and tall person. It was flanked by elephant tusks turned toward each other. Writing of his 1353 visit to the court of Mansa Sulaiman (ruled 1341–1360), Ibn Battuta included a vivid description of the decor: "The Mansa sits on a dais with three steps under a tree. The dais is covered with silk, cushions are put on it and over it is raised a silken dome-shaped parasol surmounted by a golden bird of the shape of a falcon." West Africans often attached protective amulets and fetishes to chairs and stools. This practice was especially prevalent in Hausa royal households. Royal palaces were also adorned with polychrome woven, batik, or tie-dyed tapestries.

Sources:

J. F. Ade. Ajayi and Ian Espie, eds., *A Thousand Years of West African History: A Handbook for Teachers and Students* (Ibadan, Nigeria: University of Ibadan Press / London: Nelson, 1969).

Anthony Atmore and Gillian Stacey, *Black Kingdoms, Black Peoples: The West African Heritage* (London: Orbis, 1979).

G. R. Crone, trans. and ed., *The Voyages of Cadamosto and Other Documents on Western Africa in the Second Half of the Fifteenth Century* (London: Printed for the Hakluyt Society, 1937).

Peter Garlake, *The Kingdom of Africa* (Oxford: Elsevier-Phaidon, 1978).

LEISURE ACTIVITIES

Dance. Dance was an important part of West Africans' social lives and was sometimes invested with the mystery and drama of the realm where matter and spirit meet. The people of the windward coast of West Africa (the area now occupied by the modern states of Guinea, Sierra Leone, and Liberia) expressed their religious feelings in music and dancing. The Dogon, an especially proud and independent people, were well known for their dancing. West Africans often incorporated traditional, non-Muslim ritual dances into Islamic religious celebrations. During his 1353 visit to Mali, Ibn Battuta described such a performance by masked dancers during an Islamic festival.

Music. In the royal courts of the West African empires, music was almost a constant element. During ceremonies in Mali, singers carrying golden and silver lutes preceded the ruler, who was followed by three hundred armed slaves. Court musicians of the king of ancient Ghana played on stringed instruments and sang songs of praise. Ewuare the Great (ruled 1440–1473), the most powerful oba (ruler) of Benin, invented a wind instrument similar to the fife. In some Wolof states, a *gewel* (griot, or bard) was the only person allowed to play a traditional instrument. His martial songs inspired the army, and he also entertained guests at court with performances such as playacting, acrobatic dancing, and storytelling. Long bronze trumpets and state drums with brass bells were played for the rulers of the Nupe. After Dagachi was deposed as ruler of Bornu during the first third of the fifteenth century, he is said to have introduced horse drums and trumpets (as well as flags and guns) in Kano, where he took refuge.

Magic. Performances of magic attracted great audiences in the kingdoms of West Africa. Magicians were adept at sleight-of-hand tricks, and some emitted smoke from their mouths. Sango, who ruled Old Oyo in southern Nigeria during the fifteenth century, often used such skills to increase his subjects' dread of him. Indeed, magic was much more than entertainment for most West Africans. Like religion, it was inextricably linked to all aspects of daily life. Magic was considered an important survival tool for protecting oneself from evil and the machinations of enemies. Superior magical powers were often a determining factor on the battlefield. Accounts of the decisive Battle of Kirina (circa 1235) between the armies of Susu ruler Sumanguru (ruled circa 1203 – circa 1235) and Malinke king Sundiata (ruled circa 1230 – 1255) describe it as a struggle between two powerful magicians. Whenever Sumanguru shouted, he was said to become a magical warrior with eight heads rising above his own, and his warriors were treated with a substance that was believed to help them withstand any wounds made by iron weapons. Sundiata, however, had learned Sumanguru's weakness. One of Sundiata's lieutenants threw a spear armed with a white cock's spur at the Susu leader while Sundiata shouted, "This is the spear of him who knows the ancient secrets!" When the spear struck Sumanguru, he was said to have disappeared, never to be seen again. Traditional magic, like customary religious rituals, also became linked to Islamic belief and practice.

Bronze plaques of men hunting birds and picking fruit, Kingdom of Benin, Nigeria, circa 1500–1600
(Ethnological Museum, Berlin)

Sources:

J. F. Ade. Ajayi and Ian Espie, eds., *A Thousand Years of West African History: A Handbook for Teachers and Students* (Ibadan, Nigeria: University of Ibadan Press / London: Nelson, 1969).

Anthony Atmore and Stacey Gillian, *Black Kingdoms, Black Peoples: The West African Heritage* (London: Orbis, 1979).

Naomi Mitchison, *African Heroes* (London: Bodley Head, 1968).

SPORTS

Social Life. In ancient Africa, climate, vegetation, and terrain determined the sorts of pastimes in which each ethnic group engaged. Sporting activities were generally associated with rituals and celebrations of important events in the lives of clan members or with ancestor worship. The birth of a child, the death of an elderly clan member, or a wedding ceremony was usually accompanied by elaborate sporting activity. In some cases, sporting events also preceded the waging of a war against a neighboring village.

Hunting. In the forest region of West Africa, hunting as a game or sporting activity was widespread. Sometimes different ethnic groups in neighboring villages engaged in seasonal hunting competitions. After a young man was

initiated into adulthood, he had to show his bravery by hunting alone, or as part of a larger group of his peers, for dangerous animals such as lions and wild dogs. Success in this endeavor earned him new status within the clan. A young man who killed a lion or a wild dog on his own was accorded the highest ranking in his peer group and was said to possess some sort of supernatural power and to be capable of conversing with and seeking the assistance of evil spirits during the most dangerous hunting trips. In many regions the degree to which a young man displayed his bravery in hunting games determined his chances of becoming a respected leader. Equally important, eligible young women sought out brave young men as prospective husbands. Becoming an accomplished hunter required lengthy training that started early in life, and an accomplished hunter could climb the social ladder to become a chief. As early as age four, a boy might be take on a less dangerous hunting trip.

Women and Hunting. The sport of hunting was a gender-specific activity, and women were excluded from participating in hunting trips that were considered dangerous. In some cultures, however, women played significant roles in col-

MANCALA

Still popular in many parts of West Africa and in other parts of the world as well, Mancala is widely considered the oldest game in the world. It originated in Arabia and Egypt around the fifteenth to eleventh centuries B.C.E. Muslim traders spread it through West Africa, where various versions of the game became deeply ingrained in the culture. Adults and children on all levels of society played it almost daily as an important family game, as part of a ceremonial rite of passage, or as a recreational pastime among friends. Some people believe that the New World practice of playing a version of Mancala in a house of mourning to amuse the spirit of the deceased until burial of the body derives from an ancient West African practice.

There are hundreds of variations of Mancala with different names, including *ayo*, *ti*, *kpo*, *bao*, *wari*, *azigo*, *igisoro*, and *omweso*. The two best-known versions are *ayo* from Nigeria and *wari*, which is played across West Africa. The name *Mancala* (Arabic for "to move") refers to the physical action that takes place during the game, during which objects are moved from one cup or depression to another.

Mancala is fundamentally a board game, but it can be played by making hollows or rings in the ground. The depressions or bins on a Mancala board are called *warri* or *awari* in certain West African dialects. The number of bins and the numbers of rows in which they are arranged vary from game to game and culture to culture. The game is played with counters such as pebbles, cowries, seashells, kernels, seeds, coins, or ivory balls.

In playing a typical two-row Mancala game with twelve bins and two kalahas (large depressions at each end of the board for the players' winnings), each player has twenty-four counters and places four in each of the six bins on his or her side of the board. The kalahas are empty at the start of the game. Players alternately pick up all the counters in any of their bins and distribute one in each successive bin, including their own kalaha, moving counterclockwise around the board. There are also strategies for capturing an opponent's counters and depositing them in one's own kalaha. The game ends when all six bins on one side of the board are empty. The player whose kalaha holds the most counters is the winner.

Source: "Mancala: The African game of counting and strategy" <http://www.cmi.k12.il.us/Urbana/projects/AncientCiv/africa/Mancala.html>.

laborative hunting, which was considered less dangerous than individual hunting. Apart from the danger involved, women may also have been excluded from hunting because it involved lengthy absences from the village. Also, since young men and young women were generally separated from one another until they reached marriage age, the inclusion of women in hunting groups would have violated customs.

Horseback Riding and Rowing. In the Hausa and Fulani culture young men often displayed their skills in horseback riding and rowing during celebrations to honor the ruler or on other important occasions that demanded public display of such prowess. At the start of the *Dumbar* festival, horseback riders were part of the ruler's entourage heading to the sporting site. In Senegal, riding horses was perhaps the most important sport for adult and young men. Trained to fight wars, these horsemen also provided entertainment at court during peacetime festivals. As in hunting, the display of superior skills on horseback was a sure way of gaining social recognition and higher status.

The Donga. Stick fighting was a major sporting activity among several tribes in West Africa, especially in the northwest. The Donga, annual competitive stick fights between young men, prepared them for war. The clan elder decided who was eligible to take part in the Donga and when it should take place. Many young men practiced all year long for the "Day of the Donga." Hoping to distinguish himself publicly, a stick fighter engaged in a deadly, brutal duel that ended only when he or his opponent was so severely injured that he could no longer stand. Because displaying pain was considered disgraceful and unmanly, stick fighters were not supposed to show that they were in pain. Before the Donga, young unmarried women spent several hours decorating their bodies because the event provided them the opportunity to select a marriage partner. The friends of the young men preparing to fight spent several days decorating the combatants' bodies because the more decorative they were the more they would be noticed by eligible women. These women paid particular attention to the ways the fighters moved their naked bodies, especially the lower half. At the beginning of the Donga, young women led the village in songs that acknowledged the power of the spirit world and the elders that had passed away. Clan members believed that these elders were responsible for everything from abundance of harvest to peace, prosperity, and clan stability. People asked the ancestors for protection and good harvest in the next planting season. In some cases, young men from one village competed with others from nearby villages in recognition of the bonds that historically existed between them. The winner of a stick fight was treated with deference in his village and was by custom entitled to an additional wife or wives in recognition of his sporting prowess.

Dounouba. Dounouba, another form of stick fighting, also took place in Mali among the Bambara people. Unlike the young men's yearly Donga, the Dounouba was organized as needed and primarily for the settlement of disputes between two adults. If two men refused to settle their dispute peacefully, even after the intervention of elders, they were invited to fight one another publicly in the village square. Village drummers and young women provided entertainment for the event. As in the Donga, the two opponents engaged in brutal stick fighting until only one man was left standing. If he wanted, the winner could take the wife of the vanquished man. After the Dounouba the villagers dispersed, and the dispute was considered settled forever.

Wrestling. Among the Igbo of southeastern Nigeria and other tribes in the region, wrestling was an important sporting activity in which unmarried young men could display their bravery. Wrestling matches were also training for wars against rival groups. Moreover, it was an occasion for the young men to demonstrate their masculinity, an extremely important trait for Igbo men. Failure to display one's masculinity brought social disgrace to one's family. Each match was arranged according to age level, and success signified one's readiness for adult life. As with the Donga, a wrestling match also provided an occasion for ancestor worship and mate selection. A young woman brought water and "mating cakes" to wrestling matches and offered them to a young man with whom she was particularly interested in forming a long-lasting relationship.

Sources:
Yaya Diallo and M. Hall, *The Healing Drum: African Wisdom Teachings* (Rochester, Vt.: Destiny Books, 1998).

William N. Stephens, *The Family in Cross-Cultural Perspective* (New York: Holt, Rinehart & Winston, 1963).

Carle C. Zimmerman, *Family and Civilization* (New York: Harper, 1947).

DOCUMENTARY SOURCES

Alvise Cà da Mosto (1432–1488), *Una opera necessaria a tutti li nauiga[n]ti chi vano in diuerse parte del mondo* (A Guide for All Navigators Who Wish to Travel Safely; Venice: Printed by Bernardino Rizus, 1490)—The first published account of the travels of a Venetian trader who explored Madeira and the Canary Islands, sailed along the coast of West Africa as far south as the modern nation of Guinea-Bissau, and traveled partway up the Gambia River, during two voyages, in 1455 and 1456. Cà da Mosto's book is one of the earliest known European books about West Africa.

Ibn Battuta (1304 – circa 1378), *Rihlah* (Travels)—A travel account by a wide-ranging North African Muslim traveler, who visited the Empire of Mali in 1353, recording his observations of religious practices, customs, everyday life, politics, economic relations, and topography.

Ibn Hawqal, *Kitab Surat al-Ard* (A Book on the Shape of the Earth, late tenth century)—An important geography book by an Arab who visited the ancient Empire of Ghana in the late tenth century.

Leo Africanus (circa 1455 – circa 1544), *Descrittione dell' Africa* (Description of Africa, 1550)—A travel account by a Spanish Muslim who visited the Songhai Empire of West Africa in 1507 and the Malian capital of Timbuktu in 1512.

Al-Mas'udi (died 957), *Muruj al-Dhahab wa Ma'adin al-Jawahir* (Meadows of Gold and Mines of Precious Stones, 947)—An historical-geographical work by an Iraqi Muslim, who included information about his visits to West Africa.

Brass stool made in the Kingdom of Benin, Nigeria, circa 1500–1600 (National Museum of Nigeria, Lagos)

THE FAMILY AND SOCIAL TRENDS

by PADE BADRU

CONTENTS

Sidebars and tables are listed in italics.

IMPORTANT EVENTS OF 500-1590

500*
- By this date, trade routes cross the Sahara Desert between North Africa and West Africa.
- At Nok and neighboring villages (in modern-day northern Nigeria), a massive iron-smelting culture has evolved before the same technology has been established in most parts of Europe.

800*
- West African cities such as Gao, Kumbi, and Audaghost become important trading posts.
- The states of the Yoruba (west of the Niger River) and the Hausa (toward the northeast) emerge as powerful forces in the region.
- Muslim expeditionary forces begin pushing southward from Morocco.

1052-1076
- The Almoravids, Berber Muslims from North Africa, wage war on on the Empire of Ghana (in present-day southeastern Mauritania and southwestern Mali); by 1076 the capital, Kumbi, has fallen.

1230
- The Empire of Ghana falls to Takrur warriors, who have carried on a sustained attack for several decades.

1235
- Sundiata wins a major battle against Sumanguru, the king of the Takrur people. By 1240 Sundiata has conquered the Empire of Ghana and established the Sundiata dynasty in West Africa.

1312-1337
- During his reign, Mansa Musa, king of Mali, makes a lavish pilgrimage to Mecca, seeking to legitimize his empire as a Muslim state. Mansa Musa is credited with the expansion of trade in West Africa and re-establishing the political authority of his empire over Gao.

1375
- The first comprehensive atlas of Africa is completed by Cresque, a cartographer from Majorca.

1462-1492
- During his reign as ruler of the Songhai Empire, Sunni Ali moves his seat of government to Gao, raises levies, persecutes scholars who disagree with his orthodox view of Islam, and establishes a system of provincial administration.

1471
- Portuguese navigators reach Elmina (in present-day Ghana) searching for the goldfields in the Akan forests.

***DENOTES CIRCA DATE**

IMPORTANT EVENTS OF 500-1590

1482
- Elmina Castle is built as a fortress for Portuguese traders and a symbol of Portuguese presence in the region.

1490
- The Portuguese seize the island of São Tomé in the Gulf of Guinea, where they establish sugar plantations on a scale previously unknown. Africans are captured by Portuguese slavers and transported to these plantations, where they are put to work producing sugar for European markets.

1496
- Askia Muhammad, emperor of Mali, returns home after a lavish pilgrimage to Mecca. He has been given authority to act as a caliph of Islam in the western Sudanic region.

1500
- Metallurgical techniques and iron smelting spread throughout West Africa.

1528
- Known for his extreme brutality to non-Muslims and his heavy taxation of the peasants, Askia Muhammad is overthrown in a coup by his sons, beginning decades of decline in the power of Mali, which falls to Moroccan invaders in 1591.

1548-1582
- Askia Daud rules Mali.

1553
- The first English merchants arrive in the kingdom of Benin, where they trade for ivory tusks, bronze, and spices.

1571-1603
- During his reign, Idris Alooma establishes himself as the greatest leader of the Kanem-Bornu Empire, greatly expanding its territory through a succession of military conquests. As a statesman, he maintains diplomatic relations with Tripoli and Cairo and exchanges gifts with the Ottoman Emperor in Constantinople (Istanbul).

* DENOTES CIRCA DATE

OVERVIEW

Studying Family Structure. The study of the family from an historically informed perspective is a challenging exercise. Indeed, concepts of the social unit known as the family have varied widely from time to time and place to place. Reconstructing ancient family forms is perhaps one of the historian's or sociologist's most difficult tasks, especially when it comes to studying the family and social life of ancient West Africa, from which there exist few written records other than travelers' chronicles. It is difficult to speak about a single ancient West African family pattern in the same way that one might speak about the Chinese or the European family. Despite regional variations, however, throughout West Africa people placed a strong emphasis on familial relations, and the family played a primary role in structuring social and economic relations. While African cultural forms have been distorted by colonial contact and rapid modernization, many aspects of the modern African family still remain essentially the same as they were in 1590.

Misconceptions. Until the late twentieth century most scholarly writings on Africa tended to exaggerate rather than inform, creating the perception of Africa as the "dark continent," where civilization was least developed. Recent archeological evidence, however, has revealed that great African civilizations—such as the empires and kingdoms of old Ghana, Mali, Songhai, Yoruba (Oyo Mesi), and Kanem-Bornu—either predated European civilization or emerged at the same time. While reconstructing the history of this era through the most basic social organization, the family, this chapter describes some of the significant achievements of these people.

Trade and the Family. The emergence of powerful states in West Africa is related to a remarkable degree of social and economic development in the region. There is ample evidence to suggest that with the growing political authority of kings—especially in the old Ghana Empire (in present-day southeastern Mauritania and southwestern Mali), Kanem-Bornu (around Lake Chad), and Mali—tribute in the form of taxes on exports and levies on imports propelled these empires to their greatest heights.

Family and lineage structures changed in response to increasing sophistication in trade and agriculture, giving rise to two distinct family forms. Urban family units were more likely to be nuclear (parents and their children only) than rural families, which were more often extended (including several generations linked by blood or ancestry). The arrival of Muslims from North Africa as early as the ninth century also introduced changes to the family unit and social life. These changes spread further after the Almoravids (Muslim Berbers from North Africa) waged war on the Empire of Ghana in 1052–1076. Thus, by the ninth century there were already multiple forms of West African family units, influenced by native culture or Muslim values, or both. The end result was an increasing acceptance of many different forms of marriage and cohabitation.

The Family Unit. Though there were nuclear families in West Africa, it was not uncommon for a family unit to consist not only of husband and wife but also of others related by blood and common ancestry. The family performed the function of socialization, fostering love and providing emotional support for all its members, and it was also the arena where both production and reproduction took place. Each member performed specific functions, but all worked together collectively. As the link between the present and the past, the family was also the focus of rituals, rites, and celebrations. Every occasion was marked by elaborate ceremonies. For instance, the birth of a child (considered the most important event in family life), the death of a family member, or a wedding required a public celebration and the performance of certain rites. The family unit also oversaw the rites of passage to adulthood for female and male family members.

Schooling. Education in ancient West Africa was often less formal and less organized than modern schooling. Learning was regarded as a lifelong endeavor. Older men trained boys at a young age in skills that served them throughout their lives, while girls learned values and practices from their mothers and aunts. Separating boys and girls from each other at an early age allowed for differentiated socialization. Women were taught gender-specific roles and indoctrinated to accept their place in the social hierarchy. In regions where Islam had been widely adopted, organized schools were much in evidence. These parochial schools emphasized the memorization of Islamic literature, especially the Quran (Koran). Some graduates of these schools went on to become Muslim scholars who spread the faith of Islam. Many of them were able to rise in society and become advisers to the emperors and kings.

Gender Issues. While certain tasks were gender specific, they did not carry with them the notion of superiority or inferiority. While boys and girls were socialized in gender-specific terms, their roles complemented one another. Indeed, in some cultures, for example the Yoruba of southwest Nigeria, there were no words that conveyed gender distinction. The absence of the words *he* and *she* in their language lends credence to the idea that gender distinction was not as important to the Yoruba as age or other marks of social distinction. In the Yoruba language only an understanding of the context of the speech or a prior knowledge of the subject matter allowed the listener to establish the sex of the person being discussed. Gender distinctions in language were imported at the time of European colonization.

Elders. Generally, elders in the family were accorded respect and treated with deference. Many people looked forward to old age as a time when they could sit back and let the younger generation look after them. The older a family member was, the more respect he or she commanded. Since old age also was considered to bring wisdom, elders in African culture played the role of modern-day judges. All disputes within the family were routinely referred to them for intervention, and their words normally carried the authority of the ancestors. Elders linked the living to those family members who had passed on, perform-

ing functions that contributed to the stability of the family unit, and serving as the custodians of family history and rules of blood relationship. While they no longer took part in the family's work, through the rules of reciprocity they were rewarded for all their past labor with first rights to whatever goods came to the family.

Marriage. The idea of "one man, one wife" was foreign to West African culture. Men in a position to do so often took many wives into the family unit. Women of high social status, especially unmarried daughters of a queen mother or chief, could have sexual intercourse or relationships with as many men as they could afford. The primary purpose of marriage was bringing to life many children. Companionship and proving one's masculinity were secondary to the need for having children. Any marriage that did not quickly result in the birth of a child was not considered fully consummated. Indeed, most sex was geared toward procreation. Aggressive sexuality was encouraged, especially among younger men, but promiscuity was discouraged. Sex and sexuality were rarely discussed in the public arena; such conversations took place in the privacy of one's home. Young women were expected to remain virgins until they married. However, women were encouraged to display their beauty by wearing elaborate, flamboyant clothing that revealed their bodies. Younger women went about their daily chores with their breasts on full display and only the lower sections of their bodies covered. This practice was part of a culture that celebrated the beauty of the female body. Mate selection was the exclusive preserve of the older and more knowledgeable female relatives of the aspiring spouses. Marriage was not just a union between two consenting adults but also a symbolic union of their families in a lifelong relationship. Most relatives of the husband and wife came over time to see themselves as members of one family.

TOPICS IN THE FAMILY AND SOCIAL TRENDS

ANCESTOR WORSHIP AND THE ELDERLY

Ancestor Worship. The oldest religion in West Africa is the worship of the ancestors, who were generally regarded as the link between the living and the universal being that existed outside of the realm of human understanding. The separation of earth and heaven, as in modern Christian dogmas, was most definitely foreign to African thinking. It was not unusual for a family compound or household to have a shrine containing a effigy of an ancestor who had passed away. As recognition of this forebear's continuing existence, rites and rituals were often performed daily to appease him or her. Even with the acceptance of foreign religions such as Islam and Christianity, many Africans still consider ancestor worship their central religion. Even today in the southern part of modern Nigeria, it is not unusual for pastors or imams (Muslim prayer leaders) to employ the services of native doctors (juju men) in matters they consider outside the scope of their belief. Among the Ewe in modern-day Ghana and the Vai in Senegambia, fetishism or ancestor worship is important in social and familial relations. With the settlement of Europeans during the later part of the nineteenth century, however, ancestor worship was wrongly characterized as evil worship (voodoo), and such worship was declared illegal.

Gerontocracy. Respect for one's ancestors carried over into the realm of the living. The elders were considered the link between living clan members and the world of the spirit, so they were usually treated with great reverence. Authority patterns within the family were based on age, creating a social structure known as gerontocracy. The authority of the elders was pervasive in private and public life. Any person who disobeyed the elders was considered condemned to a life of suffering in the other world, ostracized from society, and deprived of standing among his or her age group. Ranking by age was more important than factors such as economic status or gender. At village assemblies, the oldest member of the clan presided over the proceedings, consulted with the other elders, and then had the final say in whatever decision was made. In some tribes, such as the Yoruba of southwestern Nigeria and the Ewe of modern-day Ghana, parallel assemblies were held for men and for women. When joint assemblies were held, the elder of the two leaders, regardless of sex, presided over the proceedings. Seating arrangements also followed the rule of gerontocracy. Older men and women were normally seated in the front rows while younger people were seated according to age in the rows behind the elders. Upwardly mobile individuals still had to show respect to older members of the clan and give them kola nuts during public ceremonies to acknowledge their role in binding together the clan. Talking in front of elders or looking elders straight in the face was often considered disrespect, and one who did either was likely to be disciplined immediately. When one was allowed to speak in front of the elders, one had to do so with decorum and with ultimate respect for those present.

Care for the Elderly. When elderly men and women could no longer work, the clan was required to look after them. The members of the family took turns providing for the needs of the elderly, who were given priority in the distribution of food. On the death of an elder the entire family was responsible for giving the dead the proper funeral rites.

Sources:

George B. N. Ayittey, *Indigenous African Institutions* (Ardsley-on-Hudson, N.Y.: Transnational, 1991).

Yaya Diallo and Mitchell Hall, *The Healing Drum: African Wisdom Teachings* (Rochester, Vt.: Destiny Books, 1989).

Jack Goody, *Comparative Studies in Kinship* (Stanford, Cal.: Stanford University Press, 1969).

Goody, ed., *The Character of Kinship* (Cambridge: Cambridge University Press, 1973).

F. Ivan Nye and Felix Berardo, *The Family: Its Structure and Interactions* (London: Macmillan, 1973).

W. N. Stephens, *The Family in Cross-Cultural Perspective* (New York: Holt, Rinehart & Winston, 1963).

Bronze head probably used on a royal ancestral altar in the Kingdom of Benin, Nigeria,
sixteenth century (George Ortiz Collection, Geneva)

ANCESTRY AND KINSHIP: DEFINING THE FAMILY

The Kinship System. In West African societies, ancient and contemporary, kinship serves as the basis of the legal system, production, jurisprudence, politics, and rituals—as well as the basis for obligations among family members. As John S. Mbiti has observed, kinship is central to African life:

> Kinship is reckoned through blood and betrothal (engagement and marriage). It is kinship, which controls social relationship between people in a given community: it governs marital customs and regulations, it determines the behavior of individuals towards another. Indeed this sense of kinship binds together the entire life of the "tribe" and is even extended to cover animals, plants and non-living

objects through the "totemic" system. Almost all the concepts connected to human relationship can be understood and interpreted through the kinship system. This is it, which largely governs the behavior, thinking and whole life of the individual in the society of which he is a member.

The Family Unit. Unlike Europeans, most traditional African societies did not have words for *uncle*, *aunt*, *cousin*, *nephew*, or *niece* in their vocabularies. Everyone was considered brothers or sisters. To consider someone a cousin or uncle would have been an exclusion of that person from membership in one's extended family. Within the context of the African family, it was not unusual for someone to have more than one father or mother. In fact, it was customary to refer to any member of the family

TABOOS

West African social life was structured by taboos. In some cultures a man married to a flat-footed woman was not expected to live past the third year of the marriage. As a result, many eligible men stayed away from these women. The birth of a child feet first was usually considered a bad omen, not only for the baby's mother but also for the entire clan. Taboos relating to a woman's menstrual circle and sexuality were also in abundance. For example, people believed that women with irregular menstrual circles had been cursed by witches, and in some cultures women who openly expressed pleasure during or after sexual intercourse were regarded as evil. People responded to most negative happenings with elaborate ceremonies or by pouring libations. Because the ancestors were believed capable of solving most family problems, people routinely turned to them for assistance in difficult situations, usually by offering a libation. This ritual involved pouring water or wine on the mother earth and uttering incantations to communicate with elders who had passed away. Thus, libations connected the present to the past and helped allay the fears of the living about present or impending bad events.

Source: Mary Douglas, *Purity and Danger: An Analysis of Pollution and Taboo* (London: Routledge & Kegan Paul, 1966).

who was older than, or about the same age as, one's biological parents as mother or father. At the same time, those elders had parental responsibilities, such as providing emotional and financial support to a younger family member. Even outsiders residing temporarily in a village were called brothers or sisters if they stayed long enough, as a sign of their full acceptance in the family unit.

The Nuclear Family. In a nuclear family the household consists primarily of a husband and wife and their children. In West Africa the rise of the nuclear family was usually associated with the decline of old societies, though there is evidence that certain forms of nuclear families did exist in some traditional African societies. The nuclear family in its purest form—with one husband and one wife—did not exist. The number of wives a man brought to his household depended on his economic status, and many men could not afford to bring additional wives into their households. Yet, even men and women in nuclear arrangements lived within a network of other family members, some of whom they might have sexual relations with. In such situations it is extremely difficult to find the boundary where family relations stopped. Children born under nuclear housing arrangements were

still surrounded by other adults who had authority and control over them.

The Extended Family. The most common form of family grouping in ancient West Africa was the extended family, which comprised spouses and their offspring along with related members such as brothers, sisters, cousins, uncles, aunts, and older members of the clan who either could no longer survive on their own or chose to remain within the larger unit. People from other clans sometimes resided in a compound so long that they became regarded as part of the extended family. The eldest member of the extended family, male or female, usually had the power to set up living arrangements and conjugal patterns. Incest was rare.

Sources:
Paul Bohannan and Philip Curtin, *Africa and Africans*, fourth edition (Prospect Heights, Ill.: Waveland Press, 1995).

William Fagg, *Divine Kingship in Africa* (London: British Museum, 1970).

Hugo Huber, "Initiation to Womanhood Among the Se (Ghana)," *Nigerian Field*, 23 (July 1958): 99–119.

Huber, "Kinship terms and traditional form of marriage among the Se (West Africa)," *Anthropos*, 53, no. 5/6 (1958): 925–944.

John S. Mbiti, *African Religion and Philosophy* (New York & Washington, D.C.: Praeger, 1969).

Peter J. Paris, *The Spirituality of African Peoples: The Search for a Common Moral Discourse* (Minneapolis: Fortress Press, 1995).

ANCESTRY AND KINSHIP: RULES OF DESCENT

Lineage. In its most basic form lineage is a multigenerational grouping of people related through bloodline or descent from a common ancestor (consanguinity). The main function of establishing lineage was enforcing the rules of consanguinity regarding inheritance and marriage. In West Africa some ethnic groups are patrilineal and others matrilineal in establishing their rules of descent.

Matrilinealism. Among most ethnic groups in ancient West Africa, lines of descent were traced through the female side of the family. In fact, before modernization and the rise of private property, matrilinealism was far more common than patrilinealism, the tracing of descent through the male side of the family. Even in patrilineal systems there were pockets of matrilineal rule. Matrilinealism was found among the Ashanti people in what is now the modern nation of Ghana, as well as in some parts of southeastern Nigeria and the old kingdom of Dahomey (in the southern part of present-day Benin). In these cultures, daughters inherited from either their father's or mother's side of the family.

Matrilineal Inheritance. West Africans of this period had a concept of ownership that differed from that of Asian or European cultures. In West African matrilineal cultures, a person who inherited property gained control of it, not outright ownership. The eldest daughter had the rights to all property left by her parents, and she in turn could dis-

Soapstone figures of a man and woman holding weapons to indicate their authority in the community, Esie, Nigeria, circa 1100–1500 (National Commission for Museums and Monuments, Nigeria)

tribute it among her younger siblings. A daughter of the matriarch who chose to marry outside the clan automatically lost control of whatever property she inherited. By traditional law, her inheritance could not be transferred to her husband's family, where she automatically became subordinate to her husband's sisters, even if they were younger. If there were no other eligible female child, a maternal uncle inherited the property on behalf of the eldest daughter. Despite her lack of standing in her husband's family, she still retained her status within her father's compound whenever she returned home. For example, she still had the major say as to how inherited property was used or distributed within her birth family, and she presided over meetings where such decisions were made.

Patrilinealism. In certain parts of West Africa, bloodline and inheritance were traced through the father's side of the family. All male children were entitled to inherit from their father, and in some instances from their maternal grandfather and uncles. In a patrilineal society, such as that of the Yoruba, sons were considered essential to the family as they stood to inherit all the family land. The eldest male child enjoyed tremendous influence in the family, and he was most likely to inherit the bulk of the family property. Female offspring were excluded from property inheritance, and the eldest son was obligated to take care of his mother and unmarried sisters, while married sisters took up residency in their husband's compounds. The Vai people of the Senegambian region, the Idoo people of western Ivory

Coast, and the ethnic Igbo of southeast Nigeria were all rigidly patrilineal societies.

Unilinealism and Bilinealism. Some ethnic groups in Africa were unilineal, that is, they reckoned lineage from only one side of the family, usually the father's, while others were bilineal, tracing descent from both the mother's and the father's sides. The Kanuri people (of northeastern Nigeria and southeastern Niger) are an example of a people who practiced paternal unilinealism. Any boy born under this rule of descent took the name of his father or the oldest male in the line. Children born in societies that practiced bilinealism could inherit from both sides of the family and could also choose either the name of the mother's father or the name of the grandmother's father on either side of the family. Among the Akan people in Ghana, men can inherit from both sides of the family, and a female member of the same family loses inheritance rights when she marries.

Sources:

George Ellis, *Negro Culture in West Africa: A Social Study of the Negro Group of Vai-Speaking People* (New York: Neale, 1914).

Meyer Fortes, "The Structure of Unilineal Descent Groups," *American Anthropologist*, 55 (January-March 1953): 17–41.

P. A. Owiredu, "The Akan System of Inheritance today and tomorrow," *African Affairs*, 58 (April 1959): 161–165.

A. R. Radcliffe-Brown and Daryll Forde, eds., *African Systems of Kinship and Marriage* (London: Oxford University Press, 1950).

Niara Sudarkasa, "Interpreting the African Heritage in Afro-American Family Organization," in *Black Families*, edited by Harriette Pipes McAdoo (Beverly Hills, Cal.: Sage, 1981), pp. 37–53.

ANCESTRY AND KINSHIP: RULES OF RESIDENCY

Matrilocality. Residency patterns were often determined by rules of descent. In a matrilocal setting, usually in matrilineal society, the newly married couple set up residency in the bride's mother's compound. A girl born in a matrilocal setting took the name of the living matriarch or a maternal aunt. A boy would normally take the name of the matriarch's uncle or living brother.

Patrilocality. In most patrilineal groups, once a woman was married, she was obligated to move to her husband's father's compound, where the couple resided until they were able, or willing, to set up their own home. Usually, the young wife lived among the other women, and the oldest female in the compound exercised marital authority. Younger wives were placed under the control of this matriarch, or several senior wives, who established sleeping arrangements and assigned chores within the extended household. In some cases the young husband continued to live in his father's hut or compound until his father passed away. Then the eldest son, who was next in line to inherit the property, determined whether his other brothers and wives should continue their residency or not. In polygynous families (those in which the husband had more than one wife), a widowed woman could not marry another man in her husband's family and was, by agreement, required to take residency in her father's compound.

Neolocality. Neolocality is the practice by which a newly married couple sets up their own residence away from both sets of parents. In West Africa this practice is usually a feature of modernization and the rapid uprooting of people from traditional family settings. During the years 500–1590 this residency pattern occurred in urban centers, and it was common among nomadic tribes, where newlyweds built their own hut on the outskirts of the main compound of the head of the clan.

Sources:

Paul Bohannan and Philip Curtin, *Africa and Africans*, fourth edition (Prospect Heights, Ill.: Waveland Press, 1995).

William Fagg, *Divine Kingship in Africa* (London: British Museum, 1970).

Jack Goody, "Bridewealth and Dowry in Africa and Eurasia," in *Bridewealth and Dowry*, by Goody and S. J. Tambiah (Cambridge: Cambridge University Press, 1973), pp. 1–58.

ASPECTS OF COURTSHIP

Attracting a Wife. Because young women generally sought out men for their physical attraction, men in some West African cultures spent much time decorating their bodies once they reached a certain age. Many wore earrings, bangles, false eyelashes, and other decorative ornaments that might be considered feminine in other cultures. When they started wearing such adornments, it was a sign they were ready to take on the role of husband. Generally, young men married when they were able to sustain a family or were eligible to be allocated to a plot of land, usually around age twenty-one or older. Depending on their physical maturity and onset of the menstrual cycle, women married earlier than men, on average around age sixteen. In Muslim and nomadic cultures, they sometimes married as early as twelve.

Negotiations. Marriage in ancient West Africa established social bonds between families. In most parts of the region, mate selection was out of the hands of the prospective spouse. Older members of the family, especially women, were given the responsibility of arranging the marriages of eligible bachelors. Throughout West Africa, social contacts between the sexes were restricted to formal occasions, at which young men and women developed attractions for one another. Ritual dances at marriage ceremonies and festivities during the new planting season often provided the opportunity for a young man to seek out an eligible bride. Once a young man set his sights on a prospective bride, he approached his mother, who set the process in motion. The groom's mother's best friend normally served as the go-between, approaching the mother of the prospective bride, who was, however, allowed to reject prospective husbands for whom she had no liking or affection. As the bargaining over the bride-price progressed, the father of the bride was normally kept out of the picture until agree-

Upper half of a terra-cotta male figure wearing a necklace, bracelets, and a beaded belt, Owo, Nigeria, circa 1100–1500 (National Commission for Museums and Monuments, Nigeria)

ment had been reached between the go-between woman and the mother of the bride. In fact, once the bride's mother agreed to the proposal, the bride's father could do nothing to stop the union. His permission was only a formality. The family of the bride would then demand to be paid bridewealth or a dowry (what Europeans might call a dower) before the marital union could be finalized.

Bridewealth and Dowries. The bridewealth symbolized the unity of the two families in a lifelong relationship. It could be material in nature, such as goats, cattle, cowrie shells, gold and gold dust, and in more-recent times money, but service, such as labor on the bride's father's farm, was not uncommon. Even today among the Yoruba, a prospective groom can hire himself out for several years to the future bride's father, who decides when the young man has worked enough. Typically, the amount of the bridewealth was determined by the status of the bride's father and was often the subject of elaborate negotiations. The dowry was property held in trust by the bride's father, who was obligated to return it to his daughter's husband's family in cases of divorce. Payment of a dowry was far less common than bridewealth. Since they did not want their daughters to leave their households, most rich chiefs (such as those of the Okrika people) prevented such a loss by encouraging their daughters to remain in Igwe (small dowry) marriages, which kept the bride in her father's household and gave him claim to all children born of the union (who usually ended up working on his farm). Contrary to erroneous assumptions by some European scholars, bridewealth and dowry were not considered bride purchases. As Jack Goody observed in 1973, bridewealth and dowry may have had "'symbolic' aspects," but they were mainly "ways of redistributing property." For this reason, "they must always be seen in the context of the wider movement of property and its exploitation for productive and other social purposes."

Arranged Marriages. Typically, prospective mates developed a sort of affection before marriage. Arranged marriages in which the prospective spouse had no say in choosing their mate were not usually the norm in West Africa, except in Muslim cultures where some forms of arranged marriage existed. However, even in non-Muslim societies some marriages could be considered arranged. For example, a father might offer his daughter to a chief or king in return for a favor and status.

Sources:

George B. N. Ayittey, *Indigenous African Institutions* (Ardsley-on-Hudson, N.Y.: Transnational, 1991).

George Ellis, *Negro Culture in West Africa: A Social Study of the Negro Group of Vai-speaking People* (New York: Neale, 1914).

Jack Goody, "Bridewealth and Dowry in Africa and Eurasia," in *Bridewealth and Dowry,* by Goody and S. J. Tambiah (Cambridge: Cambridge University Press, 1973), pp. 1–58.

Goody and Esther Goody, "Cross-Cousin Marriage in Northern Ghana," *Man* (London), new series 1 (September 1966): 343–355.

Victor C. Uchendu, "Concubinage among Ngwa-Ibo of Southern Nigeria," *Africa* (London), 35 (April 1965): 187–197.

Kay Williamson, "Changes in the Marriage System of the Okrika People," *Africa* (London), 32, no. 1 (1962): 53–60.

ASPECTS OF MARRIAGE

The Role of Marriage. During the period 500–1590, West Africans practiced many forms of cohabitation. The institution of marriage was probably the most important means of cementing social relations between clans, preserving tradition and culture, and codifying social customs. As John S. Mbiti has observed,

> For African peoples, marriage is the focus of existence. It is the point where all members of a given community meet: the departed, the living and those yet to be born. All the dimensions of time meet here, and the whole drama of history is repeated, renewed and revitalized. . . . marriage is a duty, a requirement from the corporate society, and a rhythm of life in which everyone must participate. . . . Failure to get married under normal circumstances means that the person concerned has rejected society and society rejects him in return.

Many variations of marriage existed in ancient West Africa, and within different ethnic groups there were often several forms of multiple conjugality. Though there were instances of monogamous arrangements within the context of the extended family, polygamy was generally the norm, and it had two distinct forms: polygyny (in which a husband had more than one wife) and polyandry (in which a wife had more than one husband).

Polygyny. In ancient West Africa polygyny was common among Muslims and non-Muslims alike. One factor contributing to the prevalence of polygynous marriage in the region was a demographic distribution in which there were more women than men. Other factors that favored polygyny included common pregnancy and child-rearing practices. In general, West African women were expected to abstain from sex during pregnancy and the three-year period in which they nursed each child. While a nursing wife was unavailable for sex, a man was likely to take another wife to satisfy his sexual needs. In some instances, as a way of guarding against infidelity, nursing wives themselves brought other women into their homes to provide sexual favors for their husbands. Junior wives in polygynous family units were assigned to older wives, who served as mentors and assigned them tasks within the family unit. Each wife usually had her own living quarters; the most senior wife supervised sexual or sleeping arrangements with the husband. Children in polygynous units were raised in a communal atmosphere, with older wives having overall authority over their upbringing. In matrilineal polygynous families, the oldest female exerted even greater authority, making decisions about property rights and rules of consanguinity.

Polyandry. In some regions, it was also acceptable for a woman to take more than one husband or at least to have sexual relationships with more than one man. Polyandry was often practiced in matrilineal cultures. First daughters of chiefs in southeastern Nigeria were particularly encouraged to engage in polyandrous relationships. Because it was customary that these women should remain at home to look after their mothers in old age, these young women were encouraged to bring home men for copulation and sexual pleasure. Children born to these sexual partners belonged to the matriarch. If an eldest chief's daughter decided to marry and leave the family unit, she was required by tradition to bring into the household another woman to care for her mother. Polyandrous arrangements also took other forms. For example, a woman in a polygynous family unit might have a sexual affair with a man outside the family if she confided in and received permission from the most senior wife. To some extent polyandry was influenced by economic considerations. For example, many well-to-do chiefs or other socially powerful individuals encouraged their daughters to engage in polyandrous relationships as a means of increasing the size of the labor force

Terra-cotta funeral statuettes of a wife and husband, Komaland (modern Ghana),
circa 1200–1600 (Musée Barbier-Mueller, Geneva)

available to work their farms. In such cases, the children usually belonged to the woman's father, not their biological father. Among the Okrika people of southeastern Nigeria, Igwe (small dowry) marriage also ensured this sort of family arrangement. Among the Vai people of the Gambian region, women routinely moved from village to village without their husbands' permission for temporary sojourns in lovers' compounds. Even when a women in exogamous marriages visited their maternal villages, they were known to carry on sexual relations with men there during the duration of their sojourns. Examples of this practice were found among the Idoo tribe of western Ivory Coast.

Monogamy. The practice of having one wife or one husband was rare in West Africa. The choice between polygamy and monogamy was usually determined by the economic status of the man. A poor man who could not afford to support more than one wife usually remained in a monogamous union, but if his economic situation improved, he would often take additional wives. Property relations also influenced the choice of monogamy, espe-

cially when it came to the rights of property inheritance. Yet, in ancient West Africa, where the concept of private property was different from that of modern Western cultures, there was little social basis for monogamy.

Sources:
George B. N. Ayittey, *Indigenous African Institutions* (Ardsley-on-Hudson, N.Y.: Transnational, 1991).

George Ellis, *Negro Culture in West Africa: A Social Study of the Negro Group of Vai-Speaking People* (New York: Neale, 1914).

Jack Goody, "Bridewealth and Dowry in Africa and Eurasia," in *Bridewealth and Dowry,* by Goody and S. J. Tambiah (Cambridge: Cambridge University Press, 1973), pp. 1–58.

Goody and Esther Goody, "Cross-Cousin Marriage in Northern Ghana," *Man* (London), new series 1 (September 1966): 343–355.

John S. Mbiti, *African Religion and Philosophy* (New York & Washington, D.C.: Praeger, 1969).

Peter J. Paris, *The Spirituality of African Peoples: The Search for a Common Moral Discourse* (Minneapolis: Fortress Press, 1995).

Victor C. Uchendu, "Concubinage among Ngwa Ibo of Southern Nigeria," *Africa* (London), 35 (April 1965): 187–197.

Kay Williamson, "Changes in the Marriage System of the Okrika People," *Africa* (London), 32, no. 1 (1962): 53–60.

ATTITUDES TOWARD SEXUALITY

Privacy. Sexuality was considered a private matter and was seldom discussed in public. It was unacceptable for a person to express sexual desire by caressing or kissing someone in a public place. Parents waited until their children were ready to marry before they discussed sex and sexual pleasure with them. In most Muslim cultures sex was rarely discussed in the presence of unmarried family members, and women expressing sexual pleasure openly might be considered evil or loose. When the issue of sex did come up, the discussion was generally restricted to procreation.

Menstruation. Once a young woman reached the age at which she began to menstruate, her contacts with men were severely restricted. Like other phenomena that were not immediately explainable by common sense, menstruation was seen as the work of evildoers or "witches" and inspired fear in young women. Especially if menstruation lasted beyond its normal duration or the blood flow was unusually heavy, her mother or aunt might employ the services of magic or medicine men whom they believed were capable of expunging evil spirits that witches might have implanted in the young woman. A woman who was menstruating was not allowed to make direct contact with medicine men, or men with similar powers, because such contacts were presumed to bring bad luck to the community, which could come in the form of bad harvests, deaths of loved ones, or even wars. Generally, for the entire duration of their menstruation, women were socially and physically isolated. Sex during menstruation was considered an abomination and was severely punished.

Virginity. While sexual intercourse was not treated as "dirty" or "bad" in traditional African cultures, there were taboos associated with it. In most of these cultures, virginity was extremely important for young women. Most unmarried women were required by custom to refrain from sexual intercourse until the first night of married life, and in some cultures divorced adults were also expected to remain celibate until they remarried. On the first night of her marriage a first-time bride was required to prove to her husband that she had not had previous sexual encounters with other men. In some cases, she was required to bring a white sheet to the bedroom on her wedding night. If the groom came out of the room later with a bloody sheet, his new wife's innocence was demonstrated and was rewarded with an elaborate celebration. Her father would be held in high esteem for bringing up his daughter with authority and diligently enforcing the clan customs. If a young woman had lost her virginity before her wedding night, her mother, not her father, was blamed for shaming the family, and both mother and bride risked being exiled from the village. The family of a bride who had lost her virginity before her wedding also had to return to the groom's family all the gifts that were given as bridewealth. In societies where she was not exiled outright, the law

WIDOW INHERITANCE

In non-Muslim West Africa, widow inheritance was an age-old practice, especially among ethnic groups in southwestern Nigeria and Ghana. On the death of her husband, a widow became the wife of an eligible member of her late husband's family, usually a brother or cousin of the deceased. In some cases where the deceased had more than one wife, the older son might be eligible to inherit one of his father's wives, especially the younger ones. Widow inheritance had very little to do with property rights. In both ancient and modern African societies, marriage was seen, and is still seen, as the establishment of symbolic relations between two families. In endogamous marriages, that is, marriages where the spouse belonged to the same clan, widow inheritance was thus seen as a recognition of the continuation of the sacred link between two families. In an exogamous situation, that is, when the woman came from a different clan than that of her husband, the rules of inheritance would be different. Among the Okrika people of southeast Nigeria, a widow in an Igwe (small dowry) marriage, in which the dowry had not been fully paid, could not be inherited by a relative of her husband. By the rules of Igwe marriage, she had to be returned to her family once her husband was deceased. A woman in an Igwu (big dowry) marriage had to remain in her husband's clan, and she was likely to be inherited, especially if she was still capable of bearing children. At death, she had to be buried in her deceased husband's compound. It should be emphasized that there are regional variations regarding widow inheritance. Each clan had specific rules and customs that guided widow inheritance.

Source: Paul Bohannan and Philip Curtin, *Africa and Africans* (Prospect Heights, Ill.: Waveland Press, 1995), pp. 71–72.

required that the disgraced bride had to return to her father's compound in shame. A woman so disgraced was unlikely to find another suitor. She would either remain single for the rest of her life or become one of the concubines that rich men turned to for sexual favors. Because of this rigid emphasis on virginity, sexual intercourse was treated with utmost respect. During dating, little physical contact was allowed between prospective grooms and brides, and they were strictly forbidden to have sexual relations. Any contact between a courting couple took place in the presence of adults, mostly older women.

Illegitimate Children. Rules and moral attitudes regarding children born out of wedlock differed from one society

Bronze plaque of three young men, Kingdom of Benin, Nigeria, circa 1500–1600 (Ethnological Museum, Berlin)

to another. During early times it was more accepted than later in the period 500–1590. Generally, having illegitimate children was not condoned. Except in certain cultures, such as the Okrika people of southeast Nigeria, children born to unmarried mothers were rarely kept within the family, particularly in patrilineal descent groups, where the son stood to inherit from his father. In such groups children who were born out of wedlock were either taken to the village of the mother's father or sent to nearby villages as servants or slaves. In matrilineal descent groups, however, the matriarch usually kept illegitimate children in the family unit as her own children. In other cultures, children born out of wedlock were kept within the family unit but were automatically accorded subordinate or inferior status. A woman who had a child out of wedlock was usually subjected to abuse and isolation. She lost her social ranking among her age group and could not join the ranks of married women in the village during important celebrations. Depending on the way she became pregnant, she might also be exiled from the village. If her pregnancy was the result of sexual intercourse with a husband who subsequently rejected her because she was not a virgin when he married her, the members of her family, and the clan in general, might be sympathetic to her plight. However, if such a pregnancy was the a result of "looseness" or rape (which was rare), it would result in automatic expulsion unless the rape was not

directly the woman's "fault." Women who had children born as a result of incest were required, together with their mother and possibly other related siblings, to move entirely away from the village.

Concubinage. Concubinage, which was widespread in West Africa during the years 500–1590, is the practice of keeping several women as sexual partners outside the family unit. Even today, many West African men have concubines. If a man's wife were unable to produce a male child, then he was allowed by tradition to have extramarital affairs with other women, some of whom might eventually become his wives. A man could also take a concubine if his wife did not satisfy him sexually. In most West African cultures, male children were considered essential to perpetuate the family name and tradition. A woman's failure to bear a male child was considered sufficient reason for the man to bring another woman into the family. In ancient times, concubines performed the same functions as wives but were not allowed to take part in family ceremonies and gatherings. However, male children born to concubines had the same rights as all other children. Indeed, though illegitimacy was socially stigmatized later in this period, it was not during early times. The practice of keeping many concubines could elevate a man's social status and be seen as proof of his wealth. Widows who could not remarry and women of lower status usually formed the pool of women from which men drew their supply of concubines.

Prostitution. There is no evidence of the existence of brothels in West Africa during the period 500–1590. While rich men did indeed engage the services of unwed women for sexual pleasures in return for economic support, these women might eventually qualify as wives, especially if a relationship resulted in the birth of children. In such cases the man would be expected to bring the woman home as a wife. With increasing contacts between native Africans and Arab traders from the north, however, prostitution began to emerge in urban centers, where these traders spent weeks if not months waiting for their wares to be traded or sold. This sort of prostitution existed only during trading seasons. Men who had sexual intercourse outside marriage normally underwent purification rituals. Muslim traders were particularly likely to perform such rituals, which were required by their religion.

Homosexuality. Homosexuality was not considered a socially accepted form of sexual practice in most parts of West Africa. However, it did exist. Among pastoral and cattle-herding cultures, some forms of male bonding can generally be considered homosexual in nature. In cattle-herding tribes, young men spent several months each year searching for pasture for their herds. Because they spent such a long time away from the village, many of these herders developed bonding mechanisms that involved sexual touching, especially mutual masturbation. During initiation ceremonies a young adult man was usually placed in the care of a village elder, with whom he spent several weeks in the forest. During this period, sexual contact between the older male and the inductee was considered an essential part of the initiation ceremony. In other nonpastoral cultures, especially among the Yoruba in the southwestern part of modern Nigeria, male bonding, which usually involved touching and holding of hands or the wrapping of one's arms around a male friend's waist, was common and generally not viewed as sexual contact. Women bonded more often than men. It was not unusual for two unmarried women to lie down together, caressing one another in an intimate way as an expression of friendship. Usually this practice stopped once the women were engaged and ready to take on the responsibilities of grown women. While homosexuality was publicly frowned on, it was often practiced privately, especially between adult men and young boys. Hausa and Fulani elders in northern Nigeria and elsewhere in northwestern Africa, especially Mali and northern Ghana, were known to keep young boys as servants to satisfy their homosexual desires.

Sources:

George B. N. Ayittey, *Indigenous African Institutions* (Ardsley-on-Hudson, N.Y.: Transnational, 1991).

Yaya Diallo and Mitchell Hall, *The Healing Drum: African Wisdom Teachings* (Rochester, Vt.: Destiny Books, 1989).

F. Ivan Nye and Felix Berardo, *The Family: Its Structure and Interactions* (London: Macmillan, 1973).

W. N. Stephens, *The Family in Cross-Cultural Perspective* (New York: Holt, Rinehart & Winston, 1963).

Victor C. Uchendu, "Concubinage among Ngwa-Ibo of Southern Nigeria," *Africa* (London), 35 (April 1965): 187–197.

BIRTH CONTROL AND PREGNANCY

Birth Control. During the period from 500 to 1590, birth control was not usually a concern for West Africans. A man's social status and masculinity were often measured by the number of children he fathered. Bringing children into the family was important because they were needed to work on the family farm. Birth-control methods were used, however, especially when crop failure caused extreme famine or when giving birth might jeopardize a woman's life. Among the Yoruba, when a woman consistently gave birth to stillborn babies or infants who died shortly after they were born, she was considered a bearer of evil, and as such, she might be expected to practice birth control.

Methods. Women were taught to be aware of changes in their bodies during the menstrual cycle. In some cultures, a woman who wanted to avoid pregnancy might use locally produced contraceptive medicines or insert a sponge in her vagina before sex when she felt she was most likely to conceive. Knowledge of different birth-control methods was passed on from older women to younger girls before they reached puberty and began menstruation. However, it should be stressed that since sex before marriage was strictly forbidden, birth control for young unmarried

women was rarely an issue. Women who wanted to avoid pregnancy could also abstain from sexual intercourse. By custom most nursing mothers were not allowed to engage in sexual intercourse until lactation stopped, and breast feeding generally lasted for more than three years. The general belief was that a woman's breast milk might be polluted by sexual intercourse. In situations where women refrained from having sexual intercourse, their husbands were free to enter into sexual relationships with other women. Abortion was not an option because aborted children were believed to haunt the entire village.

Pregnancy. In some West African cultures, viewing the body of a pregnant female was taboo. Generally, a young and unmarried woman exhibited her physical beauty by going about her chores with only the lower part of her body covered, but a pregnant woman was prohibited from showing her naked body, especially her protruding stomach. The various West African ethnic groups differed in their beliefs and customs regarding pregnancy. More than any other group, the Ijaw and Okrika people of southeastern Nigeria attached much sacredness to pregnant female bodies. In their tradition a woman whose husband died while she was pregnant had to be locked away from the public until she gave birth to her baby. She was allowed to come out of her isolation to perform certain chores, such as washing dirty pots and plates, and she could wash herself weekly in a nearby river or pond. While she was bathing, no man was permitted to view her pregnant body. Any man who did so by accident was required to pick up a small stone or pebble and throw it at the woman. If the stone landed on her stomach, he had to take the woman as his wife. When born, the child belonged to the trespassing man. In other cultures, it was believed that exposure of the body during pregnancy might invite ghosts or evil spirits to enter the body and replace the unborn baby.

Sources:
George B. N. Ayittey, *Indigenous African Institutions* (Ardsley-on-Hudson, N.Y.: Transnational, 1991).

Yaya Diallo and Mitchell Hall, *The Healing Drum: African Wisdom Teachings* (Rochester, Vt.: Destiny Books, 1989).

F. Ivan Nye and Felix Berardo, *The Family: Its Structure and Interactions* (London: Macmillan, 1973).

W. N. Stephens, *The Family in Cross-Cultural Perspective* (New York: Holt, Rinehart & Winston, 1963).

CHILD BIRTH AND CHILD REARING

The Birth of a Child. In premodern African culture the birth of a child was greeted with jubilation. Indeed, childbirth was considered the most important event in family life. Older female family members were usually responsible for delivering babies, and the procedure was often less cumbersome and uncomfortable than modern birthing methods. Hardly any medication was used during pregnancy, and most pregnant women continued their usual day-to-day work. When a pregnant woman went into labor, she was secluded in a room with her husband's mother, his aunt, and the senior wife of her husband. By tradition these women were required to witness the labor. When the delivery time came, an experienced midwife was called to take over the birthing process. Through experience, the midwife could determine when the baby would arrive and if there might be complications in the delivery. Few difficult births are recorded in historical sources. Experienced female family members helped the midwife deliver the baby. By tradition men were generally not allowed to witness the delivery of a child, nor were they permitted to view the woman's naked body while she was in labor. Women suspected of practicing witchcraft were also not allowed near a woman in labor for fear that they might use their powers to complicate the delivery process or bewitch the unborn baby. After the delivery the child was immediately handed to the husband's mother, who performed a ceremony before the child was shown outside the household. Because evil spirits were believed to be ever present during labor, she appeased them with a libation once the child was successfully delivered. By custom, men were also included in the ceremony that followed the birth of a baby, and the child's father was expected to give a feast for all members of the clan in recognition of the powers of womanhood. In some African cultures, especially the Yoruba, the new mother had to remain secluded from the rest of the family until the final naming rites for her baby were performed, usually seven to nine days after its birth. Until then she was also forbidden to eat foods that contained salt, pepper, or palm oil; she was given only foods

that were supposed to purify her body. These foods were cooked without salt or palm oil and might include a soup made with white cornmeal and special herbs. According to historical sources, death from complications in labor was quite rare, perhaps because of the expertise of the older women responsible for delivery. In situations where the pregnancy was complicated, these women sometimes sought the help of medicine men, who performed rituals aimed at easing the birth process.

Delivery Complications. If the birth of the child involved complications, the mother was not allowed to see the baby until the older women had ascertained the reasons for the problems. This investigation could be a reason for postponing the naming ceremony until such time that the elders decided that it was safe to hold it. Among the Ijaw people of southeast Nigeria, children born to mothers who had severe labor pains were generally thrown into a river or pond in the hope of ensuring that no misfortune was brought upon the village. If the child surfaced, it was retrieved and brought back to the village. If it did not, it was left to drown. These practices were abolished with increasing modernization. A child whose mother died at birth was likely to be adopted by her sister, if the husband's family agreed. Otherwise, the baby might be kept by the husband's mother or, in a polygamous marriage, by one of his senior wives.

Breast Feeding. In most cases lactating biological mothers breast-fed their children. In cases where the mother was physically or mentally unable to do so, any lactating adult woman in the family, or in a nearby compound could be asked to nurse the baby. Breast feeding usually lasted for a period of three years or more.

Child Rearing. It was the duty of all members of the extended family to participate in the rearing of children. The communal approach was the norm in West Africa during 500–1590, and it is still common in most parts of West Africa. Older male members of the family, including the biological father and the child's paternal uncles, usually played the paternal role. However, crucial decisions regarding proper upbringing and the transmission of values were made by older members of the family, especially older women, whose authority was based on their knowledge of the history and the tradition of the clan. Examples of this practice were found among the Ewe people of Ghana and the Idoo ethnic group in western Ivory Coast. Among the Bambara group in Mali, and the Susu and Malinke people of the Senegambian region, child rearing was a responsibility of all adult clan members, including the older men.

Child's Play and Role Socialization. In ancient West Africa, children as young as three or four engaged in the work of clearing fields and picking fruit for the family. It is difficult to classify the child's day-to-day activities as either work or play because the two were not mutually exclusive. In general, boys followed their fathers and uncles on hunt-

TWINS

Twins (Ibeji) were sometimes considered harbingers of future events. Before colonial contact, cases of infanticide involving twins were recorded, especially among the Kalabari in southeast Nigeria. In that culture, twins were treated as omens of evil that would soon befall the village. To prevent this fate, one of the twins was killed in sacrifice to the gods or ancestors of the village. With modernization and increasing contact with other cultures, this practice stopped long ago. Indeed, among the modern Yoruba, families take pride in having twins. Men were once encouraged to eat yams in the belief that they increased the libido and the ability to father twins, and women who wanted to have twins were told to carry wooden effigies of twins on their backs. Women who repeatedly gave birth to twins were accorded the greatest respect within the family.

Source: J. D. George, "Historical Notes on the Yoruba Country and Its Tribes," Colonial Papers, National Archives, Ibadan, Nigeria.

Terra-cotta statue of a mother and her children, Djenné, Mali, circa 1150–1400
(Collection of Count Baudouin de Grunne, Belgium)

HOW TWINS CAME AMONG THE YORUBA

The following folktale explains why the Yoruba revere twins as signs of good will from the gods.

In ancient times in the town of Ishokun, which later became a part of Oyo, there was a farmer who was known everywhere as a hunter of monkeys. Because his fields produced good crops, monkeys came from the bush and fed there. The monkeys became a pestilence to the farmer. He tried to drive them away. But they came, they went, they returned again to feed. The farmer could not leave his fields unguarded. He and his sons took turns watching over the fields. Still the monkeys came and had to be driven away with stones and arrows.

Because of his desperation and anger the farmer went everywhere to kill monkeys. He hunted them in the fields, he hunted them in the bush, he hunted them in the forest, hoping to end the depredations on his farm. But the monkeys refused to depart from the region, and they continued their forays on the farmer's crops. They even devised ways of distracting the farmer and his sons. A few of them would appear at a certain place to attract attention. While the farmer and his sons attempted to drive them off, other monkeys went into fields to feed on corn. The monkeys also resorted to juju. They made the rain fall so that whoever was guarding the fields would go home, thinking, "Surely the crops will be safe in such weather." But the monkeys fed while the rain fell. When the farmer discovered this he built a shelter in the fields, and there he or one of his sons stood guard even when water poured from the sky. In this contest many monkeys were killed, yet those that survived persisted.

The farmer had several wives. After one of them became pregnant an adahunse, or seer, of the town of Ishokun came to the farmer to warn him. He said, "There is danger and misfortune ahead because of your continual killing of the monkeys. They are wise in many things. They have great powers. They can cause an abiku child to enter your wife's womb. He will be born, stay a while, then die. He will be born again and die again. Each time your wife becomes pregnant he will be there in her womb, and each time he is born he will stay a while and then depart. This way you will be tormented to the end. The monkeys are capable of sending you an abiku. Therefore do not drive them away anymore. Cease hunting them in the bush. Let them come and feed."

The farmer listened, but he was not persuaded by what the adahunse had told him. He went on guarding his fields and hunting monkeys in the bush.

The monkeys discussed ways of retaliating for their sufferings. They decided that they would send two abikus to the farmer. Two monkeys transformed themselves into abikus and entered the womb of the farmer's pregnant wife. There they waited until the proper time. They emerged, first one then the other. They were the original twins to come among the Yoruba. They attracted much attention. Some people said, "What good fortune." Others said, "It is a bad omen. Only monkeys give birth to twins."

Because the twins were abikus they did not remain long among the living. They died and returned to reside among those not yet born. Time passed. Again the woman became pregnant. Again two children were born instead of one. They lived on briefly and again they departed. This is the way it went on. Each time the woman bore children they were ibejis, that is to say, twins. And they were also abikus who lived on a while and died.

The farmer became desperate over his succession of misfortunes. He went to consult a diviner at a distant place to discover the reason for his children's constantly dying. The diviner cast his palm nuts and read them. He said: "Your troubles come from the monkeys whom you have been harassing in your fields and in the bush. It is they who sent twin abikus into your wife's womb in retaliation for their suffering. Bring your killing of the monkeys to an end. Let them eat in your fields. Perhaps they will relent."

The farmer returned to Ishokun. He no longer drove the monkeys from his fields, but allowed them to come and go as they pleased. He no longer hunted them in the bush. In time his wife again gave birth to twins. They did not die. They lived on. But still the farmer did not know for certain whether things had changed, and he went again to the diviner for knowledge. The diviner cast his palm nuts and extracted their meaning. He said, "This time the twins are not abikus. The monkeys have relented. The children will not die and return, die and return. But twins are not ordinary people. They have great power to reward or punish other humans. Their protector is the orisha Ibeji. If a person abuses or neglects a twin, the orisha Ibeji will strike such a person with disease or poverty. He who treats the twins well will be rewarded with good fortune." The diviner again threw the palm nuts and read them. He said, "If the twins are pleased with life, good luck and prosperity will come to their parents. Therefore, do everything to make them happy in this world. Whatever they want, give it to them. Whatever they say to do, do it. Make sacrifices to the orisha. Ibeji. Because twins were sent into the world by the monkeys, monkeys are sacred to them. Neither twins nor their families may eat the flesh of monkeys. This is what the palm nuts tell us."

When the farmer returned to Ishokun after consulting the diviner he told his wife what he had learned. Whatever the twins asked for, the parents gave it. If they said they wanted sweets they were given sweets. If they said to their mother, "Go into the marketplace and beg alms for us," the mother carried them to the marketplace and begged alms. If they said, "Dance with us," she carried them in her arms and danced.

They all lived on. The farmer's other wives also gave birth to twins. Prosperity came to the farmer of Ishokun and his family. He was fortunate in every way.

Because of their origin twins are often called edun, meaning monkey. Likewise they are referred to as adanjukale, meaning "with-glittering-eyes-in-the-house." The first of a set of twins to be born is considered the younger of the two. He is named Taiyewo, meaning "Come-to-Taste-Life." The second to be born is named Kehinde, meaning "Come-Last." He is the older of the two. It is said that Kehinde always sends Taiyewo ahead to find out if life is worth living.

It was the ancient confrontation with the monkeys at Ishokun that first brought twins into the world.

Source: Harold Courlander, "How Twins Came Among the Yoruba," in his *Tales of Yoruba Gods and Heroes* (New York: Crown, 1973).

ing trips, carrying dummy weapons, and in the process picked up hunting skills. After returning from such trips, they imitated the adults in front of others in their age group. While this activity could be classified as play, it was also training for necessary adult work. Toys as modern people know them were not common then. Available boys' toys were generally carved of wood and included slingshots for chasing birds away from the farm or bows and arrows made for purposes of play and training for future combat. Girls played with clay pots, with which they assisted their mothers in fetching water. Smaller versions of household utensils were also made as toys for young girls to play with when their mothers or older sisters were using the full-sized implements. It was also a common practice for young girls to carry wooden baby dolls on their backs all day long as a preparation for motherhood.

Boys' Initiation Rituals. Initiation practices were extremely important to the traditional family. In most parts of West Africa the transition to adulthood required elaborate ceremonies and rite-of-passage rituals. The exact nature of the initiation rituals differed from region to region. Among some ethnic groups, such as the Malinke and Bambara, boys who were coming of age were usually housed together in the forest, near the main compound, for two to three weeks. During this period, they slept in the forest and were visited by older male clan members, who prepared them mentally and spiritually for the ordeal they were to undergo, which in some cases included genital mutilation or circumcision. (Among the Yoruba, circumcision was performed just after an infant's ninth day.) During this time in the forest the boys bonded with each other, creating a mutual support group to face their upcoming transition to adulthood. Once the ceremony was performed, the young men were permitted to set up their own huts in preparation for a new transition to married life.

Girls' Initiation Rituals. Initiation ceremonies for girls were similar to those for boys and generally took place when girls were about to marry. The most difficult part of the ritual for girls was circumcision, which varied by region. It might be restricted to clitoral excision, but in extreme cases the labia were sewn together, leaving only an opening entry for sexual intercourse. Among the Yoruba, clitoral excision was normally performed when the child was only seven days old. Other tribes of the region delayed circumcision to a later time in the child's life. In only a few instances was circumcision performed after the boy had reached adulthood or the female had reached puberty.

Sources:

William Fagg, *Divine Kingship in Africa* (London: British Museum, 1970).

Jack Goody, "Bridewealth and Dowry in Africa and Eurasia," in *Bridewealth and Dowry*, by Goody and S. J. Tambiah (Cambridge: Cambridge University Press, 1973), pp. 1–58.

Goody, *Comparative Studies in Kinship* (Stanford: Stanford University Press, 1969).

Goody, ed., *The Character of Kinship* (Cambridge: Cambridge University Press, 1973).

Hugo Huber, "Initiation to Womanhood Among the Se (Ghana)," *Nigerian Field*, 23 (July 1958): 99–119.

Huber, "Kinship terms and traditional form of marriage among the Se (West Africa)," *Anthropos*, 53, no. 5/6 (1958): 925–944.

Derrick J. Stenning, *Savannah Nomads: A Study of the Wodaabe Pastoral Fulani of Western Bornu Province, Northern Region, Nigeria* (London: Published for the International African Institute by Oxford University Press, 1959).

Victor Uchendu, "Concubinage among Ngwa-Ibo of Southern Nigeria," *Africa* (London), 35, no. 2 (1965): 187–197.

CHILDLESS AND UNMARRIED PEOPLE

Childlessness. The primary goal of marriage was bringing children to the family, lots of children. In ancient Africa children were considered assets to the family and the lineage in general. Most children above the age of four were put to work on the family farm, thereby increasing the wealth and economic standing of the family. Furthermore, most elderly parents relied exclusively on their children for economic support, so having large numbers of children was a means of ensuring comfort in one's old age, like investing

THE NAMING CEREMONY

The naming of a child was an occasion for all the members of a clan to come together to celebrate life. Unless there were complications in the delivery, the naming ceremony for a boy had to be performed within nine days of his birth. A girl's naming ceremony was usually performed within seven days.

On that day, all members of the clan or village had to be present to give their blessings to the newborn. Each immediate relative was required to come up with a name for the child, but the name given by the father's aunt was usually the name by which the child was known.

Some newborn babies were named after ancestors who had recently passed away or after particular events or occasions observed by the clan. Among the Ewe, a child was given the name of the day on which it was born. A male child born immediately after the death of an older male member of a clan was named after him, or as among the Yoruba in southwest Nigeria, he would be called *Babatunde*, which means "the father has come back." A girl born after the death of a matriarch or an aunt was named *Yeyetunde*, meaning "the mother has come back."

Source: O. Daramola and Jeje Adebayo, *The Customs and Gods of the Yoruba People* (Ibadan, Nigeria: Onibon Press, n.d.).

Mask worn during initiation ceremonies for a Mende
female society, Sierra Leone, sixteenth century
(Archives Monbrison, Paris)

uncles. Since maternal responsibilities were shared by all the women of a polygamous family, childlessness did not carry the sort of social stigma that it did in other familial systems. In some cultures, however, the body of a childless woman could not be buried in her husband's compound but was returned to her father's house, where her brothers presided over the funeral rites.

Unwed Women. While marriage was considered an important and necessary part of family life, there were some women who for one reason or another did not marry. In some cultures the first daughter of a chief did not usually marry, because she was expected by custom to remain in the household and look after her mother in old age. If a chief's eldest daughter did marry, she had to "replace" herself with another woman. This practice was not spread throughout all parts of West Africa, however; it was an exception to the rule. Other categories of women who remained unmarried included those who had difficulties finding a man because of their low social status, those whose families were subjects of taboos and stigmas that isolated them socially from the rest of the clan, or those whose husbands had rejected them for having lost their virginity prior to marriage. These women remained in the margins of the society and were forbidden from associating with married women during important events such as weddings or naming ceremonies. Their brothers or uncles monitored their activities in the community so that they would not bring further disgrace to the family. Their sexual contacts with men were kept secret, and if such a woman became pregnant, she was likely to be sent away from the village to take residence with close relatives elsewhere. Usually, if an unmarried mother were mentally ill, she and her infant were banished from the village, or her child was taken away and sent to distant relatives. If the child of an unwed mother did remain within the family unit, it most likely was looked down on and spent its life in a lowly status.

in a pension fund. Children were considered the pillar of any marital union, and bearing children established a woman as a welcome member of her husband's family. While childlessness was never regarded as the fault of a woman, in many cases it constituted a valid ground for divorce. Childlessness, which of course might have resulted from infertility on the part of either the man or the woman, was explained in various ways. In some cases childlessness or delayed procreation was blamed on some evil act the woman might have committed in a previous life. In other instances it was attributed to the work of "evil doers" in the family. A woman who was unable to give birth to children typically spent years and years looking for remedies from medicine men and sorcerers, but once all the avenues were exhausted she resigned herself to her fate. In many polygamous marriages, such a woman—if she were considered a "good" wife—was allowed to adopt children from fellow wives of her husband or from the wives of her husband's

Unmarried Men. It was not unusual for a clan to have a pool of unmarried men, whose marital status carried with it the same social stigma as it did for their female counterparts. There were several reasons why a man remained unmarried, including impotence and lack of means to support a family. Men who were not married by the usual age were not only rumored to be impotent, but they were most likely excluded from the activities of other men in their age group. These unmarried men were often ridiculed as possessing feminine characteristics, and other members of the clan avoided having social contacts with them. In some instances a family would employ the services of priests or medicine men to ascertain whether this particular problem was a consequence of sins the family had committed in the past. They often staged elaborate rituals to cure the man of his impotence or alleviate his supposed fear of the female sex. As a last resort, the unwed man might be sent away from his father's compound or village to take up residence with his mother's clan. A family was unlikely to express openly any suspicion that an unmarried male relative might have homosexual tendencies, because homosexuality would bring much greater shame on the family. An unmarried man was thus under constant pressure to prove his sexuality by taking a wife, and when he was financially unable to do so, members of his families would, as a matter of honor, raise the necessary money among themselves in order to put behind them the shame of harboring an unmarried male adult in their midst.

Sources:
George B. N. Ayittey, *Indigenous African Institutions* (Ardsley-on-Hudson, N.Y.: Transnational, 1991).

Yaya Diallo and Mitchell Hall, *The Healing Drum: African Wisdom Teachings* (Rochester, Vt.: Destiny Books, 1989).

F. Ivan Nye and Felix Berardo, *The Family: Its Structure and Interactions* (London: Macmillan, 1973).

W. N. Stephens, *The Family in Cross-Cultural Perspective* (New York: Holt, Rinehart & Winston, 1963).

DESERTION AND DIVORCE

Desertion. While desertion did not occur frequently during the period 500–1590, it did happen. Though a woman might leave her husband because of physical abuse, she brought shame to her family unless she was able to establish proof sufficient to constitute grounds for divorce. A woman who deserted her husband normally took refuge in her father's compound or village until her reasons for leaving her husband were established. If there were not sufficient evidence to justify her action, the woman's senior brothers or uncles immediately returned her to her husband's family. At this point the husband had the choice of taking her back into his household or rejecting her and asking for his dowry back. He was especially likely to do the latter if he had reason to believe that her desertion was a result of infidelity.

Infidelity. If a married woman eloped with a lover, her action was severely stigmatized, and she was subject to serious sanctions that might include the loss of her marital status and any claim to her children. The man with whom she eloped was either exiled from the village or humiliated through public flogging. Married men rarely deserted their families unless they committed acts that brought shame and dishonor to their relatives. While it was not unusual for a man to keep other women outside his household, he was unlikely to leave his family for any of these women. It was more likely that he might bring a mistress into the household and confer on her the status of wife.

Divorce. Divorce was rare but was allowed in some situations. Grounds for divorce could include physical and mental abuse and male impotence. Where dowry and bridewealth were involved, the woman could divorce her husband on any of these grounds by returning the dowry or bridewealth. If the husband refused to take it back, she could deposit it with the oldest member of the clan (or a

high chief), who in turn annulled the marriage according to established customs. In most African societies infidelity was rarely a reason for divorce because most adult males engaged in polygamous relationships.

Sources:
George B. N. Ayittey, *Indigenous African Institutions* (Ardsley-on-Hudson, N.Y.: Transnational, 1991).

Yaya Diallo and Mitchell Hall, *The Healing Drum: African Wisdom Teachings* (Rochester, Vt.: Destiny Books, 1989).

F. Ivan Nye and Felix Berardo, *The Family: Its Structure and Interactions* (London: Macmillan, 1973).

W. N. Stephens, *The Family in Cross-Cultural Perspective* (New York: Holt, Rinehart & Winston, 1963).

ECONOMIC ASPECTS OF FAMILY LIFE

The Functions of the Family. The family performed two basic functions: biological reproduction and economic maintenance of the family unit. Most family members performed assigned functions. Gender-based division of labor was more pronounced in some kinship groupings than in others. Men dominated agricultural production for the market, while growing food for the household and raising animals for noncommercial purposes were exclusively reserved for women. In patrilineal lineage systems some household functions were traditionally defined as female, and sexual division of labor was strictly enforced, but in matrilineal systems those divisions were not so clear-cut. For instance, men in matrilineal cultures dominated activities such as fishing, hunting, waging war, and goldsmithing. Yet, contrary to many scholars' assumptions, hunting was not exclusively reserved for men. In many regions of ancient West Africa, especially among the Ashanti of Ghana and the Ijaw and Urobo of southeast Nigeria, women were not excluded from hunting or farming. Gender-based divisions in these occupations developed along with modernization. Both male and female family members of the family carried out production inside and outside the home in a cooperative way. While men were generally engaged in production that led to accumulation of wealth, women were often limited to work that supported the day-to-day needs of the family.

Division of Labor. In general, women's reproductive functions did not restrict them to child rearing alone; they took an active part in economic activities that were geared toward the social and material well-being of the family. When women left the home for farmwork or other activities, they left their children with older family members, including men who were too elderly to farm or hunt. Among the Fulani and Hausa in old Mali and northern Nigeria, where cattle rearing was the basis of the economy, gender-based division of labor was more pronounced than in agricultural regions. In these cultures younger men spent several months together outside the village in search of good pastures for their cattle. The size of the herd a young man was able to tend in a given season was a major

Mother, child, and father, wooden figures from Bamana, Mali, circa 1200–1500. Left: The Metropolitan Museum of Art, The Michael C. Rockefeller Memorial Collection, Bequest of Nelson A. Rockefeller, 1979. (1979.206.121) Photograph, all rights reserved, The Metropolitan Museum of Art. Right: The Metropolitan Museum of Art, Gift of the Kronos Collections in honor of Martin Lerner, 1983. (1983.600a,b) Photograph, all rights reserved, The Metropolitan Museum of Art.

factor in his eligibility for a prospective bride. In these pastoral cultures, women stayed behind in the village, where they cared for the children, milked cows, and did agricultural work in the absence of the men. Younger women were primarily responsible for raising animals such as goats and fowl for domestic consumption.

Property Accumulation. While private ownership was not the norm, accumulation of property for the benefit of all members of the extended family was not uncommon. Most property was either used in exchanges with other tribes, especially during marriage negotiations, or for settling feuds. People also disposed of property during the ceremonial worship of ancestors. Indeed, one's social status was often measured by one's magnanimity in sacrificing possessions. With the growth of the urban centers and increasing diversification of production, women as well as men became involved in the exchange of commodities, which had the potential for increasing private accumulation, except where it was prohibited by tradition. Bartering could take place within the family or among different families or clans, with each group engaging in different spheres of production. Such activity also helped to sustain social relations among different family units and clans.

Reciprocity. Reciprocity, an ancient mechanism for property redistribution within the family unit, was common in most traditional West African societies, where the economy was at subsistence stage. The practice involved the sharing of property and goods among members of the family and lineage in accordance with established rules of gerontocracy, by which what one received was determined by one's age and personal needs, not by social standing. Generally, younger men and women tended the farm while somewhat older adults hunted for game. Whatever meat or produce the two groups brought back went into the community food bank. These goods were then distributed according to a set of standards laid down by elders who had since passed on to the world of the spirits. For example, older members of the lineage had first choice of whatever game was caught. It was against tradition for young men to keep game to themselves, and one who did so was treated with animosity by the other members of his age group. After all, the older members of the clan had at some earlier point in their life contributed to maintaining the family, and the younger age group would eventually retire from active work and enjoy the same preferential treatment as the present generation of the elderly. This knowledge that one would eventually move up the age ladder kept the sprit of selflessness alive among the younger generations.

Source:

Derrick J. Stenning, *Savannah Nomads: A Study of the Wodaabe Pastoral Fulani of Western Bornu Province, Northern Region, Nigeria* (London: Published for the International African Institute by Oxford University Press, 1959).

EDUCATION

The Role of the Elders. In traditional African societies, education of the young was largely the duty of the older women in the clan. Commonly called the wise elders, these women transmitted family history, agricultural lore, and other knowledge, norms, and values accumulated over time, playing an extremely significant role in the social perpetuation of the family unit. Basic education consisted primarily of passing on knowledge of family bloodlines and names of objects or totems that were sacred to the clan. The elders also trained young adults to identify plants and trees that had medicinal value. Before a young person reached puberty or the age of eligibility for rites-of-passage rituals, he or she had to have acquired this crucial knowledge of the social and natural forms that existed in unison in the universe. Usually this learning also prepared the younger members of the clan for the next level of education, ritual learning.

Ritual Learning. Ritual learning, which began early for young men, was taught by the older men in the village. Ritual training involved learning about the world of the elders and ancestors who had passed on to the world of the spirits. For a young man eligible for training as a priest, ritual education was lifelong. In traditional African societies, the natural world has always been explained with reference to taboos and magic. Any misfortune that could not be explained otherwise was regarded as a curse on the clan, which required immediate purification through the sacrifice of animals and, in some instances, clan members. Family or lineage members eligible to take part in this cleansing ceremony were highly regarded in the village, and their positions were hereditary. They usually came from long lines of people who were recognized as

CARE FOR THE MENTALLY IMPAIRED

Mental illness in ancient West Africa never had the same significance it has in modern cultures. Those who were mentally ill were not isolated or excluded from the family. Some mentally ill people were housed in a different part of the compound while they underwent treatment from medicine men, but they frequently came to the main house at mealtimes. Because mental illness was considered the gods' revenge for an act of "evil," treatment involved making sacrifices to the gods and the ancestors, which in many cases involved slaughtering goats, chickens, and other domestic animals. In cases where mental illness continued or recurred throughout a person's life, the family often began to overlook the affliction and to reintegrate the individual into the family.

Sources: Robert H. Nassau, "Fetishism in West Africa," *West African Mail*, 12 August 1904.

Kay Williamson, "Changes in Marriage System of the Okrika People," *Africa* (London), 32, no. 1 (1962): 53–60.

Page from an Arabic treatise on prosody by al-Suyuti (died 1505) and "The Poem of al-Khazaji," copied by
Muhammad al-Badmasi in Nupe, Nigeria (University of Washington, Collection of John O. Hunwick)

priests or chiefs and had sufficient knowledge of the history of the clan and its past mishaps. Anyone eligible to train as a priest spent most of his young and adult life living in the forest outside the village with an elderly priest, from whom he learned all the rudiments of the job. Young trainees were prohibited from having sexual intercourse until they had acquired a certain level of knowledge. Even after they married, many of them were prohibited from living in the same compound with their wives because of fear of pollution. Because of their position in the society, these men—and in some cultures, women—were supported by other members of the clan and received gifts from the chiefs. They also kept whatever was left over from sacrifices. When they died, they were buried in a special cemetery because of the belief that their souls were in perpetual search for a place to rest. Only trained members of the clan could carry out funeral rites and ceremonies, which could last several months.

Literacy. Few written records exist for West African kingdoms (except the Empire of Mali), and scholars have concluded that the level of literacy in the region was remarkably low. The elite were most likely to be literate, especially if they had sustained contact with outside traders. Elite converts to Islam became preoccupied with the need to read the Quran. The ability to read and interpret this Muslim holy book and other Islamic works was a requirement for individuals entering the class of Islamic scholars. Thus, it is not surprising that the level of literacy was higher in West African cultures where Islam had become the state religion than in cultures that still practiced traditional religions. In some Muslim regions formal schools were established for the study of Islamic texts, and graduates became *ulama'* (scholars of the Islamic religion and religious law). Literacy was sometimes discouraged as a pre-emptive measure against social unrest among the lower classes. In the non-Muslim states of Benin and the Yoruba kingdoms, literacy was restricted to the class of chiefs, who kept the palace history and recorded the ascendancy to the throne.

Oral History. In addition to literacy, competence in oral history could earn high status for an individual. Griots and marabou (oral historians and poets) were often employed by kings to give performances during celebrations of important events such as the celebration of the queen mother's birthday. In the western Sudanic region, the griots travel from one place to another, singing the praises of the kings and emperors in return for favor and means of subsistence. The existence of such traveling performers/educators was sometimes a source of concern for rulers because these oral historians were commoners and had contacts with disgruntled members of society who might challenge the authority of the king.

Sources:

George B. N. Ayittey, *Indigenous African Institutions* (Ardsley-on-Hudson, N.Y.: Transnational, 1991).

Yaya Diallo and Mitchell Hall, *The Healing Drum: African Wisdom Teachings* (Rochester, Vt.: Destiny Books, 1998).

William N. Stephens, *The Family in Cross-Cultural Perspective* (New York: Holt, Rinehart & Winston, 1963).

Carle C. Zimmerman, *Family and Civilization* (New York: Harper, 1947).

FESTIVALS

Festivals. West African communities marked many important occasions with elaborate religious or harvest rituals. Among ethnic groups of the forest and savanna regions each day of the year was set aside for the celebration of a particular god. The Yoruba had more than 365 gods, including one for each day of the year. In their cosmology there existed a universal god known as Olodumare, who created these 365 lesser gods and sent them to earth to bring love and peace to the earth's children. A family might choose to worship one or more of these lesser gods. During festivals devoted to them, animals such as goats and dogs were sacrificed to appease the gods. Dancing was also an important feature of these celebrations, which could last for several days. On rare occasions, when a medicine man considered it necessary for the general good of the clan, humans were offered in sacrifice. Usually individuals who had been taken as prisoners of war, these people were by tradition blindfolded and led into the deep forest, where they were killed according to a sacrificial ritual.

Harvest Festivals. Africans believed that the lesser gods acted through the ancestors to create good or bad harvests. Thus, it was imperative to appease these gods at the beginning and the end of each growing season. Before the bush

Chi Wara dancers at an agricultural festival in Mali, 1971; members of a centuries-old Bamana initiation association, the dancers are wearing headdresses representing male and female antelopes (Eliot Elisofon Photographic Archives, National Museum of African Art, Washington, D.C.)

was cleared for planting, medicine men and other qualified individuals poured libations in recognition of the power of the ancestors who had passed away. Feasting and dancing accompanied this ceremony, and once medicine men gave their approval, planting began. In the event of a bumper harvest, the ceremony was repeated, and if the harvest did not turn out as expected, there was an even a more elaborate ceremony to appease the gods.

Other Ceremonies and Libations. During harvest period, the Yoruba celebrated the new yam crop with an elaborate yam festival. The Igbo ethnic group in southeast Nigeria had a pragmatic approach to the worship of the gods. Every member of the clan had two gods—a *chi* (small or personal god), and *Chukwu* (the village, or big, god). Before Igbo men or women left their houses to go to the market and sell their goods, they prayed to their *chi* for good sales, and if they sold everything and returned home happy, they poured libations on their *chi*. But if they did not do well at the market, they threw their *chi* out the window and created another one as its replacement.

Sources:

George B. N. Ayittey, *Indigenous African Institutions* (Ardsley-on-Hudson, N.Y.: Transnational, 1991).

Yaya Diallo and Mitchell Hall, *The Healing Drum: African Wisdom Teachings* (Rochester, Vt.: Destiny Books, 1998).

F. Ivan Nye and Felix Berardo, *The Family: Its Structure and Interactions* (London: Macmillan Press, 1973).

W. N. Stephens, *The Family in Cross-Cultural Perspective* (New York: Holt, Rinehart & Winston, 1963).

FUNERALS AND BURIAL CEREMONIES

Rituals for Young People. In Africa, as in other cultures, a death in the family was probably the most painful experience for the members of the clan. The death of an elder called for an elaborate celebration, which in some instances—as in the Yoruba culture—might last for several months. When a younger family member died, however, the cause of death was investigated. If the medicine men determined that the person did not die of natural causes, the village had to embark on elaborate rituals to ascertain who was responsible for the untimely death. The dead body was left for several days while the village performed rites to ensure that the dead person would come back to avenge his death. Then the body was buried outside the family land with an object such as an ax or a knife attached to the corpse. People believed that the dead person would arise on the seventh day after his burial and be ready to take on whoever caused his untimely death. People who committed suicide were not allowed to be buried near the village. Their corpses were often transported at night into the deep forests, where it was believed they would assume a new life as a ghost or evil spirit. The bodies of suicides were treated with extreme caution. Only qualified medicine men were assigned to perform the burial rites while women, younger men, and children were prohibited from viewing the dead body.

Artist's reconstruction of a burial at Igbo-Ukwu, Nigeria, circa 700–1000 (from Peter Garlake, *Kingdoms of West Africa*, 1978; illustration by Roger Gorringe)

Funerals for the Elderly. The death of a person considered old was regarded as a good thing. When elders passed away, they were not considered dead in the traditional sense; that is, people believed that these elders had gone to the world of ancestors or the spirits, from which the ancestors were supposed to protect members of the family who were still living. The corpses of elderly chiefs or high priests were displayed publicly for days in anticipation of their return as spirits. After medicine men reported their arrival to the family, funeral rites began in earnest. The bodies were generally buried in front of the family compound or inside the house, where their spirits took up residence with the rest of the family. In ancient Ghana and in the Yoruba kingdom, when an *oba* (king) died, he was buried with servants to help their master on his journey. Effigies of deceased *obas* were carved from wood and erected outside the palace as reminders of their continued existence, and they ultimately became shrines where the family worshiped yearly during important ceremonies. Believing that the ancestors would bring success, people carried their effigies into battle. The Vai ethnic group of Senegambia and the Idoo of the western Ivory Coast also had elaborate ceremonies in preparation for burying an elder. In some instances, a burial could not be performed until war had been declared on adjoining villages and captives had been brought into the compound of the deceased. In recognition of the life of the deceased and his or her social status, some of the captives might be sacrificed in the belief that they would accompany the dead one to the world of the spirits.

Sources:

George B. N. Ayittey, *Indigenous African Institutions* (Ardsley-on-Hudson, N.Y.: Transnational, 1991).

Yaya Diallo and Mitchell Hall, *The Healing Drum: African Wisdom Teachings* (Rochester, Vt.: Destiny Books, 1989).

George Ellis, *Negro Culture of West Africa* (New York: Neale, 1914).

Robert H Nassau, "Fetishism in West Africa," *West African Mail,* 12 August 1904.

F. Ivan Nye and Felix Berardo, *The Family: Its Structure and Interactions* (London: Macmillan, 1973).

W. N. Stephens, *The Family in Cross-Cultural Perspective* (New York: Holt, Rinehart & Winston, 1963).

DOCUMENTARY SOURCES

Ibn Battuta (1304 – circa 1378), *Rihlah* (Travels)—The journals of a wide-ranging North African Muslim traveler, who visited the Empire of Mali in 1353, recording perhaps the best historical account of West Africa during that period. Ibn Battuta documented social events, recorded his observations on the economy, trade, and society, and wrote pointed descriptions of the Africans, their culture, and their devotion to kings, family, and clan.

Muhammad Abdul Karim al-Maghili, *The Growth of Religion Concerning the Obligations of the Princes* (circa 1470)—An Islamic advice manual commissioned by the Sultan Sarkin Muhammad Rumfa of Kano, who ruled Hausaland between 1463 and 1499; the book deals with the organization of social life, family, politics, and rulers' relationship to their subjects in accordance with the teachings and prophecies of the Prophet Muhammad. It details the relationship of the husband to his wives and children, as well as his obligation to Islam and Islamic values.

Ibn Khaldun (1332–1406)—*Kitab al-'ibar* (The Book of Historical Lessons)—A seven-volume universal encyclopedia of world history, which includes information about the rulers of the Mali Empire and the Almoravids' spread of Islam in the region. The book describes how the Almoravids ravaged the land, plundered West Africans' property, and imposed a poll tax on them.

Gomes Eanes de Zurara (circa 1410 – 1473 or 1474) *Chronica do descobrimento e conquista de Guiné* (History of the Discovery and Conquest of Guinea)—An account of the activities of Portuguese explorers in West Africa up to 1448 and their relationships with West African royalty and Arab traders; Zurara relied heavily on the diaries of the Portuguese prince known as Henry the Navigator (1394–1460).

CHAPTER NINE

RELIGION AND PHILOSOPHY

by EMMANUEL CHUKWUDI EZE with PIERRE-DAMIEN MVUYEKURE

CONTENTS

Sidebars and tables are listed in italics.

IMPORTANT EVENTS OF 500-1590

600*
- The hub of formal religious and philosophical life in West Africa is Kumbi, capital of the Ghana Empire, founded around 400. By this date the empire is a conglomeration of diverse kingdoms and cultures, and its religions include African traditional religions, Islam, and syncretic forms of traditional religions and Islam.

1000*
- Ghana is at the peak of its imperial power.

1054
- Almoravid Berbers from North Africa invade Ghana, capturing the important oasis market town of Audaghost. Puritanical, fundamentalist Muslims, the Almoravids quickly subdue various regions of Ghana over the next two decades, forcing local leaders to convert to their radical version of Islam. As a result, indigenous African religions are suppressed.

1076
- The Almoravids complete their conquest of Ghana. The empire splits into small splinter states, which are effectively under the control of an Islamic empire. The indigenous rulers of Mande and Songhai are forced to convert to Islam as a condition for retaining some of their original powers. Islam spreads to the Yoruba lands of present-day Nigeria, as well as deeper into the mass cultures of Mali and the surrounding Mande territories.

1203
- Susu forces drive the Almoravids from Kumbi, the capital of the old Empire of Ghana.

1230-1235
- A new leader, Sundiata, emerges to lead the Mande peoples in the foundation of a new empire—the Empire of Mali—from the remnants of the old Empire of Ghana. Though he professes to be a Muslim, Sundiata, who rules until 1255, creates a new political, cultural, and religious synthesis that blends foreign and native practices. The resulting religious pluralism includes syncretic movements that blend the competing faiths of Islam and traditional religions into new harmonies.

1420
- Prince Henry the Navigator of Portugal begins sending out expeditions to explore along the western coast of Africa. By the time of his death in 1460, Henry has been so successful in the propagation of Christianity (as well as the promotion of European commerce) around the world, including West Africa, that the Pope has awarded him the title General of the Order of Christ.

1434
- Gil Eannes becomes the first Portuguese explorer to navigate successfully the treacherous waters around Cape Bojador (in present-day Western Sahara, south of the Canary Islands), opening the way for European exploration of West Africa.

* DENOTES CIRCA DATE

IMPORTANT EVENTS OF 500-1590

1444
- Portuguese mariners take African captives to the Algarve in southern Portugal to serve as slave labor on sugarcane plantations.

1455
- Pope Nicholas V issues the Bull Padroado (also known as the Writ of Portugal), a legal document that, without consultation with Africans, grants the Portuguese sovereign, supreme, and complete authority over all African kingdoms.

1468
- Sunni Ali captures the major trading city of Timbuktu, marking the end of the declining Empire of Mali and the rise of a Songhai Empire to take its place.

1471
- Portuguese explorers reach what becomes known as the Gold Coast, the southern coast of West Africa, and establish a settlement at São Jorge da Mina, later called Elmina (in the modern nation of Ghana), in the gold-mining district along the West African coast.

1482
- The Portuguese build Elmina Castle, which becomes a major slaveholding fort. With this settlement the missionary drive to convert West Africans to Christianity intensifies. The origins of the radical Christianization and Europeanization of the African mind and culture date to this period.

1485
- By this date Portuguese traders and missionaries have become firmly established along the Gold Coast and have begun to expand their religious and commercial activities further east—as far as the ancient Kingdom of Benin, in present-day Nigeria. Missionary activities increase in succeeding decades.

1500-1590
- Other strong West African states rise to compete with the Songhai Empire, notably Bornu, which reaches the peak of its power in the 1580s, during the reign of the devout Muslim Idris Alooma, who controls the political and religious life of the African peoples living around Lake Chad.

1518
- Spanish slave traders ship the first African slaves to the West Indies.

1562-1564
- Englishman John Hawkins makes two slaving expeditions to West Africa.

1590
- Muslim forces from Morocco invade the Songhai Empire, completing their conquest in 1591. Spanish and Portuguese mercenaries collaborate with Moroccan invaders to destroy Timbuktu and other West African centers of learning. Such incursions of Muslims and Christians in the region have begun to spark new religious tensions and syntheses.

* **DENOTES CIRCA DATE**

OVERVIEW

Historiographical Context. Western-influenced scholars often divide West African history into "precolonial," "colonial," and "postcolonial" periods. Others divide it into "traditional" and "modern" eras demarcated by the arrival of western Europeans, who brought with them Christianity and modern science—ignoring the much earlier arrival in West Africa of Islam and Arabic learning that in many instances was more advanced than the scholarship of Europe during the same period. While these familiar classifications may be valid for studying many aspects of West African history, they are not particularly helpful for the investigation of the origins and evolution of religion and philosophy in West Africa. Unlike politics and economics, for example, religion and philosophy were the aspects of West African life most resistant to change. Peoples' religious views and folk philosophies were not automatically transformed along with changes in government and economic systems or the arrival of new religious influences. For example, when a West African ruler was forced to convert to Islam or Christianity, his subjects' religion and cultural mentality did not undergo an equally profound change, and, when they did change, the transformation occurred over a long period of time. Because religious and intellectual traditions evolve slowly, the neat division of West African history into precolonial, colonial, and postcolonial—or traditional and modern—is analytically limiting. While some aspects of a society may be (or appear to be) modern, others may still be traditional, and while some aspects of a society may have undergone a postcolonial transformation, others might still be precolonial or colonial.

Rejecting Classifications. Traditional classifications of African history often lead to excessive Arabocentrism or Eurocentrism. European historians once called sub-Saharan Africa a "Dark Continent," revealing their lack of knowledge about the ancient and medieval peoples of East, West, and Central Africa. Many of these writers—including philosopher Georg Wilhelm Friedrich Hegel in the nineteenth century—were familiar only with the Islamized parts of North Africa and relied on secondhand—or even

further removed—accounts of peoples and cultures in other parts of the continent. Even as late as the 1960s, Hugh Trevor-Roper, an Oxford University history professor, told his students not to ask him for lectures on African history because no such history existed. As he wrote in *The Rise of Christian Europe* (1965), "Undergraduates, seduced, as always, by the changing breath of journalistic fashion, demand that they should be taught the history of black Africa. Perhaps, in the future there will be some African history to teach. But at present there is none, or very little: there is only the history of Europeans in Africa. The rest is darkness . . . and darkness is not a subject of history." Views such as this one are the result of too much reliance on Arabic and European sources and not enough primary research in West African sources. By the final decades of the twentieth century, historians and archaeologists had learned much about the complex civilizations that existed in West Africa between 500 and 1590, cultures whose religious and philosophical traditions have deep indigenous roots.

Geographical and Cultural Backgrounds. The major, or most representative, religious beliefs or philosophical traditions of West Africa include those of the ancient empires of Ghana, Mali, Songhai, and Kanem-Bornu; the Hausa states Gobir, Daura, Kano, Katsina, Zaria, and Biram (most in present-day Nigeria); Ashanti kingdoms such as Fante (all in contemporary Ghana, Togo, or Liberia); the Yoruba states of Oyo and Ile-Ife (also in Nigeria); the kingdoms of Benin and Dahomey; and the Igbo federations of Onitsha, Nri, Enugu, and Nsukka (in Nigeria and Cameroon). This list of states and peoples is not exhaustive, but it does provide a cross section of basic West African religious and ethnophilosophical worldviews. They represent the diverse religious and intellectual manifestations of West African peoples in all parts of the region and over the long period of time between 500 and 1590.

African Traditional Religions. Though the traditional religions and philosophical orientations of West Africans are sometimes characterized as *indigenous*, that term is misleading. Most elements of West African traditional religions, even before the relatively modern arrivals of Islam and Christianity, may have roots in other ancient religions—including those of ancient Egypt and Nile cultures such as Meroe (the capital of ancient Ethiopia) and Kush (in the Upper Egypt); Mesopotamia (between the Tigris and Euphrates, in present-day Iraq); and Asia Minor. Cultural interactions among these areas of the world can be documented as far back as biblical times. Archaeological, linguistic, and philological studies by scholars from diverse national and ethnic backgrounds—including the Cameroonian Engelbert M'veng, the Senegalese Cheikh Anta Diop, the Congolese Théophile Obenga, the British R. E. Bradbury, and the Nigerian Jacob Egharevba—show that certain elements of religious beliefs and rituals that continue to exist even today in West Africa may have origins in, or derivation from, Pharaonic Egypt. It is also true that religious practices and philosophical ideas originating in West Africa have enriched Egyptian, Asiatic, and Judeo-Christian cultures. Terms such as *native* and *foreign* may therefore be used only with the understanding that they are historically relative.

Religion, Politics, and Economics. It is often difficult to separate the religious practices of West African empires and states from the spheres of politics and commerce. Some empires and kingdoms were founded in the name of religions or sects. Examples of such religiously motivated states include the Sanhaja Confederacy, which had its capital at the oasis city of Audaghost. This empire was created in the eleventh century by the Almoravids, a radical North African Islamic sect bent on spreading what it considered an unadulterated form of Islam. Despite its religious motivation, this powerful Islamic confederacy controlled not only the religious beliefs of the people but also—through its domination of major trade routes—the political and economic life of the region.

The Survival of Traditional Religions. The Arab-Islamic and European-Christian influences in West Africa intertwined imperial or colonial political ambitions and economic motives with the missionary zeal to propagate Islam or Christianity. Indigenous African cultures—especially ritual arts and music—were suppressed. At various times both Islamic and Christian agents competed in their efforts to displace indigenous African modes of thought.

Both used military force or economic incentives to convert not just the African rulers but also the masses. It was common, for example, for agents of either Islam or Christianity to use the political instrument of state to punish Africans who clung to their ancestral beliefs. Suppressed African rituals included the libation, ritual animal sacrifices, and the consecration of individuals as *osu* ("slaves") to various deities. The fact that some of these indigenous religious practices still exist is evidence of their resilience in the minds and the lives of the people.

The Religious Context of Philosophy. The study of the historical development of philosophy in any culture must recognize its backgrounds in religious, or quasi-religious, worldviews or myths, and it is difficult to separate philosophy from its religious roots. Though they are related, however, philosophy and religion are quite distinct. Most practitioners and theologians of West African traditional religions believe that religion is the true source—and perhaps the only source—of wisdom. Such adepts and religious thinkers may believe that submission to Olorun, Chukwu, Allah, or Jesus is the supreme act and source of knowledge. Through beliefs (dogmas) and ritual practices (worship), believers are supposed to work at bringing their minds and souls closer to God and their conduct closer to a moral ideal established by the given religious system. One way of distinguishing philosophy from religion is to say that philosophy, unlike religion, is not dogma or worship. Instead, philosophy is a formal process of reflection and argumentation aimed at rationally illuminating one or several aspects of the human experience. While philosophy so characterized does not exclude religious experience, it is not required for philosophical thought. Religion emphasizes faith and rituals. Philosophy emphasizes freedom of thought and logical reasoning. Religious truths may be forms of hidden wisdom sought through prophecy, oracles, and divination. Philosophy relies on reasoned justifications provided for or against a particular explanation or interpretation of experience. Whereas the religious person seeks salvation of the soul through proper belief and conduct, the philosopher, with or without the religious commitment, attempts to make plain the claims of reason on any dimensions of experience—including the claims of reason on reason itself.

TOPICS IN RELIGION AND PHILOSOPHY

AFRICAN TRADITIONAL RELIGIONS: FUNCTIONARIES

Religious and Political Leaders. The heads of the West African traditional religions are often powerful kings. Among the Yoruba, for example, the Ooni of Ile-Ife in Nigeria, the traditional religious center of the Yoruba people, is believed to be the political as well as spiritual head of all the Yoruba. The Yoruba religions trace the common origins of their beliefs to the same god, who is believed to have created the first humans. The secret power of all creation, the fount of divine knowledge, is invested in the Yoruba sacred book, the verses used in Ifa divination. The Ooni is considered an authoritative guardian of the Ifa, including the clerical system. A similar hierarchical system also existed among the Fon and the Igbo. The high priest of Vodon, Da Ayido Hwedo, is also the political leader of the Fon people. Among the Igbo, where monarchies are rare, the Onyishi, the oldest member of the council of elders, is also invested with religious authority. In consultation with the council, the Onyishi sets the religious calendar for the community and ensures that the necessary sacrifices are made at the appropriate times. The Onyishi is thus regarded as the religious and spiritual father of his clan or the village, and as such he is responsible for its political and spiritual welfare. He is also obligated to attend all public religious ceremonies.

Priests. Priests are regarded as intermediaries between other humans and specific deities. A priest serves a particular god or spirit and watches over the behavior and needs of its adherents. An elder member of a lineage group may be the priest of the clan's ancestral cult. A secret society may have its own priest, and a priest may also serve the guardian spirit of a compound or village. Yoruba Babalawo and Igbo Dibia serve both as doctors and as ascertainers of the unknown. They employ magical techniques to determine the causes of misfortune, illness, or death, and they sometimes call on spirits to give them knowledge about a life sit-

uation or guidance in the execution of an important office. Their magical techniques often involve the "throwing" of objects such as bones or beads and "reading" a message from the patterns in which they fall. Another form of divination involves killing a chicken and examining its entrails to obtain the information sought. In some cases diviners also have extensive knowledge of herbal remedies, which they use in treating illnesses. Divination often requires rigorous training—sometimes up to ten or fifteen years. In some societies women diviners serve as midwives, using their herbal knowledge and magical resources in the promotion of conception, the treatment of infertility or other ailments, and the delivery of babies.

Rainmakers. Other important functionaries include the rainmakers. In agrarian societies, where rain is important for good crops, the rainmakers' task is to use their herbal and magical knowledge not only to insure sufficient rainfall throughout the year but also to stop the rains if flooding threatens. Their services may also be called on to help a patron who has scheduled an important outdoor function, such as a coronation, funeral, or wedding ceremony. Rainmakers seek to manipulate the environment in meteorologically consequential ways (such as burning wood) or through more occult techniques involving sacrifices to a god or spirit thought to bring rain or stop rain. These activities may be performed at shrines, but most often they take place in the location threatened by drought or flooding.

Sources:
Wade Abimbola, ed. and trans., *Ifa Divination Poetry* (New York: NOK, 1977).

Andrew Apter, *Black Critiques and Kings: The Hermeneutics of Power in Yoruba Society* (Chicago: University of Chicago Press, 1992).

Ulli Beier, ed., *The Origin of Life and Death: African Creation Myths* (London: Heinemann, 1966).

Norman R. Bennett, *Africa and Europe: From Roman Times to National Independence,* second edition (New York: Africana, 1975).

Herbert M. Cole, *Mbari: Art and Life among the Owerri Igbo* (Bloomington: Indiana University Press, 1982).

Bronze plaque of Yoruba priests, Kingdom of Benin, Nigeria, circa 1500–1700 (British Museum, London)

J. B. Danquah, *The Akan Doctrine of God: A Fragment of Gold Coast Ethics and Religion,* second edition (London: Cass, 1968).

Basil Davidson, *West Africa Before the Colonial Era: A History to 1850* (London & New York: Longman, 1998).

Cheikh Anta Diop, *The African Origins of Civilization: Myth or Reality,* translated by Mercer Cook (Chicago: Lawrence Hill, 1974).

Diop, *Civilization or Barbarism: An Authentic Anthropology,* translated by Yaa-Lengi Meema Ngemi, edited by Harold J. Salemson and Marjolijn de Jager (Brooklyn, N.Y.: Lawrence Hill, 1991).

Diop, *Precolonial Black Africa: A Comparative Study of the Political and Social Systems of Europe and Black Africa, from Antiquity to the Formation of Modern States,* translated by Salemson (Westport, Conn.: Lawrence Hill, 1987).

Jacob U. Egharevba, *The City of Benin, Benin Law and Custom, Some Stories of Ancient Benin,* [and] *Some Tribal Gods of Southern Nigeria* (Nendeln, Liechtenstein: Kraus Reprints, 1971).

Marcel Griaule and Germaine Dieterlen, *Le Mythe Cosmogonique* (Paris: Institut d'Ethnologie, 1965).

Joseph E. Harris, *Africans and Their History,* second edition, revised (New York: Meridian, 1998).

Constance B. Hilliard, *Intellectual Traditions of Pre-Colonial Africa* (Boston: McGraw-Hill, 1998).

John Iliffe, *Africans: The History of a Continent* (Cambridge & New York: Cambridge University Press, 1995).

Edmund Ilogu, *Christianity and Igbo Culture* (Leiden: Brill, 1974).

Arthur Glyn Leonard, *The Lower Niger and Its Tribes* (London & New York: Macmillan, 1906).

John Mbiti, *Introduction to African Religion* (London: Heinemann, 1975).

John D. Murphy and Harry Goff, *A Bibliography of African Languages and Linguistics* (Washington, D.C.: Catholic University of America Press, 1969).

P. Amaury Talbot, *Life in Southern Nigeria: The Magic, Beliefs, and Customs of the Ibibio Tribe* (London: Macmillan, 1923).

Rems Nna Umeasiegbu, *The Way We Lived: Ibo Customs and Stories* (London: Heinemann, 1969).

CENTERS OF RELIGIOUS ACTIVITY

Geographical Locations. Geographically the West African locations in which practitioners of traditional religions were the most active between 500 and 1590 include Nri, Ile-Ife, Oyo, Dahomey, Benin, Ouida, and Nsukka. Centers for Islam or Christianity included Ashanti, Mali, Kanem-Bornu, and Igbo-Ukwu.

Nri. Considered the "Mecca" of Igbo religions, Nri (in present-day Nigeria) was home to and ruled by the most-respected and most-feared Dibia—clerics, healers, diviners, and rainmakers. People came from far away to consult them, and Nri priests were also known to travel long distances, sometimes for months and years, to practice their crafts. The most renowned deity in Nri was called the Long Juju.

Ile-Ife and Oyo. The Yoruba believe that they are descendants of Oduduwa, sometimes believed to be a prince who came from the east and settled in Ile-Ife in western Nigeria. From Ile-Ife, it is believed, the children of Oduduwa spread in several directions to found empires and kingdoms, including Oyo, which at its height stretched from the Niger River to Benin on the east, to the sea on the south, and to Dahomey in the Republic of Benin on the west.

Dahomey. Dahomey was the center of Vodon, which spread as "Voodoo" through the transatlantic slave trade to parts of the Western Hemisphere, particularly Brazil, Haiti, Jamaica, and Louisiana.

Benin. The ancient Kingdom of Benin (in present-day Nigeria) was, like Ile-Ife, a center of culture and learning, religion, and the arts. Its people developed elaborate rituals surrounding birth, marriage, funerals, ancestors, and the afterlife. Legend has it that the people of Benin needed a good king, so they invited King Oduduwa of Ile-Ife to send them one of his sons. Believing that only a "son of the soil" would make the best ruler for Benin, one of Oduduwa's sons, Oranmiyan, married a woman from Benin with the purpose of fathering a king. The child of this union was Eweka, who became the first oba of Benin. The Benin people, like the Yoruba from whom they claim descent, were practitioners of traditional African religion. Islam had little or no influence in this region. Portuguese Christian missionaries who arrived in the 1400s had limited success as well.

Ouida. Located in the present-day Republic of Benin, Ouida is the headquarters of the well-known Vodon shrine of the sacred python, representing Damballah, the deity of fertility and knowledge. It was also a major port for exporting slaves from the West African coast to the Americas.

Nsukka. The annual Omaba Festival, which was celebrated at harvest season to honor Ani, the goddess of plenitude, had its shrine in Nsukka (in present-day Nigeria). As early as the 1500s, the month-long rituals and trade activities attracted pilgrims from great distances.

Kanem-Bornu. Flourishing around Lake Chad and the western parts of the Nile Valley, the Kanem-Bornu Empire was ruled as early as the twelfth century by leaders who declared themselves Muslims. Yet, according to Arab historians of the empire, the peoples of Kanem-Bornu did not immediately become Muslims. In the traditional religion of the Kanuri people of Kanem the king was revered as a divinity and believed to have some sort of divine control over life and death, and health and sickness. For these reasons, even for some time after the rulers had officially converted to Islam, the king was secluded from the public to maintain the necessary reverence for, and distance from, his terrifying power. The king appeared in public only once a year, and even then he was hidden behind a mask so that his people could not see his face. By 1194, Islam had been established in this empire. Mosques were built, and the Quran (Koran) was introduced. This change was mainly the result of contacts with Arab scholars and traders, which intensified between 1194 and 1221 when fighting with neighbors, internal revolts, and fratricidal strife weakened the empire and made it vulnerable to invaders from Bulala. By 1386, Mai (king) Abdullah ibn Umar had moved what was left of his kingdom to Bornu. By the thirteenth century the Bornu Empire, which had risen to dominate the Kanem-Bornu region, was entirely Muslim in religion and systems of thought, and its Muslim warrior-kings were actively involved in empire building.

The Hausa Kingdoms. The Hausa kingdoms of Gobir, Daura, Katsina, Zaria, Kano, Rano, and Biram were geographically located between the Empires of Songhai and Kanem-Bornu. These Hausa states were each dominated by a main city, often of the same name as the kingdom. Mostly in present-day Nigeria, some of these cities still exist. Although the states were never united into one empire, there is ample evidence of frequent mutual cooperation in actions against common non-Hausa enemies. Most of these cities followed African traditional religions until about 1400, when Islamic religion and thought systems became a dominant—and unifying—force.

Akan. Now located in the southern part of the modern nation of Ghana, as well as adjacent areas of Côte d'Ivoire and Togo, the Akan peoples, who include the Ashanti, migrated to their present location from the north between 1000 and 1700. The Akan were followers of traditional religions, until Islamic and Christian influences entered the region in the early 1300s and the 1400s respectively.

Mali. The long-lived Empire of Mali was founded around 1235–1240 by the great warrior-king Sundiata and endured until the rise of the Songhai Empire in the 1460s. Sundiata and the subsequent rulers of Mali were Muslims. Yet, Sundiata is also reported to have practiced traditional religion, and the people of his empire adopted Islam more

THE OLDEST ANIMAL

The Akan trickster god Ananse, called Kwaku (uncle) Anansi in the following translation, is usually depicted as a clever and articulate spider able to outwit not only animals and humans but also other deities. In the following folktale Ananse prevails not through magic or trickery but through his ability to tell a good story.

It happened one time that the animals of the fields and the forest had a great argument about which of them was the oldest and entitled to the most respect. Each of them said, "I am the oldest." They argued at great length, and at last they decided to take the case before a judge. They went to the house of Anansi, the spider, and they said to him: "Kwaku Anansi, we are in dispute as to which of us is the most venerable. Listen to our testimony."

So Anansi called his children to bring him a cashew shell, and he sat on it with great dignity, as though he were a chief sitting on a carved stool.

The guinea fowl was the first to speak. He said: "I swear it. I am the oldest of all creatures. When I was born, there was a great grass fire. Since there was no one else in the world to put it out, I ran into the flames and stamped them out with my feet. My legs were badly burned, and as you can see, they are still red."

The animals looked at the guinea fowl's legs and saw it was true: they were red. They said: "Eeee! He is old!"

Then the parrot declared: "I swear it. When I came into the world, there were no tools and no weapons. It was I who made the first hammer that was ever used by blacksmiths. I beat the iron into shape with my beak, and it is for this reason that my beak is bent."

The animals looked at the parrot's beak, crying out, "Eeee! The parrot is old indeed!"

Then the elephant spoke: "I swear it. I am older than the parrot and the guinea fowl. When I was created, the Sky God gave me a long and useful nose. When the other animals were made, there was a shortage of material, and they were given small noses."

The animals examined the elephant's nose and shouted, "Eeeeee! The elephant is truly old!"

The rabbit gave his testimony then, saying: "I swear it. I am the oldest. When I came into the world, night and day had not yet been created."

The animals applauded the rabbit. They said, "Eeeeee! Is he not really the oldest?"

The porcupine spoke last, and he said: "I swear it. As you will all have to admit, I am the oldest. When I was born, the earth wasn't finished yet. It was soft like butter and couldn't be walked upon."

This was great testimony, and the animals cheered the porcupine. They cried, "Eeeeee! Who can be older than he?"

Then they waited to hear Anansi's judgment. He sat on his cashew shell and shook his head, saying: "If you had come to me first, I would have saved you this argument, for I am the oldest of all creatures. When I was born, the earth itself had not yet been made, and there was nothing to stand on. When my father died, there was no ground to bury him in. So I had to bury him in my head."

And when the animals heard this they declared, "Eeeeee! Kwaku Anansi is the oldest of all living things! How can we doubt it?"

Source: Harold Courlander, "Anansi Proves He Is the Oldest," in his *The Hat-Shaking Dance and Other Ashanti Tales from Ghana* (New York: Harcourt, Brace, 1957).

---

slowly than the royal court. When the North African Muslim traveler Ibn Battuta visited Mali in 1353, Muslim practices were much in evidence, but Islam had not entirely replaced traditional religions.

Igbo-Ukwu. Located in southeastern Nigeria, Igbo-Ukwu was a pre-Islamic and pre-Christian center of commerce and urbanization. In digs at the site of this city, archaeologists have found sophisticated ritual objects that suggest a major religious renaissance took place there during the 1000s. Some of these objects are associated with cults of the king, who must have been considered a god or a descendant of the gods. According to John Iliffe, bronze artifacts found in Igbo-Ukwu were made from local metals in African styles and demonstrated "superb technical skill that was both distinctive and arguably unequaled elsewhere in the world at the time." The symbolism of these objects, especially their animal motifs, is remarkably similar to that used by the Igbo people of the area a thousand years earlier. Yet, digs at Igbo-Ukwu also show that by the year 1000 West Africa was no longer isolated from the rest of the world. Among the excavated objects were more than one hundred thousand glass beads, some probably from Egypt or India.

Sources:

Andrew Apter, *Black Critiques and Kings: The Hermeneutics of Power in Yoruba Society* (Chicago: University of Chicago Press, 1992).

Sandra T. Barnes, ed., *Africa's Ogun: Old World and New*, expanded edition (Bloomington: Indiana University Press, 1989).

Norman R. Bennett, *Africa and Europe: From Roman Times to National Independence*, second edition (New York: Africana, 1975).

K. A. Busia, *The Challenge of Africa* (New York: Praeger, 1962).

W. Walton Claridge, *A History of the Gold Coast from the Earliest Times to the Commencement of the Twentieth Century*, 2 volumes (London: Murray, 1915).

Herbert M. Cole, *Mbari: Art and Life among the Owerri Igbo* (Bloomington: Indiana University Press, 1982).

J. B. Danquah, *The Akan Doctrine of God: A Fragment of Gold Coast Ethics and Religion*, second edition (London: Cass, 1968).

Basil Davidson, *West Africa before the Colonial Era: A History to 1850* (London & New York: Longman, 1998).

Cheikh Anta Diop, *The African Origins of Civilization: Myth or Reality*, translated by Mercer Cook (Chicago: Lawrence Hill, 1974).

Diop, *Civilization or Barbarism: An Authentic Anthropology*, translated by Yaa-Lengi Meema Ngemi, edited by Salemson and Marjolijn de Jager (Brooklyn, N.Y.: Lawrence Hill, 1991).

Diop, *Precolonial Black Africa: A Comparative Study of the Political and Social Systems of Europe and Black Africa, from Antiquity to the Formation of Modern States*, translated by Salemson (Westport, Conn.: Lawrence Hill, 1987).

Joseph E. Harris, *Africans and Their History*, second edition, revised (New York: Meridian, 1998).

John Iliffe, *Africans: The History of a Continent* (Cambridge & New York: Cambridge University Press, 1995).

Arthur Glyn Leonard, *The Lower Niger and Its Tribes* (London & New York: Macmillan, 1906).

John D. Murphy and Harry Goff, *A Bibliography of African Languages and Linguistics* (Washington, D.C.: Catholic University of America Press, 1969).

Roland Oliver, *The African Experience: From Olduvai Gorge to the 21st Century* (London: Weidenfeld & Nicolson, 1999).

P. Amaury Talbot, *Life in Southern Nigeria: The Magic, Beliefs, and Customs of the Ibibio Tribe* (London: Macmillan, 1923).

Rems Nna Umeasiegbu, *The Way We Lived: Ibo Customs and Stories* (London: Heinemann, 1969).

CULTS AND RITUALS

Choice and Aims. Whether they practice Igbo, Yoruba, Akan, or other West African traditional religions, believers take part in remarkably similar rituals—just as one finds similar rituals among the many denominations of Christian churches or among the various sects of Islam. During the years 500–1590—and in the present day—West Africans could choose which of the several gods and cults best suited their needs. Thus, even the people of a single culture group might worship different gods.

Choosing a Deity. Believers want to influence the intentions of a divinity in order to secure protection for themselves, their families, and possessions; to obtain blessings of spiritual, emotional, and material plenitude; to give praise and thanksgiving to the gods when such blessings are received; or to appease any gods who might have been offended. A pressing personal or familial need might influence one's choice of which god to worship. While some gods are considered expert at healing a particular illness, others might be inept at the same job. While one god might be reputed to be especially attentive to prayers and sacrifices, another might be considered intransigent and uncompromising and thus would be chosen only when he or she is considered the only one capable of solving a particular problem. For example, the Igbo lightning god,

Amadioha, and the Yoruba lightning god, Shango, are often considered powerful but temperamental deities. While ordinarily kind and gentle, they can be extremely exacting in their demands both on themselves and on devotees who wish to emulate the intellectual and moral clarity with which the gods are associated. Among the Igbo, diviners and healers (Dibia) take as their deity the god Agwu, known as a master or custodian of knowledge. Like Esu among the Yoruba or Ananse among the Akan, however, Agwu is also a trickster god, who can reveal or hide knowledge from those who seek it.

Cults. Other professions also have their own patron gods. Some gods are perpetual patrons of certain trades, so that anyone belonging to a trade guild automatically gives allegiance to its god-protector. Among the Yoruba, Ogun is the patron god of metal fabricators, such as iron smiths, and those whose trades indirectly depend on the use of metal equipment, such as hunters and warriors. Such an allegiance did not require a professional to venerate his patron deity exclusively.

Secret Societies. Throughout West Africa, there are "secret societies" that impart specialized knowledge exclusively to selected members. Unlike cults, these groups have both secular and religious functions. These groups are often custodians of important historical, literary, and professional knowledge that is essential to a community's understanding of its origins and how it governs itself. Initiations into these "secret" societies are often conducted in monastic seclusion and may include instruction in theology, history, politics, economics, law, medicine, and military strategy. The best known of these societies were founded in the capital cities of Benin, Ile-Ife, Dahomey, Nri, Mali, and Ashanti. Groups such as the Egbo Society among the Efik, the Ogboni among the Yoruba, and the Ngbe (Leopard) Society among the Igbo performed public functions such as collecting taxes, recording titles and deeds, serving as legislative advisers to the king, and sitting as panels of judges or juries. The Leopard Society was renowned for its expertise in mortuary science, its administration of mourning and burial rites, and its ceremonial drumming. The activities of the Egbo Society included maintenance of the Nsibidi (an ideographic form of writing believed to have been secretly learned from the Igbo), knowledge of which was crucial for clerical purposes such as the keeping of public financial and judicial records, as well as religious practices. The Leopard Society's symbol is *mboko*, a Nsibidi sign symbolizing the arrival of death.

Personal and Communal Gods. Some gods, known as *chi* or *ikenga*, are personal gods, but most other gods are communal. Thus, a family, clan, or entire ethnic group might have one or several gods that all the members of the group worship, either individually in times of individual need or collectively in times of communal need. In each case sacrifices and intercessions to the gods are mediated by

A priest in the 1930s paying homage to ancestral soapstone figures made circa 1100–1500, Esie, Nigeria
(photograph by H. V. Meyerowitz)

priests, who often also know how to practice divination in order to discover the nature of the problem (or blessing) so that the appropriate sacrifices can be made to the appropriate gods.

Gender Influences. Some gods are regarded as either male or female, and therefore often attract worshipers of the same gender. While clerical duties were often—but not necessarily—gender specific, nearly all West African religions did not develop rigid gender roles. Quite often men dress as women to worship a god presumed to have or like feminine attributes; and women dress in men's attire and play leading roles in the worship of deities believed to be masculine or to prefer masculine attributes.

Family Tradition. History and tradition also play a major role in one's choice of a god and cult. If one comes from a family that has always been devoted to a particular deity, the youngest members of the family often continue the tradition, especially if the family has experienced some sort of success. Worldly attainments are considered indications that the gods to whom one has professed allegiance have been attentive to one's needs. It is therefore not only natural but also prudent to continue the same ritual practice rather than risk offending the gods who have helped the family in the past by choosing a different, and perhaps

rival, deity or deities. (Rivalries—sometimes for reasons known only to the deities themselves—are not uncommon among West African gods.) A woman who marries into another family may also develop relationships with the gods of her husband. Yet, even after marriage she may be expected to return to her father's family annually to participate in a festival to the gods of her paternal clan.

Attracting Followers. A god may gain followers by various forms of revelation such as sending a signal to a person in a dream or by troubling the prospective believer until he or she consults a Babalawo and discovers that the misfortune or illness is caused by a god who needs the sufferer's attention. African traditional religions are not evangelistic, however, in the sense of proselytizing to gain converts.

Ancestral Practices. Ancestor "worship"—or, more accurately, veneration—is practiced in nearly all traditional West African religions. The spirits of the ancestors—especially of those forefathers and foremothers who are believed to have lived exemplary lives, as measured in terms of success in family life, wealth, and longevity—are considered active and functioning members of the community. In a society where individual and collective memory was preserved orally, elders were respected as bearers of the communal knowledge accumulated from a distant past and capable of providing insights into the present and the future. For the ancestors, death was not so much a departure from the world of the living as a change of status within the social group. Their continuing spiritual and emotional relationship to the group is possible because in most African belief systems there is no sharp separation between the dead and the living. In fact, a dead ancestor is often referred to as the living-dead. These ancestors are believed to be in positions of guardianship and authority over the living. They must therefore be treated with honor and respect, an extension of the traditional values of respect for the elders and honoring the wisdom they have gained with age. The living-dead have achieved still more wisdom through association with other spirits in the abode of the gods. Yet, no known ancestral spirit commands as much respect as any of the gods. The power and authority of the ancestors seem to be derived from the gods. That is, ancestral spirits exercise influence within a certain domain (farming, fertility, or the arts, for example) according to, but never against, the will of a god with power over the same domain.

Libation. The living honored the ancestors by pouring a libation (paying homage by giving them the first "taste" of drink before the living consume it), by offering them sacrifices of kola nuts, chickens, goats, or cows (and in some rare but known cases, human beings—usually criminals or condemned war captives), and by thinking and acting in ways of which the ancestors would have approved. The authority of the dead over the living gave cohesion to the kinship group and often functioned as law and moral authority, as well as enforcing social and cultural norms of behavior.

Funeral Drumming. Among all West African peoples, the death of a member of the community is announced by "talking" drums that communicate information such as the name and age of the deceased; the names of his or her parents, children, and next of kin; and his or her village. This information tells the listeners where and by whom the loss must be most acutely felt and therefore those to whom condolence visits are due. The talking drums celebrate the life of the dead, thus flattering and soothing his or her spirit for a safe passage to the realm of the ancestors. Failure to undertake this passage could mean that the departed would remain as an angry or mischievous wandering and homeless spirit to plague its family and community. After firearms began appearing in West Africa in the fifteenth century, gun salutes began to be used when an important person died to warn evil spirits trying to thwart the deceased's passage to the land of the spirits that the dead man or woman was a distinguished person and should be honored.

Welcoming a Returned Ancestor. Sometimes an ancestor returns to the land of the living through reincarnation in one of his or her descendants. When such an event is believed to have occurred, it is announced by masquerades in which the living portray notable ancestors. According to Chinua Achebe, "The masked spirits who often grace human rituals and ceremonies with their presence are representative visitors from the spiritland and are said to emerge from the subterranean home through antholes. At least this is the story told to the uninitiated." These masked "spirits" are only symbolic ancestors. "But this knowledge does not in any way diminish their validity or the awesomeness of their presence."

Magic. Magic was an important element of traditional religions. Magic could be used to do good or harm and was considered effective against or on behalf of the living, the spirits of the dead, and the gods. While sorcery may be considered an intentional use of magic in ways immoral or illegal, witchcraft is usually believed to be beyond the conscious control of the person said to be a witch or wizard.

Witchcraft. While someone claiming to be a witch or wizard may describe in dramatic detail the processes by which they perform acts of witchcraft, from an objective or external perspective these actions do not exist, except as psychic states or mental activities. While some witches may, for example, claim that at night in their sleep they transform themselves into owls or cats and roam about dispensing poisons into the bodies of sleeping victims, there is no way of establishing the credibility of such claims. West African beliefs about witchcraft during the years 500–1590 were quite similar to those of European and American cultures during the same period. The fear of being a witch or the victim of a witch was enormous. Families took great precautions to ensure that a family member did not become a witch or a target of witchcraft. Some people, however, exploited the general fear of witches for their own gain.

Sorcery. In contrast to witchcraft, sorcery is a process through which an individual or group consciously forms and executes a plan to employ magical powers to hurt a real or perceived enemy. While witchcraft relies almost exclusively on beliefs and the psychological effects of fear, claims about sorcery can be objectively and factually investigated. Sorcerers often developed and employed poisons (often manufactured from bark, grass, or the venom of poisonous snakes). While a person could unknowingly become a witch, no one could claim to become a sorcerer unknowingly. In fact, only a person with a knowledge of medicine and pharmacology could plan and execute an act of sorcery.

Healers. Such experts are usually known as "medicine men," but in fact, both men and women practiced benevolent and malevolent sorcery. Although they were largely viewed as healers who attempted to help their patients, some of them diverted their skills to harm others in pursuit of personal ends or those of the highest bidder, with little regard to the moral intentions of the patron or the consequences of the action. Medicine was sometimes dispensed as charms or amulets, with ingredients such as herbs and sacred objects—including pebbles from the sea or shells or

IFA DIVINATION

Also known as Afa, *Ifa* is the name of the Yoruba god of knowledge and of the rigidly defined and complex system of obtaining knowledge from Ifa through divination. A person consults Ifa on an occasion when he or she needs to make a significant decision, whether about a personal matter such as marriage or a political enterprise such as war. The Babalawo ("father of secrets"), a diviner and priest, consults Ifa by manipulating sixteen palm nuts, which form a large handful. He begins by holding them in both hands and then attempts to pick them all up in his right hand. If one nut remains in his left hand, he makes a double mark in wood dust on his divining tray; if two remain, he makes a single mark. Four such marks made in a vertical column constitute one half of a figure, and each half has sixteen possible forms. Following the ranking recognized in Ifa, and reading from left to right rather than from top to bottom, these sixteen forms can be presented: 1111, 2222, 2112, 1221, 1222, 2221, 1122, 2211, 1112, 2111, 1121, 1211, 2212, 2122, 1212, and 2121. The second half of the figure, marked in a parallel vertical column, has the same sixteen possible forms; and as they may combine with any of the sixteen forms in the first half of the figure, there are a total of 16 times 16, or 256, possible complete figures.

A Babalawo can arrive at the same 256 figures more quickly by a single toss of a chain of eight half seed shells, but this method is considered less reliable. He holds the chain in the middle and casts it on the ground so that four half seed shells fall in a line on each side. A seed falling with the concave inner surface upward is equivalent to a double mark. Having arrived at the correct figure, the Babalawo recites a verse associated with the particular figure that is relevant to the client's problem. The verse prescribes a sacrifice that will ensure a desired blessing or avert an impending misfortune. During apprenticeship, a Babalawo must memorize more than a thousand Ifa verses, at least four for each of the 256 figures, and he continues to learn new verses from his colleagues throughout his life. A Babalawo can also answer "Yes" or "No" questions by making two tosses of the divining chain and observing which has the higher-ranking figure. Babalawo are consulted not only by worshipers of Ifa and the other deities but by Muslims and Christians as well.

Source: William R. Bascom, *Ifa Divination Communication Between Gods and Men in West Africa* (Bloomington: Indiana University Press, 1969), pp. 4, 40–42.

horns of certain animals. These charms and amulets were believed, when properly employed, to target one's enemies or to thwart similar charms aimed at oneself. Casting a spell (or curse) on one's enemy was another well-known method of sorcery. Only an expert at magical procedures was considered capable of activating the supernatural processes required to make a spell work. The psychological methods used by a Babalawo or Dibia to manipulate individuals or groups were also considered magic. This kind of magic might be used to make a person fall in or out of love with a particular suitor, or to convince the group that certain untruths were truths.

Divination. Divination is aimed at truth telling or knowledge acquisition. Truth and knowledge were considered properties of the gods and considered accessible to humans only through the intelligence with which the gods willingly endowed humans. Divination was used by individuals whose profession was the pursuit of disinterested or applied knowledge. These experts were known by various names in different places, including the Babalawo among the Yoruba, the Dibia among the Igbo, and the Aduru among the Akan. These people were often considered medical experts as well, because they typically had knowledge of herbs and the body. The Dibia and the Babalawo were initiated into the service of gods believed to be masters or custodians of knowledge (the Igbo deity Agwu or the Yoruba deity Esu). They were also required to have mastered the science of medicine (Ogwu) and were expected, for a fee, to employ this knowledge in healing the sick or to share their skills with other healers.

Masquerades. Among the Yoruba and Igbo, there are various forms of masquerading, including the Egungun, Gelede, and Epa. In general, masquerades such as the Egungun (literally "bone" or "skeleton," that is, a man risen from the dead) are ceremonies that pay tribute to the god Amaiyegun, who is believed to have taught humans how to protect themselves from Death by wearing masks and other costumes that disguise their humanness. The Egungun masquerade has a hierarchy. The "elder egungun" is a person from the oldest age grade and may perform duties such as the execution of legal orders. The "trickster egungun" entertains spectators. The "children of egungun" are teenagers. Women may participate in Egungun rituals only if they are clothed as males. They are not supposed to know the identities of the masqueraders, and even if a woman recognizes her husband or son, she is not supposed to reveal such knowledge to others. Whereas an Egungun ceremony may require absolute secrecy about the identities of the masqueraders, Gelede and Epa are less serious about hiding the participants' identities and are generally more playful. Gelede and Epa masqueraders may wear costumes that expose some parts of their bodies, including the face, arms, or feet.

The "Staff of Oranmiyan" (top), son of the Yoruba and Fon creation god Oduduwa, erected in Ile-Ife, Nigeria, before the year 800, and an Ifa divination tray (bottom) carved circa 1500–1700 (top: from Henry John Drewal and John Pemberton III, *Yoruba: Nine Centuries of African Art and Thought*, 1989; bottom: Ulmer Museum, Ulm)

Possession. Possession is believed to occur when a nonancestral spirit or a deity enters a person's head, thereby taking control of the body. Such a person is spoken of as a "horse" or "mount" of the possessing spirit or deity. The spirit or deity may speak through the mount's voice and thrash around in the person's uncontrollable body, pleading for some form of attention or demanding a sacrifice, while predicting curses and evil that may occur if its demands are not met. At other times, however, the spirit or god may announce blessings and good fortune that will come to the mount or the initiates of a god. Not every deity "mounts" its adherents, and some do so only at special festivals where a "mouthperson" has been chosen and prepared ahead of time for being possessed. This preparation may take the form of fasting for several weeks or eating a special diet, abstaining from sexual intercourse, or shaving of one's head (to "clear" the head so the god can "mount").

Prayer. There are many forms of prayer, including prayers of praise, supplication, propitiation, and repentance, as well as pleas for intercession. For each deity there are usually prescribed liturgical hymns and chants that priests or other followers of a god must recite during a ritual. Drums are also used to summon the gods and ancestral spirits. Morning and evening are the usual times for prayer. A particular day of the week may also be dedicated to prayers to a specific god.

Sacrifices. Today, and for the most part in the past, sacrifices are ritualized. Even when a ritual is called a "human" sacrifice, a person need not be killed. Instead a symbolic execution is enacted. In some cases such rituals are re-enactments of what is believed to be an actual sacrifice of a human ancestor in the mythical past. Among the Akan it is believed that when death strikes a member of the royal family, the "bones" of the dead are restless and hungering for life until appeased by the shedding of blood, the symbol of life. Therefore, Death must be fed the blood he wants quickly, before Death strikes another member of the family or clan. In most cases a cow, a goat, or a chicken is slaughtered to appease Death.

Oracles. Usually consulted only in times of crisis (as when a decision has to be made about waging a war), an oracle is a powerful spirit housed in a shrine, usually a grotto, far from the living quarters of a community. An oracle is considered an impartial spirit and trusted ancestor able to ascertain the truth and the best course of action. For example, if the oracle rules that the cause is just, war may be prosecuted with the implicit understanding that victory is likely. If the oracle determines that the reasons for war are unjust, however, victory is not guaranteed, and even if the war is won, the people who initiate it may bring a curse on their descendants. An oracle may also be consulted in order to determine guilt or innocence in disputes among individuals. Once again the oracle, unlike human judges, is considered impartial. The priest who speaks for the oracle is usually removed from the lives of ordinary people in the community. A person of upright character, he or she is often unmarried or a widow or widower. Moreover, the oracle is believed to "choose" its priest, not the other way round.

Sources:

Wade Abimbola, ed. and trans., *Ifa Divination Poetry* (New York: NOK, 1977).

Chinua Achebe, *Anthills of the Savannah* (London: Heinemann, 1987).

Achebe, *Morning Yet on Creation Day: Essays* (London: Heinemann, 1975).

Andrew Apter, *Black Critiques and Kings: The Hermeneutics of Power in Yoruba Society* (Chicago: University of Chicago Press, 1992).

Sandra T. Barnes, ed., *Africa's Ogun: Old World and New*, expanded edition (Bloomington: Indiana University Press, 1989).

William R. Bascom, *Ifa Divination: Communication between Gods and Men in West Africa* (Bloomington: Indiana University Press, 1969).

Ulli Beier, ed., *The Origin of Life and Death: African Creation Myths* (London: Heinemann, 1966).

Norman R. Bennett, *Africa and Europe: From Roman Times to National Independence*, second edition (New York: Africana, 1975).

K. A. Busia, *The Challenge of Africa* (New York: Praeger, 1962).

W. Walton Claridge, *A History of the Gold Coast from the Earliest Times to the Commencement of the Twentieth Century*, 2 volumes (London: John Murray, 1915).

Herbert M. Cole, *Mbari: Art and Life among the Owerri Igbo* (Bloomington: Indiana University Press, 1982).

J. B. Danquah, *The Akan Doctrine of God: A Fragment of Gold Coast Ethics and Religion*, second edition (London: Cass, 1968).

Cheikh Anta Diop, *The African Origins of Civilization: Myth or Reality*, translated by Mercer Cook (Chicago: Lawrence Hill, 1974).

Diop, *Civilization or Barbarism: An Authentic Anthropology*, translated by Yaa-Lengi Meema Ngemi, edited by Harold J. Salemson and Marjolijn de Jager (Brooklyn, N.Y.: Lawrence Hill, 1991).

Diop, *Precolonial Black Africa: A Comparative Study of the Political and Social Systems of Europe and Black Africa, from Antiquity to the Formation of Modern States*, translated by Salemson (Westport, Conn.: Lawrence Hill, 1987).

Jacob U. Egharevba, *The City of Benin, Benin Law and Custom, Some Stories of Ancient Benin*, [and] *Some Tribal Gods of Southern Nigeria* (Nendeln, Liechtenstein: Kraus Reprints, 1971).

Emmanuel Eze, ed., *African Philosophy: An Anthology* (Malden, Mass. & Oxford: Blackwell, 1998).

Marcel Griaule and Germaine Dieterlen, *Le Mythe Cosmogonique* (Paris: Institut d'Ethnologie, 1965).

Joseph E. Harris, *Africans and Their History*, second edition, revised (New York: Meridian, 1998).

John Iliffe, *Africans: The History of a Continent* (Cambridge & New York: Cambridge University Press, 1995).

A. H. M. Kirk-Greene, trans., *Hausa ba dabo ba ne: 500 Hausa Proverbs* (Ibadan, Nigeria: Oxford University Press, 1966).

Arthur Glyn Leonard, *The Lower Niger and Its Tribes* (London & New York: Macmillan, 1906).

John Mbiti, *Introduction to African Religion* (London: Heinemann, 1975).

Roland Oliver, *The African Experience: From Olduvai Gorge to the 21st Century* (London: Weidenfeld & Nicolson, 1999).

P. Amaury Talbot, *Life in Southern Nigeria: The Magic, Beliefs, and Customs of the Ibibio Tribe* (London: Macmillan, 1923).

Rems Nna Umeasiegbu, *The Way We Lived: Ibo Customs and Stories* (London: Heinemann, 1969).

DEITIES OF THE AKAN RELIGION

Earthly Origins. The West African finds it quite natural to approach the gods and believes that the gods will listen and help because, with few exceptions (such as the Yoruba and Igbo sky gods Olorun and Amadioha), they are believed to have once been humans (or at least in familiar and close contact with humans) and to have at one point inhabited the earth. Yet, the gods are of a different ontological and hierarchical order from humans, so the need to worship them is far greater than, for example, the necessity to pay homage to the known ancestors of the clan.

Akan Religion. The Akan speak the Twi language and trace back their history in West Africa some nine hundred years. They are believed to have origins in the Middle East—as the Akkadian people of Babylon. The name *Akan* is believed to be a corruption of Akkane or Akkana. In 1076 the Almoravids drove the Akans from their ancient home in the Empire of Ghana to their current West African locations in the modern nation of Ghana and adjacent areas of Côte d'Ivoire and Togo.

Ideas of God. The Akan supreme being, Onyame, has many other names. Some of these names indicate Onyame's most worthy attributes, such as Amosu (Giver of Rain), Amowia (Giver of the Sun), and Amaomee (Giver of Plenitude). Onyame is often thought to be female and associated with the Moon. Like other traditional West African religions, the Akan religion is polytheistic. While Onyame is considered supreme, there are many minor deities, the *abosom*, who exercise powers over believers but are in turn subordinate to Onyame. The abosom exercise their

---

ANANSE AND THE SKY GOD'S STORIES

In the following folktale about Ananse the spider, the Akan trickster god gets some help from his wife in planning and carrying out a clever scheme. The story of how he captures Mmoatia the fairy is a source for the African American story of Br'er Rabbit and the tar baby.

Kwaku Ananse, the spider, once went to Myankonpon, the sky-god, in order to buy the sky-god's stories. The sky-god said, "What makes you think *you* can buy them?" The spider answered and said, "I know I shall be able." Thereupon the sky-god said, "Great and powerful towns like Kokofu, Bekwai, Asumengya, have come, but they were unable to purchase them, and yet you who are but a mere masterless man, you say you will be able?"

The spider said, "What is the price of the stories?" The sky-god said, "They cannot be bought for anything except Onini, the python; Osebo, the leopard; Mmoatia, the fairy; and Mmoboro, the hornets." The spider said, "I will bring some of all these things, and, what is more, I'll add my old mother, Nsia, the sixth child, to the lot."

The sky-god said, "Go and bring them then." The spider came back, and told his mother all about it, saying, "I wish to buy the stories of the sky-god, and the sky-god says I must bring Onini, the python; Osebo, the leopard; Mmoatia, the fairy; and Mmoboro, the hornets; and I said I would add you to the lot and give you to the sky-god." Now the spider consulted his wife, Aso, saying, "What is to be done that we may get Onini, the python?" Aso said to him, "You go off and cut a branch of a palm tree, and cut some stringcreeper as well, and bring them." And the spider came back with them. And Aso said, "Take them to the stream." So Ananse took them; and, as he was going along, he said, "It's longer than he is, it's not so long as he; you lie, it's longer than he."

The spider said, "There he is, lying yonder." The python, who had overheard this imaginary conversation, then asked, "What's this all about?" To which the spider replied, "Is it not my wife, Aso, who is arguing with me that this palm branch is longer than you, and I say she is a liar." And Onini, the python, said, "Bring it, and come and measure me." Ananse took the palm branch and laid it along the python's body. Then he said, "Stretch yourself out." And the python stretched himself out, and Ananse took the ropecreeper and wound it and the sound of the tying was *nwenene! nwenene!* until he came to the head.

Ananse, the spider, said, "Fool, I shall take you to the sky-god and receive the sky-god's tales in exchange." So Ananse took him off to Nyame, the sky-god. The sky-god then said, "My hand has touched it, there remains what still remains." The spider returned and came and told his wife what had happened, saying, "There remain the hornets." His wife said, "Look for a gourd, and fill it with water and go off with it." The spider went along through the bush, when he saw a swarm of hornets hanging there, and he poured out some of the water and sprinkled it on them. He then poured the remainder upon himself and cut a leaf of plantain and covered his head with it. And now he addressed the hornets, saying, "As the rain has come, had you not better come and enter this, my gourd, so that the rain will not beat you; don't you see that I have taken a plantain leaf to cover myself?" Then the hornets said, "We thank you, Aku, we thank you, Aku." All the hornets flew, disappearing into the gourd, *fom!* Father Spider covered the mouth, and exclaimed, "Fools, I have got you, and I am taking you to receive the tales of the sky-god in exchange."

And he took the hornets to the sky-god. The sky-god said, "My hand has touched it; what remains still remains."

The spider came back once more, and told his wife, and said, "There remains Osebo, the leopard." Aso said, "Go and dig a hole." Ananse said, "That's enough, I understand." Then the spider went off to look for the leopard's tracks, and, having found them, he dug a very deep pit, covered it over, and came back home. Very early next day, when objects

---

hold on the mind of the believer through *asuman,* charms, amulets, and other fetish objects associated with their powers. The Akan also have a second superdivinity, Onyankopon, who is a polar opposite to Onyame. He is male and associated with the Sun. Finally, there is a third, ultradivine element that binds itself with Onyame and Onyankopon into the one Absolute: Odomankoma, the infinite being. This Absolute has a trinitarian character: God as male, female, and relational principle; or, metaphorically speaking, Moon, Sun, and their bonding principle. Odomankoma is therefore the name Akan-language speakers use to describe the eternal entity who deserves the credit for the work of creation, including creating the concept of trinity—the idea of the union between Onyame and Onyankopon in the Odomankoma. Odomankoma is responsible for

both natural and supernatural existence and is regularly praised during worship as the "Absolute Architect" (Borebore) of Nature.

Minor Deities. Subordinate to the Absolute (Onyame, Onyankopon, and Odomankoma), the minor deities are also vulnerable to the wishes, desires, and fortunes of the individuals who believe in them. In fact, many minor deities would not exist or would not have been considered necessary if the believers did not see them as effective intercessors, intermediaries, or messengers to the Absolute. Thought to have greater access to the Absolute than humans, the minor gods bring the needs of the mortals to the attention of Onyame, Onyankopon, and Odomankoma and carry back to humans important insights and communications. The minor gods are vulnerable to the

ANANSE AND THE SKY GOD'S STORIES (CONTINUED)

began to be visible, the spider said he would go off, and when he went, lo, a leopard was lying in the pit. Ananse said, "Little father's child, little mother's child, I have told you not to get drunk, and now, just as one would expect of you, you have become intoxicated, and that's why you have fallen into the pit. If I were to say I would get you out, next day, if you saw me, or likewise any of my children, you would go and catch me and them." The leopard said, "O! I could not do such a thing."

Ananse then went and cut two sticks, put one here, and one there, and said, "Put one of your paws here, and one also of your paws here." And the leopard placed them where he was told. As he was about to climb up, Ananse lifted up his knife, and in a flash it descended on his head, *gao!* was the sound it made. The pit received the leopard and *fom!* was the sound of the falling. Ananse got a ladder to descend into the pit to go and get the leopard out. He got the leopard out and came back with it, exclaiming, "Fool, I am taking you to exchange for the stories of the sky-god." He lifted up the leopard to go and give to Nyame, the sky-god. The sky-god said, "My hands have touched it; what remains still remains."

Then the spider came back, carved an Akua's child, a black flat-faced wooden doll, tapped some sticky fluid from a tree and plastered the doll's body with it. Then he made *eto,* pounded yams, and put some in the doll's hand. Again he pounded some more and placed it in a brass basin; he tied string round the doll's waist, and went with it and placed it at the foot of the odum tree, the place where the fairies come to play. And a fairy came along. She said, "Akua, may I eat a little of this mash?" Ananse tugged at the string, and the doll nodded her head. The fairy turned to one of the sisters, saying, "She says I may eat some." She said, "Eat some, then." And she finished eating, and thanked her. But when she thanked her, the doll did not answer. And the fairy said to her sister, "When I thank her,

she does not reply." The sister of the first fairy said, "Slap her crying-place." And she slapped it, *pa!* And her hand stuck there. She said to her sister, "My hand has stuck there." She said, "Take the one that remains and slap her crying-place again." And she took it and slapped her, *pa!* and this one, too, stuck fast. And the fairy told her sister, saying, "My two hands have stuck fast." She said, "Push it with your stomach." She pushed it and her stomach stuck to it. And Ananse came and tied her up, and he said, "Fool, I have got you, I shall take you to the sky-god in exchange for his stories." And he went off home with her.

Now Ananse spoke to his mother, Ya Nsia, the sixth child, saying, "Rise up, let us go, for I am taking you along with the fairy to go and give you to the sky-god in exchange for his stories." He lifted them up, and went off there to where the sky-god was. Arrived there he said, "Sky-god, here is a fairy and my old woman whom I spoke about, here she is, too." Now the sky-god called his elders, the Kontire and Akwam chiefs, the Adonten, the Gyase, the Oyoko, Ankobea, and Kyidom. And he put the matter before them, saying, "Very great kings have come, and were not able to buy the sky-god's stories, but Kwaku Ananse, the spider, has been able to pay the price: I have received from him Osebo, the leopard; I have received from him Onini, the python; and of his own accord, Ananse has added his mother to the lot; all these things lie here." He said, "Sing his praise." *"Eee!"* they shouted. The sky-god said, "Kwaku Ananse, from today and going on for ever, I take my sky-god's stories and I present them to you, *kose! kose! kose!* my blessing, blessing, blessing! No more shall we call them the stories of the sky-god, but we shall call them spider-stories."

This, my story, which I have related, if it be sweet, or if it be not sweet, take some elsewhere, and let some come back to me.

Source: Paul Radin, ed., "How Spider Obtained the Sky God's Stories," in *African Folktales & Sculpture* (New York: Pantheon, 1952), pp. 25-27.

people who choose, and in some cases create, them to ful-fill such intercessionary roles. As J. B. Danquah has observed, "The gods are treated with respect if they deliver the goods, and with contempt if they fail." A god who is perceived to have failed often is no longer wor-shiped. Among the minor Akan gods is Ananse (also spelled Anansi or Anyanse), who is often represented in myths as a spider and trickster—a mythological figure who is supposed to bridge the gap between God and humans through his divinatory and oracular wisdom. Ananse is so successful in dealing with the Absolute deity that the Akans hold him in high esteem and sometimes refer to God as Agya Ananse (Father Ananse).

Sources:

J. B. Danquah, *The Akan Doctrine of God: A Fragment of Gold Coast Ethics and Religion*, second edition (London: Cass, 1968).

Cheikh Anta Diop, *The African Origins of Civilization: Myth or Reality*, translated by Mercer Cook (Chicago: Lawrence Hill, 1974).

Paul Radin and Elinore Marvel, eds., *African Folktales & Sculpture*, revised and enlarged edition (New York: Pantheon, 1964).

DEITIES OF THE IGBO RELIGION

Roots. The origins of the Igbo, like those of many other ethnic groups in West Africa, are shrouded in myth. The best historical evidence produces two conflicting interpre-tations. One group of scholars, including Elizabeth Isichei, claims that the Igbo are original to the place where the majority of them still live, southeastern Nigeria. A second group, however, asserts that the Igbo, along with some eth-nic groups in Zimbabwe, are descended from the Jews, using linguistic and even genetic analysis to bolster their claims. J. B. Danquah and Jacob U. Egharevba point to similarities in Igbo and Hebrew customs and religious ritu-als, such as the circumcision of the male child eight days after birth, systems of marriage and inheritance, and ideas about ritual purity and impurity.

Chukwu. Transcending the multiplicity of gods in Igbo religion is a high god called Chukwu (or Chi Ukwu), whose name may be translated as "The Great Spirit." The Igbo religionist thinks of Chukwu as an all-powerful, all-knowing divinity, the maker of the cosmos as well as all the minor gods that make up the Igbo pantheon. Chukwu is not believed to have human attributes, but is often referred to as "He." Chukwu is believed to inhabit the sky and is often associated with the Sun, which is believed to be God's "eye" on the Earth. The central relationship between Chukwu and the Sun is evident in the people's cosmology and traditional prayers. According to Chinua Achebe, "Among the Igbo of Awka a man who arrives at a point in his life when he needs to set up a shrine to his chi [personal god] will invite a priest to perform a ritual of bringing down the spirit from the face of the Sun at daybreak. Thereafter, it is represented physically in the man's com-pound until the day of his death when the shrine must be destroyed." In various prayers the Sun is called "The Face

of God," "The Great Carrier of Sacrifice to the Almighty," and "The Single Eye of God," as in the following prayer in Achebe's *Anthills of the Savannah* (1987):

> Wide-eyed, insomniac, you go out at cock-crow spitting malediction at a beaten, recumbent world. Your crimson touches fire the furnaces of heaven and the roaring holo-caust of your vengeance fills the skies.
>
> Undying Eye of God! You will not relent, we know it, from compassion for us. Relent then for your own sake; for that building eye of madness that may be blinded by soar-ing motes of an incinerated world. Single Eye of God, will you put yourself out merely that men may stumble in your darkness. Remember: Single Eye, one-wall-neighbor-to-Blindness, remember! . . .
>
> Great Messenger of the Creator! Take care that the ashes of the world rising daily from this pyre may not prove enough when they descend again to silt up the canals of birth in the season of renewal.

Chukwu is also often referred to as *Chineke*—a shorter ver-sion of "Chi-na-eke," the God who creates—suggesting that Chukwu is the creator of Nature, in its spiritual and physical aspects.

Ala. Parallel to the idea of Chukwu as a masculine deity associated with the Sun is the idea that the Moon is femi-nine and closely associated with the goddess Ala—Earth. While Chukwu is in charge of creation, Ala is in charge of conserving that which is created. While Chukwu is the giver of the moral law, Ala is the enforcer of the law. Ala is also the "womb" that holds and nurtures and renews when necessary. The Igbo, an agrarian people, regard her as the "mother" of all crops. Before planting and harvest, they hold days of ritual ceremonies to appease Ala so she will facilitate the growth of healthy crops or to thank her for making possible the abundant harvest soon to begin. In a year of drought or other agricultural misfortunes, the peo-ple undertake ritual processes meant to examine how they may have angered Ala and caused her to withhold her blessings. After they look for wrongdoing on the part of humans, they seek scientific explanations for crop failures. When religious and natural explanations conflict, mythical narratives are used to overcome contradictions.

Duality. Chukwu and Ala are meant to represent the differences and complementary between the sexes in Igbo culture. This principle of duality extends to minor gods as well. Some of these deities are "male" gods associated with masculine rituals such as circumcision or with male-dominated professions such as iron smithing and carving. Others are "female" deities, such as those associated with protecting vegetable traders and cloth weavers—who in the Igbo tra-ditional world tended to be dominated by women.

Agbala. Agbala is the priestess of Ala. In addition to leading the community's ritual sacrifices to Ala, she is in charge of executing punishments against individuals who commit acts the community considers immoral (such as

Ala, the Igbo earth goddess, with her children and supporters in a traditional Mbari house built in Orishaeze, Nigeria, in 1955 (from Monica Blackmun Visonà, *A History of Art in Africa*, 2001)

murder, witchcraft, and perjury). These and similar crimes are believed to be transgressions against the earth goddess.

Chi. After Chukwu and Ala, the most important divinity in the Igbo religious worldview is Chi, the spirit believed to inhabit each individual. Chi is said to be the fractal representation of Chukwu that resides in each person. In fact, Chukwu may be translated as "The Great Chi" as well as "The Great Spirit." Because every person's Chi descends directly from the Great God, all humans share in the divine character. This participation in the divine is symbolized in the Ikenga, a statue that every adult may enshrine in his or her compound as a reminder that in everyday thought and action, one's spirit must constantly be elevated toward God. Some call Chi the "soul" of the person, but it is equally possible that the correct translation is "mind," because another word, *obi*, best approximates the English meaning of "soul."

Mmo. Spirits known as *mmo* do not necessarily belong to anyone in particular, but rather are believed to roam around either to protect people or to cause mischief to individuals. Often the wandering spirits are attributed to dead relatives whose funeral may not have been properly performed or altogether neglected. Unable to "cross over" to *ani mmo*, land of the dead or land of the spirits, the *mmo* have no choice but to hover around in limbo between this world and the next, unable to find rest. Depending on their characters when they were inhabiting human bodies, these homeless spirits are either benevolent or malevolent, but they are always unhappy because of their wandering state. It is believed that Chukwu may also send unwelcome spirits to rebuke or torment individuals who have committed evil acts or to protect the innocent. A spirit may also find a "home" by possessing or occupying a nonhuman entity such as a tree, snake, or river. This belief has led some scholars to characterize the Igbo traditional religion as animistic.

Mbari. Closely associated with Ala is Mbari, the divine guardian of a ritual form of art central to the Igbo religious existence. The character of the deity Mbari, who is considered a close associate, if not a divine messenger or personal aspect, of Ala, is best explained by describing the artistic ritual that also bears her name. Mbari art is considered a feminine endeavor—unlike other religious rituals that are, for example, associated with war or hunting. Mbari is a ritual of peace and art and an expression of the love of play, including the satiric and comic, and the love of the beautiful. Only adult Igbo can participate in Mbari, which involves several months of seclusion, during which the participants devote all their time to creating artworks. These works may be made with materials such as wood, cloth, and ink, but rarely clay. The results are sculptures that represent the full range of the experience and imagination of each artist: daily objects such as tables and chairs and people from various professions. In fact, the goal of Mbari artists seems to be re-creation of the everyday experience of an average person in the wider community. Thus, a Mbari house might contain an assembly of objects arranged to look like a miniature imaginary Igbo society. The purpose of Mbari is primarily to show off the talents of artists: their capacity for observation and reflection and their aesthetic appreciation of the beautiful. At the end of the months of seclusion, the Mbari house is opened to the public for view. Like visitors to a museum, people are supposed to feel a sense of recognition in the artistic—sometimes caricatured—rendition of their everyday communal lives. In return the visitors shower the artists with gifts, parties, and recognition. Unlike museums, however, Mbari houses are destroyed—or left to deteriorate unattended—at the end of each season. The Earth goddess Ala, who is also the god of fertility, is regarded as the divine patron of Mbari. Mbari artists must return to the beginning and renew creativity each year because—as in the cycle of nature—they regard art as highly creative but also improvisational. Thus, it seems that the Igbo valued the spontaneity of the artist and the technical processes of creativity more than the objects created. Some of the Mbari art objects, especially masks, have been rescued from destruction and are used in rituals from one year to the other.

Amadioha. Similar to the god Shango in the Yoruba religion, Amadioha is the Igbo god of thunder and lightning. He is therefore considered "Owner of the Sky." Whenever lightning kills a person or strikes an object, the event is often considered a sign or "message" from Amadioha. Dibia, or priests, are therefore asked to determine what wrong has been committed by the victim or the owner of the object. Sometimes a god warring with Amadioha is believed to have "entered" the person or the object. Amadioha himself, however, is presumed to be a gentle deity who gets violent only when provoked. Amadioha's favorite color is white, so a white ram is the preferred sacrifice to him.

Agwu. Also known as Agwusi, Agwu is the Igbo trickster god, similar to the Akan god Ananse and the Yoruba god Esu. It is not known whether any of these deities is male or female. Rather, the trickster is considered capable of being either sex at anytime, even both at once, or neither sex at all. Respected and feared, Agwu is capable of sowing confusion in the mind of even the clearest reasoner. Agwu, however, can also clarify confusion, even when it is caused by human ignorance, the finite capacity of the human mind, or the evil actions of other persons or gods. If it pleases Agwu to protect or "work with" a thinker, unparalleled lucidity may be attained. But if it pleases the god to sow confusion in someone's mind, there is nothing anyone can do about it—except work with Agwu to lift the curse or devise a technique of information gathering that overcomes the external confusion wrought by Agwu. Agwu is most dreaded by Dibia, whose success as diviners depends on clarity of mind. Dibia are therefore taught ritual sacrifices that they must make to Agwu at the beginning of every divination session. Agwu is thus the patron deity of diviners.

Ekwensu. Feared as much as Chukwu is respected, Ekwensu is the Igbo Evil Spirit, much like that of the Devil in other religions. Possession by Ekwensu can lead a person to commit acts of great evil against Chukwu or against humanity. Whenever an unfathomable act of evil is committed by someone considered incapable of such a crime, possession by Ekwensu is a common explanation. Without excusing the person's conduct, this attribution of the origins of such criminal depravity to a superhuman power allows the Igbo to acknowledge that there are some levels of inhumanity humans cannot reach on their own—a polar opposite to acts of good so astonishing that they are considered "miraculous."

Sources:

Chinua Achebe, *Anthills of the Savannah* (London: Heinemann, 1987).

Achebe, *Morning Yet on Creation Day: Essays* (London: Heinemann, 1975).

Ulli Beier, ed., *The Origin of Life and Death: African Creation Myths* (London: Heinemann, 1966).

Herbert M. Cole, *Mbari: Art and Life among the Owerri Igbo* (Bloomington: Indiana University Press, 1982).

J. B. Danquah, *The Akan Doctrine of God: A Fragment of Gold Coast Ethics and Religion,* second edition (London: Cass, 1968).

Jacob U. Egharevba, *The City of Benin, Benin Law and Custom, Some Stories of Ancient Benin,* [and] *Some Tribal Gods of Southern Nigeria* (Nendeln, Liechtenstein: Kraus Reprints, 1971).

Emmanuel Eze, ed., *African Philosophy: An Anthology* (Malden, Mass. & Oxford: Blackwell, 1998).

Marcel Griaule and Germaine Dieterlen, *Le Mythe Cosmogonique* (Paris: Institut d'Ethnologie, 1965).

Edmund Ilogu, *Christianity and Igbo Culture* (Leiden: Brill, 1974).

Elizabeth Isichei, *A History of African Societies to 1870* (Cambridge: Cambridge University Press, 1997).

Isichei, *A History of the Igbo People* (London: Macmillan, 1976).

John Mbiti, *Introduction to African Religion* (London: Heinemann, 1975).

Paul Radin and Elinore Marvel, eds., *African Folktales & Sculpture,* revised and enlarged edition (New York: Pantheon, 1964).

Rems Nna Umeasiegbu, *The Way We Lived: Ibo Customs and Stories* (London: Heinemann, 1969).

DEITIES OF THE YORUBA AND FON RELIGIONS

Vodon. Vodon (known as Voodoo in the African Diaspora) is the most important religious tradition among the West African Fon. Although the independence of this religion from that of the Yoruba is discernible, the remarkable similarities of the two religions in terms of metaphysical structures, overlapping of deities, and the affinities in cults make it possible to discuss the Fon and Yoruba religions together. The Fon, who migrated from Togo to Benin in the seventeenth century, and the Yoruba, one of the three major ethnic groups of Nigeria, have the same ethnic and cultural origins even though their geographic dispersal has located them in different modern states.

Yoruba Religions. Because of their large numbers in West Africa and their wide dispersal through slavery in the Americas, the Yoruba are probably the best-known West African ethnic culture in the world. In Africa, Nigeria and the Republic of Benin have the largest concentration of Yoruba and Yoruba religions. In the Americas, Yoruba cultural influences are most apparent in Brazil, Cuba, Haiti, Jamaica, Trinidad, and Tobago, especially in the religions of the masses, including Vodon, Santéria, Camdomblé, and Macumba, and so forth. (In 1989, it was estimated that more than seventy million African and New World peoples practiced one form or another of Yoruba religion.) Yoruba religions, or religions inspired by them, are arguably the most widely dispersed West African religions, both in Africa and in the Americas. They may also be the most theologically complex West African religions. For example, it is estimated that the Yoruba have a pantheon of as many as six thousand deities. In discussing the Yoruba idea of God, it is practically impossible to isolate a single conception that might encompass the varieties in belief systems from one country to another, or even all the local nuances within a country. The gods discussed here are not a universal Yoruba hierarchy of gods, but rather representatives of the diverse Yoruba religious worldview.

Ideas of God. One of the high-ranking Yoruba gods is Da, the god of order. Da is most prominent among Fon practitioners of Vodon. Da is believed to combine in itself the male and female principles—in fact, to represent conceptually the idea of such a combination, much as the Akan god Odomankoma binds itself with Onyame and Onyankopon, into one Absolute, infinite being. This Absolute is thus a trinitarian Idea that accounts for the creative act called Nature. The position of Da is so exalted among Vodon worshipers that some priests are assigned to minister exclusively to Da. These priests, naturally, are called *Da Ayido Hwedo* (High Priests of Da).

Olorun. Among the Yoruba of Nigeria, Olorun, also known as Olodumare, enjoys a status as exalted as Da among the Fon. *Olodu* may be translated as "someone who is a supreme head" or "one who 'contains' the fullness of excellent attributes." When the suffix *-mare* ("unique" or "perfect-in-itself") is added, the name may be loosely translated as "one who is absolutely perfect" or "absolute perfection." Olorun is called the supreme deity, and he enjoys the same exalted and exclusive position as the God in any monotheistic religion. With their emphases on perfection in areas such as power, intelligence, beauty, goodness, and justice, Olorun's key attributes point to the moral concerns of the Yoruba people, who believe that God's creative power is the source not only of Nature but also of the human moral striving for self- and social perfection. The Yoruba think of Olorun as the creator of Nature, including humans and their souls, and the creator of the lesser spirits and divinities that act as intermediaries between Olorun and humans. Olorun is both omnipotent and omniscient. Thus, he is considered the Oba-Orun (King Who Dwells in the Heavens) and the Impartial Judge, who controls the destiny of all gods and humans and gives each person his or her just deserts. Because his existence, or the idea of his reality, is above and beyond the realm of Nature, Olorun is immortal and holy. That is, Olorun is perfect in power, wisdom, and justice, because he exists in holiness beyond the realm of moral frailty and the possibility of transgression.

Other Deities. The polytheistic aspect of Yoruba religion is most evident in its proliferation of gods. Although they are ultimately subject to Olurun, these gods are more present in the day-to-day lives of believers than the supreme deity. Much as the oba, the earthly king, can be approached by a subject only through a long hierarchical network of intermediaries, Olorun, the King of All Kings, must of even greater necessity be approached in times of spiritual or material need through

Interior of a traditional Fon family shrine (from Monica Blackmun Visonà, *A History of Art in Africa,* 2001)

an equal, or even greater, chain of intermediaries. Many ancestral and other spirits, also believed to have been created directly by Olorun, fulfill the role of intercessors.

Oya. The female deity Oya, the goddess of waters, is believed to have been a daughter of the primordial gods Obatala and his wife Yemojya. Oya is associated with fertility and acts of creation—probably in recognition of the nurturing role of water in the lives of plants, animals, and humans. Women who wish to become pregnant, in addition to taking the necessary herbs recommended by the Babalawo, may also be advised to make sacrifices of food and drinks to Oya at the bank of a river. In mythology, Oya is a wife of the god Shango—the god of thunder and lightning. Thus, she is sometimes described as the strong wind that precedes a thunderstorm. As Shango's partner, Oya can be benevolent, especially to women who make sacrifices to her in return for fertility, but she can also perform acts of mischief. As a strong wind she blows off rooftops, fans Shango's fire, breaks trees, or sweeps over and destroys farm crops.

Oya's Retinue. In character with the polytheistic and hierarchical nature of the Yoruba earthly and heavenly

ESU AND SHANGO

Esu the trickster god (spelled Eshu in the following translation) had power over even mighty gods, including Shango. This folktale explains how the failure of Shango's wife Oya to follow Esu's instructions resulted in tragedy for Shango's people while making him the god of lightning as well as thunder.

The orisha Shango ruled firmly over all of Oyo, the city and the lands that surrounded it. He was a stern ruler, and because he owned the thunderbolt the people of Oyo tried to do nothing to displease or anger him. His symbol of power was a double-bladed axe which signified, "My strength cuts both ways," meaning that no one, even the most distant citizen of Oyo, was beyond reach of his authority or immune to punishment for misdeeds. The people of Oyo called him by his praise name, Oba Jakuta, the Stone Thrower Oba.

But even though Shango's presence was felt everywhere in Oyo, and even beyond in other kingdoms, he wanted something more to instill fear in the hearts of men. He sent for the great makers of medicine in Oyo and instructed them to make jujus that would increase his powers. One by one the medicine makers brought him this and that, but he was not satisfied with their work. He decided at last to ask the orisha Eshu for help. He sent a messenger to the distant place where Eshu lived. The messenger said to Eshu: "Oba Jakuta, the great ruler of Oyo, sends me. He said: 'Go to the place where the renowned Eshu stays. Tell him I need a powerful medicine that will cause terror to be born in the hearts of my enemies. Ask Eshu if he will make such a medicine for me.'"

Eshu said: "Yes, such a thing is possible. What kind of power does Shango want?"

The messenger answered: "Oba Jakuta says, 'Many makers of medicine have tried to give me a power that I don't already have. But they do not know how to do it. Such knowledge belongs only to Eshu. If he asks what I need, tell him it is he alone who knows what must be done. What he prepares for me I will accept.'"

Eshu said: "Yes, what the ruler of Oyo needs, I shall prepare it for him. In return he will send a goat as sacrifice. The medicine will be ready in seven days. But you, messenger, do not come back for it yourself. Let Shango's wife Oya come for it. I will put it in her hand."

The messenger went back to Oyo. He told Shango what he had heard from Eshu. Shango said, "Yes, I will send Oya to receive the medicine."

On the seventh day he instructed Oya to go to the place where Eshu was living. He said: "Greet Eshu for me. Tell him that the sacrifice will be sent. Receive the medicine he has prepared and bring it home quickly."

Oya departed. She arrived at the place where Eshu was living. She greeted him. She said: "Shango of Oyo sends me for the medicine. The sacrifice you asked for is on the way."

Eshu said: "Shango asked for a great new power. I have finished making it." He gave Oya a small packet wrapped in a leaf. He said: "Take care with it. See that Shango gets it all."

Oya began the return journey, wondering: "What has Eshu made for Shango? What kind of power can be in so small a packet?" She stopped at a resting place. As Eshu had presumed she would do, Oya unwrapped the packet to see what was inside. There was nothing there but red powder. She put a little of the powder in her mouth to taste it. It was neither good nor bad. It tasted like nothing at all. She closed the medicine packet and tied it with a string of grass. She went on. She arrived at Oyo and gave the medicine to Shango.

He said: "What instructions did Eshu give you? How is this medicine to be used?"

Oya was about to say, "He gave no instructions whatever." As she began to speak, fire flashed from her mouth. Thus Shango saw that Oya had tasted the medicine that was meant for him alone. His anger was fierce. He raised his hand to strike her but she fled from the house. Shango pursued her. Oya came to a place where many sheep were grazing. She ran among the sheep thinking that Shango would not find her. But Shango's anger was hot. He hurled his thunderstones in all directions. He hurled them among the sheep, killing them all. Oya lay hidden under the bodies of the dead sheep and Shango did not see her there.

Shango returned to his house. Many people of Oyo were gathered there. They pleaded for Oya's life. They said: "Great Shango, Oba of Oyo, spare Oya. Your compassion is greater than her offense. Forgive her."

Shango's anger cooled. He sent servants to find Oya and bring her home. But he still did not know how Eshu intended for him to use the medicine. So when night came he took the medicine packet and went to a high place overlooking the city. He stood facing the compound where he lived with all his wives and servants. He placed some of the medicine on his tongue. And when he breathed the air out of his lungs an enormous flame shot from his mouth, extending over the city and igniting the straw roofs of the palace buildings. A great fire began to burn in Oyo. It destroyed Shango's houses and granaries. The entire city was consumed, and nothing was left but ashes. Thus Oyo was leveled to the ground and had to be rebuilt. After the city rose again from its ashes, Shango ruled on. In times of war, or when his subjects displeased him, Shango hurled his thunderbolts. Every stone he threw was accompanied by a bright flash that illuminated the sky and the earth. This, as all men knew, was the fire shooting from Shango's mouth.

The sheep that died while protecting Oya from Shango's thunderstones were never forgotten. In their honor, the worshippers of Oya have refused to eat mutton even to the present day.

Source: Harold Courlander, ed., "Shango and the Medicine of Eshu," in his *Tales of Yoruba Gods and Heroes* (New York: Crown, 1973).

orders, Oya has a retinue of minor goddesses who are either directly subordinate to her or operate within her spheres of influence. Among the most notable of the nine minor feminine deities associated with Oya are Ibaje and Mama Water, who have limited supervisory roles over the tributaries of the River Niger at, respectively, Idah and Onitsha. Other members of Oya's retinue include Osun, the goddess of the Osun River; Olosa, the wife of the sea god Olokun, who lives with him on the ocean floor and is known to help fishermen who run into trouble with the elements; Oba, the goddess of the Oba River, who is also believed to consort occasionally with Shango; Ochumare, goddess of the rainbow; and Yemojya, Oya's mother, the moon goddess, who is believed to control the movement of the seas.

Esu or Esu-Elgeba. Like Ananse among the Akan, Esu is believed to be the god who best knows how to deliver offerings and ritual sacrifices from humans to the gods. He is known as "guardian of the crossroads"; that is, he sees in several directions at once and is therefore master of chance and indeterminacy, and he is able to take on different identities. By knowing how things could go wrong or go right, and having the ability to see possibilities that are hidden to humans and even to less clever gods, Esu is admired and dreaded by humans as well as the gods. Even people who do not have Esu as their primary deity sacrifice to Esu as a form of insurance to maximize the chance that the sacrifices made to their own personal deities are mischievously intercepted by Esu and diverted to some other spiritual agent, thus angering the god for whom the sacrifice was originally intended.

Esu as Intercessor. The Ifa, a body of literary work that may be accurately regarded as the Yoruba Bible, includes a story that illustrates how Esu tricked another god into helping a couple to conceive a child. Ede and her husband were having trouble conceiving a child and consulted a Babalawo, who directed them to make a sacrifice to the god Igunugun (whose name means "Vulture"). Unfortunately, Igunugun did not seem to like Ede and refused to honor the sacrifice brought to him, so he left his house. The couple turned to Esu for assistance. Esu ascertained that the sacrifice at Igunugun's house was adequate for the occasion, so he devised a plan to lure Igunugun back to the sacrifice. Esu took some samples of Igunugun's favorite dishes, transformed himself into a dog, tracked down Igunugun, and lured him homeward by dropping little bits of the food along the road. Little by little, while picking up the bits of food as they were dropped, Igunugun returned home and, without much thought, ate the sacrifice that Ede had served him.

Esu's Trickery. Because of Esu's capacity for assuming different identities, he is considered a master of dissimulation. He is capable of lying, playing cruel games, and

Archaic liths at Ogun Oke Mogun, Ile-Ife, Nigeria, the site of annual rites performed to Ogun, the Yoruba god of hunters, warriors, and ironworkers (from Henry John Drewal and John Pemberton III, *Yoruba: Nine Centuries of African Art and Thought,* 1989)

telling dirty jokes, or even stealing outright from humans or gods—all the while successfully pretending that he has done nothing wrong. Esu is thus the master rhetorician with whom everyone would prefer to be on good terms, even when one is never certain of his loyalty. Though one can never insulate oneself from Esu's mischief, trickery, or treacheries, one need not give Esu an excuse to be his natural self.

Esu as Creator of Confusion. Esu is also known to sow confusion in people's minds. Another story of Esu's interventionism is about two friends, whose farms were on either side of a road. Deciding to interfere with the farmers' friendship, Esu painted one side of his body white and the other side black. He then walked down the road on which sides the friends farmed. One friend said, "Did you see that very white fellow who just passed?" just as the other said, "Did you see that very dark fellow who just passed?" Soon they began arguing over whether this fellow was white or black, and the argument got increasingly intense. Just as the friends' tempers had cooled, and

Traditional shrine dedicated to Shango, the Yoruba god of thunder and lightning,
Ibadan, Nigeria, 1910 (Frobenius-Institut, Frankfurt)

they were concentrating once again on their work, Esu walked back up the road in the opposite direction. By this time, each friend was ready to apologize to the other for the "misunderstanding"—but their apologies led to even greater arguments and eventually the end of their friendship. Each told the other: "Sorry, I was wrong, you were right," and the shouting escalated to a point of name-calling ("You liar!") and the exchange of physical blows. In sum, Esu represents the Yoruba's concept of ambivalence and the perpetual human confusion that results from the ontological coexistence of the known and the unknown, the natural and the supernatural.

Odua. Odua (a shortened form of Oduduwa) is considered the creator of the Earth and the ancestral spirit of all Yoruba peoples. (The Yoruba sometimes call themselves "Omo Oduduwa," Children of Oduduwa.) Some Yoruba believed that Oduduwa once ruled all the Earth, with his capital in Ile-Ife. The king of Ile-Ife, called the Ooni, is regarded as a direct descendant of Oduduwa.

Orisala. Considered the "artisan" who molds human beings at inception, Orisala is believed to work in darkness, carving and shaping humans out of materials in the womb. For this reason, if a child is born deformed in any way, Orisala is held responsible. Likewise, anyone with a congenital deformity is believed to be under his protection. The Yoruba do not treat physical disability as a fault of nature but rather a result of the inscrutable will and

wisdom of Orisala. Some Yoruba theologians argue that at times Orisala intentionally misforms individuals as a reminder that God's will is unknowable and his power infinite. Such actions remind people to make appropriate sacrifices to Orisala so that none of their future children becomes one of these "reminders."

The Concept of Ogun. Ogun is considered to have begun as a concept and only later become a god. About two thousand years ago, *ogun* referred to a ritual ceremony held to honor a Yoruba who had distinguished himself at hunting or at war. Because the Yoruba were disturbed by violence and killing associated with these activities, the ritual was meant as a cleansing-of-the-soul process for the hunter or the warrior, so that some form of symbolic harmony could be reestablished within the individual and between him and other humans and the natural world. At a later stage in the development of the Yoruba culture, during the years 500–1590, Ogun grew into the deity known today throughout Nigeria and the Yoruba cultural diaspora.

Ogun the God. The god Ogun is considered the patron of hunters, warriors, and ironworkers (the people who make the equipment used in hunting and war). The Yoruba poet Wole Soyinka has written that Ogun is "the master craftsman and artist, farmer and warrior, essence of destruction and creativity, a recluse and a gregarious imbiber, a reluctant leader of men and deities," as well as "'Lord of the road' of Ifa."

ORANMIYAN

The son of the creator god Oduduwa and father of the powerful Shango, god of thunder and lightning, Oranmiyan was the great warrior-hero of Ile-Ife. The following story depicts the dangers of recalling such a powerful ancestor from the dead for trivial reasons.

Oduduwa ruled long over Ife. Orunmila, it is said, went to rule over Benin, where he remained for some time. But after a while Orunmila tired of his life there and returned to the sky. Affairs in Benin did not go well after Orunmila departed. The people sent messengers to Oduduwa asking him to come and take charge of Benin. Oduduwa was reluctant to leave Ife. He said, "If I go to Benin to give it a father, then Ife will have no father." The people of Benin continued to implore Oduduwa for help. At last he agreed to go to Benin. He took his son Oranmiyan with him to that city. He took charge of Benin's affairs, and he remained there until he heard he was much needed back in Ife. Oduduwa named Oranmiyan as ruler of Benin, after which he returned to govern Ife again. But Oduduwa did not live forever. When he knew he was going to die he sent for Oranmiyan. Oranmiyan made his own son ruler over Benin and returned to Ife, and as Oduduwa wanted him to do he became the oni, or oba, of that city.

By this time there were numerous kingdoms scattered across the earth, and war had come among humans. Because Ife was the first of all cities and because it was great in the minds of men it was envied everywhere. For this reason the obas of other places sought to vanquish Ife and diminish its reputation. But just as Ife's name was great, so was the name of Oranmiyan. For he was fierce and valorous in war. Whenever the enemy came to attack, Oranmiyan led Ife's warriors into battle. Wherever the heat of the battle was, that was where Oranmiyan was to be seen. Warrior heroes of many other cities came face to face with Oranmiyan in the fields and

were slain. The sunlight flashing from Oranmiyan's long sword struck terror into the hearts of those who sought to destroy Ife. Oranmiyan was the first on the battlefield and the last to leave, and his path could be seen by the corpses left behind by his weapons. The heroes of those times were numerous, but Oranmiyan was the greatest of them all, and while he lived Ife could not be subdued.

But Oranmiyan grew older. A time came when he knew that death would take him. He called the people together. He said: "Soon I must go. When I am no longer here, continue to live as heroes. Do not let our enemies make Ife small in the minds of men. Continue to be courageous so that Ife will go on living."

The people said to him: "Oranmiyan, you are the father of Ife. Reject death and remain here with us."

He answered: "No, it is not possible. Nevertheless I will not forget Ife. If great trouble comes to the city call me. I will give the old men the words to say, and when these words are spoken I will come back to help you."

He called the elders of Ife together and gave them the words. Then he went to the marketplace, all of the people of Ife following him. He arrived there. He struck his staff into the earth. It stood upright in the center of things. Oranmiyan said: "This is my mark. It will stand here forever to remind you of the courage of heroes." The staff turned into a shaft of stone which the people named Opa Oranmiyan, Oranmiyan's Staff.

Then the warrior hero Oranmiyan stamped his foot on the ground. The earth opened. He descended into the earth and it closed behind him. This was how Oranmiyan departed from his people.

Word reached far-off places that Oranmiyan no longer lived. The oba of a distant city said: "Well, now, he is gone and Ife is defenseless. It is time to bring Ife to its knees."

Ogun's Role among the Gods. According to legend, at the mythical beginning of reality, before the creation of the many gods in the Yoruba pantheon, there existed only one godhead, Orisa-nla, and his slave Atunda. When Orisa-nla became a tyrant, Atunda shattered him into pieces by rolling a rock down into the valley where Orisa-nla was tending his garden. These pieces became the thousands of gods that make up the Yoruba pantheon. (Orisa-nla, or "Great Orisa," is also a title given to Obatala, who in other Yoruba creation myths is credited with making the dry land and human forms, into whom Olorun breathed life.) After human beings were created by Olorun, the supreme deity, they had no way of communication with the gods until Ogun volunteered to trace a path through the mystical and existential chaos that separated gods and humans. For this reason Ogun is known as "Explorer," a title that also suits his protégés the hunters, who wander long distances in virgin territory searching for game and must be able to find their way home to the village at the end of the hunt. Because hunting and the harvest are both sources of food, Ogun, by stretching a metaphor, has also been characterized as the "owner" of the harvest and rainy seasons, periods when the earth in West Africa is full of abundant nourishment from vegetables and crops. Also by extension, modern people who work

ORANMIYAN (CONTINUED)

He gathered a force of warriors and sent them to destroy Ife. When the people of Ife saw the enemy approaching they went to the old men to whom Oranmiyan had given the secret words, saying, "Send for Oranmiyan quickly or Ife will die." The old men went to the marketplace and called Oranmiyan for help. There was a thunderous noise and the earth shook. The ground opened and Oranmiyan came out, his weapons in his hands. He led the warriors of Ife into battle. When the enemy saw Oranmiyan's weapons flashing in the sunlight terror overcame them. Those who were not killed turned and fled. The warriors of Ife pursued them until at last no living enemy was visible. Then they returned to the city. Oranmiyan stamped his foot on the ground of the marketplace. The earth opened. He descended. The earth closed over his head.

After that for many years Ife was not molested. People in other places said, "Ife remains great because although Oranmiyan is dead he is not truly dead."

There was a festival in Ife. There was drumming, dancing and singing. People feasted and drank much palm wine. Many of them became drunk. Darkness came. The festival went on. Someone said, "Oranmiyan should be here to dance and sing with us." Others said, "Yes, let us bring him out to lead us in our enjoyment." They went to the marketplace where Oranmiyan's staff was standing. They called on Oranmiyan to come out of the ground and join the festivities, but he did not appear. Someone said, "He will not come unless the secret words are spoken, the words that only the old men know." So they went through the city and found some of the elders to whom the words had been entrusted. They brought the old men to the marketplace and asked them to do what was necessary to bring Oranmiyan out of the ground.

The old men protested, saying: "No, it is not a good thing to molest Oranmiyan because of a festival. Let him rest. He should be called on only in times of great need. Those were his instructions."

But the people persisted, saying, "Do what is necessary, old men, for we want Oranmiyan to lead us in the dancing and singing."

The old men continued to protest. Yet at last they said the words: "Come swiftly, Oranmiyan. Ife is in danger."

The ground thundered and opened. Oranmiyan emerged, his weapons in his hands, his face fierce with the courage of a warrior. Because it was dark Oranmiyan could not distinguish one person from another. He believed that the men in the marketplace were the enemy who had come to destroy Ife. He began fighting, thrusting with his spear and slashing with his sword. He struck at anything that moved, killing many men of Ife. The city was in turmoil. People ran in every direction, Oranmiyan pursuing. The killing went on.

The dawn came. Light fell on the city. Now Oranmiyan could clearly see the corpses lying on the ground. He saw the tribal scars on the cheeks of the dead, and he knew then that he had been slaughtering his own people. Grief overcame him. He threw his weapons down. He said: "I was asked to come quickly because Ife was in danger. Therefore I came, and in the darkness of night I killed many of the people of Ife. Because of this terrible deed I will not fight again. I will never again come to Ife."

He stamped on the earth. The earth trembled and opened. Oranmiyan went down, and the earth closed behind him. Never after that was he seen in Ife.

His staff, in the form of a shaft of stone, still stands at that place, reminding people of the great warrior hero who once ruled over Ife, and of the slaughter that occurred because he was asked to help when the city was not really in danger.

Source: Harold Courlander, ed., "Oranmiyan, the Hero of Ife," in his *Tales of Yoruba Gods and Heroes* (New York: Crown, 1973).

---

with metals—including technologists and technicians such as engineers or car mechanics, as well as barbers, surgeons, and cooks—have adopted Ogun as their patron. Thus, it could be argued that Ogun is among the most traveled and longest surviving of the ancient Yoruba gods and remains a constant presence in the psyche of the religious Yoruba.

Shango. The god of thunder and lightning, Shango is said to have originated as a human being, the grandson of Oduduwa. The warrior Oranmiyan, a son of Oduduwa, is supposed to have been part of a military expedition from Ile-Ife, his father's country, to Nupeland, in northern Nigeria, where he met and married a Nupe princess. Shango is said to be the product of this marital union, but, like most other stories of origin shrouded in myths and legends, this one is not fully documented. Some scholars, including Samuel Johnson, think that Oranmiyan may have been just an able lieutenant to Oduduwa and elevated to the status of "son" by Shango's followers as a means of enhancing Shango's prestige. Johnson connects Shango to an historical king of Oyo, who was so tyrannical that his council forced him to commit suicide. After Shango hanged himself on a tree, his few, but inventive, sympathizers sought to whitewash the reputation of their leader. Perhaps in collusion with the elders of the Oyo, who would rather disguise their shame over the king's misrule, Shango's followers claimed that ever since the king had hanged himself on a tree, lightning had been randomly striking and killing some of the oldest and most valued trees in the country. These acts of nature were interpreted as a signal from the dead monarch that, unless he were appeased, he would continue to strike trees and then humans, until he had exacted enough revenge for the humiliation he had suffered. Hoping to prevent further lightning strikes, the Oyo agreed to say that Shango had not hanged himself but rather transformed himself into a deity. Thus, Shango became the god of thunder and lightning and attained almost the same level of power as Ogun. Shango resides in the sky, from where he controls the power of light—including, in modern times, electricity. The largest government-operated electric utility company in present-day Nigeria has as its national logo a statue of Shango rescuing light from the darkness. Shango is, as it were, the "Divine Electrician." Although he is generally considered benevolent, Shango is nevertheless capable of dispatching thunderstorms to destroy villages or people who have incurred his displeasure. Shango's favorite color is red. He is capable of turning against a follower who owes him a debt of regular sacrifice. Yet, he is also known as a protector of the helpless and an enforcer of justice. For example, he might pursue a doctor who misuses his expertise to kill rather than cure unsuspecting patients. Whenever a doctor, a hunter, a farmer, or someone in another walk of life is killed by lightning in the course of duty, it is often believed that Shango is fighting with the god-protector of that person's profession, or that the person owes a sacrifice to Shango, or that he had immoral motives for undertaking the task during which lightning struck.

The Cult of Shango. When a person is successfully initiated into the cult of Shango, he is considered to have been "mounted," or possessed by the god. During this mount the initiated behaves as though in a trance, perhaps jumping up and down or making uncontrollable, twisting body movements, while uttering largely incomprehensible words in a deep, guttural, thunderous voice that is considered peculiarly Shango's. This pattern of behavior is supposed to mirror Shango's temperament. The words are called "fire"; the body movements are considered the shock of the god's electricity. The initiated may be "brought back" to normal behavior only after he or she has become exhausted and a sacrifice of Shango's favorite foods—lamb with palm oil, kola nuts, and yam porridge—are prepared for the consumption, on behalf of Shango, by the exhausted and by then ravenous devotee. Probably because of the rhythmic "mounting" of the initiation, the Yoruba consider Shango the god of dance.

Sources:

Wade Abimbola, ed. and trans., *Ifa Divination Poetry* (New York: NOK, 1977).

Sandra T. Barnes, ed., *Africa's Ogun: Old World and New,* expanded edition (Bloomington: Indiana University Press, 1989).

Henry Louis Gates Jr., *The Signifying Monkey: A Theory of Afro-American Literary Criticism* (New York: Oxford University Press, 1988).

E. Bolaji Idowu, *Olodumare: God in Yoruba Belief,* revised and enlarged edition (Plainview: Original Publications, 1995).

Samuel Johnson, *The History of the Yorubas from the Earliest Times to the Beginning of the British Protectorate,* edited by O. Johnson (London: Routledge, 1921).

Wole Soyinka, *Myth, Literature and the African World* (Cambridge & New York: Cambridge University Press, 1976).

ISLAMIC AND CHRISTIAN INFLUENCES

Islam. Though some rulers and their courts converted to Islam and even made pilgrimages to Mecca and carried on wars in the name of Islam, the religion did not become widespread among the general populace until after 1590. Even some rulers who called themselves converts to Islam followed that religion most faithfully during visits from Muslim traders or diplomats and at other times practiced traditional religions. As in the Ashanti kingdom to the west, the dominant religion in the northern part of West African was animism—nature mysticism. However, Islam had already established a strong foothold in the Yoruba lands of present-day Nigeria as well as in Mali and the surrounding Mande territories. Most of what is known about Islam in West Africa, particularly Mali, comes from the writings of Ibn Battuta, a North African Muslim of the Berber ethnic group who received a formal Islamic education in the northern city of Tangier. At the age of twenty-one, he went to Mecca for further studies, distinguished himself as a scholar, and traveled widely, visiting China, Ceylon, India, Assam, and the Middle East as well as West Africa. His travels in the Empire of Mali started on 18 February 1352 at Walaha, where he observed: "these people are Muslims, punctilious in observing the hours of prayer, studying books of law, and memorizing the Koran." From Walaha he proceeded to the capital city, where he noted, "the inhabitants have a great sense of fairness, uprightness, justice, and fair dealing among themselves and with foreigners." He also wrote that the people "are careful to observe the hours of prayer, and assiduous in attending them in congregations, and in bringing up their children to them. On Fridays, if a man does not go early to the mosque, he cannot find a corner to pray in, on account of the crowd. It is the custom of theirs to send each man his boy [to the mosque] with his prayer-mat; the boy spreads it out for his master in a place befitting him and [remains on it] until [his master] comes to the mosque. The prayer-mats are made of the leaves of a tree resembling a date palm, but without fruit." According to Ibn Battuta, the Malians had a zeal for learning the Quran by heart: "They put their children in chains if they show any backwardness in memorizing it, and they are not set free until they have it by heart."

Ruins of a stone mosque built circa 900–1500 in Kumbi Saleh, a major trading center in the Empires of Ghana and Mali (from Monica Blackmun Visonà, *A History of Art in Africa*, 2001)

Mansa Musa. Of the many mansas (kings) who ruled Mali, none did more to create the reputation of the empire as an Islamic state than Mansa Kankan Musa (ruled 1312–1337). His 1324 pilgrimage to Mecca with a large and richly equipped entourage enhanced the reputation of Mali not only as a wealthy empire but also as a center of Islamic learning and religion. Musa's bureaucracy and military created the right conditions for merchants and clerics to work in peace and security throughout the empire and beyond. As Musa expanded the boundaries of the empire, he also extended the influence of Islam.

Christianity. When Christianity arrived in West Africa in the late fifteenth century, the people were initially no more eager to embrace this religion than they had Islam. According to W. Walton Claridge, they wanted to trade with Europeans but objected to a Portuguese policy of converting West Africans to Christianity. In answer to a request by the Portuguese Crown to station a permanent Christian mission among his people, one Ashanti ruler replied:

> I'm not insensible to the high honor which your great master, the chief of Portugal, has this day conferred on me. His

friendship I have long endeavored to merit by the strictness of my dealing with the Portuguese, and by my constant exertions to procure an immediate lading for their vessels. But never until this day did I observe such a difference in the appearance of his subjects; they have hitherto been only meanly attired, were easily contented with the commodities they received; and so far from wishing to continue in this country, were never happy until they could complete their lading, and return. Now I remark a strange difference. A great number richly dressed are anxious to be allowed to build houses, and to continue among us. Men of such eminence, conducted by a commander who from his own account seems to have descended from the God who made day and night, can never bring themselves to endure the hardships of this climate nor would they here be able to procure any of the luxuries that abound in their own country. The passions that are common to us all will therefore inevitably bring on disputes; and it is far preferable that both nations should continue on the same footing they have hitherto done, allowing your ships to come and go as usual; the desire of seeing each other occasionally will preserve peace between us.

Against the Ashanti king's objections, however, the Portuguese proceeded to build a church and send missionaries,

Bronze figure of a Benin court official wearing a cross pendant, circa 1500–1700. The Metropolitan Museum of Art, Gift of Mr. and Mrs. Klaus G. Perls, 1991. (1991.17.32) Photograph, all rights reserved, The Metropolitan Museum of Art.

backing the efforts with military force. In 1482 they built Elmina Castle, a fortress that not only provided protection from attacks but also served as a secure base for evangelizing and slave trading.

Sources:

Norman R. Bennett, *Africa and Europe: From Roman Times to National Independence,* second edition (New York: Africana, 1975).

K. A. Busia, *The Challenge of Africa* (New York: Praeger, 1962).

W. Walton Claridge, *A History of the Gold Coast from the Earliest Times to the Commencement of the Twentieth Century,* 2 volumes (London: Murray, 1915).

Cheikh Anta Diop, *Civilization or Barbarism: An Authentic Anthropology,* translated by Yaa-Lengi Meema Ngemi, edited by Harold J. Salemson and Marjolijn de Jager (Brooklyn, N.Y.: Lawrence Hill, 1991).

Ibn Battuta, *Travels in Asia and Africa, 1325–1354,* 3 volumes, translated by H. A. R. Gibb (London: Routledge, 1929).

Edmund Ilogu, *Christianity and Igbo Culture* (Leiden: Brill, 1974).

Elizabeth Isichei, *A History of African Societies to 1870* (Cambridge: Cambridge University Press, 1997).

METAPHYSICAL AND MORAL IDEAS IN TRADITIONAL RELIGIONS AND PHILOSOPHY

Life after Death. Most West African traditional religions teach that there exists life after death. "Spirits" by the Senegalese poet Birago Diop expresses the animist belief that the spirits of the dead remain among the living:

> Those who are dead are not ever gone;
> They are in the darkness that grows lighter
> And in the darkness that grows darker.
> The dead are not down in the earth.
> They are in the trembling of the trees,
> In the groaning of the woods,
> In the water that runs
> In the water that sleeps.
> They are in the hut, they are in the crowd.
> The dead are not dead.

Death may claim the body and disintegrate it into primordial matter, but the soul—and perhaps the mind or spirit, too—is believed to persist either in the land of the ancestral spirits or in an intermediate world of wandering spirits that neither inhabit human beings nor are admitted to the esteemed world of the ancestors. Some ethnic groups, including the Igbo, however, believe that there exists another, invisible, world, the *ani mmo,* where the dead who have lived full life spans continue their lives much as they did in the visible world, practicing the same trades or professions and organizing into societies much like those in which they lived on earth. The peoples of this otherworld are also separated by ethnic groups. Since reproduction is not a viable function in this world, women reunite not with their husbands but with their father's family. Most Igbo believe that *ani mmo* is underground, or so far away that it is unreachable by the living, even if one traveled an entire lifetime. As an Igbo told Arthur Glyn Leonard, "We Igbo look forward to the next world as being much the same as this. . . . we picture life there to be exactly as it is in this world. The ground there is just the same as it is here; the earth is similar. There are forests and hills and valleys with rivers flowing and roads leading from one town to another." Life in this spirit land is not only comparable but contiguous to the land of the living, with constant coming and going between the two worlds as births, deaths, and reincarnations create a chain of endless traffic.

Ghosts. People who die before their allotted time remain on earth as ghosts. They can talk to people who did not know them when alive, and to these individuals the ghosts seem to be normal human beings. Ghosts may marry and have children, and one may marry a ghost without knowing it. If someone whom a ghost knew before death comes to town, a ghost disappears. When the day appointed by Olorun arrives, the ghost "dies" a second death and goes to heaven.

Reincarnation. Nearly all West African religions include the belief that the spirit of an ancestor can be reincarnated in a newborn child. Such an ancestral reincarnation is believed to occur at the moment of conception, when the spirit of an esteemed ancestor "passes" into the forming child and becomes the child's soul. If a child is believed to be a reincarnation of an ancestor—either because the child bears a physical resemblance to that person or because a Dibia or Babalawo has learned through divination that an ancestor intends to return to life via the child—the infant is given the same name as the ancestor. Over decades or even centuries, a renowned ancestor might be reincarnated in many descendants. All individuals with the same name in a particular clan are considered spiritual descendants of the ancestor whose name they bear, and they are expected to make annual ritual sacrifices to that ancestor.

The *Ogbanje* or *Abiku*. If a woman has several children in succession who die in childbirth, infancy, or childhood, the children are believed to be reincarnations of the same angry ancestor, known as an *ogbanje* or *abiku*, who has decided to repeatedly punish the family. A diviner is usually consulted to establish the identity of this ancestor, why he or she is angry and unsettled in the spirit world, and what must be done to stop the cyclical returns. The diviner may also work with other "medicine men" to keep the child alive. Such intervention is often believed to be a strenuous battle because the child, as a spiritual extension of the tormenting spirit, may not wish to stay alive. The doctors may design charms intended to make the *ogbanje* forget to leave this world. The parents of the *ogbanje* may also join cults devoted to interventionist sacrifices and prayers meant to protect the *ogbanje* from its spirit double. If all these interventions fail and the child dies, the corpse is often branded—with a sign on the forehead, a finger cut, or in some other way—in the belief that when the same *ogbanje* returns it will bear this identifying mark. People also believe that once an *ogbanje* is so marked, it is more reluctant to return because parents who recognize it immediately will be less susceptible to developing emotional attachment to it and will thus be less hurt by its passing.

Terra-cotta figures made in Bankoni, Empire of Mali, circa 1200–1500, usually placed on burial mounds as tributes to ancestors (Art Institute of Chicago)

Destiny. According to Segun Gbadegesin, among the Yoruba before a child is born—or reborn—the ancestral guardian soul appears before Olorun to receive a new body, new breath, and a new destiny *(iwa)*. Kneeling before Olorun, the soul is given the opportunity to choose its own destiny. It may choose its fate freely, although Olorun may refuse requests that are unreasonable or are not made humbly. One's destiny includes the fixed day on which the soul must return to heaven and the individual's personality, occupation, and luck. Though the day of one's death can never be postponed, other aspects of one's destiny may be modified by human acts and by superhuman beings and forces. If an individual has the full support and protection of his ancestral guardian soul, as well as Olorun and sometimes other relevant deities, he or she may enjoy the chosen destiny.

Fate and Character. Closely related to the idea of destiny is the concept of individual character, which is supposed to be unchanging throughout life and to account for the person's fate, his or her fortunes and misfortunes. While some cultures, such as the Igbo, believe that God endows each individual directly with a chi that determines his or her character, other cultures believe that character comes from God in a more indirect manner. Some believe, for example, that "nature" fixes the person's moral character and that any effort to change it is a waste of time. Among those who believe that character can be altered, the methods for achieving such a goal vary. Some make sacrifices and say prayers. One may also argue with one's chi. In fact, the Igbo say "onye kwe, chi ya kwe" (if one says yes, one's chi also says yes), implying that an effort of the will is sufficient to transform the course of one's life. Other ethnic groups might resort to other methods, such as pharmacology, to reorient a person's natural inclinations, with the goal of escaping a "bad" fate, or of choosing a better one.

Concepts of the Person. While the Igbo believe that the person as a whole is morally constituted of his chi, they also think that chi needs the tripartite structure of body, soul, and mind (or spirit) in order to function. Like the Akan, who have a similar tripartite conception, the Yoruba believe that a person is a composition also of at least three elements: the most important is the ancestral guardian spirit, which is associated with one's "head" and destiny and with the belief in reincarnation. The second element is the breath, which resides in the lungs and chest and is served by the nostrils. The breath is the biological essence of the person, the vital force that is responsible for the mechanics of organic life. The third element is the "shadow," or soul, which has no function during life and just follows the living body about. At death, however, the soul is the part of the individual that travels to the world of the spirits.

Purity of the Soul. For the Yoruba, the ancestral spirit who guards the purity of a person's soul is associated with the head, where the soul is presumed to reside. It is sometimes spoken of as the *ori* (head) and as the *olori* (owner of the head). A lucky person is called *olori rere* (one who has a good head), and an unlucky person is *olori buruku* (one who has a bad head). To call a Yoruba *olori buruku* is regarded as an insult and a curse against him and his ancestral guardian. At the same time, the ancestral guardian is said to remain in the land of the spirits, doing exactly the same things there that the individual is doing on earth, but—except for twins and *abiku*—the guardian is always an adult. Some Yoruba believe that there are two ancestral guardian souls, one on earth and one in heaven. Others say that one resides in the forehead—which is associated with luck, a part of one's destiny—while a second resides in the crown of the head and guards against evil, and a third resides in the occiput, facing backward and guarding against danger from the rear and the past.

Dualism. Observing the division of the sexes, the Akan created two corresponding concepts to denote them: *ntoro* (the male principle of life) and *abusua* (the female principle). Semen is believed to bestow "male" spiritual qualities. A woman's blood transmits female qualities. Only the woman's blood is believed to be passed on to the child. This idea underlies the matrilineal system of descent and inheritance. In traditional religious systems the supreme being is sometimes genderless or double gendered. In some places the most powerful God is considered male, but in others God has a feminine side that counterbalances the masculine.

Virtue and Vice. According to J. B. Danquah, among the Akan of present-day Ghana, where the good of the family is more important than the well-being of the individual, "things that are dishonorable and undignified are actions that in disgracing oneself also disgrace the family, and are therefore held to be vices." For the Akan "the highest virtue is found in honor and dignity," and tradition and social taste determine what is right and wrong. Among the Hausa-speaking peoples of Nigeria, a virtuous individual is described as *shi mutumin kirki ne* (one who has intrinsic goodness), and a bad person is a *ba shi da kirki* (one who has no *kirki*). One may also say that one's people or land is *kasar mutan kirki* (the land of intrinsically good people). As A. H. M. Kirk-Greene puts it, "The warrior-hero of Hausaland may be seven feet tall, with the heart of a lion and the strength of a bull-elephant, of heroic stature at everything, and yet never qualify for recognition as *mutumin kirki*." Yet, "another man may earn that very admiration, though he be as modest as an ostrich and meeker than a gazelle." Goodness is always good, whereas generally admirable qualities such as intelligence, toughness, and cleverness are good only when they are used wisely.

Truth. Like goodness, truth is also universally esteemed. Truth speaking and basing one's conduct on truth telling are considered of the highest priority in social interaction. The Igbo call a person who is trustworthy "Eji okwu ya eme ife" (one whose word can be relied on). The Hausa have a proverb that says "Gaskiya ta fi kwabo" (Truth is worth more than gold). A good command of language was highly valued among West Africans, probably because most West African cultures did not have sophisticated systems of writing, making the spoken word crucial in many aspects of society. Proverbs were one of the most effective ways to convey complicated ideas in the shortest possible manner.

Generosity. Sharing with others was essential in the agrarian West African societies. A rich person's sin was avarice. A proverb that was common throughout West Africa says "Avarice is not a trait that calls for honour."

Patience and Prudence. Many West African cultures have sayings such as "No condition is permanent"; "Whatever the trouble, it always has an end"; and "Whatever you have endured, you will always see one with a worse fate." All these adages are meant to counsel the virtue of patience. A person with good judgment and common sense is not only patient but also prudent in the organization of his or her personal life and in dealings with others. The Hausa term *mai hankali* and the Igbo phrase *onye nwere uche* describe the prudent and well-behaved person. Conversely, *ba shi da hankali* and *onweyi uche* describe someone who lacks common sense or mature judgment.

Propriety and Respect. A person who has no sense of shame is usually considered lacking empathy and a sense of morality. That person tends to be avoided by others who are more attentive to the feelings of others. A person who is not lacking in shame is able to display propriety and the appropriate level of self-respect and respect toward others.

Sources:

Chinua Achebe, *Anthills of the Savannah* (London: Heinemann, 1987).

Achebe, *Morning Yet on Creation Day: Essays* (London: Heinemann, 1975).

Ulli Beier, ed., *The Origin of Life and Death: African Creation Myths* (London: Heinemann, 1966).

J. B. Danquah, *The Akan Doctrine of God: A Fragment of Gold Coast Ethics and Religion*, second edition (London: Cass, 1968).

Emmanuel Eze, ed., *African Philosophy: An Anthology* (Malden, Mass. & Oxford: Blackwell, 1998).

Segun Gbadegesin, *African Philosophy: Traditional Yoruba Philosophy and Contemporary African Realities* (New York: Peter Lang, 1991).

Gbadegesin, "Individuality, Community, and the Moral Order," in *African Philosophy: An Anthology*, pp. 130–141.

Constance B. Hilliard, *Intellectual Traditions of Pre-Colonial Africa* (Boston: McGraw-Hill, 1998).

Ellen Conroy Kennedy, ed. and trans., *The Negritude Poets: An Anthology of Translations from the French* (New York: Viking, 1975).

A. H. M. Kirk-Greene, "'Mutumin Kirki': The Concept of the Good Person in Hausa," in *African Philosophy: An Anthology*, pp. 121–129.

Kirk-Greene, trans., *Hausa ba dabo ba ne: 500 Hausa Proverbs* (Ibadan, Nigeria: Oxford University Press, 1966).

Arthur Glyn Leonard, *The Lower Niger and Its Tribes* (London & New York: Macmillan, 1906).

John Mbiti, *Introduction to African Religion* (London: Heinemann, 1975).

Robert Farris Thompson, *The Flash of the Spirit: African and Afro-American Art and Philosophy* (New York: Random House, 1984).

MYTHOLOGY

Stories of a Culture. In all cultures, myths are important sources of philosophical thought. Myths are not false stories. They are, however, stories whose meanings may not be construed literally. Their truths, like those derived from novels or short stories, need to be extracted through interpretation. Mythology illuminates the human condition, sometimes at a particular place and time and sometimes for all time. Many myths, for example, are about the founding of a particular village, town, or nation, but there are others that aim to provide answers about questions such as the origins of life and death, why the earth is round, why time exists, or why there are different sexes. Philosophers in all cultures have imagined nonexistent entities and assigned motives and activities to them in order to explain why natural or social realities exist. Myths educate a people about the various meanings their society has assigned to their existence. Myths also legitimize cultural practices in regard to key experiences such as circumcision, marriage, and burial rights, and they provide moral and ethical guidance by articulating and promoting virtue and discouraging vice. The stories myths tell are enjoyable in themselves, helping to ensure that they are passed on from one generation to another. When myths present themselves as fairy tales, however, they are meant to educate. The following are examples of different kinds of myths.

A Causal-Explanatory Myth. As recounted by Oyekan Owomoyela, the Yoruba sky god once had his abode close to the world of men. During these days, the sky was almost in arm's reach, and fruits and other delicacies were available in abundance to be plucked by humans. But in their greed humans gathered more than they could eat, causing the sky god considerable pain over all the waste. Moreover, when humans pounded yams in their mortars, they deliberately raised their pestles so high that they kept hitting the sky, his sacred abode. Thus doubly alienated, the sky god retaliated. Instead of expelling humans from the abundance on earth, the sky god removed himself from humans, making his new abode far away from human waste, insensitivity, and thoughtlessness.

A Myth of Ethnic Origin. The Yoruba believe that they are direct descendants of Oduduwa, the god who

AN ORIGIN MYTH

The Efik and Ibibio peoples of present-day Nigeria tell a story that explains "Why the Sun and the Moon Live in the Sky":

MANY YEARS ago the sun and the water were great friends, and both lived on the earth together. The sun very often used to visit the water, but the water never returned his visits. At last the sun asked the water why it was that he never came to see him in his house. The water replied that the sun's house was not big enough, and that if he came with his people he would drive the sun out.

The water then said, "If you wish me to visit you, you must build a very large compound; but I warn you that it will have to be a tremendous place, as my people are very numerous and take up a lot of room."

The sun promised to build a very large compound, and soon afterward he returned home to his wife, the moon, who greeted him with a broad smile when he opened the door. The sun told the moon what he had promised the water and the next day he commenced building a large compound in which to entertain his friend.

When it was completed, he asked the water to come and visit him the next day.

When the water arrived, he called out to the sun and asked him whether it would be safe for him to enter, and the sun answered, "Yes, come in, my friend."

The water then began to flow in, accompanied by the fish and all the water animals.

Very soon the water was knee-deep, so he asked the sun if it was still safe, and the sun again said, "Yes," so more water came in.

When the water was level with the top of a man's head, the water said to the sun, "Do you want more of my people to come?"

The sun and the moon both answered, "Yes," not knowing any better, so the water flowed in, until the sun and moon had to perch themselves on the top of the roof.

Again the water addressed the sun, but, receiving the same answer, and more of his people rushing in, the water very soon overflowed the top of the roof, and the sun and the moon were forced to go up into the sky, where they have remained ever since.

Source: Paul Radin, ed., "Why the Sun and the Moon Live in the Sky," in *African Folktales & Sculpture* (New York: Pantheon, 1952), p. 41.

The Origin of All Things. The Yoruba believe that in the beginning there was the god Orisa-nla. As in other cultures, he is God as the Uncaused Cause who enables all else to exist.

Origins of Life and Death. The Vai of Sierra Leone believe that Death once lived with God, continually pleading to be allowed to go to Earth and live among humans. God had promised humankind that although he had allowed Death to exist, humans would not die. Thus, God had a dilemma: How could he let Death go wherever it pleased and still give humans the protection he had promised? God decided to send humans new skins that would protect them from natural elements and therefore save them from Death. Unfortunately, the messenger carrying the new skins was waylaid by a snake who stole the skins. From that day humans have always had a grudge against snakes and tried to kill them whenever possible. In turn snakes avoid humans and live alone. Because the snake still has the basket of skins, he is able to shed one skin and wear a new one. In addition to offering explanations for why humans dread snakes, and why snakes shed their skins and stay away from humans, this story accounts for how death came to be and why humans cannot protect themselves from dying.

Creation of the World. The Fulani of northern Nigeria believe that the world came into existence by the power of the Word. In the beginning, they recount:

the sky was large, white, and very clear. It was empty; there were no stars and no moon; only a tree stood in the air and there was wind. This tree fed on the atmosphere and ants lived on it. Wind, tree, ants, and atmosphere were controlled by the power of the Word. But the Word was not something that could be seen. It was a force that enabled one thing to create another.

Sources:
Chinua Achebe, *Anthills of the Savannah* (London: Heinemann, 1987).

Achebe, *Morning Yet on Creation Day: Essays* (London: Heinemann, 1975).

Ulli Beier, ed., *The Origin of Life and Death: African Creation Myths* (London: Heinemann, 1966).

Harold Courlander, ed., *A Treasury of African Folklore* (New York: Crown, 1975).

J. B. Danquah, *The Akan Doctrine of God: A Fragment of Gold Coast Ethics and Religion*, second edition (London: Cass, 1968).

Basil Davidson, *West Africa Before the Colonial Era: A History to 1850* (London & New York: Longman, 1998).

Cheikh Anta Diop, *The African Origins of Civilization: Myth or Reality*, translated by Mercer Cook (Chicago: Lawrence Hill, 1974).

Jacob U. Egharevba, *The City of Benin, Benin Law and Custom, Some Stories of Ancient Benin*, [and] *Some Tribal Gods of Southern Nigeria* (Nendeln, Liechtenstein: Kraus Reprints, 1971).

Emmanuel Eze, ed., *African Philosophy: An Anthology* (Malden, Mass. & Oxford: Blackwell, 1998).

Leo Frobenius and Douglas C. Fox, *African Genesis* (Berkeley, Cal.: Turtle Island Foundation, 1983).

created the Earth and once ruled it from Ile-Ife. Many historians hypothesize that Oduduwa may have been an Eastern prince who migrated to West Africa to found a kingdom. Yoruba mythology, however, explains that the Yoruba have always lived in Nigeria, because God made their ancestor Oduduwa and deposited him there.

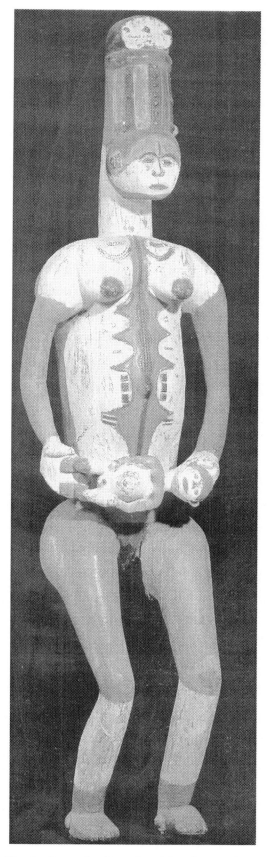

Wooden figure of an Igbo minor deity who served as a deputy of the high god Chukwu (Private Collection)

Segun Gbadegesin, *African Philosophy: Traditional Yoruba Philosophy and Contemporary African Realities* (New York: Peter Lang, 1991).

Marcel Griaule and Germaine Dieterlen, *Le Mythe Cosmogonique* (Paris: Institut d'Ethnologie, 1965).

Constance B. Hilliard, *Intellectual Traditions of Pre-Colonial Africa* (Boston: McGraw-Hill, 1998).

E. Bolaji Idowu, *Olodumare: God in Yoruba Belief*, revised and enlarged edition (Plainview: Original Publications, 1995).

A. H. M. Kirk-Greene, trans., *Hausa ba dabo ba ne: 500 Hausa Proverbs* (Ibadan, Nigeria: Oxford University Press, 1966).

John Mbiti, *Introduction to African Religion* (London: Heinemann, 1975).

Oyekan Owomoyela, *Yoruba Trickster Tales* (Lincoln: University of Nebraska Press, 1997).

Paul Radin and Elinore Marvel, eds., *African Folktales & Sculpture*, revised and enlarged edition (New York: Pantheon, 1964).

Wole Soyinka, *Myth, Literature and the African World* (Cambridge & New York: Cambridge University Press, 1976).

P. Amaury Talbot, *Life in Southern Nigeria: The Magic, Beliefs, and Customs of the Ibibio Tribe* (London: Macmillan, 1923).

Robert Farris Thompson, *The Flash of the Spirit: African and Afro-American Art and Philosophy* (New York: Random House, 1984).

SOCIAL AND POLITICAL PHILOSOPHY

Individualism and Communalism. While some West African societies, such as the Igbo, are generally considered individualistic, others, such as the Yoruba, are often characterized as communalistic. In societies where the individual is provided the incentive to excel, tensions always exist about how to maintain social harmony in the midst of disparities in wealth and status. In societies that emphasize the welfare of the group over that of the individual, there are invariably anxieties about stifling the individual creativity necessary for innovation and renewal of the social whole. The societies of West Africa between 500 to 1590 were a mixture of different social forms—from feudalism in the Muslim north and the kingdoms of Ashanti, Ile-Ife, and Oyo to the republican confederacies of the Igbo.

Socialization. Basing his observations on fieldwork, Segun Gbadegesin has observed that, among the Yoruba, the socialization of the individual starts at birth: "The new baby arrives into the hands of waiting elders of the household: the waiting family members introduce the baby to the world with cheerfulness and joy, often with songs and controlled jubilation, *Ayo abara tintin*—This is a little thing of joy." Seven days after its birth the infant has a naming ceremony, a proper welcome into the clan. Once given a name, the child becomes a recognized and entitled member of the group and is expected to realize his or her individual potential —his or her "destiny"—within this community. Other initiations that follow, such as circumcision or "secret" initiatory education, are meant to integrate the individual further into a group role—such as father, mother, warrior, iron smith, or herder.

A HAUSA SOCIAL FABLE

The following folktale from the Hausa of present-day Nigeria explains how old customs can be abandoned once they are called into question.

A certain woman had two daughters. One was married to a man who lived in a town where no one was allowed to go to sleep, the other to one in a town where no one might spit.

One day the woman cooked a dish of sweetmeats to take to the daughter who lived in the town where no one was allowed to go to sleep. As soon as the dish was ready she started off and, when she arrived, all the household said to her, "Welcome, welcome!" Food was prepared for her, for the son-in-law said, "See, my mother-in-law has come."

But the daughter said, "O parent, no one may sleep here. Do not eat too much lest sleepiness should overcome you."

But the mother said, "I knew long before you were born that sleep was not permitted here."

"Oh, very well then," replied the daughter, "I'll say no more." And the mother ate every bit of the food that was brought to her.

That night, although she lay down, she managed to keep awake. In the morning the daughter took up her jar to go to the stream for water and said to her mother, "See here, I have put the breakfast on to boil. Please keep up the fire while I am away."

But when the daughter had gone, although her mother managed to replenish the fire for a time, drowsiness over-came her in the end, and she lay down and fell fast asleep.

Just then a neighbor came to get fire and, when she saw the sleeping woman, she exclaimed, "Alas! So-and-so's mother-in-law is dead."

Then the drummers were sent for, and soon the whole town had assembled at the house and the grave had been dug. The drums were saying:

"Birrim, birrim, *get a corpse mat,*
Death's in the son-in-law's house."

But the daughter heard from where she was, and she cried out:

"Stay, oh, stay, don't get a corpse mat,
We are accustomed to sleep."

And when she had come to her house, she roused her mother, and said, "Wake up, wake up." Then the mother awoke with a start and the people were terrified, but they soon saw that it was nothing to be afraid of, and the whole town began to learn how to sleep.

Now the mother returned to her own home, and one day she cooked more sweetmeats and decided to visit her other daughter, the one living in the town where no one might spit.

When she arrived, the household said, "Welcome, wel-come!" And the son-in-law said, "My mother-in-law has come." So he killed a fowl and sent her a dish of rice. The daughter said to her mother, "Do not eat too much. You know that in this town no one is allowed to spit."

The Private Sphere. The family unit was an impor-tant—perhaps the most important—social unit in West Africa. With some notable exceptions, most of traditional West African societies were patriarchal. The head of the family, usually a polygamous male, exercised leadership and authority over his wives and children. When the head of the family was a matriarch, an equivalent hierarchy of authority was maintained. While the children were still quite young, they were educated to assist their parents not only in domestic chores but also in farmwork or selling goods at the market.

The Public Sphere. The process of socialization that began in the family continued in the larger community through age-grade associations, initiation rites, and various clubs. The child learned how older members of the commu-nity made sacrifices for the good of the whole group by tak-ing part in activities such as road building, defense, legislation, and law enforcement, as well as doing volunteer work to help

the elderly and the poor. Gbadegesin points out that among the Yoruba the family prepares the way for solidarity and selflessness within the community. What has been called African communalism in fact stems from a family structure in which an entire community is a single clan. Writing about the Akan, K. A. Busia commented: "There is, everywhere, the heavy accent on family—the blood relatives, the group of kinsfolk held together by a common origin and a common obligation to its members, to those who are living and those who are dead. . . . The individual is brought up to think of himself in relation to this group and to behave always in such a way as to bring honor and not disgrace to its members."

Communal Ownership. The organization of socio-economic life was based on the principle of the common ownership of land, which is the major source of livelihood in any nonindus-trial, agrarian subsistence economy. Ownership of land was vested in the community, which annually apportioned it to individuals on the basis of need. An assigned parcel of land

A HAUSA SOCIAL FABLE (CONTINUED)

The mother replied, "Thanks for the information! I knew that before ever you were born."

"Very well," said the daughter, and she took no more notice. The mother ate until she was full.

Now when night came, she wanted very much to spit, but she did not know where she could do so without being found out. At last she went to the place where the horses were tied, and she spat, and covered the place with some of the cut grass there. But the earth was not used to this, and the part spat upon rose up and began to complain, saying:

"Umm, umm, *I am not used to this,*
Umm, umm, *I am not used to this.*"

Soon all the people came and said, "Who has spat here?" Then they said, "Bring out the magic gourds, the small one and the large, and let everyone come here and step over them; and the gourds will catch hold of the one who has spat." So all the people of the town stepped over them, but no one was seized and they were surprised. Then someone said, "See here, there is a stranger amongst us, let her come and step over the gourds."

Immediately when she had come and had lifted up a leg to step over, the gourds seized her, and everyone said, "It is she who has spat, it is she who has spat!" And the gourds began singing these words:

"*The things which clasp and hold on,*
The mother-in-law has got them."

She could not sit down, for they held on to her body.

Now, the spider, that interfering person, met her, and said, "O mother-in-law, how lucky you are to have gourds which sing such a beautiful song. I should like to have them."

So she replied, "Very well, spit on the ground and say that it was not you who did it."

And when he had done so, he said, "There! But it is not I who have done it, if it is I, O you magic gourds, seize me."

And immediately the gourds loosed the woman and seized him. Then they began singing:

"*The things which clasp and hold on,*
The spider of spiders has got them,"

and the spider felt exceedingly pleased, and began to dance.

But soon he got tired and said, "O mother-in-law, you thing to be avoided, come and take your gourds." But she refused to do so.

Then the spider climbed a tree, and when he got high up he threw himself down on his buttocks, so as to smash the gourds. But they moved to one side, and so the spider's back was broken and he died. Then the magic gourds returned to where they had come from, and all the townspeople began to spit, for they saw that there was no harm in it.

Source: Paul Radin, ed., "The Town Where None Might Go to Sleep," in *African Folktales & Sculpture* (New York: Pantheon, 1952), pp. 247–249.

---

reverted automatically to the community once the crops were harvested. Even in the case of a homestead, the community understood that a person "owned" a house for only as long as he or she resided in it and maintained it.

The Political Economy of Sharing. There were consequences, some of them negative, to the communal sharing of wealth that existed in West Africa. Writing about the Akan, Busia described how it could be wasteful and detrimental to individual initiative: "When an African earns a pile of money, it is not his alone. He belongs to a tribe and a family. That money, under the law, is as much his sister's children's as it is his own. In fact, his first duty is towards his sister's children. . . . At once, before he can derive any personal benefit from it, his relatives descend upon him, making demands which, under the family system in Africa, he cannot refuse. They cling to him like leeches, demanding [goods such as new houses, clothes, and food]. The man is soon broke. But he does not worry. The system of native African communism saves him from

want, for all he has to do is go to another relative and sponge on him."

Political Authority. During the period 500–1590, most West African kings and emperors justified their authority in theological terms, using arguments much like the "divine right of kings" theory employed by Europeans. This idea presupposed an established political and social hierarchy that mirrors the order of Nature and creates a great chain from the lowliest slave through the head of the family, the earthly ruler, and spirits and god-mediators, culminating in the Great God who rules and presides over all existence. In most traditional West African religions, the king partakes in the divine and never really dies. Instead his soul becomes a part of that in which it resided before it was born, the God of the Sky, often represented by the Sun.

Female Authority Figures. The positions of the queen and other female authority figures were also justified in theological and metaphysical terms. In Ashanti, Yoruba, and Igbo traditions, the most powerful female

Bronze plaque of a bull sacrifice at the funeral of a ruler of Benin,
circa 1500–1700 (British Museum, London)

was often considered, and respected as, the daughter of the Moon, which is believed to have given birth to the Sun. Thus, the Sun is the king and the Moon the queen. Female rulers could have coequal status with kings. Among the Akan, the "Queen Mother" had the right to veto many of the men's actions, and on the death of the chief or king, she, in consultation with advisers, selected a new head of the clan or state. Because she menstruated, however, the Queen Mother (like women in general) was considered periodically "unclean" and thereby disqualified from participating in decision making during her menstrual periods.

Sources:
Andrew Apter, *Black Critiques and Kings: The Hermeneutics of Power in Yoruba Society* (Chicago: University of Chicago Press, 1992).

K. A. Busia, *The Challenge of Africa* (New York: Praeger, 1962).

Cheikh Anta Diop, *Black Africa: The Economic and Cultural Basis for a Federated State*, translated by Harold J. Salemson (Westport, Conn.: Lawrence Hill, 1974).

Diop, *Civilization or Barbarism: An Authentic Anthropology*, translated by Yaa-Lengi Meema Ngemi, edited by Salemson and Marjolijn de Jager (Brooklyn, N.Y.: Lawrence Hill, 1991).

Emmanuel Eze, ed., *African Philosophy: An Anthology* (Malden, Mass. & Oxford: Blackwell, 1998).

Segun Gbadegesin, *African Philosophy: Traditional Yoruba Philosophy and Contemporary African Realities* (New York: Peter Lang, 1991).

Gbadegesin, "Individuality, Community, and the Moral Order," in *African Philosophy: An Anthology*, pp. 130–141.

Joseph E. Harris, *Africans and Their History*, second edition, revised (New York: Meridian, 1998).

Constance B. Hilliard, *Intellectual Traditions of Pre-Colonial Africa* (Boston: McGraw-Hill, 1998).

Elizabeth Isichei, *A History of African Societies to 1870* (Cambridge: Cambridge University Press, 1997).

SIGNIFICANT PEOPLE

AHMAD BABA

1556-1627
ISLAMIC SCHOLAR AND JURIST

Scholar and Book Collector. Born to a prominent family near Timbuktu, Ahmad Baba was educated there in Islamic theology and religious law. During his lifetime he wrote more than fifty-six books on those subjects, as well as history and Arabic grammar. About half of his works have survived, and some are still used by Islamic scholars. Ahmad Baba was also a book collector and had a personal library that included several thousand volumes. Because it was home to Ahmad Baba and other great scholars, Timbuktu was considered a major center of learning, not just in the Songhai Empire but throughout the Islamic world.

The Moroccan Invasion. When the Moroccans conquered the Songhai Empire and took Timbuktu in 1591, Ahmad Baba and other scholars in the city refused allegiance to the invaders. In 1593 he and other prominent people of the city are said to have instigated a rebellion, and the following year, they were deported to Marrakech, the capital of Morocco. The Moroccans also confiscated books from several scholars' libraries, including some 1,600 belonging to Ahmad Baba.

Exile. While in Marrakech, Ahmad Baba was allowed to write and practice law. Among the books he wrote there was a biographical dictionary of well-known jurists in the Maliki school of Islamic law, which is still considered a valuable historical source. Around 1607 he was allowed to return to Timbuktu.

Final Years. After returning home, Ahmad Baba wrote a catalogue of West African peoples practicing Islam and traditional religions, an important contribution to the religious history of the region. He also wrote an Arabic grammar book, which is still used in some parts of northern Nigeria.

Sources:
"Ahmad Baba," Encyclopaedia Britannica Online <http://www.search.eb.com/eb/article?eu=4179>.

Elizabeth Heath, "Ahmad Baba," in *Africana: The Encyclopedia of the African and African American Experience,* edited by Kwame Anthony Appiah and Henry Louis Gates Jr. (New York: Basic Civitas Books, 1999), pp. 53–54.

OBATALA

RULER-DEITY

Human Origins. Part of the creation mythology of the Yoruba people, Obatala is one of several Yoruba deities thought to have been living people. In the Yoruba cosmology he is one of the sixteen envoys (*orisa,* or deities) whom the Supreme God assigned "to create some order out of the confused watery mass on earth below." According to what Omofolabo S. Ajayi describes as "the sacred myth," Obatala was in charge of creating "solid earth" and human forms, which he then presented to Olorun "to breathe life into." According to one myth, Obatala got intoxicated one day, after drinking palm wine offered him by Ogun, and started being sloppy in his creation. He fell asleep, and when he woke up, Oduduwa had usurped his place, becoming the ruler of all the Earth from his capital at Ile-Ife. Thereafter, "Obatala's people became known as the 'Igbo' while Oduduwa's were the 'Ife.'"

Earthly Ruler. A "civic myth" about Obatala's earthly role suggests that he may have been one of Oduduwa's lieutenants. Resenting his fate after failing to topple the usurping Oduduwa, he went into exile in Igbo's grove, his friend Obawini's settlement. Obatala later returned to Ile-Ife, and he is believed to have been its fourth ruler.

Figure of Peace and Order. Because of his exploits on Earth and the peace he brought to his people, Obatala was deified after his death. Thus, his earthly heroic deeds became part of his godly attributes. As a deity, Obatala exemplifies humility and purity. According to Ajayi, the trials Obatala underwent during his lifetime made him humble and pure, "turning him into the archetypal symbol of peace and (balanced) social values." Ajayi recounts a story about Obatala's meekness. On his way to visit his friend Shango (the god of thunder and lightning), Obatala became the object of mischief by the trickster god Esu. As a result Obatala was falsely accused of stealing a horse from the angry Shango, who, unaware of the alleged thief's identity, threw Obatala into jail without due process under the law. The humble Obatala did not reveal his identity and remained imprisoned for seven years. During that time Yorubaland was plagued by "diseases, famine, wars, infertility, premature deaths, and other disasters." Finally, the Ifa system (whose messenger was Esu) revealed the truth; Obatala was released, and peace returned to Yorubaland.

Source:
Omofolabo S. Ajayi, *Yoruba Dance: The Semiotics of Movement and Body Attitude in a Nigerian Culture* (Trenton, N.J.: Africa World Press, 1998).

DOCUMENTARY SOURCES

Amina, Sarauniya Zazzau (Amina, Queen of Zazzau)—An anonymous account of the Hausa great warrior-queen Amina (1533?–1610), who ruled a kingdom in northern Nigeria; the work includes information about Hausa religious practices during the period.

Al-Bakri, *Kitab al-masalik wa-'l-mamalik* (The Book of Routes and Realms, 1068)—A geographical work by a Spanish Muslim who never visited West Africa and based his detailed descriptions of the region on oral and written accounts by travelers; al-Bakri included information on the religion, politics, and culture of the Empire of Ghana.

The Epic of Sundiata—This orally transmitted history of how Sundiata (ruled 1230–1255) created the powerful Empire of Mali reveals much about how Islam existed alongside traditional religions; although this poem makes frequent references to Allah, the underlying actions that sustain the structure of the narrative are animist, magical practices that were prevalent in traditional West African religions.

Ibn Battuta (1304 – circa 1378), *Rihlah* (Travels)—A generally reliable account of twenty-four years of travel through much of the Muslim world, including eyewitness reports on the practice of Islam in the Empire of Mali during the mid fourteenth century.

Abd al-Rahman al-Sa'di (1569 – circa 1655), *Tarikh al-Sudan* (Chronicle of the Western Sudan, circa 1650)—A history of West Africa by a Muslim native of Timbuktu, which chronicles the Songhai Empire and its fall to the Almoravids in 1590–1591.

SCIENCE, TECHNOLOGY, AND HEALTH

by DONNA J. DAVIS

CONTENTS

Sidebars and tables are listed in italics.

IMPORTANT EVENTS OF 500-1590

500*
- Hammered copper is in use in Djenné.
- The sickle-cell trait, an inherited blood condition that prevents malaria, begins to appear among forest-dwelling peoples in West Africa.

500-800*
- Copper metallurgy includes hammered, welded, cold-spun, and hollow-casted methods; the metal is used alone or alloyed with lead, tin, or zinc.

600*
- Alluvial gold is found in West Africa.

600-700
- Iron-ore smelting begins in the Kano area.

600-1100*
- Salt-production techniques include mining bars of rock salt, evaporation of sea salt, collection of surface salt, and leaching from the ashes of xerophilous plants (plants that require little moisture).

660-1085*
- The Brong people smelt iron and make comb-marked pottery.

700-800
- Iron tools make the construction of dikes and earthen dams easier, which leads to surplus agricultural production.
- The city of Koumbi-Saleh begins keeping gold for the trans-Saharan trade.
- Lost-wax (hollow-casted) molds are used in Tegdaoust.

700-1000*
- Highly detailed bronze items are produced in Igbo-Ukwe.

700-1600*
- Arabic serves as the language in which science, mathematics, and medicine are taught in West Africa.

773
- The Arab scholar al-Fazari, living in Baghdad, is the first to name the Kingdom of Ghana "the land of gold." He also popularizes the Hindu decimal system by translating *Surya Siddhanta* (a Hindu astronomical handbook of the fourth or fifth century) into Arabic.

* DENOTES CIRCA DATE

IMPORTANT EVENTS OF 500-1590

800-1400*
- Iron-smelting furnaces are in use in the Ufe-Ijumo region.

833*
- The Arab scholar Abu Ja'far Muhammad ibn Musa al-Khwarizmi writes the book *Kitab al-jabr wa al-muqabalah* (Large Book on Calculation by Completion and Balancing, circa 833), a systematic collection of various scholars' teachings on ways of solving math problems in which at least one value is not known; he also uses Hindu-Arabic numerals. His book makes algebra a formal branch of mathematics and is later used in the universities in Timbuktu and Djenné.

900-1000
- Cotton textiles develop in Senegal.
- Gold dug from mines is added to the stocks of alluvial gold in circulation.

960*
- Ile-Ife craftsmen make life-like bronze, iron, and terra-cotta sculptures.

1000*
- Indigo is imported into West Africa from the Maghrib (present-day Morocco, Algeria, and Tunisia) to dye cloth.
- Thin-walled, decorated, and high-fired pottery in a large variety of shapes is in use in West Africa.
- The city of Ife uses vertically-imbedded potsherds for paving walkways and courtyards.

1000-1100*
- In the Tellem caves region, clothing is made from woven strips eleven inches in width.

1067-1068
- Al-Bakri makes a record of the Sudan (Arabic for "black people") with extensive economic and technical information, called *Kitab al-masalik wa-'l-mamalik* (The Book of Routes and Realms).

1100*
- Gold from forest areas of West Africa is sold to North African merchants.

1100
- Ibadi historian al-Wisyani reports on an anecdote of a man who requested eye medicine from a doctor named 'Abd al-Hamid al-Fazzani who was visiting Western Sudan.

1200*
- Sundiata, the future king of Mali, is born with a disability; braces are later made to aid him in walking.

* DENOTES CIRCA DATE

IMPORTANT EVENTS OF 500-1590

1200-1300
- The city of Jenne (present-day Djenné in Mali) flourishes. Its university becomes renowned for the teaching of medicine and surgery, and it attracts scholars from West and North Africa for five hundred years.

1200-1400
- A Rao burial mound containing a large disk of gold with ornate decorations is constructed in present-day northwestern Senegal.

1300-1400
- An Ile-Ife smith named Iguegbae is brought to Benin by its king to teach the lost-wax method of brass casting to local smiths.

1326-1330
- The Sankore mosque (later the home of Sankore University) is built in Timbuktu (located in present-day Mali). It has flat walls, flat-topped roofs, and *torons*, exterior horizontal posts projecting from the walls, in order to facilitate annual repairs after the rainy season.

1330
- Copper is so valued in the countries south of Mali that traders sell it there for a price equal to 66 percent of its weight in gold.

1337
- Al-Umari, basing his comments on reports from a man who lived there for thirty-five years, writes that buildings in the capital city of Mali (probably Niani) are made of sun-dried clay blocks two-thirds of a cubit high with domed roofs made of lumber and reeds.
- Poison-tipped arrows are reportedly used by Malians hunting wild buffalo.

1347-1351
- The bubonic plague sweeps through Europe; yet, it does not affect people in West Africa where the climate is hostile to the plague vector, the louse.

1374
- Trypanosomiasis (sleeping sickness), a tropical disease caused by the bite of the tsetse fly, kills Mansa Mari-Djata II, ruler of the Kingdom of Mali.

1391
- King Richard II of England is given a geomancy chart based on the fractal geometry used in divination charts from the Kingdom of Benin; African cowrie shells are apparent on the king's gift.

* **DENOTES CIRCA DATE**

IMPORTANT EVENTS OF 500-1590

1400	• Timbuktu is widely known as a center of learning, and scholars come for both Islamic studies as well as instruction in science, mathematics, and medicine.
1415	• Anselm d'Isalguier returns to France from Gao in West Africa with his wife, a Songhai princess; their African servant is a doctor who helps heal King Charles VI.
1450*	• Some twenty-five thousand scholars reside in Timbuktu. Sanhaja scholars, many of whom studied in Mecca or Egypt, dominate in numbers over Sudanese ones.
	• The city of Benin builds a massive defensive wall to protect its residents from marauders; the wall is nearly seven miles long and fifty-seven feet high.
1468	• Timbuktu falls to Songhai ruler Sunni Ali; his soldiers use poison arrows and padded-cloth body armor.
1475*	• After contact is made with Europeans along the Atlantic coast, new diseases begin to decimate local populations in West Africa.
1492-1528	• Askia Muhammad I rules the Kingdom of Songhai. He standardizes currency, weights, and measures throughout his domain, bringing continuity to the trade of the empire and more exchange of technological and other information.
1495*	• Because of trade and religious pilgrimages, West African gold represents the majority of gold in circulation in Europe.
1526	• Leo Africanus devotes a large section of his book *The History and Description of Africa* to the architecture of Timbuktu.
1570-1580*	• Muhammad Sa'di, brother of the chronicler al-Sa'di, receives effective eye surgery under the care of a *tabib* (doctor) called al-Tabib Ibrahim al-Susi, then visiting Timbuktu.

* DENOTES CIRCA DATE

OVERVIEW

Independent and Interdependent. The circumstances that affected the state of science, technology, and health before and during the period 500 to 1590 C.E. in West Africa include both independent and interdependent developments of technical and scientific achievements and encounters with related technological or scientific obstacles. Discoveries do not happen in a vacuum, and since the kingdoms of West Africa were communal rather than individualistic societies, the word *independent* refers more to those skills and technologies that seemed to arise in the region separately from significant influences originating outside the area. Similarly, *interdependent* refers to those scientific and technological achievements and losses that were significantly affected by contact with other cultures.

Encoding Knowledge. Science in this period in West Africa was often based on practical, functional, need-based tasks, observation, and problem solving, in addition to serendipitous discovery. Trial and error with oral, performance, and material encoding of successful practices without formal written notation may have dominated until their literacy in Arabic, which was required for the serious practice of Islam, gave 3 to 5 percent of the population both a common language among their many languages and another way of recording, retrieving, and passing on scientific and technological learning. Even before formal writing, the peoples of the kingdoms of West Africa were able to gain and transmit scientific, technical, mathematical, and health-related knowledge and skills by means of castes that served as guilds with apprentices and masters; through griots (oral historians); by means of secret societies of medicine men and women, diviners, and priests; and the codifying of communal wisdom and religious or social law inscribed in prized, sculpted weights used for the gold trade.

Metals and Metallurgy. Among the more independently arising technologies was metallurgy. Prior to 500, metallurgy developed at different speeds in different areas of Africa. For example, the first iron smelting and reduction are believed to have occurred in West Africa by 500 B.C.E. Substantial iron use took place in the Jenne-jeno area on the Niger River from 250 B.C.E. onward. However, the use of iron near Kainji Lake in the Niger Valley came later, around 130 B.C.E., and in Daboya, later still, around 100 to 1 B.C.E. The first known surface mining of copper in West Sudan occurred in 2000 B.C.E. around Takedda (now Azelick) in what is now Niger. Once discovered, iron technology had interdependent consequences: by 400 C.E., iron tools, especially the hoe and sickle, led to expansion of the amount of land under cultivation due to clearing of forestland and extension of productivity of each person. This development, in turn, made possible the production of enough food so that not all of the people needed to grow their own crops. By 500, surplus food production through more extensive agriculture, in the sense of growth beyond the immediate need of one's own family, contributed to the rise of towns and cities where people could live and trade. Further, because of iron technology and toolmaking, weapons for protection of the community and for dominating other communities created the right climate for the rise of states and kingdoms in West Africa.

Important Resource. Salt was a precious resource to the people inhabiting the torrid climes of West Africa. The need for this commodity, combined with its scarcity in the forest and Sahel (semi-arid pastureland) regions, created a demand that contributed significantly to interregional trade and the concomitant exchange of scientific and technological information. In 250 B.C.E. the drying of the once-lush savanna region known as the Sahara Desert expanded and yielded salt that could be harvested from surface deposits. Later, miners from Taghaza and other towns extracted salt from underground sites and generated the mineral most in demand among West Africans themselves. Yaqut, a Muslim of Greek origin who traveled widely and chronicled his observations, reported that the treasure-houses of the king of KuKu in the Western Sudan were filled mainly with salt.

Demand for Gold. Though the West Africans' need for salt was strong and long-standing, after 700 C.E. the demand from Europe and Southwest Asia for the rich natural resources of West Africa's gold-mining territories was equally powerful. That demand significantly influenced the mining areas at the southern edge of the Sahel and in the forest regions, generating more production for trade and a need for protection from would-be marauders. The rising and falling of the kingdoms of West Africa were based on how successfully they managed to protect and control gold mining, trade, tributes, and taxes.

Camels. The use of camels to replace donkeys and horses helped the trans-Saharan trade expand, leading to the increased exchange of information, science, technology, and innovation between West Africa and Arab and North African traders and travelers. At the beginning of the Christian Era, from the late first to early second centuries, the camel began to replace the horse substantially as the means of transportation across the Sahara. With this change, travel and trade among Western Africans and Northern and Northeastern Africans and people from adjoining continents improved and expanded, with the greatest frequency and volume of travel, trade, and exchange of scientific and technological information coming after 900, when Islam began to be successfully entrenched in West Africa.

Trans-Saharan Trade. Extensive long-distance trade among the regions of the Sahel, the forests to the south, and North Africa and Egypt developed and flourished during the entire period under discussion. Different regions held one or more of West Africa's extensive natural resources in gold (first found in 600 C.E.), copper (known since 2000 B.C.E.), iron, salt, ivory, and kola nuts. At the same time, many regions wanted the materials and products of others that both natural endowment and technological knowledge made available. Sophisticated iron metallurgy produced the weaponry that enabled the conquest of less technologically equipped peoples, which in turn led to the building of larger and stronger states able to secure areas rich with resources in exchange for tribute. Kingdoms made powerful through iron technology could also protect trade routes, generating more revenue in the form of a tax on trade and controlling international relationships with commercial contacts from other countries. The rise and expansion of Islam into Africa required pilgrimages to Mecca by well-to-do African converts and their extensive entourages, again advancing the exchange of information and technological innovation among all social and economic classes. Finally, trade routes allowed exchange of enslaved peoples taken in raids or war for criminal acts, or for refusing to convert to Islam. Thus, North African merchants sold African slaves in Spain while the Egyptians and other Middle Eastern traders exchanged their African human possessions with other Arabs and Europeans, leaving the greatest wealth of West Africa—her people and their skills and technological knowledge—in strangers' hands.

Mathematics. During the period 500–1590 C.E. distinct and not necessarily interchangeable systems of count-

ing, record keeping, and fractal geometry continued to evolve within and among the tribes of West Africa. The separation of tribes by language groups, religion, and geography may have contributed to these separate counting systems. However, once the common language of Arabic became available and, indeed, was required of converts to Islam in the larger, northern Sahel cities, the Islamic universities created opportunities for study of the rapidly expanding Arabic mathematical and scientific scholarship.

Governance. Among the policies that came out of the Great Assembly that Sundiata called before leading the Mande tribes against the Sosso to regain Mali (circa 1235), some had a significant impact on the successful exchange of information and technology. Political protection of followers of Islam helped keep information flowing between them and the followers of traditional religion. Establishment of trade clans as inherited castes (smith clans, griots, and shoemakers) maintained the importance of those essential skills. Perhaps the most insightful provision was the one that made people of different clans pseudorelatives, reducing interethnic rivalry and increasing the interclan transmission and sharing of technological and other knowledge. For example, a person from the Diop clan was considered a brother to members of the Traore clan, a ruling that made a secular brotherhood regardless of religion, and a practice still viable among Mande-speaking peoples. In governance, the administrative system included a network of *farin* (governors appointed by the emperor) who worked directly with the chiefs in their home districts, learning of the cultural and technological uniqueness of each, passing that information up to the emperor and supporting and representing the interests of the local districts. Also, after Sundiata's rise to the throne, military stations were scattered throughout the Malian Empire, helping unite the Western Sudan and insuring the protection and control of all West African trans-Saharan trade routes so essential to the exchange of information and technological knowledge as well as of material goods.

Internationality. Starting with his bringing the Andalusian architect, Abu Ishaq al-Sahili, back to Mali from his trip to Mecca (1325), Emperor Mansa Musa generated an international exchange of scholarly, professional, and technical information. Arab scholars were invited to teach at the universities established at the mosques in Timbuktu and Djenné; Sudanese scholars were sent to other countries' universities, and embassies were opened. Scholars and professionals brought to the Empire of Mali were supported by the king to teach and practice their profession at universities housed at the mosques Mansa Musa had built.

Indigenous Construction and Architecture. Widely varying available materials and climate generated largely impermanent homes for pastoralists and sedentary farmers alike. Local construction techniques utilized mud and acacia limbs and domed or conical roofs for protection against the rainy season. West African communities close to the coastal regions, where European slave raiders and their indigenous accomplices stalked most often, showed a significant inward-facing cluster pattern or even extraordinarily large city walls, as in the case of Benin.

Islamic Influences. The impact of Islamic worship requirements and building styles was reflected in the rainy-season-adapted mosques and mansions of al-Sahili. Elements of al-Sahili's contribution to West African architecture include the *torons*, or horizontal wooden poles, set in the straight walls to provide support for the post-rainy-season scaffolding needed for repair of the sun-dried, mud-brick walls.

Universities. Arabic and West African Islamic universities influenced Western African science, technology, and health practices. The most notable Arabic influence—through the universities—shows up in the fields of mathematics, medicine, and surgery, courses which were commonly taught at the universities of Timbuktu and Djenné.

TOPICS IN SCIENCE, TECHNOLOGY, AND HEALTH

CONSTRUCTION TECHNOLOGY AND ARCHITECTURE

Stone Circles and Monoliths. The stone circles of the Senegal-Gambia region, dated circa 750, were produced to honor kings, chiefs, and perhaps other important individuals. Iron laterite (naturally cemented iron-filled sandstone), plentiful in this area, was the source material for these great stones. The numbers of stone circles are particularly high in this region, outstripping concentrations in other parts of the world. Stones number from ten to twenty-four per group or circle. Shapes of pillars are generally round, though some are square or rectangular, and others taper toward the top. There are also circles with V-shaped stones (known as lyre stones). Heights of stones usually remain the same within a particular circle. However, stones in different circles may range in height from twenty-four to ninety inches, in diameter from twelve to forty inches, and in weight up to ten tons. The West Africans transported the stones from the quarry, where they probably had been shaped, using logs for rollers or perhaps hammock-style slings. In the latter case many people would have been required. Next, workers had to tip and lift the piece into place by hand or with a rope system. The stone-raising systems had already been used elsewhere in West Africa. Farther south and east, in Ife (Nigeria), stands an eighteen-foot-high monolith of granite in honor of Oranmiyan, the founder of the Benin line of rulers and the kingdom of the Yoruba Oyo. Its estimated date is before 1000. Though intertribal trade may have allowed the communication of stone-raising techniques, it is more likely that the local community generated their own systems.

Traditional Settings. Traditional West African construction technology and architecture met the needs of people in a wide variety of climates with an extensive range of building-material resources, including branches, sun-dried mud, stone, textiles, and grasses. All buildings were the work of cooperative design and labor.

Nomadic Shelter-Building. Operating in areas in what is now Mauritania and Mali and relying on the foraging needs of their animals in the savanna and near-desert areas, the Tuaregs and other nomadic peoples of North and West Africa had to adapt their housing to the herd's requirements. The building, dismantling, and reassembling of the portable, sturdy, durable, wind-resistant homes of the nomadic pastoralists of the Sahel (semiarid pastureland) and Sahara were (and remain) the work of the women. Built of flexible wooden (probably acacia) branches lashed together to make aerodynamically sound frames, then covered with skins, mats, or lighter textiles made of twenty-inch widths of camel's or goat's wool sewn together into a wide cloth, the desert dwellings had to resist the harshest winds and sandstorms. Shelters with a grass dome or conical roof continued to be used for centuries in the Sahel, even to the present.

Earthen Dwellings in Settled Communities. The functional adaptation of many West Africans before the 1300s in constructing traditional cylindrical huts with

Portion of the excavated Benin city wall

rounded conical or dome-shaped roofs is striking. Often made of mud, the most easily shaped and molded of indigenous building materials, traditional earthen buildings in West Africa were round or ovoid. Commenting on this shape, architects and mathematicians have pointed out that the dimensions of a round building not only reflect nature's forms but also provide larger actual living area per perimeter measure than square or rectangular buildings. Mud walls also lend themselves to surface design and decoration. Roofs were usually heavily thatched dried grasses over a branch frame. The family compound in a settled farming village would often consist of several round rooms, each with separate purposes, looking inward to a compound courtyard; the rooms were connected by curving wall segments. Depending on the degree of extension of the family, these compounds could be small or large and complex.

Conical Thatched Roof. The conical thatched roof is a technology that has continued for centuries and remains today in Togo and other West African countries. First, the sides of the house are built up—whether of laterite adobe mud, stone and mud, or of flexible and strong acacia branches and mud daub. Then, the cone shape is begun with three branches tied together at one end, and spread apart at the other end, with the wide ends set on top of the walls. More vertical branches are added to complete the cone shape. Next, approximately six-foot-tall straw bundles are tied with rope into a continuous mat. The thickest part of the bundle mat is what will become the bottom of the mat on the roof. The mat is rolled up and hoisted to the top of the walls, unrolled, and formed around the cone of branches. The steep pitch of the cone of thatch allows heavy rains to escape and not linger in the straw mat; however, it still must be replaced every two years. Ample headroom and ceiling height for allowing heat to rise above the human height level are available since the cone of thatch needs no truss. In other communities, such as the Dogon, the entire roof—cone plus thatch—is assembled before being lifted to the housetop.

Dogon Architecture. A notable exception to the widely used circular or oval-shaped buildings (and entire compound) is the design and construction of the Dogon peoples. In their second homeland, the highlands, nearly two hundred miles south of the Niger River bend and the Tellem cave area, the Dogon residences are square-rectangular, taller than wide, with cone-shaped roofs. Moreover, these are set high up in the mountains for the safety of the community.

Stone Dwellings. Referring to the non-Muslim part of the capital city of the Kingdom of Ghana a few years before 1067, al-Bakri said it was called *al-Ghaba* (Arabic for "forest") and its houses were made of stone and acacia wood. The king's palace was, like his subjects', a group of similar domed houses but with the addition of a wall around the structures. Further, al-Bakri noted, the priests or diviners lived in houses with domes, too, but near the thickets and woods. Perhaps these woods were where some of them extracted their medicines.

Islamic Influence. During his trip to Mecca in 1324, Mansa Musa formed a friendship with Abu Ishaq al-Sahili, a Moor from Andalusia who was both an architect and a poet. When Mansa Musa returned to the Kingdom of Mali, he invited the Moor to accompany him. Al-Sahili did so and designed the *Djingereyber* (Great Mosque) in 1327 and a palace for the king. The mosque was described by the Arab philosopher Ibn Khaldun as "a square building with a dome" with an exterior with plaster and patterns decorated in colors. Among all the round buildings of the Western Sudan, the flat walls and square (or rectangular) shape of Islamic architecture stood out. *Banco*, the material with which it was built, was soil mixed with wood, dried grass, and other fiber allowed to dry in the sun. In the absence of adequate stone for building materials, *banco* was often the material of choice in West Africa. The contributions of al-Sahili's construction technology and architectural gifts to West Africa are not only the shape of the buildings but also the horizontal wood projections coming out of the exterior walls. These *torons* were developed for hanging scaffolding when adobe mud walls needed repair after the rainy season. Al-Sahili also designed a mosque in Gao, the first building in which fired brick was used in West Africa south of the Sahara. Overall, the adaptability of the Islamic architecture to the region's climate may have been less effective compared to the indigenous architecture. However, the large size needed for the prayer center for hundreds, and later thousands, of converts to Islam might not have been accommodated by an enlarged version of the indigenous architecture.

THE IMUHA (TUAREG) CLANS

Pastoralists and semipastoralists, the Imuha (Tuareg) clans in the West African desert and Sahel (semiarid pastureland) have since circa 1000 B.C.E. built, disassembled, and rebuilt their dwellings each time they have moved to different areas for food and forage. Their homes are made of a lashed framework of acacia covered with cloth and/or leather. Built with space acuity in mind (the efficient use of space in a dwelling or other building), the shelters must protect extended families from desert heat, wind, and sandstorms. Ibn Khaldun in *Kitab al-'Ibar wa-diwan al-mubtada' wa-'l-khabar fi ayyam al-'arab wa-'l-'ajam wa-'l-barbar* (The Book of Examples and the Register of Subject and Predicate [or, of the Origin and History], on the Days of the Arabs, the Persians, and the Berbers, 1374–1378 C.E.) refers to the "veil-wearers" (the men cover their faces below the eyes with cloth), calling the different clans in West Africa by the following names: *Gudala, Lamtuna, Watrika, Masufa, Lamta,* and *Targa.* These Berber-speaking camel breeders were the original Imuha peoples. At the time of his writing in the late fourteenth century, the clans served as a buffer for the Western Sudanic kingdoms against Arab invaders from the north. These nomads were also known to hold hostages and to demand tribute from travelers on the trans-Saharan trade routes. In later years, the federations of clans included the Kel Tademaket who moved around the Timbuktu region; the Iwellemmeden Kel Ataram who were based around what is present-day Menaka; the Kel Ayr, dark-skinned peoples near the Ayr region; the Kel Adrar in the Adras N-Foras mountain area of what is now northern Mali; and the Kel Geres, the most democratic of all the clans, located south of the Kel Ayr. Throughout the centuries the women have had complete responsibility for the design, building, and seasonal dismantling and rebuilding of their dwellings.

Sources: Ibn Khaldun, "The Book of Examples . . ." / "Kitab al'Ibar . . .," in *Corpus of Early Arabic Sources for West African History,* translated by J. F. P. Hopkins and edited by Nehemia Levtzion and Hopkins (Cambridge & New York: Cambridge University Press, 1981), pp. 317–342.

Labelle Prussin and others, *African Nomadic Architecture: Space, Place, and Gender* (Washington, D.C.: Smithsonian Institution Press, 1995).

Salt-Block Buildings. Buildings and city walls composed exclusively of salt blocks were unusual construction phenomena found in the salt-mining desert town of Taghaza. Indeed, all the buildings in this town, even the mosque, were composed only of blocks of salt. Camel skins usually made the roofs. Salt was so valuable to the people of the kingdoms of Ghana and Mali and south of them that its reported prices ranged from 100 dinars per camel-load to an even trade, weight for weight, for gold. Salt to those in desperate need for themselves and their livestock was, literally, worth its weight in gold, yet buildings were made of it in the desert, when it was the only plentiful wall-building material available.

Benin City Walls. In what appears to be a response to slavers and other marauders, around 1450 the people of Benin made an enormous, highly organized effort to produce an effective defense system. The community dug a massive ditch and built banked-earth walls more than fifty-seven feet high (17.4 meters) and nearly seven miles long (11.6 kilometers). Historians estimate that it would have taken many thousands of people working more than ten hours per day if the defenses were finished in one dry season. Moreover, several other local villages wanted the same defense and so were connected to Benin and one another with similar ditch and earthen-wall systems.

Potsherd Pavement. Around 1000 the city of Ife constructed paved sidewalks or passageways and courtyards of a common material. Shards of terra-cotta pottery were wedged together on their edges in carefully placed rows. The origin of the urban improvements, according to Yoruba lore, occurred when Queen Oluwo became annoyed with dirt getting on the edges of her robes. More than 750 years later, the Frenchman Pierre Tresaguet used a similar idea, constructing roads by putting fieldstones on edge, instead of flat, and covering them with layers of crushed rock. His work was considered "pioneering" to the Europeans because, unlike Roman road design, it put the weight of foot, horse, wagon, and carriage on a well-drained subsoil, not stone slabs, and was much more economical both with time and materials. The famed English road builder, John McAdam, later modified Tresaguet's technique.

Sources:

Momodou Camara, "Stone Circles of the Gambia" (13 October 2002) <http://home3.inet.tele.dk/mcamara/stones.html>.

Graham Connah, *African Civilizations—Precolonial Cities and States in Tropical Africa: An Archaeological Perspective* (Cambridge & New York: Cambridge University Press, 1987).

Ibn Khaldun, "The Book of Examples . . ." / "Kitab al'Ibar . . .," in *Corpus of Early Arabic Sources for West African History,* translated by J. F. P. Hopkins, edited by Nehemia Levtzion and Hopkins (Cambridge & New York: Cambridge University Press, 1981), pp. 317–342.

Baba Kiabou, "Timbuktu: The Mythical Site" (12 October 2002) <http://whc.unesco.org/whreview/article7.html>.

Levtzion, "The Early States of the Western Sudan to 1500," in *History of West Africa,* volume 1, edited by J. F. Ade Ajayi and Michael Crowder (New York: Longman, 1976), pp. 114–151.

Metropolitan Museum of Art, "Ife, Pre-Pavement and Pavement Era" (13 October 2002) <http://www.metmuseum.org/toah/hd/ife/hd_ife.htm>.

Kelly Jon Morris, "Tin and Thatch in Togo," in *Shelter,* edited by Shelter Publications (Bolinas, Cal.: Shelter, 1973), p. 10.

Elizabeth Newhouse, ed., *The Builders: Marvels of Engineering* (Washington, D.C.: Book Division of National Geographic Society, 1992).

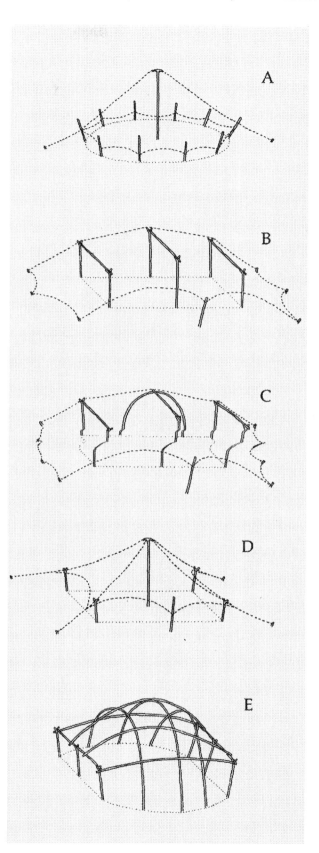

Drawings of Tuareg Berber tent structure styles (from Monica Blackmun Visonà, *A History of Art in Africa,* 2001)

Labelle Prussin and others, *African Nomadic Architecture: Space, Place, and Gender* (Washington, D.C.: Smithsonian Institution Press, 1995).

Norbert Schoenauer, *6,000 Years of Housing*, revised (New York: Norton, 2000).

Frank Toker, "Learning from Architecture, II: What Only History Can Determine" (13 October 2002) <http://www.pitt.edu/~tokerism/0040/syl/learning.html>.

UNESCO, "African Nomads" (13 October 2002) <http://whc.unesco.org/exhibits/afr_rev/africa-c.htm>.

Claudia Zaslavsky, *Africa Counts: Number and Pattern in African Culture* (Boston: Prindle, Weber & Schmidt, 1973).

COSMOLOGY AND ASTRONOMY

Oriented to the Heavens. In several West African cultures, family homes were built so that the entrances faced west. In the north of present-day Ghana, the Mamprusi people follow this practice in order to insure that the light of the sunset falls on the seating location designated for the oldest members of the family. The oldest members' task, then, was to assess from the location of light on the wall the important aspects of the seasons for planting and harvesting. The Batammaliba people of present-day Togo and Benin Republic wanted the sunset light to fall on the shrines of the ancestors, so that the sun god, Kuiye, would talk with the ancestors about the concerns of their family. Ogotemmeli, a twentieth-century Dogon sage and oral historian of astronomical secrets going back to 1283, reported that Dogon granary stairways were oriented to Orion's Belt (southern stairway), the Pleiades (northern stairway), or the morning star (eastern stairway). Similar cosmological orientations were also found in the granaries of the Bambara people.

Calculating Time. The moon, more than the sun, seems to have been the important factor by which to measure time in most early West African societies. Seasons were measured by the sun, and solstices were observed and inscribed with a zigzag pattern on public agricultural buildings of the Bambara. However, every West African culture used the lunar month as a way to calculate the passage of time. West African counting sticks, similar to the famed South-Central African Ishango bone, were used for reckoning time thousands of years before 500.

The State and the Cosmos. Throughout the continent of Africa the leaders of the tribe or state were assigned or assumed for themselves the power to connect with the cosmos. Sun images or sun-related names supported leaders'

DOGON CONTROVERSY

The priest-astronomer caste of the Dogon people, located in present-day Mali in a mountain area about two hundred miles south of Timbuktu, report that they have been observing cosmos-related activity since approximately 1283 C.E. The observations of this secret society include the most important object in the sky for them, what modern astronomers call Sirius B, usually nearly invisible to the naked eye and located in the solar system of the bright star Sirius A. The Dogon astronomical celebrations occur every fifty to sixty years, when this star they describe as small and dense, and which they liken to a seed, orbits in the Sirius solar system in such a way as to be visible. In the 1930s the Dogon priests claimed to possess a more-than-440-year-old object that showed the orbit of Sirius B and a third star. Some Western astronomers have looked on these assertions with disbelief, partially because they only identified Sirius B, a white dwarf (a small whitish star of low brightness but extremely high density), in the nineteenth century. In addition, some professional astronomers believe the mathematical calculations involved in the orbital observations are too sophisticated for the Dogon. Other astronomers claim it is impossible to see this phenomenon with the naked eye, though evidence of visibility under certain circumstances and at certain times of the year for some of their observa-tions (for example, Jupiter's moons and Saturn's rings) have been confirmed. Interestingly, the visual magnitude range of light-eyed, light-haired persons versus brown-eyed, dark-haired persons shows a wider spectrum for the latter. The factors of low or no light pollution and clear mountain atmosphere also are known to improve sky viewing conditions. Moreover, the Dogon's claim first occurred more than 250 years after Arab mathematician and physicist Ibn al-Haytham wrote about how physical, mathematical, and other factors influence the human capacity to see. It is important to note that since al-Haytham's optical concepts spread wherever Arab texts or their translations were in use, including West Africa, they may have been available to Dogon priest-astronomers. Finally, it has been noted that glass spheres were present in Egypt many thousands of years ago. Perhaps the Dogon—who claim descent from the Egyptians—acquired similar spheres and made a rudimentary telescope that they have kept secret. It is known that the Ife peoples, not far south of the Dogon, had accomplished the manufacture of glass beads.

Sources: Hunter Havelin Adams III, "African Observers of the Universe, the Sirius Question," in *Blacks in Science: Ancient and Modern*, edited by Ivan Van Sertima (New Brunswick, N.J.: Transaction, 1983), pp. 27–46.

Adams, "New Light on the Dogon and Sirius," in *Blacks in Science: Ancient and Modern*, pp. 47–49.

Granite monoliths, Wassu, Gambia, circa 600–700 (photograph by George Gerster/Network)

roles as persons of power. The loss of the presence of the sun through a solar eclipse was considered cataclysmic and reflective of the king's loss of power. The phases of the moon were also related to leadership and royalty with, for example, a month of rest for new Igbo kings. An organization named the Iwo-Uki (Rising Moon) used their knowledge of the cosmos and the seasons to recommend to the king of Benin the scheduling of events and announcements for when to harvest yams and other crops.

Islamic Astronomy. From the 1400s onward Islamic astronomical studies were available in the university at Timbuktu. Materials covered included weather observations, important issues relating to the Niger River and its floods, and discussions of the relative merits of the various lunar and solar calendars. Astrology and its uses as a divining tool were also popular.

Sources:
Hunter Havelin Adams III, "African Observers of the Universe, the Sirius Question," in *Blacks in Science: Ancient and Modern,* edited by Ivan Van Sertima (New Brunswick, N.J.: Transaction, 1983), pp. 27–46.

Adams, "New Light on the Dogon and Sirius," in *Blacks in Science: Ancient and Modern,* pp. 47–49.

Nicholas T. Bobrovnikoff, *Astronomy before the Telescope, Volume II, The Solar System,* edited by Roger B. Culver and David Meisel (Tucson, Ariz.: Pachart, 1984).

S. M. Cissoko, "The Songhay from the 12th to the 16th century," in *UNESCO General History of Africa, Volume IV: Africa from the Twelfth to the Sixteenth Century,* edited by D. T. Niane (Berkeley: University of California Press, 1984), pp. 186–210.

M. Goldsmith, "On the Companions of Sirius," *Monthly Notices of the Royal Astronomical Society,* 23, no. 5 (June 1863), pp. 243–244.

PBS, "Islam: Empire of Faith, Medicine" (24 November 2002) <http://www.pbs.org/empires/Islam/innomedicine.html>.

Carl Sagan, *Broca's Brain–Reflections on the Romance of Science* (New York: Random House, 1979).

Keith Snedegar, "Astronomical Practices in Africa South of the Sahara," in *Astronomy across Cultures: The History of Non-Western Astronomy,* edited by Helaine Selin and Sun Xiaochun (Boston: Kluwer Academic, 2000), pp. 455–473.

Peter Tompkins, *Secrets of the Great Pyramid* (New York: Harper & Row, 1971).

HEALTH

Medical Education. In addition to the traditional long apprenticeships (lasting a minimum of three years) of West African secret guilds or societies of medicine men and women and diviner/priests, medical education became available through the Islamic universities in Timbuktu and Djenné. As early as the eleventh century C.E., the Islamic scientist and philosopher Ibn Sina (also known as Avicenna) wrote his *Qanun fi at-tibb* (Canon of Medicine) in Arabic. It was destined to become the most famous medical book in the known world. Ibn Sina compiled earlier Greek and other cultures' medical and surgical treatises along with his own medical observations, theories, and discoveries. This work became available in the Islamic universities and their related health centers located at Timbuktu and Djenné.

THE SOURCE OF DISEASES

According to an Akan folktale, diseases spread among human-kind because of jealousy and competition between Nyankonpon the sky god and Ananse the trickster god:

Now there lived Kwaku Ananse, the spider, and he went to Nyankonpon, the sky-god, and said, "Grandsire, take your sheep called Kra Kwame, the one which you keep to sacrifice to your soul on a Saturday, and let me kill and eat it, that I may go and bring you a beautiful girl in exchange."

The sky-god gave him the sheep, and Ananse set out and returned to his village and killed the sheep and ate it. The spider then went to a certain village. In that village there was not a single male—all were women. Ananse married them all and he and they lived there.

One day, a hunter came and saw them. When he left, he went and said to the sky-god, "As for Ananse and that sheep of yours which he received, he has killed it and given it to some women to eat and then married them."

The sky-god said, "Is it true?"

The hunter said, "Grandsire, it is the truth."

The sky-god then sent messengers, telling them to go to that village and bring to him all the women who were there.

The messengers went off, met the women, and, with the exception of one woman who was ill, took them all to the sky-god.

Ananse said, "You who remain, what can I do with you? You can't do anything for me?"

The sick woman said, "Go and bring me a gourd cup." Ananse went and brought a gourd cup.

She said, "Bathe me, and take the water you have used and pour it into this gourd."

Ananse bathed her body and poured the water he had used into the gourd. She then became very beautiful; there was no woman like her in the tribe. Then Ananse married her again, although she was already his.

Now the hunter came again, and he saw this woman. He went off and reported to the sky-god, saying, "Ananse has made a fool of you, he sent you the ugly women and has kept the beautiful one for himself."

The sky-god sent messengers and directed them to go to the village where the spider was and bring the woman to him.

They delivered the message of the sky-god to Ananse. He said, "Would he not like me to come also?"

The messengers said, "The sky-god said we must take the woman to him."

Ananse said, "That is she sitting there, take her away."

After she had been taken, Ananse went and got the gourd into which all the diseases he had taken from the woman had been poured, and he stretched a skin over the mouth of it. Then he stretched a skin over another gourd and gave it to this child, Nti-kuma, and Ananse beat on the drum he had made and sang:

"Y'odende dende den,
Y'odende den,
   Aso Ya-e!
Y'odende dende den,

Y'odende den.
   Your eyes are red in vain!
Y'odende dende den,
Y'odende den.
   You are bandy-armed!
Y'odende dende den,
Y'odende den.
   Is that Aso Ya?
Y'odende dende den,
Y'odende den.
   You are knock-kneed!
Y'ondende dende den,
Y'odende den.
   Your nose is a lump on your face!
Y'odende dende den,
Y'odende den.
   Your feet are large as paddles,
     like those of a slave!
Y'odende dende den,
Y'odende den.
   Your head is like a cow!
Y'odende dende den,
Y'odende den."

Ntikuma drummed and sang:
"Beautiful maiden,
Beautiful maiden!"

And Afudotwedotwe or Belly-Like-to-Burst and Nyiwankonf-wea or Thin-Shanks, Ananse's children, danced. Anene, the crow, ran with speed and told the sky-god, "Ananse has a dance which is fitting for you but not for a spider."

Immediately the sky-god sent messengers there to Ananse to go and bring him this dance.

Ananse said, "This dance of mine, we perform it only in the harem, and if the sky-god agrees then I shall bring it along."

The messengers returned and told the sky-god. The sky-god said, "That is nothing, let him bring it to the harem." Ananse went with the drums to the harem, and the sky-god came and danced, and all his wives danced.

Now, there remained the one who had been sick. When she saw that Ananse had stretched a skin over the gourd in which were all her diseases, because of that she said she would not dance. And now the sky-god forced her, and she came; and when she was about to dance, Ananse lifted up the gourd and struck the woman with it, and the diseases scattered with a sound like *tese!*

This is how syphilis, stomach-ache, headache, leprosy, Guinea worm, smallpox, yaws, fits, diabetes, and madness came among the tribe. Once there was no sickness among mankind. It was the sky-god who was the cause of Ananse's bringing diseases among the tribe.

Source: Paul Radin, ed., "How Diseases Came to the Ashanti," in *African Folktales & Sculpture* (New York: Pantheon, 1952), pp. 64–66.

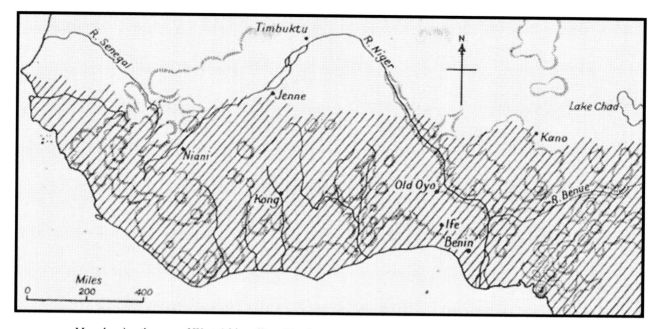

Map showing the area of West Africa affected by the tsetse fly, carrier of the tropical disease trypanosomiasis, or sleeping sickness (from Basil Davidson, *The Growth of African Civilisation*, 1965)

Doctor-Patient Relationship. Scholars can extrapolate from more-recent information about the interaction of doctor and patient in traditional West African medicine. As medical practitioners have discovered and reported in the late twentieth century, the trust and belief of the patient are imperative for an optimal result. With close, attentive observation of the patient and a thorough knowledge of his or her physical, mental, and emotional environment, the medical professional has a significant advantage as he or she works to benefit the person seeking good health. Similarly, the West African medicine man or woman living in the same village as the patient during the period 500–1590 knew more of the medical, mental, communal, and spiritual circumstances of the individual and was, therefore, able to help the person heal from within as well as from without. Both physical and psychological methods were employed by the medicine man or woman. In addition to pharmacology, the dance, which helped the individual and the community "draw down the spirit" and which put the community's focus on the person's recovery, became a powerful tool for healing.

Braces and Bones. Around 1217 braces were made for the legs of the seven-year-old prince Sundiata, who had had a walking disability since birth. The braces, plus an iron rod, helped him walk upright rather than on all fours (his determination reflected the drive that later helped him become the first king of Mali). The braces may have been made from the bones of an animal, from branches softened with plant fiber and tied around the limbs, or from iron. Oral tradition maintains that Sundiata bent a large rod of iron when he first stood up. As for the setting of bones and the reducing of fractures, substantial archaeological evidence, in the form of bones from burial places, is available

to show that those procedures were commonly practiced in early West Africa.

Surgery and Cautery. Surgical equipment that allowed delicate operations like cataract removal, mentioned as occurring at Djenné, could have been manufactured by West African smiths if they were able to produce fine enough and hard enough metal, such as carbon steel. Since there is no irrefutable evidence of carbon steel production in West Africa between 500 and 1590, it is likely they imported steel from kingdoms to the east or from the Egyptians through the North African trade. During this period the Arabic chronicler al-Bakri commented indirectly on the infibulation surgical procedure. Infibulation was the sewing of a female's labia to make a narrower opening, though there was also a procedure that could apply to males. In his comments on the inhabitants of the town of Audaghost, al-Bakri wrote of slave girls with "sexual organs so narrow that one of them may be enjoyed as though she were a virgin indefinitely." However, surgery, when it occurred, was often an emergency effort. Cautery, too, was for extreme treatment. For example, a man who had not heeded warnings about handling poisonous snakes was bitten while on caravan with Arab traveler and author Ibn Battuta. To help him, the Masufa guides cauterized the finger where the snake bite occurred, in hopes of reducing the pain from the venom. When that failed, the injured man killed a camel so he could put his hand in the water of its stomach; that procedure also failed, and the finger had to be amputated.

Environment and Disease. The tropical areas of Africa are perhaps the most fertile places for diseases carried by insects and parasites, especially if there is much standing rainwater or condensate. Malaria, yellow fever, schistosomi-

Terra-cotta figure covered with pustules, Djenné,
circa 1100–1400 (from Jean-Baptiste Bacquart,
The Tribal Arts of Africa, 1998)

asis (bilharzia or blood fluke), yaws, dengue, West Nile virus, onchocerciasis (river blindness), internal parasites, and trypanosomiasis (sleeping sickness) are common to a hot or hot-and-humid region where such insects as the anopheles mosquito, tsetse fly, and black fly can flourish and where frost never comes to keep the disease-carrying insect populations in check (with the exception of the high mountains). In that regard it is heartening to see al-Bakri's comment on the western city of Sijilmasa in the mid eleventh century: "There are no flies and none of its inhabitants falls ill with leprosy (*judham*). When anyone suffering from this complaint enters the town his illness does not develop further." However, al-Bakri also reported that some kings in that area wore clothes made from a flax-like, fireproof material that also was used for ropes for animals *(tamatghast*, or asbestos). Its use was certain to have affected people's respiratory health, though certainly so slowly that no connection was made between the two. Although lice did not flourish in the tropical region of West Africa, thus saving people there from the risk of exposure to bubonic plague, Ibn Battuta wrote that body lice did exist in what he called "the wilderness" between Taghaza in the desert and the Sudan (probably the northern part of the Sahel). The cure was to have containers of mercury attached to the body by a neck cord—a potentially dangerous solution, considering the toxicity of mercury. As for the role of animals in the health of West Africans, people on caravan would, when they ran out of water, kill a camel and drink the water stored in its belly.

Disease Resistance. Because of the tsetse flies in the rain forests and the sleeping sickness they carried, which killed animals as well as people, it was not possible for forest dwellers to keep the large range of domesticated animals that were popular on the savanna. However, there were exceptions in the form of certain resistant cows and a small variety of goat. Similarly, over a period of 1,500 years before 500, people whose ancestors had lived in the forest evolved the sickle cell trait in their blood, which made a person immune to malaria and, when present in only one parent, was not fatal, as it was when inherited from both parents.

Contact with Outsiders. Because Africa from latitude twenty degrees north to twenty degrees south has always had some of the widest ranges of diseases in the world, and because these are especially virulent for outsiders, the region enjoyed relative isolation for thousands of years. Indeed, the coast of West Africa south of Cape Vert (present-day Senegal) was called by Europeans "the white man's grave" because the Europeans' immune systems had no resistance to the diseases of the tropical and subtropical environment. By the time Europeans began arriving and trading in the fifteenth century, many West Africans' natural immune systems had already been weakened by the rise of cities and the density of human habitation there. Smallpox was carried into Africa by Europeans. Because it was an unknown factor to which they had no immunity, it devastated the people on the southwestern coast of West Africa.

Pharmacology. Observation and secret testing of local materials from plants, animals, and other sources led to a huge materia medica committed to memory and used by astute West African physician-priests who had carefully learned the knowledge from older doctors. Among biologicals occurring naturally in the rich resources of the rain forest and savanna one could find kaolin clay for diarrhea. For treatment of malaria, the most frequently experienced disease of the period 500–1590, West African doctors used parts of certain plants of the *Rubiacea* and *Apocynacea* families, plus steam inhalation of neem oil, lemongrass, pawpaw, or mango. For fever and jaundice they used *Morinda lucida* (methylanthraquinones) found from Burkina Faso eastward. Soapberry or *Balanites aegyptiaca* (desert date) was useful in every part: the bark for schistosomiasis; the root and fruit for treatment of parasitic worms, poison arrows, malaria, and herpes. To quote a Bornu saying: "A bito (soapberry) tree and a milk cow are just the same." The much-requested kola nut was the source of a stimulant popular with West Africans and their trading partners; the trade in kola nuts northward and northeast certainly helped feed the European craving for a bright, energetic feeling. The kola nut also provided a slight diuretic effect. For diabetes the Africans used the Madagascar periwinkle; for heart and blood-pressure conditions, *Strophanthus* and *Rauwolfia* (similar to reserpine but with fewer side effects). The leaves of the latter plant were also used in treating smallpox. In 1415, Anselm d'Isalguier returned to France from Africa. He brought with him his wife, who was a Songhai princess, as well as an African servant who was also a doctor. The physician subsequently provided medical assistance to King Charles VI, astonishing and upsetting the French medical community whose medicine was not effective for his mental condition.

Immunization. West Africans also made advances in immunization. In the earliest known attempt to vaccinate against malaria, a heated iron poker with a bit of infectious material on the tip was used to make a small hole in the skin of a person. There are also reports of this procedure being done with a thorn to inoculate people against smallpox. Oral traditions identify this latter procedure as occurring centuries before vaccination for smallpox in Western medicine.

Poisons. West Africans amassed a substantial collection of special knowledge on poisons used in warfare and hunting and their antidotes. Plants for poison included *Euphorbia hirta, Strophantus hispidus, Bridelia ferruguinea,* and *Erythrophlem guinese.* Poison-tipped iron arrows were reportedly used by Malians hunting wild buffalo. Around 1337 C.E. Syrian scholar al-Umari noted that the poisonous gall bladder of a slain Niger River crocodile, for which there was no known antidote, was taken to the king's storehouse of valuables.

Sources:

Bala Achi, "Biologically-based Warfare in Pre-Colonial Nigeria," in *Science and Technology in African History with Case Studies from Nigeria, Sierra Leone, Zimbabwe, and Zambia,* edited by Gloria Thomas-Emeagwali (Lewiston, N.Y.: Edwin Mellen Press, 1992), pp. 23–31.

Al-Bakri, "The Book of Routes and Realms" / "Kitab al-masalik wa-'l-mamalik," in *Corpus of Early Arabic Sources for West African History,* translated by J. F. P. Hopkins, edited by Nehemia Levtzion and Hopkins (Cambridge & New York: Cambridge University Press, 1981), pp. 62–87.

Graham Connah, *African Civilizations—Precolonial Cities and States in Tropical Africa: An Archaeological Perspective* (Cambridge & New York: Cambridge University Press, 1987).

Charles S. Finch, "The African Background of Medical Science," in *Blacks in Science: Ancient and Modern,* edited by Ivan Van Sertima (New Brunswick, N.J.: Transaction, 1983), pp. 140–156.

Ibn Battuta, "Journey" / "Tuhfat al-nuzzar fi ghara'ib al-amsar wa- 'aja' ib al-asfar" or "Rigla," in *Corpus of Early Arabic Sources for West African History,* pp. 279–304.

Maurice M. Iwu, *Handbook of African Medicinal Plants* (Boca Raton, Fla.: CRC, 1993).

Leo Africanus, *The History and Description of Africa, and of the Notable Things Therein Contained,* 3 volumes, edited by Robert Brown (London: Printed for the Hakluyt Society, 1896).

Patricia McKissack and Fredrick McKissack, *The Royal Kingdoms of Ghana, Mali, and Songhay: Life in Medieval Africa* (New York: Holt, 1994).

K. David Patterson and Gerald W. Hartwig, "The Disease Factor: An Introductory Overview," in *Disease in African History: An Introductory Survey and Case Studies,* edited by Hartwig and Patterson (Durham, N.C.: Duke University Press, 1978), pp. 3–24.

PBS, "Islam: Empire of Faith, Medicine" (1 December 2002) <http://www.pbs.org/empires/islam/innomedicine.html>.

Renee L. Pennington, "Disease as a Factor in African History," in *Encyclopedia of Precolonial Africa: Archaeology, History, Languages, Cultures, and Environments,* edited by Joseph O. Vogel and Jean Vogel (Walnut Creek, Cal.: AltaMira, 1997), pp. 45–48.

Al-Umari, "Pathways of Vision in the Realms of the Metropolises"/ "Masalik al-Absar," in *Corpus of Early Arabic Sources for West African History,* pp. 252–276.

MATHEMATICS

Sociomathematics. In the history of mathematics, sociomathematics (or ethnomathematics) provides succinct and reliable rules about arithmetic, algebraic, and geometric calculations and strategies. When few formal written systems are available, archaeology, architecture, oral tradition, and observed practices and usage provide scholars with clues about a society's understanding of mathematics. This observation is especially true in the case of West Africa, where the people's skill and capacity in mathematics are quite evident.

Number and Counting Systems. Commerce and trade, keys to so much of the life of West African kingdoms and empires, required that people of many different languages be able to communicate effectively with one another. As a consequence, there arose a consistent system of hand signs (also called gesture counting) and sequenced anatomical locations designated to represent numbers. Furthermore, counting of pebbles, seeds, segments of cloth, standard-sized bars of salt, kola nuts, or cowrie shells from the Maldives (all of which served as currencies) and several different base-number systems have been in use in West African history and continue to the present. Most common number systems in West Africa include: quinary (base 5), decimal (base 10), or vigesimal systems (base 20); others include base 6, and base 5-and-20. In the cities, by the eleventh century, reflecting the spread of Islam, Arabic numerals augmented traditional number systems, and in both regular and Islamic schools Arabic numerals were taught and used in math education.

Commerce and Currency. The Akan gold weights were in use before the Portuguese came to the coastal area of the Ashanti about 1471. The weights, themselves usually made of alloyed semiprecious metals, were used to accurately measure the gold dust harvested from post-rainy-season alluvial fields. Finely tuned jewelers' balance scales held the weight or weights on one side, and the gold dust was ladled with a fine, specially designed spoon onto the other side. The weights had an enormous variety of human and animal figures, representing cultural wisdom in proverbs or legal regulations. Other nonrepresentational weights might reflect numerical or geometric systems. Other West African currencies included gold dinars and bars and copper bars. Standardization of currency and weights and measures did not occur until the reign of Songhai ruler Askia Muhammad I (1492–1528 C.E.), a significant accomplishment in the largest empire in the history of all of Africa.

Fulani wedding blanket with a geometric design (from Ron Eglash, *African Fractals*, 1999)

Geometry. Symmetry in art and design, from mats and pottery decoration to edifices, gives insight into the abstract logic and geometrical calculations used in the practical problem-solving issues that arose in constructing objects. Modern mathematicians' analyses of repeated patterns in West African art show that they can be classified as twenty-four types for plane surfaces, broken down into strip patterns in one direction, and five-sided and six-sided symmetries appearing on curved surfaces, such as baskets. An example of the latter is the hexagonal weaving pattern in basketry.

Fractals. Knowledge and use of a non-Euclidian geometry called fractal geometry was widely employed in early West African mathematics, design, art, and architecture. Fractal geometry (plainly seen in the logarithmic spiral on a sunflower seedhead) involves all of the following elements: recursion of a pattern; varying scales of that pattern (larger or smaller); self-similarity; and potentially infinite continuation (up or down). Fractal geometry provided the basis for divination work in Nigeria and Benin for many centuries. In fact, a Nigerian divination chart with cowrie-shell shapes appeared in a geomancy chart used for English king Richard II in 1391. Extensive use of fractal geometry occurred in pattern repetitions in West African art, math games, building design, and in layouts of multiple community dwellings.

Algebra. The formal teaching of algebra in West Africa occurred through the Arabic-speaking scholars in the universities in Djenné and Timbuktu. Their text was certainly that of the "father of algebra," Abu Ja'far Muhammad ibn

Musa al-Khawarizmi. The *Kitab al-jabr wa al-muqabalah* (Large Book on Calculation by Completion and Balancing, circa 833) was a compendium of various Arab, Hindu, Hebrew, and Greek scholars' teachings, including the use of Hindu-Arabic numerals and all known methods for solving math problems in which at least one value is unknown.

Math Games. The people of West Africa played simple and complex math games, including the world's oldest game, *mancala* ("transferring" in Arabic), also known as *wari, oware, ayo,* and *adi.* A favorite with children and men to this day, it is played either on the ground or on finely made wood or metal boards. There are two parallel sets of six small holes and one hole at either end of the sets for scoring. The twelve small holes each contain four seeds, and the object of the game is to remove and place seeds into successive holes, one at a time. Memory, counting skills, mental arithmetic, and probability calculations are all involved in this often high-speed game of strategy. Reference to the gameboard even appears on some Akan gold weights.

Sources:

Leonard C. Bruno, "Al-Khwarizmi," in *Math and Mathematicians: The History of Math Discoveries Around the World*, volume 1, edited by Lawrence W. Baker (Detroit, Mich.: UXL, 1999), p. 18.

Ron Eglash, *African Fractals: Modern Computing and Indigenous Design* (New Brunswick, N.J.: Rutgers University Press, 1999).

Paulus Gerdes, "Mathematics in Africa South of the Sahara," in *Encyclopedia of the History of Science, Technology, and Medicine in Non-Western Cultures*, edited by Helaine Selin (Boston: Kluwer Academic, 1997), pp. 611–613.

Gerdes, "On the History of Mathematics in Africa South of the Sahara," *AMUCHMA (African Mathematical Union Commission on the History of Mathematics in Africa) Newsletter*, #9 (9 October 2002) <http://www.math.buffalo.edu/mad/AMU/amu_chma_09.html>.

Richard Hooker, "Civilizations in Africa: Songhay" (1996) (15 September 2002) <http://www.wsu.edu:8080/~dee/CIVAFRCA/SONGHAY.HTM>.

Beatrice Lumpkin, "Africa in the Mainstream of Mathematics History," in *Ethnomathematics: Challenging Eurocentrism in Mathematics Education*, edited by Arthur B. Powell and Marilyn Frankenstein (Albany: SUNY Press, 1997), pp. 101–117.

Georges Niangoran-Bouah, *L'Univers Akan Des Poids a Peser L'Or: Les Poids non-figuratifs* (Abidjan, Ivory Coast: Les Nouvelles Editions Africaines-MLB, 1984).

Niangoran-Bouah, "Weights and Measures in Africa: Akan Gold Weights," in *Encyclopedia of the History of Science, Technology, and Medicine in Non-Western Cultures*, pp. 1005–1007.

Claudia Zaslavsky, *Africa Counts: Number and Pattern in African Culture* (Boston: Prindle, Weber & Schmidt, 1973).

MINING AND METALLURGY

Wealth of Metals. Africa's wealth of metals made it a natural place to develop mining and metallurgy technologies. Iron, gold, copper, and salt are among the most notable of West Africa's resources mined between 500 and 1590. Lateritic iron (iron on or near the surface of the soil) was exploited throughout West Africa from at least 1000 B.C.E. (Laterite soil contains both iron oxide and iron hydroxide and has been formed from the humus soil of tropical rain forest areas.) Al-Bakri noted the availability of iron resources in the Western Sudan when he wrote that a series of mountains called *Adrar an Wuzzal* (Mountain of Iron) by the Berbers was located between Sijilmasa and Koumbi-Saleh. In addition, Ibn Battuta described areas near Takadda, called *ahsa,* where wet sand was found on top of flat rocks. If a white cloth were dropped on the sand, the cloth would turn black from the iron dissolved in the water.

Iron Smelting. Archaeological sites containing iron-smelting slag heaps are located all over modern Africa, including the Sahel (semiarid pastureland) and sub-Saharan sections where the kingdoms of Ghana, Mali, and Songhai were located. The earliest date for iron slag heaps in this region is approximately 500 B.C.E. Iron-smelting furnaces are commonly found where ceramic pottery firing is also done; certainly the use and knowledge of kiln and furnace building and the sophisticated firing processes could overlap. The level of sophistication of the smelting furnaces in West Africa was advanced. Types of furnaces included *tuyeres,* forced-air tubes often made from termite-mound soil, which was more impervious to water because of its silica and alumina content. These tubes, plus leather bellows, allowed preheating of the air in the furnace, thereby saving fuel and achieving the high temperatures required for smelting iron.

Smiths of High Caste. As an indicator of the value of technology and technicians, the Mande-speaking peoples valued the smith caste more highly than any other artisan group. Their work was considered magic, and the forge was called the *fan* (cosmic egg). The smith caste was given an honorific name that, translated, means "The First Sons of the Earth." Included in that artisan group were blast-furnace workers, blacksmiths, and workers in precious metals. Indeed, some rulers were members of smith castes.

Impact on the Military. Warriors, hunters, farmers, fishermen, leather workers, and builders all benefited from the availability of iron tools. Because of iron, the Kingdoms of Ghana, Mali, and Songhai all developed and flourished. Iron weapons included iron-pointed spears, daggers, and swords, which allowed the military of the Kingdom of Ghana to be enormously successful over other peoples. Warriors were rewarded with high pay and caste. The significance of the weapons technology of the Ghanaian army is vividly evident in the Arab chronicler al-Bakri's description of the defeat of the Bambara and Amima peoples because they had nothing but clubs made of ebony wood to fight against "swords and spears." Large military forces (as many as two hundred thousand warriors under one king) needed the best weapons available. Metal arrowheads tipped with poison and lightweight, thick, cloth-padded body armor were used in the Songhai conquest of Timbuktu in 1468. Technology changed the military parameters, and iron weapons generated the need to protect against the same.

Impact on Hunting, Fishing, and Agriculture. Iron weapons also made for successful hunting. Al-Bakri described the use of sharp-pointed iron javelins with rings attached to ropes that were used to spear and retrieve a hippopotamus in a river. Fishhooks were made of iron, as were harpoon tips and knives used in processing the catch. Iron hoes, sickles, and long knives made agriculture easier, more productive, and quicker. Knives, axes, and small scythes allowed people to expand the savanna by clearing part of the rain forest for more farmland. These implements, in combination with earth dams, irrigation dikes, and terraced plots, considerably advanced agricultural production in the period 700–800. Iron farm tools made it possible to pro-

duce a surplus beyond the needs of family or community. This surplus, in turn, generated the capacity for more specialization and for the development of cities, since not everyone was needed for food production.

Domestic Technologies. Iron eating utensils, needles, and scissors also existed. In the early part of the period under consideration, before trade expanded, many pastoralists used leather for clothing. Notably, leather workers from Takrur, a Western Sudan town on the Niger, and Kakadam, a staging place of the Masufa nomads, had both learned to make an iron-impervious shield and a leather cuirass from the hide of the oryx antelope. The tanning process involved soaking the hides for a year in a special combination of milk and ostrich eggshell, according to the traveler-chronicler Yaqut. These items were, for obvious

Bronze bowl, Nigeria, tenth century (National Commission for Museums and Monuments, Lagos, Nigeria)

Brass statue of a court dwarf, Kingdom of Benin, Nigeria, circa 1200–1400 (Museum für Volkerkunde, Vienna)

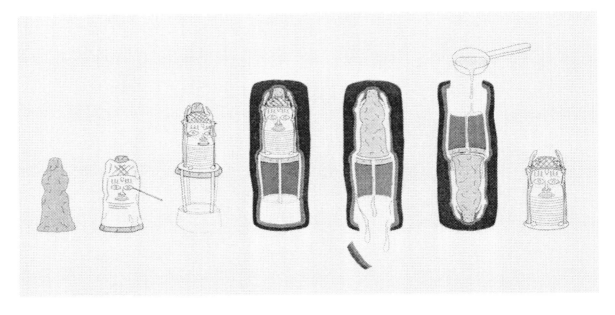

Diagram showing *Cire-perdue,* or the lost-wax process (from Monica Blackmun Visonà, *A History of Art in Africa,* 2001)

reasons, immensely valued, and cost 30 dinars each. Jewelry was also fashioned of iron. It consisted, primarily, of bracelets, necklaces, rings, and lip plugs.

Copper Mining. The first known surface mining of copper in West Africa occurred in what is now Mauritania in 250 C.E. By 500 its hammered versions were in use in the city of Jenne-jeno. Less abundant in West Africa than other parts of the continent, copper was prized. For it, people south of Mansa Musa I's Malian kingdom paid 66 percent of its weight in gold, according to al-Umari, who heard it from the king himself during the Arab chronicler's visit to that West African empire in the early 1300s. Takaddans converted their abundant copper into long bars, both thick and thin, to use as currency in trade with other peoples. Ibn Battuta observed that residents of Takadda had their male and female slaves mine the copper so plentiful there and had them smelt it in their homes. Copper's value was partly because of its malleability and the ease with which it could be combined with other metals in alloys that were easier to cast than pure copper. Alloys made in West Africa included bronze (copper with at least 5 percent tin, with or without lead) and brass (copper with 11 percent to 23 percent zinc, sometimes with lead and tin). The availability of tin from the Jos Plateau in the region that is present-day Nigeria and the importation of copper from other regions contributed to the fine bronze work done by the peoples of Ile-Ife and Benin.

High Art. By the period 500–800 all the major types of copper smithing had been achieved in West Africa. Hammering, cold spinning, twisting, and welding in combination with other metals (such as lead, tin, and imported zinc) were all known. *Cire-perdue,* a method of hollow casting dating from the third millennium B.C.E., was also employed by the West Africans. Also called the lost-wax process, it involves placing shaped wax between two heat-proof layers. The wax is then melted and drained off, and molten metal is poured into the resulting cavity. A plant native to the Sahel region and in abundant supply, *Euphorbia,* was also put to use by the artisans who made the bronze items (dated around 800) found in Igbo-Ukwe. This process involved replacing wax with latex in what is called the *Euphorbia*-latex process. Ile-Ife metalsmiths had mastered the art of lost-wax casting in the ninth century, producing some of the world's most beautiful and realistic figures. The famed bronzes of Benin were made possible, according to griots (oral historians), because of smithing techniques taught by the Ile-Ife metalsmith, Iguegbae, in the fourteenth century. (The king of Benin had arranged for the consulting service so his smiths would learn the lost-wax techniques.) Surviving Benin bronzes (actually more brass than bronze) are full-sized images of humans and animals, as well as smaller bas-reliefs.

Gold Mining. If the people of West Africa valued salt enough to put it in their treasuries and pay its weight in gold to obtain it, the traders of North Africa knew people who would pay dearly for the gold so abundant and easily bought in the Western Sudan. From contemporary reports, gold was available in alluvial deposits after the rivers flooded (near Boure and Bambouk) as well as deeper in the earth. The Kingdom of Ghana was called "the land of gold" in 773 by the Arab scholar and resident of Baghdad, al-Fazari. The people of this kingdom told no one about the whereabouts and types of availability of the gold of the area. Later, Mansa Musa I, king of Mali, while on his pilgrimage to Mecca, reportedly said to inquirers that gold grew there like plants. In a way, there was some truth to

Zinc-brass plaque of warriors with a chief holding a spear and shield, Kingdom of Benin, Nigeria, circa 1500–1600 (Ethnological Museum, Berlin)

this statement, in that fine, high-quality gold particles could be harvested both from the ground and from the surface of plants where flooding had occurred. Yet, digging deeper for gold was necessary, since the largest sources were in the ground. Work in the open-pit mines, up to five or six feet deep, was—by the reign of Mansa Musa I—performed by people of traditional religions, supposedly instead of paying tribute to the king. Later it was reported that only slaves performed this work. When Islam spread to the gold-mining areas, the activity of mining fell off badly, perhaps because of some religious laws that prevented converts to Islam from digging in the mines. Nevertheless, Muslim leaders quickly saw the value in letting people continue their traditional practices. Regardless of how the gold became available for trade, it was always a major magnet for the people of North Africa. They endured the hardships of the trans-Saharan trade from the earliest availability of gold in the seventh century C.E. onward.

Silent Trade. Part of the reason West African gold-mining and other technological practices are somewhat difficult to determine is because of the secrecy surrounding them. In order to protect mine locations and miners from being known by others, West Africans developed an unusual form of exchange called the "silent trade." In it, at a place some distance from any mining area, traders would put out whatever objects they had that might be desired by the miners. The traders would then depart; the next day they would return to find pieces of gold of various sizes by some of their wares. If the amount of gold met with the traders' approval, they would take the miners' gold and leave the trade items. If not, they would either take back their wares or add more to them in order to induce a gold exchange. Neither of the parties ever saw the others.

Big Spending. In the early fourteenth century Mansa Musa I of the Kingdom of Mali went on a pilgrimage to Mecca. He spent and gave away gold so lavishly that its price in Egypt, according to al-Umari, dropped from twenty-five *dirhams* to twenty-two and remained depressed for at least twelve years. That extravagance caught the attention of people in Europe, where a cartographer put an image of a Malian king on his map of Africa, with the king holding a very large ball of gold—considerable advertising for the riches of West Africa. West African court objects made from gold seen by Ibn Battuta included arrow quivers, sword handles, sword scabbards, and lances. An archaeological dig at a circa fourteenth-century grave site in what is present-day northwestern Senegal uncovered a disk of highly decorated gold, probably a breastplate, measuring more than seven inches in diameter.

Salt Mining. Salt was first mined from surface deposits, related to the drying of the Sahel, but the salt caves and underground reserves produced the majority of the torrid region's precious, lifesaving mineral. In Taghaza (or Teghaza), a city in the desert that was the source of large sup-

plies of salt, all the residents worked at salt production. Overseers were rotated in and out every few months, and only criminals and slaves were employed in the mines. Although the water was good, the death toll was high. Laborers assigned there were not expected to survive long, hence the phrase "going to the salt mines."

Sources:

Al-Bakri, "The Book of Routes and Realms" / "Kitab al-masalik wa-'l-mamalik," in *Corpus of Early Arabic Sources for West African History*, translated by J. F. P. Hopkins, edited by Nehemia Levtzion and Hopkins (Cambridge & New York: Cambridge University Press, 1981), pp. 62–87.

"Benin Bronzes," in *Africana: The Encyclopedia of the African and African American Experience*, edited by Kwame Anthony Appiah and Henry Louis Gates (New York: Basic Civitas, 1999), p. 223.

Graham Connah, *African Civilizations—Precolonial Cities and States in Tropical Africa: An Archaeological Perspective* (Cambridge & New York: Cambridge University Press, 1987).

J. Devisse and J. Vansina, "Africa from the Seventh to the Eleventh Century: Five Formative Centuries," in *UNESCO General History of Africa, Volume III: Africa from the Seventh to the Eleventh Century*, edited by M. Elfasi and I. Hrbek (Berkeley: University of California Press, 1988), pp. 750–793.

Eugenia W. Herbert, *Red Gold of Africa: Copper in Precolonial History and Culture* (Madison: University of Wisconsin Press, 1984).

Ibn Battuta, "Journey" / "Tuhfat al-nuzzar fi ghara'ib al-amsar wa-'aja' ib al-asfar" or "Rigla," in *Corpus of Early Arabic Sources for West African History*, pp. 279–304.

Ibn Khaldun, "The Book of Examples . . ." / "Kitab al'Ibar . . .," in *Corpus of Early Arabic Sources for West African History*, pp. 317–342.

"Iron in Africa," in *Africana: The Encyclopedia of the African and African American Experience*, pp. 999–1000.

Nehemia Levtzion, "The Early States of the Western Sudan to 1500," in *The History of West Africa*, volume 1, edited by J. F. Ade Ajayi and Michael Crowder (London: Longman, 1971), pp. 114–151.

Patricia McKissack and Frederick McKissack, *The Royal Kingdoms of Ghana, Mali, and Songhay: Life in Medieval Africa* (New York: Holt, 1994).

M. Posnansky, "Introduction to the Later Pre-History of Sub-Saharan Africa," in *UNESCO General History of Africa, Volume II: Ancient Civilizations of Africa*, edited by G. Mokhtar (Berkeley: University of California Press, 1981), pp. 531–550.

Peter R. Schmidt, *Iron Technology in East Africa: Symbolism, Science, and Archaeology* (Bloomington: Indiana University Press, 1997).

Thurstan Shaw, "The Guinea Zone: General Situation," in *UNESCO General History of Africa, Volume III: Africa from the Seventh to the Eleventh Century*, pp. 461–487.

Al-Umari, "Pathways of Vision in the Realms of the Metropolises" / "Masalik al-Absar," in *Corpus of Early Arabic Sources for West African History*, pp. 252–276.

Ivan Van Sertima, "The Lost Sciences of Africa: An Overview," in *Blacks in Science: Ancient and Modern*, edited by Van Sertima (New Brunswick, N.J.: Transaction, 1983), pp. 9–26.

Yaqut, "The Dictionary of Countries" / "Mu'jam al-buldan," in *Corpus of Early Arabic Sources for West African History*, pp. 167–175.

Al-Zuhri, "Book of Geography" / "Kitab al-jughrafiya," in *Corpus of Early Arabic Sources for West African History*, pp. 93–100.

POTTERY TECHNOLOGY

Secondary Clays and Firings. Low-fire (1,112–2,192 degrees Fahrenheit) clay pottery, such as the terra-cottas found in the Nok culture sites (500 B.C.E.) in what is now Nigeria, came from secondary clays (those containing

Two views of a ceramic vessel made of fired clay, Igbo, Nigeria, tenth century (Department of Archaeology and Anthropology, University of Ibadan, Nigeria)

impurities) that produced reddish, brownish, or even gray colors. These clays were far more widely available to West African potters than were the high-fire (2,192+ degrees Fahrenheit) primary clays, which produced white, light gray, or light pink-colored pottery. Moreover, the secondary clays were more easily molded than the primary. If the clay did not contain enough impurities to keep it from cracking or crumbling during firing, sand, plant fibers, stone grit, or grog (fine broken pieces of unglazed pottery) were added. Pottery finds in West Africa often are in the same place as the iron smiths' high-fire furnaces. It is uncertain whether the two technologies—ceramics and iron smelting—actually used the same firing process or if the potters used the furnaces at a lower temperature. However, low-fired ceramic work could also be accomplished in the open-pit kiln, where the air-dried clay pieces were

Clay urn, Djenné, Mali, circa 1100–1400 (from Jean-Baptiste Bacquart, *The Tribal Arts of Africa*, 1998)

given their first firing, to the bisque stage, under a pile of fuel, such as wood, dried grasses, or dried dung.

Vessels and Sculptures. Techniques of clay building to generate a vessel or a sculpture, such as a bowl or deep jar, include rolling and placing coils, shaping, modeling, or molding. Rolls of clay can be coiled to form the bottom, sides, shoulder (widest part), neck, and lip of a pot. Then they are joined and shaped into a vessel by pulling the clay, pinching or paddling it, and scraping the interior and exterior. Similarly, a sculpture can be made by shaping a single lump of clay. Both vessels and sculptures can also be made by the technique known as modeling, which includes forming the clay over a desired shape, or inside a shape. In West Africa that shape was usually a carved piece of wood, stone, or another already-shaped ceramic piece. Modeling could also involve making two shapes that would each be half of the final piece. Finally, adding pieces of rolls, dabs, or patches of clay were further ways to sculpt the shape desired.

Decoration Types. Various basic decoration types were in use in West Africa between 500 and 1590 C.E. The simplest was the indenting or shaping with only the potter's fingers; another was using some object—usually a pointed stick or groove-making tool—to form lines or inverted

Terra-cotta statuette probably used in a shrine or a meeting room, Djenné, Mali, circa 1000–1300 (Musee Barbier-Mueller, Geneva)

points or punctuation. The comb technique (individual incising of parallel lines) was used strikingly on sculptures of naturalistic heads in Ife pottery. Paint or ribbons of clay were occasionally added.

Sources:

Richard A. Krause, "Pottery Manufacture," in *Encyclopedia of Precolonial Africa: Archaeology, History, Languages, Cultures, and Environments,* edited by Joseph O. Vogel and Jean Vogel (Walnut Creek, Cal.: Alta-Mira, 1997), pp. 115–124.

D. T. Niane, "Mali and the Second Mandingo Expansion," *UNESCO General History of Africa, Volume IV: Africa from the Twelfth to the Sixteenth Century,* edited by Niane (Berkeley: University of California Press, 1984), pp. 117–171.

TEXTILE AND PAPER TECHNOLOGY

Materials. Evidence exists of several materials being used to produce both woven and beaten cloth between 500 and 1590 in West Africa. These include palm-tree bark from the forest region; camel and goat hair; young raffia palm-leaf fibers; bast fibers from stems of various local plants, including the hibiscus plant; cotton; flax for linen; thread produced by the West Africa native *Anaphe* silkworm; and mineral asbestos for a linen-like fireproof cloth. In addition, West Africans evidently used indigo for dyeing and gum for finishing the surface of cloth. Trade of indigo,

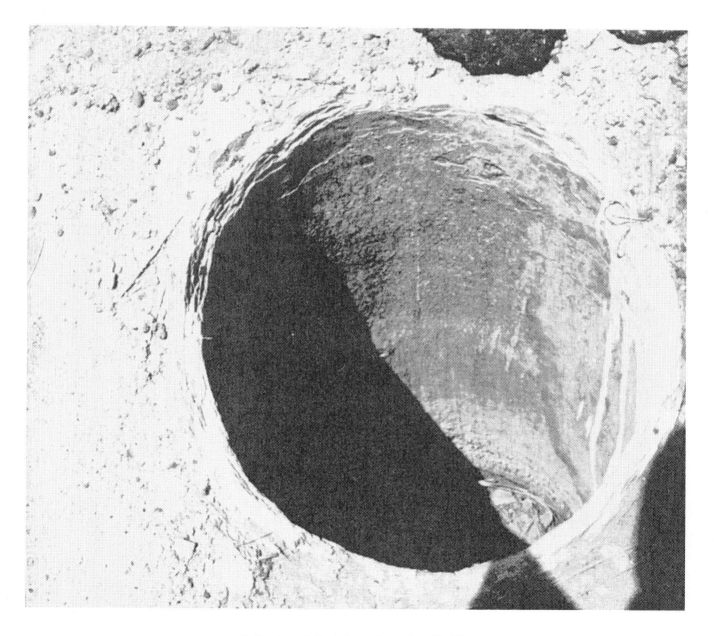

Indigo dye-pit, North Ivory Coast, circa 600–900

A TREE CALLED TWRZY

Although the Arab chronicler al-Bakri was told by some that asbestos came from a tree, those who knew more told him it came from a mineral in the ground:

Among the strange things found in the land of the Sudan is a tree called *TWRZY* which has a long thin trunk and grows in the sands. It has a big, puffed-up fruit containing white wool from which cloth and garments are made. Fire cannot damage the materials made of this wool, however long they are exposed to it. The jurist 'Abd al-Malik relates that the people of al-Lamis (a place in those parts) wear only clothes of this kind. Stone with similar characteristics is found in the Dar'a valley and called in the Berber language *tamatghust*. When rubbed in the hand it becomes so soft that it takes on the consistency of flax. Robes and hobbles for domestic animals are made of this substance and they cannot be damaged by fire in any way. The garments of some of the kings of Zanata in Sijilmasa were manufactured out of it. A trustworthy person informed me that he was acquainted with a merchant who brought a handkerchief made of this substance for Ferdinand, the ruler of the Galicians, and said that it had belonged to one of the Apostles and that fire could make no impression on it. He let the king see it with his own eyes and thus gained enormous esteem in his eyes. Ferdinand showered riches upon him and sent the kerchief to the ruler of Constantinople in order that it might be put in their greatest church. For this the ruler of Constantinople sent him a crown and commanded that he be invested with it. Several persons have related that they saw the fringes of a kerchief made of this stuff in the possession of Abu 'l-Fadl of Baghdad. When it was heated on the fire it became whiter. Fire [so to speak] washed it. It was like linen cloth.

Source: Al-Bakri, "The Book of Routes and Realms" / "Kitab al-masalik wa-'l-mamalik," in *Corpus of Early Arabic Sources for West African History*, translated by J. F. P. Hopkins and edited by N. Levtzion and Hopkins (Cambridge & New York: Cambridge University Press, 1981), pp. 83–84.

gum arabic, cotton, and flax to feed the textile craving was prodigious from the seventh century onward.

Sundiata's Influence. Less known than his military and political innovations is Sundiata's enormous influence on agricultural development. Mari-Jata (the Lion King or Sundiata) at the *Gbara* (Great Assembly) helped the tribes form a constitution that considered the interests and needs for the protection of all. Among the agricultural and technological innovations Sundiata introduced to the Empire of Mali were the extensive agricultural cultivation of cotton and the weaving of cotton. Thus he began West Africa's centuries-long and highly successful cotton textile technology, industry, and art.

Non-Spun Fibers. The process of making bark into cloth requires the hammering or beating of the material until it is flexible. In the forest regions, bark was an abundant and accessible commodity and, therefore, widely used. From excavations at Igbo-Ukwe it is known that cloth made from the fibers of the young raffia palm and from bast (or stem fibers, such as hibiscus) were both common weaving materials in the 800s.

Spinning. An excavation in West Africa uncovered a sophisticated spinning tool, a clearly distinguished spindle whorl, dated as being from the thirteenth century. However, since cloth made of spun fibers predates the Tellem cave burial date of circa 1000, hand spinning without whorls was a much older technique. In addition, the *Anaphe* silkworm spun a silk thread used by weavers in Kano for a cloth widely and heavily traded in the 1400s.

Weaving Techniques. From Igbo and other communities' archaeological evidence, it is clear that raffia palm weaving was widely used before cotton. The Tellem cave textiles are among the earliest and best available archaeological evidence of loom weaving of cotton in West Africa. Located near some of the headwaters of the Niger River in what is present-day Mauritania, the cave complex was occupied by the Dogon people before they migrated west to their present location in Mali to escape pressures to convert to Islam. The Tellem textiles are excellent examples of narrow strip weaving (ranging from four inches to fifteen inches) of the type produced by a double-heddle loom. Oral tradition from the Illorin-Yoruba weavers' caste, or guild, indicates that this kind of loom weaving goes back to the 900s. They continue to use both the vertical and horizontal loom, with warping knowledge for the former being taught and transferred entirely by oral teaching, practice, and memory from master to apprentice. While the warping of the vertical loom is done on the loom directly, warping of the horizontal loom can be done either by laying warps out following the master weaver's drawn pattern or by attaching warp yarns to spools on a pegged board and moving the board gradually back from the loom. Among these weavers women are allowed to use the vertical loom while men use the horizontal one; the justification is that the horizontal loom, which requires some pressure against the seated weaver's stomach, would be unhealthy for a female if she were pregnant.

Dyeing. According to Kano weavers and dyers' oral tradition, Hausa cloth dyeing dates from the mid 900s. Indigo, primarily *Indigofera tinctoria*, grown in the Maghrib, was the favored dye-stuff and was traded with the peoples to the south of the Sahara. Other botanicals also produce intense blue, including *Lonchocarpus*. Camwood was used in Liberia from the 1500s onward to produce a red or crimson dye for fabric. Other locally grown materials, such as kola nuts, also were used to dye cloth, though their dates of initial use are less clear. As a substitute for the natural dyeing of cloth, a laborious process that could last weeks for the fermentation process to be completed, some tribes' weavers bought or bartered for scarlet cloth—from Maghrib, Egyptian, or European sources—and raveled it to employ the red fibers in their own fabrics.

Papermaking. Papermaking, brought to Africa and Europe by the Arabs (who learned it from the Chinese), proved more economical and universally producible than papyrus, which was formed from reeds, or parchment, which was made from animal skins. Paper affected the science and technology of West Africa because it was employed to produce large quantities of scientific and other materials of wide use in Islamic academic, technological, and commercial circles, including those in Timbuktu. It was in Timbuktu during his visit in the 1520s that, according to Leo Africanus, paper books were valued more than any other object. Paper can be made from a pulp from almost any kind of plant or cloth fiber, including the inner bark of trees, rags, bast (plant stem fibers), and recycled ropes and nets; its technology made possible the scholarly life of several early West African cities.

Sources:

Lisa Aronson, "History of the Cloth Trade in the Niger Delta: A Study of Diffusion," in *Textiles of Africa*, edited by Dale Idiens and K. G. Ponting (Bath, U.K.: Pasold Research Fund, 1980), pp. 89–107.

"Dogon," in *Africana: The Encyclopedia of the African and African American Experience*, edited by Kwame Anthony Appiah and Henry Louis Gates Jr. (New York: Basic Civitas, 1999), p. 613.

Idiens, "An Introduction to Traditional African Weaving and Textiles," in *Textiles of Africa*, pp. 5–21.

Venice Lamb and Alastair Lamb, "The Classification and Distribution of Horizontal Treadle Looms in sub-Saharan Africa," in *Textiles of Africa*, pp. 22–62.

Cheryl Plumer, *African Textiles: An Outline of Handcrafted Sub-Saharan Fabrics* (East Lansing: African Studies Center, Michigan State University, 1971).

Claire Polakoff, *Into Indigo: African Textiles and Dyeing Techniques* (Garden City, N.Y.: Anchor/Doubleday, 1980).

Tellem cotton tunic, circa 1000–1100 (from D. T. Niane, ed., *Africa from the Twelfth to the Sixteenth Century*, volume 4 of *General History of Africa*, 1984)

SIGNIFICANT PEOPLE

IGUEGBAE

CIRCA 1300S
MASTER BRONZE SMITH

Royal Request. No information exists about the birth or death of Iguegbae (or Igueghae). According to the griots (oral historians) of Benin, Iguegbae was a master bronze smith from Ile-Ife who, at the request of the king of Benin, traveled there and taught the metalsmiths of that kingdom the lost-wax technique (a method of hollow casting dating from the third millennium B.C.E.). Such generous sharing of knowledge and technical skill led to the creation of many of the outstanding works of West African art, including the famed Benin brasses (which are often inaccurately identified as the Benin bronzes).

Sources:
"Benin Bronzes," in *Africana: The Encyclopedia of the African and African American Experience*, edited by Kwame Anthony Appiah and Henry Louis Gates Jr. (New York: Basic Civitas, 1999), p. 223.

"Met Timeline—Guinea Coast, 1000–1400 A.D." (27 May 2003) <http://www.metmuseum.org/toah/ht/07/sfg/ht07sfg.htm>.

ABU JA'FAR MUHAMMAD IBN MUSA AL-KHAWARIZMI

CIRCA 780–CIRCA 850
MATHEMATICIAN

Algebra. An Arab, Abu Ja'far Muhammad ibn Musa al-Khawarizmi spent most of his life in Baghdad. He served on the faculty at the famous *Dar al-Hikma* (House of Wisdom), where he not only translated scientific and mathematical documents from Greek, Sanskrit, and Hebrew into Arabic but also taught mathematics and astronomy. His most important known work was the *Kitab al-jabr wa al-muqabalah* (Large Book on Calculation by Completion and Balancing, circa 833), the earliest compendium of algebra and geometry in Arabic. His compiling of all known algebraic, geometric, and numeral resources into one volume in Arabic created the first textbook containing practical ways to make calculations for construction, surveying, and the complex system of Islamic distribution of family inheritance. The catalyst for popularizing *al-jabr* (algebra, meaning "completion" in Arabic), al-Khawarizmi's book was studied in the Islamic mosque-universities in Djenné, Timbuktu, and in many parts of the Arabic-speaking world then and, in translation, since. It also made a significant impact in medieval Europe.

Numerals, Place-Values, and Algorithm. In another volume, *On the Calculation of Hindu Numerals* (circa 825), now lost except in a Latin translation (*Algoritmi de numero Indorum*), al-Khawarizmi also provided the Middle East, North and West African Arabic-speaking areas, and Europe (through translators) with the tools to use Hindu-Arabic numerals, including zero, and place-values. *Algorithm*, a term derived from an abbreviated version of the author's last name, is used today to describe a mathematical procedure for solving a problem in the shortest effective way, by a finite number of steps that involves the repetition of a specific operation.

Other Works. Another of al-Khawarizmi's important works includes a text on astronomy, based on an Indian treatise given to the Baghdad court around 770. He evidently used the ancient scholar Ptolemy's data for a major work on geography. It listed latitudes and longitudes for more than 2,400 localities, and in many regards it was more accurate than Ptolemy's determinations.

Sources:
Leonard C. Bruno, "Al-Khwarizmi," in *Math and Mathematicians: The History of Math Discoveries around the World*, volume 1, edited by Lawrence W. Baker (Detroit, Mich.: UXL, 1999), p. 18.

J. J. O'Connor and E. F. Robertson, "Abu Ja'far Muhammad ibn Musa Al-Khwarizmi" (27 May 2003) <http://www-history.mcs.st-andrews.ac.uk/history/References/Al-Khwarizmi.html>.

PBS, "Islam: Empire of Faith, Algebra and Trigonometry" (24 November 2002) <http://www.pbs.org/empires/Islam/innoalgebra.html>.

DOCUMENTARY SOURCES

Al-Bakri, *Kitab al-masalik wa-'l-mamalik* (The Book of Routes and Realms, 1068)—Although al-Bakri did not journey to the Maghrib and Western Sudan himself, he questioned travelers who had gone there, extracting detailed information from them about the people, social and cultural activities, and political matters. Some reliance on the work of al-Warraq, from 150 years earlier, makes part of the material anachronistic, but al-Bakri also used documentation from more-recent reports on the Kingdom of Ghana and the trade and trade routes across the Sahara. Particularly useful are his discussions of textile technology relating to fireproof fabric, successful hunting and weapons technologies, epidemiological issues, and the pharmacopoeia of poisons known in Ghana.

Ibn Battuta, *Rihlah* (Journey, 1355)—The part of his work that reports on his trip to the Western Sudan is useful and relatively reliable, as he had completed it within two years before dictating this report to Sultan Abu Inan's scribe Ibn Juzayy.

Ibn Khaldun, *Kitab al-'Ibar wa-diwan al-mubtada' wa-'l-khabar fi ayyam al-'arab wa-'l-'ajam wa-'l-barbar* (The Book of Examples and the Register of Subject and Predicate [or, of the Origin and History], on the Days of the Arabs, the Persians, and the Berbers, 1374–1378)—Revised continuously until 1404, two years before the author's death. Ibn Khaldun was one of the most comprehensive Arab writers on the Kingdom of Mali, especially as it interfaced with the people of North Africa, among whom he lived, worked, and traveled for many years. The conscientious Ibn Khaldun double-checked his sources against one another, making his capture of oral traditions fairly reliable. He had a particular interest in construction and architectural matters.

Leo Africanus, *The History and Description of Africa* (1526)—Leo Africanus's work was considered to be the definitive account on West Africa for hundreds of years. It was written at the request of Pope Leo, who had converted the author (at the time enslaved by pirates and given or sold to the Pope) from Islam to Catholicism. Leo Africanus had been born in Granada in 1485, forced to leave during the expulsion of Moors and Jews in 1492, and traveled as a teenager with his uncle (a diplomat) around North Africa and to sub-Saharan cities. He then returned home and wrote extensively. The section on Timbuktu is the most famous of his writings, describing the striking visual contrast between the bell-shaped traditional West African buildings and the straight-walled Islamic buildings introduced by al-Sahili and other construction specialists, with the aid of both indigenous and updated brick technologies, including fired brick. The Timbuktu passage also reported the great international exchange of information and learning in the city, the valuing of paper books over any other object, their wide distribution and availability (made possible by the non-papyrus paper technology brought from China by the Arabs), and state support of scholarship in the university there.

Al-Umari, *Masalik al-absar fi mamalik al-amsar* (Pathways of Vision in the Realms of the Metropolises, 1338)—Al-Umari was a Syrian scholar and head of chancery of the Mamluk Empire (1339–1342). His encyclopedic work is particularly well detailed on geographic, environmental, and topographic obstacles that had to be overcome in West Africa by human imagination and technology. It contains vivid material on health and construction and agricultural technologies known and used at the time. Al-Umari's reportage on the health and cultural practices of some of the various peoples of the Maghrib and Western Sudan are highly detailed. In combination with the works of Ibn Battuta, Ibn Khaldun, and Leo Africanus, al-Umari's material provides a fairly good overview of West Africa during the period under consideration.

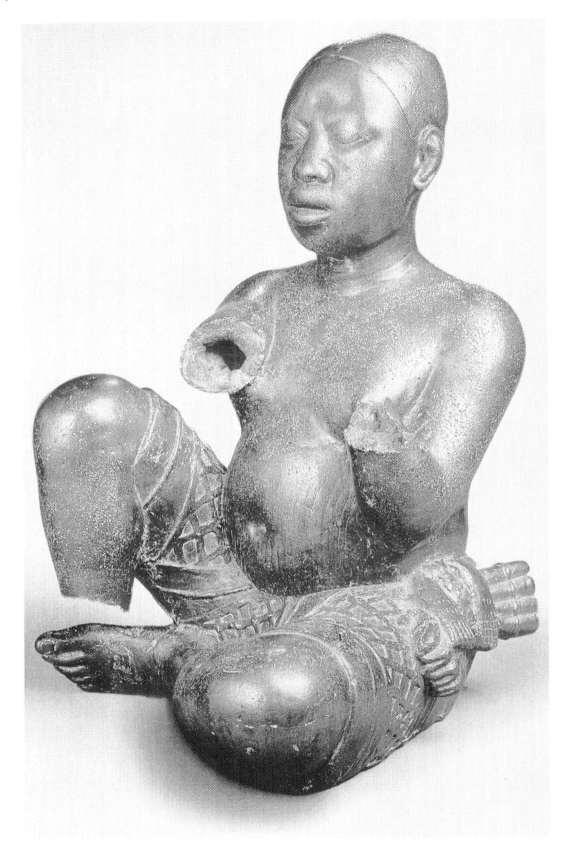

Seated Yoruba figure made of copper, Nigeria, circa 1200–1300 (National
Commission for Museums and Monuments, Lagos, Nigeria)

GLOSSARY

Abosom: **Akan** minor deities.

Acacia Wood: Also known as mimosa; a variety of the acacia plant that grows in the hot and dry climate of North and West Africa and produces a heavy but flexible wood, which can be woven into frames for houses and portable tents. Acacia wood is also the source of gum arabic, used in West Africa to finish the surface of textiles and for other purposes.

Agbala: The priestess of **Ala**, the **Igbo** earth goddess.

Age-Grade Association: A traditional social system under which people who are born within a particular period (often three to four years) are grouped together for solidarity and other purposes. Typically, men are categorized into several age grades, and specific tasks are assigned to each group. For instance, some age grades assist in the day-to-day administration of the community, while the youngest age grade (fifteen- to eighteen-year-olds) is usually responsible for environmental sanitation, such as cleaning and sweeping streets and public squares.

Agwu: The **Igbo** trickster god.

Akan: A group of peoples and languages of southern Ghana and bordering parts of Côte d'Ivoire and Togo, including speakers of the Anyi, **Ashanti,** and Fante languages—as well as the main language of the group, known as Akan (or Twi). Most of the Akan peoples migrated to their present location from the north between 1000 and 1700.

Ala: The **Igbo** earth goddess.

Almoravids: A dynasty of Berber origin (Arabic name: *al-Murabitun,* meaning people of the hermitage) that ruled in North Africa and then Spain (circa 1050–1147). In West Africa the name was often used to describe Berber invaders and marauders in general.

Amadioha: The **Igbo** god of thunder and lightning.

Amaomee: "Giver of Plenitude," one of the names for **Onyame,** the **Akan** supreme being.

Amosu: "Giver of Rain," one of the names for **Onyame,** the **Akan** supreme being.

Amowia: "Giver of the Sun," one of the names for **Onyame,** the **Akan** supreme being.

Ananse: The **Akan** trickster god, often represented in myths as a spider.

Ani-mmo: The **Igbo** land of the dead, or land of the spirits.

Ashanti: A Ghanian people and language of the **Akan** group.

Askia: The title of the ruler of the Songhai Empire.

Aso Oke: A **Yoruba** textile popular in West Africa.

Atunda: Slave of the **Yoruba** god **Orisa-nla.**

Aye: In the **Yoruba** cosmology, the word for the world of the living.

Babalawo: (Literally, "father of the secret") a **Yoruba** diviner and a priest of the deity **Ifa;** the babalawo may also be a medical practitioner.

Babatunde: A **Yoruba** name meaning "the father has come back," which is given to a male child born after the death of an elderly man in the family.

Bambara: A **Mande**-speaking people who inhabit a large area east and north of Bamako in Mali.

Banco: Sun-dried mud bricks or blocks for building. The mud was mixed with wood, fibers, and straw. The common sizes in West Africa were two-thirds of a cubit in height.

Bast: Stem fibers such as hibiscus fibers that could be woven into cloth without spinning them first.

Beaten Cloth: Bark beaten into flexible sheets for cloth.

Berbers: Pre-Arabic inhabitants of North Africa, nomads living in scattered tribes in mountainous and desert regions of Morocco, Algeria, Tunisia, Libya, and Egypt.

Bilad al-Sudan: "Land of the Blacks," the Arabic name for West Africa.

Bilineal Descent: Tracing lineage from both the mother's and the father's side of the family.

Bogolanfini, or Mud Cloth: A heavy woven and treated-cotton fabric on which **Mande** women painted elaborate images and designs.

Caliph: Anglicized version of the Arabic word *khalifah* (successor); a shortened version of Khalifat Rasul Allah (Successor of the Messenger of God; *khalifat* is the genitive form of *khalifah*). In the Islamic empire the caliph was the political and religious leader of the Muslim community.

Cengura Tree: One of the trees whose leaves are used in the making of **bokolanfini,** or mud cloth.

Chi: The spirit that the **Igbos** believe to inhabit each individual; Chi is said to be the fractal representation of **Chukwu** that resides in each person.

Chi Wara: A mythical antelope that taught the **Bambara** how to farm by using sticks to till the land; before land is cleared for planting and at harvest time, dancers wearing carved male and female Chi Wara headpieces perform ceremonies designed to make the land fertile.

Chukwu: The supreme god of the **Igbo** religion; *Chukwu* (or Chi Ukwu) may be translated as "The Great Spirit."

Cire-perdue: The lost-wax method used by West African artists to create brass and bronze sculptures; the artist first carves a figure in wax and encases it in a heat-proof substance such as clay, leaving holes at the top and bottom of the mold. The wax is lost when molten brass or bronze is poured into the mold, melting the wax, which flows out of the mold. When the molten metal cools and solidifies, the mold is broken, revealing the sculpture inside.

Consanguinity: Relationship by blood or descent from a common ancestor.

Cowrie Shells: Tropical marine gastropods with shiny, glossy, spotted surfaces and single, fixed openings. Probably imported from the Maldives Islands, they were used as currency in West Africa.

Cultural Hearth: A center of cultural origins, innovation, and creativity.

Da: The **Yoruba** god of order, highly exalted by the **Fon.**

Da Ayido Hwedo: The high priest of **Vodon.**

Dibia: A powerful **Igbo** priest, diviner, and healer.

Dieli: The **Bambara** word for minstrel, or **griot.**

Dinar: One of several units of currency (either silver or gold) used in the Arab world in the Middle Ages.

Dirham: Arabic adaptation of the Greek word *drachma;* unit of money.

Dogon: A people and language of the south-central region of present-day Mali.

Donga: An annual stick-fighting competition held to train young men for war.

Dounouba: Among the **Bambara** of Mali, a stick fight held for the settlement of disputes.

Dugutigi: A chief and priest of a village; a clan head.

Dundun Drums: Yoruba drums that mimic human speech, specifically Oyo, or standard Yoruba dialect.

Dyeli or Dieli: A ruler's public spokesman, interpreter, chief counselor, or **griot.**

Dyula: The itinerant, **Mande**-speaking merchants who served as middlemen between the trans-Saharan traders and the forest region of West Africa. Dyula is also the name for an ethnic group of Côte d'Ivoire, Burkina Faso, Mali, Ghana, and Guinea-Bissau. *See also* **Wangara.**

Efik: An ethnic group of the coastal regions of southeastern Nigeria and western Cameroon.

Ekwensu: The **Igbo** Evil Spirit, much like the Devil in other religions.

Endogamous Marriage: A union in which one's spouse belongs to the same clan.

Esu: The **Yoruba** and **Fon** trickster god.

Ewe: An ethnic group in the modern nation of Ghana, having migrated there from the north circa 1000–1300.

Exogamous Marriage: A union in which husband and wife come from different clans.

Fan: African word meaning "cosmic egg," used in reference to the forge of the blacksmith.

Farariya: A commander of the cavalry in Mali.

Farba: The slave chief of staff in a **mansa's** household.

Fari or Farin: An emperor's appointed governor who ruled alongside local tribal chiefs; a Soninke provincial chief.

Figini: Ostrich-feather fans.

Fon: An ethnic group that originated in present-day Togo and migrated to Abomey (in the modern Republic of Benin) during the seventeenth century.

Fractal Geometry: A non-Euclidian type of geometry which involves the recursion of a pattern, varying scales of that pattern (larger or smaller), self-similarity, and potentially infinite continuation (up or down).

Fulani: A pastoral people thought to have arisen in the grasslands of modern Senegal; spreading across Senegal, Guinea, Mali, Niger, Nigeria, and Cameroon, the Fulani were early practitioners and propagators of Islam.

Gerontocracy: A social structure dominated or controlled by the elderly.

Gondwana: The large prehistoric landmass that eventually split into Africa, North and South America, southern Asia, and Australia.

Griot: A French word for "minstrel"; frequently used to describe a West African storyteller/poet/musician who served as an oral historian and sometimes as a ruler's spokesman. Performing for kings and at cultural celebrations, the griot transmitted knowledge and legends from one generation to the next. He also accompanied warriors to battle, telling stories of past bravery and conquest that encouraged boldness and fearlessness among the troops. The griot's words were believed to include powerful chants and incantations that could bless or harm others.

Grog: Fine, broken pieces of unglazed pottery added to clay to make it more resistant to cracking during firing.

Guinea: A medieval European name for West Africa.

Guinea Savanna or Middle Belt: Grassland area north of the rainforests of the West African coastal area, where the grasses grow five to ten feet tall, whereas farther north toward the Sahara the grasses are shorter. *See also* **Savanna** *and* **Sahel**.

Hajj: The Islamic pilgrimage to Mecca during the month of Dhu al-Hijjah and the performance of religious rites in and around that city; every Muslim who is physically, mentally, and financially able to do so is expected to go on the hajj once in a lifetime. One who has performed the pilgrimage is called *hajji* (masculine) or *hajjah* (feminine).

Harmattan: The dry trade winds that move from the northeast across the Sahara, carrying clouds of dust and cold air into the western **savanna**. Harmattan winds contribute to the southwesterly encroachment of the Sahara Desert.

Hausa: A people of northwestern Nigeria and southern Niger.

Ibaje: A member of the **Yoruba** goddess **Oya**'s retinue and deity of the Niger River tributary at Idah, in present-day Nigeria.

Ibeji: Twins.

Iconography: Images or symbols associated with particular cultural, religious, social, or political ideas.

Ifa: The **Yoruba** god of knowledge; also the rigidly defined and complex system of obtaining knowledge from Ifa through divination and the body of literary work (Ifa verses) sometimes called the Yoruba Bible.

Igala: A Nigerian people living on the east bank of the Niger River below its meeting with the Benue River.

Igbo: A people of southeastern Nigeria.

Igwe Marriage: A "small-dowry" union, in which the groom has paid only part of the dowry; the wife remains in her family compound, and all children born of the union are the property of her father.

Igwu Marriage: A union in which the dowry is paid in full; the wife goes to live in her husband's family compound; and the children she bears are part of his family.

Ijaw: An ethnic group of southeastern Nigeria, whose subgroups include the Kalabari, Neba, and Okrika.

Imam: A leader of Muslim communal prayer rituals, who at times exercised temporal as well as spiritual control over a region.

Indigo: A deep purplish-blue dye made from plants containing a substance known as *indican*. In West Africa, indigo-dyed cloth is highly valued for its rich color and has many artistic uses.

Infibulation: A reversible practice designed to prevent or modify sexual intercourse. For males, it involves inserting a pin or a ring at the penis tip while for females it involves an incomplete sewing shut of the labia majora.

Iwa-pele: A **Yoruba** word associated with good character, a personal trait that is esteemed throughout the society. In Yoruba cosmology, Iwa-pele is a female deity associated with knowledge and wisdom.

Iwo-Uki: Rising Moon; an organization that used its knowledge of the cosmos and the seasons to recommend to the king of Benin when to schedule events and to announce harvest times for yams and other crops.

Jihad: A war in defense of the Islamic faith.

Kafu: A group of kinship-related villages ruled by a single clan head.

Kanuri: A people of the Kanem-Bornu empire, who originated east of Lake Chad but migrated west into northeastern Nigeria and neighboring regions of Niger.

Kawkaw: The Arabic name for the **Songhai** Empire and the **Sudan**.

Kaya-Maghan: The title of the ruler of **Wagadu**, the predecessor state to the Empire of Ghana.

Kente Cloth: A woven patterned cloth made by Akan and **Ewe** peoples since at least the fourteenth century.

Kidiranga Naba: The head of the **Mossi** cavalry, usually from an ordinary family.

Kirki: The **Hausa** concept of "goodness."

Kola Nut: A West African plant (*Cola nitida* or *Cola acuminata*) with nuts that are red or red-brown and aromatic. The nuts (or seeds) contain the stimulant alkaloids caffeine and theobromine and were chewed by people for energy. Today, the extract from this nut is used to make soft drinks and medicines.

Kurmina-Fari: The governor of the western region of the **Songhai** Empire, second in command to the **askia**.

Lost Wax: *See* **cire-perdue**.

Madrasah: A Muslim institution of higher learning, or college, where Islamic religion, philosophy, and law, as well as Arabic language and literature, were taught.

Maghrib: The Arabic name for the region of northwest Africa that lies south of Spain (present-day Morocco, Algeria, and Tunisia).

Malinke: An ethnic group of eastern Guinea and neighboring regions of Mali and Côte d'Ivoire. Closely related to the **Mandinka,** they speak a **Mande** language.

Mama Water: A member of the **Yoruba** goddess **Oya's** retinue and deity of the Niger River tributary at Onitsha, in present-day Nigeria.

Mancala: Considered by some to be the world's oldest game. The game is also called *wari, oware, ayo,* and *adi* in various locations in West Africa.

Mande: A branch of the **Niger-Congo** language group spoken by the **Malinke, Mandinka, Bambara, Dyula, Mende,** and Kpelle peoples.

Mandinka: A people of the Gambia and Senegal, who speak a **Mande** language.

Mansa: The chief or ruler of a large **kafu,** particularly one that grew into a heterogeneous state; the head of government in Mali.

Mansa-dyon: A trusted and loyal slave of a **mansa.**

Matrilineal Descent: Tracing lineage through the mother's side of a family.

Matrilocality: Establishment of residence in the bride's mother's compound, a practice usually found in a **matrilineal** society.

Mbari: An **Igbo** deity who is considered a close associate of the earth goddess **Ala,** even an aspect of her.

Mende: An ethnic group of Sierra Leone, which speaks a **Mande** language.

Mmintia: Ceremonial horns that communicate in a language understood by **Akan** speakers.

Mmo: The **Igbo** name for wandering spirits that may either protect or cause mischief to the living.

Mossi: The largest ethnic group of Burkina Faso; thought to have originated in present-day Ghana, the Mossi still have members living in that nation, as well as in Côte d'Ivoire, Togo, and Benin.

Neolocality: The practice by which a newly married couple sets up their own residence away from the compounds of both sets of parents.

Niger-Congo Language Family: A group of languages spoken by three-quarters of all Africans, including most West Africans.

Nsibidi: A form of ideographic writing used by the **Efik** and **Igbo** of Nigeria.

Numana: An ethnic group living primarily in the northern part of present-day Ghana, which speaks a language related to **Yoruba** and **Igbo.**

Nupe: A people of west-central Nigeria, who speak a language related to **Yoruba** and **Igbo.**

Nyama: A **Mande** term for the fiery energy that controls nature.

Nyamakala or Nyamakalaw: A **Mande** term for an occupational caste (such as smiths, griots, leather workers, or hunters). Such a group controls, or gives direction, to the **nyama.**

Oba: The **Yoruba** word for the king. In the Yoruba tradition the oba is not only the head of all chiefs and ruler of his people but also the spiritual link between the living and the world of the ancestors. In Ile-Ife, the principal Yoruba city, the oba is called Ooni Alaiyeluwa, the owner of earth and heaven. The supreme Yoruba deity, Olorun, is called the Oba-Orun, the king who dwells in heaven. *Oba* is also the name of the Yoruba goddess of the Oba River.

Obatala: The **Yoruba** god whom Olorun authorized to create dry land, the father of the goddess **Oya.**

Ochumare: The **Yoruba** goddess of the rainbow.

Odomankoma: The **Akan** infinite being, who binds himself with the gods **Onyame** and **Onyankopon** into one absolute divinity.

Odua (or Oduduwa): The mythical leader/deity who led the **Yoruba** peoples to their present homeland in southwestern Nigeria around the year 1000; as a deity, Odua is considered the creator of the Earth; the Yorubas are sometimes called "Omo Oduduwa" (Children of Oduduwa).

Ogun: The **Yoruba** god of hunters, warriors, and ironworkers.

Olokun: The **Yoruba** sea god.

Olori: In **Yoruba,** the "owner of the head"; that is, the spirit that guards the soul.

Olori Buruku: An unlucky person, one who has a "bad head."

Olori Rere: A lucky person, one who has a "good head."

Olorun (or Olodumare): The **Yoruba** sky god and supreme deity.

Olosa: The wife of the **Yoruba** sea god, **Olokun.**

Onchocerciasis: River blindness; a tropical worm infestation carried by black flies. Symptoms include node-like swelling on the skin and lesions on the eyes.

Onyame: The **Akan** supreme being, sometimes thought to be female and associated with the Moon.

Onyankopon: An **Akan** super-deity who is a polar opposite to **Onyame;** he is male and associated with the Sun.

Onyishi: The eldest member of an **Igbo** council of elders, who is given authority over the religious life of his clan or village.

Ori: The **Yoruba** word for "head," associated with the spirit that guards the purity of the soul.

Orile Oriki: Yoruba "praise poems," which were chanted at public gatherings to remind rulers and their subjects of their social responsibilities.

Orisala: The **Yoruba** god responsible for forming humans in the womb and the patron of people with congenital deformities.

Orisa-Nla: In the **Yoruba** religion, the original godhead, who was shattered into pieces that became the many gods of the Yoruba pantheon.

Orun: In the **Yoruba** cosmology, the word for the world of the spirits and the afterlife.

Orunmila: The **Yoruba** god of divination.

Oryza Glaberrima: An indigenous African rice, thought to have been first cultivated in the Middle Niger region.

Osun: A **Yoruba** goddess of wealth, power, and femininity, the giver of children; the deity of the Osun River, Osun is part of **Oya's** retinue and a wife of **Orunmila** and **Shango**.

Oya: The **Yoruba** goddess of waters, a wife of **Shango**.

Pastoralists: People who live by keeping herd animals (such as cattle, sheep, goats, deer, and camels) and who follow them from summer pasture to winter pasture as the seasons change or the availability of food for the herd declines.

Patrilineal Descent: Tracing lineage through the father's side of a family.

Patrilocality: Establishment of residence in the groom's father's compound, a practice usually found in a **patrilineal** society.

Polyandry: A marriage in which the wife has more than one husband at the same time.

Polygyny: A marriage in which the husband has more than one wife at the same time.

Potsherd Pavement: Broken pieces or shards (sherds) of terra-cotta pottery wedged together on their edges in carefully placed rows. This pavement can still be seen in Ife; it long pre-dates the similar concept used by European road builders.

Primary Clays: High-fire clays, including kaolin, which produce a white, light cream, or pink ware.

Pui: A praise song composed by Gassire, the first known **griot,** to recount the origins of the Empire of Ghana.

Qadi: A judge who applies Islamic law in civil and penal cases.

Qintar: A unit of measure used in Arabic-speaking countries during the Middle Ages.

Rak'a: Literally, the act of bowing; in Islamic prayer, a sequence of recitations and movements performed during prayer; the name of one unit of prayer.

Reciprocity: An ancient mechanism for property redistribution within the family unit, by which goods one received were determined by one's age and personal needs, not by social standing.

River Blindness: *See* **Onchocerciasis.**

Sahel: The semidesert area on the southern fringe of the Sahara from Mauritania and Senegal to Chad.

Samande Naba: The general in charge of the **Mossi** infantry, usually a slave.

Savanna: A semi-arid grassland with scattered deciduous trees, whose climate is typically rainy in the summer and dry in the winter. The African savanna, also known as the **Sudan** or Sudanic region, is a band stretching across the continent south of the Sahara Desert; the grasses here range from five to ten feet in height, and the average rainfall is twenty to forty inches, falling mostly over a period of four or five months.

Scarification: Decorative designs made on the body by scratching or cutting the skin.

Schistosomiasis: Also called bilharzia or blood fluke. One of several tropical diseases affecting both humans and animals and caused by infestation of parasitic worms or blood flukes.

Secondary Clays: Low-fire clays that contain impurities; they produce reddish, brownish, or gray-colored pots or sculpture. Secondary clays are more easily shaped than **primary clays.**

Sefawa Dynasty: A royal line established in the ninth or tenth century by an Arab hero named Sayf ibn Dhi Yazan to rule the **Kanuri** people and other nomads in the Lake Chad region of West Africa; this dynasty continued until 1846, when the last of the mais (lords) of the Sefawa was executed.

Shango: The **Yoruba** god of thunder and lightning.

Shari'ah: Islamic law and practice, the rules and regulations governing the lives of Muslims; Islamic jurisprudence.

Sickle Cell: An abnormal red blood cell that forms a sickle shape instead of the usual disc shape. This trait occurs primarily in Africans. When only one parent conveys it to the offspring, the trait is useful in making the individual resistant to malaria, but if a person gets the sickle cell trait from both parents, it leads to sickle-cell anemia, a fatal illness.

Sleeping Sickness: *See* **Trypanosomiasis.**

Songhai: A people who originated along the bend of the Niger River in Mali and spread, with the growth of the

Songhai Empire, throughout much of the **savanna** region of West Africa.

Spindle Whorl: A circular disk or sphere made of wood or clay used to aid in the process of hand spinning.

Sudan, or Sudanic Region: *See* **savanna** *and* **Bilad al-Sudan.**

Sunnah (*plural:* **sunan):** A normative custom practiced by the Prophet Muhammad or a member of the early Muslim community. In its plural form, *sunan,* it refers to several important collections of hadiths (records of the words and actions of the Prophet) and legal pronouncements.

Susu (or Soso): A people who appear to have migrated south from present-day Mali and Mauritania to the West African coastal region, especially Guinea, beginning as early as the year 900. They bear the name of a powerful kingdom that was defeated by the Empire of Mali in 1235–1240.

Tabib: Arabic word for doctor.

Tailasan: A mantle.

Termite Mound Soil: The soil used for **tuyeres** (air pipes) and for lining the walls of iron-smelting furnaces. Its alumina and silica content make its products impervious to water and thus more enduring tools.

Toron: Wooden posts horizontally jutting out from buildings; they were used to suspend scaffolding for repair of mud buildings after the rainy season. The toron was introduced by al-Sahili, an Andalusian architect brought to Mali by Mansa Musa I in the early fourteenth century.

Trephination: A rare but highly successful surgical technique known to have been used by the Berbers and others in North and West Africa (with a mortality rate of around 5 percent). This procedure involved cutting a hole in the skull of a patient in order to relieve pressure on the brain.

Trypanosomiasis: Sleeping sickness. A tropical disease transmitted by the tsetse fly and characterized by fever and inflammation of the lymph nodes, brain, and spinal cord and resulting in lethargy and frequently death.

Tungigi: A council of village headmen.

Tunka: The title of the ruler in Ghana.

Tuyere: A pipe for forcing air into a furnace to increase the heat for combustion.

Ulama' (*singular:* **'alim):** Scholars of Islamic law and religion.

Uli: A form of **Igbo** women's art painted on the body and walls. Uli designs often convey messages or indicate social status.

Unilineal Descent: Tracing lineage from only one side of the family, usually the father's.

Vai: A people of Liberia and Sierra Leone, who are related to the **Mende** and speak a **Mande** language.

Vigesimal System: A counting system based on the number 20; it probably arose from the use of **cowrie shells** for currency.

Vodon: The chief religion of the **Fon;** slaves carried it to the Western Hemisphere, where it is known as "Voodoo."

Wangara: Mande-speaking West African traders. *See also* **Dyula.**

Wolof: A people of Senegal, the Gambia, and Mauritania.

Yaws: A contagious tropical disease with symptoms that include raspberry-looking sores on the face, hands, and feet; it mainly occurs in children.

Yemojya: The **Yoruba** moon goddess, who controls the movement of the seas and is the mother of **Oya,** the goddess of waters.

Yeyetunde: A **Yoruba** name meaning "the mother has come back," which is given to a female child born immediately after the death of a matriarch or an elderly female blood relative of the father. Among some groups of Yoruba, the name *Iyabo* is used instead.

Yoruba: One of the three major ethnic groups of Nigeria, located primarily in the southwestern part of that country. Smaller groups of Yoruba are scattered in Benin and northern Togo.

GENERAL REFERENCES

GENERAL

J. F. A. Ajayi and Michael Crowder, eds., *The History of West Africa*, second edition, 2 volumes (New York: Columbia University Press, 1976, 1987).

Ajayi and Ian Espie, eds., *A Thousand Years of West African History: A Handbook for Teachers and Students* (Ibadan, Nigeria: University of Ibadan Press / London: Nelson, 1969).

Kwame Anthony Appiah and Henry Louis Gates, eds., *Africana: The Encyclopedia of the African and African American Experience* (New York: Basic Civitas Books, 1999).

William Farquhar Conton, *West Africa in History*, 2 volumes (London: Allen & Unwin, 1965, 1966).

Basil Davidson, *Old Africa Rediscovered* (London: Gollancz, 1959); republished as *The Lost Cities of Africa* (Boston & Toronto: Little, Brown, 1959; revised, 1970).

Davidson, with F. K. Buah and the advice of Ajayi, *A History of West Africa to the Nineteenth Century*, revised edition (Garden City, N.Y. : Anchor/Doubleday, 1966).

Encyclopaedia Britannica online <http://www.search.eb.com/eb>.

Encyclopedia of Islam, CD-ROM version (Leiden: Brill, 1999).

Ghana web page <www.ghana.co.uk>.

Elizabeth Isichei, *A History of African Societies to 1870* (Cambridge: Cambridge University Press, 1997).

J. Ki-Zerbo, ed., *Methodology and African Prehistory*, volume 1 of *General History of Africa* (London: Heinemann / Berkeley: University of California Press / Paris: UNESCO, 1981).

Mary Penick Motley, *Africa—Its Empires, Nations, and People* (Detroit: Wayne State University Press, 1969).

D. T. Niane, ed., *Africa from the Twelfth to the Sixteenth Century*, volume 4 of *General History of Africa* (London:

Heinemann / Berkeley: University of California Press / Paris: UNESCO, 1984).

Roland Oliver, ed., *The Cambridge History of Africa, Volume 3: from c. 1050 to c. 1600* (Cambridge, London, New York & Melbourne: Cambridge University Press, 1977).

Oliver and Anthony Atmore, *The African Middle Ages: 1400–1800* (Cambridge: Cambridge University Press, 1981); revised as *Medieval Africa: 1250–1800* (Cambridge: Cambridge University Press, 2001).

The Story of Africa <www.bbc.co.uk/worldservice/africa/features/storyofafrica/>.

G. T. Stride and Caroline Ifeka, eds., *Peoples and Empires of West Africa: West Africa in History 1000–1800* (London: Nelson, 1971).

GEOGRAPHY

Nafis Ahmad, *Muslim Contribution to Geography* (Lahore: Sh. Muhammad Ashraf, 1972).

J. F. A. Ajayi and Michael Crowder, eds., *The History of West Africa*, second edition, 2 volumes (New York: Columbia University Press, 1976, 1987).

S. M. Ali, *Arab Geography* (Aligarh: Muslim University, 1960).

Al-Bakri, *Description de l'Afrique septentrionale*, edited by William MacGuckin, Baron de Slane (Algiers, 1911).

Michael S. Bisson, S. Terry Childs, Philip de Barros, and Augustin F. C. Holl, *Ancient African Metallurgy*, edited by Joseph O. Vogel (Walnut Creek, Cal.: AltaMira Press, 2000).

Adu Boahen, with J. F. Ade Ajayi and Michael Tidy, *Topics in West African History*, second edition (Harlow, U.K.: Longman, 1986).

Ross E. Dunn, *Adventures of Ibn Battuta, A Muslim Traveler of the Fourteenth Century* (Berkeley: University of California Press, 1986).

M. El Fasi and I. Hrbek, eds., *Africa from the Seventh to the Eleventh Century*, volume 3 of *General History of Africa*, (London: Heinemann / Berkeley: University of California Press / Paris: UNESCO, 1988).

A. T. Grove, *The Changing Geography of Africa* (Oxford: Oxford University Press, 1989).

Bernard de Grunne, *Terres cuites anciennes de L'Ouest Africain*, Publications d'histoire de l'art et d'archéologie de l'Université catholique de Louvain, no. 22 (Louvain-la-Neuve: Institut supérieur d'archéologie et d'histoire de l'art, Collège Erasme, 1980)

R. Haaland, "Man's Role in the Changing Habitat of Mema During the Old Kingdom of Ghana," *Norwegian Archaeological Review*, 13 (1980): 31–46.

Ibn Battuta, *Travels in Asia and Africa, 1325–1354*, 3 volumes, translated by H. A. R. Gibb (London: Routledge, 1929).

Ibn Hawqal, *Kitab Surat al-Ard*, 2 volumes, edited by J. H. Kramers (Leiden: Brill, 1938, 1939).

Ibn Khaldun, *Prolégomènes*, 3 volumes, translated by M. Quatremère (Paris: B. Duprat, 1858).

Al-Idrisi, *Description de l'Afrique et de l'Espagne*, translated by R. Dozy and M. J. de Goeje (Leiden: Brill, 1866).

John Iliffe, *Africans: The History of a Continent* (Cambridge & New York: Cambridge University Press, 1995).

Al-Kati, *Tarikh el-Fettâch, ou, Chronique du chercheur, pour servir à l'histoire des villes, des armées et des principaux personnages du Tekrour*, translated by O. Houdas and M. Delafosse (Paris: E. Leroux, 1913).

J. Ki-Zerbo, ed., *Methodology and African Prehistory*, volume 1 of *General History of Africa* (London: Heinemann / Berkeley: University of California Press / Paris: UNESCO, 1981).

Leo Africanus, *The History and Description of Africa*, 3 volumes, translated by John Pory, edited by Robert Brown (London: Printed for the Hakluyt Society, 1896).

Al-Mas'udi, *Les prairies d'or*, 9 volumes, translated by C. Barbier de Meynard and Pavet de Courteille (Paris: Imprimerie impériale, 1861–1917).

Raymond Mauny, *Tableau géographique de l'Ouest africain au Moyen Age, d'après les sources écrites, la tradition et l'archéologie* (Dakar: IFAN, 1961).

D. T. Niane, ed., *Africa from the Twelfth to the Sixteenth Century*, volume 4 of *General History of Africa* (London: Heinemann / Berkeley: University of California Press / Paris: UNESCO, 1984).

Al-Sa'di, *Tarikh es-Soudan*, translated by Houdas and Edm. Benoist (Paris: Leroux, 1898).

R. V. Tooley, *Maps and Map-Makers* (New York: Bonanza, 1952).

Al-Umari, *Masalik al-absar fi mamalik al-amsar*, edited by Ahmad Zaki (Cairo, 1924).

Marijke van der Veen, ed., *The Exploitation of Plant Resources in Ancient Africa* (New York & London: Kluwer Academic / Plenum, 1999).

Yaqubi, *Tarikh*, edited by M. Th. Houtsma (Leiden: Brill, 1883).

THE ARTS

Rowland Abiodun, Henry J. Drewal, and John Pemberton III, eds., *The Yoruba Artist: New Theoretical Perspectives on African Arts* (Washington, D.C. & London: Smithsonian Institution Press, 1994).

J. O. Ajibola, *Owe Yoruba* (Ibadan: Oxford University Press, 1968).

Akan Cultural Symbols Project <http://www.marshall.edu/akanart/>.

Kofi Anyidoho, Abioseh M. Porter, Daniel Racine, and Janice Spleth, eds., *Interdisciplinary Dimensions of African Literature* (Washington, D.C.: Three Continents Press, 1985).

E. V. Asihene, *Apoo Festival* (Tema, Ghana: Ghana Publishing, 1980).

Jean-Baptiste Bacquart, *The Tribal Arts of Africa* (London: Thames & Hudson, 1998).

Diedre L. Badejo, *Osun Seegesi: The Elegant Deity of Wealth, Power, and Femininity* (Lawrenceville, N.J.: Africa World Press, 1996).

Peter Badejo, "The Bori Spirit Possession Dance," thesis, UCLA, 1980.

William Bascom, *African Art in Cultural Perspective: An Introduction* (New York: Norton, 1973).

Walter E. A. van Beck, *Dogon: Africa's People of the Cliffs*, with photographs by Stephenie Hollyman (New York: Abrams, 2001).

Adu Boahen, with J. F. Ade Ajayi and Michael Tidy, *Topics in West African History*, second edition (Harlow, U.K.: Longman, 1986).

Eckhard Breitinger, ed., *Theater and Performance in Africa: Intercultural Perspectives* (Bayreuth: Bayreuth University, 1994).

J. P. Clark-Bekederemo, ed. and trans., *The Ozidi Saga: Collected and Translated from the Ijo of Okabou Ojobolo* (Washington, D.C.: Howard University Press, 1991).

Herbert M. Cole, *I Am Not Myself: The Art of African Masquerade*, Monograph Series, no. 26 (Los Angeles:

Museum of Cultural History, University of California, Los Angeles, 1985).

Michèle Coquet, *African Royal Court Art*, translated by Jane Marie Todd (Chicago & London: University of Chicago Press, 1998).

Margaret Courtney-Clarke, *African Canvas: The Art of West African Women* (New York: Rizzoli, 1990).

Susan Denyer, *African Traditional Architecture: An Historical and Geographical Perspective* (New York: Africana Publishing, 1978).

Henry John Drewal and John Pemberton III, with Rowland Abiodun, *Yoruba: Nine Centuries of African Art and Thought*, edited by Allen Wardwell (New York: Center for African Art / Abrams, 1989).

Christopher Ehret, *The Civilizations of Africa: A History to 1800* (Charlottesville: University Press of Virginia, 2002).

Akin Euba, *Yoruba Drumming: The Dundun Tradition*, edited by Eckhard Breitinger (Bayreuth, West Germany: Bayreuth University, 1990).

Kate Ezra, *Art of the Dogon: Selection from the Lester Wunderman Collection* (New York: Metropolitan Museum of Art, 1988).

Ezra, *Royal Art of Benin: The Perls Collection in the Metropolitan Museum of Art* (New York: Metropolitan Museum of Art, 1992).

Angela Fagg, "Thoughts on Nok," *African Arts*, no. 3 (July 1994): 79–84.

William Fagg, *The Art of Western Africa: Sculpture and Tribal Masks* (New York: New American Library, 1967).

David Hughes, *Afrocentric Architecture: A Design Primer* (Columbus, Ohio: Greyden Press, 1994).

John O. Hunwick, "Gao and the Almoravids: Ethnicity, political change and the limits of interpretation," *Journal of African History*, 35 (1994): 251–273.

Hunwick, *Timbuktu & the Songhay Empire: Al-Sa'di's Ta'rikh al-Sudan Down to 1613 and Other Contemporary Documents* (Leiden: Brill, 1999).

Marion Kilson, ed., *Royal Antelope and Spider: West African Mende Tales* (Cambridge, Mass.: Press of the Langdon Associates, 1976).

Hans-Joachim Koloss, ed., *Africa, Art and Culture: Masterpieces of African Art, Ethnological Museum, Berlin* (Munich, Berlin, London & New York: Prestel, 2002).

Phyllis M. Martin and Patrick O'Meara, *Africa* (Bloomington: Indiana University Press, 1977).

R. J. McIntosh, "Early Urban Clusters in China and Africa," *Journal of Field Archeology*, 18 (1991): 199–212.

Susan Keech McIntosh and Roderick J. McIntosh, *Jenne-jeno, An Ancient African City* <http://www.ruf.rice.edu/~anth/arch/niger/broch-eng.html>.

Laure Meyer, *Black Africa: Masks, Sculpture, Jewelry* (Paris: Terrail, 1992).

James L. Newman, *The Peopling of Africa: A Geographic Interpretation* (New Haven & London: Yale University Press, 1995).

François Neyt, with the assistance of Andrée Désirant, *The Arts of the Benue: To the Roots of Tradition* (N.p.: Editions Hawaiian Agronomics, 1985).

D. T. Niane, *Sundiata: an Epic of Old Mali*, translated by G. D. Pickett (London: Longmans, 1965).

Ernest E. Obeng, *Ancient Ashanti Chieftaincy* (Tema, Ghana: Ghana Publishing, 1988).

Akinwumi O. Ogundiran, "Filling a Gap in the Ife-Benin Interaction Field (Thirteenth - Sixteenth Centuries A.D.): Excavations in Iloyi Settlement, Ijesaland," *African Archeological Review*, 19 (March 2002): 27–60.

Isidore Okpewho, ed., *The Oral Performance in Africa* (Ibadan: Spectrum Books, 1990).

John Pemberton III and Funso S. Afolayan, *Yoruba Sacred Kingship: "A Power like that of the Gods"* (Washington, D.C. & London: Smithsonian Institution Press, 1996).

Tom Phillips, ed., *Africa: The Art of a Continent* (Munich & New York: Prestel, 1996).

Paul Radin and Elinore Marvel, eds., *African Folktales & Sculpture*, revised and enlarged edition (New York: Pantheon, 1964).

Doran H. Ross, *Wrapped in Pride: Ghanaian Kente and African American Identity* (Los Angeles: UCLA Fowler Museum of Cultural History, 1998).

Peter Kwasi Sarpong, *The Ceremonial Horns of the Ashanti* (Accra, Ghana: Sedco, 1990).

Paul Stoller, "Social Interaction and the Management of Songhay: Socio-Political Change," *Africa*, 51, no. 3 (1981): 765–780.

Barbara Thompson, *The Earth Transformed: Ceramic Arts of Africa*, The Virtual Research Center for African Ceramics Project, 2000 <http://bailiwick.lib.uiowa.edu/african-ceramic-arts/>.

Robert Farris Thompson, *Flash of Spirit: African and Afro-American Art and Philosophy* (New York: Random House, 1983).

Monica Blackmun Visonà, Robin Poynor, Herbert M. Cole, and Michael D. Harris, *A History of Art in Africa* (New York: Abrams, 2001).

COMMUNICATION, TRANSPORTATION, AND EXPLORATION

Akan Cultural Symbols Project <http://www.marshall.edu/akanart/>.

Carrie Beauchamp, *Social Fabric: Exploring the Kate Peck Kent Collection of West African Textiles*, University of Denver Museum of Anthropology, 2002 <http://www.du.edu/duma/africloth/>.

Brian Catchpole, *A History of West Africa in Maps and Diagrams* (London: Collins Educational, 1983).

Basil Davidson, with F. K. Buah and the advice of J. F. A. Ajayi, *The Growth of African Civilisation: A History of West Africa 1000–1800*, revised edition (London: Longmans, 1967).

Leo Africanus, *The History and Description of Africa*, 3 volumes, translated by John Pory, edited by Robert Brown (London: Printed for the Hakluyt Society, 1896).

Nehemia Levtzion, *Ancient Ghana and Mali* (New York: Harper & Row, 1973).

Levtzion and J. F. P. Hopkins, eds., *Corpus of Early Arabic Sources of West African History*, translated by Hopkins (Cambridge: Cambridge University Press, 1981).

Pekka Masonen, "Trans-Saharan Trade and the West African Discovery of the Mediterranean," in *Ethnic Encounter and Culture Change: Papers for the Third Nordic Conference on Middle Eastern Studies*, edited by M'hammed Sabour and Knut S. Vikor (Bergen: Nordic Society for Middle Eastern Studies, 1997), pp. 116–142.

Patricia and Fredrick McKissack, *The Royal Kingdoms of Ghana, Mali, and Songhay: Life in Medieval Africa* (New York: Holt, 1994).

M. P. Motley, *Africa—Its Empires, Nations, People* (Detroit: Wayne State University Press, 1969).

Ivan Van Sertima, *They Came Before Columbus* (New York: Random House, 1976).

Van Sertima, ed., *Blacks in Science, Ancient and Modern* (New Brunswick & London: Transaction Books, 1983).

SOCIAL CLASS SYSTEM AND THE ECONOMY

J. F. A. Ajayi and Michael Crowder, eds., *The History of West Africa*, second edition, 2 volumes (New York: Columbia University Press, 1976, 1987).

Al-Bakri, *Description de l'Afrique septentrionale*, edited by William MacGuckin, Baron de Slane (Algiers, 1911).

Michael S. Bisson, S. Terry Childs, Philip de Barros, and Augustin F. C. Holl, *Ancient African Metallurgy*, edited by Joseph O. Vogel (Walnut Creek, Cal.: AltaMira Press, 2000).

Adu Boahen, with J. F. Ade Ajayi and Michael Tidy, *Topics in West African History*, second edition (Harlow, U.K.: Longman, 1986).

Robert O. Collins, *Western African History* (Princeton: Wiener, 1990).

G. R. Crone, trans. and ed., *The Voyages of Cadamosto and Other Documents on Western Africa in the Second Half of the Fifteenth Century* (London: Printed for the Hakluyt Society, 1937).

Basil Davidson, *Old Africa Rediscovered* (London: Gollancz, 1959); republished as *The Lost Cities of Africa* (Boston & Toronto: Little, Brown, 1959; revised, 1970).

M. El Fasi and I. Hrbek, eds., *Africa from the Seventh to the Eleventh Century*, volume 3 of *General History of Africa*, (London: Heinemann / Berkeley: University of California Press / Paris: UNESCO, 1988).

Timothy F. Garrard, *Akan Weights and the Gold Trade* (London & New York: Longman, 1980).

R. Haaland, "Man's Role in the Changing Habitat of Mema During the Old Kingdom of Ghana," *Norwegian Archaeological Review*, 13 (1980): 31–46.

A. G. Hopkins, *An Economic History of West Africa* (Harlow, U.K.: Longman, 1973).

Ibn al-Faqih, *Mukhtasar Kitab al-Buldan*, edited by M. J. de Goeje (Leiden, 1885).

Ibn Battuta, *Travels in Asia and Africa, 1325–1354*, 3 volumes, translated by H. A. R. Gibb (London: Routledge, 1929).

Ibn Hawqal, *Kitab Surat al-Ard*, 2 volumes, edited by J. H. Kramers (Leiden: Brill, 1938, 1939).

Ibn Khaldun, *Histoire des Berbères et des dynasties musulmanes de l'Afrique septentrionale*, 4 volumes, translated by William MacGuckin, Baron de Slane (Paris: P. Geuthner, 1925–1946).

Ibn Khaldun, *Prolégomènes*, 3 volumes, translated by M. Quatremère (Paris: B. Duprat, 1858).

Al-Idrisi, *Description de l'Afrique et de l'Espagne*, translated by R. Dozy and M. J. de Goeje (Leiden: Brill, 1866).

John Iliffe, *Africans: The History of a Continent* (Cambridge & New York: Cambridge University Press, 1995).

Al-Kati, *Tarîkh el-Fettâch, ou, Chronique du chercheur, pour servir à l'histoire des villes, des armées et des principaux personnages du Tekrour*, translated by O. Houdas and M. Delafosse (Paris: E. Leroux, 1913).

J. Ki-Zerbo, ed., *Methodology and African Prehistory*, volume 1 of *General History of Africa* (London: Heinemann / Berkeley: University of California Press / Paris: UNESCO, 1981).

Leo Africanus, *The History and Description of Africa*, 3 volumes, translated by John Pory, edited by Robert Brown (London: Printed for the Hakluyt Society, 1896).

Nehemia Levtzion, *Ancient Ghana and Mali* (London: Methuen, 1973).

Al-Mas'udi, *Les prairies d'or*, 9 volumes, translated by C. Barbier de Meynard and Pavet de Courteille (Paris: Imprimerie impériale, 1861–1917).

Raymond Mauny, *Tableau géographique de l'Ouest africain au Moyen Age, d'après les sources écrites, la tradition et l'archéologie* (Dakar: IFAN, 1961).

D. T. Niane, ed., *Africa from the Twelfth to the Sixteenth Century*, volume 4 of *General History of Africa* (London: Heinemann / Berkeley: University of California Press / Paris: UNESCO, 1984).

Al-Sa'di, *Tarikh es-Soudan*, translated by Houdas and Edm. Benoist (Paris: Leroux, 1898).

Al-Umari, *Masalik al-absar fi mamalik al-amsar*, edited by Ahmad Zaki (Cairo, 1924).

Yaqubi, *Tarikh*, edited by M. Th. Houtsma (Leiden: Brill, 1883).

POLITICS, LAW, AND THE MILITARY

J. F. A. Ajayi and Michael Crowder, eds., *The History of West Africa*, second edition, 2 volumes (New York: Columbia University Press, 1976, 1987).

A. K. Ajisafe, *Laws and Customs of the Yoruba People* (London: Routledge, 1924).

J. N. D. Anderson, *Islamic Law in Africa* (London: Cass, 1970).

Bolanle Awe, ed., *Nigerian Women in Historical Perspectives* (Lagos: Sankore / Ibadan: Bookcraft, 1992).

George B. N. Ayittey, *Indigenous African Institutions* (Ardsley-on-Hudson, N.Y.: Transnational, 1991).

John A. A. Ayoade and Adigun A. B. Agbaje, eds., *African Traditional Thought and Institutions* (Lagos: Center for Black and African Arts and Civilization, 1989).

Al-Bakri, *Description de l'Afrique septentrionale*, edited by William MacGuckin, Baron de Slane (Algiers, 1911).

Paul Bohannan, *Justice and Judgement among the Tiv of Nigeria* (London: Oxford University Press, 1957).

E. W. Bovill, *The Golden Trade of the Moors* (London & New York: Oxford University Press, 1958).

George E. Brooks, *Landlords and Strangers: Ecology, Society, and Trade in Western Africa, 1000–1630* (Boulder, Colo.: Westview Press, 1993).

Lester Brooks, *Great Civilizations of Ancient Africa* (New York: Four Winds Press, 1971).

Ronald Cohen, *The Kanuri of Bornu* (New York: Holt, Rinehart & Winston, 1967).

J. B. Danquah, *Gold Coast: Akan Laws and Customs and the Akim Abuakwa Constitution* (London: Routledge, 1928).

Basil Davidson, *African Kingdoms* (New York: Time-Life, 1966).

Davidson, *Old Africa Rediscovered* (London: Gollancz, 1959); republished as *The Lost Cities of Africa* (Boston & Toronto: Little, Brown, 1959; revised, 1970).

Davidson, with F. K. Buah and the advice of J. F. A. Ajayi, *The Growth of African Civilisation: A History of West Africa 1000–1800*, revised edition (London: Longmans, 1967).

J. C. De Graft-Johnson, *African Glory* (London: Watts, 1954).

Cheik Anta Diop, *Precolonial Black Africa: A Comparative Study of the Political and Social Systems of Europe and Black Africa, from Antiquity to the Formation of Modern States*, translated by Harold J. Salemson (Westport, Conn.: Lawrence Hill, 1987).

Robert Edgerton, *The Fall of the Asante Empire: The Hundred Year War for Africa's Gold Coast* (New York: Free Press, 1995).

Jacob U. Egharevba, *A Short History of Benin*, second edition, revised and enlarged (Benin: Published by the author, 1953).

T. O. Elias, *Government and Politics in Africa*, revised and enlarged edition (Bombay & New York: Asia Publishing House, 1963).

Elias, *Groundwork of Nigerian Law* (London: Routledge & Kegan Paul, 1954).

Elias, *The Nature of African Customary Law* (Manchester: Manchester University Press, 1956).

Elias, *Nigerian Land Law and Custom* (London: Routledge & Kegan Paul, 1951).

J. D. Fage, *An Introduction to the History of West Africa*, third edition (Cambridge: Cambridge University Press, 1962).

M. J. Field, *Social Organization of the Ga People* (Accra: Government of the Gold Coast Printing Press, 1940).

Sylvia C. Finkley, *Africa in Early Days* (New York: Odyssey Press, 1969).

M. Fortes and E. E. Evans-Pritchard, eds., *African Political Systems* (London: Published for the International Institute of African Languages & Cultures by the Oxford University Press, 1940).

Asaf A. A. Fyzee, *Outlines of Muhammadan Law,* fourth edition (Delhi & London: Oxford University Press, 1974 [i.e., 1975]).

Thomas A. Hale, *Scribe, Griot, and Novelist: Narrative Interpreters of the Songhay Empire* (Gainesville: University of Florida Press, 1990).

William Burnett Harvey, *Law and Social Change in Ghana* (Princeton: Princeton University Press, 1966).

J. F. Holleman, *Shona Customary Law with Reference to Kinship, Marriage, the Family and the Estate* (Cape Town: Published in association with the Rhodes-Livingstone Institute and the Beit Trust by Oxford University Press, 1952).

P. P. Howell, *A Manual of Nuer Law: Being an Account of Customary Law, Its Evolution and Development in the Court Established by the Sudan Government* (London: Oxford University Press, 1954).

Ibn Battuta, *Travels in Asia and Africa, 1325–1354,* 3 volumes, translated by H. A. R. Gibb (London: Routledge, 1929).

Ibn Khaldun, *Histoire des Berbères et des dynasties musulmanes de l'Afrique septentrionale,* 4 volumes, translated by William MacGuckin, Baron de Slane (Paris: P. Geuthner, 1925–1946).

Al-Kati, *Tarikh el-Fettach; ou, Chronique du chercheur,* translated by O. Houdas and M. Delafosse (Paris: E. Leroux, 1913).

Hilda Kuper and Leo Kuper, eds., *African Law: Adaptation and Development* (Berkeley: University of California Press, 1965).

Henri Labouret, *Africa Before the White Man,* translated by Francis Huxley (New York: Walker, 1963).

Robin Law, *The Horse in West African History* (Oxford: Oxford University Press, 1980).

Phyllis M. Martin and Patrick O'Meara, eds., *Africa,* third edition (Bloomington: Indiana University Press, 1995).

Laura Nader, ed., *Law in Culture and Society* (Chicago: Aldine Press, 1969).

D. T. Niane, *Sundiata: An Epic of Old Mali,* translated by G. D. Pickett (London: Longmans, 1965).

Wale Ogunyemi, *Queen Amina of Zazzau* (Ibadan: University Press, 1999).

Roland Oliver, ed., *The Cambridge History of Africa, Volume 3: from c. 1050 to c. 1600* (Cambridge, London, New York & Melbourne: Cambridge University Press, 1977).

Oliver, ed., *The Dawn of African History* (London: Oxford University Press, 1968).

Oliver and Anthony Atmore, *The African Middle Ages: 1400–1800* (Cambridge: Cambridge University Press, 1981); revised as *Medieval Africa: 1250–1800* (Cambridge: Cambridge University Press, 2001).

Oliver and J. D. Fage, *A Short History of Africa* (Harmondsworth, U.K.: Penguin, 1962).

Oliver and Caroline Oliver, *Africa in the Days of Exploration* (Englewood Cliffs, N.J.: Prentice-Hall, 1965).

N. A. Ollennu, *Principles of Customary Land Law in Ghana* (London: Sweet & Maxwell, 1962).

Charlotte A. Quinn, *Mandingo Kingdoms of the Senegambia: Traditionalism, Islam, and European Expansion* (Evanston, Ill.: Northwestern University Press, 1972).

John Reader, *Africa: A Biography of the Continent* (New York: Knopf, 1998).

Walter Rodney, *A History of the Upper Guinea Coast, 1545–1800* (Oxford: Clarendon Press, 1970).

Ricky Rosenthal, *The Splendor That Was Africa* (Dobbs Ferry, N.Y.: Oceana Publications, 1967).

A. F. C. Ryder, *Benin and the Europeans, 1445–1897* (Harlow, U.K.: Longmans, 1969).

Elias N. Saad, *The Social History of Timbuktu: The Role of Muslim Scholars and Notables, 1400–1900* (Cambridge: Cambridge University Press, 1983).

Al-Sa'di, *Tarikh-es-Soudan,* translated by O. Houdas (Paris, 1900).

Margaret Shinnie, *Ancient African Kingdoms* (London: Arnold, 1965).

G. T. Stride and Caroline Ifeka, *Peoples and Empires of West Africa: West Africa in History, 1000–1800* (New York: Africana Publishing, 1971).

John Spencer Trimingham, *A History of Islam in West Africa* (London: Published for the University of Glasgow by Oxford University Press, 1962).

Bala Usman and Nur Alkali, eds., *Studies in the History of Pre-Colonial Borno* (Zaria: Northern Nigerian Publishing, 1983).

Jan Vansina, *Kingdoms of the Savanna* (Madison: University of Wisconsin Press, 1966).

LEISURE, RECREATION, AND DAILY LIFE

J. F. Ade. Ajayi and Ian Espie, eds., *A Thousand Years of West African History: A Handbook for Teachers and Students* (Ibadan, Nigeria: University of Ibadan Press / London: Nelson, 1969).

Anthony Atmore and Gillian Stacey, *Black Kingdoms, Black Peoples* (London: Orbis, 1979).

Edward McNall Burns and others, *World Civilizations: Their History and Their Culture,* seventh edition, 2 volumes (New York: Norton, 1986).

G. R. Crone, trans. and ed., *The Voyages of Cadamosto and Other Documents on Western Africa in the Second Half of the Fifteenth Century* (London: Printed for the Hakluyt Society, 1937).

Yaya Diallo and Mitchell Hall, *The Healing Drum: African Wisdom Teachings* (Rochester, Vt.: Destiny Books, 1998).

G. S. P. Freeman-Grenville, *Chronology of African History* (London: Oxford University Press, 1973).

Peter Garlake, *The Kingdom of Africa* (Oxford: Elsevier-Phaidon, 1978).

Ibn Battuta, *Travels in Asia and Africa, 1325–1354,* 3 volumes, translated by H. A. R. Gibb (London: Routledge, 1929).

Naomi Mitchison, *African Heroes* (London: Bodley Head, 1968).

Roland Oliver, ed., *The Cambridge History of Africa, Volume 3: from c. 1050 to c. 1600* (Cambridge, London, New York & Melbourne: Cambridge University Press, 1977).

Oliver, ed., *The Dawn of African History,* second edition, revised (London: Oxford University Press, 1968).

Oliver and Anthony Atmore, *The African Middle Ages: 1400–1800* (Cambridge: Cambridge University Press, 1981); revised as *Medieval Africa: 1250–1800* (Cambridge: Cambridge University Press, 2001).

William N. Stephens, *The Family in Cross-Cultural Perspective* (New York: Holt, Rinehart & Winston, 1963).

FAMILY AND SOCIAL TRENDS

George B. N. Ayittey, *Indigenous African Institutions* (Ardsley-on-Hudson, N.Y.: Transnational, 1991).

John W. Blake, *European Beginnings in West Africa, 1454–1578: A Survey of the First Century of White Enterprise in West Africa, with Special Emphasis upon the Rivalry of the Great Powers* (London & New York: Published for the Royal Empire Society by Longmans, Green, 1937).

Paul Bohannan and Philip Curtin, *Africa and Africans,* fourth edition (Prospect Heights, Ill.: Waveland Press, 1995).

E. W. Bovill, *Caravans of the Old Sahara: An Introduction to the History of the Western Sudan* (London: Published for the International Institute of African Languages & Cultures by Oxford University Press, 1933).

John Desmond Clark, *The Prehistory of Africa* (London: Thames & Hudson, 1970).

Philip Curtin and others, *African History from Earliest Times to Independence,* second edition (London & New York: Longman, 1995).

Basil Davidson, *Africa in History* (New York: Collier, 1991).

Davidson, *African Kingdoms* (New York: Time-Life, 1966).

Yaya Diallo and Mitchell Hall, *The Healing Drum: African Wisdom Teachings* (Rochester, Vt.: Destiny Books, 1998).

Gomes Eanes de Zurara, *Conquests & Discoveries of Henry the Navigator; Being the Chronicles of Azurara,* edited by Virginia de Castro e Almeida, translated by Bernard Miall (London: Allen & Unwin, 1936).

William Fagg, *Divine Kingship in Africa* (London: British Museum, 1970).

M. Fortes, "The Structure of Unilineal Descent Groups," *American Anthropologists,* 55 (January–March 1953).

C. Magbailey Fyle, *Introduction to the History of African Civilization* (Lanham, Md.: University Press of America, 1999).

Jack Goody, "Bridewealth and Dowry in Africa and Eurasia," in *Bridewealth and Dowry,* by Goody and S. J. Tambiah (Cambridge: Cambridge University Press, 1973), pp. 1–58.

Goody, *Comparative Studies in Kinship* (Stanford: Stanford University Press, 1969).

Goody, ed., *The Character of Kinship* (Cambridge: Cambridge University Press, 1973).

Goody and Esther Goody, "Cross-Cousin Marriage in Northern Ghana," *Man* (London), new series 1 (September 1966): 343–355.

Hugo Huber, "Initiation to Womanhood Among the Se (Ghana)," *Nigerian Field,* 23 (July 1958): 99–119.

Huber, "Kinship Terms and Traditional Form of Marriage among the Se (West Africa)," *Anthropos,* 53, no. 5/6 (1958): 925–944.

Ibn Battuta, *Travels in Asia and Africa, 1325–1354,* 3 volumes, translated by H. A. R. Gibb (London: Routledge, 1929).

Robert A. Lystad, "Marriage and Kinship among the Ashantis and Agai; A Study of Differential Acculturation," in *Continuity and Change in African Cultures,* edited by William R. Bascom and Melville J. Herskovits (Chicago: University of Chicago Press, 1959).

Daniel McCall, *Africa in Time-Perspective* (Boston: Boston University Press, 1964).

F. Ivan Nye and Felix Berardo, *The Family: Its Structure and Interactions* (London: Macmillan, 1973).

Roland Oliver and Brian Fagan, *Africa in the Iron Age; c. 500 B.C. to A.D. 1400* (Cambridge & New York: Cambridge University Press, 1975).

P. A. Owiredu, "The Akan System of Inheritance Today and Tomorrow," *African Affairs*, 58 (April 1959): 161–165.

Derrick J. Stenning, *Savannah Nomads: A Study of the Wodaabe Pastoral Fulani of Western Bornu Province, Northern Region, Nigeria* (London: Published for the International African Institute by Oxford University Press, 1959).

W. N. Stephens, *The Family in Cross-cultural Perspective* (New York: Holt, Rinehart & Winston, 1963).

Niara Sudarkasa, "Interpreting the African Heritage in Afro-American Family Organization," in *Black Families*, edited by Harriette Pipes McAdoo (Beverly Hills, Cal.: Sage, 1981), pp. 37–53.

Victor Uchendu, "Concubinage among Ngwa-Ibo of Southern in Nigeria," *Africa* (London), 35 (April 1965): 187–197.

Kay Williamson, "Changes in the Marriage System of the Okrika People," *Africa* (London), 32, no. 1 (1962): 53–60.

Carle C. Zimmerman, *Family and Civilization* (New York: Harper, 1947).

RELIGION AND PHILOSOPHY

Wade Abimbola, ed. and trans., *Ifa Divination Poetry* (New York: NOK, 1977).

Chinua Achebe, *Anthills of the Savannah* (London: Heinemann, 1987).

Achebe, *Morning Yet on Creation Day: Essays* (London: Heinemann, 1975).

Andrew Apter, *Black Critiques and Kings: The Hermeneutics of Power in Yoruba Society* (Chicago: University of Chicago Press, 1992).

Sandra T. Barnes, ed., *Africa's Ogun: Old World and New*, expanded edition (Bloomington: Indiana University Press, 1989).

William R. Bascom, *Ifa Divination: Communication Between Gods and Men in West Africa* (Bloomington: Indiana University Press, 1969).

Ulli Beier, ed., *The Origin of Life and Death: African Creation Myths* (London: Heinemann, 1966).

Norman R. Bennett, *Africa and Europe: From Roman Times to National Independence*, second edition (New York: Africana, 1975).

K. A. Busia, *The Challenge of Africa* (New York: Praeger, 1962).

W. Walton Claridge, *A History of the Gold Coast from the Earliest Times to the Commencement of the Twentieth Century*, 2 volumes (London: Murray, 1915).

Herbert M. Cole, *Mbari: Art and Life among the Owerri Igbo* (Bloomington: Indiana University Press, 1982).

Harold Courlander, ed., *A Treasury of African Folklore* (New York: Crown, 1975).

J. B. Danquah, *The Akan Doctrine of God: A Fragment of Gold Coast Ethics and Religion*, second edition (London: Cass, 1968).

Basil Davidson, *West Africa Before the Colonial Era: A History to 1850* (London & New York: Longman, 1998).

Cheikh Anta Diop, *The African Origins of Civilization: Myth or Reality*, translated by Mercer Cook (Chicago: Lawrence Hill, 1974).

Diop, *Black Africa: The Economic and Cultural Basis for a Federated State*, translated by Harold J. Salemson (Westport, Conn.: Lawrence Hill, 1974).

Diop, *Civilization or Barbarism: An Authentic Anthropology*, translated by Yaa-Lengi Meema Ngemi; edited by Salemson and Marjolijn de Jager (Brooklyn, N.Y.: Lawrence Hill, 1991).

Diop, *Precolonial Black Africa: A Comparative Study of the Political and Social Systems of Europe and Black Africa, from Antiquity to the Formation of Modern States*, translated by Salemson (Westport, Conn.: Lawrence Hill, 1987).

Jacob U. Egharevba, *The City of Benin, Benin Law and Custom, Some Stories of Ancient Benin*, [and] *Some Tribal Gods of Southern Nigeria* (Nendeln: Kraus Reprints, 1971).

Emmanuel Eze, ed., *African Philosophy: An Anthology* (Malden, Mass. & Oxford, U.K.: Blackwell, 1998).

Leo Frobenius and Douglas C. Fox, *African Genesis* (Berkeley, Cal.: Turtle Island Foundation, 1983).

Segun Gbadegesin, *African Philosophy: Traditional Yoruba Philosophy and Contemporary African Realities* (New York: Peter Lang, 1991).

Marcel Griaule and Germaine Dieterlen, *Le Mythe Cosmogonique* (Paris: Institut d'Ethnologie, 1965).

Joseph E. Harris, *Africans and Their History*, second edition, revised (New York: Meridian, 1998).

Constance B. Hilliard, *Intellectual Traditions of Pre-Colonial Africa* (Boston: McGraw-Hill, 1998).

Ibn Battuta, *Travels in Asia and Africa, 1325–1354*, 3 volumes, translated by H. A. R. Gibb (London: Routledge, 1929).

E. Bolaji Idowu, *Olodumare: God in Yoruba Belief*, revised and enlarged edition (Plainview: Original Publications, 1995).

John Iliffe, *Africans: The History of a Continent* (Cambridge & New York: Cambridge University Press, 1995).

Edmund Ilogu, *Christianity and Igbo Culture* (Leiden: Brill, 1974).

Elizabeth Isichei, *A History of African Societies to 1870* (Cambridge: Cambridge University Press, 1997).

Isichei, *A History of the Igbo People* (London: Macmillan, 1976).

Samuel Johnson, *The History of the Yorubas from the Earliest Times to the Beginning of the British Protectorate,* edited by O. Johnson (London: Routledge, 1921).

A. H. M. Kirk-Greene, trans., *Hausa ba dabo ba ne: 500 Hausa Proverbs* (Ibadan: Oxford University Press, 1966).

Arthur Glyn Leonard, *The Lower Niger and Its Tribes* (London & New York: Macmillan, 1906).

John Mbiti, *Introduction to African Religion* (London: Heinemann, 1975).

John D. Murphy and Harry Goff, *A Bibliography of African Languages and Linguistics* (Washington, D.C.: Catholic University of America Press, 1969).

Roland Oliver, *The African Experience: From Olduvai Gorge to the 21st Century* (London: Weidenfeld & Nicolson, 1999).

Paul Radin and Elinore Marvel, eds., *African Folktales & Sculpture,* revised and enlarged edition (New York: Pantheon, 1964).

Wole Soyinka, *Myth, Literature and the African World* (Cambridge & New York: Cambridge University Press, 1976).

P. Amaury Talbot, *Life in Southern Nigeria: The Magic, Beliefs, and Customs of the Ibibio Tribe* (London: Macmillan, 1923).

Robert Farris Thompson, *The Flash of the Spirit: African and Afro-American Art and Philosophy* (New York: Random House, 1984).

Rems Nna Umeasiegbu, *The Way We Lived: Ibo Customs and Stories* (London: Heinemann, 1969).

SCIENCE, TECHNOLOGY, AND HEALTH

Nicholas T. Bobrovnikoff, *Astronomy before the Telescope,* 2 volumes, edited by Roger B. Culver and David D. Meisel (Tucson, Ariz.: Pachart, 1984, 1990).

Leonard C. Bruno, *Math and Mathematicians: The History of Math Discoveries Around the World,* 2 volumes, edited by Lawrence W. Baker (Detroit: UXL, 1999).

Graham Connah, *African Civilizations—Precolonial Cities and States in Tropical Africa: An Archaeological Perspective* (Cambridge & New York: Cambridge University Press, 1987).

Ron Eglash, *African Fractals: Modern Computing and Indigenous Design* (New Brunswick, N.J.: Rutgers University Press, 1999).

Gerald W. Hartwig and K. David Patterson, eds., *Disease in African History: An Introductory Survey and Case Studies* (Durham, N.C.: Duke University Press, 1978).

Eugenia W. Herbert, *Red Gold of Africa: Copper in Precolonial History and Culture* (Madison: University of Wisconsin Press, 1984).

Dale Idiens and K. G. Ponting, eds., *Textiles of Africa* (Bath, U.K.: Pasold Research Fund, 1980).

Maurice M. Iwu, *Handbook of African Medicinal Plants* (Boca Raton, Fla.: CRC, 1993).

Leo Africanus, *The History and Description of Africa,* 3 volumes, translated by John Pory, edited by Robert Brown (London: Printed for the Hakluyt Society, 1896).

Patricia and Fredrick McKissack, *The Royal Kingdoms of Ghana, Mali, and Songhay: Life in Medieval Africa* (New York: Holt, 1994).

Elizabeth Newhouse, ed., *The Builders: Marvels of Engineering* (Washington, D.C.: Book Division of National Geographic Society, 1992).

Georges Niangoran-Bouah, *L'Univers Akan Des Poids a Peser L'Or: Les Poids non-figuratifs* (Abidjan, Ivory Coast: Les Nouvelles Editions Africaines-M.L.B., 1984).

Cheryl Plumer, *African Textiles: An Outline of Handcrafted Sub-Saharan Fabrics* (East Lansing: African Studies Center, Michigan State University, 1971).

Claire Polakoff, *Into Indigo: African Textiles and Dyeing Techniques* (Garden City, N.Y.: Anchor/Doubleday, 1980).

Labelle Prussin, *African Nomadic Architecture: Space, Place, and Gender* (Washington, D.C.: Smithsonian Institution Press, 1995).

Peter R. Schmidt, *Iron Technology in East Africa: Symbolism, Science, and Archaeology* (Bloomington: Indiana University Press, 1997).

Helaine Selin, ed., *Encyclopedia of the History of Science, Technology, and Medicine in Non-Western Cultures* (Boston: Kluwer Academic, 1997).

Selin and Sun Xiaochun, eds., *Astronomy Across Cultures: The History of Non-Western Astronomy* (Boston: Kluwer Academic, 2000).

Gloria Thomas-Emeagwali, ed., *Science and Technology in African History with Case Studies from Nigeria, Sierra Leone, Zimbabwe, and Zambia* (Lewiston, N.Y.: Edwin Mellen Press, 1992).

Ivan Van Sertima, ed., *Blacks in Science: Ancient and Modern* (New Brunswick, N.J.: Transaction, 1983).

Joseph O. Vogel and Jean Vogel, eds., *Encyclopedia of Precolonial Africa: Archaeology, History, Languages, Cultures, and Environments* (Walnut Creek, Cal.: AltaMira, 1997).

Claudia Zaslavsky, *Africa Counts: Number and Pattern in African Culture* (Boston: Prindle, Weber & Schmidt, 1973).

CONTRIBUTORS

Pita Ogaba Agbese is a professor in the Department of Political Science at the University of Northern Iowa, Cedar Falls. He was educated in Nigeria and the United States and holds a Ph.D. in political science from Northwestern University. He widely publishes on Third World politics and teaches courses on African politics and international relations and law.

Edwin Kwetu Andoh is a sociologist who earned an M.A. degree in Spain; he was also educated in Ghana. He is currently a program director for a nongovernmental organization focused on the social, health, and recreational development of children in Ghana. Among his publications are "Black Americans and Police Vigilante Justice," "Employee Turnover in Banking Institutions in Accra," "Revisiting Ali Khan's Theory on Terrorism," and "Sexual Harassment in Banking Institutions and Judicial Bias."

Diedre L. Badejo is a professor and the chairwoman of the Pan African Studies Department at Kent State University. She holds a Ph.D. in comparative literature from the University of California, Los Angeles. Her areas of research include African American and African literatures, women's studies, and African religion and mythology. In addition to several articles, she is the author of Òsun Sèègèsì: The Elegant Deity of Wealth, Power, and Femininity (1996).

Pade Badru is associate professor of sociology and pan African studies and the codirector of the Center for Educational Policy Analysis and Social Research at the University of Louisville, Kentucky. He graduated from the State University of New York at Stony Brook and the London School of Economics and Political Science. Dr. Badru's specializations are in race and ethnic relations, international economical development with specific focus on sub-Saharan Africa, political and economic history of Africa, political economy, historiography, and the sociology of developing societies. He is the author of Imperialism and Ethnic Politics in Nigeria, 1960-1996 (1998) and International Banking and Rural Development: The World Bank in Sub-Saharan Africa (1998).

Donna J. Davis holds an M.A. from the University of Michigan in American Studies and an M.A. from the University of Northern Iowa in English, with a specialty in multicultural literature. Her Africanist interests are lifelong. Currently she is employed as a professional writer for a nonprofit organization in Iowa. She has published in a variety of fields including health, human services, and multicultural literary studies.

Emmanuel Chukwudi Eze is an associate professor in the Department of Philosophy at De Paul University in Chicago and specializes in critical theory of race and culture. He was educated in Nigeria, Zaire (present-day Democratic Republic of Congo), England, and the United States. He has taught at Bucknell University and Mount Holyoke College and has been a visiting scholar at St. Edmund's College and a research associate at the African Studies Center, University of Cambridge. In 1996 he was the Diamond Distinguished Visitor in Philosophy at the New School for Social Research, New York. His teaching and research interests include modern African and European philosophy, social and political philosophy, philosophy of anthropology, postcolonial theory, and philosophy of race. He has edited several books, including Postcolonial African Philosophy: A Critical Reader (1997), Race and the Enlightenment (1997), and African Philosophy: An Anthology (1998). He is the author of Achieving Our Humanity: The Idea of the Postracial Future (2001). He is a member of the American Philosophical Association and an elected member of the association's Committee on Philosophy and the Black Experience.

David L. Horne is associate professor of critical thinking, history, and graduate public policy in the Pan African Studies Department at California State University, Northridge. He is the executive director of the California African American Political Institute, cochairman of the Reparation Platform Coalition in Los Angeles, and a member of the Los Angeles Redistricting Commission. He participated in the United Nations Human Rights Commission Conference on Racism, Xenophobia and Related Intolerances. He is the editor of *The Journal of Pan African Studies*. He has written *Straight to the Point: A Primer for a Logical Introduction to Critical Thinking, The State of the Race: A 21st-Century Analysis of Black Americans, Achieving College Student Success,* as well as several articles.

Pierre-Damien Mvuyekure is associate professor of English and African American literature and culture in the Department of English Language and Literature at the University of Northern Iowa, Cedar Falls. He holds B.A. and M.A. degrees in letters (English) from the National University of Rwanda, where he taught English and American literature as a junior lecturer between 1986 and 1989, and M.A. and Ph.D. degrees in English (American and African American Literature) from the State University of New York at Buffalo. He is a Fulbright alumnus. Previously, he taught at Idaho State University in Pocatello as a visiting assistant professor of English until the war and genocide in Rwanda forced him to seek political asylum and permanent residence in the United States. His research areas include African American literature and culture, rap and hip-hop music, African Diaspora literatures and cultures, African literature and culture, African religion and dance aesthetics, postcolonial theory and literatures, multiculturalism, American multicultural and ethnic literatures and cultures, Rwandan ancient oral literature, and the 1994 genocide. He has published several journal articles and book chapters on the Rwandan genocide,

Ishmael Reed, Alice Walker, Jewell Parker Rhodes, Gloria Naylor, Walter Mosley, Paul Laurence Dunbar, Melvin B. Tolson, Patricia Grace, Velma Pollard, and Tupac Shakur. He is the editor of the casebook on Ishmael Reed's *Yellow Back Radio Broke-Down* (2003). His complete book-length critical study *Ishmael Reed's Literary Neo-HooDooism: Post-Colonial Textual Resistance, African Diaspora Re-Connection, and Multicultural Poetics* is being circulated for publication. He is also a poet and is writing a novel on the Rwandan genocide. In the past, he has been on the board of the NAACP (Pocatello branch), and he is now a member of the board of the African American Historical and Cultural Museum of Waterloo as well as the National Association of African American Studies and Associates.

Carole Shelley Yates graduated from the University of Nebraska, Lincoln, with a degree in journalism and teaching. She is a writer for the University of Northern Iowa InTime (Integrated New Technologies into the Methods of Education) project for their promotional CD and accompanying print materials, websites, and research documents. Her primary research and publication fields are education and alternative energy uses. She was a writer and producer for the "Energy in Iowa" series, KUNI Public Radio, between February and July 2002. This program received first place as a documentary from the Associated Press competition (2003), a merit award for a series from Northwest Broadcast News Association (2003), and a Renewable Energy Leadership Award from Iowa Renewable Energy Association (2002).

INDEX OF PHOTOGRAPHS

INDEX

This index is sorted word by word. Page numbers in bold type indicate the primary article on a topic.
Page numbers in italics indicate illustrations.